INSIDE LIGHTV

New
Riders

BY
Dan Ablan

201 West 103rd Street, Indianapolis, Indiana 46290

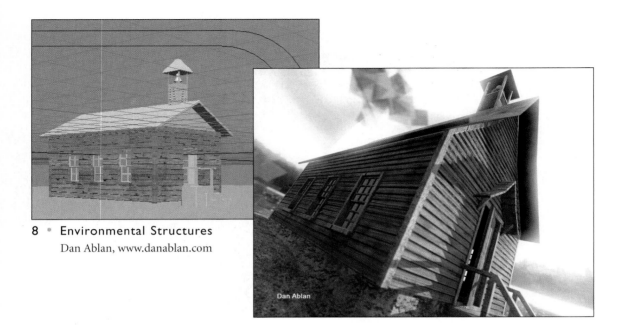

8 • Environmental Structures
Dan Ablan, www.danablan.com

9 • Environmental Lighting
Dan Ablan, www.danablan.com

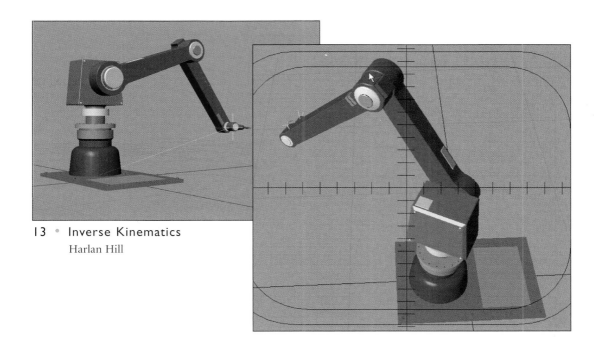

13 • Inverse Kinematics
Harlan Hill

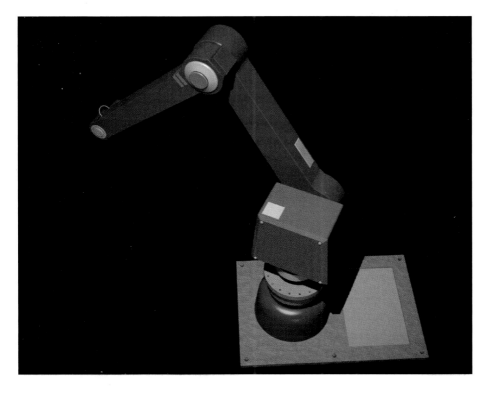

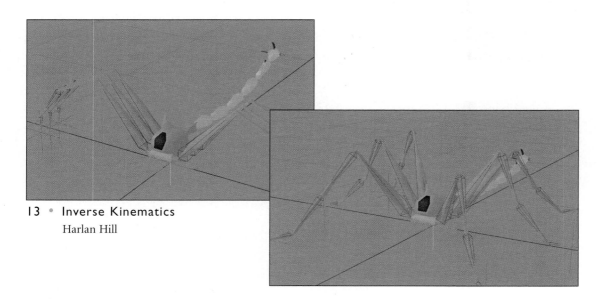

13 • Inverse Kinematics
Harlan Hill

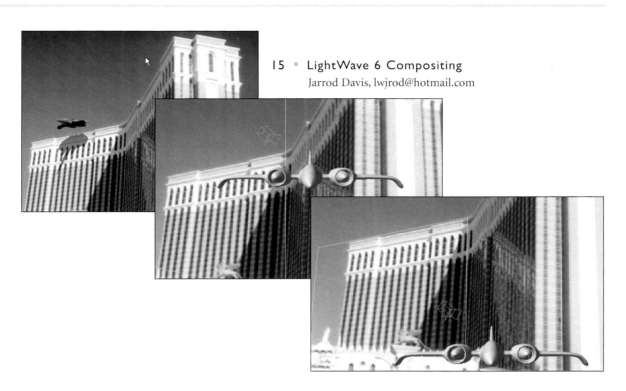

15 • LightWave 6 Compositing

Jarrod Davis, lwjrod@hotmail.com

16 • Broadcast Animations
Dan Ablan, www.agadigital.com

16 • Broadcast Animations
Dan Ablan, www.agadigital.com

Explore the Possibilities...

Poster_1280 and Poster2_1280
Terrence Walker, www.studioartfx.com

"Into Thin Air"
Gregory Duquesne, gregory_duquesne@newtek.com

TVR_Tuscan
James Hans, www.infinite-detail.com

Table of Contents

Part II   A Project-Based Approach to Creating and Building 3D Scenes

7   Lighting and Atmospheres   201

Part III   A Project-Based Approach to Animating Scenes

About the Author

Dan Ablan, a graduate of Valparaiso University and author of *LightWave Power Guide* and *Inside LightWave 3D*, is president of AGA Digital Studios, Inc. in Chicago. He has been using LightWave for over 10 years, since version 0.9 on the trusty old Amiga 2000. He has had columns in *Video Toaster User* magazine, *LightWave Pro*, and *3D Magazine*, and has taught LightWave around the country at various trade shows. Dan has worked on animation projects for Coca-Cola, Radio Disney, Motorola, Xerox, AT Kearney, NBC, FOX Television, and many others. His company is an authorized NewTek LightWave training facility.

Dedication

For Maria and Amelia.

Acknowledgments

This is my third book for New Riders. In the four years I've been working with them, I've had nothing but respect for their tireless efforts and dedication. Laura Frey and Audrey Doyle juggle more every day than anyone can imagine, while still remembering what I'm talking about on each and every page. Thank you both for your continued support and trust in me to get this thing finished! Barbara Terry, Jennifer Eberhardt, Linda Seifert, Gina Rexrode, Amy Parker, Michael Thurston, John Rahm, Sarah Kearns, and Steve Weiss all deserve my sincere thanks for helping pull this book into shape, under very tight deadlines. You guys are great! A big thank you to my friends at NewTek for getting me a beta copy of the software after I complained and nagged them for months on end. Thanks to Brian Freisinger, Brad Peebler, and especially Philip Nelson for your correspondence and assistance.

Additional thanks goes to Kenneth Woodruff, Michael Ash, and the other members of the beta team that were willing to lend a hand. Not to go unmentioned is Doug Nakakihara, my safety net…uh, I mean, tech editor. Thanks, Doug! This book has been made even better with the help of Stu Aitken, Bob Hood, Prem Subramanyn, Harlan Hill, Julian Kain and J-Rod himself, Jarrod Davis—thanks guys for lending a hand! Not enough thanks can go to my wife Maria, and daughter Amelia. In the midst of all that was going on, you let me get it all done! I'll be around a bit more now. Lastly, for all of you who sarcastically tell me "thanks for mentioning me in your book," I am now mentioning you. This includes my big, soft, grape of a brother Jerry; the rest of my family; Mark Voss; Tom Burkholder; Adrian Dinu; the Burkey's (Kelley, too); Jimbo the brother-in-law; Keith Brock; Shane Williams; that Paul Holtz guy; and all the rest of you. Don't mention it again.

New Riders Acknowledgments

New Riders would like to thank NewTek for allowing us to include the NewTek LightWave icon throughout this book. (The NewTek LightWave icon is a trademark of NewTek and is used with permission.)

A Message from New Riders

As the reader of this book, you are our most important critic and commentator. We value your opinion and want to know what we're doing right, what we could do better, in what areas you'd like to see us publish, and any other words of wisdom you're willing to pass our way.

As the Executive Editor for the Graphics team at New Riders, I welcome your comments. You can fax, email, or write me directly to let me know what you did or didn't like about this book—as well as what we can do to make our books better. When you write, please be sure to include this book's title, ISBN, and author, as well as your name and phone or fax number. I will carefully review your comments and share them with the authors and editors who worked on the book. For any issues directly related to this or other titles:

Please keep in mind that I didn't write this book and am probably not the best person to bring technical issues to. If you run into a technical problem with how the book explains something, it's best to contact our Customer Support staff, as listed later in this section. Thanks.

For any issues directly related to this or other titles:

Email:	steve.weiss@newriders.com
Mail:	Steve Weiss
	Executive Editor
	Professional Graphics & Design Publishing
	New Riders Publishing
	201 West 103rd Street
	Indianapolis, IN 46290 USA

Visit Our Website: www.newriders.com

On our website you'll find information about our other books, the authors we partner with, book updates and file downloads, promotions, discussion boards for online interaction with other users and with technology experts, and a calendar of trade shows and other professional events with which we'll be involved. We hope to see you around.

Email Us from Our Website

Go to www.newriders.com and click on the Contact link if you

- Have comments or questions about this book
- Want to report errors that you have found in this book
- Have a book proposal or are otherwise interested in writing with New Riders

- Would like us to send you one of our author kits

- Are an expert in a computer topic or technology and are interested in being a reviewer or technical editor

- Want to find a distributor for our titles in your area

- Are an educator/instructor who wishes to preview New Riders books for classroom use. (Include your name, school, department, address, phone number, office days/hours, text currently in use, and enrollment in your department in the body/comments area, along with your request for desk/examination copies, or for additional information.

Call Us or Fax Us

You can reach us toll-free at (800) 571-5840 + 9+ 3567. Ask for New Riders. If outside the USA, please call 1-317-581-3500 and ask for New Riders. If you prefer, you can fax us at 1-317-581-4663, Attention: New Riders.

Technical Support and Customer Support for this Book

Although we encourage entry-level users to get as much as they can out of our books, we appreciate keeping in mind that our books are written assuming a non-beginner level of user-knowledge of the technology. This assumption is reflected in the brevity and shorthand nature of some of the tutorials.

New Riders will continually work to create clearly written, thoroughly-tested and reviewed technology books of the highest educational caliber and creative design. We value our customers more than anything, but we cannot guarantee to each of the thousands of you who buy and use our books that we will be able to work individually with you through tutorials or content with which you may have questions. We urge readers who need help in working through exercises or other material in our books—and who need this assistance immediately—to use as many of the resources that our technology and technical communities can provide, especially the many online user groups and list servers available.

- If you have a physical problem with one of our books or accompanying CD-ROMs, please contact our customer support department.

- If you have questions about the content of the book—needing clarification about something as it is written or note of a possible error—again please contact our customer support department.

- If you have comments of a general nature about this or other books by New Riders, please contact the executive editor.

To contact our customer support department, call 1-317-581-3833, from 10:00 a.m. to 3 p.m. US EST (CST from April through October of each year—unlike most of the rest of the United States, Indiana doesn't change to Daylight Savings Time each April). You can also access our tech support website at http://www.mcp.com/support.

Introduction

New Riders Publishing is a leader in the graphics publishing industry. Its *Inside* series of
books has been at the forefront of the creative
community. *Inside* books live on just about all
artists' desks as permanent residents. Usually
the *Inside* series of books is updated when software is upgraded, but *Inside LightWave [6]* is a

completely new book. NewTek, Inc., makers of LightWave 3D, spent more than two years rewriting one of the 3D industry's most popular and powerful animation programs. Because of that, it is only fitting that this book be completely written from the ground up, making it the most comprehensive LightWave book published.

Getting the Most from *Inside LightWave [6]*

Inside LightWave [6] is designed differently from other books on the market. Each chapter is tuned to key information about a specific topic. The project-based chapters in Parts II and III teach you how to create entire animations, not just portions of them. In certain situations, you'll model, texture, light, and animate—all within one chapter! Because of this approach, you can gain valuable information through just one chapter. However, taking the book as a whole from start to finish will allow you make the most of this book.

Use the LightWave 6 Software with This Book

Due to LightWave 6's complete rewrite, it is recommended that you have the LightWave 6 software to take full advantage of the information within these pages. You will not be able to apply the tutorials in this book to previous versions of LightWave.

Read the LightWave 6 Manuals

Inside LightWave [6] is designed to be a companion to the three manuals supplied with your LightWave software from NewTek. Read the Introduction and Tutorials manual, and then move on to the Surface and Light manual. When you're comfortable with the information there, move on to the Animate and Render manual. From there, dive into this book to become the best LightWave animator on your block. Although previous LightWave books, such as *LightWave Power Guide* and *Inside LightWave 3D 5.5*, have a tremendous amount of information, the radically different architecture of LightWave 6 makes the information in this book unique. To get the most out of this book, it is strongly recommended that you study your software manuals and keep them nearby for quick reference.

Start at the Beginning of the Book

Unless you are somewhat familiar with LightWave 6, it is important for you to start at the beginning of this book and not skip directly to a project chapter. Although it's tempting to dive right in, LightWave 6 has a completely new structure and there are changes throughout LightWave's Modeler and Layout modules that you should be familiar with. Do yourself a favor and read about these changes.

Experiment with the Software

One of the best things you can do as an animator learning LightWave is to experiment. This is stressed throughout this book. However, consider this a warning: Experimentation takes you to places within the program that you might not normally go. That's why this book provides many screenshots of the topic at hand. It is important to not only have a comprehensive understanding of techniques, but also a visual reference as well.

Practice Your Craft

There is no substitute for practicing your craft. If you happen to be driving down the road and notice an interesting tree, practice re-creating it in LightWave. If you decide that you'd love to visualize your dream house, build it in LightWave. Don't wait until you have a paid project or assignment to work in LightWave. All the extra time you spend modeling and animating will help give you that extra edge.

Use Other Books with This Book

No single book can deliver it all, although we'll try! And because no single book has all the answers, it's to your advantage to use additional and, sometimes, more specific references. For example, character animation is a driving force for many of the changes within this program, as well as the reason many of you got into 3D animation. *Inside LightWave [6]* covers as much of this topic as possible, but a great number of other resources are available to you. Some of these resources include books on facial muscles, character design, motion and body studies, and lighting. Books and magazines, along with the Internet, can provide much information; studying it all practically gives you no time to accomplish your animation goals! The Internet also provides many downloadable animations that you can study, use as references, or use to get ideas. Be sure to flip through Appendix C, "Plug-Ins and References," to check out some valuable resources. Remember, knowledge is power!

Checking Out the Organization of This Book

Inside LightWave [6] is organized into five parts:

Part I, "Getting Started with LightWave 6," is an overview of the new features and functions of LightWave 6. This includes 3D terminology, methodology (such as the HUB), and other important information about the many changes in the new version. This section introduces you to the new way of creating objects, new interfaces, and customizable buttons. You'll also learn how the redesigned software integrates Modeler and Layout.

Part II, "A Project-Based Approach to Creating and Building 3D Scenes," takes you through the real-world process of creating animations. The chapters bring you through the necessary steps in LightWave 6's new modeling functions and features, surfacing techniques, lighting, and cameras.

Part III, "A Project-Based Approach to Animating Scenes," shows you how to push your LightWave software even further through the use of LightWave 6's new Expression engine, and advanced inverse kinematics. You'll learn compositing techniques, and work through a real-world project creating broadcast-style graphics. Part IV, "Animation Post," is dedicated to helping output your animations and edit them with audio using NewTek's Video Toaster NT. Add to the information you need to create a killer demo reel, from content information, length, and many other important considerations.

Part V, "Appendixes," includes an appendix on LScript, and an appendix of some necessary third-party information, such as plug-ins and finding LightWave-related information on the Internet.

Identifying the Conventions Used in This Book

Throughout this book, you'll come across Warnings, Tips, and Notes. These areas are marked with a small LightWave logo icon, similar to the one that appears on your desktop when you install LightWave. Any control area that opens will be referred to as a *panel*. Fields where you enter values will be referred to as *requesters*, while buttons that have a small upside-down triangle will be referred to as *drop-down menus*. That's simple enough, isn't it?

There's one more thing to remember—always work with the Caps Lock key off. Throughout this book, you will come across many keyboard shortcuts, and there are significant differences between a lowercase shortcut and an uppercase shortcut. The essential and immediate shortcuts used regularly are assigned to lowercase keys, while less-used commands are assigned to uppercase keys. What's important to remember is that some of the uppercase commands are more complex functions, and if you're not prepared to execute such a command, you may cause problems for yourself.

System Considerations

LightWave 6 is definitely a more robust program than any previous version of LightWave. Because of this, a good strong system is your best bet for enjoying the full benefits of the program. However, LightWave still takes fewer resources to run effectively than its competing applications. As always, the more RAM (system memory) you have, the better. *Inside LightWave [6]* recommends that you have at least 128MB of RAM or more in your system. This greatly enhances your workflow. Larger memory requirements are needed because computations in LightWave 6 are done with floating-point accuracy rather than integers. What this means for you is better renders! Please note that you should consult your LightWave 3D Reference Guides supplied by NewTek for specific requirements.

If you are planning to buy a new system or upgrade your existing one, you can get help through a number of resources. The Internet is your best bet for finding the most up-to-date pricing, power, and performance information. You also can find recommended systems through 3D workstation vendors such as SGI, Hewlett-Packard, or Intergraph. The graphics and computer industry is constantly changing, and if the price you find for a system is too high, just wait a few months and the costs will most likely decrease. However, you should not be too frugal when upgrading or purchasing a system. Be smart, but don't wait thinking that a new and faster processor will be out soon. There will always be a faster, cheaper, and stronger system. Inevitably, you could be waiting forever! Buy a good system, and start making great animations.

Video Memory

Don't think that because you have the latest processor on the market, or the fastest Mac available, you'll have the best computer for animation. Processing power is only one part of the computing process when it comes to creating with LightWave. Your system memory—in this case, 256MB of RAM or more—is very important to a productive system. However, your video memory is just as important.

Given LightWave 6's expansive interface enhancements, you should have a decent OpenGL-compatible video card with at least 32MB of RAM or more. LightWave's Modeler and Layout allow great control over viewports, shading, and interface color, all of which will rely heavily on your video memory. Not only can you model in full color in a perspective window, you also can see your texture maps, UV maps, specularity, and shading all in real time. Take advantage of the ridiculously inexpensive video cards available today and upgrade your system. Some recommended cards are the Oxygen VX1 from 3D Labs or the Matrox G400 Max, both of which are designed for 3D graphics and cost less than $300.

The Matrox G400 and the more expensive Evans & Sutherland Tornado support dual monitors from one computer. What this means is that you can have two monitors side by side with your information panels open on one, while you work on the other. Or, set up one monitor with Modeler and the other with Layout, the choice is yours. Other programs such as Adobe's Photoshop, In-Sync's Speed Razor, and NewTek's Aura can definitely benefit from a dual display. With a strong video card, you can move, rotate, and select with instant feedback and no delays. Primarily, you'll want a video card that is fully OpenGL compliant. Also, video cards change often, so be sure to check with NewTek about any new card recommendations the company may have.

Dual Monitors

LightWave 6's new nonmodal panels might not mean much to the single-monitor user. But, if you have installed a video card such as a Matrox G400 Max or, better yet, an Evans & Sutherland Tornado, you can take full advantage of the nonmodal feature. A nonmodal panel is one that can remain open while you work. For example, if you've ever worked in Adobe Photoshop, you can leave certain panels open while you work—for example, the brush panel. With a dual-monitor setup, you can open any of LightWave 6's panels and move them over to your second monitor, leaving the primary monitor full screen for optimal visibility. As you work, the panels are updated in real time. Ask your computer dealer for more information on dual-monitor setups.

 Note

Windows 2000 supports multiple monitors natively, so you may not need to invest in an expensive video card. Check with your system manufacturer and operating system developer for more details.

Words to Work By

It wasn't too long ago that most of you didn't even know what 3D animation was all about. Now, if you're one of the lucky ones, it's your hobby, or better, your livelihood. I've seen LightWave grow from a fun and cute little Amiga program to a rich, powerful, and robust animation package. Like many of you, my background in video and photography has helped me excel with LightWave to create the types of images I couldn't create in the real world. For others just starting out, you've come on board at a marvelous time. LightWave 6 is for all of you. We wrote this book to help you learn the nuances of LightWave 6, from its keyboard shortcuts to its powerful character animation and modeling tools. But more importantly, you'll gain a valuable resource for just about any project that comes across your desk with the information on these pages. Whether you are a continuing reader from my first two LightWave books, or are brand new to the game, welcome to *Inside LightWave [6]*.

Part I

Getting Started with LightWave 6

Chapter 1

Introducing LightWave 6

LightWave 6 has many new features and improvements. However, before you dig into those new features, take a quick look at the new user interface and the historical and architectural changes within the program. When you purchase LightWave 3D, you actually get two programs that NewTek calls Modeler and LightWave. For clarity, this book will refer to the two programs as Modeler and Layout.

Specifically, this chapter teaches you about:

- Layout's Graph Editor
- Layout's Groups
- The Layout Display Options Panel
- The Modeler Display Options Panel
- The Modeler General Options Panel
- Metaball Resolution
- Undo Levels

A Quick Look at Layout and Modeler

To start your relationship with LightWave 6, look at the two user interfaces: Layout and Modeler. Figure 1.1 shows Layout, and Figure 1.2 shows Modeler.

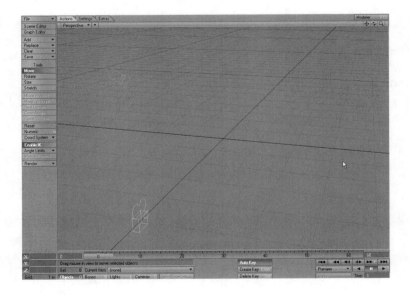

Figure 1.1   Layout at start up.

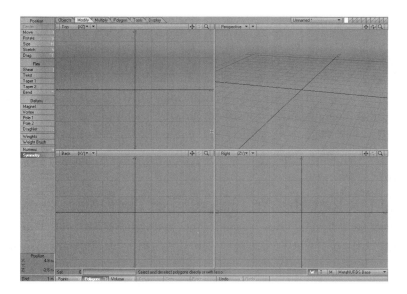

Figure 1.2   Modeler at start-up.

Note

When you purchase LightWave 3D, you actually get two programs that NewTek calls Modeler and LightWave. For clarity, this book will refer to the two programs as Modeler and Layout.

These interfaces may look similar to previous versions of LightWave, but don't let the similarities fool you—they are actually quite different. What's more is that the interfaces can look different than the ones pictured here. LightWave 6's interfaces are customizable and partially removable. Imagine working in a full frame shaded Perspective mode in Modeler, or using a Quad view in Layout—this is all possible. You learn how to customize interfaces in Chapter 3, "LightWave 6 Modeler," and Chapter 4, "LightWave 6 Layout."

A Brief Look at the History of LightWave

LightWave 6 is the program's third generation. The first generation of LightWave was available only on an Amiga computer bundled with a video card called the Video Toaster. That first generation of LightWave introduced 3D animation to an entirely new group of users who could not previously afford the technology.

The second generation of LightWave occurred with version 4.0 when NewTek modified the architecture of the program to work independently of the Video Toaster board as well as run identically on multiple platforms such as IBM PC, Macintosh, or Silicon Graphics. That second generation of LightWave also opened up the software to third-party developers with a plug-in architecture, greatly enhancing LightWave's position in the marketplace as well as strengthening its power by allowing small programs to be added on a user-by-user basis. These plug-ins included image filters for post-processing renders, particle systems, motion effects, and more.

A Brief Look at the Architecture of LightWave

When you install LightWave, you'll see multiple executable files in the LightWave\Programs\LightWave_Support directory, such as LightWav.exe (LightWave Layout), Modeler.exe (LightWave Modeler), and Hub.exe. The Hub program runs automatically when you start Modeler or Layout. Once running, you'll see a small icon in your taskbar on the Windows or Mac interface similar to an audio or system icon. When you right-click on this icon, you can launch it, or you can launch Layout or Modeler. The Hub is a link between Layout and Modeler.

In previous versions of LightWave, you had to use the Get and Put commands in Modeler to load and save objects from Layout. Now, the Hub automatically keeps information available in both programs. For example, you've loaded your scene into Layout. You realize that some objects you created need modification. Jump into Modeler (F12), and next to the Layers buttons on the top-right corner of the screen is a drop-down menu. This menu shows you the objects that are loaded in Layout. Select an object, adjust, and your object in Layout is modified. When you make an adjustment to your model, it is automatically updated in Layout. However, you also can use the Send Object to Layout command, found in Modeler under the Additional drop-down list.

Tip

Mac users: To simulate the right-click commands used in Windows, you need to hold down the Ctrl/Command key while you click the mouse button.

The Hub also allows you to monitor LightWave activities, including how many processes have occurred, how many times LightWave and Modeler have been launched, Memory Block Synchronization records, and File Asset Synchronization records. You have the option to choose how long the Hub runs, from 5 Minutes, 30 Minutes, 1 Hour, or Never. By default, Never is selected; you do not need to set any of these options for LightWave or Modeler to run. You also can set an Automatic Save from the Hub properties.

NewTek, Inc. has been working on this version of LightWave since the release of version 5.5. The company has rewritten the software from the ground up and has established a significant programming force. NewTek still listens to user requests, and the feedback is reflected in the functionality and customization of this robust new version. Of particular value are these changes:

- Customizable interfaces
- Groupable interfaces
- Multiple viewport configurations
- Shortcut navigation
- Redesigned panels

The sections that follow discuss these architectural changes.

Customizable Interfaces

The user interface is at first the most noticeable change. With completely configurable buttons and toolbars, and an updated look, both Layout and Modeler are streamlined but offer enhanced workflow. Once again, NewTek, Inc. has kept to its original workflow pattern and not succumbed to nonsensical icons. The buttons are still clearly named but now are even easier to access. Toolbars are customizable and can be moved to the left or right side of the screen or hidden completely for maximum visibility. Figure 1.1 shows Layout's toolbar at startup, and Figure 1.3 shows a customized version of the toolbar.

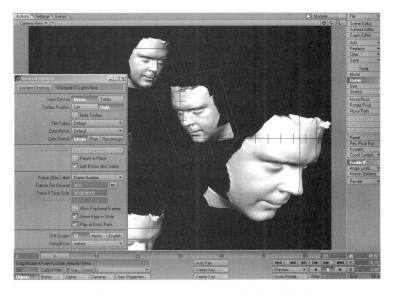

Figure 1.3   Layout's toolbar has been moved to the right side of the interface.

Tip

Pressing F1 in Layout brings up the Configure Keys menu. You can assign a key (such as F3) to Hide Toolbar On/Off.

Groupable Interfaces

Not only are the toolbars customizable, you can customize or create your own groupings. Imagine starting up LightWave and seeing only the tools you use. Figure 1.4 shows the three default Menu Groups in Layout on startup and two additional customized Menu Groups.

Figure 1.4   Menu Groups can be customized and new Menu Groups can be created to house just the specific tools you need.

Warning

To ensure you can follow the exercises and projects in this book, please use the default program settings for all groups and menus unless otherwise specified.

Multiple Viewport Configurations

The new Layout and Modeler offer more to you than simple customization. You also can work in any interface, in any mode such as Wireframe, Sketch, or even Smooth Shaded. Figure 1.5 shows Layout with multiple independent views.

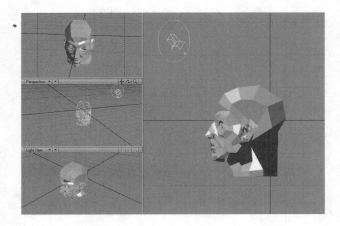

Figure 1.5   Layout now supports multiple independent viewports.

Viewports (or quadrants) in Modeler have multiple configurations and can have varying modes, such as Wireframe, Sketch, Weight Shade, and more. Access these modes by selecting your choice from the drop-down list in the Viewport title bar. Turn on the Viewport title bar through the Display Options panel (press the **d** key). Figure 1.6 shows the LightWave 6 Modeler with its four viewports reconfigured with various modes set to each view.

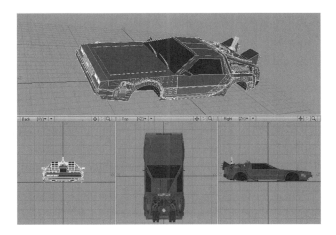

Figure 1.6   The viewports in this configuration of Modeler have a different mode set to each view.

   Note

> The capability to have multiple configurations in both Layout and Modeler means that you can make each viewport different. Each viewport's varying mode is its render style, such as Wireframe, Sketch, Smooth Shaded, and so on.

Don't let the similarities between LightWave 6 and previous versions of the software fool you. The new user interface of LightWave 6 has much more to it than meets the eye. Over the years, NewTek has taken some heat for having two separate programs, Layout and Modeler, rather than one combined interface. By developing the Hub as the link and giving Layout and Modeler similar tools (such as the Surface Editor), NewTek has made LightWave easier to use. Having two programs allows your system resources to be better utilized and keeps the interface clutter to a minimum.

Shortcut Navigation

Part of the power to reconfigure your user interface also includes the capability to hide all tools and access the commands through mouse and keyboard strokes. To hide the tools and reduce interface clutter, follow these quick steps:

1. Open Layout and press the **o** key to access the General Options panel.
2. Click Hide Toolbar to leave the Layout Interface visible.
3. Close the Options panel.
4. To access any of the buttons you've just hidden, hold down both the Control and Shift keys, and click the left mouse button.

You will see a list of the file commands, such as Load Scene, Save Scene, and actions such as Load Object, Save Object, and so on.

Holding down the Control and Shift keys while clicking the right mouse button gives you access to window commands such as Scene Editor or Graph Editor. Holding down the Control and Shift keys also functions with the middle mouse button to access the Command History.

Using the mouse to access the hidden tools may take some time getting used to, but the payoff is an uncluttered user interface.

Redesigned Panels

Besides the customizable Menu Groups, or the easily configured viewports, the panels have been redesigned throughout the program as well. The panels in LightWave are the information areas you'll access often to control item properties, such as light or camera settings. You can have many panels open at once, which is where dual monitors come in handy. Figure 1.7 shows the new Surface Editor panel, which looks similar to the other panels throughout the program, and is identical in both Modeler and Layout. Chapter 2, "LightWave 6 Surface Editor," is dedicated to enlightening you on the functionality of the new Surface Editor. If you take a look at Figure 1.8, you can see many panels open at once. You don't need to close a panel to see its effect on your item in Layout. This is beneficial for adjusting surfaces, or editing motions in the Graph Editor covered in Chapter 5, "LightWave 6 Graph Editor."

Figure 1.7   Layout's Surface Editor panel. The panels throughout LightWave 6 are similar in design and functionality.

Note

In addition to keeping multiple panels open when you're using dual monitors, you also can keep them open during rendering.

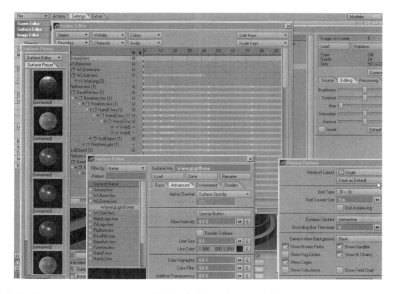

Figure 1.8   Layout now supports multiple independent panels.

While the new panel design throughout the program appears streamlined, panels are more functional than ever before. As you read on through this book, you'll discover how intuitive this new design truly is.

Notable Enhancements to Layout

Layout has many enhancements that can help you streamline your creative process.

Graph Editor

The Graph Editor within LightWave's Layout has always been the black sheep of the program. Figure 1.9 shows the new Graph Editor expanded to full screen.

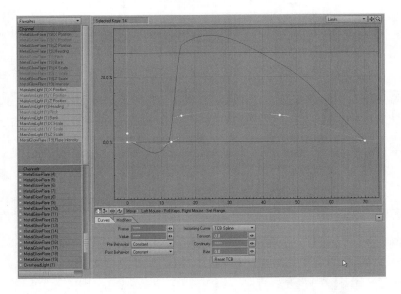

Figure 1.9   LightWave's new Graph Editor is your new best friend.

With the new Graph Editor, you'll have more control over your motions than you'll know what to do with. Keyframes can be copied, pasted, and modified in a variety of ways. You can store sets of keyframes for use in other projects. You can adjust or set offsets by dragging entire groups of keyframes.

The new Graph Editor supports multiple curve types in a single animation channel, such as TCB (Tension, Continuity, and Bias), Hermite, Bézier, Linear, and Stepped. A multiple curve evaluation and modification function has been added so you have control over dissimilar items. For example, you simultaneously can view and edit any curve in a scene. With an interactive cut and paste of keyframes, you can adjust any keyframe within the scene with little time and effort. LightWave 6's Graph Editor is resizable so you can expand the window to full screen for maximum visibility. As you update your curves in the Graph Editor, your changes happen in real time in Layout. Are you thinking about setting up a dual monitor system now?

Figure 1.10
Three tabs sit atop LightWave's Layout interface. They incorporate all the program's controls.

Don't worry about how complex this new area of LightWave is; we'll discuss the Graph Editor in detail and step you through some tutorials in Chapter 5. You'll be up to speed in no time.

Groups

Layout's new design is definitely confusing at first. If you're familiar with a previous version of LightWave, you'll see that many of the controls buried within panels are now easily accessible from the left side of the screen. The many panel buttons across the top of the interface, such as Objects, Images, Options, and so on, have been simplified. You now have three default tabs, which are called groups, and are labeled Actions, Settings, and Extras, as seen in Figure 1.10.

Rearranging the groups and the tools within them can help you bring up a setting that is buried deep in the default interface, such as a generic plug-in. You can create your own groups, and assign just the controls and functions you like to that group. For example, try the following:

1. Start LightWave Layout, or clear your current scene from the drop-down File menu at the top-left side of the screen.

2. Press **F2**. You'll see the Configure Menus panel, as in Figure 1.11.

The left column of the panel is home to the commands, or functions, and the right column, the menus. Commands that are ghosted are already assigned to a menu or group; commands that are bold, are not. Take a close look at the right column. The first item listed is Main Menu. These are the group tabs along the top of the Layout interface: Actions, Settings, and Extras.

3. Create your own group tab by selecting Actions and clicking the New Group button on the right side of the Configure Menu panel. You'll see that a line labeled New Group now sits between Actions and Settings.

4. Select it, and click Rename. Rename it to whatever you like. Click OK, and you'll see the new group tab appear on the top of the Layout interface. You can rearrange the groups by simply clicking and dragging them—you'll see a small line appear as a guide.

What will appear strange after you create your group is the blank area on the left side of the screen. Figure 1.12 shows the Layout interface with a new group created, but no commands.

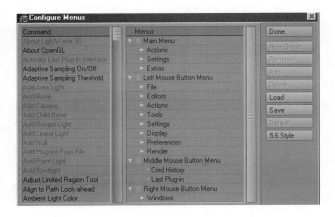

Figure 1.11   The Configure Menus panel pops up when you press F2.

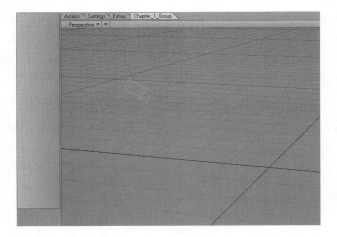

Figure 1.12   A new group now lives with the others at the top of the LightWave Layout, but has no commands, as you can see by the large blank area on the left side of the interface.

You need to assign some commands to the group that you've just created. You can do this by first pressing **F2** on the keyboard, then selecting a command in the left column (your desired Group in the right column), and then clicking Add. Or, you can drag a command to the menu window. Instantly, you'll see the command on the left side of the interface, at the top.

Note

At any time, you can always press **F2** to call up the Configure Menus panel, and click Default to return to LightWave's default Grouping configuration.

Creating a group is only one way to customize your Layout interface. You also can reconfigure the interface by adding or removing commands from existing groups and menus. In the right column of the Configure Menus panel, you'll see a small white triangle before each group. Clicking this expands the group, allowing you to see the commands set for each. You can add, remove, or even rename any one of these. Also, you can save and load different configurations as you like. Click around, create new groups, and don't worry; you can always click Default to return to your original configuration.

Note

These grouping instructions apply to LightWave Modeler as well, but not by pressing **F2**. Configure menus in Modeler by selecting the Objects tab, and selecting Edit Menu Layout from the Preferences drop-down menu.

Enhanced Layout Display Options Panel

Pressing the **d** key in both Modeler and Layout brings up the Display Options panel, shown in Figure 1.13.

The Display Options panel allows you to adjust, activate, or deactivate settings for LightWave Layout's appearance. At the top of the panel, you can tell Layout what the Viewport should look like, such as a single panel or quad view. You also can set your favorite Viewport Layout as a default so the next time you start LightWave, your settings will be applied. Figure 1.14 shows the drop-down menu choices for Viewport Layout settings.

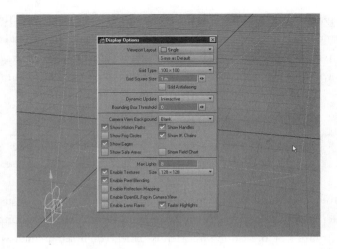

Figure 1.13   Pressing the **d** key in Layout brings up the Display Options panel.

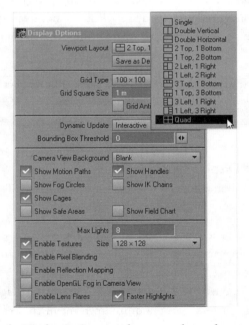

Figure 1.14   Within the Display Options panel, you can choose from many Viewport Layout options.

Camera View Background

A simple but notable new Display Options feature in LightWave 6 has to do with the Camera view Background in Layout. When you are in Camera view mode in Layout, you tell LightWave to show a Blank background, a Colored Background, an Image, or a LightWave preview file. These settings are handy for compositing, text and logo placement, or simple reference.

You have the option of seven check boxes for additional view properties. Show Motion Paths shows a visible line representing the motion of an object, light, or camera. Show Fog Circles shows a visual representation of the fog radius settings. Show Cages shows the SubPatch cages of your objects. Show Safe Areas and Field Chart are visible only when in Camera view. The other settings can be used in the top, side, or front views.

Note

LightWave 6 allows you to load SubPatch objects directly into Layout. You no longer need to change the objects (or freeze the curves) into polygons.

Show Safe Areas adds two rounded squares to the Camera view. These represent a video safe area (outer line) and a title safe area (inner line). Safe areas are a valuable reference when setting up animations for video or broadcast. Show Handles displays the position, size, and rotation handles on items in the viewport that you can drag. Show IK Chains displays a thin dotted line in Layout, which represents the relative setup of your Inverse Kinematics chain. Figure 1.15 shows a wireframe view of a simple IK robotic arm with Show Handles and Show IK Chains turned on.

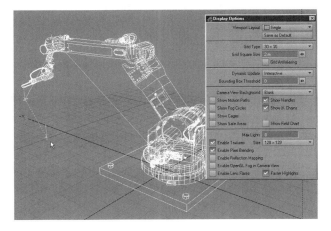

Figure 1.15   Setting Show Handles and Show IK Chains on an Inverse Kinematics setup helps control each element's movements and direction during an animation.

When you select Show Handles, and you select Move for the object, you'll see three arrows—one green, one blue, and one red—extending from the specific selection. You'll notice this throughout LightWave 6. These colored handles will vary in shape depending on if you select rotate or size. The green arrow that points upward is pointing toward the positive Y axis. Clicking and dragging it limits the selected items' motions to Y-axis movements only. Similarly, clicking and dragging on the blue arrow (which points toward positive Z) limits movements to just the Z axis. The red arrow points toward the positive X axis, and limits movements to just the X axis. This is very helpful and time-saving, compared to previous versions of LightWave in which you needed to lock and unlock the certain axes you wanted to work with. If you want to have free movement in all axes, you can click on the center yellow pivot point of the joined arrows. Figure 1.16 shows a simple null object with move handles showing.

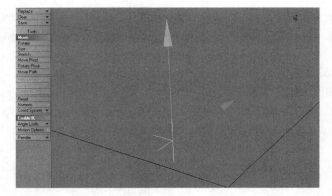

Figure 1.16   Selecting Move for any Layout item displays handles for axis control.

Like the handles that appear for movement of a Layout item, rotation handle will appear as well. Figure 1.17 shows the same null object when Rotate is selected. Clicking and dragging on the colored circular handles limits its axis rotations.

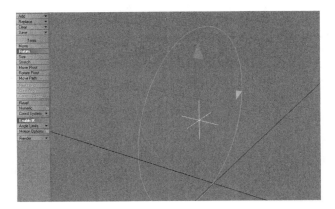

Figure 1.17   Selecting Rotate for any Layout item displays round handles for axis control.

Grid Types

Within the Display Options panel, you can change the Grid Type, Grid Square Size, and set the Grid Antialiasing. Grid Type allows you to increase the size of the visible grid in Layout. This is handy for larger scenes such as landscapes, cityscapes, or space shots. Grid Square Size sets the individual grid square. For example, the default Grid Square Size is 1m. This means that every square within the visible Grid in Layout is 1 meter is size. This is extremely important when it comes to modeling, setting up surfaces, camera shots, and more. You'll reference the Grid Square Size throughout the tutorials in this book. Clicking on Grid Antialiasing eliminates the jagged lines often associated with the grid lines farther from view in Layout.

More Display Options

Because LightWave 6 is essentially two programs, Modeler and Layout, users often confuse the function of each program. LightWave 6 integrates the two programs more than any previous version, yet each has very different functions.

The Modeler portion of LightWave is where you create and build your models. You now have full access to the Surface Editor in Modeler as well! The Layout portion of LightWave is where you set up your scene. Setting up a scene not only requires that your objects are in place, but that lights, textures, and atmospheres are set as well. Typically, you have to render a frame or two to see many of these settings. LightWave 6 Layout gives you the option to turn on OpenGL Textures (from the Display Options panel, press **d**) in your Camera view to see how your textures are being applied. Setting the Size (from the drop-down menu) tells LightWave the resolution to display textures.

Note

Enabling Textures within the Display Options panel in Layout and setting a specific size has no bearing on your final render. This size setting is for display purposes only. The resolution of the textures when rendered depends on the initial resolution of the image map. This applies to all the OpenGL display options as well.

You also can Enable Reflection Mapping in Layout to view reflections on your object above 50%. If you have fog added to a scene, Enable OpenGL Fog in Camera View turns on visible fog in Layout—a great timesaver. Enable Lens Flares allows you to see your lens flare settings in real time. You'll also see a button called Faster Highlights, which speeds up the quality of the Layout display, but might slow down the system.

If you're working with OpenGL-shaded objects in Layout, it's handy to see how the lights in your scene are working. Within the Display Options panel, you can tell LightWave to display up to eight lights when using OpenGL. However, you might have more than eight lights in a scene, perhaps twelve. In each light's properties settings, you can set Affect OpenGL, essentially telling Layout which light to use for OpenGL previews.

Note

As a rule, the Layout display settings for OpenGL Textures, OpenGL Reflection Mapping, and so on, are only approximations. You should get in the habit of test rendering everything before you commit to a final render.

Dynamic Update

In the center of the Display Options panel is a drop-down menu labeled Dynamic Update. Here, you can tell Layout to update interactively, with a delay, or not at all. Dynamic Update offers more control to you as an animator. If you are working with a strong computer system, a decent amount of system memory (RAM), and a powerful video card, setting Dynamic Update to Interactive will show you your panel changes instantly. For example, if you have the Surface Editor panel open and change the color of a surface on an object, you'll see the change right away. If your system resources are limited, having Interactive set might make panel adjustments sluggish. With a more sluggish response, change your Dynamic Update setting to Delayed, which will not update Layout until you finish making changes within the panels. Or, you simply can turn this feature off. By doing so, your Layout display will update after any open panels are closed.

Bounding Box Threshold

A key Layout component is the Bounding Box Threshold. LightWave, by default, creates a bounding box, or bounding region to represent your object. Setting this value tells Layout when to draw bounding boxes for your objects and when not to. If you create an object that is 6500 polygons and need to see your texture placement in real time, set a Bounding Box Threshold value of 6501. Any object that is less than 6501 points or polygons will not be displayed by a bounding box and remain solid. Any object made up of more than 6501 points or polygons will be displayed by a bounding box when selected and adjusted. The value here is just an example and will vary depending on your models. Keep in mind that if your object is large in size, setting a larger Bounding Box value will slow down your system.

You can determine what Bounding Box Value to set by selecting the particular object in Layout, and pressing the **w** key. This brings up the selected object statistics panel. With the current object selected, you can press the **p** key to call up the Object Properties panel to see its values.

Note

Often, the best way to work is with a Bounding Box Threshold set to 0. This gives you very quick feedback and redraw speeds in Layout.

Notable Enhancements to Modeler

This section guides you through the many options and setup features available in LightWave 6 Modeler. You'll learn that having the capability to customize the interface is a great asset to your creative workflow. As you work through this book, you can refer to this section as a reminder.

The Modeler Display Options Panel

With the enhancements to each LightWave interface, you will find similar functions in each. Pressing the **d** key in Layout brings up the Layout Display Options panel as previously discussed. The **d** key in Modeler also brings up the Display Options panel. This area allows you to set up and configure your Modeler interface. Figure 1.18 shows the Modeler Display Options panel.

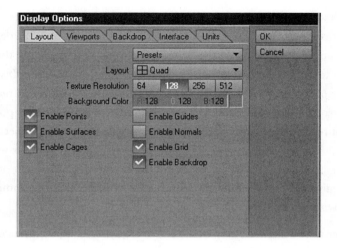

Figure 1.18   Pressing the **d** key in Modeler brings up the enhanced Modeler Display Options panel. Here the Layout tab is selected, referring to Modeler's Layout views, not to be confused with the Layout portion of LightWave.

This panel gives you complete control over Modeler's appearance, viewports, backdrop, interface, and the units of measurement. When the panel comes up, you'll see five tabs labeled Layout, Viewport, Backdrop, Interface, and Units.

Layout Tab

As a default, the Layout tab is selected. Here, you can set the initial layout of Modeler, such as a quad view, single view, double vertical, and more. Figure 1.19 shows the Layout drop-down selections from which you can choose.

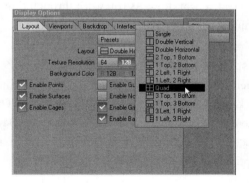

Figure 1.19   The Layout drop-down menu within Modeler's Display Options panel lets you select from many Viewport Layout options just like LightWave's Layout.

Directly above this drop-down menu is a preset drop-down menu. This menu allows you to choose presets for your Modeler's layout, such as a Quad Logo (XY) view, which puts the XY or Back view in the bottom-left quad; the XZ or the Top view in the upper-left quad; and the ZY or Right view in the bottom-right quad. These were default settings in previous versions of LightWave, where Back view was called Face, and the Right view was called Left. The upper-right quad is a preview or perspective view. Experiment with the presets to see some different configurations. Two important groups of options on this tab are

- **Texture Resolution.** These options let you set the resolution of surface textures visible in Modeler. This resolution setting is helpful for creating objects on images where there is fine detail. Setting a higher resolution here shows finer detail, but it will use up more system resources.

- **Background Color.** These options let you change the Background Color for all viewports. If you're an experienced LightWave Modeler, you know that always working in a wireframe mode can sometimes slow you down. When you set any viewport in LightWave 6 to a shade mode, such as wireframe shade or smooth shade, you now will see the background color. This option is simple, but gives you the control you need to model better and faster.

More Display Options

Among the Layout tab options within the Modeler Display Options panel are seven additional selections. You have seven choices for greater control over your Modeler setup. Remembering that this is the Display Options panel, you have the choice to Enable Points, Enable Surfaces, or Enable Cages, which are all display functions. Selecting or deselecting any of these settings will show the change in each Modeler view.

When working with a complex SubPatched model, you can deselect the Enable Surfaces option, which shows only the SubPatch cage. These Display options are visibility options that, depending on the model at hand, you may decide to use. Additionally, you can set Enable Guides, which will help you see and work with your SubPatch cage better. Note that the more complex your model is, the less likely it is that you would use this function as it might clutter your view. However, because this feature is independent of the cage, you can turn off Show Cages and work with just the guides to shape your model. The choice is yours! Within the Display Options panel, you can turn the grid on or off for better visibility, use Enable Normals to see in which direction your surface is facing, and also use Enable Backdrop to view backdrop images.

Note
SubPatch will be discussed throughout the modeling chapters in this book. Chapter 3 will get you started.

At first, the multiple options available to you throughout Modeler and Layout might be overwhelming, but as you work through models and projects, you'll come to appreciate their control.

Viewports Tab

The second tab option available to you within the Modeler Display Options panel controls the viewports. While previous versions of LightWave Modeler didn't allow for much variation, LightWave 6 Modeler gives you independent viewport control. Figure 1.20 shows the Display Options panel with the Viewports tab selected.

Note
Settings within the Viewports tab can override the global settings on the Layout tab, such as the Enable commands.

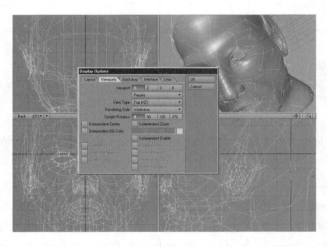

Figure 1.20 The Viewports tab in the Display Options panel allows for independent control over your viewports.

When working with a quad layout and the Viewports tab is selected, you'll see four selections across the top numbered clockwise from the top-left viewport: 1, 2, 3, and 4. These represent Viewport 1, the upper-left quadrant; Viewport 2, the upper-right quadrant; Viewport 3, the lower-left quadrant; and Viewport 4, the lower-right quadrant. You can customize each viewport in this area. Try it yourself by following these steps. When not using a quad layout mode, names will be given to each viewport.

1. In LightWave Modeler, press the **d** key to call up the Display Options panel. Then, select the Viewports tab.

2. Select the first Viewport button, labeled 1. This controls the upper-left quadrant, which until LightWave 6, was typically the Top (XZ) view only.

   You can choose a preset for this quadrant from the drop-down menu list, or set up a customized viewport.

3. The third selection area from the top in the Viewport tab is the View Type selection. Use this area to choose if the selected quadrant will be a Top (XZ) view, Bottom (XZ) view, or a perspective view. Choose Perspective view.

Tip

If you choose to set the current viewport to any of the orthogonal view types (Bottom XZ, Left ZY), the Upright Rotation options appear. Use these to rotate your view 90, 180, or 270 degrees. This is helpful for visual control depending on the model at hand.

4. Next, tell LightWave Modeler what Rendering Style to make the viewport. The choices are Wireframe, Wireframe Shade, Smooth Shade, Sketch, Flat Shade, Weight Shade, and Texture. Set the current viewport to Smooth Shade.

Experiment with different options and different views. You will find that as your projects change, you'll appreciate the flexibility of configuring each viewport. But there is more control here for you to investigate.

Note

If you have Viewport Titles selected from the Interface tab, you can change the View Type and Rendering Styles directly in each viewport.

Independent Controls

There are more controls for each viewport than just the visuals listed previously. LightWave Modeler now understands independent control over each viewport. You have the choice of setting Independent Zoom, Independent Center, Independent Background Color, and Independent Control over your layout visuals listed earlier, such as Enable Guides, Enable Surfaces, and so on. With Independent settings enabled, such as Independent Zoom, you can specifically control keyboard commands by placing the mouse pointer in the specific view. If Independent Zoom is active, and you press the period (.) key, only the current viewport will zoom. If you move the mouse pointer outside of this independent-enabled view, the zoom function will apply to all views as it normally does. As you work, you'll discover what settings work best for you, whether only select viewports are independent, wireframe, shaded, and so forth.

The Backdrop Tab

Next on the list of tabs within the Modeler Display Options panel is the Backdrop tab. Figure 1.21 shows the selection.

Figure 1.21   The Backdrop tab within the Display Options panel allows you to load images to be placed in each viewport.

The Backdrop panel is straightforward. It allows you to load an image, and select in which viewport it will be seen. You would do this if, for example, you had to build a 3D logo from artwork, or needed to create a character from an artist's sketch. Within this panel, you can adjust the brightness and contrast and set the size and image resolution. You'll use this feature later in Chapter 3.

The Interface Tab

The Interface tab has a few key functions for your working Modeler environment. This is the place to tell Modeler if you're using a mouse or tablet input device. You also can select the position of your toolbar—the right or left side of the screen. You also can turn off the toolbar, increasing Modeler's screen visibility.

The Interface tab has a few more options. These options, however, are often set and left alone.

- **Viewport Titles.** This feature should be on all the time. Having it on displays each viewport's ViewType and Rendering Style at all times. This means that you can quickly and easily change your perspective window from Smooth Shaded to

Wireframe, or make it a Top view with Smooth Shaded, and so on. Having
Viewport Titles on saves a lot of time by eliminating the need to go deep into
panels and menus to make interface changes.

- **VBFileRequester.** A nice enhancement to LightWave 6 is a varied File Dialog
  requester. Figure 1.22 shows the default file requester for a Windows-based system. Figure 1.23 shows the new VBFileRequester option, using a more robust
  selection method.

Note

When using the VBFileRequester, you can choose to view your files as a list, or as icons,
making navigation and selection fast and easy.

Figure 1.22   The Interface tab within the Display Options panel offers the choice of a standard file requester, pictured here, when loading an object.

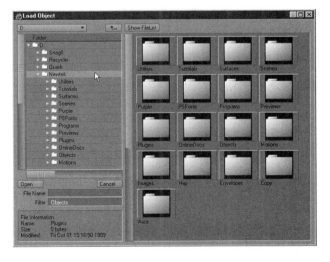

Figure 1.23   In addition to the default file requester, LightWave 6 offers a newer, visually
enhanced file requester.

Tip

When using the new VBFileRequester in Modeler, you can resize the window for better visibility. Additionally, you can choose from a file view or icon view. What's better, when using the VBFileRequester, you can hold down the Shift key to load multiple objects into Modeler. Further, right-click for additional controls.

- **LW_ColorPicker.** Along the lines of a newer file requester, you also can use the LightWave color picker instead of your system's standard color picker. This setting also is found within the Interface tab in the Display Options panel. Figure 1.24 shows a default Windows color picker, while Figure 1.25 shows the new LW_ColorPicker option.

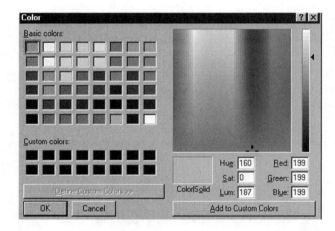

Figure 1.24   The default Windows color picker is available to you through the Interface tab in the Display Options panel.

Figure 1.25   LightWave's new color picker offers much more control over the type of selection, such as this Quick Color view for instant RGB or HSV color values.

The LW_ColorPicker offers the Quick Color picker as shown in Figure 1.25, or an HSV to RGB visual selector. In addition, you have the choice of Tint & Shade, Wavelength, or Kelvin. Using Kelvin as a color picker allows you to put in the degree of a Kelvin temperature, such as the sun, which is 6000 degrees Kelvin, or in technical terms, "really hot." This is an excellent way to match real-world lighting. Figure 1.26 shows the Kelvin color selection.

 Tip

The color selection appears when you choose to edit colors from the Surface Editor or the Background Color from the Display Options panel.

Figure 1.26   Using the new LW_ColorPicker, you can choose to set colors in degrees Kelvin to match real-world light temperatures.

 Note

Chapter 2 will give step-by-step instructions for the new color selection options.

- **Color Format.** The final option available to you in the Interface tab within the Display Options panel is the Color Format selection. You can choose between Integer, Float, or Percentage options. These functions allow you even greater control over the way Modeler handles your color selection. This color format changes the RGB/HSV color units, and is shared through the Hub.

The Units Tab

Throughout this book, you'll be instructed to set specific measurements, and you'll be asked to refer to the Grid size often. To set up your Modeler with a unit of measurement, you can select the Units tab in the Display Options panel (see Figure 1.27).

The Units tab is important for you to understand. First, you have the choice of selecting a Unit System of measurement. This is Metric, English, or SI measurement. SI is the System International unit of measurement that is the recommended default setting. This measurement system uses microns, millimeters, meters, kilometers, and mega meters. You can choose any of these as your Default Unit as well. As you begin the tutorials later in the book, you'll be instructed which default unit to use.

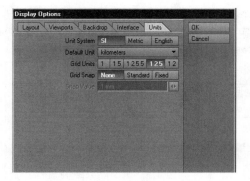

Figure 1.27   The Units tab within the Display Options panel is where you set your system measurements.

You also can set the Grid Units in this tab area. You'll see settings of 1, 1 5, 1 2.5 5, 1 2 5, and 1 2. These settings refer to the way your grid increases or decreases when zooming in or out. If you set the Grid Unit to 1 5, for example, when you zoom in, your Modeler grid squares will increase by 1, then 5, then by 1 again, and so on. Lastly, you can define the Grid Snap as None, Standard, or Fixed. This is used for controlling your mouse movements while moving or dragging points and polygons. If you have a Fixed value set, you can enter a setting of 1mm, for example. Dragging a point around in Modeler would make the point snap in place every 1mm. Use this setting for more precise modeling.

 Tip

If you are modeling more organic objects, such as a character, you should turn the Grid Snap off. Having this on will hinder your control when shaping your curves by not allowing you to precisely position selections.

The Modeler General Options Panel

Earlier in this chapter, the General Options panel in Layout was discussed. Pressing the **o** key in Layout brings up the panel that allows you to change various settings for your Layout workflow. While you'll visit the General Options in Layout often, you'll only use the General Options in Modeler to set a few key options. Figure 1.28 shows the General Options panel. Pressing **o** in Modeler also calls up this panel.

Figure 1.28   The General Options panel in Modeler gives you access to initial polygon creation values, curve divisions, as well as the Content Directory similar to Layout.

Polygons

The Polygons selection allows you to tell Modeler what type of polygons you would like to create, such as quadrangles or triangles. This is good for creating primitive shapes. As a recommended rule for this book, work with quadrangles. The reason for this is because you can always turn a quadrangle into a triangle by using the Triple command. You cannot turn triangles into quadrangles. Also, you will have much better control over the shape and contour of your models in LightWave by working with quadrangles. Quadrangles are simply polygons that are made up of four points. Triangles are made up of three points. You also can set this to Automatic, and Modeler will generate the necessary polygons depending on your model.

The other options within the General Options panel are usually set once and most of your modeling is done with these variables. Try making a few objects with various settings to see the differences.

- **Flatness Limit.** When polygons are created, they have a general flatness to them. The Flatness Limit is the minimum angle before a polygon is considered non-planar. You can change the value of this through the Flatness Limit option. In most cases, this value stays at its default of 0.5%.

- **Surface.** Each time you create polygons in Modeler, whether it's from points, extrusions, or text, a default surface is applied. This default surface is typically slate gray, and named default. If you choose, you can set a specific name to all default surfaces. Within the Change Surface dialog box **q**, you can make a default from any existing surface. You can find the Change Surface button under the Polygons tab. This default name will be applied to any unnamed surfaces. However, it's a good idea to leave this setting named "default" for clarity. If you decide to be clever and name your default surface something like "AlphaBeta," you can easily confuse things later when you add multiple surfaces.

Curve Divisions

When you build curves in Modeler for objects such as Rail Extrusions, you can set an initial Curve Division. As a common value, the Curve Division is left at Medium, but you also have the choice of Coarse or Fine. Depending on the complexity of your spline curve, you can set this value to increase or decrease smoothness of the curve.

Patch Divisions

This is the one area of the General Options panel that you will access regularly. When building objects with SubPatch (which will be discussed further in Chapter 3), you need to set the Patch Divisions. A SubPatch smoothes an object by subdividing the selected polygons. The Patch Division determines the amount of subdivision. Each region or patch of an object will be subdivided by the value you set in the General Options panel for Patch Division. For example, a Patch Division value of 4 will subdivide one selected polygon four times. A typical setting is about 3 or 4. The lower the value, the less smooth your object will be. The higher the value, the smoother and more complex your model will be. Patch Division also affects the smoothing you see in viewport displays.

 Tip

LightWave 6 can load SubPatched objects into Layout for animating. There are two Patch Division settings in Layout as well, which can greatly help workflow. This feature allows you to set a Display SubPatch Level, which can be a low value to help save system resources. You can set a Render SubPatch Level for rendering for smoother objects. These settings can be set to any level.

Metaball Resolution

LightWave 6 has a powerful new creation method called Metaballs. Yes, there were Metaballs in previous versions of Modeler, but not like this. One tip for using Metaballs is to see what HyperVoxels will look like. HyperVoxels, discussed later in the book, only display when rendered. Metaballs appear in OpenGL. These Metaballs are interactive and definitely much more powerful. You can set a Metaball resolution in the Data Options panel. The default value is 10.0, but you can increase this value for smoother, cleaner Metaball shapes. Be sure to read more about Metaballs in Chapter 3.

Undo Levels

Undo Levels is a control that you really don't need to set. Having the option to set undo levels is handy, but often not necessary. For example, why would you set an undo level of 5? What if you need to undo something you did 6 or 7 steps back? Set this value to a high value and leave it. You never know when you'll need all the undo levels available to you.

Note
You can set a maximum undo of 128.

Content Directory

If you're an experienced LightWave animator, you are familiar with the Content Directory in Layout. LightWave 6 now adds the Content directory to Modeler. It tells LightWave where to look for scenes, objects, images, and any other necessary content. Now that Modeler directly integrates with Layout, and that you have complete surfacing control in Modeler, you need to set up a Content Directory. You only need to set the Content Directory once for both Modeler and Layout, as the Hub will update both programs for you.

The Next Step

When preparing to create, a last bit of advice is to be comfortable. Yes, it's been said before, but it is something that is often overlooked by animators and employers. 3D animation is one of the hottest growing markets in the world, from kiosks to video games, to television and movies. It is a very creative industry and as any creative person knows, the surroundings and mood you are in play a key role in your creative success.

So, turn off the awful overhead fluorescent lights, adjust your chair so you're not hunched over your keyboard, grab a cool drink, and head on into Chapter 2.

Summary

You've just been through the key preparation and configuration you'll need to get rolling in LightWave 6 Layout and Modeler. The similarity between the two programs will help you greatly, even when it comes to keyboard commands.

Chapter 2

LightWave 6
Surface Editor

What was the first thing that piqued your interest in 3D? Was it a movie? Maybe it was a video game. Perhaps you took a class in school or a friend or colleague

introduced you to 3D. Whichever the case may be, it is often the realism of 3D animation that is so eye-catching. Realism in 3D is created by two key factors, lighting and surfacing. Both of these factors play an extremely important role throughout your 3D
creations, and they will help bring your animations to life.

This chapter introduces you to LightWave 6's Surface Editor. Specifically, it covers the
following:

- Organizing surfaces
- Setting up surfaces
- Working with image map references on surfaces

If you are familiar with the Surface Editor in previous versions of LightWave, you'll find
the new Surface Editor quite different. Figure 2.1 shows the Surface Editor interface at
startup.

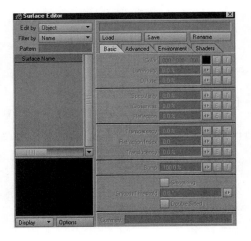

Figure 2.1   LightWave 6's Surface Editor at startup.

LightWave 6's Surface Editor is a smart addition to the software. In previous versions of
LightWave, the process of setting up surfaces for your models began when building the
models, in Modeler. But, you could only make basic surface changes in Modeler. From
there, you needed to apply any image maps or procedural textures in Layout. Essentially,
the real surfacing was always done in Layout. Now with LightWave 6 you have the choice
of using the Surface Editor in either Modeler or Layout. It's the same panel in both programs, so this chapter applies to both Modeler and Layout.

To find the Surface Editor in Modeler, go to the Objects tab at the top of the interface. From there, the Surface Editor button is the fifth button from the top on the left side of the interface (see Figure 2.2).

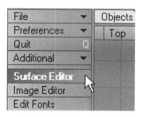

Figure 2.2
LightWave 6's Surface Editor can be accessed through the Objects tab in Modeler.

To access the Surface Editor in Layout, either select the Settings tab or the Actions tab at the top of the interface, and you'll see the Surface Editor button on the left side of the interface, three buttons down (see Figure 2.3).

 Tip

Using the Surface Editor in Modeler does not give you access to a new feature in LightWave 6 called VIPER (Versatile Interactive Preview Render, discussed in detail later in this chapter). So for major surfacing projects, use the Surface Editor in Layout and take advantage of VIPER.

 Note

Remember that LightWave 6 enables you to completely customize the user interfaces in both Modeler and Layout. However, you should be working with the LightWave default Configure Keys (F1) and Menu Layout settings throughout this book.

Figure 2.3
LightWave 6's Surface Editor can be accessed through the Settings tab in Layout.

Using the Surface Editor

As you begin to explore and use the Surface Editor either in Layout or Modeler, you should be familiar with the new features. Many enhancements have been made to make surfacing your objects easier.

Organizing Surfaces

The Surface Editor makes it easy for you to manage your surfaces. Figure 2.4 shows the Surface Editor with an object loaded that has multiple surfaces.

If you enter the Surface Editor after a scene has been loaded, the scene's surface names are listed alphabetically, as you can see in Figure 2.4. The Surface Name list enables you to easily manage your surfaces by grouping individual surfaces as a drop-down list from each object. Clicking on the small triangle next to the object name expands the list, showing the surfaces associated with that object. Figure 2.5 shows the same scene as in Figure 2.4, but with a surface of the first object selected.

Figure 2.4 The Surface Editor allows you to manage your surfaces easily, either by Object name or Scene selection. You also can Filter your surface names for organization.

When you drop down a surface list of an object, your surface settings won't be available, such as color, diffusion, or texture maps, until you click on a surface name. You must select one of the surfaces in the list before you can begin to work with it. When you select a surface, you see the surface properties change. Working with a hierarchy like this is extremely productive, enabling you to quickly access any surface in your scene.

Selecting Existing Surfaces

Do you like to be in control? It's good if you do because LightWave 6 is all about control. It gives you these three modes to aid you in quickly selecting the surface or surfaces you want:

- Edit By
- Filter By
- Pattern

Figure 2.5
Surfaces are grouped with their respective objects.

The Edit By mode, found at the top-left corner of the Surface Editor panel, has two selections: Object or Scene. Here, you tell the Surface Editor to control your surfaces by just that, the Objects or the Scene. For example, you have 20 buildings in a fantastic-looking skyscraper scene and eight of those buildings have the same surface on their faces. If you choose to Edit By Object, you would need to apply all the necessary surface settings eight times.

Tip

The Edit By setting is saved from session to session in LightWave. You might accidentally overwrite previously saved surfaces by switching between Edit By Object and Edit By Scene settings. To avoid this, always make each surface name unique.

However, you also can set the Edit By feature to Scene, and any surface with the same name in the scene only requires you to set the surface once. So, in the case of the 20 buildings with eight identical surfaces, one setting will take care of all eight surfaces.

At the top-left corner of the Surface Editor panel, you'll see a Filter By listing. Here, you can choose to sort your surface list by Name, Texture, Shader, or Preview. Most often, you'll select your surfaces by using the Name filter. However, say for example you have

100 surfaces and out of those 100, only two have texture maps. Instead of weeding through a long list of surfaces, you can quickly select Filter By and choose Texture from the drop-down list. This displays only the surfaces that have textures applied. You also can select and display surfaces that use a Shader, or Preview. Preview is useful when working with VIPER because it lists only the surfaces visible in the render buffer image.

In the space just beneath the Filter By setting, you have a space available to type in a Pattern. Pattern enables you to limit your surface list by a specific name. Think of this as an "include" filter. Any surface that does not "include" the Pattern won't show up in the surface list. Have you ever created an object with multiple surfaces and found yourself wasting time looking for one of those surfaces? You spent quite a bit of time scrolling up and down a surface list in the past, where now you can type in a keyword. For example, you created a scene with 200 different surfaces. You have six surfaces named carpet, and for some crazy reason you can't find them. By entering "carpet" into the Pattern requester, only the surfaces named carpet will appear in the Surface Name list. Pretty cool, eh?

Working with Surfaces

After you select an existing surface, you are ready to work with it. LightWave has four commands that are fairly common to software programs: Load, Save, Rename, and Display.

The first command, Load, does what its name implies. It loads surfaces. NewTek has provided a number of premade surfaces that you can load, use, or even modify. You can load your own surfaces as well. For example, you've been working hard to surface a nice wood-planked wall, and it took hours of tweaking to make it look just right. You can reuse this surface again on different objects. To do so, you need to first save the surface.

The second command, Save, tells the Surface Editor to save a file with all the settings you've set. This includes all texture maps, bump maps, image maps, and so on. Having the capability to save your surfaces is handy because you can create an archive of surfaces. For example, you made a shiny silver surface for a corporate client and you know that this client comes in every quarter and wants a big animated silver metallic logo. The client tells you "make it just like last time!" and you suddenly draw a blank. By having that surface saved, you can load it and not have to worry about matching something you did three months earlier.

Note

A visual representation is always a good choice for previewing surfaces. Because LightWave 6's Preset Shelf saves and organizes all your surface samples, it might be more productive to use it instead of Save. The Preset Shelf is discussed in more detail later in this chapter.

Too often, you'll create a complex object with dozens, even hundreds of surfaces. Stressed throughout this book is the importance of organization. With the third command, Rename, you can rename any of your surfaces. This helps keep things in order.

The fourth command is Display. While you're working with the Surface Editor, you'll often want to see how your surface and textures are coming along. Without going through the process of a full frame render, you can simply point your eye to the Display window in the bottom-left corner of the Surface Editor interface. Here, you can see your surface changes instantly. This is especially useful for luminosity and specularity settings. Yet, you might need to look at these or other channels independently. The Display command allows you to choose what type of display you'll see. Figure 2.6 shows a sample surface in the Display window.

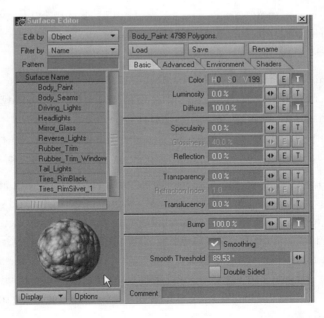

Figure 2.6 The Display window within the Surface Editor can show you your selected surface.

The drop-down list for the Display command offers many choices, the first of which is Render Output mode. This is the default display, and it is the most common. The Render Output mode of Display shows what the rendered surface will look like. This includes color, texture, bump, and any other surface settings you've added. With a surfaced object loaded, Figure 2.7 shows the full surface sample, the Render Output in the Display window.

Perhaps you have a situation in which you don't want to preview the entire render output in the Surface Editor's display window. Maybe you just want the Color Channel. You can do this by selecting the Color Channel option from the drop-down list (see Figure 2.8). The Color Channel shows the color component of the surface. This component can be a texture image, gradient, procedural, or a combination. You'll see that color appears, rather than a complex surface with specularity, bumps, and more.

Selecting the Luminosity Channel shows only the amount of luminosity of the surface, as in Figure 2.9. If you are using a procedural texture for luminosity, you might want to just display the Luminosity Channel.

Note

Except for Render Output and Color, all the channels are grayscale, with pure white representing 100% of that surface attribute and black being 0%.

When creating surfaces, you can use LightWave's Preset shelf to save and load surfaces visually and instantly. From the Surface Editor, you can click the Options button at the bottom of the screen and turn on Use Preset Shelf. To save a surface to the Preset Shelf, double-click the display window, and the currently selected surface is added. To copy a surface setting from the Preset Shelf to another selected surface, double-click in the Preset Shelf.

If you right-click in the Preset Shelf window, you can create new libraries for organizing your surface settings. You also can copy, move, and change the parameters.

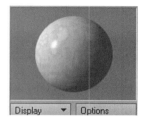

Figure 2.7
Choosing Render Output as the Display shows the current surface's attributes such as Color, Diffuse, Specularity, and Glossiness.

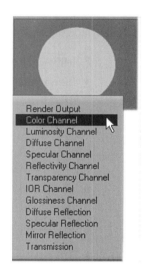

Figure 2.8
The same surface in the Display window with the Color Channel selected. Notice that the bump texture and specularity do not display as in Figure 2.7.

Setting Up Surfaces

The main functions you use to set up and apply surfaces in the Surface Editor are located within four tabs. These tabs are Basic, Advanced, Environment, and Shaders. Each tab controls varying aspects of the selected surface. This chapter introduces you to the most commonly used tab areas, the Basic and Environment tabs.

 Tip

As a quick reference, keep the LightWave "Shape: Model, Surface, & Light" user guide available while working through this book's tutorials.

Figure 2.9
The same surface in the Display window with the Luminosity Channel selected. No luminosity is set for the object, so you will not see anything in the Display other than a black circle.

Aptly named, the Basic tab is home to all your basic surfacing needs. These are the most commonly used surface attributes, and usually act as a basis for any advanced, environmental, or shaded surface. Within the Basic tab, you can assign:

- **Color.** The color of the selected surface.

- **Luminosity.** The brightness, or self-illumination, of a surface.

- **Diffuse.** The amount of light the surface receives from the scene.

- **Specularity.** The amount of shine on a surface.

- **Glossiness.** The spread of the shine on a surface. A high Glossiness setting keeps the Specularity, or shine, to a tight hotspot, similar to glass.

- **Reflection.** The amount of reflection of a surface.

- **Transparency.** The amount of transparency in a surface.

- **Refraction Index.** The amount that light bends through a surface, such as water or glass.

- **Translucency.** The ability of light to pass through a surface, such as a thin leaf or piece of paper.

- **Bump.** A visual displacement based on procedural textures or image maps.

- **Smoothing.** A shading routine to make a surface appear smooth.

- **Double Sided.** The placement of a front and back on single-sided surfaces.

If you were familiar with LightWave before this current version, you'd know to click the Reflection Options button next to Reflection for setting values. That option has been replaced by Environment, an entire tab of settings. Within the Environment tab, you can assign:

- **Reflection Options.** The type of reflection applied to a surface, either spherical or raytrace, or backdrop.

- **Reflection Map.** What the surface will be reflecting.

- **Refraction Options.** The type of refraction applied to a surface, either spherical or raytrace.

- **Refraction Map.** The image file used (if any) for refraction.

The best way for you to get a feel for using the Surface Editor and the Basic and Environment tabs is to try them out for yourself. An excellent way to observe the effect of the settings you choose is to use the LightWave 6 VIPER feature.

Exercise 2.1   Using VIPER

A new feature in LightWave 6 that you will soon learn to appreciate is VIPER. VIPER stands for Versatile Interactive Preview Render, and it gives a preview of your scene within certain areas of adjustments in Layout, such as Volumetric settings, or the Surface settings. It's important to point out that because VIPER does not do a full-scene evaluation, some aspects of your surfacing are not calculated, such as UV Mapping. However, it is very useful for most of your surfacing needs such as color and texture. As you adjust your surfaces, you'll see what's happening and how the surface looks on the object in the scene you have set up without rerendering. VIPER is available in Layout only.

Note

Surfacing objects can be as simple or as complex as you want. A key role in how your surfaces appear when rendered has to do with the light and surroundings in the 3D environment. This chapter takes you through the key features in the Surface Editor. Later in the book you will use these techniques, along with proper lighting, for ultimate images.

To give you an example of how useful VIPER is, try this quick tutorial:

1. Start Layout, or if already running, from the File menu select Clear Scene. Be sure to save any work you've completed thus far.

2. Load the 02Rose_Lit.lws scene from the Chapter 2 folder within this book's CD Projects directory.

   You'll see a pedestal with a rose sitting on it. The scene is lit and has a simple backdrop.

3. Turn on Enable VIPER through the Render Options panel, found in the Render drop-down list.

4. Select the camera, go to the Camera Properties panel, and then click the Properties command at the bottom of the interface. (You also can press the **p** key to access Properties.)

5. Once in the Camera Properties, turn off Antialiasing, be sure that the Resolution is set to VGA (640 × 480), and set the Resolution Multiplier to 50%.

   This renders a 320 × 240 image—50% of the VGA resolution.

6. Press **F9** to render the current frame.

   You see that the backdrop for the small scene is a bit too messy. The Procedural Texture (Layer Type) is too busy. But instead of changing the surface and rerendering this scene, you can just use VIPER. Figure 2.10 shows the interface with VIPER active.

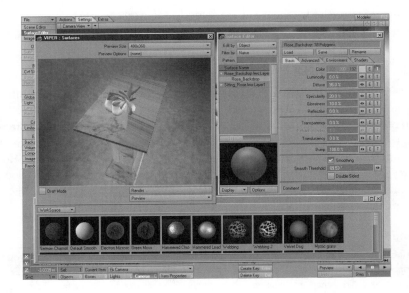

Figure 2.10   Pressing **F9** renders the current frame and stores the information in LightWave's internal buffer. Because of this, you can see your surface changes through VIPER.

7. Go to the Surface Editor, and from the list on the left side of the panel, select the Rose_Backdrop surface.

   You'll see the surface settings appear throughout the commands on the right, on the Basic tab. The T button, which stands for Texture, should be highlighted next to Color on top of the list. The color is set to a dark eggshell or off-white color.

8. Click the T button to enter the Texture panel for the backdrop surface.

   You'll see that the Layer Type is set to Procedural. A procedural texture is computer-generated, meaning it has no end, no seams, and can often be just what the doctor ordered for organic-looking surfaces.

   The Blending Mode is set to Additive, which tells LightWave to add this procedural texture to the selected surface.

   The Procedural Type is set to Fractal Noise, used by LightWave animators for years.

   Adding Fractal Noise to the current surface color adds color variances to the surface.

9. Make sure the VIPER window is open.

   If it's not, click the Options button beneath the sample render display at the bottom of the Surface Editor interface. Clicking Options calls up the Preview Options window, where you can tell LightWave to use VIPER.

   You rendered the scene in Step 5, and LightWave remembers that by storing the data in an internal buffer.

10. Click once directly in the VIPER window so that your render appears. (You can click the Draft Mode button for faster redraws.)

Note

Remember that if you change the Preview Size resolution in the VIPER window, you'll need to rerender the image by pressing **F9**.

11. Make certain that the Texture Editor is still open (you got to the Texture Editor by clicking the T button next to Color in the Surface Editor).

12. Because the procedural fractal noise texture was a little too busy, change some of the parameters, such as the Size. Click and drag the X, Y, and Z values, and watch VIPER redraw your image with the surface changes.

13. Experiment with the other procedural settings for Fractal Noise. From there, try to use other procedurals and adjust their properties as well.

VIPER will quickly become one of your best friends *inside* LightWave 6 (no pun intended!). VIPER saves you time. Not only that, many of you are not mathematical wizards and know what every value means within the surface settings. Explaining all these values would defeat this book's purpose—to teach you LightWave 6. Using VIPER can answer many of your questions when it comes to surfacing because you can instantly see the results from changed values. It's guaranteed that at some point during your practices, you'll utter a loud "Oh, that's what that does" from time to time.

Warning

Be sure to disable VIPER from the Render Options panel when rendering final images or animations because it slows processing time.

Using the Environment Tab Settings

To take you even further into the Basic tab of the LightWave 6 Surface Editor, try the following exercise. Remember to set up your preview display within the Surface Editor and to enable VIPER in the Render Options panel to help you along.

Exercise 2.2   Creating Everyday Surfaces

More often, you'll have a project that requires you to use a vehicle, whether it's a space-age design you've created yourself, purchased from third-party companies such as Viewpoint Digital (http://www.viewpoint.com) or Zygote (http://www.zygote.com), or downloaded from public archives on the Net. Follow these steps to load a surface:

1. Be sure to save any work you've completed thus far. Start Layout, or if already running, choose File, Clear Scene.

Note

At this point, it's a good idea to assign LightWave's Content Directory to the book's CD-ROM. Insert this book's CD-ROM into your computer. You can either install the project files, or select the Cancel button to work from the CD. Press the o key in Layout to access the General Options panel. At the top, click Content Directory, and set it to the Projects folder on the CD. Now, LightWave knows where to look for this book's tutorial files.

2. From the CD that accompanies this book, load the 02Rental_Car.lwo object from the Projects/Objects/Chapter2 folder. To load the object, go to the Actions tab, and then select Add from the drop-down list on the left side of the interface.

Tip

Super-cool tip here folks: You can hide all the toolbars and menus in Layout and work with just the keyboard and mouse. Press o on the keyboard to access the General Options panel. Select Hide Toolbar. Now when in Layout, you can access the Surface Editor (or any other panel) by holding the Ctrl and Shift keys, then clicking either the left or right mouse button. Doing this will pop up the list of commands and menus you've just hidden away (see Figure 2.11)! Press o again to access the General Options panel to unhide the toolbar.

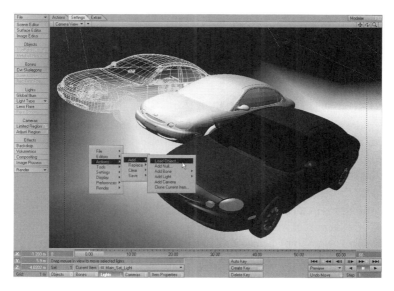

Figure 2.11   Load objects into Layout from the Add drop-down menu, found under the Actions tab, or by holding the Ctrl and Shift keys, then clicking in the Layout window with the left mouse button as show in this example.

> **Note**
>
> Remember that you should be using LightWave 6's default interface configuration for all tutorials in this book. To make sure you are, press **F2** on the keyboard to call up the Configure Menus panel. Click the Default button on the right side of the panel's interface. If it is ghosted, you already have the default interface set. Select Done to close the panel.

3. After the 02Rental_Car.lwo object has been loaded, select the Settings tab from the top of the interface. Next, select the Surface Editor button on the left side of the interface.

You'll see that by default, the name of the object appears in the Surface Name list within the Surface Editor.

4. Clicking the small triangle to the left of the 02Rental_Car.lwo filename opens and closes the surface list.

All the surfaces associated with the car appear, as shown in Figure 2.12.

5. If you have more surfaces than you do space in the Surface Name list, a scroll bar will appear. Simply click and drag to view the entire surface list.

Figure 2.12
Clicking the object's filename in the Surface Name list area within the Surface Editor shows all the surfaces associated with that object.

Tip

Naming your surfaces is half the battle when building 3D models. If you name your surfaces carefully, you'll save oodles of time when you have many surface settings to apply. Organization is key!

6. Select the first surface in the list, Body_BlackGlass.

When the surface is selected, the name appears in the information display of the interface next to Surface Info. The polygons associated with that surface will also appear. In this case, the Body_BlackGlass surface has 463 polygons. A display at the top of the surface list displays the amount of polygons associated with each surface.

Because this rental car is from the "El Cheapo" car rental company, there is no interior. Given that, you don't need to make the glass transparent. You'll want the color of the glass to be black (R,G,B: 0,0,0), hence the surface name Body_BlackGlass.

 Note

Don't worry about glass surfaces. They are easier to create than you might think, and quite cool to look at too! A glass-surfacing tutorial is coming up later in Chapter 9, "Environmental Lighting."

There are a few ways to set a color to the glass. Under the Basic tab within the Surface Editor, you'll see the Color listing at the top. There is an RGB value indicator, with a small color sample. This small area offers you a lot of control:

- Left-clicking on the small, colored square next to the RGB values makes the standard Windows color palette appear. Here, you can choose your color via RGB (Red, Green, Blue), HSL (Hue, Saturation, Luminance), or from custom colors you may have set up previously.

- Right-clicking on the small colored square next to the RGB values in the Surface Editor draws a render display of the current settings. The sample display is at the bottom-left corner of the Surface Editor interface.

- Clicking and dragging the left mouse button on either the red, green, or blue numeric value and dragging left or right increases or decreases the color value. You will instantly see the small color square next to the RGB values change. You'll also see the sample display update.

 Note

Your sample display has a number of options, and they may need to be set up to see your color surface adjustments. Be sure to check them out by right-clicking directly in the display window, as was shown in Figure 2.8.

- If you're not keen to setting RGB values and prefer HSV values instead, rest easy. Clicking once on the RGB values with the right mouse button changes the selection to HSV. Figure 2.13 shows the change.

Figure 2.13
Right-clicking on the RGB value in the Surface Editor (Basic tab) changes the settings to HSV values.

> **Note**
>
> HSV is the Hue and Saturation Value. It describes colors by their overall color directly, unlike RGB values, which are three discrete subcolors. HSV produces more accurate color.

With the Body_Glass surface set to the color black, you still need to make the glass shiny. This next part of the tutorial discusses surfacing the car, while introducing you to the rest of the Surface Editor. Remember that you will create many more surfaces throughout the chapters in this book.

7. Make sure the Body_BlackGlass surface is still selected as the current surface in the Surface Editor. Now go down the list of options and set each one accordingly.

8. Make sure that the value of Luminosity (the option just underneath surface Color) is zero.

Luminosity is great for objects that are self-illuminating, such as a lightbulb, candle flame, or laser beam.

9. Set the value of Diffuse to roughly 80% to tell the Body_BlackGlass surface to accept 80% of the light in the scene.

The Diffuse value tells your surface what amount of light to pick up from the scene. For example, if you set this value to 0, your surface would be completely black. And although you want the glass to be black, you also want it to have some sheen and reflections. A zero Diffuse value renders a black hole—nothing appears at all.

10. Set the value of Specularity to 75%.

Specularity in simple terms is a shiny reflection of the light source. 0% is not shiny at all, whereas 100% is completely shiny.

When you set Specularity, you almost always adjust the Glossiness as well. Glossiness, which becomes available only when the Specularity setting is above 0%, is the value that sets the amount of the "hot spot" on your shiny (or not so shiny) surface. Think of Glossiness as how much of a spread the hot spot has. The lower the value, the wider the spread. For example, Figure 2.14 shows a bumpy object, with a Specularity setting of just 10%, with Glossiness set to 10%. The result is a silky-looking cloth.

Figure 2.15, on the other hand, has a Specularity setting of 80%, and Glossiness of 20%. The result looks more metallic. A higher Glossiness setting gets you polished metal in this case. There will be a lot of surfacing ahead in this book for you, such as glass, metal, human skin, and more. This section however, should give you a brief overview.

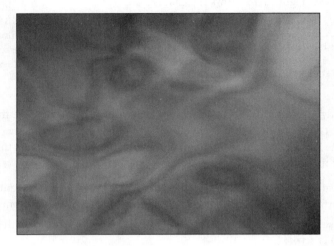

Figure 2.14   A low Specularity and a low Glossiness setting results in a surface that looks like a silky fabric.

Figure 2.15   Higher Specularity settings combined with moderate Glossiness settings results in a copper, or metal type surface.

11. Now, back to our car surface. Set the value of the Glossiness to 40%.

    This gives you a good, working glass surface for now.

12. Set the value of Reflection for the Body_Glass surface to 15%.

A glass windshield reflects its surroundings. In this case, the glass windshield has no surroundings, so instead, it can reflect some fractal noise.

Tip

It's a good idea when setting reflections to balance the Reflection value and the Diffuse value to roughly 100%. The Body_Glass surface has Diffuse at 80%, and Reflection at 15%, for a total 95%. This is not law, but just a guideline to start with.

13. Click one more option—Smoothing. Click this button on to use Phong Shading to smooth the Body_Glass surface.

Note

Phong is a shading method developed by Bui Tuong-Phong in 1975. Essentially, it interpolates the vertex normals of the object, rather than the intensity. The result is a smooth surface that is good for plastics, metals, or glass.

14. Click the Environment tab within the Surface Panel.

    Figure 2.16 shows the Environment tab.

15. Set the Reflection Options to Spherical Map.

    This sets an invisible sphere around your entire scene, which is wallpapered with whatever image you choose. In this case, use the 02Fractal.tga image from this book's Chapter 2 directory on the CD-ROM.

Figure 2.16
The Environment tab is where you set up reflection options in LightWave 6.

16. Click the Reflection Map drop-down list, select Load Image shown in Figure 2.17, and choose the 02Fractal.tga image from the Chapter2/Images directory.

    Because LightWave can calculate true reflections, setting a reflecting image helps create a more realistic surface. A small thumbnail image appears in the panel.

 Tip

LightWave 6 allows you to adjust the image properties, such as contrast and brightness through the Image Editor. You can access the Image Editor by clicking on the button just below the thumbnail image.

Figure 2.17
The Environment tab is where you set up reflection options in LightWave 6.

If your display options are set up, you should see the texture sample update in the lower-left corner of the Surface Editor interface.

Exercise 2.3   Painting a Car Body

With an object such as a car, one of the toughest things to do is match the real-world properties of the clear-coat paint applied to today's vehicles. Believe it or not, this is very easy to do within LightWave 6. This next section takes you through surfacing the painted body of a car. Figure 2.18 shows the unsurfaced car.

Figure 2.18   This rental car model needs a new coat of paint.

1. Select the Body_Paint surface of the 02Rental_Car.lwo object. Set the Color to your favorite, such as midnight blue.

   You should see the surface sample display update, as well as the car object in Layout. Figure 2.19 shows the car with just the Body_Paint color set to midnight blue. The surface looks pretty flat and plain.

2. Set the Diffuse to 60%, the Specularity to 65%, and the Glossiness to 80%.

3. Set Reflection to 30%, and then in the Environment tab, set up a Spherical Map as you did with the Body_Glass surface earlier in this chapter. However, instead of using the 02Fractal.tga image, load the 02Swamp.tga image.

   Figure 2.20 shows the rendered car at this point.

Figure 2.19   A coat of paint on the rental car looks good, but more surfacing needs to be applied.

Figure 2.20   The car now has surfacing set up for its glass and body paint. It's starting to look like something more than clay!

At this point, the paint and the glass of the rental car are about complete. Remember that other factors play a role in surfacing, such as surroundings and lighting.

4. Select the Body_Seams surface, set the Color to a deep blue, or black, and set the Diffuse value to about 85%. Leave all other settings alone.

Body_Seams is a surface set aside for the small grooves between the car's panels and doors.

5. Select the Body_OpenGrills surface, set the color to a soft gray, about 172 for all RGB values, and set Diffuse to 65% and Reflection to 25%. Turn on Smoothing, and set a reflection map of the 02Fractal.tga image.

Body_OpenGrills is the area that can be set to either the body's paint color, or better, to a chrome surface.

6. Select the Rubber_Trim and the Rubber_Trim_Windows surfaces and set each one to a dull black color, like rubber.

Figure 2.21 shows the rental car object at this point with paint, trim, and glass windows surfaced.

Figure 2.21   The car is slowly coming together. Here you can see that a full coat of paint has been added, along with window glass and trim.

Next, you will surface the hubcaps.

7. Select the Tires_RimSilver1 surface in the Surface Editor, and set the color to a medium gray, about 185 RGB value. Diffuse should be set to 40%, no Specularity, and Reflection should be 50%. Use the same 02Swamp.tga image as a Spherical Map in the Environment tab's Reflection Options setting.

This creates nice chrome on the hubcaps.

8. Save your object by choosing Actions, Save, then Save All Objects. If you've hidden the toolbars from the General Options panel, you can use Ctrl and Shift with the left mouse button to select Items, then save directly in the Layout window.

Note

Remember that simply saving a LightWave scene file does not save your surfaces. You must save your object in addition to saving your scene if you want to keep the surfaces applied.

You'll often come across a situation where you need to use the same surface settings on multiple surfaces. With so many variables being set within the Surface Editor, keeping track of identical surfaces could be a problem. Not to mention, you might want a quick reference to the changes you've made to the current surface. This is where the Preset Shelf comes in.

Exercise 2.4   Using Preset Shelf

If you noticed, there are two hubcap surfaces, Tires_RimSilver1, and Tires_RimSilver2. You've just set up a few parameters, and used multiple tabs to do so. To repeat this would be tedious, and often not accurate. Instead, you can use the Preset Shelf to review surface changes, or copy and paste surfaces.

 Tip
Loading and saving surfaces works as well, yet the Preset Shelf shows you a small thumbnail of the surface.

The Preset Shelf defaults to a tall thin column that appears when you access the Surface Editor, as seen in Figure 2.22.

Note
All the Presets from this chapter's tutorials are on the CD-ROM. Go to the Projects/Scenes/Presets/ directory on the CD, and you'll find the INLW 6 Chapter2 preset category. Copy this to the LightWave/Programs/Presets folder on your hard drive. Be sure to copy them to the Surface Editor preset list. You'll now have all the surfaces on your system that were used to create this chapter.

If your Preset Shelf does not appear, you can access it in two ways.

- You can right-click on the render display sample within the Surface Editor. Doing so calls up a number of options from which to choose, as in Figure 2.23.

- You can click with the left mouse button directly on the Options button in the Surface Editor to call up the preview options. There you can turn on the Preset Shelf, as in Figure 2.24.

If you don't care for the tall narrow look of the Preset Shelf, you can click and hold one of the corners of the panel and resize it to

Figure 2.22
The Preset Shelf by default opens as a tall window, but can be resized to fit your screen.

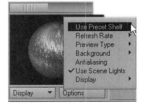

Figure 2.23
Accessing the options for the Preset Shelf is one right mouse click away.

your liking. A good option is to stretch the shelf out across the interface from left to right, and move it to the bottom of the screen. Because all your Preset Shelf samples remain in the shelf, you also can open up the panel to fit your entire screen. The choice is yours.

Figure 2.24   The Preview Options window also allows you to turn the Preset Shelf on and off.

Tip

Using LightWave with a dual-monitor system is great when setting up surfaces. Simply set the Preset Shelf wide open on the additional monitor, maximizing preset visibility and workflow real estate.

You set up a chrome hubcap, and now you need to duplicate it using the Preset Shelf. To do this, just follow these steps:

1. Double-click on the sample render display in the Surface Editor.

   You'll see that surface sample appear on the Preset Shelf.

2. Select the second surface you need to apply surfacing to, such as the Tires_RimSilver2.

   All hubcaps are named Tires_RimSilver2, so you need to set the surface only one time.

3. Go back to the Preset Shelf, and double-click the sample you recently added.

   A small window appears asking you to load the current settings. This is asking you if you want the settings from the Preset Shelf sample to be applied to the currently selected surface in the Surface Editor. In this case, you do.

4. Click Yes, and all hubcaps are surfaced.

All the parameters you've set on the previous surface will be copied over. With the click of a button, you've just copied and pasted the surface. Figure 2.25 shows the completed rental car surfaced, with a couple of lights added.

Figure 2.25   The rental car now looks like a showroom car, thanks to some basic surfaces. Load this scene from the Chapter 2 folder on the book's CD-ROM, 02Rental_Car.lws.

 Tip

If you are sure that you like a surface setting and want to copy it to another surface and do not need to preview it, you have an option other than the Preset Shelf. In the Surface Name list, right-click the surface name and select Copy. Then, right-click the target surface name and select Paste. Try it!

As you can see from the previous examples, the body of the car is starting to look really good. The next step is to continue surfacing the car on your own, using the few simple parameters outlined in the previous pages. If you like, you can load the 02Rental_Car_Complete object from the Projects/Objects/Chapter2 folder on the book's CD-ROM to study.

Color, Diffuse, Specularity, Glossiness, and Reflection will be the base for just about all the surfaces you create. Once you have a handle on setting up the basics, it's time for you to create surfaces that are more advanced.

Making a 3D Surface from a 2D Image

Too often when working on a project, your client will demand, or politely ask, for a particular surface. And although you may have many texture CD-ROM surface collections, they sometimes do not match your specific needs and are only a base to work from. For example, your big corporate client comes in and needs its new testing division's logo animated. "No problem," you say. The client tells you it needs to be completed in three days. Again, "No problem," you reply. Then the client tells you that it must be on green marble. You scramble for words as the hard drive in your head scans your memory for any images of green marble. As you begin working on the project, there is none! What will you do? You can use LightWave's Surface Editor and all will be well.

In your archives, a high-resolution earth-tone marble image is found. But the client needs green. Toning the image in an imaging program like Photoshop could work, but by adjusting the image in LightWave, you'll have more control over the final scene. Follow along in this next tutorial to take a single 2D image and make it a different colored 3D image.

Exercise 2.5   Using the Texture Editor for Bump and Specularity Maps

Marble, granite, and stone are great surfaces for 3D animation. Terrific images for logo backgrounds, floors, sidewalks, and more, they are often easy to find on the Internet and in the world around you. Figure 2.26 shows the earth-tone marble image used as the base for the animation.

Figure 2.26   An everyday earth-tone marble image.

In this project, you'll start with a picture and use it to create bumps and specular highlights on a surface. To do this, follow these steps:

1. Select Clear Scene in Layout from the File requester. Remember to save any work. Next, load the 02EarthMarbleBKD.lwo object from Chapter 2 of this book's CD-ROM. Select camera, and then press 6 on the numeric keypad to switch to Camera View. Then, move the camera in toward the 02EarthMarbleBKD.lwo object so that it fills the frame. Press the Enter key twice to create a keyframe at frame 0, which will lock the camera in place.

2. Go to the Surface Editor and select the EarthMarble surface, and set the RGB Color value to deep green, RGB 55, 100, 065.

3. With the proper color set, look to the Diffuse area, and click the T button to access the Texture Editor.

4. Starting at the top of the Texture Editor, make sure that the Layer Type is set to Image Map.

You're selecting an image map because you're using an image to enhance the surface. Image maps can be used on all types of surfaces, as an alternative to Procedural textures that are strictly computer generated.

Here, you are mapping an image onto the flat object—think of image mapping like wallpapering. Other layer types you can set are Procedural, computer-generated surfaces that do not use image maps. Or, you can choose to set a Gradient layer type, which enables you to use a spectrum of colors as a texture. Gradients in LightWave 6 are quite complex and will be used more throughout the book. They are surface translation filters. Figure 2.27 shows the Texture Editor interface.

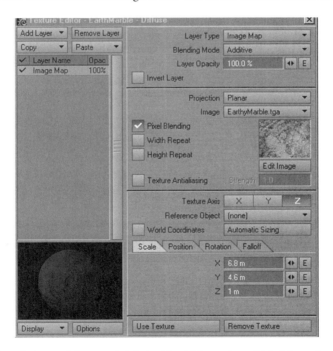

Figure 2.27   All the small buttons labeled with a T throughout LightWave take you to this panel, the Texture Editor.

5. Set the Blending Mode to Additive, from the drop-down list.

Additive uses the texture to its full extent for the selected surface. You also can choose Subtractive, which subtracts the full extent of the image from the selected surface. Choosing Difference as the Blending Mode determines how a layer affects underlying layers, similar to Adobe's Photoshop.

6. Experiment with Blending modes to see what results you can come up with.

Note

Every surface layer can have a different blending mode.

7. Return the Blending Mode to Additive, and keep the Layer Opacity set to 100% for now.

A setting of 100% tells LightWave to use this texture map completely. Because you are in the Texture Editor for Diffuse, you are using the brightness values of the image for the diffuse channel, and the Color setting is disregarded.

8. Leave Invert Layer turned off.

In this instance of an Image Map, inverting the layer would reverse the image.

9. Set the Projection to Planar.

Remember, with an Image Map layer type, you are wallpapering. Planar tells LightWave to keep the wallpaper flat. You also can choose to set Projection to Cylindrical, Spherical, Cubic, Front, and UV. These additional values enable you to surface on tubes, balls, boxes, composited backgrounds, and organic surfaces.

Note

You will get to try the different types of Projection modes such as UV later in Chapter 10, "Organic Animation."

Now you need to tell LightWave what image you want to Image Map as a diffusion texture.

10. Next to the Image drop-down list, select Load Image and from the book's CD-ROM, load the 02EarthyMarble.tga file.

You'll see the image appear in the small thumbnail window.

11. Keep Pixel Blending checked (turned on) to smooth out the pixelization that can occur if the camera gets too close to the surface.

12. Set Width Tile and Height Tile to Reset. These settings allow you to repeat or mirror the image map.

These two settings are used if you were tiling a floor, for example, and wanted a texture to repeat.

13. Uncheck Texture Antialiasing.

Turning this off is important when applying textures. When you render animations, you will turn on Antialiasing in the Camera Properties panel. This setting smooths out jagged edges throughout your scene. Setting Antialiasing within the Texture Editor will do the same thing. However, when you add that to a final render that is antialiased, you end up with a blurry image. Too much antialiasing can sometimes be a bad thing.

You told LightWave to set an image map and keep it flat (planar). Because this is a 3D animation program, you also need to identify to what axis you want to apply this image.

14. Set the Texture Axis to Z, the axis that is in front (positive Z) and in back (negative Z) of you.

Note

You do not need to set a Reference Object for this surface. Setting up a Reference Object, such as a null object, allows you to interactively control the position and size of the image map in Layout. However, LightWave 6 enables you to animate a texture's Position, Scale, and Rotation. The choice is up to you.

15. Click the Automatic Sizing button.

LightWave looks at the polygons of the selected surface and applies the currently selected image to them as best as possible. The size parameters change under the Scale tab at the bottom of the Texture Editor interface. In most cases, Automatic Sizing works like a charm. When it doesn't, use a null object as a reference object to obtain precise image placement.

16. Leave World Coordinates unchecked.

When you tell LightWave to Image Map, you are wallpapering an image onto the surface of an object. If you move the object, the image should move with it. But imagine if you wallpapered a bumpy wall and decided to move the wall. When you did this, you wanted the wall to move, but not the wallpaper, making the bumpy wall move through the wallpaper. Clicking on World Coordinates does just that.

Now your texture surface is set up, but you have a few more things to do.

17. Go to the top of the interface and choose the Copy drop-down list. Select the Current Layer choice, and then click Use Texture to close the panel. Copying the Current Layer enables you to apply all these settings to another aspect of the surface, such as a bump map.

18. In the Layout window, select the single light in the scene, press y to rotate, and point it toward the 02EarthMarbleBKD.lwo object. Also, move it up and back slightly to fully illuminate the object. Press the Enter key twice to create a keyframe and lock the light in place at frame 0. Press **F9** on your keyboard to see the marble image blended with the green color set earlier, as in Figure 2.28.

Tip

Be sure that your Render Display is set to Image Viewer within the Render Options panel to see the F9 render.

19. Before you go any further, click the Actions tab at the top of the Layout interface, and select Save All Objects from the Save drop-down list on the left side of the screen.

This saves the surface properties to your object thus far.

Figure 2.28   The Texture Editor is used to diffuse an earth-toned marble image with a deep green color.

Exercise 2.6   Applying Bump and Specularity to a Surface

The rendered result at this point doesn't look like much, does it? In LightWave, you can apply as many textures as you'd like. However, you have to use the Texture Editor to do so. To use the Texture Editor for Bump mapping, follow these steps:

1. In the Surface Editor, click the T button next to Bump.

    The Texture Editor appears again. And while this is the same editor where you applied a Diffuse texture, it has different results. Instead of resetting all the same parameters, you only need to paste them. Remember the Copy Current Layer command you selected earlier? This copied all the Texture Editor settings for Diffuse.

2. From the top of the Texture Editor interface, choose Paste and then Replace Current Layer.

    All the parameters are now aligned.

    You'll see that the same 02EarthyMarble.tga image has been loaded into the thumbnail window. Changes only need to be made to two areas—which is easier than changing all the settings. This is why you copied and pasted the settings.

3. From the Image drop-down list, select Load Image, and load the 02EarthyMarbleBump.tga image.

    This is a high-contrast grayscale image made just for a bump map. The other parameter to change is the Texture Amplitude.

Note

Bump maps are a way of creating surface detail. It is a shading function that perturbs the surface of an object, not the physical geometry even though it appears so. Using a grayscale image interprets the incident light angles: the dark areas less and brighter areas more.

4. Set the Texture Amplitude to 2.0. Essentially, this is the amount of Bump the Texture Editor applies.

5. Copy this surface, and then click Use Texture.

6. Be sure to select Save All Objects again; then press **F9** to render a test frame. Figure 2.29 shows the surface with both Diffuse and Bump maps applied.

Figure 2.29   By adding a bump map to the surface, it starts to take on more depth.

Tip

It is not always necessary to use a grayscale image for bump mapping. If your color image has good variations in contrast, it will often work well as a bump map image.

7. With the bump texture copied, now enter the Texture Editor (T) for Specularity.

    This is where you can take an average surface and make it exceptional. Because you copied the bump texture, simply paste it here. You are not trying to apply the bump map as a Specularity texture; that isn't how it works. By copying, you are taking the grayscale value of the image and its settings such as size and position. Copying saves you the trouble of resetting all the values.

8. Paste the copied surface to the current layer in the Specularity Texture Editor. This will use the same settings, but make the surface more shiny where the image is brighter, and less shiny where the image is darker.

The last step you need to take to make this surface look great is to adjust the Specularity and Glossiness.

9. After reading more about LightWave[6] lights in Chapter 7, change the single light in the scene to a spotlight. This will help direct the light more accurately on the marble surface. Leave the Specularity at 0%, and set the Glossiness to roughly 15% or 20%.

   Because the Specularity Texture Layer Opacity is set to 100%, the base (the 0% setting) is meaningless. This creates a nice wide gloss on the surface. However, you can play with the amounts to find a setting you might like more.

   Figure 2.30 shows the three textures applied to the single surface, which is just one polygon. You can load this scene from the book's CD-ROM, 02GreenMarbleBKD.lws.

Figure 2.30   Adding a Specularity texture map helps bring this surface to life, all from a flat image.

Note

You also can use LightWave's gradients to apply specularity maps and help control contrasts. Look for more on gradients in Chapter 8, "Environmental Structures."

Specularity maps are useful any time you have bump maps. If you look at even the slight imperfections on your desktop, or your computer monitor, you can see that there are bumps, but the light falls in and out of them. This is what a Specularity map will do for your surface. And similar to the bump map properties, it also bases its calculations on the grayscale image—the darker areas do not allow as much Specularity where the lighter areas allow more.

The techniques are a foundation for your entire real-world surfacing projects. Anything from a plastic toy, to a telephone, to a dirt road, can benefit from setting these three texture maps. As another example, read on to create a dirty metal surface with a few more involved steps.

Applying Image Map to Surfaces

Surfacing that rental car earlier in this chapter was no big deal, right? Well, it wasn't. You used basic, everyday surfacing techniques and a couple of simple reflection images. This is great for logos and colored balls, but in today's marketplace, if you want to stay competitive, you need to make things look not so clean. In the early days of 3D animation, shine and reflection were big crowd pleasers, but now it's a different story and you need to be aware of it. The trick is to use LightWave's Surface Editor to apply texture maps, bump maps, and procedurals to achieve the "not so perfect" surface.

What happens when you need to create a dirty and rusty piece of metal pipe? Fortunately, you can apply these surfacing techniques to anything you want, such as metal grates, steel, wood, fences, and much more. How? You can use image maps.

When you begin creating a 3D object, you most often work from some sort of reference, whether it's a physical model or a photograph.

The same would apply to surfacing your model, but most people don't consider it. When you begin to surface an object, you will save yourself hours of frustration and headaches by having a photograph or digital image of the surface you want to create. In this particular case, an image has been photographed and scanned into a computer at a high resolution. This single image is used as a reference to create an entire 3D surface. Figure 2.31 shows an image you can use as a reference.

Figure 2.31   The starting point to any decent surface is a decent image.

There are a number of resources available to you for gathering image maps. One of the best resources is your own eye and a camera. Taking photographs of the world around you is the best way to get the original and real textures into your 3D environment. Not to mention, they are your images and royalty free. You don't need an expensive digital camera, and frankly, you're better off with a traditional 35mm film camera. Unless you spend a lot of money, most digital cameras have average quality. If you are using images in 3D for surfacing, you should always go for the highest quality. Instead of a digital camera, take photographs with a 35mm. The quality of the film has a much nicer look to it than the digital, especially when applied as image maps. Not to go unmentioned is the Kodak PhotoCD. You can have any of your photographs created on a PhotoCD which can be read in your computer's CD-ROM drive. Check your local photo shop for more information.

If you can't take your own photos, you can buy some wonderful sets of real-world textures. Marlin Studios (www.marlinstudios.com) has more than half a dozen CDs available with some of the best-looking rocks, foliage, wood, and more available today. You can buy these discs from Safe Harbor computers at 1–800–544–6599 or online at www.sharbor.com. A few sample images are provided for you on this book's CD-ROM to experiment with. With Figure 2.31 as a reference, Figure 2.32 shows the base image you can start with.

Figure 2.32   A flat, dirty metal image is a great starting point for making a realistic surface.

To achieve a complex look as in Figure 2.31, you can use LightWave's Layered surfaces in combination with your base image. This next exercise shows you the techniques to use LightWave's powerful texture layers to blend multiple textures on a single surface.

In the previous exercise, you mixed surface Color with an Image Map through a Diffuse texture map. In this instance, you are going to replace surface Color all together.

Exercise 2.7   Setting Up the Image Map and Layers

LightWave's Texture Editor looks simple at first, but actually runs deep with control. This next tutorial steps you through setting up a base image and adding layers of procedural textures to create a rusty surface.

1. Save any work you want to keep, and then select Clear Scene from the File drop-down menu.

2. From the book's CD-ROM, load the 02MetalPlate.lwo object into Layout.

   This is a simple polygon box with a seam in it for variation. The textures will be applied to the entire object.

3. Open the Surface Editor, select the MetalPlate surface, and click the T button next to Color.

   All the default values in the Texture Editor are settings you can use. The Layer Type is an Image Map, the Blending Mode is Additive, Layer Opacity is 100%, and because the object is flat in front of the camera, you want the Projection set to Planar.

4. From the Image drop-down menu, select Load Image. Load the 02MetalPlate.tga image file.

   A thumbnail image appears as representation.

5. Select Z as the Texture Axis, and click Automatic Sizing.

6. Press **F9** to draw a quick render preview of your surface.

   The image should be mapped on similar to Figure 2.33. Now you can add Layers to this surface for more complex surfacing.

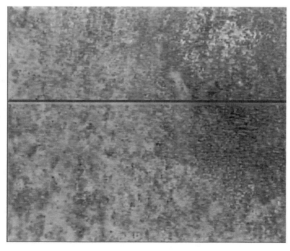

Figure 2.33   The flat image is now applied as a texture map to the surface. This is only one layer of surfacing.

7. From the top of the Texture Editor interface, click and hold down the mouse button to display, and choose Add Layer, then Procedural.

You'll see the right side of the interface change, and a small thumbnail of fractals appears, as in Figure 2.34.

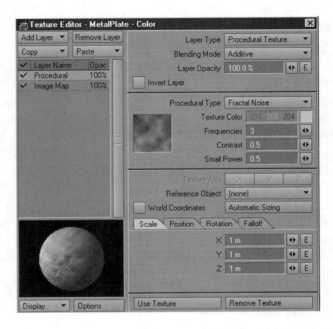

Figure 2.34   Adding a Procedural Layer to your surface displays a similar Texture Editor display.

As you add Layers to your surfaces, you'll see a list begin on the left side of the Texture Editor interface, as in Figure 2.35.

Note

LightWave's surface layers are stacked on top of each other. Lower layers can be obscured if the upper layers show through, either by Layer Opacity or certain procedural textures set to less than 100%.

If you look at the Layer Type selection, you'll see that it is set to Procedural. Blending Mode is still set to Additive, as you want to add this procedural on top of the Image Map layer.

8. Set the Procedural Type to Fractal Noise.

This is a random fractal pattern that can be used for creating dust, dirt, rust, or just a simple variation in a surface. At this point, it's a good idea to turn on VIPER to preview your surfacing. Remember to enable VIPER through the Render panel, and then turn it on through Surface Editor options selection.

9. Select Render Options from the Render drop-down list, and be sure to Enable VIPER. Close the Render Options panel, and press **F9** to render one frame.

This puts the render into LightWave's buffer, for use with VIPER.

10. After the render is complete, click the Texture Editor and under the preview Options button, select Use VIPER.

When VIPER pops up, click the Render button on the VIPER window. Your render appears, as shown in Figure 2.36.

11. Back in the Texture Editor, you can begin adjusting the Fractal Noise procedural color. Because this will be rust, select an RGB value close to 140, 110, 75.

12. Move down to the bottom of the Texture Editor panel, and select the Scale tab to change the size of the procedural texture, making the X value 150mm and the Y value 6m.

You'll see the updated image appear instantly in VIPER. Notice how the rusty orange color looks more like dripped rust.

13. Click the Rotation tab, and set the B (bank adjustment) to 20 degrees.

The procedural texture is now slightly angled across the surface.

14. Click the Falloff tab, where you can tell the texture to simply end—fall off.

Because the texture is primarily on the Y axis (up and down), you want to make the rust look like it's dripping.

15. Set the Y falloff value to –40%, and set Linear Y from the drop-down Type list.

Figure 2.35
You can easily select which layer you want to work on by selecting the Layer Name from the list on the left side of the Texture Editor interface.

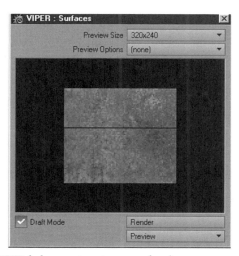

Figure 2.36   Using VIPER helps you to set your surface layers more precisely.

Figure 2.37 shows a full-frame render of the adjusted surface layer.

Note

Falloff is the rate at which the visible brightness decreases from the center to the edge of the texture.

Figure 2.37   Two surface layers, an Image Map and a Procedural, make an ordinary polygon look more like rusted metal.

The Next Step

Using VIPER in combination with the Scale, Position, Rotation, and Falloff tabs is a great way to work. Now you can interactively set these values. Additionally, before LightWave 6, you could not rotate a surface like this without messy Layout setups.

From this point on, you can experiment on your own. Add more layers. As a matter of fact, add as many as you like. Your only limitations are time and system memory! Try adding some of the other Procedural surfaces, such as Smokey, Turbulence, or Crust. Keep adding these to your rusty metal surface to see what you can come up with. Now if you remember the copy and paste commands you used earlier with the Bump mapped marble tutorial, you can repeat those same steps. Try selecting the Copy All Layers from the Color Texture and applying them as Bump and Specularity textures. The results are endless.

Summary

This chapter gave you a broad overview of the main features within LightWave 6's Surface Editor, including the Texture Editor. There are literally countless surfaces in the world around us, and it's up to you to create them digitally. As the book progresses, you will use the information and instructions in this chapter to create even more complex and original surfaces such as glass, water, and dirt. But from here, read on to Chapter 3, "LightWave 6 Modeler," to begin the creation process.

Chapter 3

LightWave 6 Modeler

It's been said that necessity is the mother of

invention, and when you get into Modeler 6,

you'll see that this statement has never

been truer. The LightWave 6 Modeler has

all the features, ease of use, and control you'd want in any 3D-modeling package. You can create everything from simple shapes, to famous architecture, to complex characters.

Of course, necessity *and* significant suggestions from the LightWave community have made this version of Modeler what it is today. There are enhancements upon enhancements in Modeler, from a customizable interface to interactive controls to brand-new modeling tools. This chapter guides you through Modeler with practical working examples. Some major issues discussed in this chapter include:

- Points, Polygons, and Volume
- Objects
- Weight Modeling Mode
- Texture Modeling Mode
- Morph Modeling Mode with Endomorphs
- SubPatching objects
- Splines
- Skelegons
- Spline Curves and backdrop images

The exercises in this book are not only a simple cookbook of techniques, but also a thorough explanation of what is happening when you choose a specific command. However, don't mistake this for a long, drawn out description of the Modeler toolset—that's what the manuals are for! Building anything requires that you start with a good working knowledge of your software and what you are trying to accomplish.

How you work, where you work, and the people you work with all play a part in your projects. When you sit down to create a 3D model, you choose to expand your creative sense and style. Interruptions can block your creative process. Try to make your work environment as comfortable as possible, even if 3D modeling is just a hobby to you.

Just as important as your working environment is your model management. While you may just sit down to see what you can create with LightWave Modeler, it is always more productive to know where you are going. For example, if you decided to build and animate a singing alien, you first need to decide what the alien should look like. You don't need to be an artist to make a simple sketch of your idea. Flush out any variations on paper, before you start your modeling.

From there, what will the character do in the animation? LightWave 6's modeling tools are designed for ease of use when it's time to animate. This means that you need to plan your animation so that your model can be animated appropriately. There is nothing worse than trying to make a bad model move the way you want it to. Plan your motions, and know how the character will react to its surroundings. Realizing what you are trying to do and where you are trying to go will help you get there that much faster. For some, getting a new software package and diving right in is a common practice. For others, reading the manuals cover-to-cover is the norm. As with anything, moderation is the key and either of these extremes may not be the best way to tackle this new program.

Understanding Modeler 6

Before you begin to figure out where you are going with your models and animations, it's a good idea to be familiar with the tools you have available to you. While this chapter cannot take you through each panel in Modeler, it will describe how to quickly create any type of model you want. You'll use the information in this chapter (and your LightWave user guides) as reference for the remainder of this book. Figure 3.1 shows the LightWave 6 Modeler interface at startup.

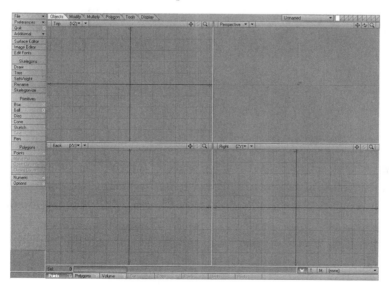

Figure 3.1 LightWave 6 Modeler at startup looks similar to previous versions of LightWave, but don't let that fool you.

LightWave 6 Modeler is quite different from previous versions of LightWave in many ways. It is a better way to work, not only because of the many new tools, but also because you can work faster through numerous interactive tools. You can customize keyboard shortcuts and menu bars to fit your specific needs.

To begin, you should be familiar with the way Modeler 6 creates objects. While points, polygons, and splines are all still a part of the object creation process, Modeler now integrates many animation setup routines. These routines were left for Layout in the past, but now you can fully build, surface, and set up hierarchies for your objects directly in Modeler.

Note

LightWave 6 Modeler enables you to create full bone structures for your objects, which you can save with your objects. Learn more about bones in Chapter 11, "Character Construction," and inverse kinematics in Chapter 13, "Inverse Kinematics."

Click around the Modeler interface and try to make a few simple objects, even just boxes and balls. You'll learn right here that this version of the software is different from any other version of LightWave. Aside from interactive tools and a streamlined interface, you should be aware of an entirely new object structure. Objects now have their own layers, allowing a single object to have multiple independent parts. Features commonly used in Layout are now updated and available in Modeler, such as a robust Surface Editor and the creation of bones. Click further to see what buttons are hidden within panels and try them. Doing so will spark your curiosity when reading through the LightWave 6 manuals.

Points, Polygons, and Volume

At the bottom left of the Modeler interface, you'll see three selections available to you: Points, Polygons, and Volume. By selecting Points, you are telling Modeler that you want to work with the *points* of an object. By selecting the Polygons button, you're telling Modeler that you want to work with the *polygons* of an object. Points make up polygons, sort of like connecting the dots. You can't have polygons without points. Although moving points that make up an object also moves the polygons, there are times when you will work with one selection over the other. Working in Point mode, you'll gain finer control over adjusting details of a model. Working in Polygons mode allows you to adjust other parameters of an object, such as Bevel or Smooth Shift. You'll be instructed to work in both of these modes throughout the exercises in this book.

Volume mode allows you to make a selection either within a set-bounding region or outside of it. With Volume mode set, you can drag out a region for your object, press the **w** key to bring up the Volume Statistics, and select the points to include or exclude polygons on the border of the volume. You will constantly work between Points and Polygons modes, but will only occasionally work in Volume mode. Instead of using the Volume Statistics, you can select an area in any view. But it's there when you want it! Please read through your LightWave 6 manuals for more information on these selection modes. It is important for your success with Modeler to understand the difference between the Points, Polygons, and Volume selection modes.

Objects

3D modeling must begin somewhere, either with a few points, a curve, or more commonly, a primitive object. Look around you—most everyday shapes are based on primitive geometric shapes. The desk you work at can be created from a box. The walls around you, the windows, all can be created from boxes. Cups, plates, and other kitchen items can be created from discs. You see, the more you pay attention to something, even something as simple as a coffee mug, the more you will understand how to re-create it in LightWave Modeler. You can use the Primitive Objects, Box, Ball, Disc, and Cone tools as the basis for even the most complex 3D models.

With a major upgrade like LightWave 6, it can be overwhelming to find a starting point for creating. One of the improvements and upgrades within this rich program is a new object-creation standard. Understanding this is vital to your success with LightWave.

Loading, Saving, and Creating Objects

Loading objects has not changed since previous versions of LightWave. Pressing l on the keyboard opens the Load Object command window. Here, you can load LightWave objects (lwo), 3D Studio objects (3ds), AutoCAD objects (dxf), and Alias|Wavefront objects (obj). You also can choose to use the mouse to load objects. With the Objects tab selected, you can select Load Object from the File drop-down menu.

Although loading objects is straightforward, you must be aware of the changes made to Modeler in respect to its multidocument capability. Previous versions of Modeler enabled you to create a new object on each layer. Modeler 6's objects now have their own set of layers. If you've created a big red ball and decide to create a big yellow box, you need to tell Modeler that you are creating a New Object using the File menu. This moves the existing object and sets up a new object layer set. The existing object is still loaded, just not selected.

As you read through this book, many of the tutorials will use LightWave Modeler's New Object standard, MultiMesh. MultiMesh is what LightWave calls an object with multiple layers.

The File menu also lets you save objects, close objects, and create new objects. By the way, pressing **Shift+n** creates a new object instantly.

Because objects themselves have layers, you need to inform LightWave that you want to begin creating a new object. You can select New Object from the File menu. Doing so will create a fresh set of layers. A single object file can have unlimited layers, so don't be confused when your current object suddenly vanishes—it is still loaded in Modeler, just not within the new object's layer set. Creating a new object does not delete any other work. As the modeling tutorials progress, you'll understand how this functionality is used. When you create new objects, you'll see the object selections are added as "unnamed 1," "unnamed 2," and so on. You can find these in the object selection drop-down menu at the top of the Modeler interface, to the left of the Layer buttons.

Earlier versions of LightWave Modeler only required you to either clear or delete an object to discard it for good. LightWave 6 requires you to select Close Object from the File menu. Simply deleting an object in Modeler 6 only hides it from view. If you only delete the object, Modeler keeps the object's layer information. Selecting Close Object removes the object and closes its layers. Later in the chapter you'll learn more about managing objects, interface enhancements, and functionality to streamline your workflow. For now, read on to learn about how Modeler 6 creates objects.

Creating Object Layers

If you've worked in any version of LightWave Modeler, you should be familiar with layers.

These layer buttons live atop the Modeler interface in the upper-right corner. Before Modeler 6, you could create different objects or parts of objects on each layer. Essentially, each layer in previous versions was its own object. Now in Modeler 6, all the layers relate to the current object.

If you're familiar with Adobe's Photoshop, you often use layers there to build your images. The same idea applies to Modeler. For example, you've created a large mechanical robotic arm. The base and main arm of the robot are complete, but to build the extended arms that move on their own pivots, you need to create a separate part of the same object—this is where the use of layers in Modeler 6 is key.

A secondary use for layers relates to references. Using layers, you can set one or more layers as a background reference layer, and work in a clean foreground layer without harming your other model(s). Modeler 6 works like this, but the functions run much deeper. Now, each object has its own layer set, and you can have unlimited layers. Figure 3.2 shows the Modeler 6 interface with objects loaded in both the foreground and background layers.

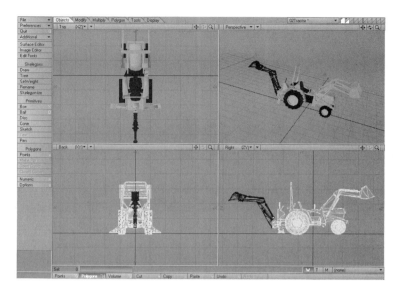

Figure 3.2   Objects can be put in different layers for reference and safety.

The layers in Modeler have more than just one function. They also are used for model-ing using Booleans, creating curve extrusions, and more. You will use multiple layers later in this chapter to create various objects. Layers can be visible or invisible. To help control layer visibility, select the Layers command from the Display tab. This panel enables you to select (or multiselect with the Shift key) any and all layers. A check mark under the F heading refers to an object in a foreground layer, while a check mark under the B heading refers to an object in a background layer.

But beyond the basics, the layers within Modeler 6 are very powerful and can be confus-ing at first. As with anything, the best way to understand this is to try it out. Before that can happen, you need to know how Modeler 6 creates different types of objects.

Modeling Methods

All versions of LightWave before LightWave 6 were simple in comparison when it came to modeling objects. Because the final work, such as deformations, surfacing, and mor-phing, was all accomplished in Layout in the past, all you needed to do in Modeler was build. Now, many of the tasks performed in Layout can be done in Modeler, such as sur-facing, morph targets, and bone setups. This is because Modeler 6 offers three different types of vertex maps. At the lower-right side of the Modeler interface, you'll see three small buttons labeled W, T, M (see Figure 3.3). These letters stand for Weight Map, Texture, and Morph, respectively.

Note

A vertex map is additional data that can be hung on points.

Figure 3.3
Three types of vertex maps can be created in Modeler: Weight, Texture, and Morph.

Weight Modeling Mode

The first button is W (Weight Map), and is usually active by default when you start Modeler. However, the default vertex map is "none" as seen in the Weight Map drop-down list. "None" signifies that the Weight Map is off. In a basic sense, a Weight Map is a set of values associated with the points in an object. A point can have a value, 0, or no value in a map. There are two types of Weight Maps: General and SubPatch Weight. If you create a General map, you can assign different values to points for this map. Then you can do things like bend an object with bones using the map rather than just the bone. Maps can also be used for falloff with most modeling tools. Chapter 11 will take you further into using Weights. The SubPatch Weight Map is a predefined special map that controls the bias of a control point. See Exercise 3.1 for an example of using weights.

Note

A SubPatch is a surface that is subdivided until it is smooth. Pressing the Tab key creates results similar to MetaNURBS in previous versions of LightWave. SubPatch in LightWave 6, however, is like a real-time MetaForm tool (the complex subdivision tool in past versions of LightWave), allowing you to create smooth organic objects from simple primitives such as automobiles, humans, or even flowers. SubPatch is discussed later in this chapter.

Exercise 3.1   Using Weights

Weights are mentioned often through this book, but to give you a good headstart, create your own Weight object.

1. Start Modeler and be sure that you are using the default interface settings.

   You'll see the buttons change on the left side of the screen. These are all the commands that allow you to create objects.

2. Click the W button at the lower-right corner of the interface.

   This puts Modeler in Weight creation mode.

3. In the drop-down menu next to the W, T, and M buttons, click and hold down the mouse button to select SubPatch Weight from the list.

   Your other choices are None or New, which will be used later. Figure 3.4 shows the SubPatch selection.

4. Select the Box command under the Objects tab.

5. In the top viewport in Modeler, click and drag to draw a box. The box at this point is flat, so click in the Back viewport (bottom-left quad) above and below the flat box. The box object expands to meet your mouse.

6. Once the box has depth, tap the space bar to turn off the Box command.

Figure 3.4
The SubPatch Weight is selected from the drop-down menu at the bottom-right corner of the interface.

 Note

The box you just created was LightWave 6's new way of building objects. You no longer need to press Enter on the keyboard to "make" the object. Simply turning off a tool keeps the object and deselects the tool. When you draw out a box as you did here, you are truly drawing a box, not just an outline representation. There is no "Make" button. This applies throughout Modeler.

 Tip

Because you can set up your own keyboard equivalents in LightWave 6, try to set up Deselect for the Enter key because it is no longer needed to "make" an object.

7. Press the comma (,) key once to zoom out. Press **Tab** to apply a SubPatch to this box.

   You'll see the square box turn into a control cage for a smooth-surface object. This is the SubPatch at work, as in Figure 3.5.

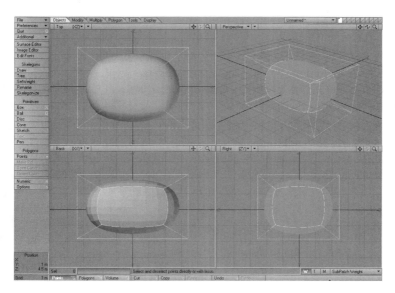

Figure 3.5   Pressing the Tab key activates SubPatch for the current object. This is a simple box, but SubPatch smoothes it out.

8. Be sure that one of your Modeler views is set to Perspective. Make that Perspective view's mode Weight Shade, as in Figure 3.6. You can do this through the Viewport Titles, or through the Display Options (**d**) panel.

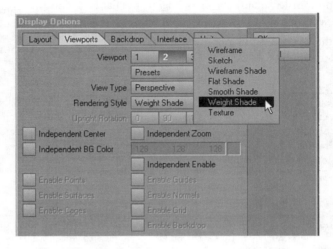

Figure 3.6   You can specify a Weight Shade mode in any of the Modeler views from the Viewport Title bar, or here in the Display Options panel.

9. Select the Modify tab from the top of the Modeler interface.

   Toward the bottom on the left side of the interface, you'll see the Weights and Weight Brush commands. Figure 3.7 shows the toolbar.

10. Select Weights, and move your mouse over to the Perspective Viewport. With the left mouse button, click and drag to the right on one of the corners of the SubPatch box.

    You'll see three things happen: a percentage change will appear in the info display, the corner will sharpen, and it will turn red.

11. To see the Weight Shade being applied, you need to have your Viewport Rendering Style set to Weight Shade. This is not necessary for Weight control to work, but necessary for color representation.

    Now if you click and drag a point to the left of the box, you'll see the SubPatch object smooth out and turn blue. Access the Viewport Rendering Style through the small drop-down arrow atop each viewport.

A Weight object enables you to sharpen or smooth a SubPatched object without the need to create more geometry. Figure 3.8 shows a simple box with Weights applied. This shape is only six polygons.

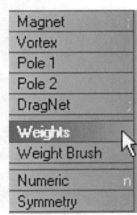

Figure 3.7
When a SubPatch Weight is active, the Weights tool becomes available.

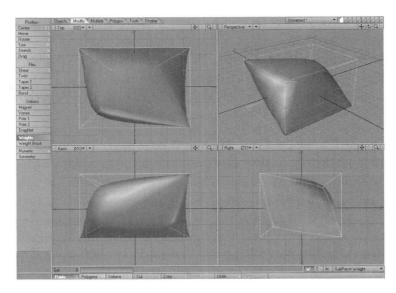

Figure 3.8   Using Weights to adjust your SubPatch model allows for complex shapes with a very low geometry count.

However, if the object in Figure 3.8 did not have Weights applied, it would take nearly 400 polygons to create this shape. It is very easy to create a shape like this by using Weights. Without using Weights on your objects in your scene, you'll find that there is a lot of wasted geometry. The more geometry there is, the longer it will take to render your animation. The redraw speed in Layout will also be affected. Additionally, Weights give you very precise control in areas of your model not previously possible.

Texture Modeling Mode

Not to be confused with the Texture Editor or an applied texture, the Texture button in Modeler offers to you another control for creating models. Figure 3.9 shows the T button at the bottom of the Modeler interface.

Texture enables you to create a texture map for your object. This is not a traditional texture map, but a texture UV map. UV mapping is a new addition to LightWave 6, and can be useful for applying images to complex objects.

Morph Modeling Mode with Endomorphs

You may have heard the term "endomorphs" when information became available about LightWave 6. An endomorph is an embedded morph. A morph is a displacement of points from one position to another, like a marching band forming different

Figure 3.9
The Texture modeling mode button at the lower right of the Modeler interface.

shapes. Points, of course, make up an object and, in turn, morphing reshapes your object. In previous versions of LightWave, morphing between objects required that you model separate objects
for each target. Now in LightWave 6, morph targets are all part of
one single object via the Morph modeling mode, also known as
endomorphs.

Figure 3.10
The Morph modeling
mode button at the
lower-right corner of
the Modeler interface.

Figure 3.10 shows the **M** button at the lower-right corner of the Modeler interface. Select
this mode to begin creating an object with endomorphs.

Exercise 3.2   Preparing a Morph Object

Creating a morph object is easy. You don't need to make a new object to create endomorphs—any existing object will work. The first step is that you need to be sure that you
are in Morph mode. Be sure to select the **M** button pictured in Figure 3.10 before you
begin modeling. The .next step is to understand the difference between Absolute and
Relative morph settings. An Absolute morph setting tells Modeler that any newly created
endomorph stands on its own and is not affected by any changes to the base model. A
Relative morph setting then reflects any changes made to the base model. Follow along
with this next example to see how easy it is to create morph objects.

Note

You create morph objects with endomorphs to be animated in Layout. A primary use for
endomorphs is animating character expressions. This will be covered in detail in Chapter
12, "Organic Animation."

1. With your default Modeler configuration active, start Modeler and press the **l** key
   (lowercase L).

   The **l** key opens the Load Object command window.

Tip

The Grid is part of LightWave's coordinate system. Its size determines the scale with
which you'll be building objects. In Modeler, the Grid size is visible through the information panel at the lower-left corner of the interface. For more information on the Grid,
refer to your LightWave user manuals.

2. Load the 03Facial.lwo object from the Projects/Objects/Chapter3 directory.

3. Press the **a** key to fit the model into all views.

4. Click the M at the lower-right of the screen to tell Modeler you'll be working
   with Endomorphs.

5. To the right of the M key selection, you'll see the word "base" in the drop-down menu.

This tells Modeler that the current object, and the way it looks right now, is the base morph target.

Figure 3.11 shows the full Modeler screen with the 03Facial.lwo object loaded, and the M button selection.

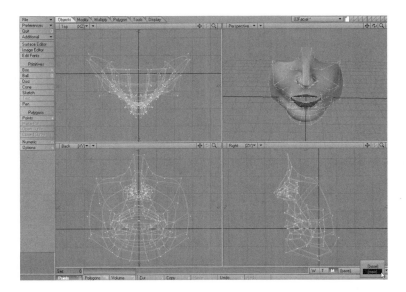

Figure 3.11   Once your model is loaded from the book's CD-ROM, select the **M** button at the lower-right corner of the interface. This puts Modeler in Morph mode to create endomorphs.

6. Click and hold the same drop-down menu and you'll see the selection labeled "new." From this drop-down menu you can select your "base" as well as any new endomorphs you create, and you can select "new" to create a new endomorph. Select the option labeled "new," and you'll see the Create Morph Map panel come up, as in Figure 3.12.

Figure 3.12   Choosing to make a new endomorph calls up the Create Morph Map requester.

7. In the Create Morph Map requestor, type a new name, such as Mouth.open.

It's important to add the period between the name, as this creates a group called

Mouth, which has a control called Open. When you use the MorphMixer plug-in in Layout, you'll be able to see your groups and control your morphs.

> **Note**
>
> MorphMixer is a Layout Displacement plug-in that enables you to morph between any of the morph targets you've created. It produces a window of morph sliders that you can adjust and keyframe. This is similar, but much better than the Morph Gizmo plug-in in previous versions of LightWave.

Before you click OK in the Create Morph Map panel, you need to decide if this Morph Map will be Absolute or Relative. Choosing Absolute tells Modeler that the Morph Map you create will not be affected if you make changes to the base object. Therefore, a Relative Morph Map will be affected if you make any changes to the base object. Of course, any changes you make to the geometry, such as adding or deleting, will affect all morph targets. You will use a Relative type setting most of the time when creating endomorphs.

8. For the Mouth.open Morph Map, choose Relative, and click OK.

9. Now, select the points encompassing the lower portion of the mouth and jaw, as shown in Figure 3.13. With the lower jaw points selected, in the Right view (lower right) move the mouse to the back of the face. Press the **y** key to select the Rotate command.

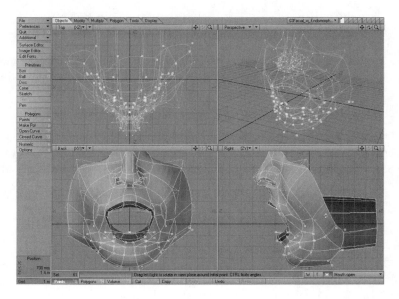

Figure 3.13   After you have created a new Morph Map, adjust the model's points to a new position. This becomes an endomorph—an embedded morph target.

10. When your mouse cursor changes to two small curved arrows, click and drag slightly and rotate the group of points to open the mouth.

11. After you've moved the points into a position you like, deselect them by first tapping the space bar to turn off the Rotate command, then clicking a blank area of the interface.

12. Now, from the drop-down menu next to the M button, select "new" as you did in Step 7, and create additional absolute Morph Targets. Set the new name to Mouth.pucker. Keep the Type set to Relative.

13. Select the points of the mouth area and move them into a pucker position using the Size tool (**Shift+h**) in the Back view (bottom-left view).

14. Once you've puckered the lips, you may need to Move the selection forward to make sure the puckered lips are not too far back into the face.

 Note

If you create a new Morph Map and do not adjust the model in some way, and then select another Morph Map, the new Morph Map will not be created. This is because vertex maps can have a value (including zero) or no value. A map has to have at least one value for at least one point to exist.

You've now created two Morph Maps.

15. Save the object as a new object, making sure not to save over your original.

16. Continue making new Morph Maps, and save your changes as you go. Experiment with this feature, with modifications to a simple ball, just to get the hang of it.

Exercise 3.3   Testing Morph Maps

To test your Morph Maps, select a map from the drop-down list. In the previous example, you created Mouth.open and Mouth.pucker. You should now see these names in the list, along with "base" and "new." Continue making as many Morph Maps (endomorphs) as you need.

You can use endomorphs to make phonetic shapes for lip-syncing and speech animation. You also can make changes to eyelids, cheeks, brows, and so on. Having individual Morph Maps for these things allows greater flexibility when animating.

1. You can put each Morph Map into motion at any time. If you decide to animate another part of the face, such as the eyes, set your Morph Map name to Eyes.*xxx*, where the Eyes will become a group, and the *xxx* will be the position you choose to name.

2. Load the 03Facial_w_Endomorphs.lwo object to see additional Morph Maps. When this object is loaded, select the name list at the lower-right corner of the Modeler interface.

3. Select any of the morph targets to see a particular object's various facial positions.

SubPatching Objects

You'll be hearing the term SubPatch a lot throughout this book. As a matter of fact, you might get sick of hearing about it, but the truth is, this is one of the most powerful tools within LightWave 6 Modeler. A SubPatch is what used to be a MetaNURBS. MetaNURBS were LightWave's version of Non-Uniform Rational B Splines. In LightWave 6, a SubPatched object turns quadrangles (polygons made of four points) and triangles (polygons made of three points) into curves. Think of SubPatch as digital clay, which enables you to mold objects.

Exercise 3.4   Creating SubPatches

Perform the next steps to get a feel for how LightWave 6's SubPatches work.

1. From the File drop-down menu in Modeler, select Close All Objects.

> **Note**
>
> Unlike older versions, there is no longer a Clear button in Modeler. In previous versions of LightWave, you would select the Clear button to completely reset Modeler and clear all layers. Now you must select Close All Objects. Be sure to save any work you want to keep before you do this.

2. Press the **a** key to fit all views.

    Although there is no data in Modeler, pressing **a** resets Modeler to a default 500mm Grid size. This assures that any measurements in this book match up with your system.

3. Be sure you are using the Default Modeler configuration and select the Box primitive from the Objects tab, or press **Shift+x** at the same time. From the Top view (Viewport 1), draw out a flat rectangle, similar to Figure 3.14.

    Notice that the rectangle is already visible in the Preview viewport. This is because LightWave 6 Modeler no longer requires you to make an object. Once you draw out the tool, the box is generated.

4. Once you've drawn out a rectangle shape you like, press the space bar to turn off the Box tool.

    Your rectangle has been created. All you need to create a box, ball, or any other primitive is to select the particular tool, draw it, and turn off the tool. There is no longer a "make" button.

5. Next, press the **Tab** key. Your rectangle will suddenly become an oval, as shown in Figure 3.15.

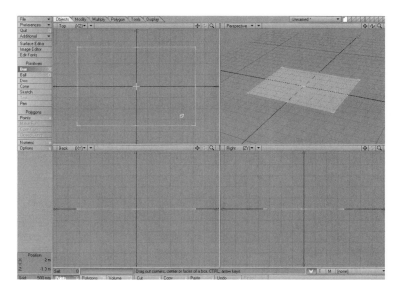

Figure 3.14   The Box primitive can be used to draw out a rectangle of any shape.

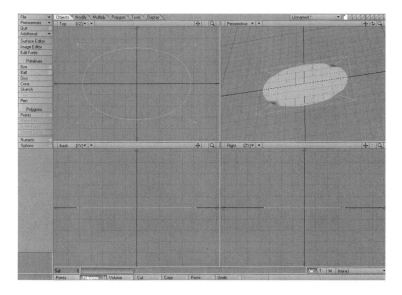

Figure 3.15   Pressing the Tab key activates SubPatch mode, smoothing active polygons.

This shape can be the basis for many types of objects such as a potato chip or leaf. If you wanted to make a leaf, you might need a little more control.

6. Press **Shift+d** to bring up the Subdivide Polygons panel as in Figure 3.16.

Figure 3.16   Subdivide Polygons can add more geometry to your existing shape for added control.

7. Make sure that Faceted is chosen in the Subdivide Polygons panel. Click OK. This adds polygons to create an object now totaling four polygons.

 Note

SubPatched polygons require either three- or four-sided polygons. However, try to always work with four-sided polygons for best results. Three-sided polygons can sometimes create undesirable results when rendering smooth surfaces.

8. Press **Ctrl+t** to activate the Drag tool (also found in the Modify tab). Now click and drag the corners of the polygon in the top view to round out the shape on the left side, similar to Figure 3.17.

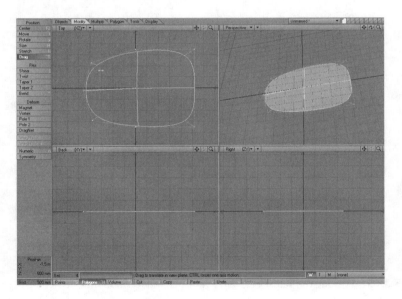

Figure 3.17   Use the Drag tool to shift points of the polygon into more of a curve.

9. For the other side of the polygon on the right, use the Drag tool to make a sharper point, as this will be the tip of the leaf. Just to see how this is working, press the **Tab** key to turn off SubPatch mode. You can see how simple polygons are turned into smooth flowing curves with SubPatch mode on.

10. From the Back view (Viewport 3), drag the right side points up to give the leaf some curves. You also can drag the left side points down.

Figure 3.18 shows the adjustments.

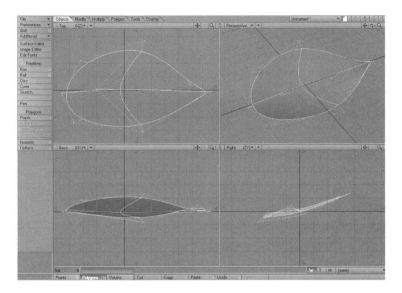

Figure 3.18   Adjusting just a few points on this simple box creates a smooth-flowing leaf.

From this point on, the leaf needs color and texture, and a stem. Later in Chapter 8, "Environmental Structures," you'll learn how to build a simple tree and its leaves, and surface them. The quick example showed you how a simple flat box can be made into something natural and organic, such as a leaf. While this is just a hint of what SubPatch can do, the principles are the same regardless of the complexity of your object. You start with a simple primitive, such as a box or a ball. You can even begin with a few points. Using SubPatch you can mold and shape your model into anything you can imagine. Chapter 10, "Organic Modeling," will show you how these simple techniques can take you far enough to create a stunningly realistic human face.

Splines

With LightWave 6's SubPatch mode, rich toolset, and full OpenGL interface, it is easy to create any shape you can imagine. However, there is yet another way for you to create and shape your models. A spline is a curve defined by mathematical functions such as Bezier, B-Spline, Hermite, and NURBS (or SubPatch). Spline modeling can help you create additional shapes like tubes, tunnels, staircases, and more. It is also useful for creating 3D geometry from background images. The next two exercises show you how to create and shape a spline, and build a simple object from a background image.

Before the capability to mold shapes with SubPatch, splines were often used to create smooth-flowing objects, such as curtains, or the hull of a boat. This type of modeling is still available in LightWave and may serve better for your specific modeling needs. This next tutorial shows you how to create a rowboat with spline curves.

Exercise 3.5   Creating a Rowboat

In this exercise, you build a rowboat using splines and the Skin tool. Its curves are simple but too complex for primitive shapes. These techniques also can be used to create cloth, landscapes, or even characters.

1. Save any work in Modeler, and then select Close All Objects from the File menu. Press the **a** key to fit all views.

2. Select the Points command from the Objects tab.

   This enables you to create points—points that make up a curve.

3. In the Top view (Viewport 1), click with the right mouse button to instantly create a point to the right of the X axis.

   You can line up a point with the left mouse button, then click the right button if you like.

Note

Mac users: Use the Command button along with the single mouse button to simulate the right mouse button functions.

4. Create five points, similar to Figure 3.19.

   These points will represent an outline of one-half of the rowboat. LightWave's splines will make the curve, and the Skin feature will be used to create a surface.

5. Press **Ctrl+p** to create an open curve.

   Pressing **Ctrl+o** creates a closed curve.

6. With the single open curve created, call up the Clone tool by pressing **Ctrl+c** (the Clone tool also is found under the Multiply tab). Using the Clone tool, duplicate the spline curve for the rest of the boat's right side.

7. For Number of Clones, enter 4.

   This creates four more splines in addition to the original, totaling five.

8. Set the Offset Y to 250mm.

   This spreads the curves up 250mm from the original.

9. Set the Offset Z to 150mm.

   This shifts each clone down the Z axis, creating the curve needed for the front of the rowboat. Figure 3.20 shows the Clone tool's interface.

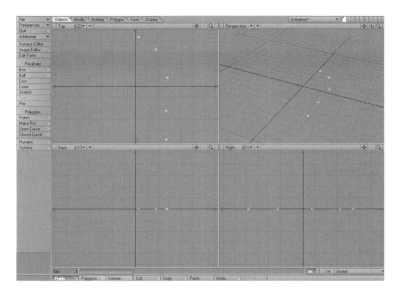

Figure 3.19   Create points with the right mouse button to begin making a spline curve.

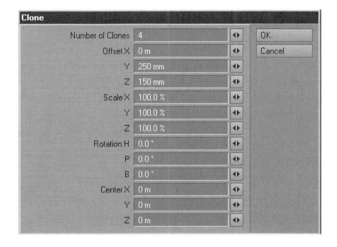

Figure 3.20   The Clone tool duplicates the curve, allowing you to set offsets.

10. Click OK to see your curves.

Feel free to adjust the curves if you like, and to try various Offset values. Figure 3.21 shows the cloned curves. Then, deselect all curves.

11. Select the Mirror tool (**Shift+v**) from the Multiply tab and with the left mouse button, click and drag the mouse on the center X axis in the Top view.

LightWave 6's tools are interactive, and holding the mouse down while slightly moving the mouse shows where the mirrored objects will be placed.

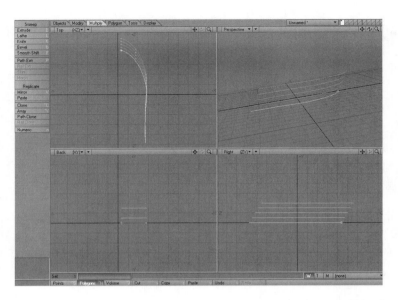

Figure 3.21   The Clone tool duplicated the single curve, creating a framework for the row-boat.

12. Line up the mirrored curves with the original curves.

13. Let go of the mouse button to set the new curves.

14. Press the spacebar to turn off the Mirror tool. Figure 3.22 shows the mirrored curves.

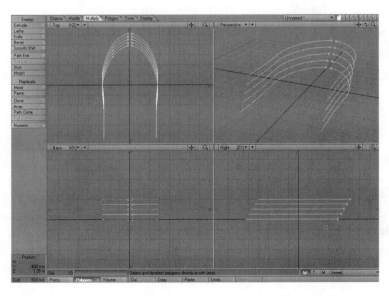

Figure 3.22   The interactive Mirror tool is used to create a duplicate of the curves on the opposite side of the X axis.

If the front points of the curves do not line up, don't worry—you can align them to make sure your boat won't have any leaks.

15. Switch to Points mode at the bottom of the Modeler interface, and select the 10 points that make up the curves in the front of the boat, as shown in Figure 3.23.

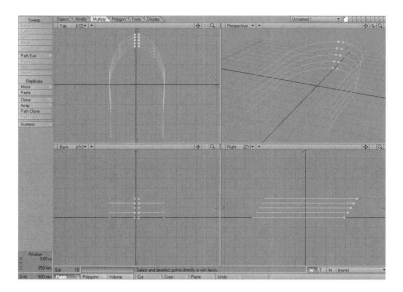

Figure 3.23   Working in Points mode, make sure the 10 points in the front of the boat are selected.

16. With the 10 points selected, go to the Tools tab, and select the Set Value command (also **Ctrl+v**).

    This enables you to precisely set any selected points to a specific location.

17. Select the X Axis, and the Value (the Modeler measurement you want to move the points to), to **0**.

18. Click OK.

    Now it looks like you only have five points selected, as in Figure 3.24.

    Even though it looks like only five points are now remaining, if you look at the small information window above the Points mode button at the bottom of the Modeler interface, you'll see that it reads Set 10. This tells you that you have 10 points selected. Figure 3.25 shows this area.

    Keeping the 10 points in the exact location does you no good. When you create a surface for the boat, the front side will not connect. Modeler still sees the curves as separate entities.

19. To remedy this, set the points to an equal location using the SetValue command.

20. Now eliminate the duplicate points by pressing the **m** key for Merge Points.

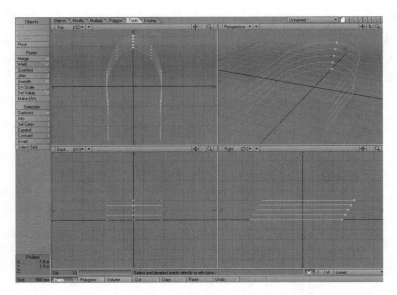

Figure 3.24   The SetValue command can move selected points to a specific location in Modeler.

21. When the Merge Points panel comes up, select Automatic, and click OK.

    A message should instantly pop up telling you that five points were eliminated.

    Press the / key to deselect the points.

22. From here, all you need to do is create a surface on top of the curves. You do this by using the Skin tool, found under the Multiply tab. But first, you need to tell Modeler what to skin.

23. In any of the Modeler viewports, select half of the curves in order, one after the other, being sure not to skip any.

    Make sure you are working in Polygon mode (from the bottom of the Modeler interface (see Figure 3.26). The curves are highlighted with bright yellow when selected.

24. Once the first set of curves is selected, select the Skin tool, and Modeler will generate a surface or skin for the curves.

    Because these were open curves, Modeler will try to connect the end of the curve with the start. You'll see a straight section of new polygons on the inside of the boat.

25. Press the / key to deselect the curves, then select the extra polygons on the inside of the boat, as shown in Figure 3.27.

26. With the extra inside polygons selected, press the **z** key to delete them.

Figure 3.25
While it appears as though only five points are selected, the numeric info accurately tells you that 10 points are selected.

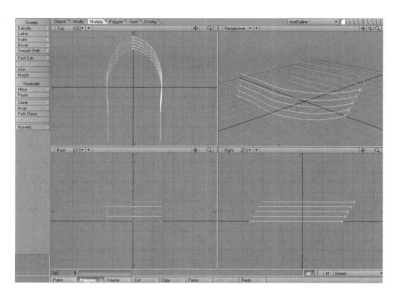

Figure 3.26   The first set of curves is selected, ready to have a skin applied.

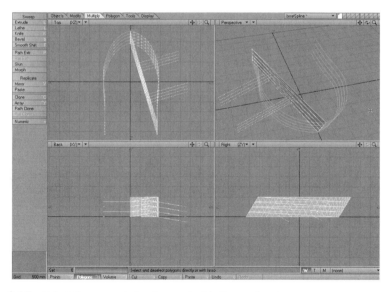

Figure 3.27   Select the unwanted polygons inside the rowboat.

27. Press the **f** key to flip the existing surface outward, if the polygons don't seem to be facing outward.

    When surfacing, you can make the boat's surface double-sided, so that both the inside and outside have visible polygons. Figure 3.28 shows the final surface on one side of the rowboat.

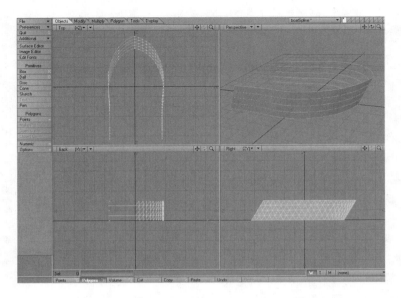

Figure 3.28   Once the unwanted polygons are removed, pressing the **f** key flips the remaining polygons outward. Here you can see half of the boat now has a surface.

There's nothing glamorous about spline modeling. It's tedious, and not often the best method to use when creating specific shapes. The idea here is that you have all the tools you need to create whatever you can imagine. This section introduces you to the basic tools and functions that will be used throughout the chapters in this book. There are even more features to LightWave 6 Modeler that you should be aware of. Read on through the rest of this chapter to learn about the Additional functions.

 Note

You also can create a skin for the rowboat using LightWave's Patch command, found under the Curves heading within the Polygon panel. Using the same techniques described in the previous exercise, you can skin splines with the Patch command. Additionally, you also use the Skin command to "skin" a series of polygons.

Additional Functions

Even if you are a seasoned veteran in LightWave Modeler, there will always be some tool or function that you don't use or didn't know about. Version 6 is no exception, and as your modeling hours accumulate, you may find that there are even more functions you didn't know about.

Go to the Objects tab in Modeler, and toward the top-left side of the interface you'll see the Additional drop-down menu. If you are familiar with LightWave Modeler previous to version 6, you may remember this area as the Custom selections. There was also a Custom selections in the Tools tab as well, helping to confuse you. But because LightWave 6 is customizable, the Additional selections are simply a place for tools and plug-ins that don't have a home. As you work through your projects, you'll find what tools you might need from this Additional list, and give them their own interface button or keystroke. Refer to Chapter 1, "Introducing LightWave 6," for information on configuring menus and buttons. Take a look at some of the cool tools in the Additional drop-down menu.

Send Object to Layout

This command is not the first in the list of Additional tools, but perhaps one of the most important. Figure 3.29 shows the selection from the drop-down list.

Send Object to Layout does just that. However, it is ghosted until the current object is saved. Once saved, the command becomes available and you can instantly send it to Layout for animation. This is a command that you might consider creating a button for, or better, a hotkey on the keyboard.

Figure 3.29
One of the first commands you might consider assigning to a button is the Send Object to Layout command.

Synchronize Layout

Directly above Send Object to Layout is the Synchronize Layout command. This automatically updates Modeler and Layout so that your project is current in both programs. You wouldn't want to be working with an older model in Modeler and override the newer model in Layout by mistake.

 Note
Send to Layout and Sync Layout only work if the Hub is active. You also must save an object before you can use the Send to Layout command.

Create Weight, Texture, Morph Maps

Here is a family of tools that are worthy of buttons they can call their own. Earlier in this chapter, Weight, Texture, and Morph Maps were discussed, as well as their creation process. Instead of selecting the W, T, or M buttons at the lower-right corner of the screen, and then selecting New from the drop-down menu, you can assign a button or keystroke to the commands from the Additional menu selections.

These are only options for you to work with. If you create Weight Maps from the Additional menu, or from the W button commands at the bottom of the interface, there is no difference.

Bone Weights

Bone Weights are a powerful new addition to LightWave 6. Because you can set up full skeletal structures for your characters directly in Modeler, you can also assign Bone Weights. These are just general Weight Maps used for bone influences. When you create a character and set up a bone structure, the bones deform the geometry to create a moving character without any seams. Often, areas like fingers are troublesome to animate due to influences bones have on surrounding geometry. Now with Bone Weights, you can tell each bone to have a certain amount of falloff and influence. This subject will be covered with a detailed tutorial later in Chapter 11. Figure 3.30 shows the Make Bone Weight Map panel which appears when you select the tool.

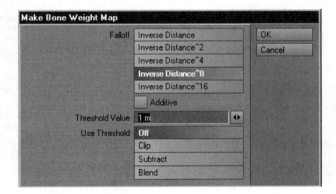

Figure 3.30   Bone Weights can be found in the Additional drop-down menu and offer more control over bone influences.

Skelegon-ize

Skelegon-ize, also found under the Additional selections, can quickly create skelegons from curves. Skelegons are placeholders for bone structures. Figure 3.31 shows a full bone structure created in just 15 seconds! Using the Gear tool (also found under the Additional selections), a simple gear object has been created. Then, running Skelegon-ize, Modeler created a bone structure around the points of the object. Using the points of an object, Skelegon-ize can create a full bone hierarchy. This, too, will be covered in Chapter 11.

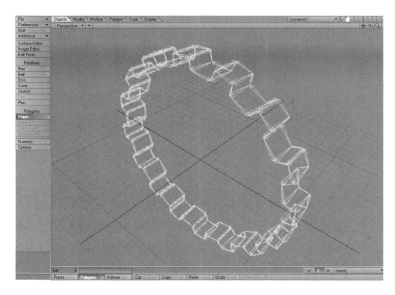

Figure 3.31   A gear-shaped skeleton of bones can be created in seconds with the Skelegon-ize command found under the Additional selections.

Draw Skelegons

You can also find the Draw Skelegons command in the Additional menu selection list. Selecting this command enables you to quickly and easily draw a skelegon structure in Modeler, which can be converted to a bone structure in Layout. You can work with your model in a background layer while building the bones in another. Because LightWave 6 saves all layers with each object, your model will have the bones saved with it as well. Load the single object into Layout for animation and the bones will be there as well.

 Note

Once Skelegons are converted to bones in Layout, they cannot be changed back.

More Commands

There are a number of handy tools in the Additional selection list, from Capsule, which creates a perfect capsule object, to centering functions, to LScripts. As you find free moments while working with Modeler, be sure to check out the tools and commands in the Additional selection list. Find your favorites, and map them to their own buttons. Try everything! The more aware you are about what tools are in your tool chest, the more prepared you'll be on your next project.

Note
Find out all you need to know about LScripts in Appendix B, "LScript and LSIDE."

You may even have projects that require you to create a complex object or shape from nothing more than an image. And although it would be nice to have a command in the Additional list that was labeled "Make Cool Object," you're simply not going to find it. This next project will quickly step you through the process of using splines to create a logo from a backdrop image.

Spline Curves and Backdrop Images

More often than not, a client will want you to create an abstract 3D object or a simple logo creation from a sketch he or she has made. Whatever the case, you will not always be fortunate enough to be supplied with 3D data that you can covert and manipulate— leaving you to create from the ground up.

Exercise 3.6   Using Spline Curves

Exercise 3.6 shows you how important your knowledge of spline curves is, and how you can bring a flat piece of art to life. Figure 3.32 shows the original artwork your client wants you to make 3D.

Figure 3.32   The image your client provided is small and plain. It's your job to make it a 3D object.

Your first step in creating 3D geometry from flat art is to get the flat art into the computer. You can do this with a scanner or maybe video capture.

   1. Input your flat art into the computer.

Note

From the Additional drop-down list in Modeler, you can use the EPSF loader to load EPS (Encapsulated PostScript) files into LightWave. Often, programs such as Adobe Illustrator are used to create logos and artwork. The EPSF loader converts the file to flat geometry that you can extrude and animate.

2. In Modeler, select the Display tab.

3. From the commands on the left side, select the Backdrop button. The Backdrop tab of the Display Options panel opens.

   You can quickly access this area as well by pressing the **d** key, then selecting the Backdrop tab.

   It's a good idea to work in the Back/Front view (Viewport 3) for any nondescript object, such as the clip art you're using here.

4. Select the Viewport 3 button in the Backdrop tab under Display Options.

5. From Image, select Load Image.

6. Load the 03splat.tga image from the Projects/Images/Chapter3 folder. Figure 3.33 shows the Backdrop tab with the image loaded.

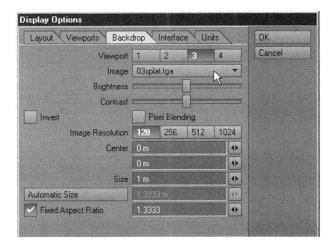

Figure 3.33   You can load one image and place it in each viewport's backdrop, or load a different image for each viewport. Here, the image 03splat.tga is loaded and assigned to Viewport 3.

7. Click OK to close the Display Options panel.

   You'll see the image appear in the Back (Viewport 3) display. Figure 3.34 shows the image loaded. If you zoom into the view, because of the low resolution, creating precise spline curves might be tough to do.

8. Go back into the Display Options panel (press **d**) and in the Backdrop tab, set the Image Resolution for Viewport 3 to 512.

You'll see the backdrop image sharpen.

 Note

You might at some point grab an image from video and have a different aspect ratio. For example, a video frame in your computer will appear more rectangular in shape than a generic computer-generated image. Chapter 6, "LightWave 6 Cameras," has more information on aspect ratios.

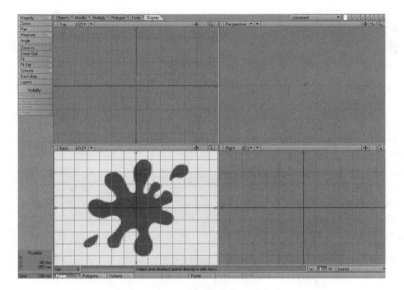

Figure 3.34   Although the image now appears in the viewport, its low resolution might be a problem for precise curve creation.

Now that the image is loaded and sharp, you can begin creating curves.

9. From the Objects tab, select Points, and begin creating points around the image.

You can't do anything to the image—it's only a backdrop reference.

10. Continue making points around the main splat picture, similar to Figure 3.35.

You don't want too many points, only enough to control the curves. Too many points will create less smooth curves at this stage. For this model, create about 70 points.

 Tip

Feel free to use the Contrast adjustment in the Display Options panel under the Backdrop tab to make your points and curve more visible.

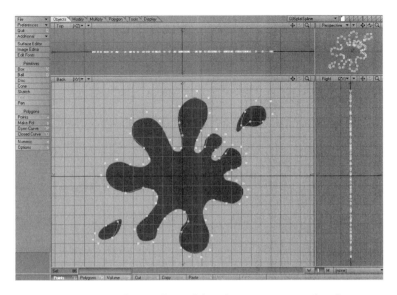

Figure 3.35   Points are created around a Backdrop image to create a closed curve.

11. Once you have the rough outline of points, use the Drag tool (**Ctrl+t**) to move each point into place, using the image as a reference.

12. When you've come full circle and created the points, press **Ctrl+o** to create a closed curve.

    Figure 3.36 shows the final curve. Note that the Brightness and Contrast were brought down even more to make the curve visible.

13. Save the original spline curve. You never know if you'll have to readjust is later.

14. Freeze the curve, either under the Polygon tab, or by pressing **Ctrl+d** key.

    This makes the curve into a flat polygon.

15. Save this as well, but as a separate object.

    The more points you have created in your curve, the more points will be created when you freeze the curve.

 Note

Always save your work in stages. Never wait until something is finished before saving.

16. Extrude, bevel, and surface the newly created object. Figure 3.37 shows the final 3D splat.

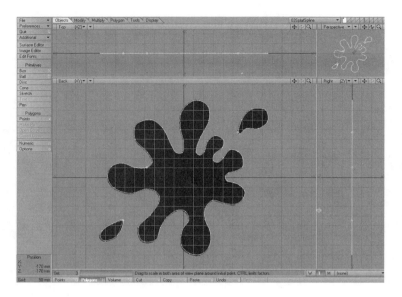

Figure 3.36   The final closed curve matches the original artwork.

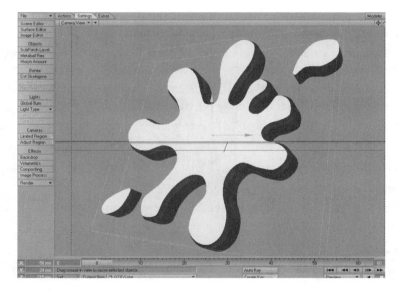

Figure 3.37   See how far a simple image can take you? One small image is now a 3D object, thanks to Splines and Backdrop Images.

The Next Step

Exercise 3.6 is straightforward, but it shows you how to: create closed curves; use the backdrop image feature; adjust the backdrop image contrast and brightness; create polygons from curves. Anytime you have to create a 3D object from an image, you can use this technique. This is especially useful for creating logos from business cards. Later in Chapter 16, "Broadcast Animations," you will create high-quality graphics from fonts. Often, a client will have an EPS or AI (Adobe Illustrator) file of his original artwork. This is an excellent way to import artwork into Modeler to create instant and perfect geometry. Try loading some of the EPS files from the book's CD using the EPSF loader in Modeler.

Summary

The exercises in this chapter took you through some of the key features of Modeler 6. You were introduced to many new functions and revisited old ones as well. The steps provided here will help guide you through the upcoming chapters and the tutorials within them. It is important that you understand the methods and principles of how LightWave 6 Modeler functions and how objects are created. If you're okay with that, turn the page and head on into Chapter 4, "LightWave 6 Layout."

Chapter 4

LightWave 6 Layout

In LightWave 6, just about everything can be animated. Because of this, it is crucial for you to plan your projects. Knowing ahead of time what you want to create helps you decide how to create it. The tools in LightWave 6 are extraordinary and powerful, and knowing what they can do and how they do it is a benefit to you and your projects. Before that, however, you need to be familiar with the basic Layout environment, keyframing, and animation setup. This chapter steps you through the simpler aspects of Layout. Specifically, this chapter discusses:

- The Animation environment
- Keyframing
- Constructing scenes
- Using the Scene Editor

Although these aspects are simple, the concepts here are the foundation for moving ahead and creating more complex objects and animations.

In the simplest terms, 3D objects are created in LightWave's Modeler. LightWave's Layout is used to put these objects in motion.

Understanding the Animation Environment

Understanding the environment in which you are creating animations is key to your success as an animator. Knowing how to create an effect, or where to make the right adjustments, not only saves you time but also aggravation. This chapter instructs you on:

- The LightWave 6 Layout environment
- Keyframe animation
- Constructing scenes in Layout
- Using Layout's Scene Editor

LightWave 6 has a lot of power and it's up to you to harness it. If you are familiar with previous versions of LightWave, the LightWave 6 Layout interface should look familiar to you. It is uncluttered, yet functional. Many programs fill up the screen with useless icons—LightWave names buttons clearly. Figure 4.1 shows the Layout window at startup. The default interface is in Layout's Perspective view—sort of a bird's-eye view of the environment.

Think of Layout as your very own television studio. Figure 4.1 shows the studio layout with a camera and a light. By default, one camera and one light are in the scene.

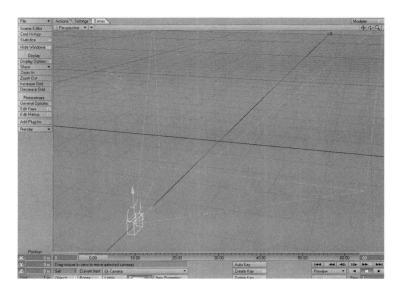

Figure 4.1   Layout opens to the Perspective view at startup.

Note

The colored arrows visible on selected items represent axis control handles. Clicking and dragging the green arrow limits movements to the Y axis. Clicking and dragging the blue arrow limits movements to the Z axis, and red, to the X axis.

The Layout Interface

Too often when a program opens, it's as if you're staring at a blank canvas. Where do you go from here? What's next? Or even if you know what's next, what should you create? If you look at the default startup of the Actions, Settings, and Extras tabs, you'll notice that the Actions tab is selected. This is where you begin to bring objects into Layout, adding lights and moving items. Think of the Actions, Settings, and Extras tabs as your steps to creating. What Actions will you take? What Settings are you going to apply? And what Extras do you need? Beginning with Actions, you can add items to a scene. A scene contains movements, lighting, and camera arrangements.

When you select the Actions tab, controls appear on the left side of the interface.

Note

You should be using LightWave's default interface settings for this chapter. The controls for each tab can be moved from the left to the right or hidden. A default setting puts them on the left side of the interface.

Here, you can add whatever element you might need for your scene. You can control position with the Move and Rotate commands. Selecting the Settings tab changes the controls on the left side of the screen, and gives you access to the Surface Editor, the Image Editor, and the Effects panels. Selecting the Extras tab changes the controls again, allowing you control over editing keyboard commands, adding plug-ins, and so on. You will use most of the tools in these three tabs throughout this book. If you refer to your LightWave 3D user guides, or Chapter 1, "Introducing LightWave 6," of this book, you can add your own tabs and controls, and rearrange everything to your liking. For now, stick with these default settings.

The Timeline and Fractional Frames

At the bottom of the Layout interface, you'll see more controls. The timeline for your animations, referred to as the frame slider in LightWave 6, appears here and cannot be moved. Don't think of this as just a timeline for your animations, think of it as your lifeline. All the elements of 3D animation are important, from lighting, to cameras, to special effects, but the timing and movement you employ is what brings it all to life. Figure 4.2 shows the default Layout timeline.

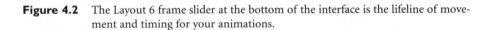

Figure 4.2   The Layout 6 frame slider at the bottom of the interface is the lifeline of movement and timing for your animations.

If you click and drag the frame slider, you can shuttle through your animation. By default, the timeline ends at frame 60. In most cases, you'll need more than 60 frames for your animations. In the General Options panel, accessed by pressing **o**, the frames per second (fps) is set to 30. NTSC video is 30fps, and is the most common setting for rendering. If the timeline ends at 60, and there are 30fps, you have a 2-second animation. To change this, double-click the number 60 at the end of the timeline to highlight it, and enter a new number, such as 300. At 30fps, 300 frames will give you a 10-second animation. Once entered, the numbers in the timeline adjust automatically, as in Figure 4.3.

Figure 4.3   The Layout timeline adjusts accordingly when you make the total animation length longer.

Although the default fps value is 30, you can change this to whatever you like. For example, if you're creating animations for film, change this value to 24. You might need an animation rendered at 15fps for a corporate PowerPoint presentation. Whatever fps you set, the default value will be used the next time you run Layout. Saved scenes with different fps values retain the information.

A new feature in LightWave 6 is the capability to view fractional frames in the timeline. Activating Allow Fractional Frames lets a user input frame numbers with decimals, like frame 4.23. Back in the General Options panel (accessed by pressing the **o** key), click the Allow Fractional Frames button and you'll see values appear between the increments in the timeline (see Figure 4.4).

Figure 4.4   Fractional frames can be turned on in the timeline for added control and timing.

The Coordinate System

Animating in 3D takes some getting used to. You need to realize that although you are looking at a flat computer monitor, elements in a 3D environment have X, Y, and Z axes. This is the 3D world in which your animations live. The world, per se, is the environment around your animation. Each animation you create will have its own environment and its own coordinate system. LightWave 6 allows you to choose between three coordinate systems: World, Parent, and Local. Previous versions of LightWave used only a Parent coordinate system that allowed you to move objects along the axes of a selected item's parent. This was a real problem when working with complex hierarchies and inverse kinematics bone chains. LightWave 6's Local coordinate system eliminates this problem by allowing an object to be moved or rotated upon its own axis.

The Coordinate System setting affects movements and what happens when you drag your mouse. The easiest way to see this is to add a null, rotate it on Heading (H), Pitch (P), and Bank (B), and then parent the default light to it. You can turn on the Show Handles option to indicate the movement axes. If World is used, the axis will be along the grid. With Parent, it will be the same as the null's local axes. With Local, it will be the light's own axes. Only World is really new. In LightWave 5.6, you could move an item along its local axes by holding the Ctrl key. However, World is an incredible addition. If an item is deep within a hierarchy of rotated parents, movement along its parents or local axes can be confusing. The capability to move the item along the world axes is a lifesaver.

Pivots

Every item in Layout has a pivot. Think of a pivot as an item's root. Movements, rotations, parenting, or targeting all work based on an object's pivot. LightWave 6 enables you to interactively move pivots in Layout as in previous versions, but now you have the capability to rotate pivots as well. To understand this further, follow along with this next exercise.

Exercise 4.1   Moving Pivots

Building multiple objects in Modeler, such as machinery or industrial equipment, requires you to have individual parts that rotate independently but remain assembled to a single object. A tractor, for example, requires that the wheels rotate upon their own pivots and the main lift rotates upon its own pivot. The arm extending from the main lift also needs to rotate, as does the main body of the tractor. The main body also needs to move and rotate upon its own pivot. This tutorial shows you how to load a single object with multiple pivot points (something you couldn't do before version 6) and move each pivot into place. Doing this will allow you to animate your model correctly.

1. From the Add command, load the 04Tractor_Layers.lwo object file from the CD that accompanies this book into Layout.

   A generic tractor object loads on the X axis.

2. At the bottom of the Layout interface, click and hold the Current Item dropdown list.

   You'll see that the single object you loaded is comprised of five layers. Each layer contains a separate part of the object.

3. Press 1 on the numeric keypad to switch to the Front view.

   This is the view looking down the Z axis. Figure 4.5 shows the view.

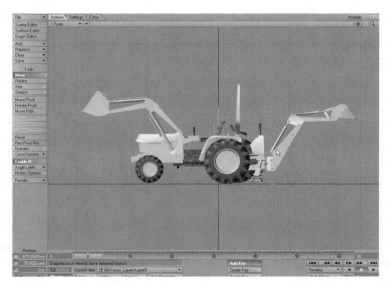

Figure 4.5   The tractor object has five layers, which means there are five parts (four wheels and the main body) to the object, each with separate pivoting parts.

Note
The numeric keypad is preprogrammed in Layout. 1 is Front view (z), 2 is Top view (y), 3 is Side view (x), 4 is Perspective view, 5 is Light view, and 6 is Camera view.

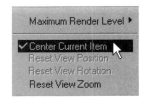

Figure 4.6
The Center Current Item function helps you align your view.

You can use the period key (.) to zoom in to the view, or the comma key (,) to zoom out.

4. From the top of the viewport, click and hold the small arrow, and select Center Current Item.

   The view centers on the currently selected item's pivot. Figure 4.6 shows the Center Current Item function. Note that this feature toggles on and off—select it again to turn it off.

   To place the pivots correctly, start with the wheels.

5. Select Layer 2 of the tractor object, as shown in Figure 4.7.

   When Layer 2 is selected, you'll see the front left wheel is highlighted with a yellow bounding box.

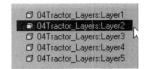

Figure 4.7
Select a layer of a particular object from the Current Item drop-down list at the bottom of the Layout interface.

Tip
If your object continually jumps to the representational Bounding Box mode when object layers are selected, increase the Bounding Box Threshold. Press **d** on the keyboard to enter the Display Options panel. Set the Bounding Box Threshold to 42000. This keeps all layers drawn when selected.

Warning
Higher levels of the Bounding Box Threshold can slow system resources.

At this point, you can begin to move the item's pivot into position. Positioning pivots in orthogonal views is important for accuracy. This is why you are in the Front (z) view.

6. With Layer 2 of the tractor selected, choose Move Pivot from the Actions tab.

   The object's handles, shown as arrows, will appear: a green arrow pointing upward, a red arrow from left to right, and a blue arrow pointing away (which is not visible in the Front view). The handles are centered on the object's origin along the X, Y, and Z axes. The wheel is off to the left of the 0 axis. The 0 axis is where the X, Y, and Z axes meet, sort of like an intersection. Each axis has 0, represented in Modeler by the dark line in the center of the grid. For example, in the Back view, the dark line running up and down is the 0 Y axis. To the right of the 0 Y axis is the positive X axis, and to the left of the 0 Y axis is the negative X axis. Rotating the wheel in this position would rotate the wheel around the 0 axis, and not its center. Figure 4.8 shows the wheel rotated with the existing pivot.

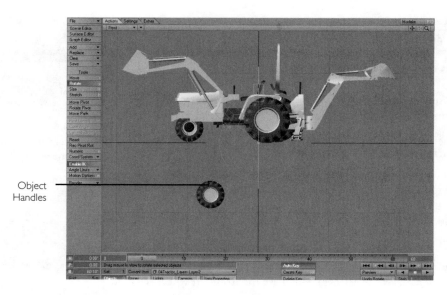

Object
Handles

Figure 4.8   Rotating the wheel's pivot instead of moving it produces a wide rotation around
the 0 axis. The wheel should rotate around itself.

7. With the wheel in its original position, Move the pivot by dragging the red
   arrow.

   This moves the pivot on the X axis. Use the period key (.) to zoom in if needed.

> **Tip**
>
> To quickly move into a closer view of the wheel, position the mouse pointer over the
> wheel. Press the g key to instantly center the mouse position. Then, zoom in with the
> period key (.). Note, this works only in the Front, Side, or Top view.

   Be as precise as possible centering the pivot.

8. When the X-axis pivot movement is in place, press **3** on the numeric keypad to
   switch to the Side view (x).

9. Select the green arrow and move the pivot up and over, centering it on the wheel
   for the Z and Y positions. Figure 4.9 shows the movements in Bounding Box
   Mode.

10. If you cannot get your pivot movements to be precise enough, you might need to
    adjust your Grid Square Size.

    You can do this through the Display Options panel (**d**) or press the left-bracket
    key ([) for a smaller grid and the right-bracket key (]) for a larger grid.

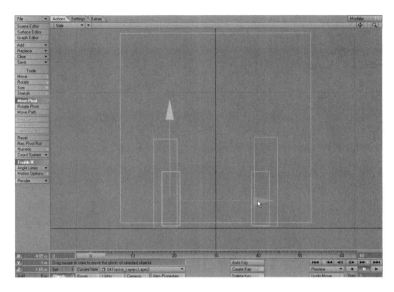

Figure 4.9   Use the Side view to align the pivot's position for the Y and Z axes.

 Tip

If you do create a smaller grid square size, you'll need to zoom out your view using the comma (,) key. A smaller grid square size allows you to create more precise movements.

You've just moved the pivot for the front wheel, Layer 2.

11. To test its position, select the Rotate command for the selected item, then use the right mouse button to click and drag to rotate the wheel on its bank position.

Because the tractor is positioned on the X axis, selecting Bank for rotation makes the tire rotate upon its center.

If you notice that the spinning of the wheel is unaligned, reposition the pivot point. When you have it to your liking, save your scene and your objects. From here, select the other layers of the tractor object and move the pivot points into place. Experiment with different pivot point positions, and even try rotating them for various results. You can load the tractor object into Modeler, select the scoop area, and place it on another layer. Resave the object, and you'll be able to set a pivot point for the rotation of the scoop. You can do this for any object. Remember that pivot points are the roots of the object and/or layer. All movements, centering, and even rotation are based on the pivot. For example, the pivot for a door swinging on a hinge would be the edge of the door where it meets the frame. The door rotates on this pivot point.

Setting Pivot Points in Modeler

You also have the capability to set a pivot point in Modeler. Setting the pivot point in Modeler is much easier than in Layout. To do so, choose the object you want to adjust and follow these steps:

1. Under the Tools tab, select Pivot, and you'll see a blue crosshair appear in your Modeler views.

2. Move this pivot point into your desired position, and save the object.

   This is a smart way to create complex objects with many moving parts. Once you have a pivot point set, it is recorded.

   If you were to Rotate the pivot in Layout, you can use the Rec Pivot Rot (Record Pivot Rotation) command to lock the new pivot location.

   This eliminates rotation problems often found in complex hierarchies and works well for LightWave 6's new multilayer objects.

Understanding Keyframing

Many of the new features in LightWave 6 are discussed and used throughout the projects in this book. Because this is the first chapter to dive into Layout, it's necessary that you understand the importance of keyframing and timing. After you've mastered proper keyframing, you'll be equipped to move into more advanced techniques and concepts.

Keyframing is the act of setting or marking an animatable attribute in time. When you want a ball to move from point A to point B over two seconds, you need to set keyframes to tell the computer "stay here" at this point in time. You will quickly get a feel for timing the more you set keyframes. You can set keyframes yourself or let LightWave manage them for you.

Keyframing goes beyond just animating position and rotation. It encompasses light intensity, color, various surface attributes, and virtually anything in Layout that has a value that can be changed.

Exercise 4.2   Auto Key

By default, LightWave's Layout has the Auto Key button on at the bottom of the Layout interface. It will adjust the values of existing keyframes. For the Auto Key feature to automatically create keys, you need to turn on Auto Key Create (General Options), which is off by default. Any commands such as Move, Rotate, Size, or Stretch will be remembered for selected items at the current frame. The following exercise explains this feature further.

1. Clear your scene in Layout, and load the 04IsoBall.lwo object from the book's CD-ROM.

2. With the 04IsoBall.lwo object loaded, be sure the frame slider at the bottom of the Layout interface is at 0, be sure Auto Key is enabled, and activate Auto Key Create in the General Options panel (o) to have keyframes created automatically.

3. Select All Motion Channels from the selection area of the Auto Key Create command.

   In the Layout window you'll notice that there is always a key at frame 0, by default. Thus, an object is locked in place, even without Auto Key. Auto Key merely lets you make an adjustment at frame 0 without having to re-create the key.

4. Move the 04IsoBall, shown in Figure 4.10, out of view in Layout.

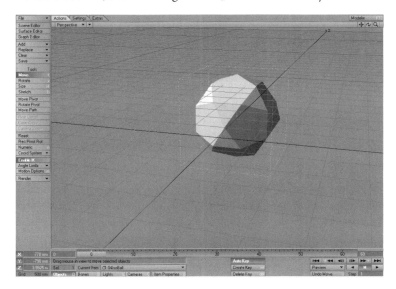

Figure 4.10   The Auto Key is on, and when the 04IsoBall is moved, it will remain in the position where it is moved to, without the need to create a keyframe to lock it in place.

5. Move the timeline slider to frame 10.

6. Move the object to a different position or rotation.

7. Click and drag the timeline slider.

   The object doesn't move. This is because Layout has automatically locked it in place at frame 10, thanks to Auto Key.

8. Drag the timeline slider to frame 20.

9. Move the object to a different position, and give it some rotation.

Note

When setting up keyframes, LightWave automatically draws a motion path. When the keyframe is set at frame 20, you will see a line appear representing the object's path of motion if Show Motion Paths is enabled from the Display Options panel (**d**).

10. Move the timeline slider to frame 40, and then move and/or rotate the object again.

11. Press the Rewind button (see Figure 4.11), which has the two small arrows pointing to a line on the left, and then press the Play Forward button, which is the small right-pointing triangle above the Step value entry.

Figure 4.11
The Rewind button takes you back to frame 0 and resets your timeline.

The three buttons underneath the Rewind buttons are the Play Forward, Play Reverse, and Pause buttons. You should see the 04IsoBall object move and rotate between keyframes 20 and 40. You can shuttle through the animation by grabbing the timeline slider and dragging.

Auto Key can make your animation work go smoother, but if you're not careful, it can damage your work. There may be situations where your keyframing needs to be precise. Having Auto Key enabled and accidentally moving the wrong object, or moving the right object the wrong way, could potentially cause you more work. Work with caution when using the Auto Key feature.

A great time to use Auto Key is when setting up character animation.

Exercise 4.4   Manual Keyframing

Manual keyframing is often a more common way to work, yet the choice is yours. Keyframing requires that you develop a keen sense of timing, and while this can't be done overnight, a few practice animations can get you started.

Tip

A good way to work is to turn off Auto Key Create in the General Options panel, and work only with Auto Key enabled. Auto Key adjusts existing keyframes without the need to create them again after any changes are made.

1. Load the 04Leaf_2.lwo object into a clear Layout scene. Be sure to turn off Auto Key.

2. Press 6 on the numeric keypad to switch to Camera view.

    If the leaf object is not selected, click it with the left mouse button. A bounding box highlights around the leaf, and its handles show, as in Figure 4.12.

3. With the left mouse button, click and drag the green arrow up, moving the leaf up on the Y axis.

    Move the leaf until it just leaves the frame. This is where you want the leaf to start off in the animation. Now you need to tell LightWave to make the leaf stay at this location.

4. Press the Enter or Return key once to call up the Create Motion Key requester.

    The current frame will be highlighted, as in Figure 4.13. You also can select the Create Key button at the bottom of the interface.

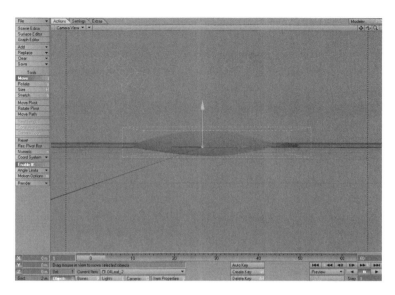

Figure 4.12   Selecting 04Leaf_2.lwo shows the bounding box representation and the object handles. The box in the upper-left portion of the screen is a light.

Figure 4.13   Pressing Enter or Return calls up the Create Motion Key command.

If the timeline slider was at frame zero, a 0 will appear in the Create Key At command window.

5. If the timeline slider is not at frame zero, enter 0 and press the Enter or Return key again.

The keyframe is now set.

Tip

You might be in the habit of clicking in each numeric window and erasing the existing values, then reentering them. This is not necessary. When you open the Create or Delete key requester, the existing value is already selected. All you need to do is enter the desired value. This saves time.

Note

You do not need to move the timeline slider to set keyframes throughout an animation if you are manually setting keyframes. However, it helps to move it to keep yourself organized and aware of the current animation frame.

6. Move the leaf down to the grid plane where it originally was, as shown in Figure 4.14.

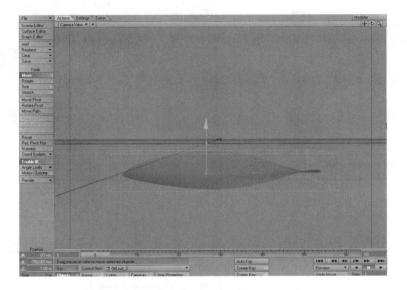

Figure 4.14   Move the leaf down to the ground plane or just below.

7. Press the Enter or Return key to call up the Create Motion Key command.

8. Type 60 from the numeric keypad and press Enter.

Too often, users are in the habit of using the number keys across the top of the keyboard. While this works just as well, you will save time by using the numeric keypad.

Tip

Because you want the leaf to end at frame 60 where it originally was positioned, you could have created a key when it was in that position, but for frame 60. You can use the single position of an object to create various keyframes by entering the desired keyframe values in the Create Motion Key dialog.

9. Press the Play button (right arrow icon) at the bottom right of the Layout interface.

The leaf should fall into the screen and land.

Okay, that was really basic and will be the simplest thing in this book, but it's important for you to get the hang of how to keyframe and understand what you are doing. You told the leaf to be at a certain position at frame 0, the beginning of the animation. Then, you moved the leaf to its resting position at the end of the animation. You told LightWave that the last position of the leaf is frame 60, creating a 2-second animation. LightWave will interpolate the frames between 0 and 60.

Deleting Keyframes

You also can delete keyframes just as easily as you create them. Pressing the Delete key on the keyboard calls up the Delete Motion Key box, with the cursor set at the Delete Key At requester and the current frame already selected, as shown in Figure 4.15.

Figure 4.15   Delete unwanted keyframes by pressing the Delete key on the keyboard to call up the Delete Motion Key command.

As with creating keyframes, the timeline slider does not need to be on the specific keyframe to delete a key. Enter the key you want to delete when the Delete Motion Key command window opens. Again, use your numeric keypad to save time!

Note

You can make this leaf land more gently using spline controls. Chapter 5, "LightWave 6 Graph Editor," explains it all.

Following the Keyframing Rule

You should know a few more things about keyframing in LightWave. A common misunderstanding with keyframes is that the more you have, the more control there will be in a scene—wrong! Setting up keyframes creates a motion path. That motion path is a curve, controlled by the keyframes you set.

A good rule of thumb to use when setting keyframes is to initially make two keyframes: your first keyframe and your last one, then set your frames that fall in between. For example, you want an object to move down a path and around an obstacle. The movement needs to be smooth, and trying to guess the timing might be tough to do. Set the beginning keyframe, then the ending keyframe to create the initial motion path. If you drag the timeline slider, the object moves between the two keyframes. If you move the timeline slider to the point where the object would move around the obstacle, you'll have the exact frame to set your next key. By creating the keyframe at this point in time, you've adjusted the motion path evenly. You can load the 04Move_2keys.lws and 04Move_5keys.lws scenes as examples. Also, load the 04LeafFall_1.lws scene to see a variation on the previous exercise. In this scene, the leaf had two mid-keyframes added, but notice that the motion is smooth and even between each of the keyframes.

Later, in Part III, "A Project-Based Approach to Animating Scenes," you'll have many more opportunities to work with advanced keyframe techniques.

Constructing Scenes

With the necessary basics on keyframing out of the way, it's time for you to begin learning how to build 3D scenes in LightWave 6. A scene in LightWave is comprised of objects, lights, and cameras, sort of like the real world. But with LightWave, you have no limitations—a virtual world you can call your own.

Setting up scenes often requires that you plan what it is you are trying to accomplish. Plan it, organize, and you'll be much better off. Remember the motto, "Work smarter, not harder."

Surfacing Objects

Sometimes it can be overwhelming when starting a big project. Where do you begin? What should you do first? From the start, you should know where you want to end up. This is, of course, if you're creating an animation for a client or your boss. There is much to be said about letting your creativity flow and see where it takes you—just don't do this on paying jobs. Time is money! Nevertheless, you should be aware of the entire project and begin by creating models.

When you set up a scene, a good place to start is to load your objects into Layout. However, because LightWave's object files retain their surface information (surfacing is not saved with a scene file), it's a good idea to load an object, surface it, save it, and then continue. Don't load all your objects at once, and don't try to surface them all together. Surface objects one at a time. From there, you can concentrate on movements and lighting.

 Note

LightWave 6's Modeler now supports surfacing and texture mapping, so much of your object's surfaces can be created there, as well as Layout. The choice is yours. Be sure to check out Chapter 10, "Organic Modeling," for more surfacing information.

Loading and Saving Objects

Earlier in this chapter you followed the steps to load objects into Layout. However, you also can load objects from other scenes. Additionally, because you have the capability to change object properties and shapes, you can save objects as well.

At some point in your career as an animator, you will come to know the Load Items From Scene command. This handy option enables you to load just the objects and their motions from one scene into another. You also have the option to load another scene's lighting into your existing scene.

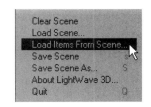

Figure 4.16
The Load Items From Scene command allows you to load objects, motions, and lights from one scene into another.

For example, let's say you've set up a complex scene of city streets, cars, elevated trains, and more. Now you need to add a pigeon or two flying across the street. You could load the pigeon and its wings into this scene and set the bird in motion. However, you'd need to do that twice, once for each bird, and you'd be working in a crowded scene, which might slow down things. Additionally, you don't want to accidentally change any of the other objects' settings. Instead, you can set up the bird in a scene all its own. You can test the wings, make sure they flap, and so on. From there, you can save the scene, and load the complex city scene. Then, all you need to do is select the Load Items From Scene command (see Figure 4.16) to load the bird and its motions into your current scene.

LightWave will ask you if you'd like to load the lights as well. In most cases, you won't load the lights because you already have a scene with active lights. You really only want the objects and their motions to be added into your current scene. But there are times that all you do want is the lights, such as a scene where the light source is a key element. You can create a scene with only the specific lights you need, and load those lights with their motions into your current scene, also with the Load Items From Scene command.

Adding Cameras to a Scene

Without a camera in your scene, you would never see anything render. LightWave 6 lets you add multiple cameras. Adding additional cameras is very useful for animations that need multiple angles of a single animation event. For example, perhaps your client has contracted you to re-create a traffic accident. It is required that you show the animation from all views: top, side, front, back, and a traveling aerial view. You can add five cameras and place them all once, in their respective positions. This eliminates the need to move the camera to different angles. Instead, you can simply switch between any of the multiple cameras. Chapter 6, "LightWave 6 Cameras," explores multiple cameras further.

Note

It's important to remember that in LightWave, rendered animations are always seen through whichever camera is selected at the time of rendering. Therefore, it's a good idea to get into the habit of using camera views to set up your scenes and keyframes.

1. Clear the scene by selecting Clear Scene from the File menu.

2. Click and hold down the Add drop-down menu.

3. Select Add Camera, as shown in Figure 4.17.

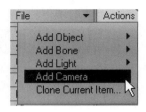

Figure 4.17
Adding a camera is as easy as adding objects.

Before the camera is added, a requester comes up asking you to name the camera. If you choose not to name the camera, LightWave names it Camera (1) (additional cameras are automatically named Camera (2), Camera (3), and so on). If you are creating a scene with more than two cameras, take the extra three seconds and name them. Figure 4.18 shows the 04MultipleCams.lws scene's cameras.

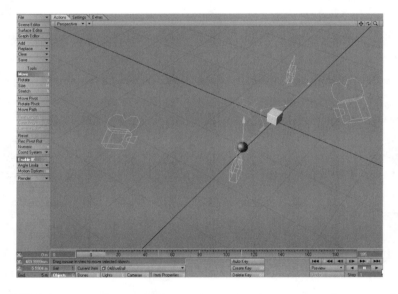

Figure 4.18 When scenes have multiple cameras, rename the cameras so that you can keep track of which camera is which.

You can rename your existing cameras by first selecting the specific camera, clicking the Replace drop-down menu, and choosing Rename Current Item.

Adding Lights to a Scene

Even if your scene is a virtual set, you need to add a light or two to see what's going on. By default, Layout has one light, which cannot be removed. It can be turned off, but not deleted from the scene. To add a light to a scene, all you need to do is select Add, then Add Light, then the type of light you want to add. With a light selected, pressing **p** on the keyboard takes you to the Light Properties panel where you can color each light, change the type of light, and add lens flares, volumetrics, and more.

Lights in Layout respond the way objects do when selected. They can be moved or rotated, and they, too, will show control handles. You can also select lights (as you can with objects) directly in Layout by clicking them. If you hold down the Shift key, you can select multiple lights. When you have multiple lights or objects selected, your movements and rotations apply to each selection. Multiple selections are great if you have to place your lights or objects perfectly and need to adjust their positions. However, if you were smart and planned out your scene, you would have parented the items to a null object.

Parenting

Parenting your lights or objects in Layout is a good way to help keep things organized and save time. This next brief tutorial will show you how to parent a few lights to a null object.

A null object is nothing more than a representational point in Layout used for various control issues. It does not show up in the render, and it is very useful for texture references, visual references, motion tracking, parenting, or targeting. Here's how it works:

1. Clear the scene.

   Start by adding two more lights, making a total of three including the existing default light.

2. Select Add, then Add Light, then Add Distant Light, as shown in Figure 4.19.

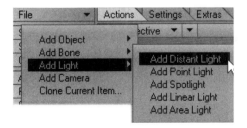

Figure 4.19   Add lights directly from Layout.

 Tip

Remember that you also can access the Add menu by pressing the Ctrl and Shift keys, then clicking directly on the Layout interface with the left mouse button. This brings up the mouse button menus.

Note

A name requester appears asking you to give the light a name. You also can choose not to name the light and click OK, or press the Enter key.

The second light appears directly in the middle of Layout at the 0 XYZ axis. Now it's time to add a null object.

3. Select Add, then Add Object, and then Add Null.

4. Just like adding a camera or light, a name requester appears. Click OK or press Enter to leave the default name Null.

5. The Null object also loads at the 0 XYZ axis. Select the second light in the center of the screen and move it off center, similar to Figure 4.20.

    Don't forget to create a keyframe for it after you've moved it to lock it in place! Otherwise, it will jump back to the previous position once the timeline slider is adjusted.

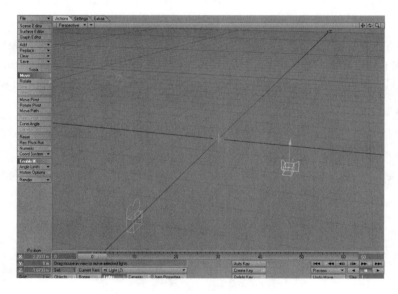

Figure 4.20   The second light is moved off center to make the Null object more visible.

6. With the second light still selected, press the **m** key to access the light's Motion Options panel.

7. Select Null for the Parent Item, as in Figure 4.21.

8. Select the child item (the item that is to be parented).

9. Parent the first light and the camera to the same Null object.

10. Select the Null object, and move and rotate it.

    You'll see that the items parented to it move along with it.

Figure 4.21
The Motion Options panel holds the commands for parenting your objects.

Parenting items is useful in so many ways. You can create great variations in reflections by parenting objects and rotating them during an animation. You can organize your scene and group items, such as lights and cameras.

This is a traditional way of selecting and parenting objects. However, LightWave 6 now allows you to parent items directly in the Scene Editor. In addition, you can parent multiple items at once, which is handy for characters with bone structures, or other complex hierarchies. Later in Chapter 12, "Organic Animation," you'll discover how parenting is essential to properly setting up skeletal structures for character movement, and more. But for now, you can load the 04Parent.lws scene as an example of simple parenting. Use this scene to parent items to other objects, and even un-parent items to get a feel for parenting.

Targeting

Targeting is different from parenting in that parenting attaches one item to another. Targeting only points one item to another. For example, if you parented a camera to a moving car the camera would move with the car, wherever it traveled. If you target a camera to a car, the camera will remain stationary, but it will always point at the car, following it wherever it goes.

Although targeting is different from parenting, the two processes are similar. From the Motion Options panel of a selected item, you can choose to have an item target another. Figure 4.22 shows the Motion Options panel and Target Object selection.

When setting up targets, the camera's pivot will point at the pivot of the object. This is great for many types of animations, such as a character's eye movements, a simulation rifle to target animation, and much more. Try targeting the camera to a null object and move the null around. The camera will point at the null no matter where it goes.

The exercises in this chapter have given you an idea of the relationship between objects in that each individual item, such as an object, camera, or light, can be grouped together or individually through parenting and targeting. Larger scenes incorporate the same usefulness of hierarchies, but managing them becomes difficult in Layout. No worries, though, the LightWave 6 Scene Editor keeps track of your complex setups.

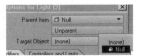

Figure 4.22
The Motion Options panel for the selected item allows you to target other items.

Using the Scene Editor

Managing any scene you put together requires that you are aware of everything going on in your animation. From time to time, however, you will need a visual reference of your setup, and the capability to control items and make changes to them. Figure 4.23 shows the LightWave 6 Scene Editor with a scene loaded.

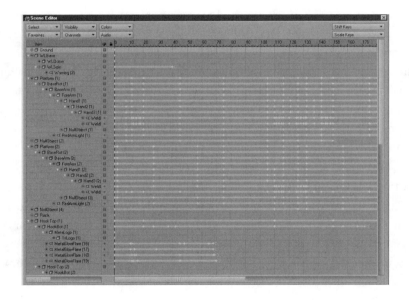

Figure 4.23   A complex scene shows each item's hierarchy and keyframes.

The Scene Editor also can be considered the scene manager. You can use this to parent and un-parent items, instead of the Motion Options panel. To do so, drag the selected item underneath the item to which you want to parent it. Figure 4.24 shows the line that appears representing the parenting position.

Tip

Although the Motion Options panel can be used to parent items, the Scene Editor is a better way to go. By working in the Scene Editor, you have a hierarchical view of your object, and it allows for multiple parenting of items.

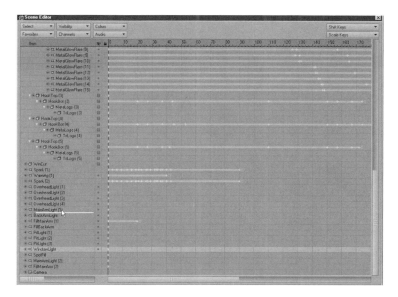

Figure 4.24   You can use the Scene Editor to parent and un-parent items. The line represents the parenting position.

In Figure 4.24, the highlighted item, WindowLight, has been selected and dragged up underneath MainArmLight1. The line represents where the selected item will be parented. If you move the mouse slightly over the parent, the line will indent, signaling you that the selected item will become a child of the parent. Otherwise, you are simply re-arranging an item, which also makes the Scene Editor useful. Any item that is parented to another will be indented.

Keyframe Adjustments

In addition to the organization of your Layout items, the Scene Editor also can help you change the pace of your entire animation, or just one item. Figure 4.25 shows the Scene Editor with a small scene loaded. The shaded lines on the right side of the interface represent items that are in motion. The small plus signs within them represent keyframes.

Also, you can see in Figure 4.25 that 04BlueBall.lwo and the Follower_Camera have been expanded. By clicking the small plus sign in front of any item, you can expand the item's properties to show its XYZ values for Position, Rotation, and Scale. Across the top of the main Scene Editor window, you'll see numbers. These numbers represent time in your animation. If your scene is 300 frames long, you'll see these numbers listed up through 300.

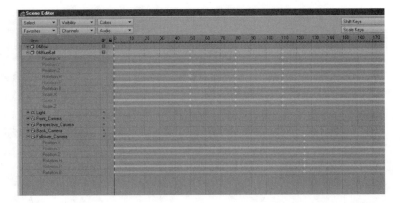

Figure 4.25   The Scene Editor displays items that are in motion (the shaded lines on the right side of the interface) as well as keyframes (small plus signs).

You can click a shaded motion track and drag it to adjust its timing. Figure 4.26 shows the 04BlueBall.lwo object with its motion now starting 40 frames into the animation, rather than at 0. This was accomplished by dragging the motion track.

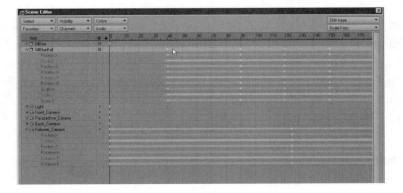

Figure 4.26   The Scene Editor allows you to move the entire motion of an item.

You also could move this motion to negative 40 frames. Perhaps you've set up a perfect motion for a flying logo. The only problem is, you need it to animate to its resting place much sooner. If you set up new keyframes, the perfect rotations and timing with other elements will be off. Instead, you can drag the motion to a value less than 0. When you begin rendering the scene at frame 0, the flying logo would already be in motion.

Later in Chapter 16 "Broadcast Animations," you'll use the Scene Editor in a project to adjust the timing of animations.

Visibility

The Scene Editor also controls the visibility of your Layout items in that you can choose to view which items are seen as wireframes, points, or shaded. Figure 4.27 shows the section of menus available for adjusting your scene's visibility.

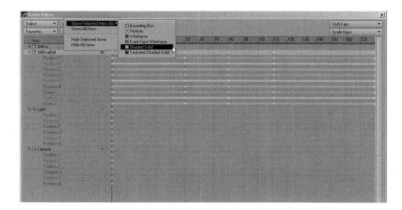

Figure 4.27   The Scene Editor gives you the power to adjust any item's visibility.

With these menus, you can choose what to select, such as Objects, Lights, Cameras, or Bones, and how to view them, such as Wireframe or Solid. You can select various items and hide them to help keep Layout clutter to minimum. Also, you are given the capability to make each item a separate color for organization.

While the visibility controls in the Scene Editor are straightforward, take some time and click around in there. Try various selections and colors. Expand and collapse the channels of items while experimenting with parenting and rearrangement.

Audio Files

Audio files also can be loaded from the Scene Editor panel. Figure 4.28 shows the Audio drop-down menu requester.

When you load an audio file (.WAV file), you can instantly play it by choosing the selection from the menu list. By default, the Fixed Frequency option is turned on (checked). This keeps the pitch of the audio file constant as you scrub through it on the timeline. You will use this feature extensively in Chapter 11, "Character Construction."

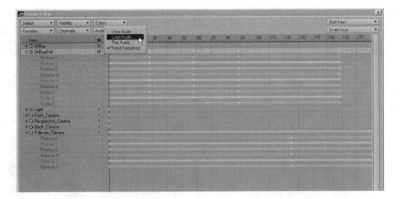

Figure 4.28   Audio files can be loaded from the Scene Editor panel.

Shift and Scale Keys

The Scene Editor also allows you to Shift or Scale selected keyframes. For example, your client loves the animation you've created and is ready to sign the check. But, before that happens, the entire animation needs to be exactly five seconds shorter. By using the Scale keys function, you can scale the entire scene to exactly the length you need. This is handy because throughout the animation, elements have varying keyframes, and resetting each of them would be quite tedious. Shift and Scale allow you to adjust timing without resetting keyframes. Chapter 16 will give you a step-by-step explanation of these features.

The Next Step

This chapter introduced you to LightWave 6's Layout and its core functionality. There is much, much more to learn within this program, and the rest of this book will help take you there. The MultiMesh object format introduced here will be a stepping stone for all the objects you create in Modeler. The keyframing information can be applied to any project you encounter, while the coordinate system information is important for every model and animation you create. Use the information in this chapter as reference for the rest of this book, and any future projects you take on. You can never have enough information!

Summary

In this chapter, you learned about keyframing, both manual and automatic; the importance of pivots and how to adjust them; parenting and targeting; adding multiple cameras; and the Scene Editor. All these elements are foundations for the projects you'll work on in LightWave, but there's just one more area you need to be familiar with before you really get into the meat of things. Chapter 5 introduces you to the incredible control you can have over every aspect of your scene. You will learn about modifiers, curves, channels, and footprints. Once you've worked through Chapter 6, step up to Part II, "A Project-Based Approach to Creating and Building 3D Scenes."

Chapter 5

LightWave 6 Graph Editor

LightWave 6's powerful new Graph Editor

offers you complete control over a specific

item's motion and timing. This can be a

camera, object, light, or any other editable

parameter. The Graph Editor in LightWave 6 offers you control over every channel of an item, such as the Position.X, Position.Y, Rotation Heading, and so on. Each channel can be controlled through the use of expressions, modifiers, or even keyframes, all from within the Graph Editor. The Graph Editor is used to edit any type of envelopeable parameter, from surface color, light intensity, object dissolves, and more. In this chapter, you will learn about:

- Using the Graph Editor
- Multi-curve editing with the Graph Editor
- Exploring additional commands
- Editing color channels

Navigating the Graph Editor

From Layout's interface, you can access the Graph Editor by clicking the Graph Editor button at the top left of the screen, under the Actions Tab. Figure 5.1 shows the Graph Editor at start-up, with a scene loaded.

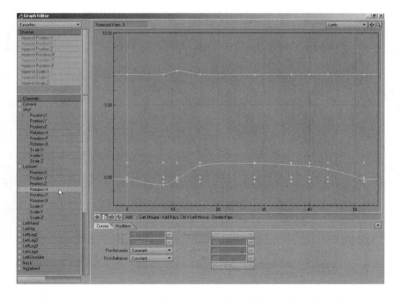

Figure 5.1   The LightWave 6 Graph Editor is radically different than the editor in previous versions of LightWave. Here, the Graph Editor shows all the items in Layout on the bottom left and individual editable channels on the upper left.

Note

Any of the small buttons labeled E throughout LightWave Layout can also access the Graph Editor. You can find them next to the values of items that can be edited in the Graph Editor, such as Surface Color.

When you open the Graph Editor, you'll notice four areas called zones.

- The Curve Bin zone is in the top-left quadrant. This is the area of the Graph Editor where you set the specific channels you want to edit.

- The Curve Window zone is in the top-right quadrant. This is the area where you edit curves. You can adjust values, edit keyframes, and more.

- The Curve Controls zone is in the bottom-right quadrant. Here you can apply specific controls and modifiers. This area enables you to set expression plug-ins, spline controls, and so on. This area will be discussed in Chapter 14, "Expression Animation."

- The Scene Display zone is in the bottom-left quadrant and shows your current scene elements. Lights, cameras, and objects are listed here, and you can select any or all of their channels, bring them into the Curve Bin, and begin editing.

You will work with each zone to adjust, modify, or create various motions, timing, and values for LightWave elements. You can control all Layout items here—from the camera, to lights, to objects—including color, light intensities, morph envelopes and more. You may be asking yourself where to begin in the Graph Editor and what does it really do. Good questions! The Graph Editor is a complex part of Layout, one that is best explained through examples.

Note

An envelope in LightWave is an animatable feature via the Graph Editor. Many settings throughout Layout have a button labeled with an E. This E represents "envelope," which leads you into the Graph Editor.

The following exercise provides an explanation of how to navigate through the Graph Editor interface. As a note, you can maximize the Graph Editor window to make full use of your screen's real estate.

Exercise 5.1   Working with Channels

When you begin creating an animation, you will often need specific control over one or a group of keyframes. The Graph Editor gives you this control, but you first must understand how to set up the channels with which you want to work. This exercise introduces you to working with the position and rotation channels from a light and a camera.

1. Open Layout, and select the default Distant light.

2. Select the Actions tab at the top of the interface and click the Graph Editor button to enter the Graph Editor.

   You don't need anything loaded into Layout to follow along here.

   Look at Figure 5.2, and you'll see that the attributes in the Curve Bin relate to the currently selected item in Layout, the Light. All the appropriate channels are listed here.

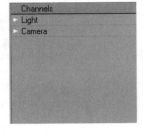

Figure 5.2
When an item is selected in Layout, such as an object, camera, or light, its attributes are automatically entered into the Curve Bin in the Graph Editor.

Tip
You can maximize the Graph Editor window by clicking the small square next to the X in the top right of the panel. Clicking this square opens the Graph Editor to full view. Mac users can resize the window as well.

Note
You can rearrange the order of items in the Curve Bin by clicking and dragging them. This does not effect your scene.

3. Hold down the Shift key and double-click the Camera label in the Scene Display area. This is in the lower-left corner of the Graph Editor interface.

   Double-clicking the Camera label adds all its channels to the Curve Bin, which can now be edited.

4. Go back to the Scene Display area, and expand the Camera's channels by clicking the small white arrow to the left of the Camera label.

   This shows all the camera's available attributes, as shown in Figure 5.3.

5. Double-click any of the Camera's channels.

   The channel is now added to the Curve Bin and overrides any other channels. However, you can add more channels to the Curve Bin without overriding the existing channels.

6. To add the Position.X and Rotation.H channels to the Curve Bin, hold down the Shift key and select the two channels. Then, drag the selected channels up to the Curve Bin. You've now added channels instead of replacing them.

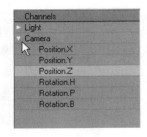

Figure 5.3
Clicking the small white arrow next to an item's label in the Scene Display area expands its channels.

Note

If you have noncontiguous channels to select, use the Ctrl key rather than the Shift key to make your selections in the Scene list.

Now that you know how channels are added to the Curve Bin, the next thing you can do is modify or edit them in many different ways.

Working with the Graph Editor

Navigating through the Graph Editor is straightforward. You select which channels you want to edit, and add them to the Curve Bin. From the Curve Bin, you select channels and then edit the curves in the Curve Window. Editing curves is one of the primary functions of the Graph Editor.

Editing Curves

The Graph Editor is probably most commonly used to edit curves. Editable curves are motion paths that you've created in Layout to control lights, objects, cameras, and other animatable Layout attributes, such as textures or intensities. The preceding section talked about the Scene Display. The Curve Window is discussed in this section.

Figure 5.4 shows the Graph Editor in full frame with the same leaf scene from Chapter 4 loaded (05LeafFall_2.lws). You can find this scene in the Projects/Scenes/Chapter5 folder.

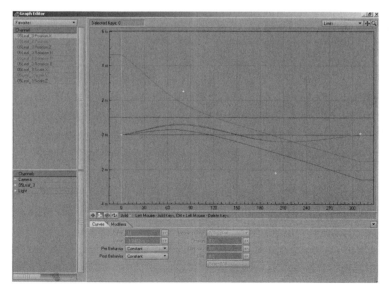

Figure 5.4   With a scene loaded into Layout, opening the Graph Editor reveals all motion channels already in place in the Curve Bin for the selected leaf object.

In Figure 5.4, the first channel (Position.X) in the Curve Bin is selected. In the Curve Window, the channel that represents the leaf's X position is highlighted. On your computer, you'll notice that each channel has a specific color in the Curve Bin: X is red, Y is green, and Z is blue. The same color represents the corresponding curve in the main Curve Window. If you move your mouse pointer over one of the small white dots (which represent keyframes) on an active curve, numeric information will appear, as shown in Figure 5.5.

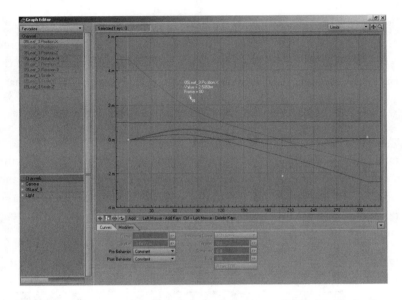

Figure 5.5   Moving the mouse pointer over a keyframe instantly displays the keyframe number, the value, and what channel (such as Position.X) you're working with.

Your LightWave manuals take you step by step through the necessary buttons in the Graph Editor. *Inside LightWave [6]* takes you further with practical tutorials. Exercise 5.2 requires you to load a scene from this book's CD-ROM and adjust various channels. You will create and delete keyframes in the Graph Editor, adjust timing, and even adjust multiple channels at once. Later, you will apply Graph Editor Modifiers to existing keyframes.

Positioning the Graph Editor

Before you begin working with the Graph Editor, you should know that you can configure the window so that it is visible along with Layout. Figure 5.6 shows a possible interface configuration.

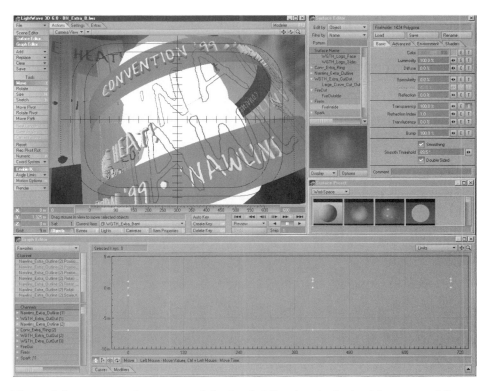

Figure 5.6   You can resize Layout and the Graph Editor, keeping both of them open while you work, thanks to LightWave 6's non-modal panels.

To resize the Graph Editor:

1. Move your mouse pointer over the lower portion of Layout until small arrows appear. Click and drag the Layout window to a smaller size.

2. Click and drag the Layout window from the top of the panel, and move it to the upper-left of your screen, as shown in Figure 5.6.

3. Open the Graph Editor and resize it as well. Move it beneath the Layout windows.

Additionally, you can now keep the Surface Editor and Preset Shelf open while working in Layout. This is beneficial because you can make a change, see the result in Layout, and continue working. You do not have to continually open and close panels—just leave them open. A large monitor is helpful for screen real estate when setting up configurations like this.

Graph Editor Timing

The Graph Editor enables you to do many things, such as create, delete, or adjust keyframes for specific channels. You can also modify various entities within LightWave such as surface color and light intensities. One of the more common uses for the Graph Editor is for timing. You can use the Graph Editor to adjust the timing of elements in your LightWave scenes.

Exercise 5.2   Adjusting Timing in the Graph Editor

The Graph Editor has many uses, which you will inevitably use at some time during your career as an animator. One of the more common uses of the Graph Editor is the ability to adjust the timing of your Layout animations.

Figure 5.7
Opening the Graph Editor with a selected object in Layout reveals all its channels in the Curve Bin.

1. Load the 05FontLogo.lws scene into Layout from this book's CD-ROM.

    This loads a simple background animation that can be used for animated logos.

2. Select the 05LWFont.lwo object, and open the Graph Editor.

    You'll see that all the object's channels are automatically loaded into the Curve Bin. However, in this tutorial, you are adjusting only the object's timing on the X axis, therefore, the remaining channels are not needed. Figure 5.7 shows the Graph Editor with Position.X selected.

3. To remove the remaining channels, first select Position.Y in the Curve Bin. This is identified in green, and should be the second channel in the list.

4. Holding down the Shift key, select the Scale.Z channel.

    This selects all the channels between Position.X and Position.Y, as shown in Figure 5.8.

5. Right-click the selections and click Remove From List, as shown in Figure 5.9.

Tip

You can do more than just remove items from the list with the right mouse button. You also can Replace, Save, Copy, Paste, Show Velocity, Show Speed, and Show Modified channels, as well as apply Footprints.

You should now be left with only the Position.X channel in the Curve Bin.

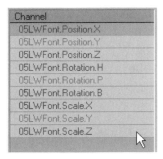

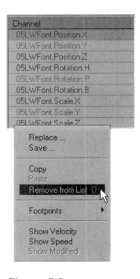

Figure 5.8
To select multiple channels, hold the Shift key and select the first and last channel in the Curve Bin.

6. Select the Position.X channel to highlight it in the Curve Window.

   This represents the motion of the X position for the object. The tall white vertical line is the current frame.

7. Move your mouse over the first white dot (the first keyframe) on the curve for Position.X to see the information for that keyframe (see Figure 5.10).

   The information tells you what curve it is, which in this case is Position.X for the 05LWFont.lwo object. It also tells you the current frame and the value. The value is the object's position. For example, the value in Figure 5.10 reads 1.07m. You are working with the Position.X channel, so this means the object is 1.07m away from the 0 axis on the positive X axis.

Figure 5.9
Right-clicking selected channels in the Curve Bin offers control such as Remove From List.

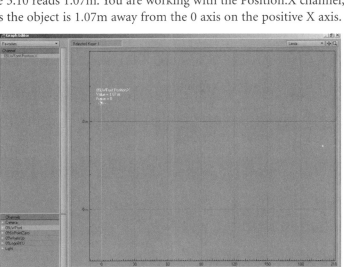

Figure 5.10 Holding the mouse over any keyframes in the curve window shows the channel, value, and frame number.

8. Click the first keyframe in the Curve Window to select it. Be sure the Move edit mode button is selected. It is the first button located above the Curves tab, beneath the Curve Window.

   You'll see it highlight slightly, and the values throughout the Curves tab at the bottom of the screen will appear, as shown in Figure 5.11.

Figure 5.11   When a keyframe is selected, the commands in the Curves tab area become available.

The middle of the Graph Editor interface offers four tools from which to choose: Move, Add, Stretch, and Roll. These are small icons. When you select them, information is displayed to the right, explaining what the function will do via a keyboard legend. Figure 5.12 shows the area.

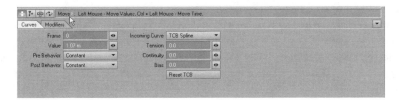

Figure 5.12   Selecting a specific tool displays the appropriate keyboard legend. Here, the Move tool is selected, allowing you to move selected keyframes in the Curve Window.

The Move tool can be used to select and move single or multiple keyframes in the Curve Window.

9. Select the Move tool, and click and drag the first keyframe in the Curve Window.

   Notice how you can only move its value. Doing this changes the position of the object in Layout.

10. Move the keyframe to set the value at 2m.

    Perhaps you do not want the 05LWFont.lwo object to move until frame 100. It's easy to do in the Graph Editor.

11. Make sure the Move tool is selected. While holding down the Ctrl key, click and move the keyframe to the right. You'll see the frame number appear over the keyframe, as shown in Figure 5.13.

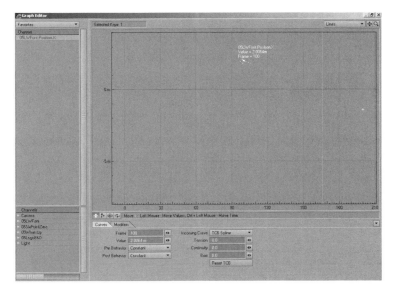

Figure 5.13   Holding the Ctrl key and moving selected keyframes adjusts timing.

Tip

If you don't care to hold down the Ctrl key and use the mouse, you can numerically enter the specific keyframe. At the bottom of the screen under the Curves tab, you can set the selected keyframe numerically. You can set the value numerically as well.

12. Adjust the value and keyframes of selected objects and return to Layout to see the effects. You can adjust values by dragging the keyframes in the Curve Window, or numerically in the Curves tab area. You will soon get the hang of editing in the Graph Editor.

There's much more to the Graph Editor than this. The first part of this chapter guided you through basic navigation and editing of channels and keyframes. Moving forward, you have the capability to move groups of keyframes, adjust curves, and add modifiers.

Multi-Curve Editing

Multi-curve editing is useful when you want to edit multiple curves simultaneously or use curves of different items as references. By selecting desired curves in the Curve Bin (as demonstrated earlier in this chapter), you can edit them together as one in the Curve Window. You easily can drag and drop curves from the Scene Display window into the Curve Bin. For example, the Position.X of an object, with the Rotation.Y of a Light, and the Scale.Z of a camera—any channel you want.

Foreground and Background Curves

When you add selected curves to the Curve Bin, you can see them in the Curve Window and view them as either foreground or background curves. Curves that are selected in the Curve Bin will become editable foreground curves in the Curve Window. Conversely, the curves unselected will be uneditable background curves in the Curve Window.

There are benefits to working with foreground and background curves. You can interactively cut and paste keyframes from one curve to another. You also can replace an entire curve with another, or lock areas of curves together. By having multiple curves selected when you create keys, the curves can be identical at those selected areas during an animation. Additionally, you have the capability to compare one curve to another, such as a light intensity to the H rotation of a camera. This next tutorial demonstrates some of these features.

Exercise 5.3   Adding Keys to Multiple Curves

1. Clear Layout and open the Graph Editor.
2. Move Camera Position.X and Light Position.Y to the Curve Bin.
3. Holding down the Shift key, select both channels in the Curve Bin.

   You'll see both curves highlight in the Curve Window. Right now there are only straight lines as the channels have no motions applied.

 Note

You can click and drag on the bar between the Curve Bin and the Scene Display windows in the Graph Editor to quickly resize the two windows.

4. Select the Add key button beneath the Curve Window, as shown in Figure 5.14.

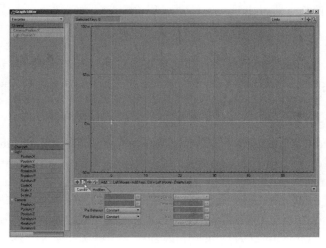

Figure 5.14   You can choose to add a key from the Graph Editor window, as well as Move, Stretch, and Roll.

5. Click once in the top area of the Curve Window, once near the bottom right, similar to Figure 5.15. You'll see the curve adjust to the keys you just created.

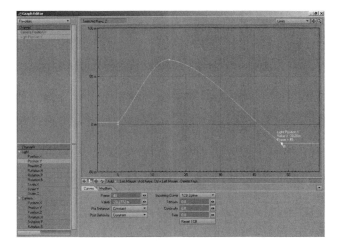

Figure 5.15   You can create keyframes for the selected motion channels directly in the Curve Window.

Navigating the Curve Window

By selecting Multiple Curves, you can edit them together, create keyframes together, and so on. However, you also can adjust one of these curves based on the background curve, simply select only the curve you want to adjust in the Curve Bin. The remaining curves in the Curve Bin appear slightly darkened in the background of the Curve Window. From there, you can select the Move tool, and click and drag a keyframe to change its value. Following are a few quick steps to try when working in the Graph Editor:

- Select the Move keyframe button and click and drag to adjust a key's value.
- Select the Move keyframe button and click and hold the Ctrl key to adjust a key's position in time—for example, to move a keyframe from frame 5 to 15.
- Hold the Alt key and click in the Curve Window to adjust the entire Curve Window view.
- Press the period (.) key to zoom into the Curve Window; press the comma (,) key to zoom out.
- Press the **a** key to fit the Curve Window to view—for example, if you zoom into the Curve Window, press the **a** key to instantly fit all keyframes of curves to the full window.

- Select Automatic Limits from the top right of the Graph Editor window to fit the Curve Window to view. This limits the Curve Window to the length of the entire animation. You also can just press the **a** key on the keyboard.
- Select Numeric Limits from the top right of the Graph Editor window to set the minimum and maximum frame for the Curve Window. **Ctrl+Alt** drags and zooms the Curve Window. You also can set a minimum and maximum value. Figure 5.16 shows the Numeric Limits panel.

Figure 5.16   You can set Numeric Limits to control the frame and value settings in the Curve Window.

Exploring Additional Commands in the Graph Editor

As with much of LightWave 6, the Graph Editor has some additional commands that you should be aware of. Using these commands can increase your efficiency. Like much of LightWave 6, clicking the right mouse button in certain areas gives you access to additional tools, which enable more control.

Key Pop-Up Menus

In both the Curve Bin and Curve Window, you can access additional controls with the right mouse button. Figure 5.17 shows the key pop-up menu in the Curve Bin. Figure 5.18 shows it in the Curve Window.

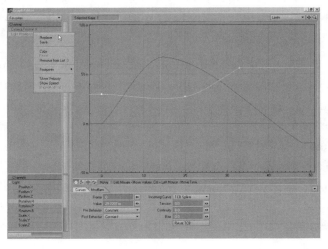

Figure 5.17   Right-clicking a selected channel opens the key pop-up menu for additional control.

Selecting a specific channel and right-clicking it in the Curve Bin gives you controls to perform a number of tasks. You can Replace a channel with a preexisting one. You can Save a specific channel's properties. This is useful when you want to save and reuse the motions, such as a flickering light or a rotating globe. Instead of setting up new keyframes, you can save the channel motion and reload it later.

You also can Copy and Paste a specific channel's motion if you want to create a duplicate. Other controls include Show Velocity, which you can use to add a visual representation of the selected channel's velocity in the Curve Window; Show Speed, to make the speed of the selected channel visible in the Curve Window; and Remove From List, to delete a channel from the Curve Bin.

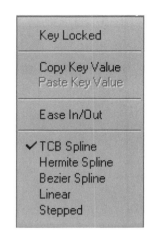

Figure 5.18
Right-clicking on a selected keyframe opens the key pop-up menu for control in the Curve Window.

Footprints

Part of the charm that comes with the LightWave 6 Graph Editor is the capability to create Footprints for a selected channel. Because you are not always sure of the adjustments you might make to a keyframe or curve, setting a Footprint helps you visually remember the shape of your curve before it is adjusted. You can then return your curve to the Footprint. Follow this next tutorial to learn more about Footprints.

Exercise 5.4   Working with Footprints

1. Open Layout, Clear the Scene, and open the Graph Editor.

2. Select the Light in the Scene Display, and drag it to the Curve Bin.

    All the motion channels for the Light are added to the bin, as shown in Figure 5.19.

3. Select the Light Rotation P, which is the Pitch rotation for the Light. Of course, any selected channel will do for this exercise.

    When a channel is selected, you'll see it highlight in the Curve Window.

4. Select the Add key command, and click throughout the Curve Window to create some keyframes for the Rotation P channel. Figure 5.20 shows the channel with a few keys added.

Figure 5.19
Selecting just the Light from the Scene Display area and dragging it to the Curve Bin adds all its motion channels.

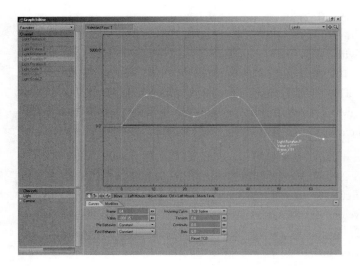

Figure 5.20   A few keyframes are added to the Light's Rotation P channel in the Curve Window.

5. Go back to the Curve Bin, and with the Rotation P channel still selected, right-click it to open the pop-up menu.

6. Select Footprints, and then select Leave Footprints.

   Figure 5.21 shows the selection. It won't look like much has happened in the Curve Window, but wait.

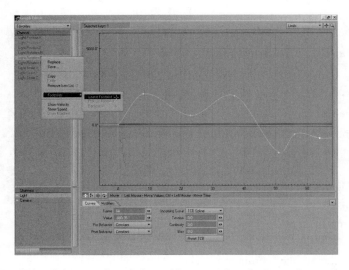

Figure 5.21   Right-clicking a selected channel lets you select the Footprints option.

7. With the right mouse button, click and drag to select a region over all your keyframes in the Curve Window.

This selects all keys, as shown in Figure 5.22.

Note
You also can hold the Shift key, and double-click in the Curve Window to select all keys. Move mode must be selected.

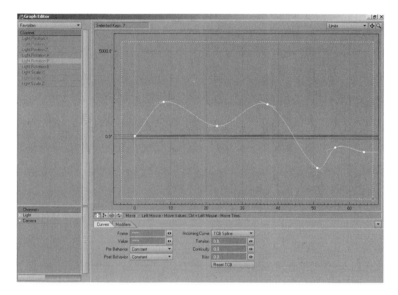

Figure 5.22   Right-clicking and dragging in the Curve Window lets you select multiple keyframes.

8. With all the keyframes selected, click and drag in the Curve Window to move the entire motion curve up, as shown in Figure 5.23.

You'll see a faint line underneath the curve you just moved. This is the footprint that tells you where your curve was.

9. Go back to the Curve Bin, right-click again, and choose to Pick Up Footprint or Backtrack.

Picking up the Footprint removes it from the Curve Window. Selecting Backtrack resets any channel adjustment to the original Footprint position.

Footprints are a way for you to keep track of what you're doing and where you've been while working in the Graph Editor. It is easy to make too many changes and lose your place when adjusting various channels. Using the Footprint option helps you organize your steps.

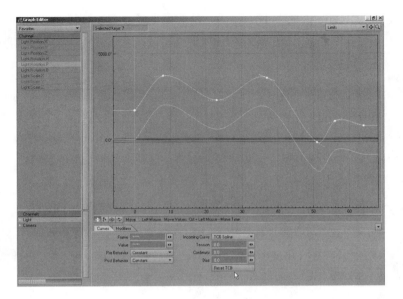

Figure 5.23   After a Footprint is created, moving either single or multiple keyframes reveals the Footprint.

Using the Curves Tab

At the bottom of the Graph Editor interface is the Curves tab. Here you can adjust the value of a selected keyframe and its pre- and post-behaviors. This area is ghosted until a keyframe is selected. For example, say you have created a spinning globe that takes 200 frames to make a full 360-degree revolution. Your total scene length is 600 frames and the globe needs to rotate throughout the animation. Instead of setting additional keyframes for the globe, you can set the post-behavior to repeat. Once the globe completes its 200 frames of motion, the Graph Editor's post-behavior takes over. You can also set pre-behaviors. A pre-behavior is what happens before the first keyframe. You can set either pre- or post-behaviors to:

- Reset, returning the motion to frame 0.
- Constant, where values are equal to the first or last frame's value.
- Repeat, which will repeat the motion from the first to the last keyframe.
- Oscillate, which mirrors the channel repeatedly. For example, you can make a spotlight rotate from frame 0 to frame 30 on its heading rotation. Set post-behavior to Oscillate, and the motion will sway back and forth between the two keyframes like a searchlight.

- Offset Repeat is similar to Repeat but offsets the difference between the first and last keyframe values.

- Linear, which keeps the curve angle linearly consistent with the starting or ending angle.

The Curves tab also is home to Spline controls. If you are familiar with previous versions of LightWave, you may have used either Tension (T), Continuity (C), or Bias (B) to control keyframes' splines. LightWave 6 now offers more control than simple TCB splines.

Spline Controls

Spline controls come in many varieties, and give you the control you need over your curves. When an item is put into motion in LightWave, it instantly has a curve. The Graph Editor gives you control over the individual channels of an item's motion. You can adjust the keyframes of the curve that is created with various types of splines. Figure 5.24 shows the Incoming Curve types. An Incoming Curve is the type of curve that precedes a keyframe.

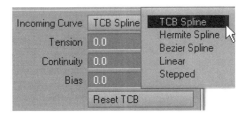

Figure 5.24   LightWave 6 has numerous curve types from which to choose.

TCB Splines

Easy to set, TCB splines are useful for creating realistic motions. The values for each spline range from 1.0 to −1.0.

A tension with a value of 1.0 is often the most commonly used TCB spline because it allows items to ease in or out of a keyframe. For example, a 3D, animated car needs to accelerate. Setting it in motion would make the car move at a constant rate. By adding a Tension setting of 1.0, the car would ease out of the keyframe and gain speed. By setting a negative value, the car would speed away and toward the keyframes.

Setting Continuity enhances a break or change in an item's path. You might not really use a positive continuity setting, as it overcompensates an item as it passes through a keyframe. Negative continuity, however, can be used to create a sharp change in an item's motion between keyframes, such as a bouncing ball.

Bias is great for anticipation. A positive Bias creates slack after a keyframe—great for a fast-moving car around a corner. A negative Bias creates slack before a keyframe. This could be used for keyframing a roller coaster around a sharp turn.

TCB splines are not the only spline controls you have over keyframes in LightWave 6. This version of the software employs Hermite and Bezier spline curves as well.

Hermite and Bezier Splines

While TCB splines are often used for common, more everyday animated elements, such as flying logos or animated cars, Hermite and Bezier splines offer a wider range of control. Hermite splines have tangent control handles that allow you to have control over the shape of a curve. Figure 5.25 shows three keyframes with Hermite splines added to the middle keyframe. Its handles are adjusted.

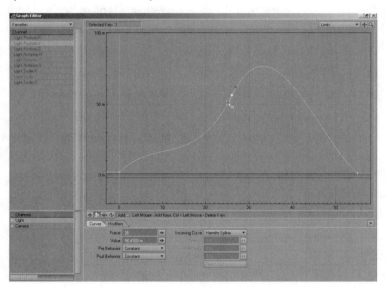

Figure 5.25   Hermite splines are added to the middle keyframe. Such splines offer more control than regular TCB splines.

Figure 5.25 shows three keyframes, one low, one high, and one low again—sort of a bell shape. However, the middle keyframe has a Hermite spline applied and the left handle of it has been pulled down quite a bit. The figure shows how an adjustment to one keyframe can have a drastic affect on the shape of a curve.

Now if you applied a Bezier curve, you will have different control than you would over a Hermite spline. A Bezier spline is a variant of a Hermite spline, and also will shape the curve. Figure 5.26 shows the same bell curve of three keyframes with one handle of the Bezier curve pulled up drastically.

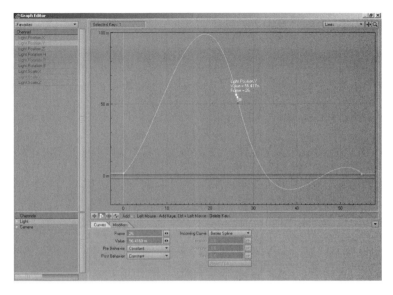

Figure 5.26   Bezier splines, although a variant of Hermite splines, enable control over a spline before and after a keyframe.

Both Hermite and Bezier splines can help you control your curve. It's up to you to experiment and try both when working with the control of an item's motion.

Stepped Transitions

Using a stepped transition for an incoming curve simply keeps a curve's value constant, and abruptly jumps to the next keyframe. Figure 5.27 shows a few keyframes with a stepped transition applied.

Stepped curves are usable when you want to make drastic value changes between keyframes for situations such as lightning, interference, or blinking lights.

Whether you create motions in the Graph Editor, or simply adjust preexisting ones, you should understand the amount of control the Graph Editor gives you. The Graph Editor in LightWave 6 even allows you to mix and match spline types for individual channels. Follow along with Exercise 5.5 to make and adjust curves in the Graph Editor.

Note

Pressing the **o** key in the Graph Editor opens the Options panel for the Graph Editor. Here, you can set the Default Incoming Curve as well as other default parameters.

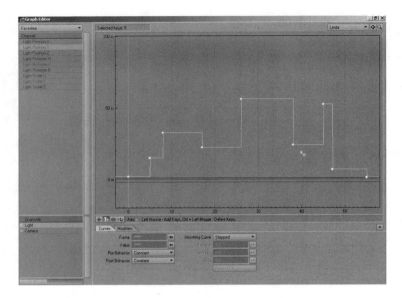

Figure 5.27   Stepped transitions for curves abruptly change your motion from one keyframe to the next.

Exercise 5.5   Creating Matching Curves

To begin, start by saving anything you've been working on in Layout, and then clear the scene. These next few steps provide the information to create curves and adjust them so that certain areas perfectly match. These techniques can be used with any of your projects.

1. Open the Graph Editor, and in the Scene Display, select the Camera Z position and double-click it.

   The Camera Z position is now added to the Curve Bin and your Graph Editor interface should look like Figure 5.28.

2. Expand the channels for the light in the Scene Display by clicking the small white triangle.

3. Hold down the Shift key and double-click the Light Z position to add it to the Curve Bin.

4. In the Curve Bin, hold down the Shift key and select both the Camera Z and Light Z positions.

5. Select Add mode and in the Curve Window create three keyframes to the right of the first keyframe at zero.

   Figure 5.29 shows the Graph Editor with the additional keyframes.

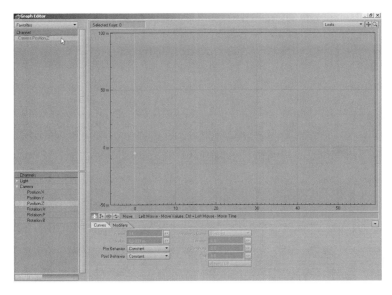

Figure 5.28 Double-clicking the Camera Z position adds it to the Curve Bin.

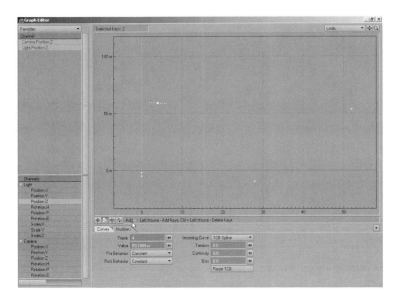

Figure 5.29 With multiple curves selected, you can create identical keyframes for both keyframes at once.

6. Select just the Camera Z position channel in the Curve Bin. This automatically deselects the Light Z position channel.

7. Select Move mode, and move up the last keyframe.

You'll see the Light Z channel in the background. What you've done here is created similar motions on the Z axis for both the camera and light, but toward the end of the motion, the value has changed. Figure 5.30 shows the adjusted channel.

Note

When modifying identical channels on one keyframe, you'll need to compensate surrounding keyframes slightly. Due to the spline curves, one keyframe affects another. You can see the slight shift in the curve in Figure 5.30.

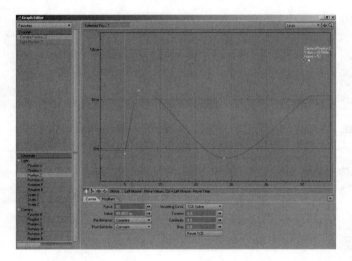

Figure 5.30   One keyframe of matching channels is adjusted.

A more realistic use for matching curves is a formation of flying jets. Each jet flies in unison, swooping, looping, and twisting in perfect sync. After the formation, one or two jets might need to fly off from the pack. Using the preceding example, you can easily select the appropriate channel, and adjust the value at the desired keyframe.

It's easy to see where you would move the jet in Layout, but in the Graph Editor, translating the visual motion to a value might take a little more work. Don't worry, this next exercise helps you adjust values in the Graph Editor.

Exercise 5.6   Adjusting Graph Editor Values

  1. Close the Graph Editor from the previous exercise, select Clear Scene from the File menu in Layout, and then reopen the Graph Editor.

  2. Click the small white triangle in the Scene Display window to expand the Camera channels.

3. Double-click the Camera Y position channel.

Because only one channel is in the Curve Bin, it is automatically selected.

4. In the Curve Window, create a few keyframes. Figure 5.31 shows the additional keyframes.

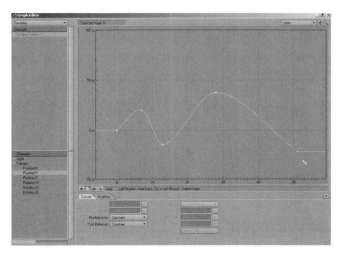

Figure 5.31   One channel is added to the Curve Bin and additional keyframes are created in the Curve Window.

5. With Move mode selected, hold the Shift key and double-click in the Curve Window to select all keyframes, as shown in Figure 5.32.

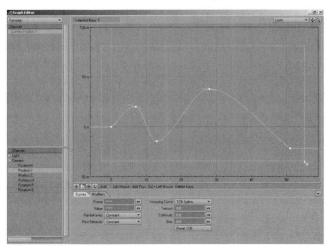

Figure 5.32   The right mouse button is used to draw a bounding box to select multiple keyframes in the Curve Window.

Take a look at the Frame and Value areas under the
Curves tab. Instead of values, they are highlighted with
asterisks, as shown in Figure 5.33. This means that the
currently selected keyframes have different values.

6. In the Value area, enter 10.

You'll see all selected keyframes jump to the same
value. This is useful when you need to adjust many
keyframe values. Instead of selecting a keyframe and
adjusting individual values, you can change values in
one step.

Figure 5.33
Because multiple keyframes
are selected, asterisks represent the Frame and Value
areas.

Note

By selecting multiple keyframes with the bounding box selection, you can also set spline
controls all at once.

Editing Color Channels

A cool new feature in LightWave 6's Graph Editor is the capability to animate color channels. This is great for animating colored lights for animations such as stage lighting, or a
gradually changing sunset.

Exercise 5.7   Animating Color Channels

1. Clear the LightWave scene, and select the scene's default light.

2. Press the **p** key to enter the light's Properties panel.

   You will see a series of small buttons labeled E. These are envelopes, and anywhere you see them throughout LightWave they will guide you right back to the
   Graph Editor. However, when you access the Graph Editor in this manner, you
   will only have control over the specific area you have selected an envelope from,
   such as Light Color.

   It's important to note that entering the Graph Editor through the E buttons tells
   LightWave that you want to perform a specific function. For example, if you click
   the E button next to Light Color, you are telling LightWave you want to animate
   the Light Color, and the Graph Editor opens accordingly. Entering the Graph
   Editor on its own from the Layout interface would not enable you to animate the
   Light Color.

3. Click the E button next to Light Color, as shown in Figure 5.34.

   Once you've clicked on the E button, you'll be in the Graph Editor. It looks similar to the Graph Editor you've been reading about in this chapter, but there is a
   strip of color along the bottom. LightWave 6 enables you to use the Graph
   Editor's capabilities on color channels as well as motion channels. Figure 5.35
   shows the Graph Editor with the color channel.

Figure 5.34   The E button (envelope) guides you to the Graph Editor for specific control over Light Color.

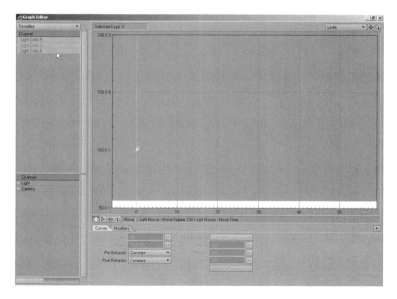

Figure 5.35   Color channels can be animated in the Graph Editor, along with motion channels. Here you can see the separate RGB channels in the Curve Bin, while the default Light Color, White, is visible in the Curve Window.

In Figure 5.35, the Curve Bin doesn't have position, rotation, or scale channels, but rather, color channels.

4. Select all the color channels by selecting the LightColor.R, then holding down the Shift key and selecting LightColor.B.

5. Create a few keyframes in the Curve Window and then click in one of the small circles that appears next to each keyframe.

The color requester appears, as shown in Figure 5.36.

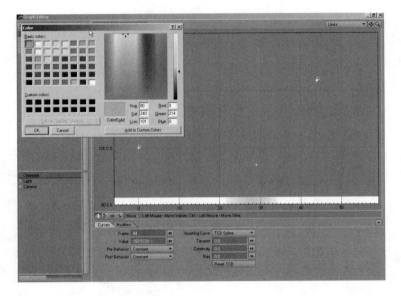

Figure 5.36   Selecting a keyframe when editing color channels calls up the color requester.

6. Choose a color and click OK.

You'll see the color you've selected appear as a gradual change in the Curve Window.

7. Set colors for the other keyframes, and adjust their values accordingly to set precise timing. Experiment with these values to see the different types of results you can achieve.

Note

Remember that you can keyframe individual color channels for Light Color.

The Next Step

The Graph Editor is a home base for your animations and envelopes. Before long, you will be using it with most of your animations, and might even consider keeping it open while you work. Try using the Ctrl+Shift+right mouse button in the Curve Window to access more control over your keyframes. And remember, LightWave 6's panels are non-modal which means you can shrink the size of Layout, and configure your computer screen to show Layout, the Graph Editor, and even the Surface Editor all at once. You'll find yourself using the Graph Editor for adjusting timing, clearing motions, saving motions, creating object dissolves, or animating color channels. Practice creating, cutting, and adjusting keyframes and channels in the Graph Editor. When you're confident of your ability, read on to begin creating amazing models and animations with LightWave 6.

Summary

Don't let the Graph Editor overwhelm you. Although much of this chapter introduced you to the many features and functions of the Graph Editor, you don't always need to use it for keyframing. A good way to work is to use traditional keyframing methods directly in Layout. Then, use the Graph Editor for tweaking and adjustments. As with much of LightWave, you have multiple ways to achieve the same result. Reference this chapter any time you need to control your keyframes with splines or specific modifiers, or if you need specific control over individual channels. The power of the Graph Editor will become more evident throughout this book, specifically in Chapter 14.

Chapter 6

LightWave 6 Cameras

Learning the art of 3D animation involves more than creating models, applying textures, and setting keyframes. 3D animation is an art form all its own, and it's still in its infancy. But part of learning the new and fascinating art form is understanding the digital camera. Not the kind of camera you use to take snapshots of your family, but the kind *inside* the computer—your digital eye.

This chapter introduces you to everyday camera techniques that you can apply to your LightWave animations. The camera in LightWave is a significant part of every animation you create, from simple pans, to dollies and zooms, to dutch angles. If you have any experience in photography or videography, the transition to "shooting" in LightWave will be smooth.

The title of this chapter is plural because LightWave 6 now offers multiple cameras. LightWave has always been a digital studio, and just like in a television studio or movie set, you can now set up multiple cameras in your scenes. This chapter instructs you on the following:

- The Camera Properties panel
- Basic real-world camera principles
- Setting up and using LightWave's cameras
- Applying various camera techniques to animations

Setting Up Cameras in LightWave

As you work through LightWave, you'll become familiar with the Item Properties panels associated with objects and lights. The Camera Properties panel controls camera settings, such as resolution, focal lengths, and more.

Take a look at the Camera Properties panel in Layout. Figure 6.1 shows the Camera panel, accessed by first selecting Cameras at the bottom of the Layout interface, and then clicking the Item Properties button.

At the top of the Camera Properties interface, you'll see a small window that is labeled Resolution. Figure 6.2 shows the available selections from the Resolution drop-down list.

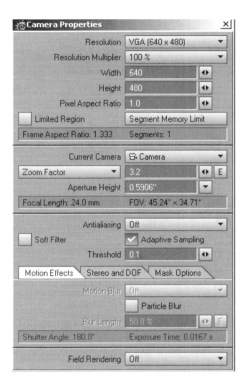

Figure 6.1   The Camera Properties panel gives you the control you need to set up cameras in Layout.

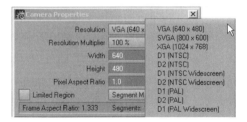

Figure 6.2   From the Resolution window you can automatically set the width, height, and pixel aspect ratio for your renders.

Multiple Cameras

Multiple cameras in LightWave are easy to set up, and they can be very useful for any type of scene. More specifically, they can be used when you have a large scene that has action that needs to be covered from various angles, such as an accident re-creation. Exercise 6.1 shows you how to add multiple cameras to Layout.

Exercise 6.1   Adding Multiple Cameras to Layout

Multiple cameras can help you save time setting up animations that need to be viewed from different angles. And although you can't switch between specific cameras during rendering (in the initial LightWave 6 release), you can render passes from any camera in the scene. Here's how to add cameras to Layout:

Figure 6.3
You can add more cameras to your scene from the Add drop-down list in Layout.

1. From the File menu in Layout, select Clear Scene.

2. Select the Add drop-down list, and choose Add Camera, as in Figure 6.3.

   When you select Add Camera, a small requester comes up, asking you for a name. Clicking OK keeps the camera name as "Camera," which appears with a number next to it, such as "Camera (2)," for the second camera added, and so on.

   You can choose whether to rename the cameras you add. You can always rename them later if you don't want to rename them now. Clicking OK sets the default name, Camera, and adds another camera to Layout.

3. Click OK to add an additional camera to Layout.

   Now you want to tell Layout that you want to set up your cameras, but first you must select a specific camera.

   With multiple cameras in a scene, you need to choose which camera you are currently using.

4. Select the camera by first clicking the Cameras button at the bottom of the interface.

5. From the Current Item selection, choose which camera you want to work with.

6. To rename a camera, select the camera and choose Replace, then Rename Current Item from the Replace drop-down list under the Actions tab.

Working with multiple cameras is as easy as working with one camera. Simply point and shoot! To get the most out of multiple cameras, set them up in a way that will be most beneficial to your animation. For example, you need to re-create a traffic accident and the client wants to see the accident from a bystander's viewpoint, an aerial viewpoint, and the driver's point of view. By adding three cameras to your scene and setting them in the desired positions, you can render the animation from any view. Try it!

Resolution

Resolution is the first selection within the Camera Properties panel, and for good reason. It is the width and height of your rendered images. LightWave also will set the appropriate pixel aspect of your rendered images when a specific resolution is set.

Note

Rendering is a generic term for creating or drawing an image. This is done in LightWave by pressing the **F9** key for single frames, and **F10** for multiple frames.

The resolution you set here determines the final output size of your images and animations. The default resolution is VGA mode, which is 640 pixels wide by 480 pixels tall. This resolution is of a medium size, common for most computer work. You also can choose SVGA, which is 800 by 600 pixels, or XVGA, which is 1024 by 768 pixels. These are good resolutions to work with if your images or animations are being used in a computer environment, such as in QuickTime or AVI formats. Although these three resolutions might be too large for most QuickTime or AVI files, you can use the Resolution Multiplier to change the output size. This is discussed later in the chapter.

Note

QuickTime is Apple Computer's animation format, now common on both Macintosh and Windows computers. Rendering an animation to a QuickTime movie creates a playable computer file. AVI (Audio Video Interleaved), developed by Microsoft, also is another type of animation format.

If you are creating animations that will eventually end up on videotape, you'll want to use the D1 or D2 NTSC resolution settings (in the United States), or the D1 or D2 PAL resolution settings (in Europe).

Note

In 1953, the National Television Standards Committee (NTSC) developed the North American television broadcast standard. This standard is 60 half frames, or fields, per second, with 525 lines of resolution. PAL stands for Phase Alternate Line. This standard, which most of Western Europe uses, is 625 lines of resolution at 50 fields per second.

Resolution Multiplier

The Resolution Multiplier is a welcome addition to LightWave 6, because it can help you more accurately set up animations in different sizes. In earlier versions of LightWave, setting up an animation in low resolution (to work faster) and rendering in a higher resolution (for quality) did not produce the same results. For example, you've created a scene that uses a lot of stars, made with small individual points. You set your resolution to a low setting to make your test renders quick. The individual points are modified and adjusted to look right. When a higher resolution is set, the stars are barely visible. This is because the actual resolution of the image is changing. What looks large on a small image is not the same size on a larger image. This problem also occurs when setting up lens flares. Now, LightWave 6 uses a Resolution Multiplier, as shown in Figure 6.4. The Resolution Multiplier keeps the same resolution settings but multiplies the value by 25%, 50%, 100%, 200%, or 400%. 100% renders an image the exact size of the set width and height, whereas 50% renders an image half the size.

Pixel Aspect Ratio

The difference between VGA modes and D1 or D2 modes, aside from the resolution difference, is the pixel aspect ratio. The pixel aspect ratio is the shape of the individual pixels the computer draws. A pixel is a tiny picture element that is always rectangular and is comprised of colored dots that make up the computer graphic image. Computer images use square pixels, which means a pixel aspect ratio of 1.0. Television images, generally 720 by 486, or 349,920 pixels, use rectangular pixels. NTSC D1 video is 0.9 pixels tall. Because the pixel aspect ratio is the ratio of the width to the height, 0.9 is narrower than it is tall. Try Exercise 6.2 to get a better idea of pixel aspect ratios.

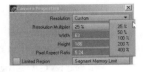

Figure 6.4
The Resolution Multiplier increases or decreases resolution while keeping the width, height, and pixel aspect ratios correct.

Exercise 6.2   Working with Pixel Aspect Ratios

Throughout most of your animations, setting the appropriate resolution automatically sets the proper pixel aspect ratio. By default, LightWave shows the Perspective view. To see the change in camera settings, you need to switch from Layout to Camera view. Pixel aspect ratio (PAR) is merely the shape of the pixel on the target display device. If the images will be viewed on a PC, you always want 1.0 because PCs use square pixels. If the images will be shown on a video device, such as a normal TV, you need a PAR that is .86 to .9. Say you have a perfect square in your image. If you use a PAR of 1.0, LightWave will render the square using the same number of pixels for its width and height. This looks cool on your PC monitor, but if you showed the image on a TV, it would look tall. This is because televisions have tall pixels and although the same number of pixels make up the square's height and width, because they are "tall" they make the box tall. You need to compensate for this. If you use a PAR of .9, LightWave automatically scales the pixels it uses to make the image with the assumption of "tall" pixels. A television pixel aspect ratio might not always be exactly .9, but it won't be 1.0. To give you an idea of how the different aspect ratios work, open LightWave Layout and perform the following steps:

  1. Select Camera View in the selection mode in the top-left corner of the Layout window, as in Figure 6.5.

 Note

Safe areas are important to use as shot reference. The outer line represents the Video Safe area—any animation elements outside this area will not be visible on a normal television monitor. The inner line represents the Title Safe area, and any text in your animations should not travel beyond this bounding region. Keeping within these guidelines will help your relationship with video editors as well.

Figure 6.5
Resolution and the results of setting the pixel aspect ratios can be seen only through the Camera view in Layout.

  2. Make sure that Show Safe Areas is selected and then press the **d** key to enter the Display Options panel.

3. Select Show Safe Areas toward the middle left of the interface, as in Figure 6.6.

4. Close the Display Options panel by pressing the **d** key again, or **p** (for panel).

Figure 6.7 shows the Camera view with the safe areas enabled. This represents the Title Safe and Video Safe areas of your view. You should set up animations with this feature enabled to ensure that your animation is viewed properly when recorded to videotape.

Figure 6.6
Selecting the Show Safe Areas from the Display Options panel turns on a visible outline through the Camera in Layout.

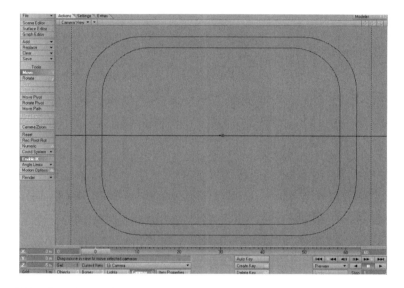

Figure 6.7 When Show Safe Areas is enabled, you'll see a television-style shape around your field of view through the camera.

5. Select Camera from the bottom of Layout, and then press the Item Properties panel, or the **p** key. Move the Item Properties panel over to the far right of the screen, revealing more of your Layout window.

6. Go to the Resolution drop-down list and select D1 NTSC Widescreen, as in Figure 6.8.

This resolution changes the width to 720 and the height to 486, with a pixel aspect ratio of 1.2.

7. Press the **p** key to close the Camera Properties panel.

Figure 6.9 shows the safe areas with a different pixel aspect ratio. Notice how the view looks stretched?

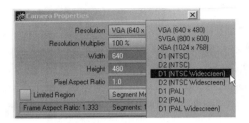

Figure 6.8   You have a number of choices when it comes to resolution, such as LightWave's Widescreen settings.

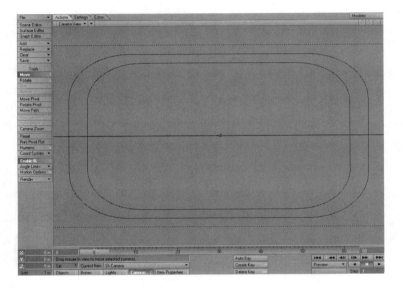

Figure 6.9   Setting a resolution to D1 NTSC Widescreen changes the pixel aspect ratio to 1.2, making the safe area viewed through the Camera panel appear stretched.

8. Press **p** again to open the Camera Properties panel. Grab the slider button next to Pixel Aspect Ratio, and drag it back and forth.

Figure 6.10 shows the slider button. You should see the Safe Area field of view changing in Layout.

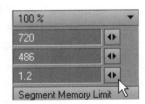

Figure 6.10
You can interactively control the width, height, and pixel aspect ratio by clicking and dragging the small slider buttons.

It's important to note that the pixel aspect ratio will affect your renderings. Changing the resolution changes the size of the image, whereas changing the pixel aspect ratio changes the target pixel shape—which also can distort your final output if not set properly. As an animator, it's important for you to remember what the target display device is, such as a video recorder, and set your resolution and aspect ratio accordingly. For example, if you are rendering an animation for video and accidentally set to D1 NTSC Widescreen resolution, your final animation when imported into an animation recorder or nonlinear editor will appear squashed. The computer will take the full image and squeeze it to fit the television-size frame your nonlinear editor or animation recorder uses. This is because Widescreen resolution is the incorrect resolution for the standard video recorder. And because setting resolution also sets the pixel aspect ratio, both are the wrong version for widescreen to video.

Limited Region

Every now and then, there might be a situation in which the resolution settings are not the exact size you need for rendering. You sometimes might need to test-render just an area of an animation, saving valuable time rendering. For example, if you have an animation that has many objects, textures, reflections, and more, test-rendering the full image might take up too much of your time—especially if you want to see how one small area of the scene looks in the final render. Using the Limited Region setting helps you accomplish this. Figure 6.11 shows the selection in the Camera Properties panel.

Figure 6.11   Limited Region lets you control the area of the screen to be rendered.

When using Limited Region, you can easily turn on a limited region directly in Layout by pressing the l key. A yellow dotted line encompassing the entire Layout area appears. From here, you can click the edge of the region and resize it to any desired shape. Figure 6.12 shows a limited region for a small area of a scene. Figure 6.13 shows how the final rendered image with this Limited Region setting would look.

Limited regions also are useful for creating images for websites using LightWave. Perhaps you want to animate a small spinning globe or a rotating 3D head. Rendering in a standard resolution draws unwanted areas, creating images that are not only the right size, but also larger as well. Setting up a limited region can decrease file size and create renders in the exact size you need, such as a perfect square. Try using a Web GIF animation program and render out a series of small GIF files, set up with a limited region. The GIF animation program imports the sequence of images to create one playable file. Limited Region works differently from a custom resolution. A limited region can be made to any size visually and set for any area on the screen. Setting a custom resolution sets only the specific size for the center of the screen. Also, Limited Region enables you to render limited regions of very high-resolution images if you wanted. A custom resolution would not work this way.

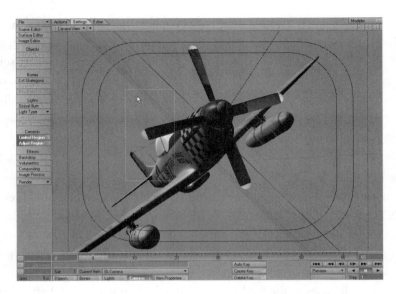

Figure 6.12   You can resize the Limited Region directly in Layout to render a selected area of the animation.

Figure 6.13   The Limited Region-rendered image is just the area assigned in Layout.

Segment Memory Limit

Too often, you'll run out of RAM. RAM, or the memory in your computer, can get used up quickly with many images, large objects, and hefty render settings. The Segment Memory Limit feature lets you tell Layout how much memory to use for rendering. Lower values will render a frame in segments, and might take a bit longer. The tradeoff is that you don't need as much memory. For faster renders, you can increase the segment memory. Setting the segment memory to 20000000 bytes, or 20MB of RAM, will often enable you to render D1 NTSC resolutions in one segment. Although this setting is only an example, LightWave 6's Segment Memory setting is a maximum setting. This means you can set this value to the same amount of RAM in your system, and LightWave will only use what it needs, and often eliminates the need for your system to use virtual memory, or a scratch disk.

Note

Remember that higher resolution settings require more memory.

When you click the Segment Memory button, a small requestor pops up allowing you to enter a value. You can enter a value as large as you want, provided you have the memory in your system. When you click OK, LightWave will ask you if this value should be the default limit. Click Yes, and you won't have to change this value when you start creating another animation scene. Figure 6.14 shows the Segment Memory Limit requester.

Figure 6.14   Setting a segment memory limit tells LightWave how much memory is available for rendering. Setting a higher value allows LightWave to render animation frames in one pass.

Current Camera

Because LightWave 6 allows you to add multiple cameras to your scene, you'll need a way to select them to adjust each item's properties. The Current Camera selection list is in the Camera Properties panel. If you have not added any cameras to your scene, all you will see is the listing "Camera." If you have added multiple cameras, they will be listed here, displayed as Camera (1), Camera (2), and so on, if you have not set a name for them. Cameras added with names also appear in the list, as in Figure 6.15. These cameras listed are all available for selection in the Current Item selection list at the bottom of the Layout interface. You don't need to enter the Camera Properties panel to select a different camera.

Figure 6.15   All your scene's cameras can be selected within the Camera Properties panel, from the Current Camera selection list.

Zoom Factor

The zoom factor is probably one of the most overlooked areas when it comes to cameras in LightWave. The zoom factor is essentially the camera's lens. Have you ever worked with a telephoto zoom lens on a real camera? This is the same thing, only in a virtual world. Pretend you are videotaping a family party with your camcorder. You probably pan around and constantly zoom in and out to cover the action. In LightWave, you can do the same thing! Changing the zoom factor over time not only gives your animation a different look, but also adds variation to your animations.

The default zoom factor is 3.2, as seen in Figure 6.16.

Figure 6.16   LightWave's default zoom factor is 3.2, or the equivalent of a 24mm focal length.

This setting is fine for most projects, but to make something come alive in 3D, you should lower this value. 3.2 is equivalent to a focal length of 24mm, or a standard camera lens. Figure 6.17 shows a scene with the default zoom factor. It looks good, but the scene lacks depth. But take a look at Figure 6.18, where the same shot has a zoom factor of 1.5. Notice how wide the shot looks and how much depth is in the image. Now the image looks three-dimensional. This setting is only an example, and you should try different zoom factors on your own to see what works best for you.

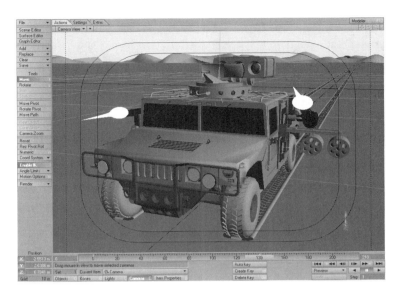

Figure 6.17   A scene rendered with the default zoom factor looks fine but lacks depth.

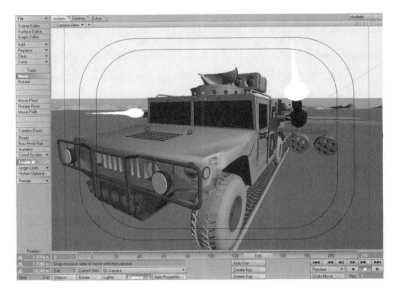

Figure 6.18   The same scene with a zoom factor of 1.5 gives the shot a lot more dimension, and makes it much more interesting.

The camera in LightWave is just as important an element as your objects. Don't overlook the possibilities of changing the zoom factor over time, either. Using LightWave's Graph Editor, you can animate the zoom factor with stunning results.

Focal Length

Zoom factors directly relate to lens focal lengths. Focal length is measured in millimeters. The larger the focal length number, the longer the lens. For example, a telephoto lens might be 180mm, and a wide-angle lens might be 12mm. Because focal lengths represent everyday camera settings, just like your 35mm camera, you may be more comfortable working with lens focal lengths instead of zoom factors. You can do this by selecting the desired option from the Zoom Factor drop-down list, as seen in Figure 6.19.

Figure 6.19   You have the option to choose Lens Focal Length instead of Zoom Factor in the Camera Properties panel.

Note

Each camera you add to Layout can have different zoom factors. For example, in the Camera Properties panel, you can select one camera and set the zoom factor so that it renders like a telephoto lens. Then, you can select another camera in the Camera Properties panel and make it render like a wide-angle lens. Each camera in LightWave can be set differently.

FOV

In addition to zoom factor and lens focal length, you can set up a camera's field of view (FOV) using the Horizontal FOV or Vertical FOV settings. Changing the values for zoom factor automatically adjusts the lens focal length, the horizontal FOV, and the vertical FOV. The horizontal and vertical fields of view give you precise control over the lens in LightWave. The two values listed next to FOV are the horizontal and vertical fields, horizontal being the first value. This is useful when you are working in real-world situations and need to match camera focal lengths, especially when compositing. Don't let all these settings confuse you, however. The Zoom Factor, Lens Focal Length, Horizontal FOV, and Vertical FOV settings enable you to set the same thing. Users should use the one with which they are familiar, or perhaps what is called for to match a real-world camera. There is no inherent benefit in using one over the other.

Antialiasing

When you render an animation, it needs to look good. The edges need to be clean and smooth, and no matter how much quality you put into your models, surfaces, lighting, and camera technique, you won't have a perfect render until you set the antialiasing. Antialiasing cures the jagged edges between foreground and background elements. It is a smoothing process that creates cleaner-looking animations. Figure 6.20 shows a rendered image without antialiasing. Figure 6.21 shows the same image with a low antialiasing setting applied.

Figure 6.20   Without antialiasing, the rendered image looks jagged and unprofessional.

Figure 6.21   After antialiasing is applied, even at a low setting, the image looks cleaner and more polished.

Antialiasing can really make a difference in your final renders. Figure 6.22 shows the available Antialiasing settings.

Figure 6.22 You can choose to add a Low antialiasing setting to your animations, all the way up to Enhanced Extreme.

The higher the antialiasing setting is, the more LightWave will clean and smooth your polygon edges. But of course, higher values mean added rendering time. The Enhanced Antialiasing setting smoothes your image at the sub-pixel level. It takes a bit more time to render, but it produces better results. In most cases, Medium to Enhanced Medium antialiasing produces great results.

Adaptive Sampling

Although you can set up an antialiasing routine for your renders, you still have to tell LightWave how it should be applied. Adaptive sampling is a flexible threshold that LightWave employs to evaluate the edges in your scene. Lower values evaluate more, enabling a more accurate antialiasing routine. Higher values evaluate less. A default setting of 0.1 is an average threshold value. Changing this to 0.01, for example, adds to your render times but helps to produce a cleaner render. A good way to work with adaptive sampling is to set a higher antialiasing, with a not-so-low threshold. For example, Enhanced Medium antialiasing, with a Threshold of 0.1, renders reasonably well (depending on your scene) and produces nice-looking images. For more details on adaptive sampling, refer to your LightWave 6 manuals.

Soft Filter

As an additional help to eliminate sharp, unwanted edges in a scene, you can turn on the Soft Filter option in the Camera Properties panel. As an alternative to setting higher antialiasing routines, you can set a lower antialiasing with Soft Filter applied.

Motion Effects

At the bottom of the Camera Properties panel, there are three tabs. Each tab offers even more control over your camera's settings. The first tab, Motion Effects, is home to some common, more everyday functions.

Motion Blur

When Antialiasing is turned on (set to at least Low), the Motion Blur option becomes available. From time to time, you may need to create motions that mimic real-world properties, such as a speeding car or a fast-moving camera. To give things a more realis-tic look, you can apply motion blur to your scene. Motion blur in LightWave combines several semidissolved images on each frame to give the effect of blurred motion. Motion blur mimics real-world actions. You can see an example in Figure 6.23.

Figure 6.23   Motion blur is applied to the Hummer scene. It helps give realism to the bullets being fired and the wheels turning. Motion blur helps add the feeling of move-ment because in real-world cameras, the shutter speed is not fast enough to freeze the action.

Motion blur should be used anytime you have something fast-moving in your scene. Even if it's only a slight motion blur, the added effect will help "sell" the look. If your animation is perfectly clean, perfectly smooth, and always in focus, it will look better with some inconsistencies, such as motion blur.

Motion blur also is important to set for things like a bee's wings flapping, an airplane's propellers, and so on. Many animated objects moving at this speed will require you to set Motion Blur. If you look at spinning propellers in the real world, all you see is a blur. To re-create that look in LightWave, turn on Motion Blur in the CameraProperties panel.

Blur Length

Simply put, blur length is the amount of motion blur when applied. Default is set to 50%, which produces nice results. Depending on the animation, you may want to set this value slightly higher—say, to 60% or 65%—for more blurring. When you apply the Blur Length, corresponding Shutter Angle and Exposure Time values display beneath the Blur Length window. Most of your motion-blurred animations should have a 50%

blur length set. This is because the blur length relates to the amount of time the theoretical film is actually exposed. Because of the physical mechanism, a film camera can't expose a frame for 1/24 of a second, even though film normally plays back at 24 frames/sec. It turns out that this rotating shutter mechanism only exposes the film for 50% of the per-second rate; thus, 50% blur length is right on.

Particle Blur

Along the lines of motion blur is particle blur. Use this anytime you have an animation whose particles need to blur, such as explosions, fast-moving stars, snow, rain, and so on. A blur length of 50% works well for particle blur.

Field Rendering

At the bottom of the Camera Properties panel is the Field Rendering selection. In NTSC video, there are 30 frames per second, or 60 fields per second. Applying field rendering to your animations is useful when your objects need to remain visible when moving swiftly and close to the camera. This setting is targeted for video, and it allows you to mimic the effect of video's interlaced fields. Motion will seem smoother on the video display. Field rendering makes the final output crisp and clean, especially when there are visible textures. Video draws half the frame first, one field, and then the other half, second field. There are two fields per frame. You can set LightWave to render the even or odd fields first. Motion can occur between the time it takes to display these fields, just as it does from frame to frame, and applying field rendering accounts for this.

Stereo and DOF

Setting up additional camera properties can further enhance the final look of your animations. The second tab area at the bottom of the Camera Properties panel is the Stereo and DOF tab, as seen in Figure 6.24.

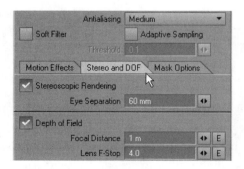

Figure 6.24   The Stereo and DOF tab offers stereoscopic rendering and depth of field functions to your cameras.

Stereoscopic Rendering

Within the Stereo and DOF tab in the Camera Properties panel, you can turn on Stereoscopic Rendering. Stereoscopic rendering is yet another way for you to change the look of your animations. Applying this setting to your camera results in an image that looks separated, as if two images are blurred together. Simply put, this setting creates left and right stereoscopic image files. Changing the Eye Separation value tells LightWave how far apart to render the left and right stereo images.

Depth of Field

You see it every time you look through a camera lens. It's used in movies, television, and now, animation. Depth of field (DOF) is defined as the range of distance in front of the camera that is in sharp focus. Depth of field is a fantastic way to add real depth to your animations. Without DOF, everything will be in focus, as in Figure 6.25.

Figure 6.25   Without depth of field applied, everything in your scene will be in focus.

By adding a DOF setting, you tell the camera where to focus. Anything before or after that focal point will be out of focus. Figure 6.26 shows the same image with DOF applied. Notice how the background is out of focus.

Depth of field can dramatically add to your LightWave renders, as it enables you to set a focal distance for any of your LightWave cameras. The focal distance tells the camera in Layout where to focus when DOF is applied. The default setting is 1m. To use depth of field in your animations, you must have an Antialiasing setting of at least Medium quality.

Figure 6.26   With depth of field applied, the image is out of focus farther away from the set focal point.

Using LightWave's grid, which is the system of measurement in Layout, you can easily determine the focal distance from the camera to your objects in a scene. Figure 6.27 shows the information window in the bottom-left corner of the Layout interface. You'll see the grid measurement at the bottom. The default of 1m appears.

The grid measurement relates to every square in the Layout grid. If the default grid size of 1m is present, each square of the grid in Layout equals 1m. Therefore, you can count the number of grids between the camera and the focal point in the scene. Figure 6.28 shows a scene where the camera is 4 grid squares away from the front of the object. With a grid measurement of 1m, the focal distance setting should be 4m. This makes any object before or after the 4m mark out of focus.

In addition to focal distance, you also can set an f-stop for any of your LightWave cameras. You do this through the Stereo and DOF tab.

The human eye automatically adjusts to brighter or darker lighting situations. Under low light, the human eye's iris and pupil open to allow in the maximum amount of light. Bright sunlight, on the other hand, makes the human eye close to protect the eye.

By the same token, cameras also have an iris and pupil that allow in more or less light. While the human eye smoothly opens and closes to control incoming light, cameras need to have this control set. This is done through f-stops.

X	9.5528 mm
Y	0 m
Z	-4.997 m
Grid:	1 m

Figure 6.27
Using LightWave's grid measurement, you can easily determine where to set the focal distance from the camera to the objects in the scene.

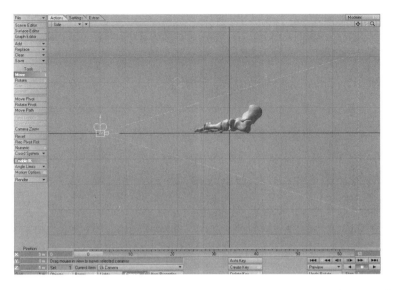

Figure 6.28 Using the grid as a visible measurement, you can count the grid squares from the center of the camera to the focal distance. Here, there are four grid squares equaling 1m each, between the camera and the object. Therefore, the focal distance is 4m.

F-stops are numerical values that represent the amount of varying degrees of light transmission. A smaller f-stop allows more light into the camera, while higher values allow less light into the camera. Here are the common f-stop numerical values used in the real world:

- 1.4   Softest focus, allowing a lot of light into the camera
- 2.0
- 2.8
- 4.0
- 5.6
- 8
- 11
- 16
- 22   Sharpest focus, allowing little light into the camera

Here's how it all comes together. When you have a higher f-stop number (which equates to a smaller iris opening), your depth-of-field value will be greater. So, the depth of field on a LightWave camera set to an f-stop of 11 will be larger and less blurred, creating a flatter image. If you set an f-stop of 2.0, you will have a smaller depth of field, making items behind and in front of the focal distance out of focus. Be sure to check the NewTek LightWave 6 manual, Motion, Animate, and Render, for instructions on calculating the Pythagorean theorem for computer focal distance for depth of field.

Mask Options

The final tab available for enhancing the LightWave camera is the Mask Options tab. Here, you can tell the camera in LightWave to render certain areas while masking out others. The remaining areas are defined by a color. This option is great for setting up pseudo wide-screen renders, or a letterbox effect. You can set values for left, top, width, and height, as well as the mask color. Figure 6.29 shows the Mask Options tab. Figure 6.30 shows a rendered image with the mask option applied.

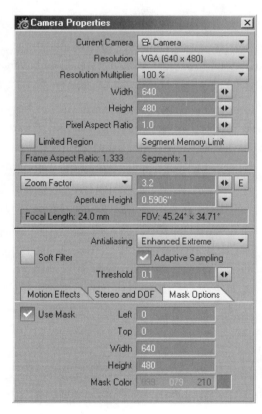

Figure 6.29   The Mask Options tab within the Camera Properties panel enables you to mask areas of your camera view for rendering.

Figure 6.30   Mask options are great to use for rendering only portions of animations while setting a color for the unmasked area.

Note

Remember that masking covers up your rendered image based on the parameters you set. It does not resize your image.

You can see that the control available to you for LightWave's cameras can be a significant element in the animations you create. Too often, the camera is ignored and left in place. Remember the camera! Animate it as well as your objects.

Camera Concepts

You may find yourself in situations where you don't know how to frame a shot or simply where to place the camera. This next section will provide you with some basic instruction that you can use throughout any of your animations.

View in Thirds

To many animators, looking through a camera lens is like looking at a blank canvas. Where should you begin? How should you view a particular shot? Your first step in answering these questions is to get a book on basic photography and cinematography. References such as these can be invaluable to animators as well as a great source of ideas.

When you look through the camera in LightWave, try to picture the image in thirds. Figure 6.31 shows a sample scene as viewed through LightWave's default camera. However, lines have been painted in to demonstrate the concept of framing in thirds.

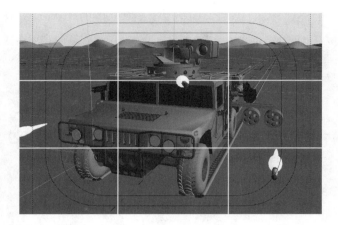

Figure 6.31   Framing your shot in thirds can help you to place the camera more accurately.

By framing your shot in thirds in the vertical and horizontal views through the camera, you have areas to fill with action. Now remember, you need to visualize this grid when setting up camera shots in LightWave. There is not an option to do this. By visualizing, you can begin to think more about your shot and framing. Figure 6.31 is an example of a bad camera shot. Figure 6.32 is the same scene with a decent camera angle.

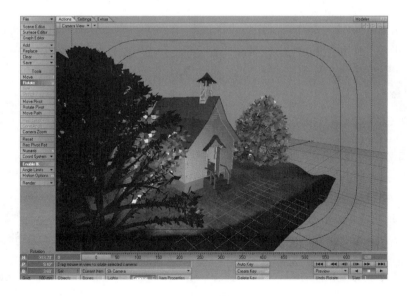

Figure 6.32   A good scene gone bad because the camera is set up poorly. The schoolhouse is centered in view, a common mistake many animators make. This is bad because there is too much open or "dead" space on the top and right of the frame.

Figure 6.33   The same scene looking much better because the camera is set up properly, placing action within the frame. Notice that the dead areas at the top and right of the frame are now filled with subject matter.

If you visualize in thirds, you can see that the action in Figure 6.33 feels better—it is aesthetically pleasing. Although Figure 6.32 had the main focus, the schoolhouse, centered, the rest of the frame was ignored. Figure 6.33 takes into account not only the main focus, but also the surrounding areas of the frame. If you visualize the image in thirds, as in Figure 6.34, you can see that areas of the scene fit into place.

Figure 6.34   This shows Figure 6.33 with lines drawn in thirds for the horizontal and vertical views. Notice how all areas of the scene seem to have a place in view.

Visualizing your camera shot in thirds is a way to help frame the entire field of view. Don't be afraid to try different camera angles and different perspectives.

Camera Angles

After you get the hang of framing a scene, the next thing you should think about is the camera angle. Consider what you are trying to portray in the render. Do you want the subject to look small, or should it be ominous and looming? What you do with the camera in LightWave helps sell the mood of your animations to the viewer. As good as your models and textures might be, your shot needs to work as part of the equation as well. Figure 6.35 shows the schoolhouse from a bird's-eye point of view.

Figure 6.35   Setting your camera to a bird's-eye point of view makes the shot unthreatening.

But perhaps you need to convey that the schoolhouse is not a pleasant place to be. You want to convey a feeling that the schoolhouse is overpowering. Figure 6.36 shows how a different camera angle changes the feel of a shot.

Taking your scenes one step further, you can also employ dutch angles to your cameras. Adding a dutch angle will convey the feeling of uneasiness, or a creepy mood. Figure 6.37 shows a shot similar to Figure 6.36, with the camera rotated on its bank, or dutched.

Figure 6.36   A wider camera angle, set low in front of the schoolhouse, gives a grander look and feel to the shot.

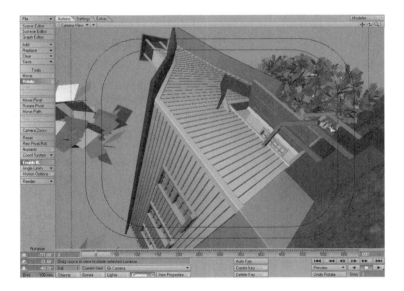

Figure 6.37   Rotating the camera on its bank sets up a dutch angle that conveys the feeling of something being wrong, creepy, or uneasy.

The Next Step

The cameras in LightWave are as powerful as the software's modeling tools. When you model, you create shapes and animate them. When you animate, your motions create a mood, and without the proper camera angles, your work will not be as powerful. Practice setting up different types of shots. Load some of the scenes from your LightWave directory that installed when you bought the program. Study the camera angles used there and try creating your own. Use reference books from real-world situations, mimic the cinematography in movies, and most importantly, experiment.

Summary

This chapter introduced you to the cameras in LightWave Layout. You learned how to add multiple cameras and set their parameters. Concepts were presented to you to change the way you look through the camera to make your animations more powerful and expressive.

This chapter concludes Part I, "Getting Started with LightWave 6." You read about the new features, navigating the interfaces, surfacing, cameras, and using the Graph Editor. When you are ready and feel that you have a solid grasp on the concepts in this section, move ahead into Part II, "A Project-Based Approach to Creating and Building 3D Scenes," where you will put this information to the test with real-world projects.

Part II

A Project-Based Approach to Creating and Building 3D Scenes

Chapter 7

Lighting and Atmospheres

You might consider lighting to be one of the less important aspects of your 3D animations, or perhaps it is an area you are just not comfortable with. Lighting is crucial to your success as an animator. Lighting can be used for so much more than simply brightening a scene. Lighting and the atmosphere it resides in can convey a mood, a feeling, or even a reaction. Lighting is vital in film, photography, and 3D animation.

Project Overview

Basic lighting can add warmth or cool off your animations. It can improve your animations. But you need to be aware of some basic real-world principles before you can put it all together. This chapter instructs you on:

- Basic lighting principles
- Using LightWave's Global Illumination
- Using different light sources
- Animating lights
- Adding atmospheres

Before you begin working through lighting setups in this chapter and throughout the book, you should be aware of the types of lights LightWave has to offer as well as their uses.

Lighting for Animation

The great thing about LightWave is that its lights work in a fashion similar to lights in the real world. They do not exactly mimic lights in the real world, but with a few settings and adjustments, you can make any light realistic.

Five lights are available in LightWave Layout. Each has a specific purpose, but each is not limited to that purpose:

- **Distant lights.** Used for simulating bright sunlight, moonlight, or general lighting from a nonspecific source.
- **Point lights.** Used for creating sources of light that emit in all directions, such as a candle, light bulb, or spark.
- **Spotlights.** Used for directional lighting such as canister lighting, headlights on cars, studio simulation lighting, and more. Spotlights are the most commonly used type of light.
- **Linear lights.** Used to emit light in elongated situations, such as fluorescent tubes.

- **Area lights.** The best light to use for creating true shadows, area lights create a brighter, more diffuse light than distant lights and can create the most realism. They do, however, take longer to render than spotlights, distant lights, or point lights.

The environment in which your animation lives is crucial to the animation itself. Color, intensity, and ambient light are all considerations that you should be aware of each time you set up a scene. Light and the use of shadows are as much an element in your animation as the models and textures you create.

Light Intensity

By default, there is always one light in your LightWave scene. It has a light intensity of 100%, and is a distant light. The light intensity of 100% is a placeholder for you to adjust. Although you can use this one light and its preset intensity as your main source of light for images and animations, it's best to adjust the light intensity to more appropriately match the light and the scene at hand.

Light intensities can range from negative values to the thousands. Yes, thousands! You can set a light intensity to 9000% if you want! The results might not be that desirable, unless you're animating a nuclear holocaust. In general, if you were to create a bright, sunny day, a point light, which emits light in all directions, can be used with a light intensity of 150% or so for bright light everywhere. Conversely, if you were lighting an evening scene, perhaps on a city street, you can use spotlights with light intensities set to around 60%.

Negative Lights

Negative lights can be handy depending on the scene you're working on. As lights with a positive light intensity can brighten a scene, negative lights can darken a scene. You might be asking why you would darken a scene with a negative light instead of just turning the lights down. For example, you might have to add a lot of light to make areas appear properly lit. Depending on the surfaces you've set, the extra light might make one area look perfect, while making other areas too bright. This is where negative lights come into play. Adding a negative light (any light with a negative light intensity value) will take away light from a specific area.

Light Color

The color of the light you use is important and useful in your images and animations because it can help set tone, mood, and feeling. No light is ever purely white, and it's up to you to change LightWave's default 255 RGB light color.

In LightWave, you can even animate colored lights. Say you're animating a rock concert, for example, and need to have fast-moving lights shining on the stage. By animating the light color, you can change the colors over time at any speed you want. The light color in LightWave 6 can now be enveloped, meaning you can use the Graph Editor to set changes to the color over time.

Adding Lights

Adding lights in LightWave 6 is different from previous versions. Follow these simple steps to add lights to LightWave Layout. And remember, unless you are working with Auto Key enabled, you'll need to create a keyframe to lock your lights into position after they're moved.

1. Open Layout or select Clear Scene from the File drop-down menu.

   This sets Layout to its default of one distant light.

2. Make sure you are in Perspective view so you have a full view of Layout. Under the Actions tab, select the Add drop-down button, Add Light, and then Add Spotlight. Figure 7.1 shows the menus.

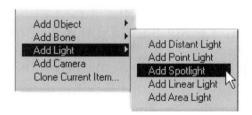

Figure 7.1   You can add lights directly in Layout under the Actions tab.

   You have the choice to add any type of light you want.

3. For this exercise, select Add Spotlight.

   Before the light is added to Layout, a Light Name requester appears, as shown in Figure 7.2.

4. Type in the name you want to give the new spotlight.

Figure 7.2
After a light is added, the Light Name requester appears, enabling you to set a specific name for your light.

> **Note**
> You don't have to change the name of a new light. Instead, you can accept LightWave's default light name by clicking OK when the Light Name requester appears. By default, LightWave names new lights Light (1), Light (2), Light (3), and so on.

The added light is placed at the 0 axis, or the origin, as shown in Figure 7.3.

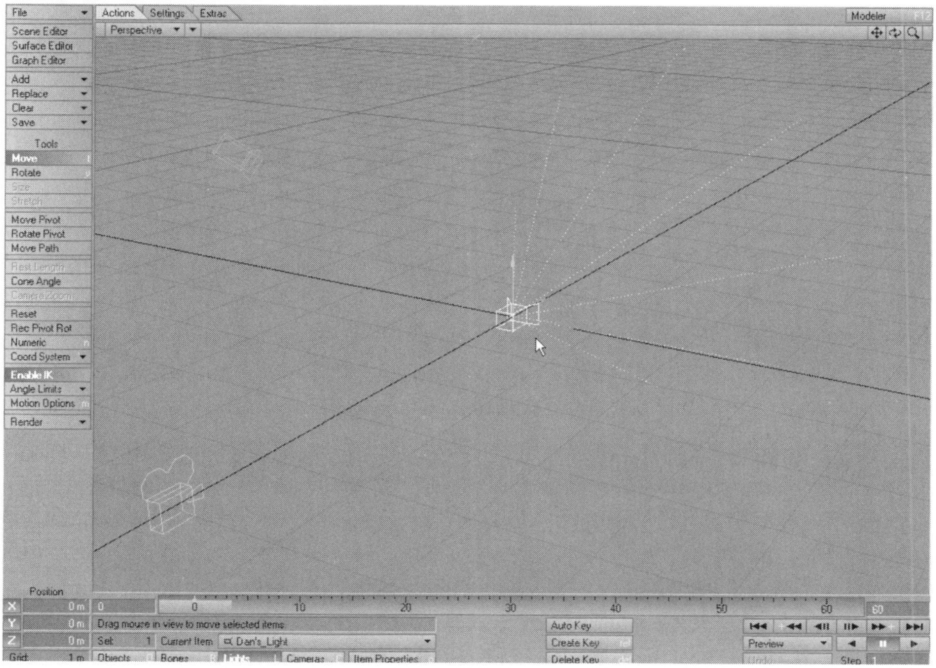

Figure 7.3   Added lights are placed at the 0 axis (the origin) in Layout.

Adding lights this way is intuitive and saves time. In addition to adding lights like this, you also can clone lights. Cloning a light creates an exact duplicate of a selected light. This includes the light's color, intensity, position, rotation, and so on. Any parameter you've set will be cloned. Cloning lights is as easy as adding lights. To clone a light, first select the light to be cloned, and then use the Add drop-down list under the Actions tab, but instead of selecting Add Light, select Clone Current Item. The selected light is cloned.

Global Illumination

The space around you, whether at your desk, in your living room, or outside, has global luminosity properties. The following global properties—Global Light Intensity, Global Lens Flare Intensity, Ambient Light, Ambient Color, Radiosity, and Caustics—can be controlled in the Global Illumination panel. You can find the Global Illumination panel under the Settings tab in Layout. Figure 7.4 shows the panel.

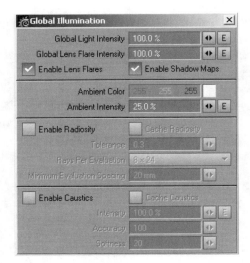

Figure 7.4   The Global Illumination panel, found under the Settings tab in Layout, is where you can control such properties as Global Light Intensity, Global Lens Flare Intensity, Ambient Light, Ambient Color, Radiosity, and Caustics.

Global Light Intensity and Global Lens Flare Intensity

Global Light Intensity is an overriding volume control for all lights in a scene. This can be useful for scenes that have multiple lights that need to get brighter or dimmer over time. Say you're animating a rock concert, for example. You have 20 spotlights shining on the stage. All their intensities are randomly and quickly changing to the beat of the music. At the end of the song, you want all the lights to fade out equally. Instead of setting the light intensity 20 times for each light, you can ramp down the Global Light Intensity. Similarly, if you have lens flares applied to these lights, you can change the Global Lens Flare Intensity.

Ambient Light and Ambient Color

The light around you is either direct or ambient. Direct light comes predominantly from a light source. Ambient light has no specific source or direction.

Within the Global Illumination panel, you can set the intensity of your ambient light. A typical setting is around 5%. LightWave defaults to 25%, which is often too high a value for most situations. It is better to lower the value, sometimes to 0%, and use additional lights for more control. Don't rely on ambient light to brighten your scene. Instead, use more lights to make areas brighter.

You also can set the color of your ambient light so that the areas not hit by light still have some color to them. Say you have a single, blue light shining on an actor on a stage, for example. You can make the side of the actor not hit by any light visible by using an Ambient Light setting; with the Ambient Color set to blue (like the light), the shot will look accurate. You'll use Ambient Light and Ambient Color later in this chapter.

Radiosity and Caustics

Also within the Global Illumination panel are the Radiosity and Caustics settings. These two new features in LightWave 6 enable you to take your 3D creations even further by adding more real-world lighting properties.

Radiosity is a rendering solution that calculates the diffused reflections of lights in a scene. It is the rate at which light energy leaves a surface. This also includes the color within all surfaces. In simpler terms, radiosity is bounced light. A single light coming through a window, for example, can light up an entire room. The light hits the surfaces of the objects and bounces, lighting up the rest of the room, in turn creating a realistic image. You'll use radiosity and learn more about the setting in Chapter 9, "Environmental Lighting."

Caustics are created when light is reflected off a surface or through a refracted surface. A good example is the random pattern often seen at the bottom of a swimming pool when bright sunlight shines through the water. Another example of caustics are the ringlets of light that can appear on a table as light hits a reflective surface, such as a gold-plated statue. The light hits the surface and reflects. Chapter 9 steps you through an exercise explaining this technique further.

Lens Flares

Introduced in LightWave 3.0, lens flares are a popular addition to animated scenes. Too often when you add a light to a scene, such as a candlestick, the light source emits, but no generating source is visible. By adding a lens flare, you can create a small haze or glow around the candlelight. Other uses for lens flares are lights on a stage, sunlight, flash-lights, and headlights on a car. Anytime you have a light that is in view in a scene, you should add a lens flare so that the viewer understands the light has a source. Lens flares in LightWave 6 also can be viewed directly in Layout before rendering. You'll be setting up lens flares later in this chapter.

Volumetric Lights

You need to be aware of one more area when it comes to LightWave lighting before you start working through exercises. Volumetric lighting is a powerful and surprisingly fast render effect that can create beams of light. Have you ever seen how a light streaks when it shines through a window? The beam of light that emits from the light source can be replicated in LightWave with *volumetrics*. Volumetric settings give a light source volume. Additionally, you can add textures to a volumetric light to create all sorts of interesting light beams. Coverage of volumetric lighting can be found in Chapter 9.

Applying Lights in LightWave

You will encounter many types of lighting situations when creating your animation masterpiece. This next section steps you through a common lighting situation that you can use for character animation tests, product shots, or logo scenes.

Lighting for Video

One of the cool things about LightWave is that you don't have to be a numbers person to make things happen. You can see what's happening throughout the creation process from object construction, to surfacing, to lighting. This exercise introduces you to basic three-point lighting often used in everyday video production. You can apply this lighting style to LightWave and create a photographer's backdrop (or psych) to act as a set for your objects. Creating a set in LightWave is a good idea so that even simple render tests are not over a black background. By rendering objects on a set, you add more depth to your animation.

Exercise 7.1   Simulating Studio Lighting

The goal of this project is to introduce you to a common lighting setup that can be useful in just about any type of render situation when simulating studio lighting. You'll use a premade set object that was created in LightWave Modeler with a segmented box, which is smoothed out by applying a SubPatch.

1. In Layout, load the 07Set.lwo object from the accompanying CD-ROM.

   This loads the MultiMesh object, which includes the set and a statue object. Figure 7.5 shows the object loaded in Layout from the Perspective view.

2. Select the default light that is already in the scene. This is a distant light and is not useful for the current lighting situation.

3. Press the **p** key to enter the Item Properties panel for the light.

4. Just below the middle of the panel interface, change the Light Type to Spotlight, as shown in Figure 7.6.

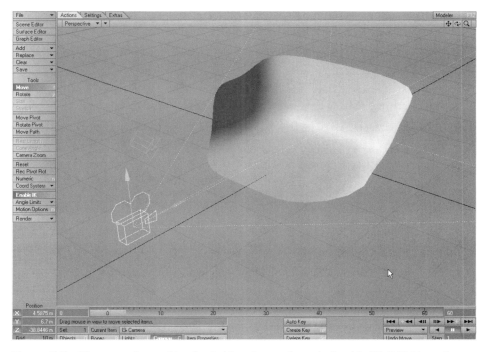

Figure 7.5   The premade set object loaded into Layout from the book's CD-ROM is perfect
for casting light onto.

Figure 7.6   For studio lighting, spotlights work best. Start by changing the default distant
light to a spotlight.

The spotlight becomes the key light, or the main light in the scene setup. You'll be creating a three-point lighting situation in this scene.

5. Change the Light Intensity to 95%, and the Light Color to off-white, about 245, 245, 220 RGB.

You've set the Light Color to off-white because light is never purely white. In a studio setting, the key light burns with a slight off-white tint.

Note

Three-point lighting is a common lighting setup used in most studios. It consists of a key light, which is the primary source of brightness; a fill light, which is less bright than the key and used opposite the key; and a backlight, sometimes referred to as a hair light, which is used to separate the subject from the background.

6. Set the Spotlight Cone Angle to 40 and the Spotlight Soft Edge Angle to 40.

This creates a nice edge falloff for the key light.

7. Lastly, set the Shadow Type to Shadow Map, which creates softer shadows than ray-traced shadows.

8. Change the Shadow Map Size to 2000, which tells LightWave to use 2MB of RAM for calculating shadows. Leave Shadow Fuzziness set to 1.0.

9. Be sure the Fit Cone option is selected, and press **p** to return to Layout.

Warning

You can use Shadow Maps only with Spotlights. This is because LightWave uses the same procedure to calculate areas that are hidden from the camera view by objects as it does for a spotlight. The result is a soft shadow.

Note

The larger the Shadow Map Size, the more memory LightWave uses to calculate the shadow. Larger Shadow Map Sizes produce cleaner shadows. About 2000 is a good size to work with. If you want to increase the Shadow Fuzziness to, say, 8, the Shadow Map Size should be increased to 3000 or higher.

10. Back in Layout, press **5** on your numeric keypad to switch to Light View. Looking through the light to set it in position is the quickest and most accurate way to set up lights.

11. Right-click directly in Layout view and move the light up on the Y axis about 10m.

When you load the 07Set.lwo object, the Grid Size in Layout changes to 10m. You're now moving the light up 1 grid square. LightWave 6 shows the grid squares for the Y axis when in the Side and Front views.

12. On the numeric keypad, press **1** for Front View or **3** for Side View to see the light position.

13. Switch back to the Light View (**5**). With the left mouse button, move the light back away from the set, so that it has a larger coverage area, as shown in Figure 7.7.

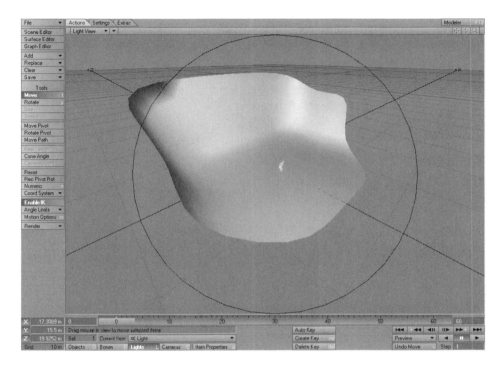

Figure 7.7   Setting the position of the spotlight from the Light View is quick and easy. Because of the way the object is shaded, you can see that the light is in front and to the upper left of the set.

14. Save your scene as LightSetup.lws.

Before you add the other lights, you need to rename this light to keep your scene organized.

15. From the Actions tab, and with the existing light selected in Layout, choose Replace, and then Rename Current Item. Rename the light to Key_Light, and click OK.

Now you need to add another light to create the fill light.

16. From the Actions tab, select Add, and then Add Light, Add Spotlight. After you add the light, LightWave asks you to name it. Name this light Fill_Light.

17. Enter the Item Properties for the Fill_Light, and change the Light Intensity to 65%. Change the Light Color to a soft blue, 135, 170, 230 RGB.

Adding a blue light as a fill light is often a nice touch when setting up lights, either in a studio or in outside situations. It helps create the feeling of distance.

18. Change Shadow Type to Shadow Map for this spotlight, as you did with the Key_Light; change the Spotlight Cone Angle to 40; and change the Spotlight Soft Edge Angle to 40.

19. Press **p** to close the Light Item Properties panel, move the Fill_Light to X 11.5m, Y 3.15m, Z -14m, and Rotate the light to: H −47, P 20, B 0.0. Figure 7.8 shows a view of the set from the Fill_Light. Figure 7.9 shows a perspective view of the Layout setup.

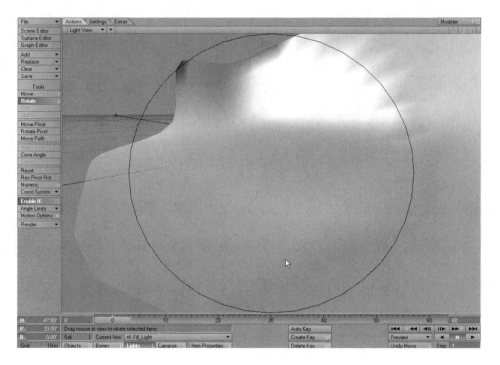

Figure 7.8   The Fill_Light's view of the set.

You need to add one more light to the scene to set up the backlight. This also will be a spotlight.

20. Based on the settings for the Key_Light and Fill_Light, add another spotlight and set the values similar to the Key_Light. Position the new spotlight above and to the back of the set, facing into the set. Be sure to create keyframes at zero to lock the lights in place. Save the scene.

Note

You also can Clone a light in Layout by first selecting the particular light, then selecting Clone Current Item from the Add drop-down menu.

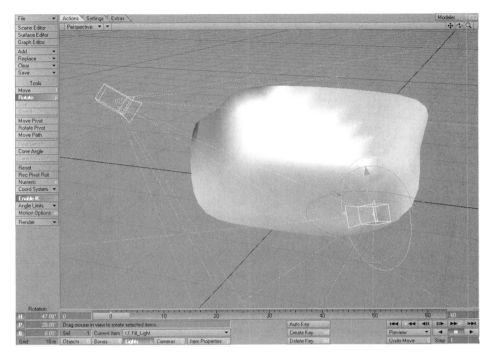

Figure 7.9   In this overview of the scene thus far, you can see the Key_Light to the left and the Fill_Light to the right.

Exercise 7.2   Finishing Touches for Studio Lighting

Now that you have some basic lighting set up, you need to have something to cast light onto. You have a set and lights, but no objects. This exercise shows you how to adjust your lighting situation to accommodate objects and the rest of the set.

1. Be sure the scene you've been working on is loaded in Layout. If not, use the one from this book's CD-ROM, labeled 07LightSetup.lws.

2. Also from the book's CD-ROM, load the 07Betty.lwo object file.

   This is a statue that you can use as a template for adjusting your lights. The object should load directly in the middle of the set, as shown in Figure 7.10.

   The object has a default gray surface to which you can add a texture, such as marble or granite.

3. Switch to Camera View (**6**), Move the Camera into the set, and Rotate the camera so that the statue fills up the frame, as shown in Figure 7.11.

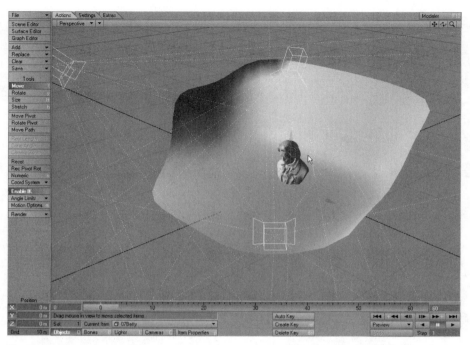

Figure 7.10   The 07Betty.lwo object loads right into the set in Layout because both objects were saved at the 0 XYZ axis. The 07Betty.lwo object is resting on the 0 Y axis.

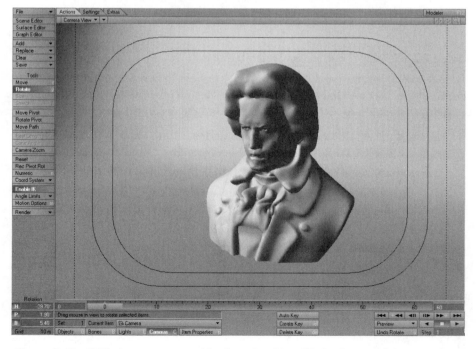

Figure 7.11   With the camera moved in close, the object fills the frame and the set creates a nice backdrop.

Note

The view in Figure 7.11 shows the camera view with Safe Areas enabled to help frame the shot for video. You can find out more about Safe Areas in Chapter 6, "LightWave 6 Cameras." To turn on the Safe Areas, press the **d** key for Display Options, and click Show Safe Areas.

At this point, you can finesse the scene with light adjustment.

4. Press the **d** key to enter the Display Options for Layout. Set the Max OpenGL Lights to 4.

   This enables you to set up effects of lights directly in Layout. The maximum number of lights you can set for OpenGL visibility is 8.

5. Close the Display Options panel.

6. To get a feel for how your lighting looks, press the **F9** key to render a frame. You should see something similar to Figure 7.12. This lighting is harsh and too bright, and should be softened.

Figure 7.12 This initial render of the setup shows lighting that is too bright and somewhat harsh. This is fine, as it is a good place to start finessing the scene.

7. Select the Key_Light and press the **5** key on the numeric keypad to switch to Light View.

8. Move the Key_Light toward the 07Betty.lwo object so that the light is focusing directly on the object, as shown in Figure 7.13. To light the statue with the Key_Light and not the rest of the set, create a keyframe at 0 to lock the Key_Light in place.

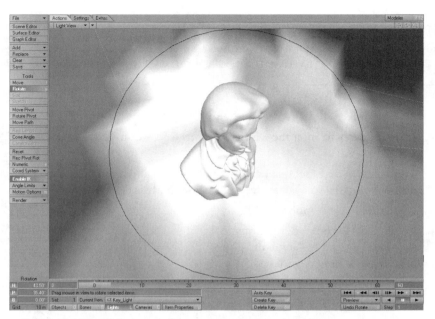

Figure 7.13   The Key_Light is moved in to encompass just the object.

9. Select the Fill_Light, and move and rotate it so that it covers the entire set, as shown in Figure 7.14. Remember: This is the blue light added to simulate distance and to fill the darker side of the object.

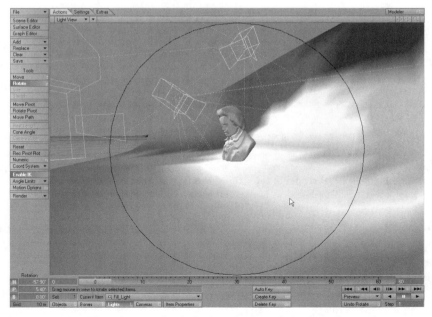

Figure 7.14   The Fill_Light is used to light the scene, simulating light from a distance.

10. Press **F9** to test-render the scene.

It's looking better, but perhaps the shadow from the Fill_Light is too strong.

11. To remedy this, do the following two things: Go to the Global Illumination panel and change the Ambient Intensity from 25% to 0% to help create more contrast between lit and unlit areas; and turn off the Shadow Map for the Fill_Light. Figure 7.15 shows the render thus far.

Figure 7.15 With Ambient Intensity now at 0% and the Shadow Map for the Fill_Light off, the focus is now on the statue.

12. To further enhance the scene, Move the Back_Light in to encompass the statue, change its Light Color to orange, about 235, 155, 55 RGB, and change the Light Intensity to 65%. Figure 7.16 shows the position of the Back_Light, as viewed through the light.

You can load this final scene into Layout from the book's CD-ROM and take a look at the final settings if you want. The scene is called 07LightStatue.lws. Take a look at it and modify it for your own scenes.

Projection Images with Spotlights

Exercise 7.2, although basic in design, is the core lighting situation for many of your LightWave projects. Equipment, figures, generic objects, or any element that is not rendered in an environment can benefit from this basic three-point lighting setup. But you are not limited to using just three lights for these types of situations. You can start with the basic three, and then add more light to highlight certain areas, brighten dark areas, or use additional lights as projection lights.

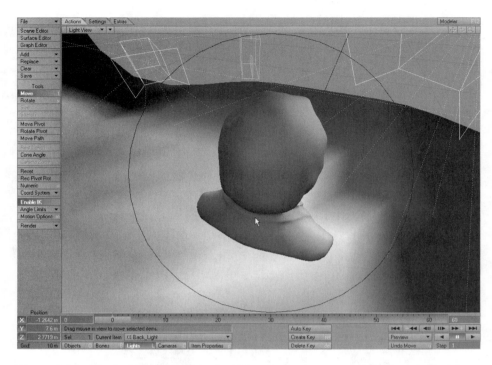

Figure 7.16   The Back_Light is adjusted to shine on the statue as a hair light, separating the object from the background.

Exercise 7.3   Creating Gobo Lights

This exercise will show you how to use LightWave 6's Projection Image feature. This is a useful lighting tool that mimics real-world lighting situations where "cookies" or "gobos" are used to throw light onto a set. A *gobo* is a cutout shape that is placed in front of a light, sort of like a cookie cutter. Certain areas of the gobo hold back light, while other areas let light through. For this exercise, you will use a gobo that creates the look of light coming through a window.

1. Load the 07ProjectionSetup.lws scene from the book's CD-ROM. This is the statue three-point lighting scene from Exercise 7.2.

   Figure 7.17 shows the gobo you'll use to create the effect. This image is nothing more than six white squares on a black background. When this image is applied to a spotlight, the white areas allow light to shine through, while the black areas do not.

Note

Gobo images can be created with a paint package such as Adobe's Photoshop, Jasc Software's Paint Shop Pro, or better, NewTek's Aura 2. The image should be 24 bits and the size should match your render resolution. For example, video-resolution gobo images should be a pixel size of 720×486. Images smaller than 320×340 resolution do not produce the best results.

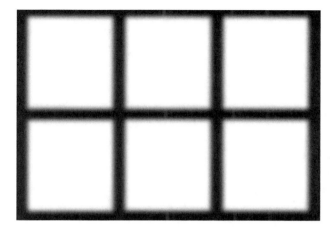

Figure 7.17   A painted image with white squares can be used as a Projection Image in the Lights panel to create window lighting effects.

2. Add a spotlight, and when prompted, name it Gobo_Window_Light. Then, go to the Item Properties for that light.

   The default intensity for added lights is 50%, which is fine for this type of light.

3. Change the Spotlight Soft Edge Angle to 30, matching the Spotlight Cone Angle of 30.

4. Under the Spotlight Soft Edge Angle value, select the Projection Image drop-down list. No images are loaded, so select Load Image from the list, as shown in Figure 7.18.

   After you select Load Image, the system Load Image File requester appears.

5. Select the 07windowGobo.tga file from the book's CD-ROM.

   This is the image pictured in Figure 7.17. After you select the file, it appears in the Projection Image list.

6. Close the Item Properties panel, returning to Layout.

7. Select the Gobo_Window_Light, and press 5 on the numeric keypad to switch to Light View. Move the light up from the center axis about 11m on the Y axis, and then move it over to the left of the statue on the X axis, about –10m.

8. Rotate the light so that it is pointing on the set area behind and to the left of the statue object. Also, move the light back on the Z axis, about –10m.

   Figure 7.19 shows the Light View. You are setting up the light to cast onto the backdrop.

Figure 7.18
You can load the specific gobo image directly from the selected light's Properties panel.

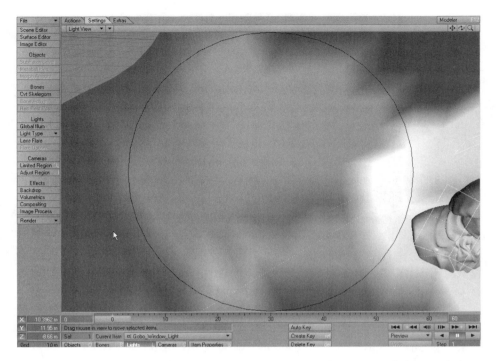

Figure 7.19   This is the Light View for the Window_Gobo_Light, set to cast light on a darker area of the set.

   9. After the light is lined up and in position, create a keyframe at frame 0 to hold it in place. Press **F9** on the keyboard to see how it looks. Figure 7.20 shows the render.

Figure 7.20   The added light has a Projection Image applied and gives the look of a true-to-life studio gobo.

Adding gobos is easy. But it's probably a more powerful feature than you realize. Creating windowpanes on a set is nice, but you can accomplish much more with gobos:

- Use a black-and-white image of tree branches to simulate shadows from a tree.
- Use color images for added dimension. Darker areas will hold back more light, and lighter areas will shine more light. For example, you can create the effects of light through a stained-glass window.
- Use softer, blurry images for added effects.
- Use animation sequences as projection images.

You also can apply volumetric effects for projection images. Later in this chapter, you'll learn about volumetric lighting and the cool things you can create with this feature.

Area Lights

Distant lights and point lights can produce hard-edged, ray-traced shadows. Ray-traced shadows take more time to calculate, which of course means more time to render. Spotlights also can produce ray-traced shadows, but with spotlights you have the option to use Shadow Maps, which take less time to render than ray-traced shadows. Softer than ray-traced shadows, Shadow Maps use more memory to render than ray-traced shadows. Ray-traced shadows use more processing power.

Area lights also can produce realistic ray-traced shadows, but to do so they require more rendering time. For example, say a person is standing outside in bright sunlight. The shadow that the person casts has sharp edges around the area by the subject's foot, where the shadow begins. As the shadow falls off and away from the subject, it becomes softer. Ray-traced shadows from distant lights, point lights, and spotlights cannot produce this effect—and neither can Shadow Maps. Area lights can produce these true shadows, and create a softer overall appearance to animations.

Exercise 7.4   Applying Area Lights

Spotlights are the most common lights and they are the most useful for your everyday animation needs. But on occasion, the added rendering time generated from area lights is worthwhile. An area light is represented in Layout by a flat square and emits light equally from all directions except for the edges, producing very realistic shadows. This next exercise introduces you to using area lights.

1. Load the 07AreaSetup.lws scene file from the book's CD-ROM. This is the scene created for the previous exercises, and it has only one default distant light.

2. Select the Light and press **p** to go to the Item Properties panel. Change the Light Type to Area. Change the Light Intensity to 60%. Keeping the default 100% Light Intensity would be too bright, and the image would appear washed out.

3. Close the Item Properties panel and return to Layout.

4. If the new area light is not selected, select it and change your Layout View to Perspective to get an overall view of the scene. The area light appears as a small box outline. Position this above and in front of the statue object and create a keyframe to lock it in place.

Note

To help set up lights in Layout, change the Maximum Render Level to Smooth Shaded or above. Make sure Max OpenGL Lights is set to 1 or above, and turn on Affect OpenGL for the light in the Light Item Properties panel. This makes the light source's effect visible in Layout, and helps you line up the direction of the light source.

After the light is in place, you need to tell LightWave to calculate the shadows. The Item Properties told the light what kind of shadow to use, Ray Trace, but now you need to turn on the feature.

5. Under the Actions tab, click and hold the Render drop-down menu. Select Render Options. Click Ray Traced Shadows to have LightWave calculate shadows for the Area Light, as shown in Figure 7.21.

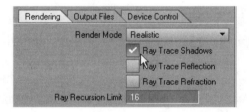

Figure 7.21   You tell LightWave to calculate Ray Traced Shadows while rendering from the Render Options panel.

Tip

While you're in the Render Options panel, make sure the Show Rendering in Progress feature is checked. This enables you to see the render as it's being drawn.

6. Close the Render Options panel and press **F9** to test-render the current frame. Figure 7.22 shows the render with an area light applied.

Area lights can give your animations a professional look. The time it takes to render such lights will be increased, but the results are often worth it. Here are a few more things to remember when using area lights:

- Quality settings can be adjusted. The default Area Light Quality of 4 results in 16 samples per area light. Values of 2 and 3 result in 4 and 9 samples per area light, respectively.

- Linear lights perform like area lights but emit light from a two-point polygonal shape, similar to a fluorescent tube.

- You can mix spotlights, distant lights, point lights, and linear lights with area lights for added effects.

Figure 7.22 Adding just one area light to the scene creates a soft, realistic-looking light with shadows. Notice the soft shadows under the folds of the statue, and how the shadow and light fall off onto the set.

Adding Atmospheres

When you create scenes in LightWave, whether they consist of logos, characters, or architecture, you can create an atmosphere for added value. Atmospheres in LightWave can be created through various methods, such as backdrops, fog, or LightWave's SkyTracer plug-in, to name a few. These next sections introduce you to the different types of atmospheres you can create in LightWave.

Backdrops

The Backdrop panel in LightWave is where you can set up background and gradient colors, or add environmental shaders. Setting a backdrop creates an infinite world inside Layout. By default, the backdrop color is set to black, as seen in Figure 7.23.

Figure 7.23   The default Backdrop Color is black; however, this can be easily changed.

Think of LightWave Layout as one infinite world. When you set a backdrop color, the color is, in effect, wallpapered to this world. You cannot cast shadows onto it, nor can you pass through it or have it affected with lights. To set a backdrop color, all you need to do is click the Gradient Backdrop button. This turns off the solid backdrop color and creates a colored backdrop, defined by four color variables:

- **Zenith color.** This is the top-most region of the "infinite world." If you were setting up a daytime scene, this color would be deep blue, simulating space through the Earth's atmosphere.

- **Sky color.** This is just what it implies: the color of the sky. This color blends smoothly with the zenith color.

- **Ground color.** This setting, by default, is brown, simulating a ground plane below the 0 Y axis. However, because it's labeled ground color does not mean that this is all it's used for. If you set the color values of ground color to those of sky color, you'll create a smooth transition of color.

- **Nadir color.** This is the bottom-most region of the "infinite world." The ground color will blend smoothly with the nadir color.

If you look through the book's CD-ROM, you'll find a few scenes with backdrop settings. Take a look to see some of the variations possible.

Sky Squeeze and Ground Squeeze

Because the backdrop color is applied as an infinite world, you might need to shrink the world from time to time. The Sky Squeeze and Ground Squeeze settings default to 2.0, but if you increase them, the ground color and sky color will, in essence, squeeze together. This is useful for sunsets, for example, where you can set a larger Ground Squeeze to make the ground color smaller, while the sky color remains larger. Check out the 07Sunset.lws scene on the book's CD-ROM for some examples of Sky Squeeze and Ground Squeeze.

Adding Environments

Add Environment, a new selection available in the Backdrop panel of LightWave 6, is an environmental setting that enables you to add environmental shaders to your backdrop. Figure 7.24 shows the drop-down list.

Figure 7.24   The Add Environment selection in LightWave 6 offers more control for creating various backdrops.

LW_ImageWorld

This handy environment plug-in enables you to use an image as a backdrop within LightWave's virtual world. You can use LW_ImageWorld as an environmental mapping solution often used in radiosity situations. This feature adds the capability to apply an image using a spherical warp technique used by high dynamic-range images as an environment wrap. Radiosity is covered in Chapter 9.

To set up LW_ImageWorld, select it from the Add Environment tab within the Backdrop tab. After LW_ImageWorld is loaded in the list, double-click it. This calls up a requester enabling you to apply an image.

LW_ImageWorld creates a spherical image map around your entire LightWave scene. This is not visible in Layout, but it will be when rendered. It's useful for creating reflections and radiosity lighting.

LW_TextureEnvironment

Wouldn't it be cool if you could do more with your backdrop than add color and a single image to it? Wouldn't it be useful to apply LightWave's powerful procedural texture engine to the backdrop, or apply complex layers of gradient colors? All this is possible with the LW_TextureEnvironment handler. Adding this environment gives you access to LightWave's Texture Editor. The results are put into the backdrop.

Exercise 7.5   Adding a Texture Environment

This feature is simple to use, but powerful. You can create realistic-looking backdrops for your animations, or cool computer screen backgrounds, or textures that can be reloaded and mapped onto surfaces of your objects. To begin, save any work you've been doing, and then Clear Layout.

1. Under the Settings tab, select Backdrop from the Effects heading on the left side of the screen. First select the LW_TextureEnvironment plug-in from the Add Environment list, then double-click it to open the interface control.

   You'll see a set of controls appear just below the listing, as shown in Figure 7.25.

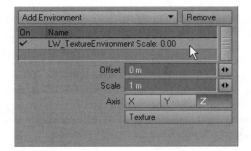

Figure 7.25   Double-clicking the LW_TextureEnvironment listing brings up its controls.

2. Leave the Offset at 0 and the Scale at 1m. The Z axis should be selected because you want the texture to be applied down the Z axis.

3. Begin to set up the texture environment by clicking the Texture button for the LW_TextureEnvironment.

   You'll see LightWave's Texture Editor appear.

4. Change the Layer Type to Procedural Texture. Leave Blending Mode set to Additive and Layer Opacity to 100%.

5. Change the Procedural Type to Cyclone and the Texture Color to something other than white, such as blue or purple. Press **F9** to see what happens. Figure 7.26 shows the Cyclone texture applied as a background.

Figure 7.26   The LW_TextureEnvironment plug-in enables you to use LightWave's texture editor as backgrounds for your animations. Here, a procedural texture, Cyclone, has become an animated backdrop.

This is just a taste of what the LW_TextureEnvironment can do. You can use multiple images, gradient textures, and other procedural textures such as Ripples, Puffy Clouds, and of course, Fractal Noise. This is a great way to make complex textures as well. If you have a large scene with lots of surfaces, for example, you can use the LW_TextureEnvironment feature to create full-screen procedural texture images. Render the images, and then map them onto your surfaces. LightWave will not have to calculate multiple procedural textures—image maps render much faster than procedurals. Try experimenting with these settings and various combinations!

SkyTracer

Too often, you'll need to create a realistic sky. Sure, you can load in an image map or sequence of a sky or clouds, but it's more fun to generate your own. This next exercise takes you through setting up a SkyTracer sky.

Exercise 7.6   Using SkyTracer

SkyTracer can add beautiful clouds and skies to your LightWave environments. SkyTracer is cool because it creates more than a pretty backdrop—it actually creates a full environment so that wherever you rotate the camera in Layout, you'll see the sky. This is why the feature is found under the Add Environment listings in the backdrop panel.

1. Begin by saving any work and selecting Clear Scene in Layout.
2. Under the Settings tab, go to the Backdrop panel, and from Add Environment select SkyTracer to add it. Double-click the listing to start SkyTracer. Figure 7.27 shows the SkyTracer panel at startup.

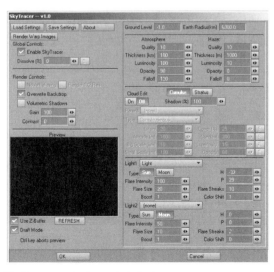

Figure 7.27   The SkyTracer control panel at startup.

The SkyTracer control panel contains numerous controls that you can use to set up SkyTracer and quickly generate great-looking environments. First, look at the default settings by clicking the Refresh button beneath the Preview window. Notice how a sky with some clouds appears. Figure 7.28 shows SkyTracer with the preview pane refreshed.

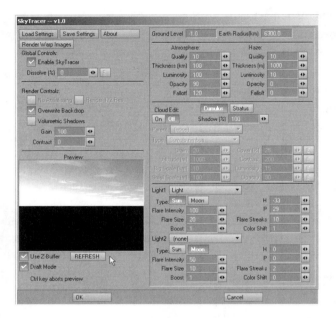

Figure 7.28   By pressing the Refresh button underneath the Preview window in SkyTracer, you can see a nice blue sky.

You'll use this Preview window to see how your sky is coming along. Notice that in this window, the sky appears only in the top half. This is because LightWave sees the ground plane, and SkyTracer is generating the sky from above the 0 Y axis. It's up to you to create a ground in Layout.

The next step is to adjust your settings. The best method for setting up a decent sky with SkyTracer is to utilize the Preview window. Make an adjustment, and see the result in the Preview window. This is your fastest route to animated skies.

3. Adjust the Atmosphere settings by changing the Quality to 50 and the Thickness to 50.

   This makes the sky a clearer and deeper blue.

4. Change the Luminosity to 80, which lessens the overall brightness of the sky. The Opacity should be set at 90, but a lower setting can create a deep, rich-looking sky.

5. Set the Falloff to 50, and click the Refresh button under the Preview window to see how the sky looks at this point.

It needs some clouds! The following settings show your how to create an overcast day with SkyTracer.

6. Click the On button for Cloud Edit, and you'll see the controls become active, as shown in Figure 7.29.

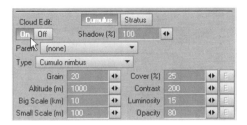

Figure 7.29   Turning on Cloud Edit enables the Cloud Edit controls.

7. Select Cumulo Nimbus as the Cloud Type.

   Cumulous clouds are big and puffy; sometimes they're tall when a storm is near.

8. Set the Grain to 10.

   This adds nice variations to the clouds.

9. The Earth Radius set by default at the top-right corner of the screen is 6300km. Therefore, set the Altitude in the Cloud Edit area to 1500m.

   This creates a low-lying cloud layer.

10. To change the cloud's size, set Big Scale to 30km and Small Scale to 10m. Set Cover to 75% because you want things mostly cloudy.

11. Set Contrast to 50 to add contrast between the sky and the cloud layer. Set Luminosity to 15 to make the clouds duller and less bright. And then, set Opacity to 80 to set the strength of the cloud layer. Click the Refresh button under the Preview window to see the clouds.

Note

When using the Preview window in SkyTracer, you can stop any Refresh by pressing the Ctrl key. Also, you can speed up the Refresh previews by clicking Draft Mode. The Use Z-Buffer button remembers the last render you performed in Layout.

SkyTracer takes a little getting used to, but the advantage is that you can create full environments with it. The downside is that it can be an exhaustive render process. To make your life a little easier, SkyTracer has a feature called Render Warp Images.

Render Warp Images

The Render Warp Images feature in SkyTracer enables you to create your sky environment and save out five seamless images. Instead of rendering every frame, SkyTracer can generate a front, back, left side, right side, and top image that it seamlessly maps together on a cube. Simply import this cube into Layout, and you have your rendered sky. Figure 7.30 shows the Render Warp Images interface.

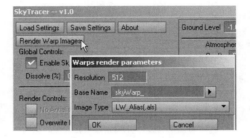

Figure 7.30   Render Warp Images creates a rendered view of your environment from SkyTracer.

After you have the sky settings the way you like them, you can click Render Warp Images and tell it where to save the files. From there, use LightWave's Load Items From Scene feature to load the scene it generates. Then, add your objects!

The Next Step

The information in this chapter can be applied to any of the exercises and projects in this book. These basic lighting setups and core functions will apply to all your LightWave work in some way. Use the information here to branch out on your own and create different lighting environments. Use lights to your advantage—remember, there are no wires or electric bills to worry about when creating virtual lighting situations. You won't need to worry about light bulbs burning out either! Experiment by adding more lights to your everyday scene, or perhaps take some away. Use negative lights, colored lights, dim lights, overly bright lights, and whatever else you can think of to make your animations stand out.

Summary

This chapter guided you through common lighting situations, including three-point lighting, area lights, and environments. In Chapter 9, you'll create more advanced lighting situations with volumetric lighting, lens flares, and radiosity. This chapter can be a good reference for you in any of the lighting situations you may encounter. To go further, use the information in the other chapters to fully enhance your lighting environments. The combination of textures, motion, models, and light is what makes great animations.

C h a p t e r   8

Environmental
Structures

3D animation is so much fun. Hopefully
the information throughout these pages
gives you enough knowledge and insight
that you enjoy it! This book was created to

help you stop scratching your head for a moment and concentrate on a goal—creating with LightWave. Up to this point, you've learned about many of LightWave 6's cool features and powerful creation tools. This chapter gives you a chance to use many of those tools and introduces you to some new ones.

Project Overview

Too many books just tell you how to create one object in an animation, such as a cup, but what about the saucer? Or they instruct you on creating trees, but what about the landscape? This chapter takes you step by step through the creation of a nineteenth-century schoolhouse. In this chapter you'll:

- Model the schoolhouse
- Texture the schoolhouse
- Apply lighting and various surfaces
- Create the exterior of the schoolhouse
- Build the land that the schoolhouse sits on, and add a foggy environment

That's a lot to cover, so stock up on the caffeine and let's get started!

Exercise 8.1   Building a Schoolhouse

The first portion of this project begins in LightWave's Modeler. The schoolhouse design is simple and based on some old schoolhouse structures in upstate New York. The model you will create is a duplicate of the one built for the Fox television special "Night of the Headless Horseman" produced by CAT, in Dallas.

Before you begin any real-world project like this, you must have an outline of your project. What is the final output? Video? Film? Television broadcast? Also, what should the model look like? How will it be used in the final animations? All these questions are important to answer up-front because the answers can help you determine the level of complexity you need to add. For this project, the goal is to create a weathered, old building for television. Textures needed to be of high quality, and the idea of using only bump maps to create some of the "old wood" look was out of the question. Certain shots would require the camera to get close to the walls and floors, revealing the smallest of details. However, much of this model is made with boxes, and that helps ease the complexity of the model.

It also is crucial to have concept sketches if possible. Figures 8.1 and 8.2 show concept sketches for the schoolhouse, created by Dori McBride. These concept sketches are often all you need to start creating your masterpiece.

Figure 8.1   A perspective view of the schoolhouse as a concept sketch.

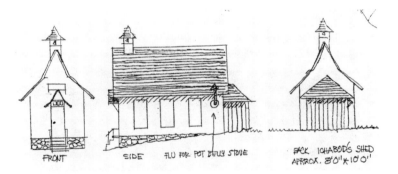

Figure 8.2   A front, side, and back view of the schoolhouse as a concept sketch.

1. Open Modeler and change the Grid size to 1m if it's not already set to this. Do this by pressing **a** to fit all views.

This resets Modeler's viewports. You'll see the Grid size change in the bottom-left corner of the screen.

To create the schoolhouse, you'll start by building a box shape. Boxes, balls, and the other primitive shapes really do make up much of your everyday modeling. Soon, you'll wonder how you ended up where you are from just a simple box!

2. Select Box from the Objects tab, and press **n** (for numeric). In the Numeric Box Tool, select Activate from the drop-down list, and enter the following values:

Low X	–2m
Low Y	0m
Low Z	–3m
High X	2m
High Y	3m
High Z	3m
Segments X	2
Segments Y	1
Segments Z	1

Note

When using a tool such as Box, pressing **n** opens the Numeric panel. Pressing **n** again instantly switches you to Activate mode.

These values are not based on real-world measurements of an actual schoolhouse, but rather, the characters that might inhabit the schoolhouse. Characters for the Fox television special were built at approximately a 1m scale. Given that, the buildings in the special were 3m tall and 6m long—the measurements of your schoolhouse.

3. Close the numeric window by pressing **n**. Press the spacebar to keep these measurements. Figure 8.3 shows the object at this point.

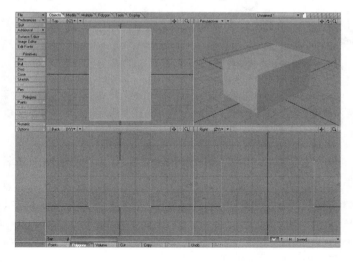

Figure 8.3   The initial structure for the schoolhouse built with the Box tool.

4. Select the Drag tool (**Ctrl+t**) and grab the center point on the top of the box from the Back view. Drag this point up 1m on the Y axis, as shown in Figure 8.4.

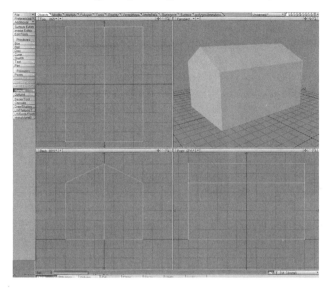

Figure 8.4   You created a box with two segments on the X axis so that you can grab one point and drag it up to create a vaulted ceiling.

5. Copy this object by pressing **c**, and go to a new layer. Press **v** to paste the copy into the new layer.

6. Select the Size tool (**Shift+h**), and size (or scale) the copied object down 10%.

   When you begin scaling an object, the information panel in the bottom-left corner of the Modeler screen displays the percentage. Scaling down 10% represents an information display showing 90%.

Tip

You can also use the Smooth Scale (Sm Scale) from the Tools tab to evenly scale objects.

7. Click the bottom half of the layer button where the first object resides so that you can see it as a background layer.

   Figure 8.5 shows the original object in the background, represented by a black wireframe, and the copied object, which is the object scaled down 10%, in the active (or foreground) layer. You might need to center the scaled-down object to fit directly inside the object in the background layer.

   Using the two layers serves two purposes: It helps you visually line up the scaled object and create an inside of the schoolhouse.

   Now you must subtract the scaled object from the original object so that you can cut out the inside of the schoolhouse. To do this, you need the cutting tool (the smaller object) in a background layer.

8. Press the single quote key (') to instantly reverse the foreground and background layers.

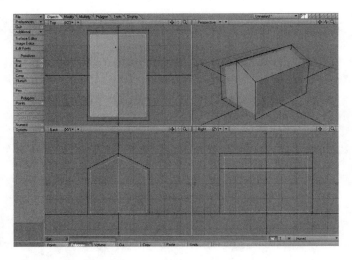

Figure 8.5   The original object is in the background, and the copied object, which is scaled down, is in the foreground.

9. Press **Shift+b** to call up the Boolean CSG panel (also found under the Tools tab). Figure 8.6 shows the panel.

Figure 8.6   The Boolean CSG panel will help you cut out the inside of the schoolhouse.

10. Select Subtract and then press OK.

You'll see a quick jump on your screen and the schoolhouse will now have interior walls. Figure 8.7 shows the schoolhouse with the inside cut from Boolean Subtract. On the outside, it looks as though nothing changed, but if you pay close attention to the wireframe, you can see that the object now has polygons inside as well.

11. Save your object as SchoolhouseShell.lwo.

At this point, you no longer need the smaller object that you used to cut the interior, as it was just a tool for Boolean operations.

12. Press the single quote key (') again to reverse layers, and then press **z** to delete the smaller object. Press the single quote key (') again to reverse layers and bring the main schoolhouse object to the foreground layer.

You need to create the windows and then the doors for the schoolhouse. But before you get too far into that, it's a good idea to begin naming your surfaces.

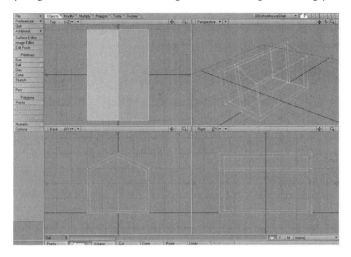

Figure 8.7   After the Boolean Subtract is performed, the schoolhouse has interior walls.

13. Be sure you're in polygon mode by selecting Polygon at the bottom of the Modeler interface (or press **Ctrl+h**), and then click the inside bottom polygons of the schoolhouse.

    If additional polygons are selected, let go of the mouse button and click again on the unwanted selection. Selection and deselection are toggled with the mouse button. Figure 8.8 shows just the inside floor polygons selected.

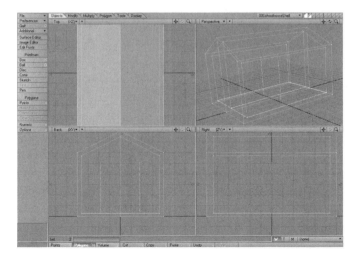

Figure 8.8   Just the inside polygons are selected to assign the surface name for the floor.

14. While the floor polygons are still selected, press **q** on the keyboard to call up the Change Surface dialog. Name the surface School_Floor, and press OK. Press the **?/** key to deselect the polygons.

15. Select the walls on each axis, such as the –X and X, press **q**, and enter the surface names you'll need, such as School_Walls_X. Type in the following names:

School_Walls_X

School_Walls_Z

School_Ceiling

School_outwall_X

School_outwall_Z

School_outroof_Y

Note

You can create all your surface names first and then apply them, or you can select and apply a surface name from polygon to polygon.

For this project, you are going to create the surface names first and then apply surfaces to them.

16. Select the polygons on the X axis of the inside of the schoolhouse, as shown in Figure 8.9. Press **q**, and from the Change Surface list, select the School_Walls_X surface. Figure 8.10 shows the list of surfaces created as they appear in the Change Surface requester.

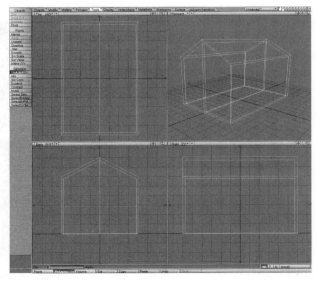

Figure 8.9   The polygons on the inside of the schoolhouse on the X axis are selected and ready for a surface name.

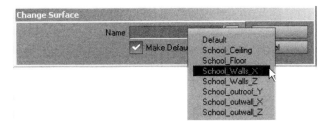

Figure 8.10   You can find any surface you create in the Change Surface requester list. You can apply these surfaces to any selected polygon.

This exercise got you up to speed creating the schoolhouse structure. You made the initial structure from a box, copied it, and named the appropriate surfaces so that later, when it's time to apply image maps, you'll have control over every wall. Go ahead and repeat the previous steps to create surface names for the rest of the structure as you see fit.

Creating the Exterior

You can build in LightWave Modeler with the same types of tools you might use in the real world, such as a lathe. But often, the method you use to build in everyday life is different inside the computer. The next exercise shows you how to create the exterior siding, or wood planks, that make up the outside walls. From there, you'll create and cut out the windows.

Exercise 8.2   Creating the Schoolhouse Exterior

Because many of the shots in the final animation will be close-ups, you'll want to create the exterior of the school with as much detail as possible. This means you should build the wood planks that make up the siding rather than use a bump or image map.

To begin, be sure the schoolhouse structure you created in Exercise 8.1 is in a background layer, and a new blank layer is selected.

The siding for this structure is made from a series of boxes. You need to make only one box for each exterior axis.

   1. Start by creating a box in layer 2, representing one of the pieces of lumber you'll use to build the exterior of the schoolhouse. Create the box using the following measurements:

Low X	−2.0577m
Low Y	−1.504mm
Low Z	−3.0003m
High X	−2m

High Y   209.4396mm

High Z   2.9928m

Segments X   1

Segments Y   1

Segments Z   1

Figure 8.11 shows the result.

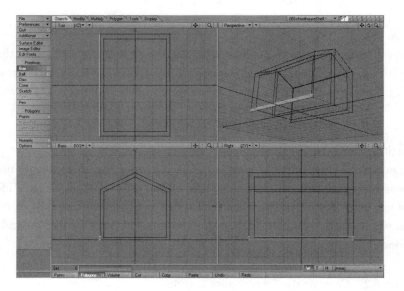

Figure 8.11   A single piece of lumber (actually, it's a long box) is created to make the siding on the exterior of the schoolhouse.

When you build real-world objects in Modeler, especially buildings, you never want to have a sharp edge. Look at the corners of the walls around you—even straight corners are slightly rounded. This is especially true for the siding that makes up a structure. Therefore, before you duplicate the piece of lumber you just created, you need to bevel it.

2. To prepare the lumber object for beveling, start with the long box you created in the foreground layer, and move the mouse over the Perspective viewport (Viewport 2) in Modeler.

3. Press **0** on the numeric keypad to make this quad full screen, and press the period (.) key to zoom into the lumber object.

4. Center the object in view by moving the mouse over it and pressing **g**. Pressing **Alt**, click and rotate the object to see its edge, as shown in Figure 8.12.

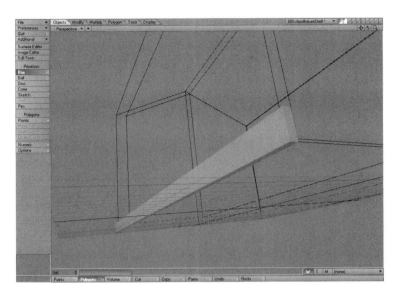

Figure 8.12   Making the preview window a full screen, and using the Alt key, you can position your view to a nice close-up of the object.

5. When you can see the object from a good perspective, press **b** to activate the Bevel tool. Click and drag up and to the right slightly to bevel the long box. Bevel about 5.5mm for the Shift and Inset. (You can set this manually through the Numeric Bevel panel (**n**) if you want.)

   You're now working with LightWave 6's new interactive bevel. It's a bit tricky to get the hang of at first, so remember to use the Undo command (**u**) if the bevel gets out of hand.

   If you look at old homes and notice how the lumber is stacked, or even how aluminum siding is applied on new homes, you'll see that the individual pieces are not exactly perpendicular to the structure. Therefore, the last touch you need before duplicating the siding is to angle it.

6. Press **0** on the numeric keypad to return Modeler to a quad view setup. Press **a** to fit the model into all views.

7. Activate the Zoom tool by press **Ctrl+z**. Place your mouse pointer at the center of the board in the Back viewport and drag out a bounding box surrounding the board using the left mouse button.

   This instantly zooms you into the edge of the object, as shown in Figure 8.13.

8. In the Back view, select the Rotate tool (**y**), and from the top of the lumber object, rotate about −10 degrees, as shown in Figure 8.14.

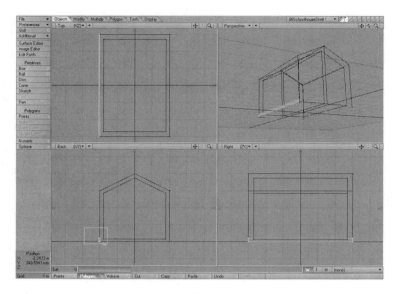

Figure 8.13   The Zoom tool can quickly zoom you into any region of an object in any view.

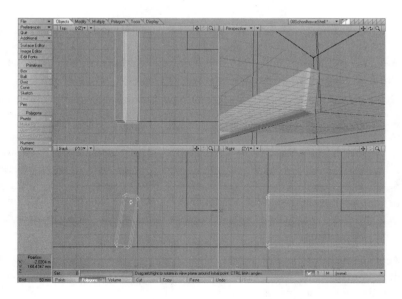

Figure 8.14   Use the Rotate tool to rotate the single piece of lumber about 10 degrees.

9. Save the object.

If you save your schoolhouse structure, the layer with the single long box will save with it. This is part of LightWave 6's MultiMesh system, which you'll use later in this chapter.

At this point, you need to duplicate the single piece of lumber so that it covers the full wall of the schoolhouse.

10. Select the Clone tool from within the Multiply tab. Figure 8.15 shows the panel.

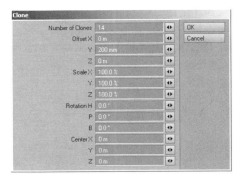

Figure 8.15   The Clone tool multiplies your selected object in various degrees.

11. Enter 14 for the Number of Clones, and set an Offset on the Y axis of 200mm.

This duplicates the single box 14 times up the side of the structure. Figure 8.16 shows the duplicated boxes.

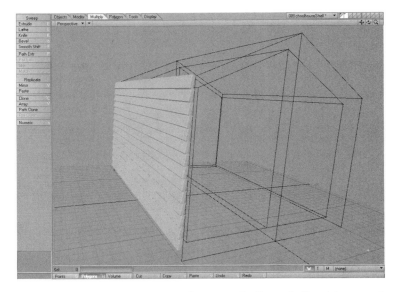

Figure 8.16   The Clone tool makes it easy for you to duplicate similar objects evenly, such as siding on a structure.

You can create the siding for the other walls of the structure by repeating these steps. However, an easier way is to copy and paste the lumber object.

12. To do so, be sure the cloned items are in the Active layer and press **c** to copy
them. Then move to an empty layer and press **v** to paste them. Move the mouse
over the center of the object in the Top view, and press **e** to instantly rotate them
90 degrees counterclockwise (the **r** key rotates 90 degrees clockwise). Figure 8.17
shows the top view before rotation.

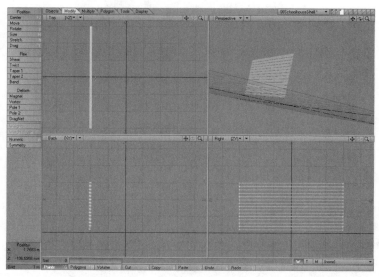

Figure 8.17   Modifications in Modeler work based on the position of the mouse. Centering
the mouse over the top of the cloned objects and pressing **e** rotates the object 90
degrees counterclockwise around the mouse pointer position.

13. Make the shell of the schoolhouse a background layer, and use the Move tool to
line up the rotated item for the siding on the short wall, as shown in Figure 8.18.

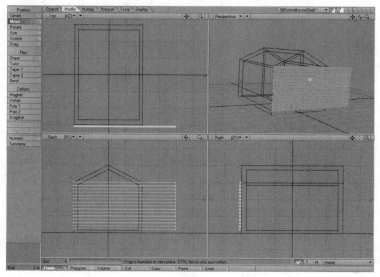

Figure 8.18   Making the schoolhouse object a background layer helps you line up the siding.

As you can see from Figure 8.18, the copied and rotated siding is too long for the front of the schoolhouse.

14. Switch to Point mode, and in the Back view (looking down the Z axis), click and hold the right mouse button and draw around the extruding edge of the siding to select the points, as shown in Figure 8.19.

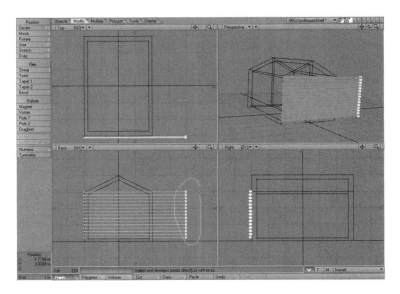

Figure 8.19   Using the right mouse button to make a selection will lasso-select the points in the Back view to adjust the size of the siding.

15. Move the extruded points inward so that they fit the schoolhouse.

   This is where using different layers is handy—you can adjust one model based on another, without disturbing the existing structure.

16. Use the period key (.) to zoom in closer for accuracy, if you need to. Figure 8.20 shows the moved points. The Back view is full screen for better viewing.

   The next step is to mirror the siding object across the Z axis.

17. Deselect all points by pressing the **?/** key. Then, in the Right (or side) view, press **Shift+v** to activate the Mirror tool. Click the center Y axis and move the mouse up a bit. You will see the object instantly mirror across the Z axis. But don't let go of the mouse button just yet.

18. To be sure the line is straight so that the mirrored object is lined up along the Z axis, let go of the mouse button, click the mirror line representation, and move the mouse to adjust the position of the mirror.

19. When the mirrored object is lined up, press **Shift+v** again to turn off the Mirror tool and keep your settings. Figure 8.21 shows the mirrored object.

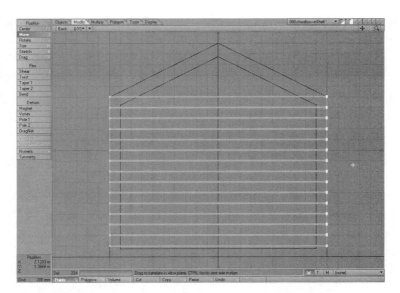

Figure 8.20   Using the Back view as a full view in Modeler, the points of the siding are moved and lined up to fit the schoolhouse structure.

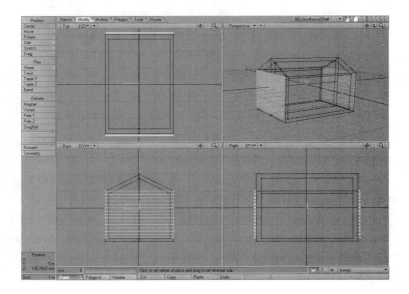

Figure 8.21   The Mirror tool is used to duplicate the cloned siding object to the other side of the schoolhouse structure.

20. Follow Step 19 to duplicate the original siding object on the long wall (x axis). Assign surface names to these objects as well, such as School_Siding_X and School_Siding_Z. Save the objects!

From this point, you have a structure and the siding for the outside. You still need to create windows, doors, and trim, and then put on a roof. After that is complete, you can begin surfacing the structure.

Creating Windows and Doors

This phase of the project guides you through creating windows and doors for the schoolhouse. These objects, like the schoolhouse structure and the siding, also are created from primitive boxes. Like the siding, the objects will be beveled to enhance the overall appearance and take away some of the sharp edges.

Exercise 8.3   Building and Installing Windows and Doors

Using most of the same techniques you used to create the base model, you can create the windows and doors for the schoolhouse structure. The first step is to build the window, then use it to cut out the window area from the schoolhouse structure.

1. Select the schoolhouse structure and the siding by holding the **Shift** key while individually selecting the objects' layers. Center the objects by pressing **F2**.

2. With the schoolhouse object you created in Exercise 8.1 in a background layer, create a box with the following measurements:

Low X	1.6385m
Low Y	−1.0709m
Low Z	−1.9069m
High X	2.2612m
High Y	196.1565mm
High Z	−1.1768m
Segments X	1
Segments Y	1
Segments Z	1

    This creates a box in the shape of a window and places it in position. You'll use this box to cut and then build the windows. Figure 8.22 shows the box, with the schoolhouse structure in the background as reference.

3. In Polygon mode and using the right mouse button, lasso around the box object to select it. Press **c** to copy it, and move it to the center of the schoolhouse structure, as shown in Figure 8.23.

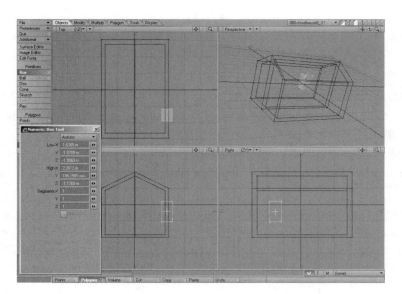

Figure 8.22   To create a window, start by creating a box.

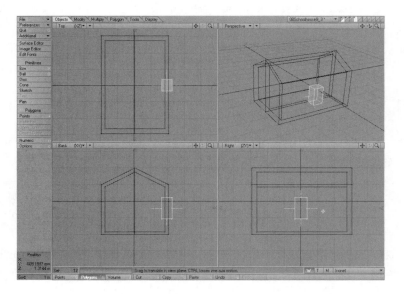

Figure 8.23   The box is selected, copied, and moved for duplication.

4. Press **v** to paste the original back into place.

   Now the box should be in its original position, and the copied box should be in the center of the schoolhouse.

5. With the center box still selected, press **c** to copy one more time, and move this box to the right about 1.5m. Press **v** to paste the copy. Figure 8.24 shows the copied objects in position.

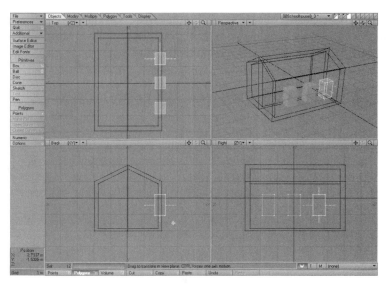

Figure 8.24   All the boxes are copied and moved into place evenly to create the windows.

Note

You're copying and pasting the position of the window object rather than eyeballing it so that it is not exactly symmetrical. It's okay to space the windows unevenly, as this more closely mimics the real world and will help to sell the final animation.

6. Deselect any selected polygons, then with the three boxes in place, mirror them over to the other side of the structure, as shown in Figure 8.25.

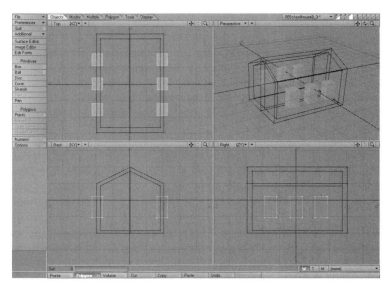

Figure 8.25   The three boxes used to create windows are now mirrored to the other side of the structure.

7. Press the single quote key (') to reverse the layers, putting the schoolhouse in the foreground and the window boxes in the background. Press **Shift** and select the layers with the siding, making them foreground layers.

The only background layer you should have is the one containing the boxes for the windows. Figure 8.26 shows the selections.

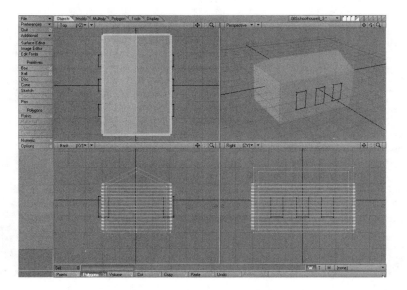

Figure 8.26   The schoolhouse structure and the siding layers are in the foreground, while the boxes for the windows are in the background.

 Note

The boxes to create the windows are in the background because you will use them to cut out the windows from the schoolhouse, which includes the siding. Remember that to use Boolean functions, you need the cutting tool (the boxes, in this case) in a background layer. The objects to be cut (the schoolhouse and siding) should reside in a foreground layer.

8. Press **Shift+b** to call up the Boolean CSG tool. Select Subtract, and click OK.

You'll see the status bar working at the bottom of the Modeler interface, just above the Point, Polygon, and Volume mode.

 Note

If you encounter a Polygon Partitioning Error message, you need to adjust your model slightly. All you should have to do is move the windows slightly, either up, over, or down.

9. Holding the **Shift** key, press the background layer button where the window boxes are to take them out of view. Figure 8.27 shows the cut windows from layers 1 and 2, the schoolhouse structure, and the siding.

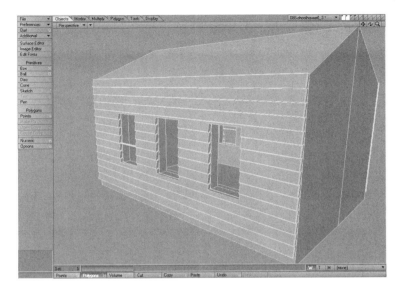

Figure 8.27   The schoolhouse and the siding in layers 1 and 2, with the windows cut out.

Now it's time to create the front door.

10. In a new layer, create a box with the following settings:

Low X	−387.2765mm
Low Y	−1.2266m
Low Z	−3.2648m
High X	465.0731mm
High Y	270.2572mm
High Z	−2.4125m
Segments X	1
Segments Y	1
Segments Z	1

Figure 8.28 shows the box for the door. This creates the door centered on the front Z wall (closest to the camera in Layout). The schoolhouse has stairs that will be built later, leading up to the front door.

11. Use the Boolean CSG function (**Shift+b**) to cut the door out of the schoolhouse and the siding, just as you did for the windows. Select the three layers containing the schoolhouse, the x wall siding, and the z wall siding. Press **x** to remove them; then select the first layer (or an empty layer) and press **v** to paste them all together. This helps to consolidate your model. Save your object!

You should still have two layers available: one with the boxes used to cut the windows, and one with the box used to cut the door.

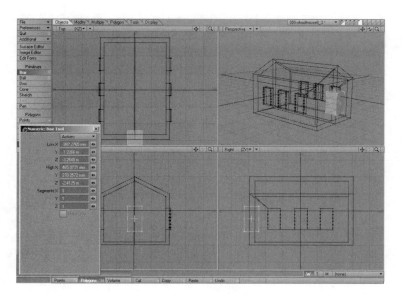

Figure 8.28   Another box object used to create the front door.

12. Select the window box layer. In Polygon mode, select one of the window boxes, as shown in Figure 8.29.

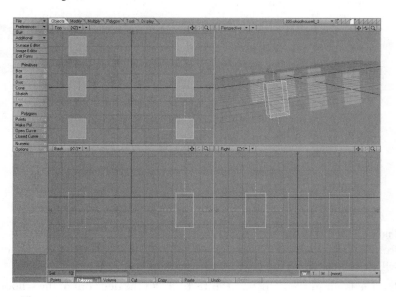

Figure 8.29   One of the boxes used to carve out the window shapes is selected in Polygon mode.

13. Press **x** to cut this object from the layer. Move to an empty layer and press **v** to paste it. Also, paste it into another layer so that you have two copies. Make one copy a background and one copy a foreground.

14. Using **Shift+h**, size one of the copies down about 90%.

    You might find that the Stretch command (**h**) works better for scaling accurately around all sides. Don't be afraid to move the scaled copy so that it lines up evenly with the background layer.

15. Select the points on one edge and move them out on the X axis so that this scale object completely intersects the background layer, as shown in Figure 8.30.

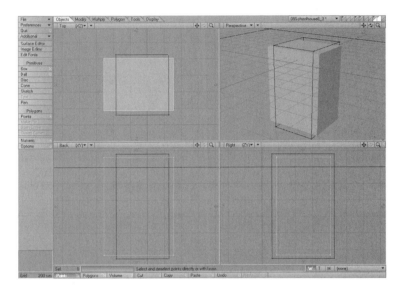

Figure 8.30   The window box object is copied and scaled down in an empty layer to make windowpanes.

16. Press the single quote key (') to reverse the layers, putting the smaller version in the background. Boolean-subtract the smaller box from the larger one, leaving just a frame, as shown in Figure 8.31.

    Now you need to move the frame points so that the frame is resting inside the window well of the schoolhouse in the background layer.

17. Reverse the layers and delete the cutting tool for the window. Go back to the window frame layer and select the schoolhouse as a background layer. Select the points of the window frame on either side and move them in so that the window frame is about 75mm in depth on the x axis. Working with the points only rather than stretching the object helps you control its shape. Figure 8.32 shows the result.

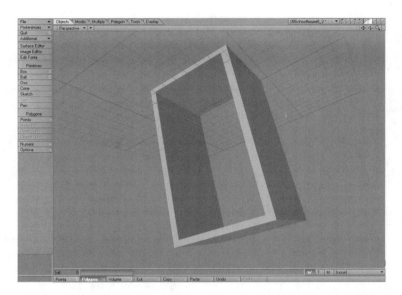

Figure 8.31   One box is subtracted from another to begin making window frames.

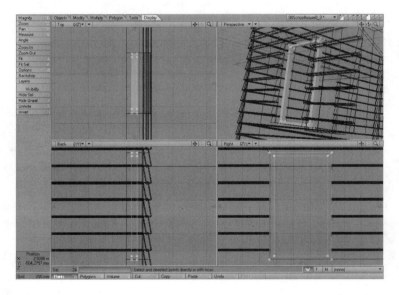

Figure 8.32   The window frame is sized and positioned based on the schoolhouse background layer.

At this point, you're ready to create the inner frame of the window that will hold the glass panes.

18. Select the points at the bottom of the window frame and move them up half the distance of the window itself, as shown in Figure 8.33.

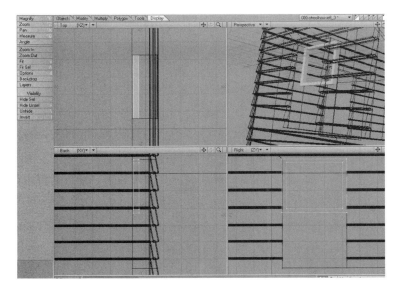

Figure 8.33 The points of the window are moved up to create a double window that can slide open in an animation.

19. Place the window frame in a background layer as a reference, and in a new layer create a thin, vertical box roughly equal to the outer frame of the window.

20. Copy the box, rotate it 90 degrees, and paste the copied box object back down. This gives you the same-sized beams horizontally and vertically. Select and adjust the points on the edges of the frame to fit the outer window frame. Figure 8.34 shows the window's inner frames.

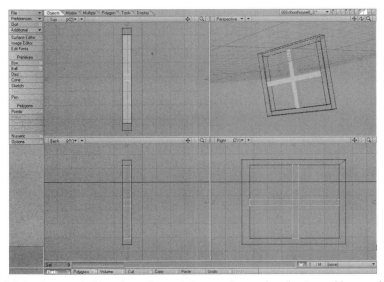

Figure 8.34 One vertical box is made, copied, rotated to make a horizontal box, and pasted to make the frames for the windowpanes.

Now it's time to bevel the object.

21. Press **Shift+b** to call up Boolean CSG. Select Union to bring the foreground and background window frames together as one. Using the Bevel tool, bevel the frames about 3mm for both the Shift and the Inset. Change the surface name (**q**) to School_WindowFrame. Save your work. Figure 8.35 shows the beveled frame.

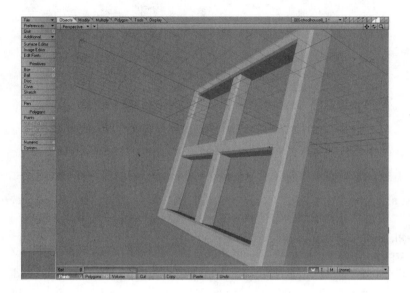

Figure 8.35   Beveling the window frame adds a soft touch.

Rather than follow these steps to create additional window frames, you can use the Mirror tool.

22. Make a new layer the foreground, and put the window frame in the background. Create a flat box between one of the frames, and change the surface name to School_Window_Glass. Figure 8.36 shows the single pane of glass.

23. Mirror the pane of glass to the other three framed areas within the window. Figure 8.37 shows the copied panes of glass.

Note

You also could have created one large piece of glass that encompasses the entire window. However, because the schoolhouse has many windows that will use refraction and transparency, individual panes are more efficient. LightWave will not have to calculate the glass areas hidden through the window frame. Additionally, individual windowpanes enable you to vary their placement, adding more realism to the scene.

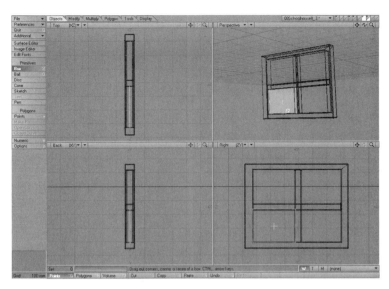

Figure 8.36   A single polygon is created for the pane of glass.

Figure 8.37   Panes of glass in the window.

24. Cut and paste these two layers together, making the glass and the window frame one complete object.

 Note

These are simple objects, so cut and paste can work well. Although a Boolean Union (as shown in Step 21) eliminates unnecessary polygons that can slow down rendering, it also can take away some polygons that it shouldn't.

25. With the full window as an active layer, place the schoolhouse as a background layer for reference. Copy this window frame, and then move it down and into the schoolhouse slightly so that you create the inside window.

26. Paste the copied objects and individually select each to adjust their positions. Size and stretch the windows as well so that they fit perfectly in the window opening. Place them as shown in Figure 8.38.

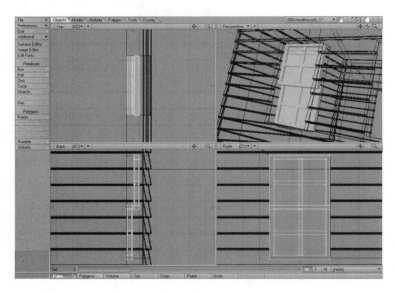

Figure 8.38   The window is copied, moved, and pasted to create two windows: an inner window that can slide up and down and an outer window that remains stationary.

27. When you have the windows in place, copy and mirror them to fit the other window openings in the schoolhouse. Leave them on their own layer, and the schoolhouse on its own layer. Save the object.

The techniques in this exercise are useful for creating any type of building. Most of the homes and buildings in which you live and work are built from square pieces of lumber that are cut, sized, and shaped to make a structure—just like you've done here.

Exercise 8.4   Adding Trim and Structural Details

Exercise 8.4 guides you through adding the finishing trim and details to the outside of the schoolhouse. This includes fascia, stairs, and windowsills. You can continue working with the model you created thus far, or use the 08Schoolhouse8_3.lwo model on the book's CD-ROM.

I. With the schoolhouse in a background layer, select an empty layer as the foreground. Create a box with the following measurements:

Low X	−2.0616m
Low Y	−1.8296m
Low Z	−3.0735m
High X	−1.9269m
High Y	1.0299m
High Z	−2.9245m
Segments X	1
Segments Y	1
Segments Z	1

Move the box (if needed) to fit the corner edge of the schoolhouse, as shown in Figure 8.39. This image shows the box created to make trim on the corners of the schoolhouse. You don't want the siding to stick out!

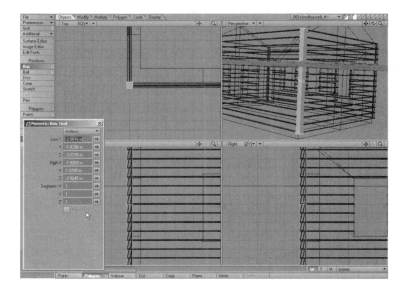

Figure 8.39   A long box is created to fill in the corner trim of the schoolhouse.

2. Bevel this box to soften the edges and change the surface name to School_Corner_Trim. Copy and paste this box to the other corners of the schoolhouse, making sure to select and move each corner trim, zoom in on it, and precisely line it up if your mirroring is not exact.

3. When all four corners have trim, cut and paste them to the schoolhouse. Figure 8.40 shows the trim, beveled and added to the corners of the schoolhouse. Be sure to save your object at this point.

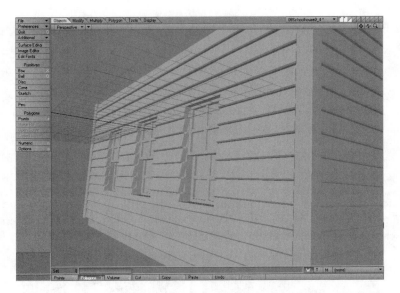

Figure 8.40   The trim, windows, and siding all come together to make the schoolhouse start looking like something useable in an animation!

4. In a new layer, create yet another box with the following measurements:

Low X	1.8432m
Low Y	−1.1507m
Low Z	−1.9064m
High X	2.2098m
High Y	−1.1056m
High Z	−1.128m
Segments X	1
Segments Y	1
Segments Z	1

This creates a small windowsill that you can copy and place in all the windows.

5. As you did with the trim, bevel this box slightly and copy it to the other window layers. Remember to apply a surface name, such as School_Windowsill. Figure 8.41 shows the windowsill, with the schoolhouse and the windows together. Save your object.

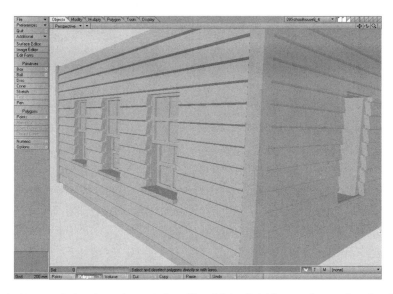

Figure 8.41   Small details, such as windowsills, add the finishing touches to the schoolhouse model.

6. To create a roof for the schoolhouse that hangs over the edges of the walls, create a large box with the following measurements:

Low X	−14.0545mm (remember, millimeters!)
Low Y	2.1886m
Low Z	−3.4588m
High X	2.6729m
High Y	2.2969m
High Z	3.367m
Segments X	1
Segments Y	1
Segments Z	1

7. Place the mouse over the bottom-left point in the Back viewport. Rotate this box 27 degrees downward to match the slope of the roofline, as shown in Figure 8.42.

8. Move half of the roof down so that it is resting on the existing structure. You can see the existing structure because it is selected as a background layer for reference. Mirror the roof to cover the other side of the schoolhouse.

9. In the Back view, lasso-select the points that make up the center edges of the roof, as shown in Figure 8.43.

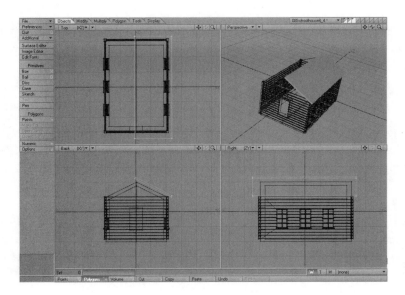

Figure 8.42   One half of the roof rotated into place.

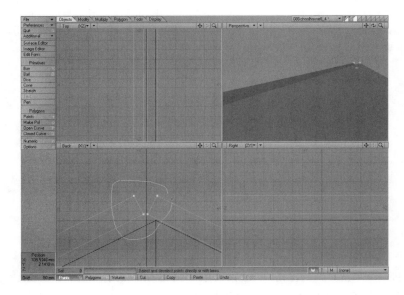

Figure 8.43   Lasso-select the points that make up the center portions of the roof.

10. To align the roof, press **Ctrl+v** to call up the Set Value command. Select the X axis and set the Value to 0% (see Figure 8.44). Click OK and the selected points will jump to the 0 X axis equally.

Figure 8.44   Set the value for the roof alignment here.

Depending on where the center peak of your schoolhouse resides, you might need to shift the selected points (after the Set Value) for proper alignment.

11. Press **m** to Merge any points living in the same space as others. Four points should be eliminated. Bevel the roof (**b**), change the surface name (**q**) to SchoolhouseRoof, and save the object.

12. Perform a Boolean Union (**Shift+b**) to join the roof with the schoolhouse. If you encounter errors, cut and paste instead. Again, save the object. The beveled roof is shown in Figure 8.45.

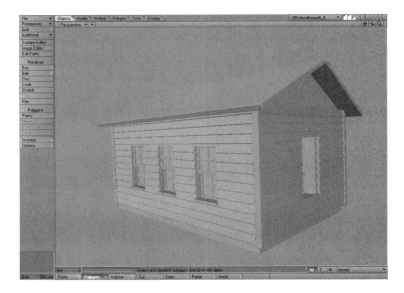

Figure 8.45   The schoolhouse with the beveled roof.

From this point, you can create a few of the other touches on your own, using the same techniques and principles applied in these exercises. You need to create a front door and some stairs. Using boxes, which are beveled, and the combination of foreground and background layers, you can create these remaining elements without much trouble. As an added touch, try creating a small bell tower on top of the schoolhouse. Using a tall box, cut out the inside with Boolean Subtract, then add a bell object. The book's CD-ROM includes a reference for you to use.

Working with Multiple Layers

Figure 8.46 shows the final schoolhouse with windows, a door, front stairs, interior stairs, and a bell tower.

Figure 8.46   The final schoolhouse with trim, windows, stairs, and a door is ready for surfacing.

If you look at the layer buttons at the top right of the Modeler interface (refer to Figure 8.46), you can see that five layers are selected. Each layer contains a separate element that can be animated independently of the school object, yet they are still part of the school-house object. The bell in the bell tower might need to sway and ring, while the door needs to swing open and closed. A window or two might need to be opened during an animation. This is part of LightWave 6's MultiMesh object standard. Later, when you load the schoolhouse object into Layout, all the layers associated with it will load as well—the door, the bell, the windows, and so on.

MultiMesh Objects, Layers, and Pivots

Because you are utilizing LightWave 6's MultiMesh object feature for the schoolhouse, you should use it to its full extent. First, go to the Display Tab, and then select the Layers button. Figure 8.47 shows the Layers panel open in Modeler.

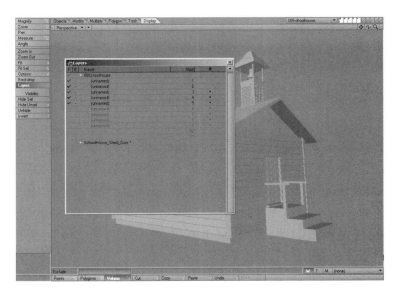

Figure 8.47   The Layers panel in Modeler, where you can control the layers within an object. Here, you can see all the layers associated with the schoolhouse.

This panel gives you all the control you need over the layers in Modeler. You can see that the 08Schoolhouse.lwo object is loaded and listed at the top of the Layer interface. The small white triangle to the left of it is pointing down, which means the object's layers are expanded, or visible.

Notice the two columns on the left with the headings F and B. Underneath are check marks. F represents foreground layers and B represents background layers. Whichever column is checked tells Modeler where the layers should be—foreground or background.

The next column is labeled Name. You can see from Figure 8.47 that the only name listed now is the object name, 08Schoolhouse. You can (and should) name the other layers. Naming all the layers helps you keep organized in Layout. For example, Figure 8.48 shows the Rename Layer command that appears when you double-click any of the layers. Add a name and click OK. The layer is now named.

You also can set up hierarchies with the Layer panel. For example, Figure 8.49 shows the layer of the schoolhouse containing the door. You can see that the name was changed to schoolhouse_door, and that it is now parented to the schoolhouse layer. When the full 08Schoolhouse.lwo object is loaded, the door will be parented to it.

Figure 8.48   Double-clicking any of the layer names calls up the Layer Name command.

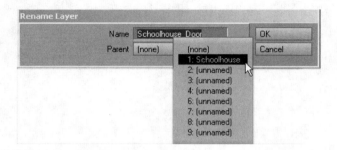

Figure 8.49   When you rename a layer within the Rename Layer command, you also can set its parent.

When you're creating a large object with many parts instead of saving out all the individual parts, you can keep them as part of a single object. In this chapter's exercises, you've been creating a schoolhouse that has a door, windows, a school bell, and soon, landscaping. Each element can be saved with the object. Be sure to use the Layers panel to control your layers.

Notice the small eye symbol toward the top right of the Layers panel. The column underneath it has small dots next to each layer. These dots represent which layer will be visible in Layout. For example, you used a lot of boxes throughout this chapter to create the cut outs for the windows and door. If you didn't delete these cut outs, you can uncheck them (turn off the dot) in the Layers panel. Those layers will not be available for selection in Layout.

Note

Although you see only 10 layer buttons across the top of the Modeler interface, you actually can have unlimited layers through the Layers panel. To add more layers, just click once on the last layer line. Figure 8.50 shows 41 layers!

Because some of the elements will animate independently of the schoolhouse but remain part of the full object, such as the door, a window, and the school bell, adjust their Pivots. You were introduced to moving the pivots earlier in this book. By going to the Tools tab and then selecting Pivot, you can set each layer's pivot. For example, the school bell's pivot can be adjusted to the top of the bell so that in that animation, it can swing properly. The same goes for the door and the window. Adjusting their pivots now in Modeler makes them ready to animate when brought into Layout.

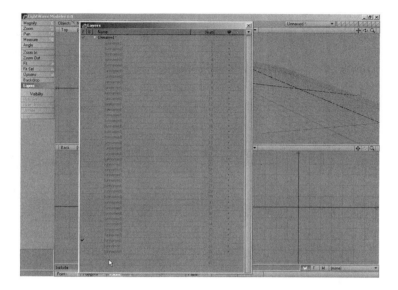

Figure 8.50   Unlimited layers are easy to add within the Layers panel.

Creating Landscapes

LightWave is your own little Hollywood set. You can build as much or as little as you want. And if you've ever been on a real television or film set, you know that much of what the camera sees is not as it seems. This can apply to your LightWave animations as well. To set up the type of shots you'll need for the schoolhouse, it will need some landscaping and an environment. But, the camera is focusing only on the schoolhouse, so an extensive landscape is not necessary. You have to build only what is needed for the particular shot.

Exercise 8.5   Modeling Trees

This exercise steps you through the creation of trees to accent the exterior of the schoolhouse. Begin in Modeler.

1. Load the schoolhouse you've been working on throughout this chapter, or load the 08Schoolhouse8_4.lwo object from the book's CD-ROM.

   Five layers should load with this object: the schoolhouse, the windows, an individual window, the front door, and the school bell.

2. Go to an empty layer and select the schoolhouse as a background layer. Press the comma (,) key to zoom out until you have a 5m grid, as shown in Figure 8.51.

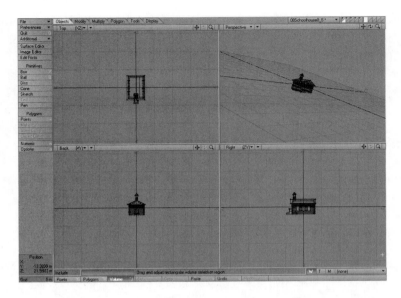

Figure 8.51   The comma key zooms you out to a 5m grid. By placing the schoolhouse in a background layer, you have a good reference from which to work.

3. Create a box in the entire Top view. Keeping the mouse over the Top view, press the up arrow once and the right arrow once to add a segment to each (Z, X) axis. Press the **spacebar** to turn off the Box tool. Finally, press **Tab** to create a SubPatched object.

4. Change the Surface Name of the ground to School_Ground. Move the ground down so that it rests under the schoolhouse, as shown in Figure 8.52.

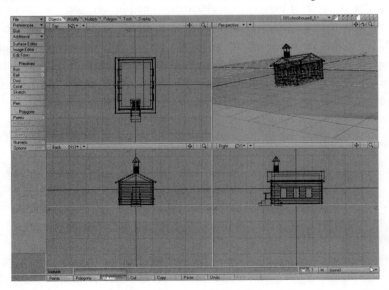

Figure 8.52   The ground object should be moved to rest beneath the schoolhouse.

The ground object looks pretty flat, but don't worry; it won't be after it's in Layout.

5. Go to an empty layer and create a box with the following measurements:

Low X	−11m
Low Y	−2.5m
Low Z	−8m
High X	−9.5m
High Y	200mm
High Z	−6.3m
Segments X	2
Segments Y	3
Segments Z	2

This box is used to create a big tree in front of the schoolhouse.

6. Press **Tab** to make the object a SubPatched object. Press **o** to call up the General Options panel. Be sure the Patch Division is set to 6.

7. From the Back view, select the bottom row of points on the cube. Select Stretch (**h**) and stretch them out in the Top view to about 200%.

You'll notice that because there are more segments in the initial cube, the base is still somewhat square. Deselect any selected points.

8. Pull every other point inward with the Drag tool (**Ctrl+t**), and pull out the corners, as shown in Figure 8.53.

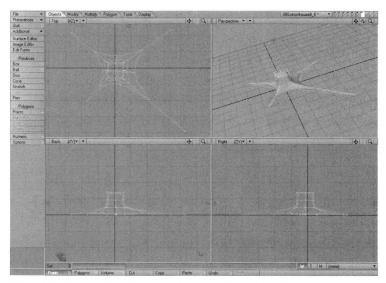

Figure 8.53   A SubPatched box is used to begin making a big, old tree. Points are pulled at the base to create the roots.

9. From the Top view, start pulling the points inward at the corners of the box. You'll see the SubPatch going to work by smoothing the curves.

10. In Polygon mode, select just the top polygons, as shown in Figure 8.54.

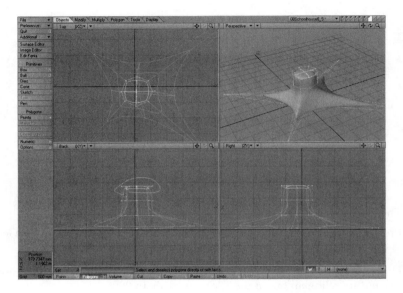

Figure 8.54   The top portion of the tree stump's polygons is selected, ready to be multiplied.

You need to expand these polygons to make the rest of the tree. Do this with the Smooth Shift tool. Smooth Shift multiplies a polygon or group of polygons equally. Bevel, on the other hand, extrudes polygons individually. You need the tree to remain solid at this point, so Smooth Shift is the right choice.

11. Press the **Shift+f** to activate Smooth Shift.

12. In the Right (or side) view, click and drag to the right and you'll see the tree grow.

Smooth Shift multiplied the selected polygon and shifted it the distance you dragged. Figure 8.55 shows the growth.

Believe it or not, that's all there is to it. Because the top of the tree has multiple segments, you can at any point Smooth Shift just one or two of those to create the branches. After you Smooth Shift, bend or rotate the points. Smooth Shift again, and continue. Figure 8.56 shows the tree with two polygons on the top Smooth Shifted one way, while two other polygons are Smooth Shifted individually.

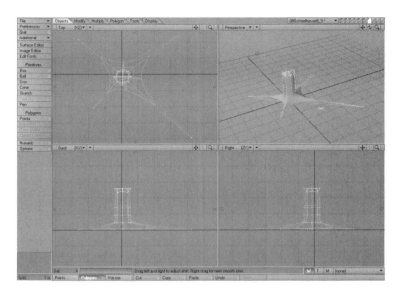

Figure 8.55   Smooth Shift is used to multiply polygons on the tree to extend its growth.

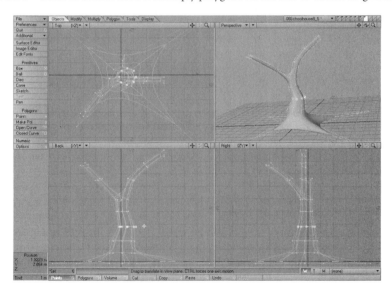

Figure 8.56   With just a few Smooth Shifts and rotates, you can start forming a very cool and unique tree. Here, the points in the center of the trunk are selected and pulled to the side to give the tree some character.

The polygons are rotated and pulled to form branches. Now it's your goal to continue multiplying polygons and building the tree—it could be endless! Remember, you don't have to select just the end polygon—you can select any of the side polygons and Smooth

Shift to create other strange branches and growths. Figure 8.57 shows a more complete tree created with this technique.

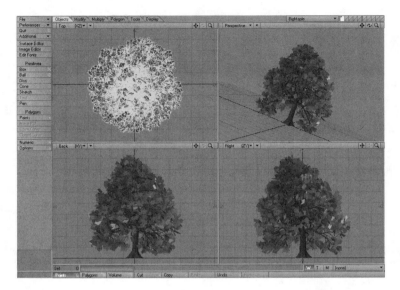

Figure 8.57   A little more tweaking and a tree is complete, ready for surfacing. Here, a clump of single polygons is created and bunched together to simulate leaves.

Note

Remember that in LightWave 6 all your tools work in the Perspective view. You can drag, rotate, move, and more in this Perspective view. To rotate the view, you must either use the viewport controls located at the top right of the viewport interface, or press **Alt** to Rotate, **Ctrl+Alt** to zoom, or **Shift+Alt** to move.

Exercise 8.6   Creating Realistic Leaves

To make realistic leaves on the tree, you have a few options. The tree in Figure 8.57 has basic, generic leaves, nothing more than single polygons. Because this tree is dense in foliage, applying fully detailed leaves would be nearly impossible. This tree has a simple random array of leaves because it will be seen in the distance. The next few steps, however, can help you create detailed leaves, which can be used for close-ups. You would put a number of these leaves on a single branch for close-up camera shots, to fool the viewer.

The best way to make a leaf is to base it on an image. Figure 8.58 shows a scan of a leaf. From this, you can build your model as well as your textures.

1. In Modeler, click the Display tab. Select the Backdrop button to open the Display Options panel. LightWave 6 enables you to place an image in any viewport to work with. For this exercise, select Viewport 3, the Back view.

Figure 8.58   A scan of a leaf is all you need to start making realistic leaves.

 2. From the Image drop-down list, select Load Image and load the 08Leaf.tga file
    from the book's CD-ROM.

    This is the leaf you will create and duplicate to make a realistic branch of leaves.
    Figure 8.59 shows the setup.

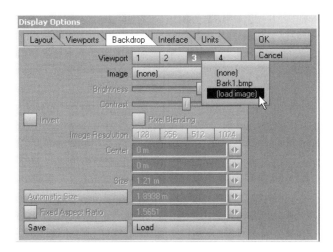

Figure 8.59   You can load the leaf image into the backdrop in Modeler through the Display
                 Options panel.

 3. Make the Back view full frame, and begin creating points around it with the
    Points tool, found under the Objects tab. Use the right mouse button to create
    points. You only need a few points at key places. Press **Ctrl+o** to make a closed
    curve. Figure 8.60 shows the leaf curve.

Figure 8.60   Points are created around the image to build a 3D leaf.

4. Tweak the curve to precisely fit the image using the Drag tool (**Ctrl+t**). If you want, go to the Display Options panel and increase the resolution to sharpen the background image. (This is for display only and does not change the original image.)

5. When you have the curve adjusted, press **Ctrl+d** to freeze the curve. Rename this surface Leaf and save it.

    Create a branch in the same way you created the tree.

6. Create with a box and use the Smooth Shift tool, but make the branch smaller and thinner. Extend a few of the branches out to an even thinner branch that will hold the leaf. You might need to size down the leaf to fit the branch, and when you do, vary the sizes of the leaves. Although leaves on a tree are generally the same size, none is exactly the same. As always, save your work.

    You don't need to actually "attach them" unless the camera will get very close. With a dense array of leaves, it is difficult to tell if the leaves are really attached.

7. When the tree is complete, select all the points that make up the areas where you want to add leaves. Copy the points (c) and paste (v) them into a new Layer. Make this layer a background layer and select the leaf you created in the foreground.

8. From the Additional drop-down list, select the Point Clone Plus tool.

    This clones the leaf object to every point in the background. Play around with the size and rotation variations to come up with a tree full of leaves.

The real trick to creating leaves is not so much in the modeling, as you can see, but in the surfacing. Shortly, you will see how to surface the leaf with color, bump maps, and procedural textures, and you will use LightWave 6's new Translucency feature. All the models you'll need for the time being are complete. For now, save all your work and get ready to surface the schoolhouse.

Surfacing Old Structures

The goal of this chapter is to take you through an entire project without taking up the entire book to do it. However, it's not a good idea to overlook what is probably the most important aspect of this particular project, the surfacing. The schoolhouse has its own style, but depending on what color and texture it has, it may take on a completely different look and feel. You want the schoolhouse to look old and weathered. The way to accomplish this is with good image maps and LightWave's procedural textures.

Exercise 8.7   Weathering the Schoolhouse

Although you can now apply surfaces directly to your models in LightWave's Modeler, you can't take advantage of VIPER there. This exercise is done in Layout so that you can use VIPER technology.

1. Open Layout and load the schoolhouse you've been building throughout this chapter. You also can use the 08Schoolhouse.lwo found on the book's CD-ROM.

    You'll see that although you loaded only one object, you have multiple objects from which to choose in the Object Current Item list. You'll also see that the other layers in Modeler have loaded with the schoolhouse, such as the door and the school bell. This is LightWave 6's MultiMesh at work.

2. Open the Scene Editor.

    You'll notice that the windows and door are parented to the schoolhouse. You did this in the Layers panel in Modeler. And because you did, you're ready to begin surfacing the walls. Figure 8.61 shows the parenting.

Figure 8.61   Because you used the Layers panel in Modeler, your objects are already named and parented to the schoolhouse.

Start with the outside of the schoolhouse for surfacing.

3. Go to the Camera View in Layout, and set up a perspective shot of the school-house, as shown in Figure 8.62.

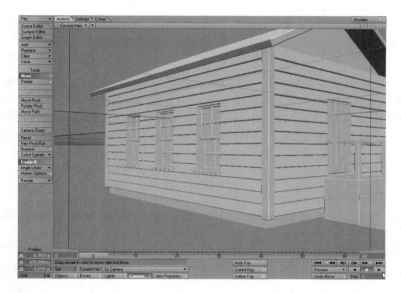

Figure 8.62   Set up a good view of the schoolhouse from the Camera View to begin applying surfaces.

4. You want to utilize VIPER, so first go to the Render Options panel and click Enable VIPER. Close the Render Options panel and press **F9** to render one frame. When the render is complete, close the render window.

Note

If your frame is rendering in two segments, such as the top half first, then the bottom half, go to the Camera panel to adjust the Segment Memory. Change the Segment Memory Limit to 20000000. This tells Layout that it has up to 20MB of RAM to use for rendering, which will allow a regular video-resolution frame to render in one pass. It saves time and is much less annoying. When you set this value, LightWave will ask you if this should be the default value—click Yes.

5. Open the Surface Editor. If the VIPER preview window does not open, click the Options button, and select Use VIPER. Click the Render button on the VIPER window so that you can see the render you created in Step 4.

It is now time to apply a texture. Figure 8.63 shows the image taken from an old barn in Long Grove, Illinois. It's been cleaned up a bit in Photoshop, but it is nonetheless a perfect image to use for the walls of the schoolhouse.

Figure 8.63   A photo of old barn wood ready to apply to a 3D schoolhouse.

6. Select the SchoolSiding_X surface.

   If you're not sure about what surface you named on your model, just click the area you're interested in surfacing from the VIPER window. That surface becomes highlighted in the Surface Editor's Surface Name List.

7. Click the T button for the Surface Color for the SchoolSiding_X surface.

   The Texture Editor panel opens. Layer Type should be Image Map. Blending Mode should be set to Additive, and Projection is Planar. The Image listing says None because no images are loaded.

8. From the Image drop-down list, load the 08StackedWood.tga file from the book's CD-ROM. Click the Render button in the VIPER window.

   You'll see the surface change update in VIPER. It probably looks streaked and messy, but this is easy to fix.

   This surface is named SchoolSiding_X because its mapping should be on the X axis. Adding the axis to your surface names in Modeler is a quick and easy way to remember to what axes your surfaces should be applied.

9. Change the Texture Axis to X.

   The texture change is applied and VIPER updates, but it will probably look too small and patterned, as shown in Figure 8.64.

10. Click the Automatic Sizing button.

    The texture updates in VIPER, and you see that the patterned look is now gone.

11. Turn off Texture Antialiasing.

    The texture now looks too big for the surface.

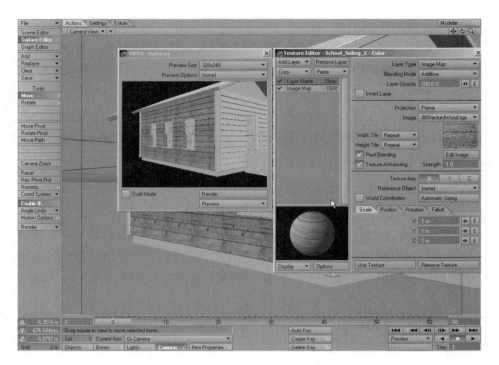

Figure 8.64   After the wood texture is applied to the X axis, it starts to look too patterned.

12. Repeat it slightly by changing the Scale X to 2m, Scale Y to 1.4m, and Scale Z to 3m. Check the update in VIPER.

The wood texture seems to fit the wall better. Before the sizing, it almost looked stretched to fit the wall. This is something you never want. Always work with an image that has a high enough resolution or can be repeated.

The surface looks pretty good, but you can make it look better and avoid any repeating lines.

13. While still in the Texture Editor for the SchoolSiding_X surface, select Add Layer, and choose Procedural.

14. Change the Layer Opacity to 50%.

Because this layer was added after the Image Map layer, it resides above (or on top) of the wood texture layer. This is fine, but you don't want it to overpower the wood texture.

15. Set the Procedural Type to Smoky2. Make the Texture Color a dark brown mud color, something about 65, 50, 50 RGB. Then, select the Scale tab and change the X value to 200mm and the Y value to 10m. Leave the Z value set at 1m.

16. Click Use Texture to return to the Surface Editor.

Figure 8.65 shows the render with this side of the schoolhouse surfaced.

Figure 8.65   Adding a procedural layer on top of the good-looking wood surface helps dirty the side of the schoolhouse.

Take this surface a bit further.

17. Go back to the Texture Editor for the SchoolSiding_X surface and copy the Image Map Layer. Again select Use Texture. Open the Texture Editor for Bump Map by pressing the T button next to it. Paste the copied layer using Replace Current Layer.

18. From the Image drop-down list, select Load Image. Now load the file 08StreakedWoodBump.tga from the book's CD.

This is a grayscale high-contrast version of the color image you mapped earlier. This image is used for the bump maps. The brighter areas appear bumpier than the dark areas.

Because you copied and pasted this layer, changing the image was one of the two changes you needed to make. The size is set right and should remain with the same values set for the color map. Otherwise, the bump map won't line up. But you can increase the Amplitude to about 4 or 5. This increases the amount of bump.

19. Click Use Texture to close the Bump Map texture panel. Save your objects!

If you are satisfied with the results of this surface, you can quickly apply it to the front of the schoolhouse.

20. From the Surface Name list, select the SchoolSiding_X surface with which you've been working. Right-click and hold to pop up the quick Copy and Paste commands. Copy this surface.

This copies all the Color Texture layers as well as the Bump and any other parameters you've set.

21. Select the SchoolSiding_Z surface, and right-click to select paste.

VIPER updates drawing the texture map and the bump map. However, you'll notice that the newly applied surface doesn't look quite right. This is because you are applying an X texture on a Z axis.

22. Go to the Color Texture Editor, and change the Texture Axis to Z. Also, click Automatic Sizing. Repeat this for the Bump Map texture as well.

The copied layers also can be applied as Specularity Texture Maps.

23. Enter the T button for Specularity, and paste the copied Image Layer down.

This allows the light to fall in and out of the bump map grooves based on the bright and not-so-bright areas of the wood image.

24. Click Use Texture, save your work, and press F9 to test-render. Figure 8.66 shows the two sides with the same wood surface.

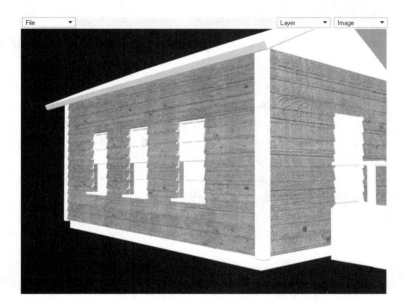

Figure 8.66   The initial X surface is copied and modified to the Z axis walls, while bump and specularity maps are applied.

 Note

You can add as many layers as you want to the surfaces in this exercise. You can continue adding procedurals for weird and really grungy surfaces, or you can add other image layers for complex looks. Whatever you decide, remember that the layers you add build on top of each other. The Opacity needs to be lowered to see all the underlying layers.

To surface the trim or the corners of the schoolhouse, you can copy and paste the SchoolSiding_X surface just as you did for the SchoolSiding_Z. But instead of changing the applied axis, change the Projection type to Cubic. This maps the texture around a cube-like surface, such as the corner of the old schoolhouse.

Enhancing with Gradients

The Gradient textures in LightWave 6 are useful and powerful. You can use them on surfacing projects, such as the schoolhouse, to change the look of the image map. Gradients enable you to vary color, luminosity, or any other settings based on parameters such as distance between objects or surface bumps. Before you get too far into surfacing more of the schoolhouse, try enhancing the existing wall you've already surfaced with Gradients.

Exercise 8.8   Surface Variations with Gradients

With the schoolhouse on which you've been working loaded in Layout, press **F9** to render one frame. Be sure you have Enable VIPER checked in the Render Options panel. When the render is complete, open the Surface Editor.

1. Be sure the VIPER window is open for the Surface Editor, and click the Render button to preview your rendered frame. Click directly in the VIPER window on the SchoolSiding_X surface.

   The surface becomes highlighted in the Surface Name list.

2. Enter the Color Texture Editor for the surface.

   You have two surfaces already: an image map with the wood texture and a procedural with Smoky2 applied for some dirt. Take this surface one step further by adding another layer on top of the existing two.

3. Select Add Layer, then a Layer Type of Gradient. Set Layer Opacity to about 40%. Because this layer is on top of the other layers, you won't be able to see the Procedural or Image Map layers with 100% Opacity on the Gradient Layer.

4. Set Blending Mode to Additive and set the Input Parameter to Bump.

   Doing the former enables you to join this layer with the existing layers, and doing the latter mixes the Gradient colors you'll set up in a moment with the bumps in the wood texture.

5. Click the tall, white Gradient bar.

   This adds a key, which is represented by a line across the Gradient bar.

6. Click again just beneath the first key to add one more. Figure 8.67 shows the two keys.

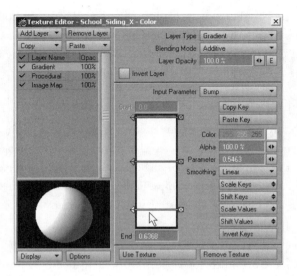

Figure 8.67   Clicking directly on the Gradient bar adds keys that you can adjust and recolor to change gradient parameters.

If you click the right end of the key, you'll remove it. If you click the left end of the key, the arrow side, you can slide and adjust it.

7. Move the keys so that they are evenly spaced within the Gradient bar.

8. Click the small arrow on the top key to select it. Then, adjust the color for this key to a deep brown, about 65, 50, 50 RGB. Select the middle key the same way, and change its color to a mid-tone brown, about 185, 175, 150 RGB. Lastly, set the bottom key in the Gradient to a deep brown color, using the same settings as the first key.

9. Select the center key again, and set the Parameter to 0.3.

This determines the position for the selected key.

10. You should see your render in VIPER. To get a really good look at this, select Save All Objects and render the frame by pressing **F9**.

Remember, surfaces are saved with objects, and you should get in the habit of always saving your objects after you've made changes to its surfaces. Figure 8.68 shows the render with the SchoolSiding_X wall surfaced.

From here, use the same image-mapping techniques on the other walls and the roof. You can load the Shingle.tga file off the book's CD-ROM for tiling the roof. Remember that you can add a procedural texture layer to dirty it up, and cover up visible repeating patterns.

To surface the trim of the schoolhouse, use the same techniques applied in the previous exercises, but use a Cubic map instead of a Planar map. Cubic wraps your textures around square items, such as corner trims. You can even get away with copying and pasting the settings you've set in the previous exercises, removing the image map, and adjusting the values.

Figure 8.68   Three layers of textures applied to the X and Z walls of the schoolhouse give the surface an old, weathered look. Gradients help discolor the wood.

There are many more surfaces to set up in the schoolhouse, but the principles in the preceding exercises can be applied to any of them. However, the glass on the windows is a different surface entirely, so follow along with Exercise 8.9 to surface the glass windows.

 Note

Coming up in Chapter 9, "Environmental Lighting," you'll learn about surfacing multiple layers of glass with refraction and caustics.

Exercise 8.9   Surfacing Glass Windows

Be sure the object you've been working on is saved. While it's loaded in Modeler, go to the Surface Editor and select the School_Window_Glass surface.

Making window glass is much easier than you might think. This type of glass really has no color because it will be mostly transparent. The default gray/white color is fine.

1. Set the Diffuse to 75% so that the glass picks up 75% of the light from the scene.

2. Set the Specularity to 90% because you want the glass to be very shiny, but set the Glossiness to 20 or so.

Although you want shiny glass, you don't want high-gloss glass. This is an old schoolhouse, so the windows might need to be a bit duller than usual.

3. Set the Reflection to 20% so that it reflects its surroundings. Also, set the Transparency to 95%. The reflections and glossiness will make it visible.

Note

Because this is windowpane glass, it's not necessary to set Refraction. Refraction is the bending of light rays, such as the distortion you see when looking through a glass of water. This will be covered in Chapter 9.

Adding a bump map helps the windows look more lifelike.

4. Click the T button for Bump Map, and set the Layer Type to Procedural Texture. Blending Mode is set to Additive, while the Procedural Type is set to Fractal Noise.

5. Lower the Texture Value to 25% to make the bump just slight—not too strong. Leave all other settings alone, and click Automatic Sizing. Click Use Texture to return to the Surface Editor.

6. Go to the Environments tab and select Ray Tracing + Backdrop for the Reflection Options. Close the Surface Editor and save your objects.

7. Go to the Render Options panel, and click Ray Trace Reflection.

   This allows the glass windows to reflect their surroundings, But the surroundings are just black.

8. Go to the Backdrop panel and click Gradient Backdrop to set up LightWave's default brown ground and blue sky. press **F9** to render a test frame. Zoom in closer to the windows to see how they look. Figure 8.69 shows the render at this point.

Figure 8.69   With some realistic-looking wood and glass now surfaced, you're ready to finish surfacing the window frames and the interior.

You'll still have to surface the wood window frames, the roof, and the interior. Also, you can use the SchoolWalls_X and SchoolWalls_Z surfaces as the foundation underneath the SchoolSiding surfaces. You can do this with the other wood textures that are on the CD-ROM, or try using procedural textures with Gradients, as you did earlier.

Surfacing Grounds

This next section shows you how LightWave 6's subdivision surfaces can make great-looking landscapes from a few polygons. The Gradient texture you applied earlier to enhance the old wood can be used to surface the landscape entirely without image maps.

Exercise 8.10 Subdivision Surface Uses

Although image maps are great to use, as you saw with the wood siding on the school-house, applying image maps to curved bumpy ground doesn't often work too well. Images can be mapped on the X, Y, Z, U, or V axis. A ground or landscape is so random; it's difficult to do without procedurals and gradients.

1. With your schoolhouse scene still loaded in Layout, load the ground object you created in the beginning of this chapter. On the CD, there is a 08School_Ground object as well.

   The ground object doesn't look like much at first, and really, it's not. But it will be.

2. Move your camera back about 10m or so, until you have a nice, wide view of the schoolhouse and grounds, as shown in Figure 8.70.

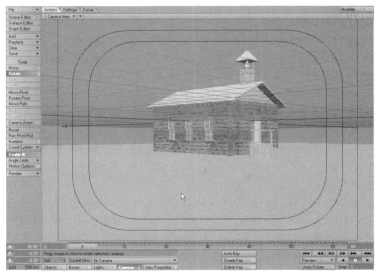

Figure 8.70 A wide shot will help you see the ground when applying surfaces.

3. With the ground object selected, press **p** to enter the Item Properties panel for it. Select the Geometry tab. Set the Display SubPatch Level to 10, and the Render SubPatch Level to 80.

A setting of 10 keeps LightWave from using too much processing power in Layout.

Setting a Render SubPatch Level of 80 subdivides the ground 80 times for each polygon, creating more than 50,000 polygons. This makes a clean render, but it can really kill Layout's performance. This is the reason to use subdivision surfaces.

Note

Depending on the speed and performance of your system, you might have trouble with a large Render SubPatch Level set to 80. Try using a setting of 30 or 40.

4. While in the Object Item Properties for the School_Ground object, go to the Deformations tab. Click the T button for Displacement Map to enter the Displacement Texture Editor.

This Texture Editor looks just like the one you used earlier, except that its effects are for Displacement.

5. Set Layer Type to Procedural Texture.

6. Displacement Axis should be set to Y because you want to create bumps in the ground. Try adding a Dented setting for Procedural Type, with a Texture Value of 0.8. Change the Scale to 2.0, which lessens the effect of the Dented procedural.

7. Set Power to 3.0, Frequency to 0.8, and Octaves to 6.0. Go to the Scale tab and set the X, Y, and Z scales to 5m. In the Position tab, change the X value to 20m, the Y to –2m, and Z to 40mm.

8. Click Use Texture and press **F9** to render. Remember to save your objects! Figure 8.71 shows the ground created from four SubPatch polygons. Now it needs a surface to call its own.

Note

Look at Figure 8.71. The shape might give you ideas. This exercise creates a springtime ground, but the default white might give you the idea of snow. With a small bump map and some smoothing applied, you have snow. On a larger scale, this landscape can be a mountain range.

9. Close the Object Item Properties panel and go the Surface Editor. Set the School_Ground surface color to a deep green, about 30, 60, 0 RGB. Then, click the T button for Color to enter the Texture Editor.

10. Change the Layer Type to Procedural Texture. Blending Mode is Additive, and the Layer Opacity should be at 100%. Set the Procedural Type to Fractal Noise, with a Texture Color of 113, 90, 50 RGB.

Figure 8.71   Using SubPatched objects allows for simple objects in Layout, but complex objects heavy with polygons in rendering. Here, a ground object with random bumps is easily rendered.

11. Set Frequencies to 3 to add more patterns throughout the ground. Contrast should be set at 1.0 to create an even blend between the ground color and the procedural texture. Also, set the Small Power to 0.5. This brings the smaller areas of the texture closer together.

12. Set the Scale to 300mm for the X, Y, and Z axes. Click Use Texture and Save your objects.

    Go a little further with this surface by applying a Bump Map.

13. Click the T button for Bump Map to enter the Bump Map Texture panel. Layer Type should be Procedural. Set Procedural Type to FBM, with a Texture Value of 80%. Set the Scale to 50mm for the X, Y, and Z axes. Frequencies are 3, while Contrast is 0, and Small Power should be set at 0.8.

14. Press **F9** to render you scene. Figure 8.72 shows the ground with the procedural surfacing.

Using procedural textures for the ground are helpful in this instance where the area to cover is large and a repeating image of grass would not look very good. A procedural can provide the right amount of randomness, while giving you control over color and texture. However, if you really want to make this ground look good, you need to take a look at a third-party plug-in from Worley Laboratories called Sasquatch. With it, you can create hair, fur, plants, and even grass right in LightWave. Find out more about this plug-in in Appendix C, "Plug-Ins and References."

Figure 8.72   A procedural color texture and a procedural bump map are often all you'll need to create a ground texture.

Setting Up Environmental Shots

The final thing you need to do is set up some lights and the camera. The figures so far have shown the work in stages, without any lighting or shadows. After the textures are in place, an atmosphere is added, and the proper lighting is set up, your project will look much more lifelike.

Exercise 8.11   Creating Finishing Touches with Environmental Lighting

To set up the environment for a project, such as the one you've been working on throughout this chapter, a good place to start is with lighting.

1. Load the scene on which you've been working. Select the default Distant light, and change it to a spotlight. Set Light Intensity to 60%, just enough to light the scene. This is not the main light. Make the Light Color a pale white, about 225, 225, 220 RGB. Set the Spotlight Cone Angle to 60, as well as the Spotlight Soft Edge Angle. Turn on Shadow Map, and increase the Shadow Map Size to 2400.

2. Back in Layout, position the light so that it is far from the schoolhouse, lighting the entire scene. Move it up about 20m, looking down on the scene. The best way to set this is from the light's point of view, so press **5** on the numeric keypad to change to Light View. Figure 8.73 shows the view of the scene through the light.

Note

You made the Spotlight Cone Angle 60 because with Shadow Maps applied a good rule of thumb is "wide and tight." Make the lights wide but close to the subject. You'll have better results with Shadow Maps.

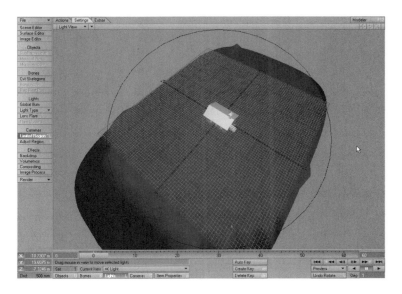

Figure 8.73   Set up the light to highlight the entire scene.

Before you add other lights, set up the surroundings to get a better idea of the overall scene.

3. Change the Background color to a flat-gray, nighttime sky. Set the Zenith to 29, 29, 44 RGB, the Sky Color to 50, 60, 75, and the same for Ground Color. Set the Nadir Color to 132, 96, 28 RGB. Save the scene.

4. Go to the Global Illumination panel under the Settings tab in Layout. Change Ambient Intensity to 5%. The default 25% is too bright.

   You should now have a dark, dimly lit scene. The reason you added just one light was to light the overall scene.

5. Add another spotlight, set its color to a pale blue and make its Intensity about 90%. Set the same Shadow Map values you did for the first light. Position the light away and in front of the schoolhouse about 15m, sort of like Figure 8.74. This light is blue to simulate a nighttime moon.

6. Move up the camera close to the schoolhouse so that it fills the frame.

   Now add Fog to give the scene some atmosphere.

Figure 8.74   Another spotlight is added and moved to the front side of the schoolhouse.

7. From the Settings tab, go to the Volumetric settings. Select Fog Type of Non-Linear2. Press **d** in Layout to open the Display Options panel. Click OpenGL Fog in Camera View.

   This lets you see the fog you're applying.

   As soon as you clicked this button, the screen probably became ghosted out. This is because you have not yet set up the Fog parameters.

8. The Grid Square Size is 500mm in the scene, so change the Min Distance and Max Distance for Fog in the Volumetrics panel.

   You can move the Effects tab over to your entire Layout and then drag the sliders for the values to see their effects in real time in Layout. Figure 8.75 shows the Effects tab open for live updates in Layout.

   Depending on where you've placed your camera, the settings will vary. However, the Min Distance is basically the starting point of the fog, while the Max Distance is where the fog is completely opaque.

9. Tweak the Fog settings to see what you like best. Because you added the eerie nighttime sky as a backdrop color, the Fog takes on this color for itself.

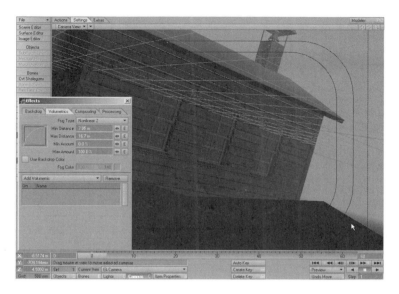

Figure 8.75   Because LightWave 6 enables you to interactively see fog in Layout, you can move the Effects panel off to the side of the screen and see any adjustments to fog settings in real time.

The Next Step

Guess what. That's it! You've now modeled, textured, surfaced, and lit a structure, and even added some fog to the scene. The techniques applied throughout this chapter apply to many types of scenes you'll encounter in your animation journeys. The advanced OpenGL architecture of LightWave 6, such as Fog in Layout, makes your job so much easier. Use the techniques in this chapter to finish surfacing the interior of the schoolhouse and the front stairs. You can use the same techniques and the same image map or load a new wood texture from the book's CD-ROM.

Summary

This chapter introduced you to modeling concepts that are common, everyday tools. For example, you created primitive shapes to make more complex shapes and used Boolean operations to carve the object you want. You learned that adding details through LightWave 6 Gradient surfaces enables you to take your surface styling even further.

Chapter 9 continues with the models from this chapter. It introduces you to radiosity and caustics, while employing useful tools such as transparency and refraction. You will use LightWave's Radiosity feature to simulate daylight inside the schoolhouse.

Chapter 9

Environmental Lighting

Perhaps at one point in your career, you've

dabbled in photography or video. If you

have, you know how important lighting is

to a shot. Light can create an atmosphere or

a mood. Light can warm a shot, or make it feel cold. Light is everything. This chapter introduces you to powerful new lighting techniques in LightWave 6. Specifically, you'll learn about:

- Proper light setups for radiosity effects
- Creating caustics for glass
- Setting up lighting for sunlight

Project Overview

In Chapter 8, "Environmental Structures," you built a structure—an old schoolhouse. You surfaced it, and you lit it with LightWave's spotlights. You added a sky and fog, and you created a realistic-looking scene. But you can go even further with such a scene, and this chapter will help you do it.

You will then take the same scene you created in Chapter 8, or use the one from the book's CD-ROM, and instead of lighting it with spotlights you'll use LightWave 6's new radiosity feature. You will light the exterior of the schoolhouse with an image. That's right, an image. This technology enables you to take the millions of colors in a photograph and use them as a light source. The result is some of the most realistic lighting you can produce in a 3D environment. This is because in the real world, light bounces. If you have a window open in your room during the day, sunlight enters and bounces everywhere, lighting up the place. In the computer, without radiosity, the light only comes in the window. Unless additional lights are added in the scene, the other areas of the shot will remain dark.

You'll also learn about the caustics feature in LightWave 6, which is a real-world property that happens everyday. A good example is the small area of light that a magnifying glass produces when light is refracted through it. Or, the patterns of light that reflect off of a shiny metal object onto another surface. Caustics add a realistic touch to your scene.

In addition to understanding and applying radiosity and caustics, you'll learn how to add volumetrics to lights for an added effect.

Understanding Radiosity

It's important to understand radiosity before you begin using it in your project. *Radiosity* is a rendering situation that calculates diffuse reflections of color and light from all surfaces in a scene. In 1984, a team at Cornell University published a paper called "Modeling the Interaction of Light Between Diffuse Surfaces." This paper described a new rendering process called radiosity, a type of global illumination. You'll find a Global Illumination panel under the Settings tab in LightWave Layout that contains the radiosity controls.

Radiosity is the calculation of the rate at which light leaves a surface. This process calculates the diffused light of an entire surface, unlike ray tracing. Figure 9.1 shows a simple room with light coming through a window. This is a typical render. Figure 9.2 shows the same setup with radiosity turned on—a not-so-typical render. You don't always need lots of geometry and complex surfaces to achieve a realistic look when applying radiosity. The project you'll do in this chapter uses the schoolhouse object from Chapter 8 and lights the interior with radiosity.

Figure 9.1   A simple room with a light shining through a window. The rest of the room is dark without radiosity.

Faking Radiosity

Although LightWave 6's radiosity feature can produce realistic results, you can fake radiosity effects. The benefit of faking radiosity is to cut down render times. The calculations LightWave needs to process for radiosity effects can often be time-consuming. When rendering multiple frames for an animation, your computer might be tied up for days calculating!

Figure 9.2   Turning on radiosity makes the light bounce off of the floor and walls, lighting up the entire room. The light is soft and diffused.

You can fake radiosity effects by adding colored lights shining on the areas where the bounced light would be. For example, a light is shining through a window onto a wood floor. The walls are white. In the real world, the light would hit the brown wood floor and bounce to hit the walls and ceiling. A soft light matching the color of the floor can be pointed up toward the ceiling from the floor to simulate the bounced effect. Additionally, a smaller colored light can be pointed to the wall surface to give the appearance of the brown wood color bouncing.

Faking radiosity is common in many animation houses, and often quite effective. However, with processor speeds on PCs and Macintoshes reaching beyond 1000MHz, you will eventually not need to worry about render times. Won't that be nice?

Understanding Caustics

Caustics are all around you. A caustic happens when light is reflected off a surface, or shines through a transparent surface and creates a small area of light. A glass of water on a table in the sunlight will have caustics on the table because the light that is refracting through the glass, and then the water, focuses onto a small area of light. The reflections of light at the bottom of a pool, or the hotspot generated from a magnifying glass, are caustics. In this chapter, you'll place objects on a table in the schoolhouse scene and enable caustics to add to the scene's realism. Figure 9.3 shows a glass of water lit on a set without caustics. Figure 9.4 shows the same setup with caustics turned on. Like radiosity, this feature is found in the Global Illumination panel.

Figure 9.3   Here is a glass of water on a set, without caustics. Nothing happens to the light when it passes through the glass and water surfaces.

Figure 9.4   Turning on caustics takes the refracted light through the glass of water and creates an area of small light on the set.

Understanding Volumetrics

Volumetrics are lighting effects used for special effects and dramatic scenes. In the world around you, volumetrics can be seen on a sunny afternoon, when light streaks through a living room window. The visible beams from car headlights on a foggy road are volumetrics. Animators use volumetric lights to mimic real-world properties. Setting up volumetrics in LightWave 6 is as easy as pushing the Volumetrics button, found within the Lights panel.

Interior Daylight

One of the great things about using radiosity is that it makes your job a lot easier when simulating indoor lighting. Wherever you are—at home, at work, in the car—the light sources around you bounce off everything. In the daytime, the light shining through your window can easily light up the entire room. To simulate this in a 3D environment requires a lot of lights, cleverly diffused and lighting all the areas in your 3D environment. Instead, a scene with radiosity not only makes your project look more real, but also saves you the headache of setting up multiple lights.

The lighting you choose to create in your 3D animations does more than just light your scene. It also creates a mood. Mood lighting is used in films. It's that soft, hazy light shining through a café window in the morning. This light is warm and creates a mood that otherwise would be hard to produce. This next exercise guides you through creating a mood in a 3D environment using radiosity and volumetrics.

Exercise 9.1   Using Radiosity Lighting

This exercise requires only that you be patient and have a room with a view. That is to say, you need an object that has some surfacing inside and a window to the outside. This exercise uses the schoolhouse object created in Chapter 8, which also is on the book's CD-ROM.

1. Open LightWave Layout, and load the schoolhouse scene labeled 09School.lws from the book's CD.

   The model on the CD is based on Chapter 8's exercises, with some added detail and an extra room in back.

Warning

This scene uses a lot of memory for the amount of geometry and image maps. Be sure that you have other RAM-intensive programs closed when working with this scene.

Figure 9.5 shows the schoolhouse interior with benches and desk. An old stove was added for character. If this were really an old schoolhouse, you wouldn't have any electricity and, of course, no lights. The light inside would require either candles or sunlight.

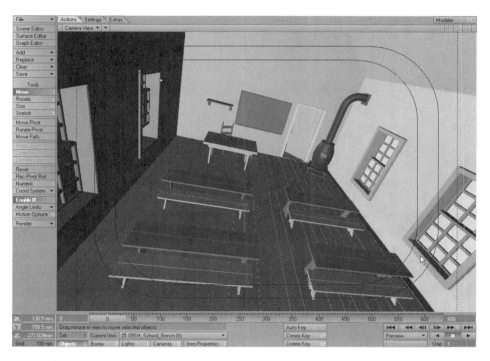

Figure 9.5   The interior of the schoolhouse as seen through Layout, with some benches, desks, and a stove added.

2. Switch to Light edit mode by selecting the Lights button at the bottom of the Layout window. Select the Light from the current item list at the bottom of Layout, and press **5** on the numeric keypad to select Light view. This scene is the complete schoolhouse with one default light source. Set the light to:

Position X   827mm

Position Y   445mm

Position Z   –245mm

Heading X   –75°

Pitch Y   25°

Bank Z   0°

Figure 9.6 shows the view from the light source now in position with the preceding settings.

Figure 9.6   One distant light in position, ready to calculate some radiosity lighting inside the schoolhouse.

This light source simulates sunlight coming through the windows inside the schoolhouse. The position you've set for the light is a good working position, as it will cast shadows from the windowpanes inside the schoolhouse.

3. With the light still selected, press the **p** key to enter the Light Item Properties panel.

   A distant light exists by default and is the best light to use in this situation.

   Point lights do not direct the light with as much intensity as a distant light or spotlight. The controlled direction of a distant light or spotlight helps charge up the surface, meaning it will bounce light better. A point light will emit light in all directions.

4. Change the Light Intensity to 1400%.

   Even though the Light Intensity slider only brings the setting to 100%, you can manually enter values much higher. Remember, the sun is really, really bright (that's a technical term). Because this light needs to simulate sunlight, a brighter light is needed.

   The walls, floors, desks, and so on, in this scene can't have pixel colors that are brighter than 100% (which is 255, 255, 255 RGB, or pure white), but with an intense light source (such as the one in this scene at 1400%), the bounced light fills the room. This is because the radiosity in LightWave can carry unlimited pixel luminosity data.

5. Set Shadow Type to Ray Trace.

6. Set the Light Color to 250, 240, 200 RGB for a warm off-white color.

   If you were to render the frame now, you would see something such as Figure 9.7. The light is falling nicely throughout the schoolhouse, but the rest of the interior is still dark. Now you need radiosity.

Figure 9.7   A single point light on the outside of the schoolhouse works well to cast light through and create shadows from the windows. However, the rest of the room needs more light.

7. Click the Global Illumination panel, from either the Lights panel or the Settings tab directly in Layout.

8. Click Enable Radiosity, which is in the middle of the Global Illumination panel.

   This tells LightWave to calculate the diffused lighting when rendering. You won't see the effects in Layout's OpenGL display.

9. Set the Tolerance to 0.5.

   Tolerance allows LightWave to save rendering time by storing the radiosity information. A value higher than 0, with 1.0 being the highest, will apply the tolerance to your scene.

10. Change the Rays Per Evaluation to 12×36.

    The Rays Per Evaluation setting represents the number of sides and segments of the projection area. As discussed in Chapter 4, "LightWave 6 Layout," LightWave Layout has a sort of invisible world around it. Reflections can be wallpapered on this invisible world, for example. This is how LightWave calculates, so when you apply the Rays Per Evaluation, it works based on this projection hemisphere. You can set values from 2 × 6 to 16 × 48. This determines the number of radiosity rays sent out for evaluation. With a higher value, the quality is much better because LightWave is sending out more radiosity rays for evaluation—this, of course, requires more render time.

Radiosity is bounced light. So, in the example of, say, the cover image of this book, a luminous polygon is placed in front of the face. The polygon isn't really a light source. With radiosity applied, the surface knows to be lit by the polygon. This feature places these hemispheres on surfaces that shoot out rays to detect illuminated surfaces. The Rays Per Evaluation setting determine the number of rays, and the Min Evaluation Spacing controls the spacing of these hemispheres. The hemisphere data is evaluated and the surface is lit accordingly.

Note

A good rule of thumb is to set up your radiosity scene with a low Rays Per Evaluation setting, then increase the value for final renders.

The higher the setting for Rays Per Evaluation, however, the better the quality. Of course, this comes with a price. A higher value also will generate higher render times. Often, the results are worth it.

11. Set the Minimum Evaluation Spacing to 10mm.

   The default setting is 20mm, and a lower value will make a better image but create longer render times.

12. Turn on Cache Radiosity.

   This is useful when rendering an animation, as it caches radiosity data for multiple render passes and frames. If you are antialiasing your final render (which you should), cache radiosity will help save time during antialiasing passes.

   When lights or objects are moving, however, this setting might produce inaccurate results because it is using the radiosity information from the initial frame rendered. If you are animating only the camera, the radiosity will still be the same. Therefore, it is more useful to have this feature turned on.

13. Save the scene, and make a preview.

   As a note, the settings you've applied here are for high quality, so you might want to set a lower resolution for testing. Press **F9** to test the frame. Figure 9.8 shows the final frame.

Radiosity can add realism to your scenes. This example shows how one single light source can help illuminate the interior of a building. Often, structures such as the schoolhouse are dark inside, and due to the way LightWave's radiosity engine works, you might need to add a few fake radiosity lights to help illuminate the interior. This is because the textures within the schoolhouse are dark and not very luminous. You should work with brighter surfaces when possible, and also try adding additional light sources. Your experimentation is key to the final image!

Figure 9.8   The interior of the schoolhouse is now lit to photorealistic quality, thanks to radiosity. One point light outside the windows of the building is creating all the lighting in this shot. Cool, huh?

Volumetric Lighting

With radiosity being such a cool thing, it's hard to imagine that you can enhance the visuals of a scene even more. But you can with volumetric lighting. This feature in LightWave 6 enables your light to have physical volume. Some examples of this are the huge search beams soaring into the sky at a movie premier or a searchlight in a storm. Figure 9.9 shows a simple volumetric example with one spotlight.

Volumetrics can have shadows, which is especially cool for realistic effects. For example, a spotlight behind a logo with volumetrics applied can have the beam of light broken where the geometry is—in effect, making the light "spill" out from behind the logo.

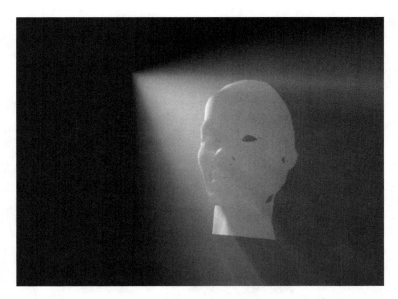

Figure 9.9   A single spotlight with volumetric lighting applied. Notice how the beam of light is visible but breaks where the object is.

Exercise 9.2   Applying Volumetric Lighting

This exercise will continue using the same scene from the first exercises in this chapter. The use of volumetric lighting along with radiosity can produce realistic images.

  1. In Layout, load the 09VolumeSetup.lws scene from the book's CD-ROM. This is the schoolhouse scene from Exercise 9.1 with radiosity applied.

  2. Make sure that Enable Radiosity is off, in the Global Illumination panel.

  3. Back in Layout, select the light and go to its Item Properties (**p**).

  4. Click Volumetric Lighting for the light. When the Light Properties become available, click the Volumetric Light Options button to enter the Volumetric Options for Light panel, as seen in Figure 9.10.

   Instead of adjusting the settings in the panel and guessing what the outcome will be, you can use VIPER to see firsthand what the values do.

  5. Move the open Volumetric panel to the side of the screen and press the **F9** key to render a single frame.

   This enters the scene information into VIPER.

  6. When the render is finished, return to the Volumetric Options for Light panel and click Open VIPER at the bottom of the panel.

   The VIPER window opens, and your last render appears. Don't be alarmed when the image looks washed out—remember that shadows do not show up in VIPER.

Because the light source is outside the window, the rendered volumetric is partially blocked by the window and schoolhouse walls—this creates the streaks of light.

Now, when you make changes to the volumetric settings, the result will update in VIPER, giving you instant feedback.

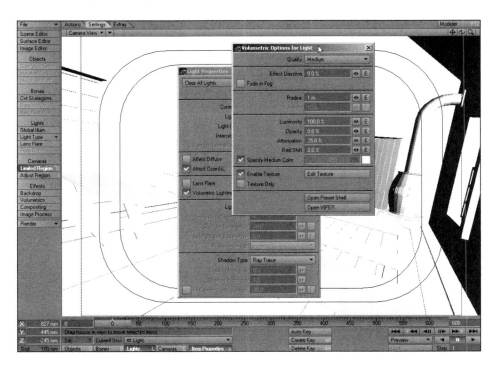

Figure 9.10   The Volumetric Options for Light panel, accessed through the Light Properties panel.

7. In the Volumetric Options panel, set the Quality to Good.

You'll always want to start out at low quality, test the render, and then increase the quality as needed. The Good setting is neither low nor high quality, sort of right in the middle. The higher the quality, the more render time you'll need.

Now it's time to adjust the Radius to see how large the volumetric light will be. The Grid Square Size for this scene (found in the information panel at the bottom left of the Layout interface) is 100mm.

8. Set the Radius to 2m to make the volume light glare halfway into the VIPER frame.

The radius setting is available because a point light is being used in the scene. A point light is omnidirectional, so it requires a radius. Distant lights also will use a radius setting along with height, while a spotlight will use only height values. These two settings determine the size of the volumetric light.

9. Change Luminosity to 250%.

   This will make the volumetric source nice and bright.

10. Leave the Opacity setting at 20%.

    This setting tells LightWave how transparent the volumetric is. The setting of 20% tells LightWave to create somewhat transparent volumetrics. A setting of 100% would make a completely transparent volumetric, and a negative value would make it appear very dense.

11. Change Attenuation to 75%.

    This setting is a falloff setting for the volumetric. Attenuation makes the volumetric effect fade off from the origin. In this scene, the volumetric light needs to be bright at the window, but then dissipate as it reaches the other side of the room. A higher attenuation fits the bill.

12. In conjunction with Attenuation, set the Red Shift to 10.

    This controls the activity of the light similar to the real world. Essentially, during a sunset, for example, the atmosphere does not diffuse the red colors, nor do they have attenuation—they don't fall off. Setting the Red Shift above 0% tells the volumetric to allow the color red from the source to bleed through.

13. Leave the Specify Medium Color setting for the volumetric at its default white. For special effects, such as green oozing light coming from a dungeon, you can set the color of the volumetric.

14. Press **F9** to test the volumetric.

    Figure 9.11 shows the render with the volumetric lighting applied. If you apply radiosity to the image, you'd add significantly to your render times, but enhance the image. Add some interior lights, such as candles, and faked radiosity lights for an even greater appeal.

Volumetrics are quick to apply in LightWave 6, especially with VIPER. If you are familiar with the Steamer volumetric plug-in previous to LightWave 6, you'll appreciate the easy controls and fast results.

Besides adding simple volumetric effects to your lights, you also can add textures. At the bottom of the Volumetric Options for Light panel is the Edit Texture button. Clicking this button guides you into the ever-familiar Texture panel you see throughout LightWave. Here, you can apply procedurals, images, or even gradients to volumetric lights. Here's a great example: A movie projector is playing a film. It's projecting on a screen in the 3D movie house you made. You can load a sequence of frames, or a QuickTime or .AVI movie, and apply it as a projection image to the light. Turn on volumetrics and the sequence will shine through the volumetric light, picking up colors and shapes, as it would in the real world. Try it out!

Figure 9.11   Volumetric lights applied to a point light, creating glares of light streaking through windowpanes.

Environmental Radiosity

You're probably reading the word "environmental" a lot in this chapter, but it has important meaning to many aspects of LightWave 6. This next section will shed some light (figuratively) on the uses of environmental lighting.

Environmental lighting is a fantastic way to light your 3D worlds with real photographs and the result is photorealistic lighting. Figure 9.12 shows the schoolhouse used throughout this chapter, rendered with some generic lights. It's nice, but honestly, it's boring. Figure 9.13 shows the same shot, with no lights! That's right, no lights. The lighting in this scene uses an environmental map of a real photograph. Using radiosity, LightWave takes the millions of colors and variations in the image and uses them to light the geometry in the scene. Read on to set this up yourself.

HDRI: High Dynamic Range Images

Computer systems represent color on a 24-bit spectrum. All the colors of the spectrum at their highest values for RGB are 255, such as Red, Green, and Blue. High Dynamic Range (HDR) images can store more data than the standard 24 bits per pixel. With HDR images, luminosity is separate from color. You can't see this much information onscreen, but the information is used for situations such as radiosity for added brightness from a surface. LightWave can load HDR images such as Flexible Format, TIFF LogLuv, or

Radiance HDR images. You also can create your own HDR images with the HDR Expose plug-in to create an image in one of these formats. HDR Expose normalizes the extra data within the image.

Figure 9.12   The schoolhouse lit with conventional lighting. It's not a bad image, but it can look better with radiosity.

Figure 9.13   The same shot but with no lights. The schoolhouse is now lit from the image surrounding it.

Lighting with Images

The downside to radiosity is that it takes more time to render. But if you consider the results, it is often the only way to go for photorealistic rendering. Lighting with images is so easy; the time you save setting up lighting can be used to render! The process is simple, requiring only a few steps, outlined here.

Exercise 9.3   Environmental Lighting

For this exercise, you're going to use the existing schoolhouse structure from the book's CD-ROM. You'll use a pleasant sunset image to achieve the effect for this exercise, but other images are there for you to experiment with on your own.

This exercise lights the scene using an image rather than lights. The effect is similar to creating many colored lights.

1. To begin, load the 09School_nolights.lws scene into Layout.

   This is the schoolhouse scene with no lights added to the outside (other than LightWave's default light).

2. Select the default light, and press **p** to go to the Item Properties panel. Change the Light Intensity to 0%.

3. Close the Light Item Properties panel, and return to Layout. From the book's CD-ROM, load the 09Enviro.lwo object.

   This is merely a large ball with its surfaces facing inward. A ball was made in Modeler large enough to encompass the schoolhouse exterior and its landscape, then the **f** key was pressed to flip the polygons inward.

4. Go to the Surface Editor and select the Enviro_Sphere surface. Click the T button for Color to enter the Color Texture Editor. Set Layer Type to Image Map and Blending Mode to Additive.

5. Set the Layer Opacity to 100%, if it isn't already. Change Projection to Spherical (remember, you're mapping an image on the inside of a big round ball, a sphere). Leave the Width and Height Wrap amounts at 1.0.

6. Select the Image drop-down list and choose Load Image. Load the 09Sky1.jpg image from the book's CD-ROM.

   When it's loaded, you'll see a small thumbnail appear under the Image listing.

7. Turn off Texture Antialiasing, as it will create unnecessary blurring when the final image is antialiased at rendering.

8. Set Texture Axis to Y.

   Imagine that a pole is in the center of the sphere being mapped. This pole represents the Y axis, and you're wrapping the image around it.

9. Click Automatic Sizing, and then Use Texture.

You probably can't see anything in Layout yet on the 09Enviro.lwo object. However, the luminosity of this object will be used to light the scene.

10. In the Surface Editor, change Luminosity to 160% and Diffuse to 0%.

    If you have OpenGL Textures enabled in Layout, you'll see the texture map on the 09Enviro.lwo object.

11. Now rotate the 09Enviro.lwo object 45 degrees on the heading to hide the seam of the image map. Be sure to create a keyframe to lock it in place.

12. Close the Surface Editor to return to Layout.

13. Back in Layout, press the **4** key on the keyboard to view the scene from the Perspective view.

    You can see that the sphere encompasses the entire setup.

14. Go back to the Camera view (**6**) to tweak the camera shot. The camera for this scene is already in place with the following settings, but you can adjust them if you want to:

Position	−575mm
Position	202.5mm
Position	−768mm
Heading	−316°
Pitch	−20°
Bank	23°

    Figure 9.14 shows the shot, as seen through the camera.

15. Go to the Global Illumination panel and click Radiosity. Leave the default settings for now.

16. Close the panel and open the Camera Item Properties panel. Set the Resolution to VGA. Change the Resolution Multiplier to 50%, and turn off Antialiasing. Press **F9** to test-render the frame.

    Depending on the speed of your system, your render shouldn't take more than a few minutes. Figure 9.15 shows the render without radiosity applied. It doesn't look much different than the OpenGL layout view in Figure 9.14. Figure 9.16 shows the same scene with radiosity turned on.

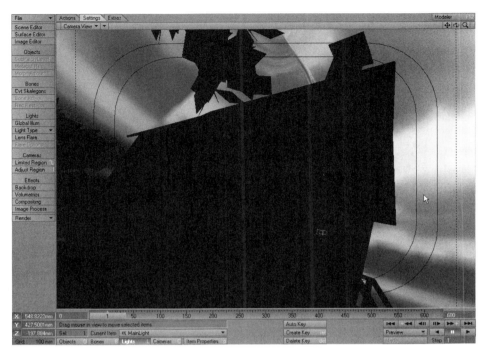

Figure 9.14   The camera is in place in front of the schoolhouse. The shot is dark because no lights are on the structure. Rendering with radiosity will light the scene.

Figure 9.15   With the camera in place and a test render, the image of the schoolhouse is dark.

Figure 9.16   When radiosity is applied, the brightness and color of the image map on the
sphere light the geometry in the scene.

Creating Shadows with Radiosity

Although the radiosity solution is being used to light the entire scene globally with a single image, you can use LightWave's lights to cast more distinct shadows. Radiosity produces soft shadows because the light is coming from a variety of directions as in the real
world, and not a concentrated light source. For an exterior shot such as the schoolhouse,
you might want harder shadows, especially on a sunny day.

Exercise 9.4   Shadows and Radiosity

You can enhance this render even further. The light in the scene is in position from the
previous exercise. It is in front of the schoolhouse and off to the right of the camera. That
is where the sun is in the mapped image on the Enviro_Sphere object.

   1. Turn up the Light Intensity to 100% or so, and turn on Ray Traced Shadows
   from the Render Options.

   While you are adding a light, the radiosity will still work, coloring and lighting
   the schoolhouse structure. The light casts shadows, enhancing the realism. Figure
   9.17 shows shadows added to the image.

   But wait! There's more! Take this image to the full extent.

   2. From the Settings tab in Layout, select the Image Process button to access the
   Effects panel. From the Add Image Filter selection, choose the LW_Bloom Image
   Filter. When the plug-in loads, double-click it to open its interface.

Figure 9.17   Although the radiosity is being calculated to light the structure, a light can be
added to cast shadows.

   3. Set the Bloom Threshold to 30%, Strength to 30%, and Size to 60%.

   This creates a natural bloom or glow from hot areas in the image, similar to real-
   world properties.

As an added effect of realism, you can apply depth of field to the camera to blur the
branches from the trees in the foreground, creating more depth in the image.

Radiosity lighting is a brilliant way to create realistic lighting in your scenes. This exercise used a sunset image to light the schoolhouse environment, but imagine if you used
an image with an overcast sky or a rich night sky. The color and brightness of these
images would be calculated for lighting the geometry in your scene.

The environment sphere you used in this exercise also was used as a backdrop. You can,
however, use an environmental map with the same techniques mentioned here, only for
lighting. You can then add a completely different image as a backdrop, or the same image
only flat, not wrapped on the sphere. To do this, select the 09EnviroSphere object from
the book's CD-ROM (which is only a ball with polygons facing inward) and from its
Item Properties under the Rendering tab, click Unseen By Camera. The LightWave scene
sees the object's radiosity, shadows, or reflections, but the rendered image does not see
the object. This is a handy tool for things such as diffused light boxes.

Adding Caustics

Caustics can produce realistic results when applied correctly. This next exercise instructs you in two areas: surfacing a glass for use with caustics, and applying caustics.

Exercise 9.5   Tabletop Realism

For this exercise, you can start with the simple glass object from the CD-ROM accompanying this book. You will set the parameters of the glass surface before loading it into the schoolhouse scene.

1. Begin by saving any work you've done in Layout, and clearing the scene. Load the 09Glass1.lwo object from the book's CD. Figure 9.18 shows the loaded object.

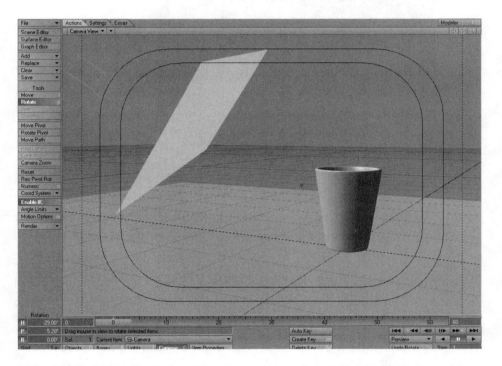

Figure 9.18   Here, a simple glass object sits on a set, a reflector object resides in front of the glass, and both are set and ready for refraction and caustics.

The 09Glass1.lwo contains three layers: a small set underneath the glass, a light reflector that is nothing more than a flat white polygon, and the glass.

2. Using these values, move the camera in close to get a good view of the glass :

Position X	−1.0278m
Position Y	1.3758m
Position Z	−2.7193m

Heading	15.40°
Pitch	18.50°
Bank	0.00°

3. Create a keyframe at frame zero to lock it in place.

4. Position the light above and to the right of the glass, about:

Position X	2.4656m
Position Y	2
Position Z	1.6135m
Heading	−119.60°
Pitch	24.20°
Bank	0.00°

5. Create a keyframe at zero to hold the new position.

6. Go to the Surface Editor and select the reflector surface. Set the Color to white, the Luminosity to 85%, and the Diffuse to 25%. Leave all other settings alone.

7. Select the WaterGlass_water surface (the surface for the water inside the glass). Make the Color a soft blue, about 168, 177, 223 RGB. Change Diffuse to 85%. Set the Specularity to 75% to make the water shiny. Set Glossiness to 40% to give it some nice hotspots. Change the Reflection to 10%. Set Transparency to 75% so that you can see through the water. Lastly, set the Refraction Index to 1.6. The higher the value, the more refraction will occur. Water is typically a refraction value of 1.33.

8. Select the WaterGlass surface. Set the Color to white, Luminosity to 0%, Diffuse to 85%, Specularity to 75%, and Glossiness to 40%, just like the water. You can vary these if you want. Set Reflection to 10% and Transparency to 100%. You might think that 100% transparent would render nothing, which it would— except that you have reflections and refraction coming into play. Set the Refraction Index to 1.33.

   You need to tell LightWave to calculate the reflections and refraction. By default, the Environment tab within the Surface Editor lists the Reflection Options as Ray Tracing and Backdrop, which is what this setup needs.

9. Go to the Render Options panel and turn on Ray Trace Shadows, Ray Trace Reflection, and Ray Trace Refraction. These are all heavy-duty render killers, but the results are worth it.

10. Turn on Radiosity to allow the reflector to light the opposite side of the glass. Press the **F9** key to render. Make a low-resolution render to save on rendering time. Figure 9.19 shows the rendered image.

Figure 9.19   A single light, glass surfacing, and ray tracing make a cool-looking image, but caustics will make it better.

11. Feel free to play with the lighting and refraction levels for different looks. When you're satisfied, save your objects and save your scene as WaterGlass.lws.

12. Go back to the Global Illumination panel and click Enable Caustics. Turn on Cache Caustics (which will save data for subsequent renders, similar to Cache Radiosity discussed earlier) and set the Intensity to 90%. This is a scaling factor for the brightness of the caustic.

13. Set the Accuracy to 120.

This value can range from 1 to 10,000, and the higher it is, the more time is required to calculate the caustic. On a simple water glass, an accuracy of 120 is fine. More complex objects with multiple caustics would require a higher accuracy.

14. Finally, set Softness to 30.

This evaluates the surrounding caustic rays when rendering. A higher softness results in blurrier caustics, while a lower softness results in sharper caustics. If the caustic appears blotchy and not so smooth, the Softness setting can be increased, but the accuracy setting needs to be increased as well.

Figure 9.20 shows the final rendered image with reflection, refraction, shadows, radiosity, and caustics applied.

Figure 9.20   All of LightWave's heavy render hogs are at work: ray tracing, radiosity, and caustics. Quite nice, but expensive rendering times.

The Next Step

Although caustics and radiosity are cool new tools in LightWave 6, using them together can cramp your style—well, at least your render times. As you work through the other examples in this book, think of ways you can incorporate the information in this chapter. *Inside LightWave [6]* shows you that radiosity is good for lighting not just interiors, but people as well. Chapter 10, "Organic Modeling," will guide you through modeling, texturing, and lighting a human face with radiosity.

Summary

This chapter not only introduced you to radiosity and caustics, but it also showed you practical, real-world examples. You've seen radiosity applied with individual lights, and you've used it to create environmental lighting for exterior structures. This can be taken further with the use of HDR images.

You also learned about caustics and saw how applying them can add realism to your scenes. With additional LightWave tools, such as the LW_Bloom Image Filter and depth of field applied, your images can look amazingly real. Just imagine what you can do with more experimentation and practice! Before you set your computer off to ren-der-render land, move on into Chapter 10, and learn how radiosity can be used to light human faces. It also shows you how to create the face that is on the cover of this book.

C h a p t e r   1 0

Organic Modeling

This chapter will carefully guide you through a project containing all the stages required to build a realistic 3D model of a young woman's head. The tutorial consists of several parts, and it might take you some time to complete. It deals with advanced modeling issues, so you should be fairly comfortable modeling with LightWave 6's toolset before tackling it.

Organic modeling is the process of creating objects that can't be created with only primitive shapes. Buildings, roads, computers, and many other objects can be built with simple boxes, balls, cones, and discs. But more organic or natural objects, such as the human form, need a different approach to be created in 3D. Figure 10.1 shows the cover model of this book, which is the subject of this chapter.

Figure 10.1   This chapter will teach you how to model, texture, and light a young woman's face. The finished model is shown here.

Project Overview

The face has been the most favored subject of artists—professional, budding, or otherwise—throughout history, and it's no different in today's world of 3D computer graphics. The reasons for this are fairly obvious. You are surrounded by people's faces every day of your life, and they are your primary means of communicating and showing your feelings—happy or sad, angry or serene. As such, people tend to be fascinated by looking at faces.

Ironically, it is this kind of ubiquitous interest and familiarity that makes re-creating faces realistically one of the hardest tasks for any artist, digital or otherwise. Everyone is an expert on the face, and everyone will sense when you've gotten it wrong.

In addition, a face, in a purely abstract sense, is actually a complex structure of interlocking shapes and forms. But don't worry. In the following sections, you're going to break down what might initially seem like a daunting task into manageable chunks that you should be able to follow relatively easily. With a modicum of artistic ability, you should soon have a new head to be proud of. In this chapter, you will learn to

- Create a photorealistic female head
- Use LightWave's advanced texture-mapping tools to create realistic surfaces
- Paint and create texture maps
- Set up lighting for a human head with radiosity

Using SubPatch Surfaces to Model the Head

The tutorial steps throughout this chapter are geared toward using Modeler's SubPatch surfaces (called MetaNURBS in previous versions of LightWave).

Although they are the easiest and most intuitive methods in LightWave for modeling free-flowing organic subjects, like most 3D tools SubPatch surfaces tend to require you to work in specific ways to make the most out of them. The first few sections of this chapter outline some basic techniques for working with SubPatch surfaces. As well as heads, this chapter will also give you a good foundation for modeling any kind of organic geometry.

Organic Model Preparation

When using SubPatch surfaces, you don't have to worry about adding more geometry to make a surface smooth, as you would with normal polygonal modeling, because the software takes care of that for you. If you need the model to be smoother, you can turn up the patch resolution (particularly now that Layout can render SubPatched objects directly in Layout). With a SubPatched object, you will create a cage, which is a simplified mesh. You can control this mesh to shape and form your object.

Controlling Curves

When modeling with SubPatch surfaces, the main way to control the curvature or tightness of a surface is to increase or decrease the number of polygons (and thus, vertices) in the control cage mesh. You can deliberately ignore point weighting here because in complex objects that method won't produce the required results as there is no control over the direction of the effect. Figure 10.2 shows an example.

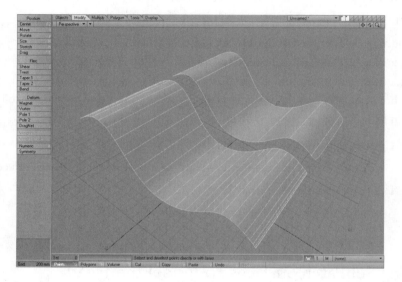

Figure 10.2   The density of the control mesh relates to the curvature of the underlying shapes.

To achieve a proper balance, tightly defined areas of a model with harder edges or a lot of detail will need several vertices to accurately define the shape. Fewer control vertices should be used to define flat or smooth areas. When working with curves, remember the following:

- Having too many control vertices in the control mesh is inefficient and makes editing or altering an object time consuming and difficult.

- Having too few vertices in the cage might make it close to impossible to accurately define the exact shape you need.

- Aim to get your model just right with just enough polygons to define the shape you want in a specific area (this often takes a bit of trial and error).

Both objects in Figure 10.2 are identically shaped, but the one farthest away uses fewer vertices to achieve the same result—this will be easier to adjust or sculpt. Because sculpting (basically, pushing and pulling vertices around) takes up the vast majority of modeling time (or should if you're doing things right), making the process as easy as possible should be a priority.

Following Contours

The next thing to consider when building organic models is that because SubPatched surfaces are built primarily from quad polygons (polygons made up of four points), they tend to form grid-like structures. How these grids or patches align with the underlying form of the surface is important. Generally you should get the grid to follow the natural contours of the model. This has several advantages:

- It leads to a more efficient use of geometry (again, the fewer polygons and vertices you can get away with using, the better).
- It makes the underlying surface much easier to follow, and therefore edit.

To better illustrate how a grid formation should follow the contours of an object, take a look at Figure 10.3. You can see that the control mesh is easier to follow because it follows the natural contours of the polygonal shape. Figure 10.3 shows how the control mesh does not follow the natural contours of the shape, making it harder to manage and edit.

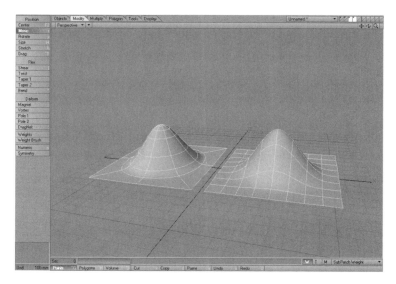

Figure 10.3   When building geometry, you should try to follow the natural contours of the model, such as the hump on the right.

To quickly recap, an easily editable cage relies on the following:

- Getting the quad patch structure of the control mesh to flow with the contours of the model
- Getting the right number of control polygons to achieve the appropriate curvature in various parts of the model

Following these guidelines will make the job of shaping the forms of the human face much easier. The more ideal the control cage structure you create for the surface at hand, the more you can concentrate solely on the sculpting process of molding the surface without having to wrestle with the inherent behavior of the SubPatch itself.

Okay, enough of the textbook stuff. How does all this work in the real world? How do you achieve this mythical, "structural" balance with models that have lots of smooth areas joining against areas with a lot more detail, where the contours of the model flow one way here, and a completely different way there, such as a human head?

Well, basically, you have to compromise. Most "real-world" approaches can be reduced to two opposing camps, with associated pros and cons.

The Box Approach

One way is to create the basic, general forms of the model first and then selectively add more detail as needed. This method is called the "box approach," as it generally entails starting with a rough box and then refining the model by dragging points, stretching, slicing, knifing, beveling, and smooth-shifting various bits as you work down to the areas of small detail.

Although generally a fast and intuitive way to model for most people, this approach can also be rather chaotic. Unless you're either very adept at it, or very careful, the polygon structure created along the way tends to favor the broader forms of the model (that is, what you started with) at the expense of the detailed areas, where things can often get a little tricky.

The Detail-Out Approach

The second way to model is to start with the detailed areas in isolation first, where it is relatively easy to construct them with an ideal polygon structure. Work your way from there, dealing with how these areas join into the whole later, as you work outward. This is called the "detail-out" method.

Modeling this way is definitely a more structured process than the box method but, again, things can sometimes get tricky when you have to join all the separate bits neatly.

Despite this limitation, the detail-out approach makes modeling complex objects and, especially human head models, a bit easier. This is the approach you'll use in this chapter.

The most important parts of the human face are the mouth and eyes because they are the most expressive. For this reason, a detail-out modeling approach works well. Additionally, these parts must usually be able to deform in carefully controlled ways if you are thinking about making expressions later on. Thus, they require an ideal control structure. By building a proper control structure, or mesh, of the expressive areas of the face first, you'll eliminate difficulty shaping and modifying the object to your desired shape. Properly modeling the expressive areas of the face first makes joining them with the rest of the head much easier.

Using Background Template Images

A potential drawback to modeling using the detail-out method is that by concentrating on smaller areas first, it is easy to lose a sense of the overall proportions of the model. For this reason it's important to use background images, as shown in Figure 10.4, to guide you as you work.

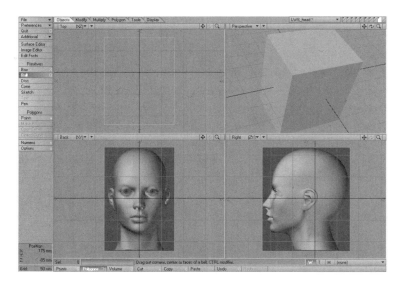

Figure 10.4   Background template images set up in Modeler.

For the purposes of this tutorial, two images—a front and side view of the head—are included on the book's CD-ROM to help you get started. They are FaceFront.bmp and FaceSide.bmp (Projects/Images/Chapter10/background_template). When following these techniques on your own projects, try to make or acquire similar templates; a simple rough sketch will do, as long as the overall proportions are correct. If you are modeling from a real-life subject, try to get photographic equivalents or use a mirror.

Exercise 10.1   Setting Up Background Images

For this exercise, begin in LightWave Modeler. You don't need Layout running right now. To set up the backdrop images in the Modeler viewports, follow these steps:

1. Select the Box tool and press the **n** key to open the Numeric panel. Select Activate from the Actions pop-up and input the following dimensions:

Low	X	–80mm
Low	Y	–120mm
Low	Z	–100mm
High	X	80mm
High	Y	120mm
High	Z	100mm

2. Leave Segments at 1 for all three axes, close the Numeric panel, and click the Box tool again. This will create a box with the right dimensions for you to automatically size your images to.

3. Press **d** to bring up the Display Options panel and select the Backdrop tab. For Viewport 3, the back view, load the FaceFront.bmp image. For Viewport 4, the right view, load the FaceSide.bmp image of the head. Use Automatic Size for each viewport. Your Modeler screen should look like Figure 10.5.

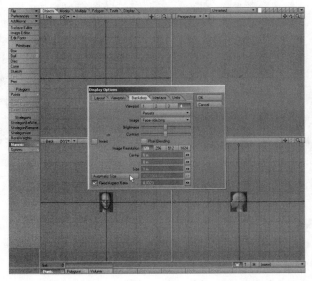

Figure 10.5   Using the Backdrop image feature in Modeler, a separate image can be placed in different viewports as references for modeling.

It's a good idea to keep the box you created as a separate object that you can load to quickly set up background images.

Building the Eyes

The first part of the face you're going to tackle is the eyelid area. But before starting the actual skin mesh, you will be building an eye object. It's much easier to shape the eyelids properly if you have an eye in another layer to make sure the lids match up properly.

Exercise 10.2   Modeling the Eyeball and Cornea

1. Close the Box tool if you haven't already, and then click Layer 2 and select the Ball tool.

2. Using Figure 10.6 and the background images as a guide, drag out a sphere over the left eyeball. It should have an approximate radius of 12.5mm on all three axes.

> **Note**
> You can hold the **Ctrl** key while creating the ball to force Modeler to create a perfect sphere. Also, if the background images seem too bright for you, remember that you can adjust the contrast and brightness in the Backdrop panel.

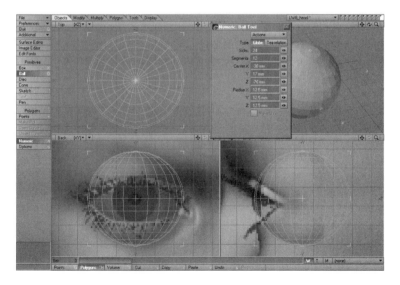

Figure 10.6   To place the eye, start by dragging a sphere over the left eyeball.

3. Rotate the sphere by 90 degrees on the X axis so that its poles face down the Z axis. This will facilitate making the pupil and iris later on. Or, you can place the

mouse pointer over the center of the object in the right viewport and press the **r** key to instantly rotate it 90 degrees. Conversely, pressing the **e** key instantly rotates it –90 degrees.

4. Press **q** and name the sphere Surface Left Eyeball.

   It's generally convenient later in Layout to have a separate cornea surface (the shiny outer coating of the eye), so that's what you're going to make next.

5. Select and then copy and paste the eyeball sphere.

   This will leave you with two copies; one of them selected. Switch to Polygon Edit mode from the selections at the bottom of the Modeler screen.

6. Press **q** to change the surface name of the selected polygon. Call it Left Cornea.

7. Next, select Smooth Scale from the Tools tab and scale this surface up by .25mm, which will leave the cornea slightly lager than the eyeball.

   It's important to have the eyeball selected first, before you copy and paste. Otherwise, when using Smooth Scale, you'll be sizing both copies of the eyeball, not just the cornea.

   A real cornea has a large bump where it covers the front of the eyeball over the iris, and it's important to model this feature. The change in curvature over this bump is the reason the eye tends to catch specular highlights from light sources most of the time, and it works the same way in the virtual 3D world. A highlight in the eye helps give the illusion of life to a 3D character.

8. To create the bump, deselect any polygons that are still selected, then select just the first two bands of polygons that face into the –Z axis for the cornea. The selection is easier in the right viewport. From the Multiply tab, use Smooth Shift to multiply the selected polygons with an offset of 0. To Smooth Shift with an offset of 0, right-click directly on the selected polygons.

9. Move these polygons –1.5mm on the Z axis and scale them by 80% on both the X and Y axes, making sure your cursor is centered on the cornea on the Z axis. You want the cornea to sort of bubble out in front of the eyeball.

> **Note**
> You might want to set Grid Snap to None under the Units tab in the Display Options panel. This will help you precisely size and move polygons in small amounts.

10. Now select the front three rows of polygons (the two rows you adjusted and the third row you created by Smooth Shifting) and scale them on the X and Y axes by 105% (again, make sure the cursor is centered on the cornea). This will help ensure that the cornea is located outside, or around the edge of the eyeball.

11. Select the entire surface from the Polygon Statistics panel and use the Knife tool to slice vertically just behind the third row of polygons, as in Figure 10.7.

    This will add some definition to where the bump blends back into the sphere of the eye. It will also help the smoothing over the front of the cornea.

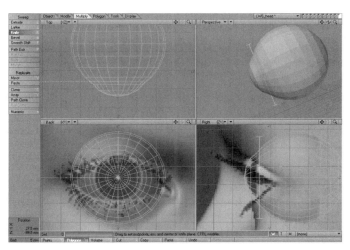

Figure 10.7   Vertically slice the cornea object at points A and B.

12. Select the back four rows of both the cornea and the eyeball and delete them. The camera will never see this side of the eyeball, so you can safely delete the geometry there for efficiency.

13. Use the Surface Editor from the Objects tab to add some preliminary colors to the cornea and eyeball surfaces. Remember to turn on smoothing. This will help you see how your eyeball model is coming along.

14. Use the Metaform tool to subdivide the eyeball and cornea once to check that everything is smoothing off nicely. This is found by pressing **Shift+d**. The eyeball and cornea should look like the ones in Figure 10.8a. Save your work.

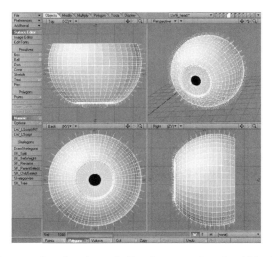

Figure 10.8a   After metaforming the eyeball and cornea, they should look like this.

Exercise 10.3 outlines the steps you need to follow to create the iris, lens, and inner cornea of the eye.

Exercise 10.3   Creating the Iris, Lens, and Inner Cornea

1. Undo the metaform you created in the preceding tutorial. Hide the cornea surface by selecting the surface named Left Cornea from the Polygon Statistic panel (**w**). Then, choose Hide Selected from the Display tab. Select the front two bands of the eyeball in the right view. Right-click to lasso select.

> **Note**
> You also can easily select polygons by clicking directly on the specific surface and then pressing the right bracket key (**]**) to activate the Select Connected command.

2. Press **Shift+Z** to activate the Merge Polygons command from the Polygon tab. This will merge these polygons into a flat disk. Next, with your cursor centered on the eye in the back view, scale this about 90% on the X and Y axes.

   Some points will be left over after you merge polygons. To eliminate these, use the Point Statistics panel (**w**), and click the white plus sign (+) next to the area labeled 0 Points. This will select any points not associated with polygons. After they are selected, you can press the **z** key to delete them.

3. Change the surface name of this polygon to Left Iris by pressing the **q** key. Next, perform the following series of bevels with the Numeric tab to give the iris the right amount of inward curvature. Press the **b** key to activate the Bevel tool. Press **n** to activate the Numeric panel and enter the following for an inner bevel:

Shift 0mm	Inset 1mm
Shift –.25mm	Inset .25mm
Shift 0mm	Inset .5mm
Shift 0mm	Inset 2mm
Shift –.25mm	Inset .25mm

4. In the back view, cut and paste the disc polygon, reselect it, and stretch it about 130% on the X and Y axes. Make sure the Numeric panel is open, and you'll see the 130% values for horizontal and vertical factors.

5. Press the **t** key, and move the disc polygon back into the eyeball by about 5mm. Rename it Lens Black. This polygon stops the camera from seeing through the eyeball when it comes time to render.

Now you will create a back surface for the cornea. This is important because you will ultimately render the eye with refraction turned on.

6. Unhide the cornea by selecting Unhide from the Display tab, or by pressing the backslash key (\). Select it, copy it, hide the cornea again, and then paste in the copy.

What you're doing here is making an inside to the cornea. Right now, the surface only faces outward, and for the cornea to properly refract, an inside needs to be created, sort of like a glass.

7. Select the copied bump and flip the polygons so that they point inward. Rename this Eye Aqueous.

8. Use the Stretch tool to scale down the Eye Aqueous until its outer edge matches up with the outer edge of the iris. Be careful where you put the cursor when scaling. Ideally the object should be the same diameter as the iris and should just butt up against it. You'll probably have to use the Move tool to properly line Eye Aqueous.

9. Unhide everything and select all the polygons, accept the Lens Black surface and Metaform (**Shift+d**) once to smooth out the eye.

10. Triple the newly subdivided geometry to get rid of any non-planar polygons. Save your work.

Your eye should look like the one in Figure 10.8b. (The cornea in this image is dissolved out so that you can see the whole eye better.) Alternatively, compare your results with the eye layer in the final model on the CD.

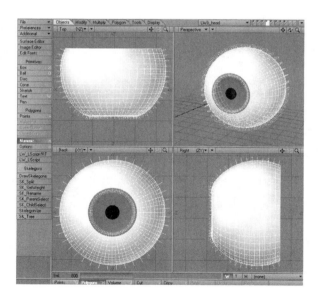

Figure 10.8b   The eye with the cornea dissolved so you can see the whole eye better.

Building the Eye Area

Now that the eye object is finished, it's time to build the eyelids.

In real life, the actual muscle structure that gives the eyelids their shape is a circular band. Therefore, in this exercise, you will build the eyelids from a shaped circular band of polygons. Building them in this manner also will enable you to sculpt the eyelids efficiently and easily, as well as deform them in a lifelike manner when building morph targets.

Exercise 10.4   Modeling the Lids

To prepare for this exercise, switch back to Layer 1, with the eye in Layer 2 as a background layer. Also, make sure you have the extender.p plug-in loaded (it's one of the standard Modeler plug-ins found in the Additional drop-down list). Map it to a keyboard shortcut or give it a button, as you'll be using it a lot over the next sections.

Begin by building a template polygon to shape the hole between the lids. Zoom into the back view to see the left eye close up.

1. Select the Pen tool and lay down 15 points, as in Figure 10.9. Note how there are more points around the areas where the shape narrows in the outer corner and around the tear duct in the inner corner. This will enable you to tightly define the surface in those areas. Rename the surface Skin, and apply a skin color of your choice.

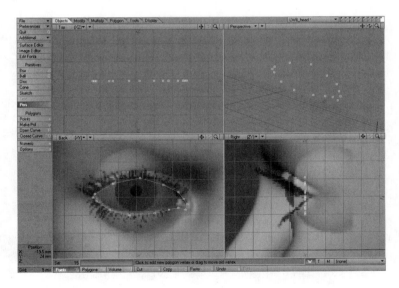

Figure 10.9   To shape the hole between the eyelids, start by laying down 15 points using the Pen tool.

Next, you will use this polygon to bevel out the bands of polygons that will form the eyelids. Don't worry about shaping the lids just yet. All you're doing here is getting the polygons in place (and in the right structure) so that you can sculpt them into nicely defined lids later.

2. Bevel the polygon four times with the following settings:

Shift 1mm	Inset 0 mm
Shift –0.6mm	Inset –1.5mm
Shift –1.5mm	Inset –1.5mm
Shift 0mm	Inset –2.0mm

The end result should look something like Figure 10.10. Delete the template, or the initial polygon. This should be the only selected polygon.

Note

To interactively bevel, press the **b** key to call up the Bevel command. Left-click on the selected polygon and drag. Dragging down insets; dragging to the left or right shifts. To multiply and bevel a new polygon from the selected polygon, simply right-click with the mouse and then left-click to continue beveling. (Macintosh users use the Command key with the mouse for right-click button functions.)

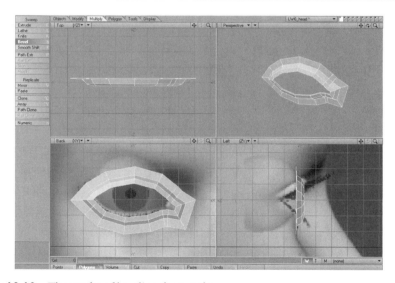

Figure 10.10   The results of beveling the template.

You'll note that the side viewport is changed to left rather than right to get a better look at the geometry in the Shaded View modes.

3. Press Tab to turn the geometry into a SubPatch surface.

4. Now select each end of the lids in turn and use Bend from the Modify tab to bend them in toward the face. The curvature should roughly match the profile of the eye in Layer 2. You can use the Move tool to help you line up the eyelid before bending if you want.

5. Use Sheer from the Modify tab in the top viewport to pull the top of the lids forward slightly.

6. Move and stretch the lid object in the front viewport so that its front profile matches up again with the background image.

You should now have something that's similar to Figure 10.11.

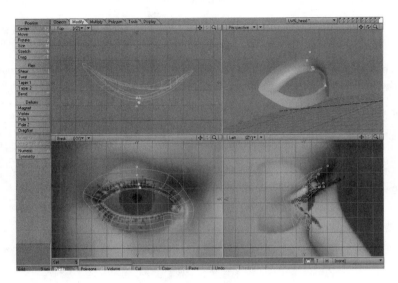

Figure 10.11   The selected points show the top lid profile.

Now it's time to sculpt the eyelid.

7. Select each radial row of points in turn on the top part of the lid and drag them in the side viewport to shape the eyelid surface. Tackle one row at a time, and always try to work in SubPatch mode. You also can switch the side view to wireframe while checking your results in a shaded perspective view. Sculpt the bottom lid in the same manner. Note that as you go from the center of the eye out, the general shape becomes softer and rounder. Aim for something that looks like Figure 10.12.

Tip

When you move the points on the inside edge of the lid, make sure you move the two innermost points on each row as a pair. The distance between them forms the thickness of the eyelid "lip" at that point, and you want to keep this fairly even along the whole of the lid surface.

Note

You'll be doing a lot of control-point sculpting when building the rest of the face. It's not really feasible to provide numerically exact instructions for doing these massaging operations. Just remember to match the background image and take it nice and slow. This is where your talent as a sculptor (as opposed to a technical 3D modeler) will shine.

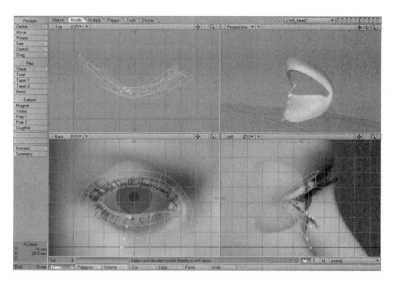

Figure 10.12   Sculpt the bottom lid by selecting each radial row of points in turn on the bottom part of the lid and dragging them about in the side and back viewports.

8. Tuck the bottom lid up behind the top lid slightly at the outer corner by selecting the points as shown in Figure 10.13 and moving them up and under the edge of the top lid.

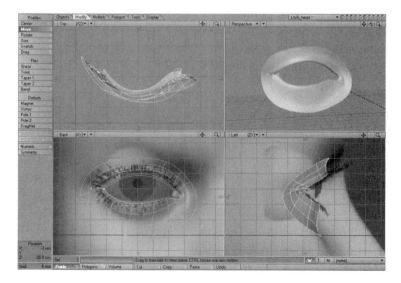

Figure 10.13   Select and move the points shown here to refine the lids.

Note

It will probably take a bit of trial and error to refine the lid corner. If you get lost as to what point belongs to which bit of the mesh, try turning on Guides or Cages in the Display Options tab. If you get really stuck, switch the surface back to standard polygons by pressing the **Tab** key, select the points you need, and then go into Poly Selection mode and reactivate the SubPatch surface with the **Tab** key. The points will still be highlighted when you change back to point selection.

Now it's time to add a bit more geometry to make the tear duct in the inner corner of the eye.

9. Select the five innermost points on the lid that surround the tear duct area. Then press **p** to make a polygon.

 Tip

An easy way to select only the inner points of the lid is to use the Statistics tab (w) to select only points with 2 polygons attached, and then deselect the ones you don't need.

10. Add a point to this polygon's inner edge and split the poly, as shown in Figure 10.14, so that you have two quads.

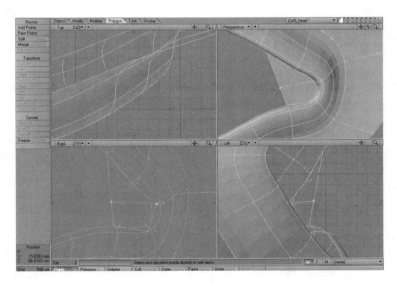

Figure 10.14   Add geometry to make the tear duct.

11. Now Smooth Shift these polygons and move them in toward the eye socket a bit.

12. Turn all this new geometry into a SubPatch surface and apply the Smooth tool a few times to help soften off the result. You will have to manually drag a few points around to get the bump in the middle, as in Figure 10.15, and to refine the shape.

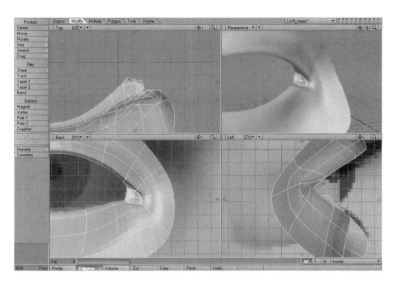

Figure 10.15   The finished tear duct.

Finally, check that the eyelids are sitting just off the surface of the eyeball.

13. Select one pair of inner lid points at a time and, with both layers one and two in the foreground, move them into place.

   The points will become transparent in any shaded view when they move behind the surface of the cornea.

14. Check the rest of the lids to make sure they look nice and smooth. Figure 10.16 shows the finished lid surface. Save your work.

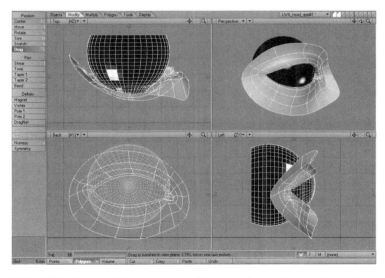

Figure 10.16   With the eye object layer in the foreground, select the eyelid surface and match the lids to the cornea.

Exercise 10.5   Extending the Lids Up into the Brow

Next is the eyebrow. Instead of creating new geometry from scratch, you will use the Extender plug-in to expand the existing mesh.

1. Select the outer points of the top lid surface in order, working from left to right, and press the Point Extender keyboard shortcut you created in the previous exercise.

   Although it appears nothing has changed, the plug-in has duplicated the points and connected them to the originals with new polygons.

2. Select the Scale tool and stretch the new points out from the center of the eye in the front viewport.

3. Using Point Extender, repeat the scaling operation two more times.

   Extender will have created three back polygons (it always forms closed loops) that you don't need. These unnecessary polygons should be much longer than the other ones, spanning from one side of the selection of points to the other.

4. Select the unnecessary polygons and delete them.

Note

You'll notice that some of the remaining polygons aren't facing the correct direction. You can avoid this minor inconvenience by making a template polygon from the selected edge points and using Bevel to create the new surface, as you did with the original eyelid geometry. Using Extender still tends to be a bit quicker to work with, though, as the new geometry is created instantly and you don't have to deselect the Scale tool in the process.

5. Select the new polygons and use Align from the Polygon tab to make sure they are facing the same way. You might need to flip them as well if LightWave aligns them to face the wrong direction.

   Figure 10.17 shows the results of the three Extender/Scale operations after the back faces have been removed and the geometry has been aligned to face the front.

6. Select the new polygons and press **Tab** to activate SubPatch mode. Shape the brow ridge, one row of points at a time. This enables you to move the selected point around in all viewports without fear of disturbing any other parts of your model accidentally. Again, you might have to switch to Wireframe mode on some viewports to select and drag all the points you need, and you might find it helpful to change the visibility options frequently (for instance, enabling Cages and Guides) while you work. Figure 10.18 shows the result. Save your work.

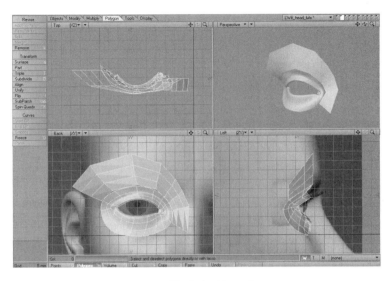

Figure 10.17   The new geometry created by Point Extender.

Note

By holding the **Ctrl** key and pressing a number on the numeric keypad, you can set up shortcuts to switch between Viewport modes.

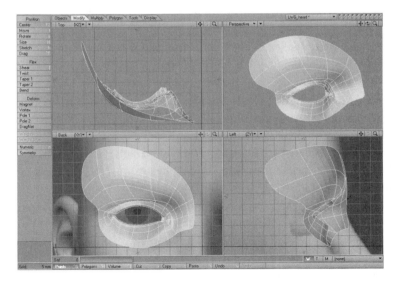

Figure 10.18   The finished brow should look something like this.

The following lists offers you important points to note while you work:

- The skin around the tear duct corner turns out quite sharply as it begins to join the bridge of the nose.

- A layer of fat and muscle just under the brow tends to hang down over the top lid, creating a distinct crease. This part can be hard to get right. Don't be afraid to move the brow control points down quite a bit over the upper lid.

- Keep the horizontal ridge of the brow distinct by keeping the rows of points there fairly close together.

Don't pay too much attention to what the model looks like in Plain Polygon mode. The SubPatch surface is what's important, not the control cage. Although as mentioned earlier, going back to Polygon mode is sometimes useful to select those hard-to-pick points. Make sure you switch back to SubPatch mode before sculpting.

Exercise 10.6   Extending the Brow Down to Form the Cheekbone

Looking at the reference pictures in the backdrop, you should be able to see how the outer brow curves around the eye and merges into the cheekbone below the eye, to complete the eye socket. To model this, you'll use Extender again, this time on the outer edge of the brow.

1. In order, select the three vertices running between the outer corner of the lids and the second-to-last outer brow row.

2. Press your Extender key, or the button you mapped in the beginning of this chapter. If you didn't map this, the command can be found under the Additional drop-down tools.

3. Use the Move and Rotate tools in the front and side views to bring the new vertices around the outer edge of the lower lid area so that the new row of polygons matches up with the lid surface above, as in Figure 10.19.

4. Repeat this process—Extender, Move/Rotate—another seven times, matching up the new row of cheekbone polygons with the next row in the eyelids each time until you reach the corner where the brow surface starts, as in Figure 10.20.

5. Once again, delete the back polygons. It might be a bit harder to select them this time. They're the ones that span from the top edge of the cheekbone to the bottom edge, as shown in Figure 10.20. The easiest way is to select them from the back in the Perspective window.

6. Make sure the remaining cheekbone polygons are aligned and facing the right direction, as in Figure 10.21. Then change them into SubPatch surfaces.

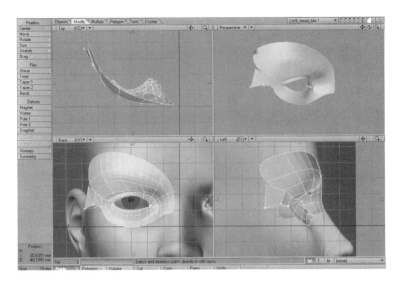

Figure 10.19   Bring the extended points down and around the lower lid.

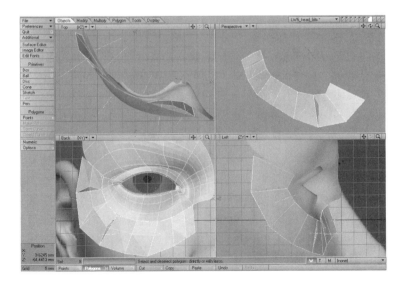

Figure 10.20   Bring the new cheekbone surface all the way around to the inner corner of the eye and then delete the back polygons, shown selected here. You can see in the Top view that surface normals are facing the positive Z axis. You only want normals facing forward.

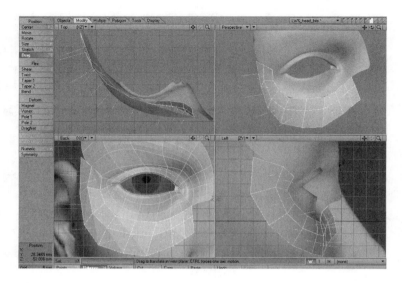

Figure 10.21   The cheekbone surface after alignment.

7. Select the edge points along the border of the lower lid and the cheekbone (see Figure 10.22) and press **m** to access the Merge panel.

8. Click Fractional. If you've been reasonably careful about matching the polygons up at the border, a value of 1 should weld everything nicely. Save your work.

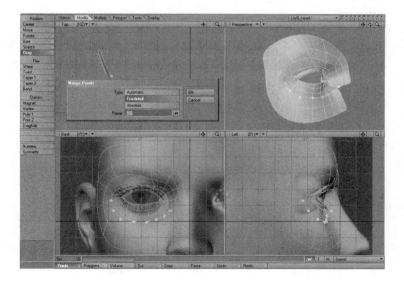

Figure 10.22   Merge the border points.

If you've been sloppy, the merge might have missed a few stray points or merged the wrong points (a small kink in the merged surface around the selected points is a sure sign of this). If this is the case, undo the merge and weld (**Ctrl+w**) the vertices in pairs manually.

Finally, take a look at the finished surface and make sure it's nice and smooth. Use the Drag tool to reshape it, if necessary.

Exercise 10.7   Building the Bridge of the Nose

The final step in building the eye area is to build the bridge of the nose.

1. Select the first four points on the extreme right edge of the brow, and then use the Extender command to duplicate them.

2. Use the Set Value command (**Ctrl+v**) to bring these new points directly to 0 on the X axis. Set Value is great for aligning multiple points to one specific location.

3. Follow the standard procedure you've been using throughout the exercises in this chapter with any new geometry—that is, kill the extra back polygon created by the Extender command, align the remaining polygons properly, use the Drag tool (**Ctrl+t**) to arrange points, and then press **Tab** to activate SubPatch mode. Your result should look like Figure 10.23.

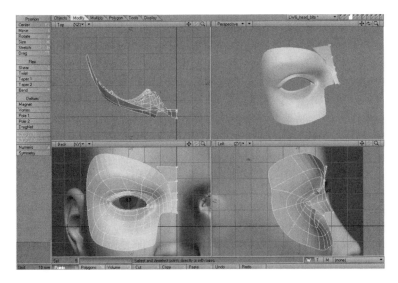

Figure 10.23   To build the bridge of the nose, kill the extra back polygon created by Extender, align the remaining polygons properly, and then press Tab.

4. Deselect any extra geometry created with the Extender tool and choose the Mirror tool (**Shift+v**). Activate the Numeric tab (**n**) and accept the default values. Mirror over the X axis centered on zero with Merge Points on.

5. Go to Layer 2 and follow Step 4 for the eye geometry to mirror the model thus far.

6. Bring both layers to the foreground. You should now have a pair of eyes and surrounding head area staring out at you. Save your work.

With the benefit of seeing both sides of the head, decide if you want to make any cosmetic changes to anything. Hopefully, if you're using the supplied background images as a guide, there shouldn't be anything amiss, but chances are something will need to be tweaked a little. Don't be put off by any inconsistencies in your model. No matter what you create in LightWave Modeler, you'll always need some tweaking here and there.

If this is the case, LightWave 6 has a great nifty new "mode" to help out with altering symmetrical objects. Look under the Modify tab and you'll see a button called Symmetry. When Symmetry is active, and as long as you have any geometry mirrored exactly over X, as you do here, anything you modify (using any of LightWave's Modify tools) on the positive X axis will be copied on the negative side. Your final image should look like Figure 10.24.

Note

Although the Symmetry tool is cool, it can also mess you up! Be aware when this tool is active, as everything you do on the positive X axis will be mirrored on the –X axis. Be sure to turn off this tool when you do not want your actions mirrored, such as centering the model (**F2**).

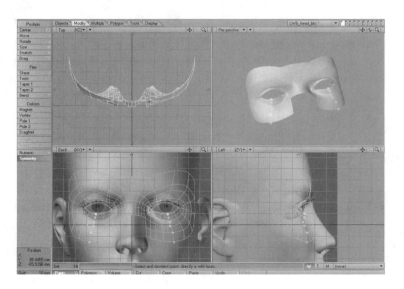

Figure 10.24   Make final modifications to the eye area with Symmetry on.

Building the Mouth

The other main area of detail on the face is, of course, the mouth, which is what you'll be moving on to next. You'll start in a way similar to the eyelids—quickly building a suitable cage structure, and then carefully molding the resulting SubPatch surface into shape. As you can see, a few key tools can help you build just about anything! Too often, LightWave animators think there is some hidden secret to making great models such as the one in this chapter. Instead, you're learning that with the right references, proper point placement, and a little time, you are creating a great-looking model.

Like the eyelids, the mouth area is also basically a circular ring of muscles. However, when modeling the lips, the difference in thickness (the side profile) along the length of each lip is much more pronounced than in the eyelids, so it's easier to start building them from the side first rather than the front.

Exercise 10.8   Modeling the Lips

Make sure only layer one is active and hide all the existing eyelid geometry. Start with the top lip first. Be sure that you have also turned off the Symmetry tool (Modify tab). Also, if SubPatch mode is active, deactivate it by pressing the **Tab** key.

1. Look at Figure 10.25 and, using the Point tool, lay down a similar group of vertices (six altogether) to make a side profile for the top lip. Try to make them in order from top to bottom. If you don't, reselect them in that order.

   Note that two points are close together at the leading edge. This is important to define the distinct ridge where the lip blends into the skin above it.

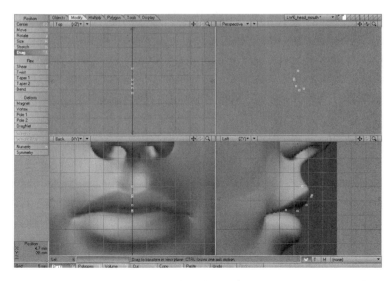

Figure 10.25   The profile points for building the top lip. You can see how easy this is with a picture reference.

2. Use the Extender tool to multiply the six points, and then in the back viewport, move the points to the left (about 6mm or so) and up slightly.

3. In the top viewport, move the points forward a couple of millimeters as well.

4. Use the Extender tool again. This time, move the points back a few millimeters in the top view and rotate them clockwise about 10 degrees. You can see why you were instructed to assign the Extender tool to a button or keyboard equivalent earlier in the chapter!

5. Move the points down slightly in the front view and rotate them counter-clockwise a couple of degrees.

6. Squash them a bit on the Z and Y axes using the Stretch tool.

7. Repeat Steps 4, 5, and 6 another three times, using Figure 10.26 as a guide, to roughly shape the surface with the Move, Stretch, and Rotate tools as you go. You should end up with a band of polygons five rows wide.

8. As you did in earlier exercises, delete the extra back polygons created by the Extender tool, and make sure all polygons are facing the forward. Press the Tab key to activate the SubPatch mode.

9. Finally, refine the top lip shape using the Drag tool. Select each row of points in turn before tweaking. Remember to pay attention to all viewports to see how your model is shaping up. Save your work!

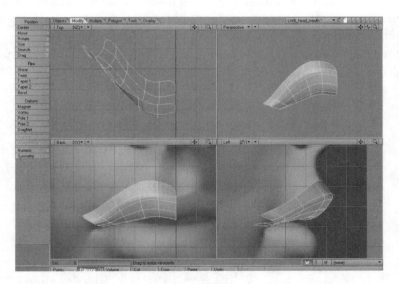

Figure 10.26   The finished top lip before it's mirrored.

10. Repeat the entire process from step one of this exercise for the bottom lip. Hide the upper lip first (Display tab) so you don't destroy the work you've done on it. Figure 10.27 outlines the point profile for the lower lip. Again, use the Point tool to put the vertices in order from top-left to bottom.

Tip

As in the top lip, the bottom profile has two points that are fairly close together and that help define the join between skin and lip. However, here the lip blends more smoothly into the skin, so keep them a bit wider apart than in the top lip.

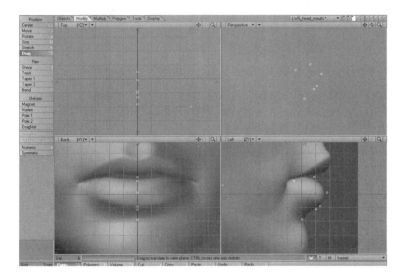

Figure 10.27   The bottom lip profile is fuller and rounder than the top.

11. Use the Extender tool to multiply the point profile in the lower lip, and then Move, Stretch, and Rotate to the selection to build out the lip surface as you did for the upper lip.

    The rows of points should gradually be rotated from a vertical to a horizontal profile as you go (use the front viewport to do this). Again, you should end up with a band of geometry five rows of polygons wide.

12. Clean up the polygons. Press **Tab**, and then use the Drag tool (**Ctrl+t**) to make sure the points are in the right position and shaped nicely based on the background reference images. Finish refining the surface. Save your object.

    Remember that the bottom lip stays thicker for more of its length than the top lip.

    Although the lip gets thinner at the outer corner, it actually retains a bit of volume. Don't make it too thin at the far edge. Figure 10.28 shows how it should end up. The end looks a lot thinner in the side view because its profile has been rotated.

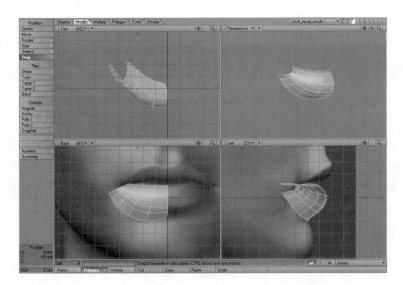

Figure 10.28   The finished bottom lip before it's mirrored.

Now that the lips have been modeled, it's time to join them together.

Exercise 10.9   Joining the Lips Together

1. To begin, unhide the top lip (if you hid the polygons in the previous exercise). Make sure only the two lip surfaces are visible and then align the outer edge vertices (shown in Figure 10.29) so that the two lips match up with each other.

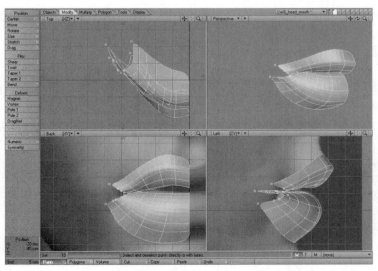

Figure 10.29   Align the two sets of outer edge vertices together before welding.

2. Select the last row of vertices on the top lip and rotate them counterclockwise in the front view so that they lie on a horizontal plane. Do the same for the outer row of points on the bottom lip, this time rotating them clockwise so that they roughly match up with the top lip vertices.

3. Select both sets of edge vertices and drag them in the top viewport so that each pair (one vertex from the top lip and the corresponding vertex from the bottom lip for each row) is aligned.

4. In the back viewport, use Stretch (**h**) to compress the two sets of vertices together. Weld each pair together in turn, and use Drag to refine the join area. It helps to select the last row of polygons in the bottom lip (shown in Figure 10.30) and slightly tuck them up, under, and behind the top lip surface.

Tip

The lip crease at the corner can be fairly tricky to shape properly. Don't pull the points in this area too close together on the X axis or you'll end up with an ugly pinch in the corner of the mouth. Do pull them close together on the Y axis (especially in the inner corner). The crease should be a lightly curved, well-defined horizontal line that continues the natural curve of the lips.

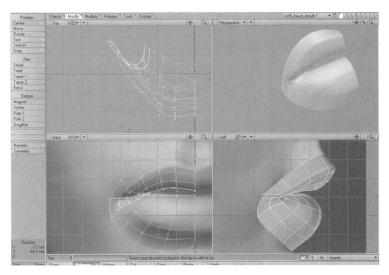

Figure 10.30 Be careful sculpting the corner of the mouth. Although it needs to be tightly defined, try not to make the area look pinched.

5. When you're happy with the corner area, select the other edge vertices of both lips and use Set Value (**Ctrl+v**) to make sure they are all sitting perfectly on the X axis.

6. Use the Mirror tool (**Shift+v**) to create the right side of the mouth. The default numeric settings should be fine. Mirror on the X axis and make sure merge points is on in the numeric mirror panel.

7. Switch to the trusty Drag tool (**Ctrl+t**) again and make any last-minute refinements to the completed lip surface. Save your work. Figure 10.31 shows the finished area.

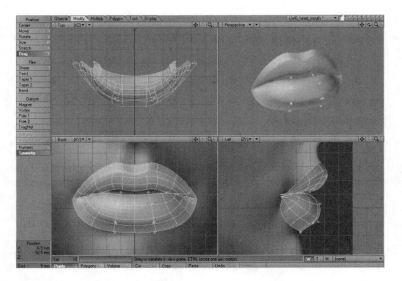

Figure 10.31   Make final alterations to the lips after both halves are in place.

Exercise 10.10   Building the Rest of the Mouth Area

To complete the mouth, you'll need a few more bands of geometry around the lips:

1. Select all the outer-edge vertices in order, going clockwise.

2. Use the Extender tool to create the first band of polygons, and then use Scale to give them some width.

3. Repeat Step 2 again.

You should now have something that looks like Figure 10.32.

Note

Don't worry about any extra back polygons this time. Because you deliberately extended a closed loop of points, everything should be fine. Just make sure all the geometry is aligned, though, before switching them to SubPatch mode.

Now it's time to sculpt the outer mouth area. This procedure should be fairly familiar to you by now.

4. Select rows of points one at a time to work on.

5. Switch the top, back, and side views to Wireframe if necessary for access to obscured geometry, but keep the Perspective window shaded so that you can accurately gauge your progress.

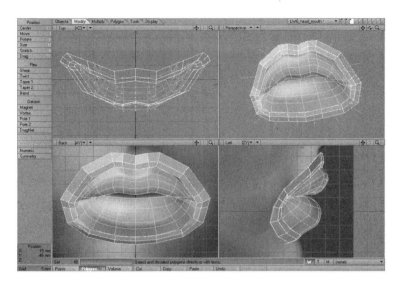

Figure 10.32   The mouth after extending the outer lip points.

6. Switch on Enable Guides or Enable Cages in the Display Options panel (**d**), or switch the surface back to Polygon mode in the viewport briefly if you have trouble working out which vertices you need to be working on.

Note

You can quickly switch between Viewport modes easily by setting a numeric preset. By changing the viewport to a certain display style, then holding the **Ctrl** key and selecting any of the numbers on the numeric keypad, you can save a view preset.

7. The mouth sits in the middle of a raised mound. Spread the outer edges back into what would be the face, making sure they form a smooth curve around the whole mouth area using the Drag (**Ctrl+t**) tool.

   A distinct notch runs from the two upper tips of the top lip all the way up to the base of the nose. Keep a bit of definition in this area by keeping the points relatively close together. There should be just the right amount of geometry to get the shape right. You can turn on Symmetry mode to mirror your actions if you want.

8. At either side of the mouth there is a small raised area and a light crease where a lot of facial muscles meet. Slightly drag a couple of points out from the face here. Save your work.

   The bottom lip will blend into the start of the chin. A defined crease in the middle just under the lip will soften out quite quickly toward the outer edges of the mouth, as in Figure 10.33.

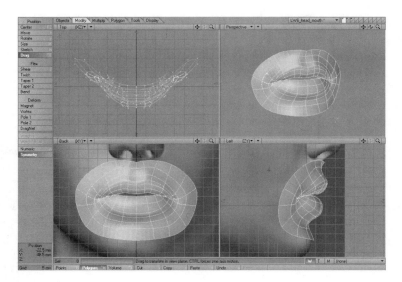

Figure 10.33   The completed mouth area.

Building the Jaw

The jaw, despite being a relatively smooth structure, defines a major contour of the face and is important in terms of overall proportion. It's a good idea to add it in at this stage as you start to see more of the face coming together.

Exercise 10.11   Adding the Jaw Line

1. Hide the polygons you've created thus far before you start building the jaw. Hiding the polygons from the Display tab does not remove them, it only makes them invisible so that you don't harm the work you've already done. Make sure Symmetry mode if off in the Modify tab, and do not have the SubPatch mode active (Tab key).

2. Use the Points tool to lay down a row of five profile points, as in Figure 10.34. These should curve in toward the neck area at the bottom. Remember to pay attention to all viewports as you build.

3. Using the Extender tool to multiply the points, rotate (**y**), stretch (**h**), and move (**t**) the points to fill out the jaw line, as in Figure 10.35.

   You should have six rows of polygons, from the start of the jaw near the ear to the center X axis.

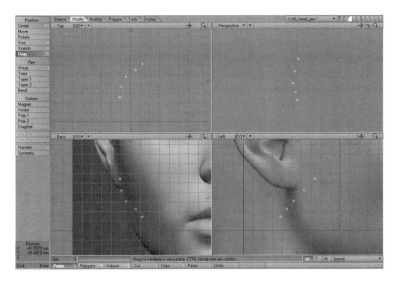

Figure 10.34   Lay down a row of five profile points for creating the jaw line.

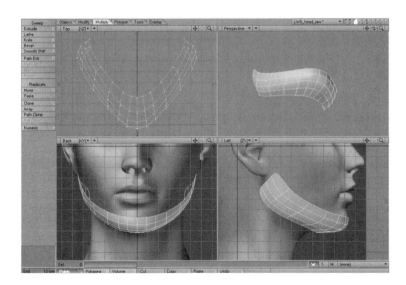

Figure 10.35   Extend the jaw line so that you have six rows of polygons, from the start of the jaw near the ear to the centerline on the X axis.

 Tip

Remember to cull those pesky back polygons from the Extender operations, and make sure the extended geometry is aligned to face the right direction.

4. Use Set Value (**Ctrl+v**) to make sure the last row of points sits exactly on the X axis. Then mirror them to create the other half of the jaw.

5. Finally, use the Drag (**Ctrl+t**) and Stretch (**h**) tools to refine the jaw shape, and press the Tab key to activate SubPatch mode to see the smooth shaped jaw, as in Figure 10.36. Save your work.

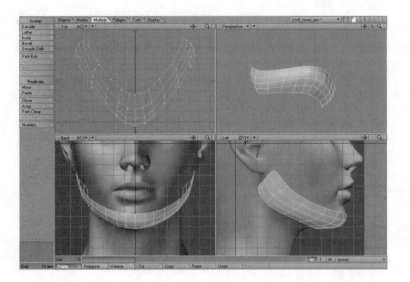

Figure 10.36   The completed jaw surface.

Exercise 10.12   Joining the Jaw and Mouth to Create the Chin

With the jaw complete, it's time to create a chin. Turn off SubPatch mode by pressing the Tab key.

1. Make sure only the jaw and the mouth area are visible by unhiding the mouth polygons, and hiding the eye areas and nose bridge polygons.

2. Align the middle seven vertices at the lower edge of the mouth and the corresponding points on the upper edge of the jaw, as in Figure 10.37.

3. Weld (**Ctrl+w**) the respective pairs of points together, or use a fractional merge (**m**) if you think you've got them close enough together.

4. Refine the chin area if needed with the Drag tool (**t**), or Stretch tool (**h**). Pay special attention to the points highlighted in Figure 10.38. They control the surface crease where the lower mouth blends into the jaw and changes direction to become the raised mound of the chin. Save your work.

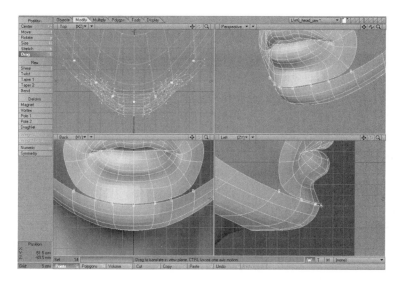

Figure 10.37   Drag the selected vertices of the mouth and the jaw so that they line up.

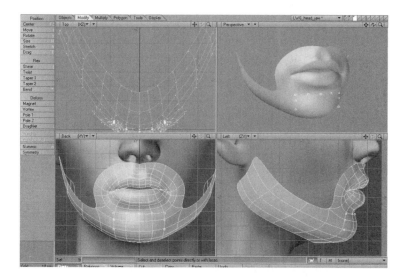

Figure 10.38   The points shown here need to be carefully positioned. Even moving them fractionally can make a big difference.

Building the Nose

The nose seemingly presents the aspiring face modeler with a few challenges, as the nose is a complex little knot of interconnecting curves and planes. However, just like all the other parts of the face you have modeled so far, after you've broken it down into smaller, easy-to-model sections, the nose is really not that hard at all to create.

Exercise 10.13   Extending the Bridge

Start by bridging the remaining gap between the cheekbones to complete the bridge of the nose.

1. Invert the visible status of your geometry by selecting Invert from the Display tab. The previously modeled eye area should now be the only thing you can see, while the mouth and nose polygons become hidden.

2. Select the vertices at the bottom of the currently existing nose bridge, between the two cheekbones, in order from left to right. There should be nine of them altogether.

3. Use the Extender tool to multiply the selection, and then move (**t**) the points down so they match up with the next row of cheekbone points. You'll have to move them forward a bit off the face as well.

4. Repeat the last step so that the points match up with the bottom row of cheekbone vertices.

5. Do one last Extend/Move operation so that you have one more row of nose bridge polygons protruding at the bottom. Check that their profile matches up with the line of the nose in the side viewport.

6. Weld (**Ctrl+w**) the border between the bridge and the cheekbones at either side of the nose and save your work. Figure 10.39 shows the results at this stage.

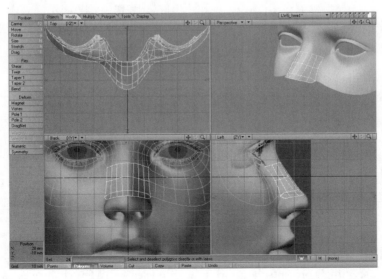

Figure 10.39   Fill in the gap between the two cheekbone sections to continue the nose line.

Exercise 10.14   Sculpting the Nostrils

Begin the left nostril by building some polygons to form the outer "wing." You should know the drill by now.

1. Lay down some profile points in order (five points should suffice this time).

2. Use Extender and a combination of Move, Rotate, and Stretch to create and roughly shape the new geometry. Remember, pay attention to the geometry you're creating in all viewports to properly shape the nostrils.

3. Delete the extra back polygons, align the remaining geometry, and turn it into a SubPatch surface by pressing the **Tab** key. Use Drag to refine the shape, as in Figure 10.40.

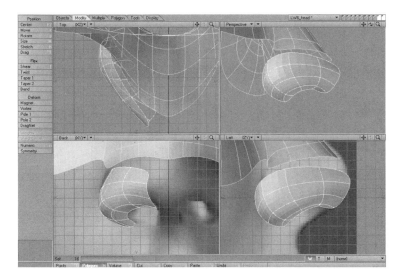

Figure 10.40   The nostril "wing" surface.

4. Start at the back of the nostril wing and begin contouring the shape of the nostril. Use the Drag (**Ctrl+t**) tool to individually adjust the points.

5. Make the shape gradually curve around until it meets the nose tip using the Drag tool, but stop short of the center X axis.

   The wing should be four poly rows wide (you will join it with the corresponding nose bridge polygons shortly).

6. Curve the lower edge of the nostril underneath itself to form the edge of the actual nostril hole.

7. Now Mirror the nostril over X.

8. Between each upper nostril edge and the lower edge of the nose bridge, a gap exists. The quickest way to fill this gap is to simply select a group of four points

at a time and then press **p** to make a polygon. Depending on the order in which you selected the points, you might need to flip some of them afterward. Try to select in a clockwise order.

9. Using the Extender tool, fill in the middle tip of the nose between the two nostrils, but leave a gap between the last two rows around the inner nostril edges.

10. Weld (**Ctrl+w**) the border points between the tip and the bridge of the nose. Your object should look like the one in Figure 10.41. Again, note that a gap should remain between the bottom nostril rows.

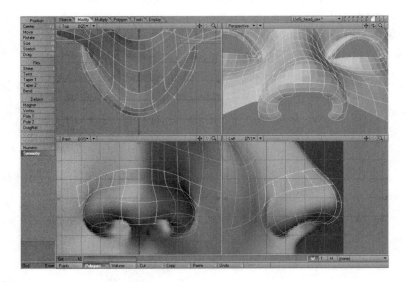

Figure 10.41   The nose after filling in the gaps.

On the left nostril:

11. Use the Extender tool on the two points at the gap edge of the lower row of nostril polygons. You need to do this four times altogether to expand this bottom row into a complete ring of polygons.

12. Use Move and Rotate to bring the points around a bit each time.

13. When the last polygon is in place, weld the seam points to make the nostril edge a continuous circle.

14. Make sure the four new polygons are properly aligned—flip them (**f**) to face forward, if they're not—and then select them and press Tab to activate SubPatch mode. Save your work.

Don't worry about the back polygons. Only one polygon is created when Extender is used on just two points. Figure 10.42 should make these last few steps more clear.

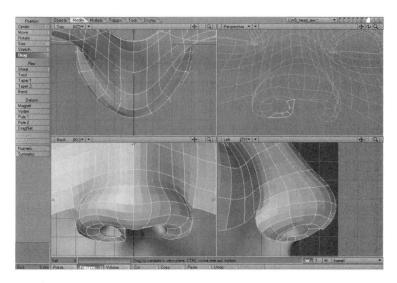

Figure 10.42   Extend four extra polygons to complete the circle at the bottom edge of the nostril.

Exercise 10.15   Joining the Nose to the Upper Lip

1. Mirror the four polygons from Step 14 in the last exercise (the polygons highlighted in Figure 10.42) over to the right side of the nose, deselect them, and do an Automatic Merge to weld them in place. (You might need to weld a couple of points manually. A small kink or tear in the surface usually indicates this.)

2. Select a set of four points for the other two rows between the nostrils and press the **p** key to create a polygon. This will complete the underside of the nose tip.

3. Unhide the mouth/jaw assembly if it's still hidden. Move the five middle points on the upper top lip edge to align them with the five middle points on the bottom nose edge. Weld theses border points in pairs, as in Figure 10.43.

4. On the left nostril, select the innermost points in the bottom nostril ring in a clockwise order (Perspective view is the best to use for this).

5. Press **p** to make a polygon, and check that it faces downward.

6. Bevel (**b**) this a couple of times, moving it up into the nose each time, as in Figure 10.44.

7. Delete the temporary polygon. Select the inner nostril polygons created by the bevel. Press Tab to switch them to SubPatch surfaces.

8. Mirror these across, deselect, and merge or weld to join them to the opposite side of the nose.

   Next, you're going to join a bit more of the nose to the top of the mouth. But as you can probably see from the model, there is a geometry mismatch between the two areas—that is, there aren't any points on the top lip edge that you can easily match up to the next free points on the bottom nose edge. Rectifying this will take a bit of low-level polygon editing on the top lip.

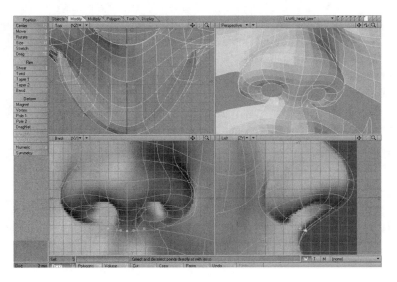

Figure 10.43   Weld the border points between the nose and the top lip surfaces.

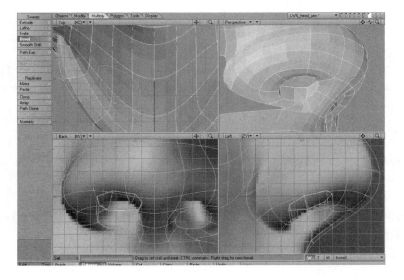

Figure 10.44   Bevel in the nostril using a temporary polygon.

9. Switch all your geometry back to Polygon mode by pressing the **Tab** key to turn off SubPatch mode.

10. Using Figure 10.45 as a guide, add two points to the top edge of the polygon shown by first selecting the polygon and then using the Add Points tool from the Polygon tab. Then, split the polygon (Polygon tab) so that it becomes two quads. To split polygons, select two points—the split also will activate. Click it, and you'll split the geometry.

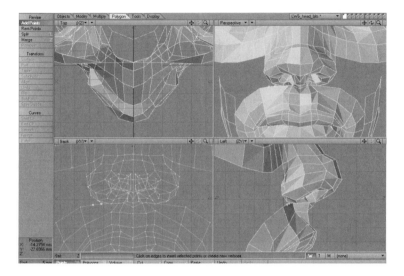

Figure 10.45   Use low-level editing to adjust the local geometry match between two surfaces.

You now have the extra geometry needed to match up the top lip with the bottom nose edge (on the left side at least).

Note

This kind of editing—splitting, merging, and adding points to polygons—is often required to match up two distinct surfaces that need to be joined together but have a different number of points along the border edge.

Most of the time it can be avoided if you can arrange in advance for the two surfaces to have the right amount of geometry to start with, knowing that they will need to match up at some point. That's one of the reasons you created various sections with specific numbers of polygons or points. But sometimes, either by accident or by design, it doesn't work out that way, and you will need to fiddle around with the border edges a bit to get them to match up properly, as you have here.

11. Align the newly split polygon with the left side of the lower nostril using the Drag tool, as in Figure 10.46. Then weld them to the nostril.

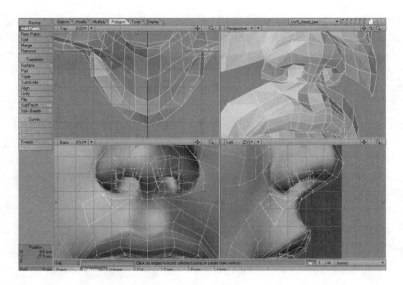

Figure 10.46   Align the new geometry to the nose.

12. Deselect and then turn everything back to SubPatch surfaces by pressing the **Tab** key, as in Figure 10.47.

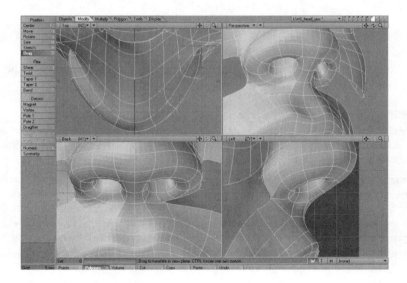

Figure 10.47   The join in SubPatch mode.

13. Now perform the same operation of patching by repeating Steps 10 and 11 on the right side of the nose. Save your work.

Completing the Face

Okay, you've modeled the eyes, eye area, mouth, jaw line, and nose. But you still need to perform a few more steps in order to complete the face.

Exercise 10.16   Creating the Cheeks

In this exercise, you will go back to where the lower cheekbone edge joins the bridge and fill in the gap between it, the nose, and the upper lip edge.

1. Use the Extender tool to multiply and duplicate the three points from the side of the nose around the bottom of the cheek (don't forget to clean up after extending).

2. Align, making sure your polygons are facing outward, and then weld the border vertices of this new geometry at both the upper edge, where it meets the cheekbone, and the lower edge, where it meets the top lip surface. Figure 10.48 shows the filled gap.

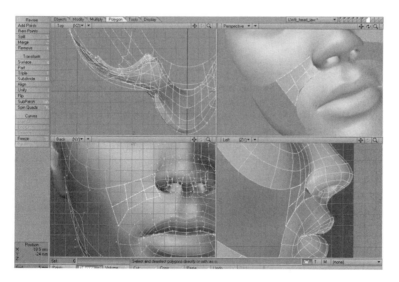

Figure 10.48   The highlighted polygons show where the gap has been filled.

Continue in a similar manner to fill in the much larger gap between the jaw and the rest of the cheekbone surface:

3. Select the five points at the left edge of the cheek/mouth area.

4. Use Extender and then move (**t**) the points to the left and back so they match up with the next row of points on the jaw and the cheekbone. Weld the border vertices at the top and bottom. Your model should look like the one in Figure 10.49.

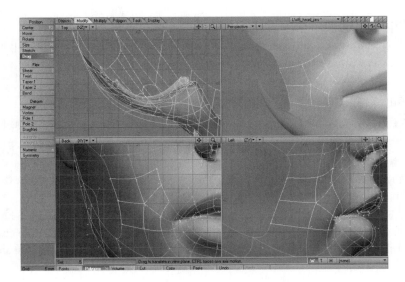

Figure 10.49   The cheek surface after filling in one row of polygons.

 Note

The polygon selection in Figure 10.49 marks an interesting structural feature. The point in the middle of the highlighted area is attached to *five* patches rather than the usual four. (Although you've actually created a few five-patch intersections already—look closely at the nostril area, for instance, where there are several,—this one is a much clearer example.) Five-patch intersections are useful for joining areas with differing contour structures or patch densities. In this case, you have the circular area of the mouth and lips joined to three much more planar arrangements of polygons that form the jaw, cheek, and cheekbone surfaces.

However, five-patch intersections can also cause a few problems of their own when sculpting a surface. Because the vertex in the middle is attached to five patches rather than the usual four, it has an unduly large influence on the local shape of the surface compared to its normal neighbors (which are only attached to four polygons). So you'll have to position this point with extra care. The surface around the intersection point doesn't tend to smooth as consistently as normal and will have a much greater tendency to crease.

With that in mind, it's a good idea to try to stick them in areas where you would expect to see a crease anyway. In this case, they lie at the natural crease zone between the mouth and the cheeks.

5. Continue to use the Extender tool and move the cheek edge points so that you completely fill the gap between the jaw and the cheekbone. Remember that you can use the Drag tool on selected points as well.

6. Clean up the unwanted back polygons and align the remaining geometry.

7. Weld the edges, select the cheek polygons, and press **Tab** when you're done to activate SubPatch mode. Figure 10.50 shows the finished cheek structure.

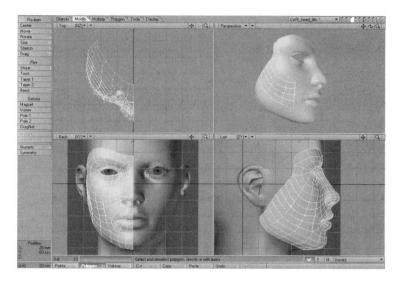

Figure 10.50   The cheek completes the face by filling the last gap.

8. Rather than repeat this for the right side, use the Volume Selection tool to delete everything on the positive side of the X axis (you should be left with exactly half a face on the left side).

9. Make sure all the points lying on the X axis are positioned exactly on the 0 X axis by using Set Value.

10. Mirror the face over X with Merge Points on.

11. Finally, go over the whole face (use Symmetry mode to update both sides at once) and make changes to the shape of any areas you feel need refining with the Drag and Stretch tools. Once again, it's generally best to select small groups of points at a time to do this. You can also Drag one point at a time. Save your work.

Specifically, it's highly likely that the area spanning from one edge of the face over the cheeks and nose to the other will need a bit of tweaking to get everything looking just right—and that's the key. Tweak and adjust until the model looks right to you.

Figure 10.51 shows the face after this process. The cheekbone profile has been cleaned up and smoothed where it blends into the lower mouth and jaw, and the nose has been reshaped slightly to give it a bit more definition around the nostrils and where it blends into the eyes and cheeks. For future revisions of the model, you can drag these cheek-bone points to make your model look heavier, or gaunter.

If you still have any unwanted kinks or bumpy bits that you are finding hard to get rid of using Drag, careful use of the Smoothing tool (Tools tab) will usually do the job. Don't go overboard with it, as overuse can remove too much definition from the face, but for the simpler areas of the face it's quite useful. Use low smoothing values/iterations, and then repeat if necessary. Also, be aware that Smooth tends to have adverse effects if used with Symmetry on. It will certainly alter the exact relationship between the two sides of the face that Symmetry relies on to work properly. Remember, to use Symmetry, the point placement must be identical on both the negative and positive X axis.

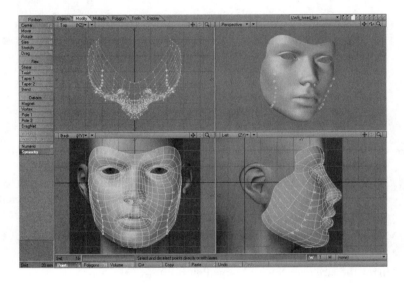

Figure 10.51   Selecting rows of points to refine the cheeks.

Building the Rest of the Head

Now that you have completed the face, the rest of the head should be easy by comparison. You should be familiar with using Extender, Drag, Stretch, and so on. And everything except the ears is fairly straightforward at this point.

Exercise 10.17   Extending the Forehead to Create the Skull

To build the skull, you first need to add a few extra polygons to the temple area on each side of the head:

   1. Using Figure 10.52 as an example, build four similar polygons off each brow edge using Extender. Remember to clean up the back polygons and align them.

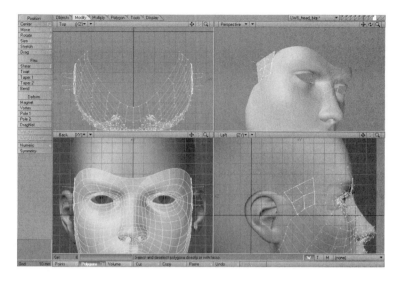

Figure 10.52   Extend four polygons from each brow edge to form the temples.

Now you can use Extender again on the whole upper brow area to sweep out the skull:

2. Select the points at the top of the eyebrows, as shown in Figure 10.53.

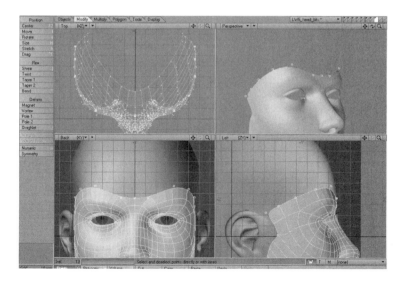

Figure 10.53   Use these points to extend the skull geometry.

3. Using the usual combination of Extender, and then the Rotate, Stretch, and Move functions, build out the skull polygons using the background image to guide you. You should be doing most of the shaping in the side viewport. Create eight bands of polygons altogether.

4. Delete the extra back polygons that Extender created, and align the remaining new geometry properly, making sure the polygons face forward. Then, turn the shape into a SubPatch surface by pressing the **Tab** key. Figure 10.54 shows what you should end up with.

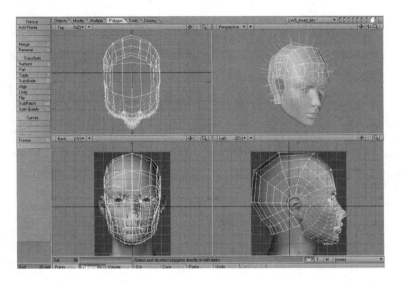

Figure 10.54   The newly extended skull polygons. Note the change in profile as the neck joins the skull.

Note

In terms of shape, the skull is basically a fairly simple, elongated sphere, widening slightly in the front profile as it curves back from the face, and then tapering in again at the base where it meets the neck muscles. There is usually a light indentation at each temple, just behind the eye socket. Also, there are some marked differences between the female skull, which you are modeling now, and the male skull. The female head tends to have a higher, more rounded forehead that blends quite smoothly into the brow. The male forehead tends to have more of a slope and a pronounced eyebrow ridge that protrudes from the skull.

Now it's time to join the skull to the edge of the jaw line:

5. Weld (**Ctrl+w**) the edges of the two polygons, as shown in Figure 10.55, on each side of the face. Save your work.

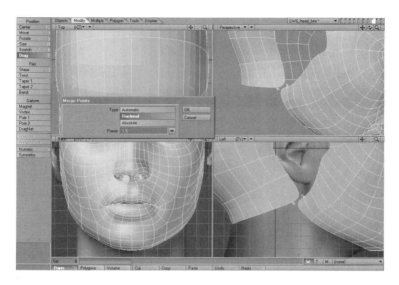

Figure 10.55   Join the jaw and the skull surfaces at the points shown here.

Exercise 10.18   Sculpting the Neck Area

Creating the neck geometry is a simple matter of extending the points around the lower edge of the skull and jaw:

1. Select the points around the lower edge of the skull and jaw in clockwise order. Use the Perspective window for this, as shown in Figure 10.56. Remember that you can hold the Alt key and left-click and drag in the viewports to precisely rotate the view.

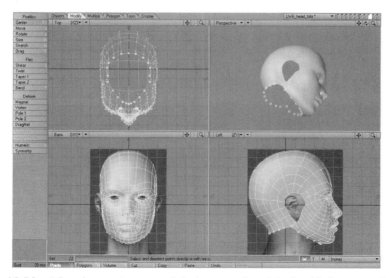

Figure 10.56   Select these points around the bottom edge of the head before extending the neck.

2. Press **p** to make a polygon and, using either Extender or Bevel, create three new bands of polygons. If you use Extender, make sure you clean up the polygon alignment afterward.

3. Roughly shape the new bands of polygons as you use the Stretch and Move tools. Use the background images to guide the profile. Figure 10.57 shows the new surface after two bevels.

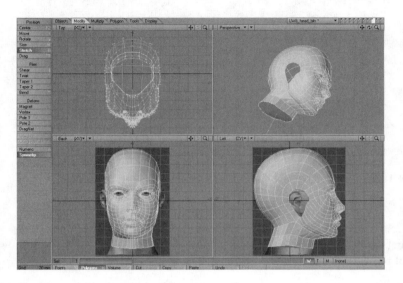

Figure 10.57   Bevel or extend out the neck as shown.

4. After you've got the three rows roughed out, start sculpting the neck into a more refined shape. You can use the Drag tool, Move, or Rotate to define the proper shape.

The fleshy part of the neck under the chin starts out quite thick and then narrows as it descends down to the collarbone. Two major tendons run along either side of the neck. You can usually see them right where they join the skull behind the ear. You should have enough geometry to easily sculpt both of these features. Refer to Figure 10.58 if you need some help.

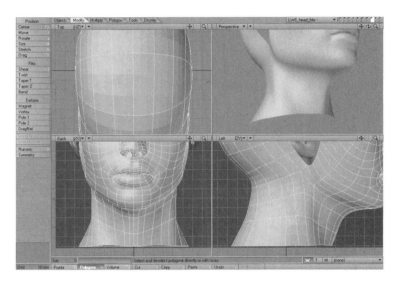

Figure 10.58   The refined neck area after sculpting.

Now all you have left to do are the ears.

Note

The ears are probably the hardest bit of modeling you'll have to do on the whole head. The problem is that the ear surface is convoluted. That is to say, it's easy to get lost in Modeler when you're trying to sculpt the surface. There are so many tight turns and overlapping polygons that selecting the points you want to work on can be a time-consuming task in itself. Try to use the Perspective window, turning it a bit to get a clearer view each time you need to select points and, particularly, when you reach the inner ear stages. You will need to regularly hide geometry to get a clearer view of things.

Luckily the ear doesn't ever have to do much, certainly in terms of deformation. People don't tend to pay too close attention to them either. This means that you can get away with slightly "rough and ready" polygon structures when building the ear that might cause problems in other, more prominent parts of the face. In addition, after you build an ear, save it and use it over and over again for future characters.

5. To create the ear, go to an empty layer and build a set of profile points, as in Figure 10.59.

6. Use the profile points, and use the Extender tool to duplicate the outer ear surface, first going around the back of the ear toward the ear lobe. Make eight bands of polygons altogether, as in Figure 10.60. Clean up the alignment when you're done. Don't worry about back polygons just yet.

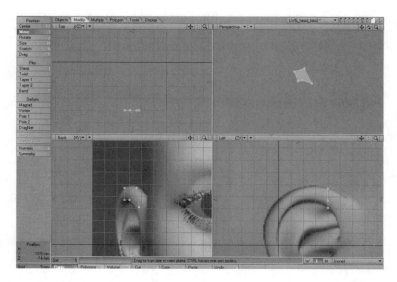

Figure 10.59   The profile for the outer ear. The polygon shown here is just to make the order of the points clearer.

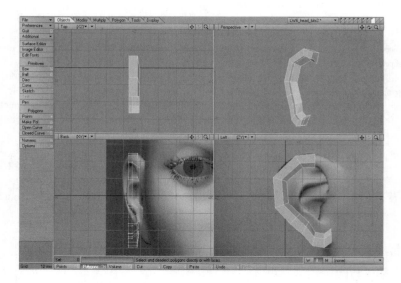

Figure 10.60   Build the back of the outer ear first.

7. Now reselect the original profile points in order again and extend the ear forward. This time create five bands of polygons going around the top corner of the ear and down where it would join the cheek. Select the band of polygons that runs around the inside edge. The easiest way to do this is to select two of them in the Perspective view and then run the Band Saw plug-in, found under the

Additional drop-down list. Leave the options for Band Saw as they are (that is, you don't want to split anything) and it will select the rest of the band of polygons for you. Then, delete those polygons. Figure 10.61 shows the correct row of polygons to select.

Note

The Band Saw plug-in might easily become your new best friend in Modeler 6. As you can see in the previous example, you can use Band Saw to select a region of intricate polygons. But what it is really good for is splitting polygons. By selecting a polygon, you can run Band Saw to instantly slice or divide the geometry.

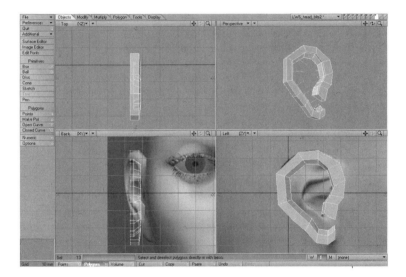

Figure 10.61 After creating the front part of the outer ear, select these polygons and delete them.

8. Now select the eight polygons at the back and side edge of the front part of the ear. Figure 10.62 shows the ones you want. Then, delete these as well.

9. Press **Tab** to activate SubPatch mode, and adjust the outer edge profile of the surface along its length, as in Figure 10.63. It should be thin at the top rear edge and fairly flat and thick at the lobe.

Next you're going to build the middle ear out of the inner edge of the existing geometry. Deselect any polygons at this point.

10. In the Perspective viewport, select the first nine vertices on the inner front edge of the ear going from the lobe around. See Figure 10.64 to see which points to select.

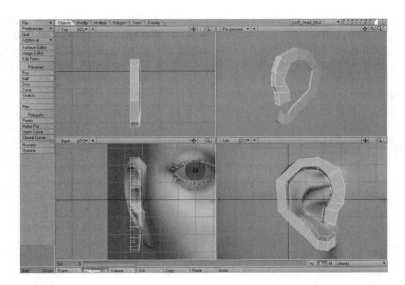

Figure 10.62   Delete the highlighted polygons at the front of the ear. Note that the Perspective view shows the back of the ear.

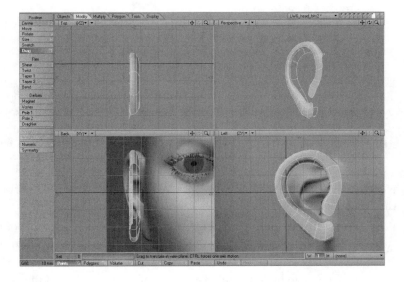

Figure 10.63   Refine the ear surface along the outer edge.

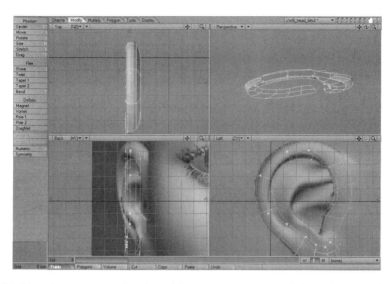

Figure 10.64   These points at the edge of the inner ear surface will form the basis of the middle ear.

11. Using Extender, create three new rows of polygons, scaling them in toward the middle of the ear (each time in the side viewport).

12. Add one additional row with Extender, this time moving the points in toward the skull in the front viewport.

13. Cut the extra back polygons (the big, long, thin ones) and align the remaining surface. You should now have something similar to Figure 10.65.

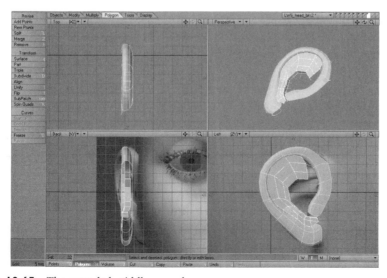

Figure 10.65   The extended middle ear polygons.

You now need to attach this new middle ear surface to the two cheek side rows of the outer ear:

14. Using the Drag tool (**Ctrl+t**), rearrange the bottom couple of rows of the middle ear so that they smoothly flow into the edge of the outer ear, as shown in Figure 10.66. It's probably best to switch all the ear geometry back to Polygon mode to do this. Press the **Tab** key to turn off SubPatch mode. Select the border vertices where they meet (also highlighted in Figure 10.66) and weld (**Ctrl+w**) the corresponding pairs together.

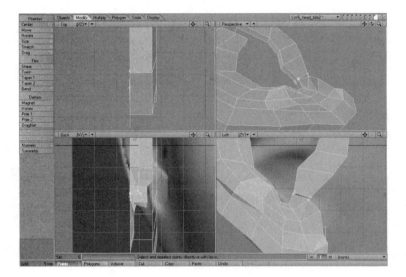

Figure 10.66   To complete the circular ear structure, join the middle surface to the outer edge in the area shown.

Return to the front top edge of the ear, as you need to add a couple of polygons to smoothly integrate the two ear parts in this area:

15. Drag the three vertices selected at the edge of the middle ear, as shown in Figure 10.67, so that they are more closely aligned with the nearby outer ear points (also highlighted). Create two new polygons to connect the two surfaces between these points. Then create a third, three-sided polygon (or tri, as it's known in the trade) to join the last innermost row of the middle ear to the edge of the outer ear.

16. Press **Tab** to make the whole ear a SubPatch surface.

17. Using the Drag (**Ctrl+t**) tool, raise the rear inner edge of the middle ear out from the head a bit so that it forms a distinct ridge.

This ridge continues around toward the earlobe where it kinks slightly and then blends smoothly into the lobe itself. The ridge on the outer ear also starts to blend smoothly into the lobe here.

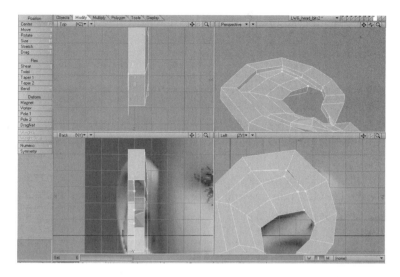

Figure 10.67   Build polygons between the highlighted points to join the top corner pieces together.

18. Weld (**Ctrl+w**) together the row of polygons that form the indent on the outer ridge over the lobe area. Delete the last four polygons on this row. Then weld the vertices on either side of the resulting hole, as in Figure 10.68.

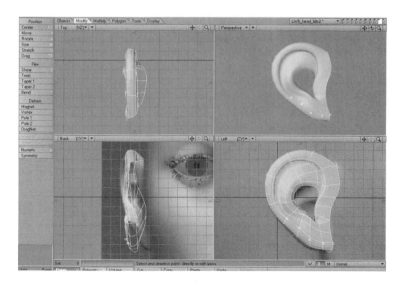

Figure 10.68   The results of welding the four polygons around the lobe.

Before going any further on the interior folds of the ear, it's a good idea to attach the ear to the skull while it's still relatively easy to see what's going where in all the viewports. It's also a good idea to save your work at this point.

19. First, angle the ear in toward the skull by rotating it 20 degrees counterclockwise in the top viewport. Then, rotate it another 10 degrees or so in the back viewport so the bottom moves closer to the jaw area.

Next, you'll use the Extender tool to create another row of polygons off the inner edge of the back part of the outer ear (that is, the polygons that face in toward the skull):

20. Select eight vertices on the back edge in order. Use the Perspective window to do this. You want only the middle eight points. Leave one unselected at either end of the row.

21. Using Extender, move the new points in toward the skull by about 15mm or so. Delete the one back polygon, and make sure the new polygons are facing outward, as in Figure 10.69.

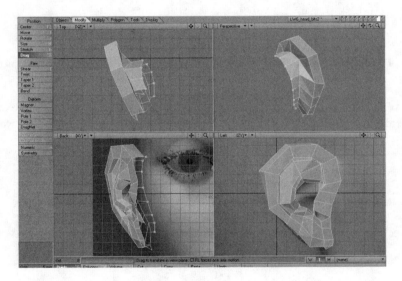

Figure 10.69   Create a row of polygons to connect the outer ear to the back of the skull.

22. Unhide the rest of the head and delete any geometry on the positive side of the X axis that might have been created using the Extender tool.

This should leave half a head and the unfinished ear on the left side. You'll do one side of the head and later mirror the whole thing across.

23. Cut the ear from its layer and paste it into Layer 1. Hide everything except the connecting ear polygons of the ear that you made a few moments ago, as well as the innermost band of skull polygons. It's important here to hide as much geometry as you can to leave yourself a clear view of the join area.

24. Weld (**Ctrl+w**) the border vertices between the ear and the side of the skull, as shown in Figure 10.70. Start from the bottom, near the lobe, and work your way around. Don't go further than the sixth skull polygon. You'll have to weld three ear points to one skull point at some point around the seam, due to the differing number of polygons in each part. Merge (Shift plus the Z key) the two resulting three-sided polygons into one quad polygon afterward (nobody is ever going to really see around here anyway, so a little structural sloppiness doesn't matter).

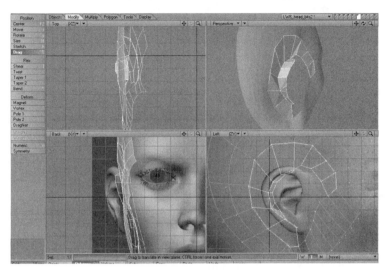

Figure 10.70   Weld the seam between the ear and skull. Note the three ear-piece polygons joined to one skull vertex just up from the lobe.

25. Next, repeat Steps 23 and 24 for the front part of the skull. This time, build connecting polygons to fill in the seam between the front edge of the ear and the cheek. Figure 10.71 shows where. Note that again there are a differing number of head and ear polygons to join at the border edge. The triangular-shaped polygon (it is, in fact, a quad) you see near the bottom of the join in Figure 10.71 takes care of that.

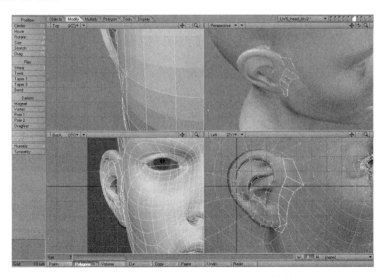

Figure 10.71   Build connecting polygons to join the seam at the front.

Note

It's probably becoming apparent that this final stage is a little messier than earlier stages. This is a side effect of the detail-out approach. This will happen with a human head model, a crazy character, or even an animal. But don't think you've done something wrong. This is all perfectly normal and part of the modeling process.

Unless you have amazing foresight, the last few parts you join to complete the overall mesh tend to mismatch slightly. Here, for example, the ear has more rows of polygons that need joining than the head does.

Although hard to avoid, the trick is to arrange for this to happen in an area of your model where a few untidy seams won't make a big difference. In this case, around the back of the ear where it joins the head is pretty much perfect because the seam will be mostly hidden or lost in a natural crease line and this area hardly needs deforming at all. Also, if you add hair to the model with third-party plug-ins such as Worley Laboratories' Sasquatch, Joe Alter's Shave and a Haircut, or Binary Arts' FiberFactory3, this area will be covered up from view as well.

To finish joining the ear to the head, you have to fill in the two gaps at the top and bottom of the seam. At this stage, it's a case of just trying to get the holes patched up any way you can. Do try to avoid tri polygons as much as possible. If you patch it one way and it creates a visible pinch or ridge in the mesh that you can't get rid of, simply try splitting a few polygons in the offending area and remerging them in a different configuration. It usually takes only a couple of attempts, at most, to get it looking okay.

The following two figures show the gaps filled in. The bottom join in Figure 10.72 is a bit messy but does the job. The top join in Figure 10.73 is actually fairly neat. Don't worry about these joins being perfect. Do the best you can. If it looks right, it is right (conversely, if you see nasty tears or pinches, try again).

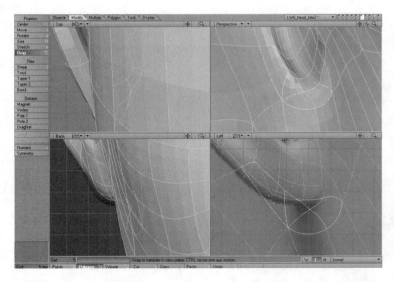

Figure 10.72   The bottom gap patched up—not too neatly, but it works. Sorting it out further would require fairly extensive re-editing of the surrounding surfaces.

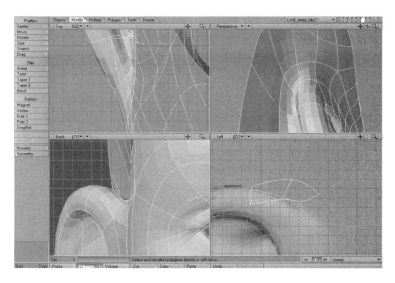

Figure 10.73 Luckily, the top gap is actually much easier to fill, requiring just three polygons to complete the join.

To finish the head model, all that's required now is to go back in and add the inner ear:

26. Select the inward-facing edge polygon halfway down the front edge of the ear hole. Bevel this polygon out three times to create the small ridge that runs into the inner ear, as in Figure 10.74.

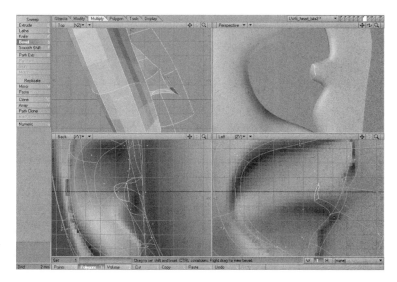

Figure 10.74 Bevel out the highlighted polygon from the forward ear edge.

27. Delete the polygon you have been beveling with. Also delete the three back polygons created by the bevels that face into the skull. Using the Drag tool (**Ctrl+T**), reshape the ridge to smooth it out toward its end, as in Figure 10.75.

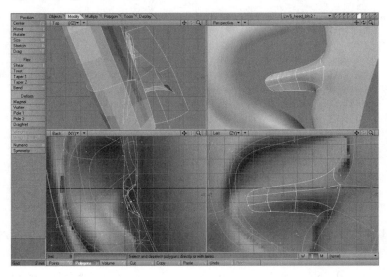

Figure 10.75   The ridge after a bit of reshaping.

28. Using Figure 10.76 as a guide, build a semicircular band of polygons to fill in the remaining gap in the ear between the ridge you just built and the rest of the inner edge. Selecting the correct points to build polygons from can be quite tricky, so take your time. Try hiding as much extraneous geometry as possible to make your job easier. After you've built them, use the Smooth tool a couple of times to iron out any kinks.

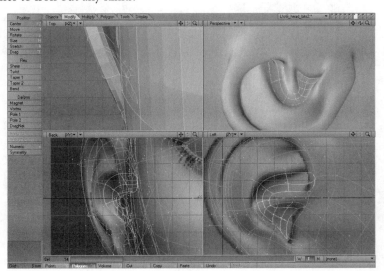

Figure 10.76   The highlighted polygons fill in the remaining gap. Watch that they join to the surrounding geometry without leaving holes in the recessed area behind the front ear.

29. Select the bottom four polygons you just made and smooth-shift them into the ear. You might have to numerically set the Smooth-Shift angle to 179 degrees for the tool to behave correctly. Move them down and forward a bit in the side view as well, as in Figure 10.77.

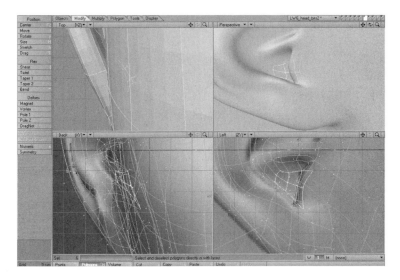

Figure 10.77   Move these four polygons in, down, and forward slightly to finish off the inner ear.

30. Zoom out a bit from the ear and make sure that it blends smoothly into the head, particularly at the front, where it joins the cheekbone and cheek. Again, use the Smooth tool to get rid of any kinks you find. The points highlighted in Figure 10.78 will probably need some attention.

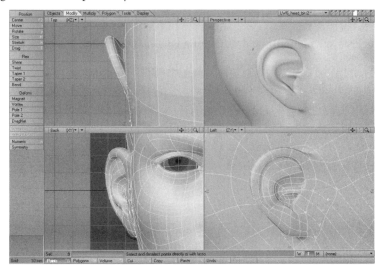

Figure 10.78   Smooth any small bumps or kinks in the front join area.

31. To finish, just mirror the half head over X. Save your work.

Note

Modeling the ear can be the hardest part of your human head-modeling career—but ears don't vary much. Taking the time to do this ear correctly will pay off—save this ear object, and reuse it on future models!

Finishing Touches

Believe it or not, the head modeling is complete! You have successfully created a young woman's face. Get ready to apply textures to the face to bring her to life. First, make some final tweaks to the model.

Final Tweaks and Asymmetry

Have another look at the whole head and refine any areas you still think aren't quite right with the Smooth and Drag tools. You can spend a lot of time at this stage changing little bits here and there. When you're happy with the model, save it! It's also a good idea to add in a little asymmetry at this point too. Although it's convenient to build a computer-generated head as two symmetrical halves, heads and faces in real life are never perfectly symmetrical. Giving your model a few tweaks to knock it out of perfect balance will give that extra hint of believability and get away from the "too-perfect" look typical of computer-generated imagery.

Some examples of what you might do:

- A lopsided nose
- One eyebrow higher or at a different angle than the other, a la Sean Connery
- One of the eyes a different shape than the other
- One ear that sticks out more
- A light twist in the lips to one side or the other

Unless you are deliberately modeling some poor, misshapen soul, don't go overboard. Subtle changes to one side of the face or the other will usually suffice.

Tip

To really see how different two sides of a face are, take a photograph of your own face. With two copies, cut the pictures in half. Put the two left halves together, and then put the two right halves together. It will look more like a relative of yours than your actual face. Think of this when creating computer-generated people in LightWave.

Eyelashes

Just to add that all-important final detail, you also need some eyelashes.

There are several approaches to eyelashes, depending on the task at hand:

- Use clip or transparency mapped polygons
- Use two-point polygons
- Build them from 3D tubes

Exercise 10.19   Building Eyelashes

Because this tutorial is about realistic heads, you're going to build your model's eyelashes from 3D tubes. If you don't have a hair generation program, such as Binary Arts' Fiber Factory 3, eyelashes can take a little while to make, and they're not good as morph targets either; however for close-up renders, the results are worth the effort.

1. To start, go to an empty layer and build a long, thin cone. It should have three segments and four sides, be about 10mm long and .4mm in diameter, and have a thin end pointing into –Z. You can use the Numeric panel for adding specific values.

2. Bend it up at the thin end and delete the cap polygon at the other side. You should have something similar to Figure 10.79.

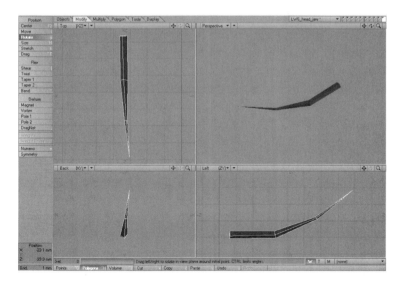

Figure 10.79   A single eyelash.

3. Change the Surface name (**q**) to Lashes and Move (**t**) it into place against the inner corner end of the left upper eyelid on the head. You'll need to place the head model in a background layer for visibility. The eyelash should be right against the lip of the eyelid. Rotate (**y**) it around its base slightly until you feel it's pointing the right way (the background images should help here).

4. Select the lash if it's not already selected and do a quick copy and paste. Rotate the new eyelash slightly and size or stretch it a bit along its length. Then move it along the length of the eyelid 1mm or so.

5. Copy and paste again and repeat the Rotation, Scale, and Move operations.

6. Repeat these steps several more times until you have a small clump of lashes, as in Figure 10.80. Around 10 lashes should be fine.

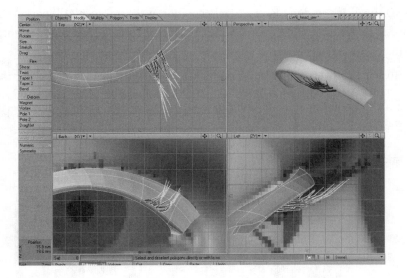

Figure 10.80   Ten lashes pasted in makes a clump.

7. Select the whole clump, copy and paste it, and move the selected clump along the eyelid edge just enough so that it butts up against the pasted clump. Rotate it slightly to account for the change in curvature of the eyelid, and stretch (**h**) it slightly outward on the Z axis.

8. Repeat this copy and paste process along the whole length of the lid. It should take about 15 or so clumps to complete the row of eyelashes. When you're past the center of the lid, start sizing (**Shift+h**) them in slightly on Z rather than out. This way, they will be longest in the middle and shorter at both ends.

9. When you're finished, go along the row using the Drag tool, and tweak the odd individual lashes a bit (that is, move, rotate, and size them slightly, just to add a bit more randomness).

10. Select the entire lash and mirror it on Y just at eye level to create the bottom set of lashes. Use the Modify tools—Magnet, Stretch, Move, Bend—to adjust the lashes' shape to fit the bottom lid. The bottom lashes are slightly sparser and shorter than the top ones, so drag out a couple of the longer lashes from the bottom set. Mirror the whole lot over X.

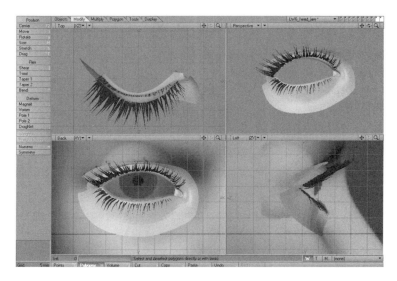

Figure 10.81   The finished lashes.

11. Use Smooth Scale to adjust the lashes if you think they're too thin or thick. Save your work. Figure 10.82 shows the finished model.

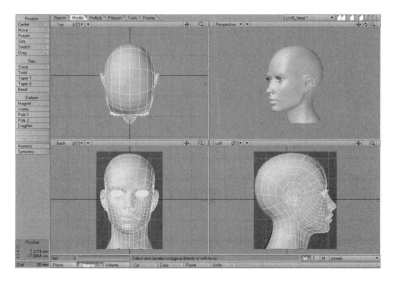

Figure 10.82   The finished head model.

Modeling Summary

Now that you've finished modeling the head, here's a brief recap of the major points of this section:

- SubPatch surfaces are great for modeling freeform organic surfaces such as heads. But to get the best out of them, give some thought to the underlying structure of the control cage. An easily editable cage relies on the following:

  Get the grid-like structure of the control cage to flow with the natural contours of the model. Your model will be easier to read in wireframe, and it makes shaping the surface predictable and straightforward.

  Get the right number of control polygons to achieve the appropriate curvature in various parts of the model. Too many and the surface will be hard to shape, too few and you won't get the definition you need.

- To tackle complex subjects such as heads, break them down first into smaller, more manageable parts.

- Prioritize which parts are the most important in the model and start with them. On a face, these are the mouth and eye areas.

- Use background templates or images so that you don't lose track of the bigger picture. This helps keep the head's proper proportions.

- Model each part independently, concentrating on achieving the optimum polygon structure.

- Quickly lay down the control cage geometry—a row of points. Spend the time on actually sculpting the SubPatch surfaces into shape. Select individual bands of points or polygons at a time to work on if you're having trouble.

- "Grow" new geometry out of the existing mesh—using the Extender tool or any other means—when you can. This helps keep your polygon structure consistent (and it's generally quicker).

- Where the separate areas eventually meet, try to find elegant ways of joining them together:

  Use five- (and three-) patch intersections of quad polygons rather than triangles.

  Plan ahead and try to get areas that will join up to have a similar number of polygons at the border edges.

  Have the seams occur in the natural creases of the model.

  If the final parts of the model are tricky to join, hide any untidy seams in places where they won't matter.

UV Mapping

Too often, when creating objects such as a human head, proper texturing becomes difficult. Textures in LightWave have traditionally been applied to the X, Y, and Z axes. Although this is perfect for most texturing applications, from time to time you might need to map around curved objects.

Often, cylindrical or spherical mapping can be used, which is a global map using a linear interpolation along two axes, such as Y and Z. This method means that the object shape has no bearing on how the texture is applied. Objects such as a human can greatly benefit from UV mapping. UV mapping sets up a relationship of not one, but two dimensions of an image, the U and the V. This relationship is combined with the three dimensions of an object, the X, Y, and Z.

> **Note**
>
> It's important to note that standard projection mapping is accurate across the surface of your model. UV mapping is technically accurate only at small sample points. LightWave interpolates the surface for the large areas in between the sample points. Adjusting the sample points so that the interpolated areas look right is often difficult to do.

Simply put, UV mapping enables you to tack an image onto your model. The points of the model act as tacks, and adjusting any of these tacks adjusts the UV-mapped image. So far in this chapter you've learned how to model a human head. Now imagine the human head was a real object that you could see and touch. If you took a large picture printed on a piece of fabric or rubber, you could stretch the image around the head model to form a perfect fit. This is essentially what UV mapping will do.

Exercise 10.20   Applying UV Mapping

This exercise will introduce you to UV mapping in LightWave 6. The process is simple and can be applied to any object you create, not just human heads.

1. Open Modeler, and load the 10BlankHead.lwo object. This is the same head model created in the beginning of this chapter, but with only one surface name applied to the entire head.

2. Press the **a** key to fit the head into view. Select just the first layer of the object. Figure 10.83 shows the object loaded with only the first layer selected.

3. Select the T button at the bottom right of the Modeler interface, between the W and M buttons. This is the Texture Map button. From the drop-down list next to the T button, select New. The Create Texture Map panel will appear, as in Figure 10.84.

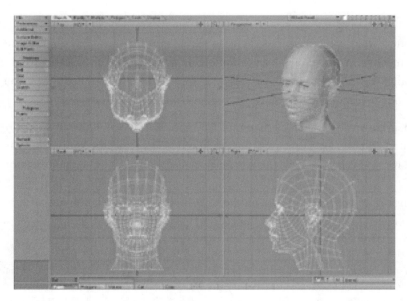

Figure 10.83   The 10BlankHead.lwo object has only one surface for the entire head. UV mapping can help you tack an image to the entire surface.

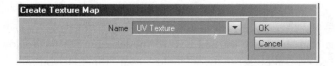

Figure 10.84   The Create Texture Map panel appears when selecting New from the Texture
mode drop-down list.

4. Type in the name UV_Head, or something similar. You do not need to add the
UV letters in the name, but it's a good habit to get into for keeping organized.
After you enter the name, click OK.

5. Set the Viewport 1 display style to UV_Texture, as in Figure 10.84. You'll see a
small grid appear in the viewport. Then set the viewport 2 rendering style to
Texture. You won't notice a change with this viewport yet, but you will when the
UV texture is applied.

6. Be sure that nothing is selected, and from the Tools tab, select MakeUV's.

This will call up the Assign UV Coordinates panel, as in Figure 10.86. Here, you
can assign what mapping type you want the UV Texture to set up a relationship
with.

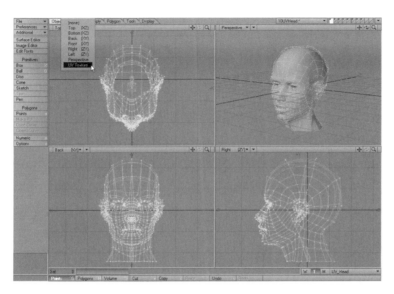

Figure 10.85   At the top of each viewport, you can determine the rendering and viewport display styles. Here, the display style is set to UV_Texture.

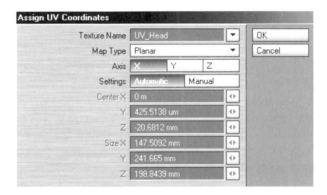

Figure 10.86   The Assign UV Coordinates panel creates the relationship between the UV and X, Y, and Z axes of the model. It will also unwrap the model as well.

You'll see that in the Texture Name area, the name you set in Step 4 now appears. If you set up multiple UV texture maps, you could select those from the drop-down list.

7. Set the Map Type to Cylindrical, and the Axis to Y. Make sure the Settings value is set to Automatic.

These values will tell LightWave that you want to tack your image around the head, as if it were a tall cylinder. However, the UV map will seamlessly map your model. This step sets up the starting values for the UV map. If you did not have this command to work with, you would have to create them from scratch, defining each point.

8. Click OK, and you'll see what looks like a flat wireframe of the front and back of the head model in Viewport 1, as in Figure 10.87.

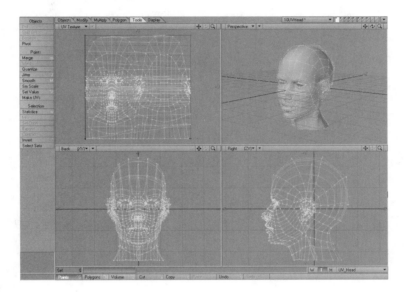

Figure 10.87   Creating a cylindrical UV map on the Y axis creates what looks like a flat, unwrapped image of the model.

Don't let this flat mesh fool you, however. Your model is not really unwrapped or changed. What you see is a representation of how the UV map will be applied. You can make this viewport full frame, and with a screen-capture program (or sometimes the print screen button on PCs) you can create a screen grab of the unwrapped UV and bring it into your favorite paint program, such as Adobe's Photoshop, or NewTek's Aura 2.0. Figure 10.88 shows the screen grab in Photoshop, cropped to just the mesh.

9. Open the Surface Editor in Modeler, from the Objects tab. Move the panel to the lower right of the interface so that the two top viewports are visible. Then, select the BlankHead_Skin surface, and click the T button for Surface Color to apply a texture map.

10. The Layer Type in the Texture Editor should be set to Image Map. Set Projection to UV, as in Figure 10.89.

11. After you've set the Projection to UV, the UVMap listing appears. From the drop-down list, select the surface you set in Step 4, UV_Head.

12. For Image, select Load Image from the bottom of the drop-down list, and load the UV_Map.tga image from the Projects/Images/Chapter10/maps/head folder on the book's CD.

The texture will appear on the head in Viewport 2. This is why it was good to set the viewport rendering style to Texture. Figure 10.90 shows the applied texture.

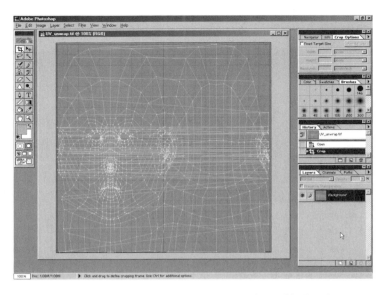

Figure 10.88   The UV texture viewport from Modeler can be grabbed with a screen-capture program and used in a paint package to make a full head image map.

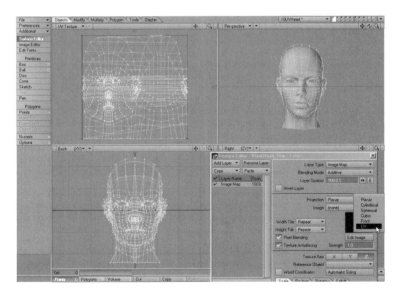

Figure 10.89   When a UV map is assigned, you can apply a texture to it in the Texture Editor, within the Surface Editor.

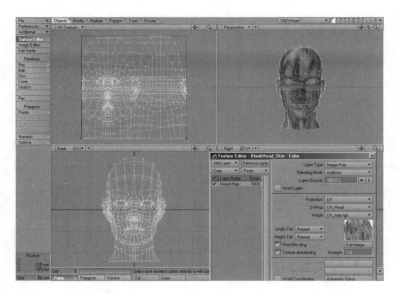

Figure 10.90   After a UV texture is applied through the Surface Editor, it is visible in the viewport with a rendering style set to Texture.

The image you loaded is a painted image, based on the screen grab, as mentioned
in Step 8. You can see from Figure 10.90 that the map lines up almost perfectly
around the entire head. This, friends, is UV mapping.

You're probably saying to yourself, "that's it?" Yes, that's it. The 12 steps listed here show
you how quickly and easily you can set up UV maps for your objects. But there are a few
more things you should be aware of to help you work with UVs.

Note

You can clear any map such as a UV map from an object by first, selecting the map from
the drop-down list at the bottom right of the Modeler interface. Then, either select
Clear Map from Vertices from the Additional drop-down list, or simply press the underscore (_) key to remove the map. This works for Weight Maps, Texture Maps, and
Morph Maps.

Adjusting UV Maps

When you created the UV map in Step 8, you generated an unwrapped mesh of your
object. Although this is only a visual representation, it is also an editable blueprint for
your map. Figure 10.91 shows a close-up of the UV map applied.

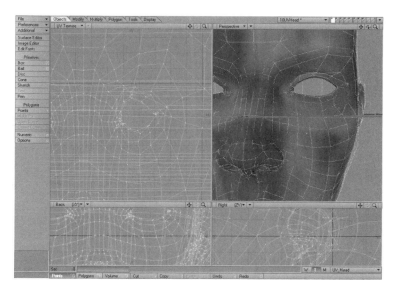

Figure 10.91   When a UV map is created based on the unwrapped polygonal mesh image, you can perfectly line up image placement with UV textures.

You can see that the painted image wraps around the perimeters of the eyes on the head object. Perhaps you'd like to extend the color around the eyes to fall across the nose. By either selecting and moving or using the Drag tool on the points of the nose in the UV_Texture view (viewport 1), you can move the UV map. Although it might seem strange to be dragging points, you must remember that you are only adjusting the placement of the UV texture—you are not changing your model. If you move points in the other views that are not set to UV_Texture, you will be moving points on your model. Figure 10.92 shows the points of the nose in the UV_Texture view selected and moved so that the color from around the eye areas extends across the nose.

> **Note**
> You can select points or polygons in both UV and non-UV viewports to help you identify the related points.

The benefits of UV mapping are obvious when you're trying to:

- Apply textures to organic shapes, such as humans, animals, rocks, and more.
- Apply textures such as labels or decals to a specific position on a model.
- Apply a single texture to an entire single surface for things such as video-game creations.

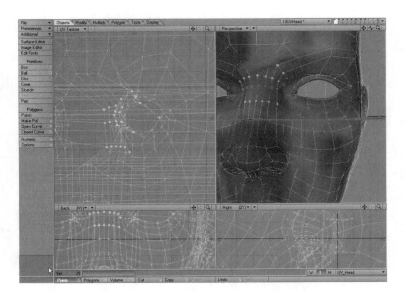

Figure 10.92   By adjusting the points of the UV map in the UV_Texture view, you can move and re-tack the applied UV texture.

You also can use UV maps to bend an object and have its surface image warp with the geometry. This would be impossible, or at the least very difficult, to do with standard projection mapping.

UVs to Weight Maps

Aside from properly placing textures, UV maps can also be converted to Weight Maps. As you build your models and create various UV texture maps, you can easily convert any UV texture to a Weight Map. The benefit of this is that not only can you apply a perfectly precise texture, but also precisely animate that texture with a Weight Map. Figure 10.93 shows the UV to Weight Maps panel. You can find this tool in the Additional drop-down list. Weight Maps are demonstrated next in Chapter 11, "Character Construction."

Figure 10.93   Although UV maps are great for texturing, you can use them for creating Weight Maps with the UV To Weight Maps command, found in the Additional drop-down list.

Select UV Seam

Also under the Additional drop-down list, you can find the Select UV Seam command, which calls up the Find UV Seam Polys panel, as in Figure 10.94.

Figure 10.94   The Select UV Seam command helps you easily select the seam of a UV map.

Why do seams occur when you set up UV maps? They occur whenever your UV map is continuous around an object, such as a head, cylinder, or ball. The problem occurs because a point can have only a single position in UV space. For one polygon, it might start at .9, for example, but it needs to end at a UV point—say, 1.1. But, for the neighboring polygon, that same point needs to start at .1. Unfortunately, the single point can have only one UV value, and .1 wins. This makes the surface use the wrong part of the image and even inverses it. UV space normally goes from 0 to 1. However, you can have points beyond this, such as 1.1.

So, the solution to eliminating seams in your UV maps is to unweld the points at the seam of the model where the image meets. This creates duplicate geometry points at the same location. You could then have different UV positions for the previously contiguous polygons.

The Select UV Seam command locates the seam polygons, but it does not create new polygons. It adjusts the surface to what it thinks the right values are and then automatically creates per-polygon UVs. These polygon-level UV values essentially lock in the UV values for the selected polygons.

Note

The Select UV Seam command selects polygons where the difference between the U's and the V's is greater than .5. It assumes these are seams, but they might not be.

Lock UVs to Poly

The Lock UVs to Poly command locks the UV values for the selected polygon's points. If you subsequently move the UV points, it will have no effect on the surface that uses those polygons. The Lock UVs to Poly command can be found under the Additional drop-down list. Figure 10.95 shows the panel.

Figure 10.95   The Per-Polygon UV Map panel appears when the Lock UVs to Poly command
is selected from within the Additional drop-down list.

UV Mapping is a great addition to the LightWave texturing toolset. Remember that you
can use this technique to apply textures to any type of model you create, especially more
organic ones. Even things such as a long winding road with hills, or the rings around a
planet, can benefit from UV mapping because it tacks an image into place. Experiment
on your own using existing models, or any from this book's CD. Try making unique textures such as clown faces for humans, cool stripes for a tiger, or spots for a dog using your
favorite paint package. Then, apply that image using UV mapping in Modeler.

Rendering the Head

Although your model is complete, the key to creating the final render is surfacing and
rendering. The next part of this chapter will take you through some quick surfacing and
texture-mapping techniques for heads and faces. You don't have to be a genius with a
graphics tablet to use these techniques. They will simply give you a rough guide on how
to best use LightWave 6's lighting features when rendering your head model.

Texture Mapping

When surfacing any object, the first step is usually to decide on how to map it. There are
several ways you could map your head object in LightWave 6—for example, cylindrical,
spherical, planar, UV as described previously—each with their own advantages and disadvantages. The techniques outlined below make use of a compound approach, using
different mapping types layered on top of each other and blended with alpha matte
images. You'll use a cylindrical map for the base layer, as it's easy to wrap around the
whole head and is well-suited to creating broad areas of texture, and then specific planar
maps for the eyes and mouth, areas that require much more accurate placement of specific detail. The technique described here is often better than UV mapping, but as always
the choice is up to you.

Exercise 10.21   Preparing the Surfaces

The easiest way to isolate the various areas for mapping purposes is just to give them a
different surface. That way, you can simply use auto-size to make sure that your texture
map will fit properly.

1. Select the entire head skin surface of the head and assign it to a new surface (**q**). Call it Skin Head.

2. Select the polygons that make up the left eye area (see Figure 10.83) and assign them to another new surface. Call it Skin Left Eye.

3. Repeat Steps 1 and 2 for right eye area. Select the same polygons on the right eye that you did for the left eye. Assign the right eye polygons to their own surface: Skin Right Eye.

4. Select the mouth area polygons and assign them to their own surface as well. Call them Skin Lips. You can see the eye and mouth areas with their newly assigned surfaces in Figure 10.96.

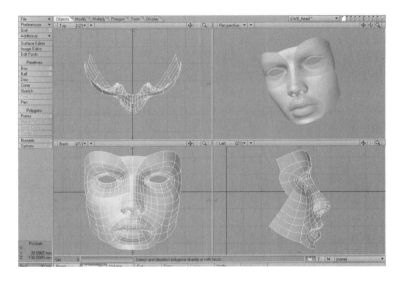

Figure 10.96   Give the eye and mouth areas their own specific surfaces, shown in gray here.

 Note

Each of the four main mapping areas on the face—the head in general, the two eyes, and the mouth—will require a template image to guide you when painting the texture maps in Photoshop. You need to make these templates in the same manner they will be mapped in LightWave—that is, a cylindrical template for the general head base layer and Z axis planar templates for each eye and the mouth.

The three planar map templates are easy to create because Modeler provides you with the needed projection in the back viewport. For each surface—Skin Left Eye, Skin Right Eye, and Skin Lips—perform the following steps:

5. Select the relevant surface and make everything else invisible by hiding (Display tab) the selected polygons. Expand out the back viewport so that it fills the

Modeler viewing area. Do this by moving the mouse over the viewport and pressing **0** on the numeric keypad. Pressing it again will return the view to the previous view configuration. Then use the Fit All command (**Ctrl+a**) to zoom instantly to selected polygons. Also, set this viewport to Wireframe Shade if it's not already, as it gives the clearest view of the geometry for painting over.

6. Press the Print Screen button on your keyboard, or use a screen capture program to grab a view of the Modeler interface.

   This will write a copy of everything you see on your monitor screen into your system's clipboard.

7. Open Adobe Photoshop and make a new image. The default parameters should already be set properly to match the clipboard, so leave everything as is and click OK.

8. Paste in the screenshot you took. You should now be looking at a copy of your Modeler screen in the Image window.

9. Flatten all layers, then crop the image to the extents of the visible geometry in the front view. Save the template image as a .psd (Photoshop) file. Figure 10.97 shows the completed template for the left eye. Treat the right eye and mouth areas in the same way.

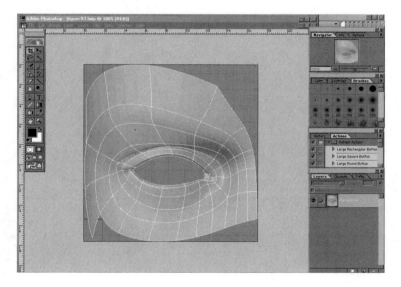

Figure 10.97   The left eye template. Crop your image so that the borders just meet the outer extents of the visible surface on all four sides.

The cylindrical map for the head surface requires the use of a small LightWave Modeler plug-in, helpfully provided by Ernie Wright. If you don't already have it installed, you will find a plug-in called unwrap.p on the CD that accompanies this book.

After installing unwrap.p into LightWave Modeler, use it to create a cylindrical template for the head:

10. Back in Modeler, select the whole head object (complete with the eye and lip surfaces) and copy this to a new layer. Press the **Tab** key to turn the SubPatch geometry on this new copy back to polygons, and then center (**F2**) it on all three axes. (For Texture Auto-Size to work properly later, the geometry needs to be absolutely centered in Modeler's coordinate system.)

11. Select Unwrap from the Additional Tools tab and enter the following into the dialog box that will appear:

   - Texture type   cylindrical
   - AXIS   Y
   - Image width   2000
   - Image height   1000

12. Click OK and Unwrap will ask you for the name and location of the 2-bit (black and white) .iff file it will save.

   If you look at this .iff file in Photoshop now, you can see that it consists of a perfectly "unwrapped" cylindrical projection of the polygons that make up the head—hopefully just like the example shown in Figure 10.98. The image needs to be quite large to hold the textural detail for such a relatively large surface area.

13. Convert the image first to grayscale, and then to RGB color and save it as a Photoshop file. Call it head_base.psd.

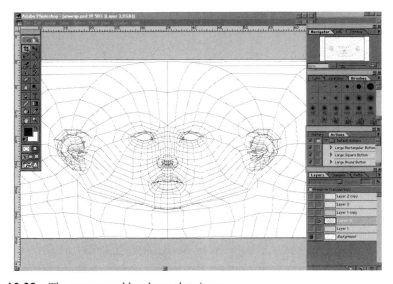

Figure 10.98   The unwrapped head template image.

Exercise 10.22   Creating the Base Texture Maps

Although it is often desirable to spend a lot of time intricately painting detailed maps for the whole face—an old man's head, for instance, would require a lot of time painting wrinkles, pores, blemishes, warts, and so on—it is not necessary for the young woman's head you have created for this tutorial. Some relatively simplistic textures that break up the surface giving the impression that the character's virtual skin is organic and imperfect, as it would be in real life, with the addition of some basic makeup techniques to pick out the eyes and lips, is all that's really needed. Remember, this is the Organic Modeling chapter after all!

The base cylindrical mapping will be used on all four surfaces—the left eye, right eye, lip area, and head—to create subtle but appropriate variations in color as well as the other texture channels across the skin. Achieving this in Photoshop is a fairly simple task. Only the eye and lip area planar maps—the detail maps—that will be applied over this base layer will require any painting work that might require a steady brush hand.

A few quick tips on using Photoshop layers when creating texture maps in general:

- Try as much as possible to paint discrete elements of any surface into their own separate layers. This enables you the make changes quickly and easily.

- You can then create all the various types of maps needed—that is, color, specular, bump, and so on—by recombining, duplicating, and altering the visibility, opacity, and overlay mode of selected layers in one Photoshop file.

- Often, you will need a feature dark in one kind of the map and light in another—for example, an eyebrow or a beauty spot would generally need to be dark in the color map and light in the bump channel because it is a raised feature. To achieve this, simply paint it once in its own layer, and then duplicate this layer and invert it.

- Working this way also allows a lot of flexibility when altering or changing things. Going back to the previous example, the beauty spot is easy to get rid of if you don't like it and without changing anything else. Just switch off or delete the relevant layers. This would be much harder to do if you had painted the beauty spot directly onto an underlying texture.

- Similarly, by using Photoshop layers as much as possible, it is a simple matter to adjust the positioning of one feature or several together on the map without damaging underlying work—for example, you could move both the bump and color versions of an eyebrow over the face as one unit simply by linking them in the Layers palette and moving them as one layer. (Click the small box next to the Visibility icon on any layer to link it to the active one. You should see a small chain symbol to denote its linked state.)

Back to the specific task at hand. If you need to see clear color examples, look at the .psd files on the CD for reference. Texturing is definitely an area where it's good to experiment a lot with combinations of various techniques—for example, photographic close-ups of skin, different combinations of noise types and filters, or, for the more artistically inclined, painting in the detail by hand. Finding your own unique methods for texture-mapping is, together with lighting, the main opportunity you have for defining your own particular look and style.

1. In Photoshop, open the cylindrical head_base.psd you saved previously and add a new layer. Call it Color Base.

   This layer will be used to give the skin color a slightly mottled look, suggestive of the way blood vessels just underneath the skin vary the color over its surface. You can do this any way you like, but the following steps will give you a good, quick result:

2. Select a foreground color approximate to a neutral skin tone. Somewhere around R 254, G 195, B 165 gives a good, light-skinned look (though you may prefer something else). Select Fill to flood the entire layer with this color.

3. Use the Noise filter on the layer, set to Gaussian. A low amount, around 10 to 20, should be fine. Now apply a gaussian blur to the layer. A radius of around 2 should smooth out the noise nicely.

4. Next, apply some grain (Texture submenu). Set the grain type to Clumped, but don't put the intensity up too high—don't make the image too grainy. You only want to add skin variations.

5. Finally, select the Paint Daubs filter from the Artistic Filter menu. Set it to Simple, brush size around 8, sharpness quite low—around 3 or so—and apply that.

   Feel free to repeat the last couple of steps a few times. The Fade Filter tool is also useful for altering the results of a filter after you've applied it. In any case, you want to end up with a subtle textured effect, with hues ranging from yellowish to reddish pink. The colors should blend to a nice, uniform skin tone if you squint at the image.

6. Now, add another layer. Call this one Blush. You're going to use this one to add some pinker hues to the underlying base, simulating areas where the face would be naturally redder (nose, ears, cheeks) or even where blusher might be applied as makeup (generally just under the cheekbones and around the outer corners of the eyes). Using a separate layer makes it easy to adjust the strength of the effect by altering the layer opacity.

7. Swap the foreground and background colors and change the foreground swatch to a shade slightly darker and pinker than the previous one: e.g., R 240, G 170, B 140.

8. Choose the Airbrush tool with a large brush—100 or above—but with a low pressure setting. Set the opacity for the previous color base layer at around 80%.

This should enable you to see the unwrapped polygon template underneath the new layers

9. Make sure the top blush layer is selected and paint on some blusher using the background template layer as a guide to where you lay down the color. Some soft strokes around the cheeks, over the tip of the nose, and earlobes should be fine.

Don't worry if you overdo it a bit. You can always lower the opacity of the blush layer to compensate. In fact, you will almost definitely need to tweak it up or down after doing the first test renders later.

10. Use the Eraser tool to remove any unwanted blusher.

As a final touch for the color layers, and because the model is a bit bald anyway, add a bit of stubble around the skull area for a newly shaved look:

11. Once again, add a new layer. This time call it Stubble.

12. Set the foreground color to a slightly bluish dark gray—for example, R 105, G 115, B 125. Fill the stubble layer with this color.

13. Press the Quick Mask Mode button at the bottom of the toolbar. Use the Airbrush with intensity set to 100% to paint in a mask over the shaved area at the top of the head, stopping where the hairline would be (remember to go around the ears!).

14. Apply a lot of noise to the quick mask. An amount of about 500 should be fine.

15. Use the Fade Filter option set at 100% Screen mode to remove the noise from the original unmasked area.

16. Press the Standard Mode button to make the quick mask into a selection. Select Cut from the Edit menu.

This will remove most of the gray, leaving behind a layer of stubble-like grain sitting on top of the base color. Again, use the layer opacity to control the strength of the effect to suit and, perhaps, a small amount of gaussian blur to smooth it out a little. Your Photoshop file should now look like Figure 10.99.

These three layers together will form the color map.

17. Make sure all the new layers are visible and that the base color's layer opacity is back at 100% and then choose Select then All (**Ctrl+a**).

18. Choose Copy Merged from the Edit menu to copy the combined layers to the clipboard.

19. Make a new image (again, Photoshop should have altered the default image sizes to suit the clipboard image) and paste the combined layers you copied in Step 18.

20. Finally, select Flatten Image from the Layer menu for the new image and save it as head_colour.png. The image format is up to you. The .png format has good lossless compression.

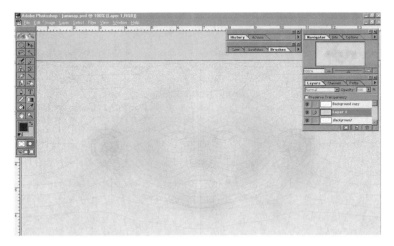

Figure 10.99   The first layers form the head color texture. Here the base layer has been reduced in opacity to see the template layer underneath.

Next, you need to add some more layers for the bump and specular features for the 3D model.

Note

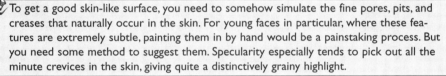

To get a good skin-like surface, you need to somehow simulate the fine pores, pits, and creases that naturally occur in the skin. For young faces in particular, where these features are extremely subtle, painting them in by hand would be a painstaking process. But you need some method to suggest them. Specularity especially tends to pick out all the minute crevices in the skin, giving quite a distinctively grainy highlight.

One way to do this is to combine several layers, each containing a different sort of detail. Figure 10.100 shows two examples that are used in the example texture maps on the CD.

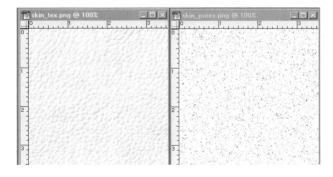

Figure 10.100   Two examples of fine detail textures used to create the skin bump map.

Note

The image on the left in Figure 10.100 is an adapted scan of some fine-detail leather grain. This has the familiar cellular look of tiny crisscrossed creases representing the fine wrinkles in the skin surface. The image on the right was made using repeated applications of the Noise, Gaussian Blur, and Grain tools, with Fade Filter frequently used with either the Screen or Multiply apply modes to modulate the effects of the filters. Both images are supplied for you on the CD: skin_tex.png and skin_pores.png.

To combine these elements into the bump map:

21. In the head_base_psd image, duplicate the base color layer. Call this copy Texture Base and desaturate it because you only need grayscale values for the other texture channels. This layer will be used as the base texture for both the specular and bump maps.

22. Adjust the tonal levels slightly so that the image is a bit darker. It's good for the base to approach a mid-gray so that you can both darken and lighten bits for the bump map. Move this new layer to the top and hide the other color layers for now.

23. Open skin_tex.png and reduce it to 200 by 200 pixels.

    This will bring it down to a more appropriate scale relative to the head map.

24. Using Photoshop's level adjustment (Image/Adjust/Levels), move the white point in slightly, compressing the tones toward white.

25. Choose Select All (**Ctrl+A**) and choose Define Pattern in the Edit menu.

    This copies the selection to Photoshop's pattern buffer.

26. Go back to the head base image and make a new layer. Call it Wrinkle Bump and set its Apply mode to Multiply.

27. Choose Fill from the Edit menu and select Pattern in the Use: Drop Down menu. Click OK. The layer should now be filled with the crease texture, which will selectively darken the underlying base texture.

    Now do the same for the pores:

28. Make a new layer for the pores. Call it Pore Bump and again set it to Multiply.

29. Open skin_pores.png, select all, then choose Define Pattern.

30. Go back to the head base psd image and fill the newly made layer with the pores pattern.

    Finally, you need a bump layer for the stubble:

31. Duplicate the color stubble layer, invert (**Ctrl+i**) the layer, and move it to the top of the Layers list. Rename it Stubble Bump.

32. Hide all the color layers (by selecting the small eye icon in the Layers list), then save a bump map by selecting the whole image and doing a copy-merged from the Edit menu. You must be in an active visible layer for copy merged to work. Paste this into a new (grayscale) image.

33. Make sure the texture base, wrinkle bump, pores bump, and stubble bump layers are visible. Click the small eye icon beside each layer to switch visibility.

34. Save the new bump map as head_bump.png.

It's good to have a way to control how much these maps affect the rendered skin in LightWave over the various surfaces—for example, the tip of the nose and earlobes, where the skin is pulled tight over underlying cartilage, tend to have much smoother skin than, say, the cheeks or forehead, where the skin has to move and crease a lot.

The simplest way to do this is to create a grayscale layer that you can use as an alpha map to modulate the effects of the fine detail bumps. Figure 10.101 shows an example.

Figure 10.101   The grayscale alpha image used to modulate the bump map.

It's usually not necessary to paint the alpha map with any great finesse. A quick 5-minute job with the airbrush should be fine. Remember to make a new layer and switch off all the layers underneath so that you get a good view of the template background layer for reference.

Use blacks and dark shades where you want to lessen the effects of the bump map (make the surface smoother) and lighten areas where you want it to be at full effect. Everyone's face is different, of course, but as a rule of thumb, the ears, nose, and chin areas should be reasonably free of wrinkles while the forehead, cheeks, and, especially, under the eyes should be at full strength.

To save the map, simply duplicate the layer to a new image, then convert this new file to Grayscale mode (Image/Mode/Grayscale).

To save memory later on, reduce the image size (say, to 25% of the original size) as well. There's no particular need for the alpha map to be at a high resolution because it doesn't contain that much detail.

Last but not least, you need a specular map.

The specular layer should be painted in the same manner as the bump alpha image. The only big difference should be around the ears where the image needs to be fairly light. Due to their waxy nature, the ears tend to be reasonably shiny (relative to the drier skin around them). The white or brighter areas of a specularity map will tell LightWave to apply more shininess where dark areas are duller.

Mix in a bit of the bump layers to break the specular map up as well. Figure 10.102 shows an example specular layer.

Figure 10.102   Treat the specular map shown here in a similar manner to the two bump alpha mattes.

Save the specular layer on its own by using the Duplicate/Layer/New command (right-click on the layer). Remember to change the image to grayscale before saving.

This map also can be used in the new glossiness texture channel to help vary the sharpness of the specular highlight across the skin. (The purists among you might want to go as far as painting a separate custom map for this too.)

Remember to save the final head template psd file as well, just in case you want to change anything after you start doing renders. In general, you will want to make changes to the psd file and then save these to the specific maps that will be used in LightWave.

Exercise 10.23   Creating the Detail Maps

With the base layer textures done, move on to the smaller, more specific maps for the eyes and mouth areas.

Start with the lips:

1. Open the mouth template .psd and create a new layer. Call it Lip Alpha.
2. Fill the new layer with pure black, and then lower the layer opacity so that you can clearly see the underlying template. Using the Pen tool, draw a shape representing the outer edge of the lips. It should encompass the area where lipstick

would be applied on a real pair of lips. Make this path a selection, with a Feather radius of 2 and antialiased.

3. Fill the selection with pure white. Deselect and blur the black/white border a bit at the outer lower edges of the bottom lip.

   You have created the alpha matte that you will use later to blend the lip textures over the base layers on the head—the skin texture. The upper left image in Figure 10.103 shows the finished alpha map.

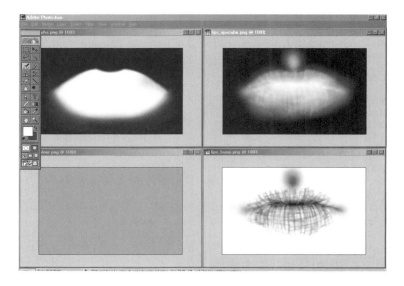

Figure 10.103   All four planar maps for the mouth area, clockwise from the top left: the alpha matte, the specular map, the bump map, and the color map.

4. The color map is easy to create. Just choose a suitable lip or lipstick color and fill a new layer with it. The alpha matte will take care of applying this color to the lips only when all images are applied in LightWave.

   The bump layer requires a bit more work. As you can see in Figure 10.103, you need to paint in a few cracks and ridge lines going from the center outward and following the natural curvature of the lips. Although tedious, this is one area that adds great realism to the final render.

5. For the bump layer, make a new layer and call it Lip Bump. Fill it with white. Using a black foreground color and a fine airbrush set at a low pressure, make short strokes from the mouth center out along each lip. A pressure-sensitive graphics tablet will really make your life easier here. Again refer to Figure 10.103.

6. Blur the cracks a bit with the Gaussian Blur filter. Go over them again, this time with an even finer brush set on Multiply mode (from the drop-down selection in the Photoshop Layers panel).

7. Repeat Step 6 until you are happy with the results.

8. Adjust the levels for this layer slightly, pushing the mid-gray arrow in the level graph toward white, compressing the layer. This helps make the strokes more crack-like in appearance.

9. To add the finishing touch, apply the Paint Daubs filter set on Simple with a brush size of about 3 or 4 and sharpness set to 2 or 3. This helps thin out your brushwork and makes the effect look a bit more organic.

   To create the specular layer, simply recombine the alpha matte layer and the bump layer:

10. Duplicate the alpha matte layer, call it Spec Base, and move it to the top of the layers list. Do the same for the bump layer, this time calling it Spec Cracks. Make sure this layer is above spec base.

11. Using the bottom graph in the Levels dialog, cap the upper-white level for the spec base layer at around 150.

    This will have the effect of leaving the lightest parts a mid-gray.

12. Blur this layer to smooth out the lip edge border. Invert the spec cracks layer and set its Apply mode to Screen.

13. Merge this layer down over its spec base. You should now have something similar to the upper-right image in Figure 10.103 that will create a nice, bright highlight on the lips.

14. Save the combined .psd file, and then save the four maps from the various layers as separate .png files. Remember to change the alpha matte, specular, and bump maps to Grayscale mode before saving, as it will save memory later.

    The eye maps are done in exactly the same sort of way as the lips. However, they will require more work.

15. Open the left_eye.psd template.

    You need to borrow some of the base color layer from the head map.

16. Open the head_base.psd file and duplicate the base color layer into the eye template image.

    This will give you a similar color base to work on, and avoid any mismatches between the color around the eyes and the rest of the face. The eye maps will blend in LightWave to reveal the skin map for the head, so the color needs to be a perfect match.

17. Create a new layer above this color base and call it Eyebrow.

18. Lower the opacity on the color base layer so that you can clearly see the eye geometry underneath. Using a fine airbrush set to Multiply, paint in individual eyebrow hairs over the appropriate area of the image—that is, along the eyebrow ridge. Start at the inner edge of the eyebrow and paint each hair outward. Use a Low pressure, and build the eyebrow mass gradually. Again, a graphics tablet is far superior to using the mouse. When you've finished, you should have something like Figure 10.104.

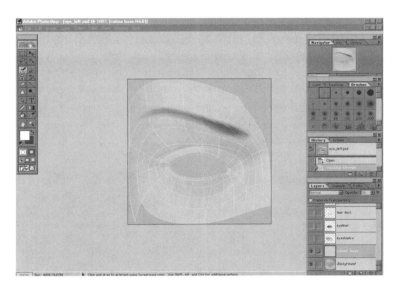

Figure 10.104   The completed eyebrow layer.

You'll be duplicating and adjusting the eyebrow layer for each mapping type later, but for now keep concentrating on the color layers by adding some makeup around the eye.

It's not strictly necessary to add makeup, of course, but it helps blend the tricky border between eyelid, eyeball, and eyelashes, which tends to look a bit unconvincing otherwise. Even adding some dark shading will help bring the eyes out when rendered.

Note

Throughout this book, reference has been a theme. You can pick up a book on basic makeup techniques and apply that information to your Photoshop image map creations.

If you don't use makeup it's probably best to get some reference for this. In today's society you are literally surrounded by images of artfully made-up women, so this shouldn't represent much of a problem:

19. Hide the eyebrow layer for now and add another new layer. Call it Eye-shadow.

20. Choose a suitably fashionable shade, such as blue-gray, and blend a bit of color from the edge of the top lid, toward the outer corner of the eyebrow. Try to get a smooth blend into the skin color as you move away from the eye. Don't worry about the eye-socket edge of the lid.

21. Bring a small amount around the edge of the bottom lid as well, and add another layer on top of the Eye-shadow layer. Call it Eyeliner.

22. Paint in some dark gray using a medium to fine airbrush, being extra careful to follow the edge of the eyelids in the background. Be fairly light in the inner corner of the eye, gradually building more tone as you reach the outer corner. The idea is to accentuate the outer edges of the eyelids. The top lid also should be denser than the bottom lid. Again, try to smoothly blend the color into the base.

23. Paint in some pink over the tear-duct in the inner eye corner on a separate layer as well, just to get rid of any makeup there. Figure 10.105 shows the eye Photoshop file at this stage.

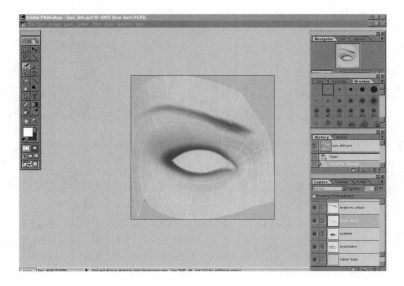

Figure 10.105   The completed color elements arranged in separate layers.

That pretty much does it for the color layers. You can see that having the screen grab reference of the texture area of the model is ideal for creating image maps. You'll see that these maps also line up perfectly when applied in LightWave.

24. To save them as one map, make sure all the layers are visible and that none of the background template geometry is showing through. Then copy-merge the combined layers to a new image. Call it eye_L_colour.png.

For the other attributes, you need to duplicate and reuse these color layers, sometimes altering or inverting them. You also will need to add a few more elements, mainly some fine lines around the bottom lid and outer eye corner for the bump map:

25. Again, borrow a base layer from the head .psd file. Copy-merge all the bump layers (except the stubble layer) and paste this into a new layer—call it Texture Base—in the eye template file.

26. Duplicate the eyebrow layer, invert the copy, and change its Apply mode to Screen (because it will be raised in the bump map). Place this above the texture base and name it Eyebrow Bump.

27. Repeat Step 26 for the eyeliner and eye-shadow layers. Add some noise to these too (makeup tends to have a slightly grainy consistency).

28. Add a new layer set to Multiply and paint in some wrinkles around the bottom lid and outer corner. Use the same techniques you used to paint the lip wrinkles. Paint in just enough to give the suggestion of extra creases and bumps around the eyes. You can see some finished wrinkles in the bump map in Figure 10.106.

29. Again, select Copy Merged on these bump layers and save to a new grayscale file. Call it eye_L_bump.png.

    For the specular map, you can reuse most of the bump map layers. The one major change is to make the eyebrows dark rather than light, as making them specular tends to enhance their texture-mapped nature:

30. Hide the eyebrow bump layer and then duplicate the eyebrows again, this time naming them eyebrow spec. Set Apply mode to Multiply this time. Also, paint in some lighter tones on another layer around the bottom of the eyelids and nose bridge to give a bit more specularity in these areas.

31. With these layers and the texture base, eye-shadow bump, and wrinkle bump layers visible, copy-merged the lot to a new grayscale image for the specular map. Call it eye_L_specular.png.

32. Finally for the alpha matte, make one last layer. Fill it with black, and then lower the opacity slightly so that you can see the layers underneath.

33. Using a pure white airbrush, paint in the matte so that it covers all the underlying eye elements. Be careful to maintain a completely black border on all sides. Figure 10.106 makes this clearer. The alpha matte is at the upper left.

34. Make this layer fully opaque when you have finished, then save it in a new file called eye_L_alpha.png.

35. For the right eye, either duplicate the procedures for the left eye or if your geometry is symmetrical enough to allow it, just flip the left eye maps over horizontally and resave them as right eye versions.

    Figure 10.107 shows the maps for the eyeballs. These are fairly straightforward, so this tutorial won't go into any detail. The figure shows from top left to right:

    - A cylindrical color map with some blood vessels for the eyeballs (they don't require any other map types).

    - Color and specular maps for the iris surface. The color map was made by painting in some rough color, adding noise and grain, and using the Radial Zoom Blur filter. The specular map was adapted from the color version by desaturating and altering levels.

- The last map is a transparency map for the inner edge of the iris—just to soften off the inner iris edge a bit. It tends to look a bit sharp otherwise.

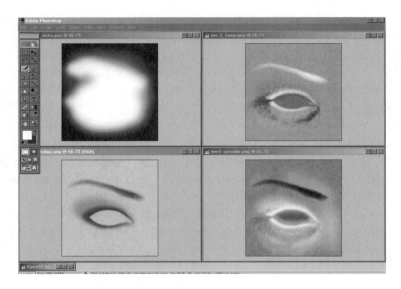

Figure 10.106   The four finished eye maps, clockwise from top left: alpha, bump, specular, and color.

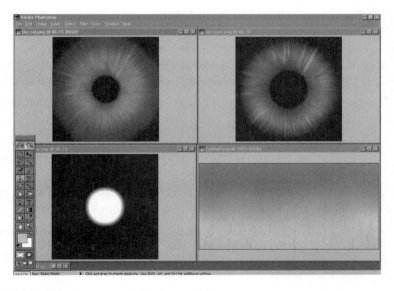

Figure 10.107   The texture maps for the eye objects.

Surfacing and Lighting the Model

Surfacing and lighting can't really be separated from one another. They both have a more or less equal play in how your rendered object will look. Because lights can have such a dramatic effect, it's important to have a decent lighting set-up before you start surfacing. LightWave's default lighting is not a desired set-up. This next exercise will teach you how to set up a basic lighting situation.

Exercise 10.24   A Basic Lighting Rig

1. Open Layout and load the layered head object.

   It should bring in the SubPatch skin mesh, the eyeballs, the corneas, and the eyelashes as separate objects.

2. Parent the corneas to the eyeballs, then parent both the eyeballs and the eyelashes to the head. You can do this in the Scene Editor, or through the Motion Options panel (press **m** for the selected object).

3. Go into the Item Properties tab for the cornea objects (press **p** with the object selected) and make sure the Shadow Casting options are turned off. Do this for both cornea objects. Although these are transparent objects, LightWave still sees their geometry and calculates shadows, making the eyeballs underneath the corneas dark.

4. In the Render panel, turn on all the Raytracing options: Ray Trace Shadows, Ray Trace Reflection, Ray Trace Refraction.

5. Aim the camera so that the girl's head fills the frame well.

   Try tilting the camera up at the subject slightly and just off to one side. Try adding a couple of bones and twisting the head around the neck slightly as well. This will give a bit of tension to the character and make the composition a bit more interesting. Chapter 11 contains more information on bones.

Okay, time to sort out the lighting:

6. Change the default light to a spotlight and change the shadow casting options to Shadow Map. Rename this light Key Light.

7. Increase the Light Intensity to around 130% and make it slightly yellow or off-white. Clone this light two times. Change the first clone's name to Fill Light. Change the second clone's name to Rim Light.

8. Decrease the fill light's intensity to around 50% and tint the color with a bit of blue.

9. Click the No Specularity button and turn off shadow casting.

10. Increase the rim light's intensity to 250%, and decrease the ambient light level to 0%.

Note

You now have the basis for a classic three-light rig. Most lighting set-ups in cinema and still-photography are based on these three types of light:

- Key light is the primary light source and will usually provide most of the direct illumination. It's the dominant source of light in the scene.

- Fill is used to lighten and, hence, soften the areas in the subject that are shadowed by the key light, playing an important part in how much contrast there is in the lighting.

- Rim light generally means light coming from the backside of the subject toward the camera at an oblique angle (usually creating a bright rim around one edge of the subject). It is used to counterpoint the key light, adding interest and drama as well as controlling how much the subject stands out from a dark background.

How you use these three kinds of light (their direction, intensity, softness, and color) together with the choice of camera angle and lens can have a dramatic effect on the mood of a scene. In general, try to come up with interesting lighting schemes. Don't be afraid to drop half the face in shadow, for instance, if it will lend your image a nice dramatic air. A common mistake, particularly when someone has spent a lot of time modeling something, is to bathe every nook and cranny in a broad, flat light from the front with little contrast.

The simplistic set-up in Figure 10.108 (three spots) can be surprisingly versatile and effective in achieving a wide variety of looks and moods. But for now, you just want a nicely lit view of the head with a reasonable amount of contrast so that you can see how the textures react across a range of light and shade.

Figure 10.108   The basic three-light setup.

11. Place the key light above and to the left of the head, just behind the camera. Use the Light view to make sure the head is centered and fills the shadow map area (the light cone angle). Narrow the cone angle if it doesn't.

Tip

You can switch Layout to Light view to help properly aim the lights. You also can change your viewport layout to a multiple view (through the Display Options panel) to keep an eye on placement and effect.

12. Place the fill light to the right and beneath the subject, again just behind the camera, making sure that it's lined up by using the light view.

13. Finally, place the rim light behind, above, and to the left of the subject, looking back toward the camera and the back of the head.

14. Activate VIPER in the Render panel and make a quick test render to make sure you're happy with the light positioning and their relative intensities. Adjust them if necessary. You might want to experiment with alternative light positions, but this set-up works reasonably well for texturing purposes (that is, the figure is well lit without looking boring). Figure 10.109 shows the result. Save your work.

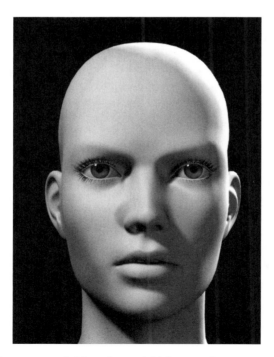

Figure 10.109   The untextured object after an initial test render.

Exercise 10.25   Adding the Maps to the Texture Channels

Now that you have a complimentary lighting rig in place, setting up your surfaces in Layout will be much easier.

1. Bring up the Image Editor and load in all the maps for the face. You should have the following images loaded into Layout when you're finished:

   - Head color
   - Head specular
   - Head bump pores
   - Head bump pores alpha
   - Head bump wrinkles
   - Head bump wrinkles alpha
   - Lips color
   - Lips specular
   - Lips bump
   - Lips alpha
   - Eye left color
   - Eye left specular
   - Eye left bump
   - Eye left alpha
   - Eye right color
   - Eye right specular
   - Eye right bump
   - Eye right alpha
   - Eyeball color
   - Iris color
   - Iris specular
   - Iris transparency

2. Open the Surface Editor and turn on VIPER in the Options panel. As you make changes to the surfaces, they will show up in the VIPER preview immediately, saving you from having to do test renders all the time.

3. Select the skin head surface for editing.

   You're going to set up the head cylindrical textures first because they will be used as a base layer for the other three surfaces.

4. Add a cylindrical map (Y axis, auto-sized) to the color channel and choose the head_colour image. Do the same thing for the specular and glossiness channels, this time using the head_specular image.

5. Again, add a cylindrical map on the bump channel (Y axis, auto-sized) and select head_bump as the image. Copy and paste (using the Add to Layers option) this layer.

6. Change the Blend mode on the copy to alpha and change the image to head_bump_alpha. This will make this map into an alpha channel for the bump below.

7. Double-click the sample sphere.

   This will put a copy of this surface into the preset shelf.

8. Right-click the preset shelf swatch and name the shelf copy Head base.

9. Select the skin lips surface and double-click the head base swatch.

    This will paste the swatch settings into the current surface.

10. Repeat Step 3 for both skin eye surfaces. Make all the skin surfaces double-sided to avoid any shadow errors (otherwise, light can creep in on the backside of the eyeballs).

    For the eyeball surfaces:

11. Apply the color map as a Z axis cylindrical map to the color channel on each eyeball (remember to auto-size).

12. Map the iris color, transparency, and specular files as Z axis planar maps to each iris (again auto-size them).

13. Make the cornea surface 100% transparent, set the cornea specularity to 200%, and set its glossiness high—around 70%.

    This will give a nice, strong highlight in each eye, which is important in creating a feeling that the character has some life.

    The cornea needs to refract the iris as well. The effects of this are particularly noticeable if you look at the eyes from the side.

14. Give the cornea a refraction index of around 1.3. 1.3 is approximately a glass refraction setting. Make the aqueous surface completely transparent. All other channels can be set to 0% (its only purpose is to set a thickness for the cornea for refraction purposes).

    And for the eyelashes:

15. Color the eyelashes a dark gray. Give them a low specularity setting—around 25%—and set the glossiness to around 25% as well.

16. In the Advanced tab, add the Transparent Edges plug-in and set the edges at 0.25 transparent to soften them a bit. Turn Double Sided on for these too. Save your work. That's all for the base skin surfaces set-up. Check the VIPER preview to make sure everything's okay, as in Figure 10.110 (obviously, the eye and lip maps will not be present because you haven't set those up yet).

Note

VIPER does have a few limitations. You'll note that due to the cornea refraction, you won't be able to see the eyeballs behind them without doing a test render.

You might want to tweak some of the surface values at this stage. You can alter the relative strength of effect the maps have on the surfaces by changing the texture layer opacities on the map layers. This works in an almost identical fashion to the way it does in Photoshop. Play these off against the numeric values for each attribute channel. Most importantly, tweak only the values on the head surface and update the mouth and eye area surfaces afterward by using the preset shelf. This ensures that all the surfaces have the same values for the base layers. You don't want a mismatch between the surfaces.

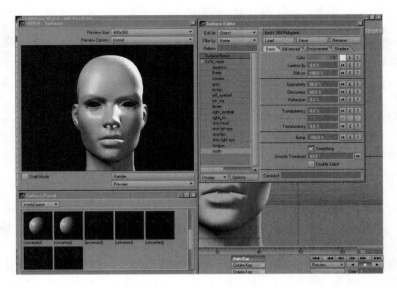

Figure 10.110   The VIPER preview panel is particularly useful when you make fine adjustments.

Here are some sample values after making careful adjustments to the surface:

Color	numeric value: N.A.	texture opacity: 100%
Luminosity	numeric value: 0%	
Diffuse	numeric value: 105%	
Specular	numeric value: 0%	texture opacity: 25%
Glossiness	numeric value: 0%	texture opacity: 30%
Transparency	numeric value: 0%	
Translucency	numeric value: 0%	
Bump	numeric value: 100%	texture opacity: 50%

Alpha opacity: 85%

You might also want to make tweaks to the actual maps themselves, in which case you can use LightWave's built-in editing capabilities in the Image Editor, which are useful for making quick adjustments to things such as map gamma or contrast. If you want to make any changes to the placement or strength of a particular element within one map, though, you'll have to re-edit the original .psd file in Photoshop and resave the texture map.

Exercise 10.26   Adding Details to the Eyes and Mouth

After you are happy with the base textures, it's time to add in the details you painted for the eyes and mouth:

1. Select the mouth surface. The base texture layers from the rest of the head should already be in place.

2. Go into the color channel and add a new layer on top of the existing head color cylindrical map. Make this layer a planar map on the Z axis and auto-size it.

3. Choose the lip color map as the image, turn off height and width repeat for this map, and copy and paste this layer.

4. Change the image in the copy to lip alpha and change the Layer mode to alpha. This layer will now effectively blend the lip color into the head color texture.

   It's the same for the specular, glossiness, and bump channels:

5. Add a new planar map to each channel using the appropriate image file on top of the existing head maps. Make sure the new layers are planar maps on the Z axis and are auto-sized.

6. Copy and paste this, changing the copy to an alpha map using the lip alpha image (make sure that the lip alpha map is the top layer). Save your work.

Again, the alpha map will ensure that the top lip maps blend smoothly into the base texture below, ensuring that there are no sudden changes in surface values.

With VIPER active, you can make any necessary changes to the new texture layer's opacity levels. Make sure that the specular and glossiness values are giving a nice sheen to the lips in particular. This will mean playing with the glossiness map opacity a bit on the lips. Try about 50%.

Applying the eye maps to their respective surfaces is an identical procedure. For each mapped channel, add a planar map with the appropriate image and an alpha layer to blend it in over the existing head maps using the eye alpha maps.

Reduce the layer opacities for the specular and glossiness maps to similar levels to the base head maps—around the 20–35% range.

Do a full-size test render (**F9**) after you've finished making adjustments, just to make sure everything is okay. Figure 10.111 shows the final texture layers applied and set.

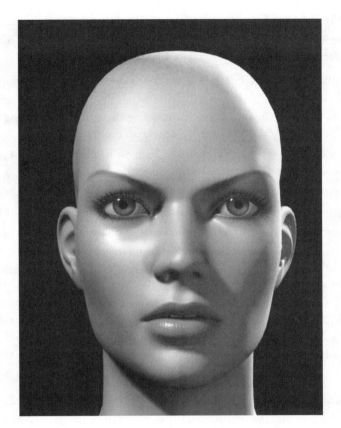

Figure 10.111   A bit of adjustment to the relative strengths of the texture maps is usually required. This test render shows the results afterward.

Realistic Shading Techniques

Although the basic spotlights you have used so far produce reasonable results, things could be better. For one thing, it's hard to get a realistic skin surface just by using standard spot, distant, and point lights. Skin, perhaps more than any other surface, is hard to simulate digitally. The way it responds to light in the real world is complex, compared to the relatively simplistic algorithms used to simulate light and surface interactions in 3D packages, which are more suited to reproducing hard plastic and metallic surfaces. The results often look distinctly less than realistic.

Luckily, LightWave 6 has a few advanced lighting options to enable more realistic shading. Some of these techniques can lead to long render times, but the results are often worth it, generating images that have a quality of light that can look stunningly real.

Area Lights

One of the problems with conventional lights is that the source of illumination is an infinitely small point, something that never happens in the real world. Even the tightest spotlight beam emanates from its source with some volume or area.

The size of this area actually defines the major character of the light, in fact. A small area gives a tight, hard shadow, whereas a large area will give off a soft light that creates diffuse shadows. In real life, you are rarely lit by hard sources of light. Even in direct sunlight, there is enough reflected light from the atmosphere to soften shadows a bit. Photographers and cinematographers often go to some lengths to soften the light falling on their subjects (unless some dramatic effect is called for). Soft light tends to flatter the human face.

LightWave's area lights can be used to give a much softer illumination. To use LightWave's area lights:

- Switch the key and fill lights from spots to area lights in the Item Properties panel.

- Area lights tend to be a bit brighter than their standard counterparts, so set the light falloff options to compensate. This also will add a bit more realism.

- For each light, set the falloff to inverse distance squared and the nominal range to 1 meter. Lower the intensities by about 25%.

With area lights, you also have to consider the size of the illumination surface. As in reality, a large area light will give much softer shading than a small one. Try experimenting with various sizes and note the different feel it gives to the image. Figure 10.112 shows two examples at either extreme. (Also note the difference to the eyes when there is no longer a highlight, as in the left hand render.)

Be prepared to wait a while for LightWave to finish rendering. Area lights take much longer to render than shadow-mapped spots. Realism takes time.

Area lights are expensive on render time, but a big improvement over the spotlights. The skin in particular looks much more realistic now.

Due to the way they are calculated, area lights tend to produce slightly grainy shading. You will notice this especially with large light areas. You can control this to some degree with the light quality setting in the Item Properties panel, but even with a high-quality setting of 4 you will get some grain. Turning motion blur on and increasing the antialiasing level will help smooth it out.

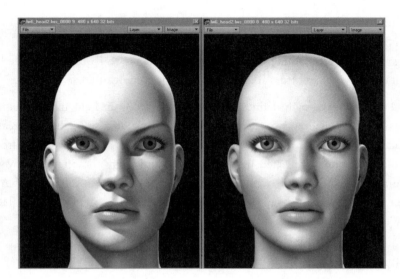

Figure 10.112   The effects of area lighting. The render on the left has the key set to 0.1 meter, the one on the right is set at around 0.8 meter.

Global Illumination

Large area lights (that is, soft lights) pose a bit of a dilemma. The grain just becomes too much of a problem. At this point it's time to use another great feature in LightWave's rendering arsenal: radiosity.

Traditionally, radiosity has been mainly associated with architectural visualization where accurate simulation of the diffuse qualities of light is necessary when designing building interiors. But it can also do wonders for realistic depiction of more human subjects, bringing a subtlety to lighting faces (or anything else, for that matter) that it is almost impossible to get any other way.

Briefly, it is a technique that models the way diffused light bounces off one surface onto another. Rather than a light ray just stopping when it hits a surface (which is pretty much what happens with normal lighting), radiosity takes into account the fact that some of this light will be reflected by the surface onto the objects around it.

Radiosity also opens a host of new options in terms of what you can use as a light source. Anything luminous, including geometry, backgrounds, and even image environments, can create light in the scene. This means that you can now re-create almost any real-world lighting effect using bounce cards to fill in shadows, a luminous box as a soft-box light, or a high dynamic range image mapped environment to re-create the exact global illumination from a real-world location.

Try the following exercise to sample some of LightWave's radiosity features.

Exercise 10.27   Applying Radiosity

1. Make a flat box in Modeler that is 1 meter square on the X and Z axes and assign it the surface bounce card.

2. Save it and load three copies into Layout. Place them so that they occupy the rough positions of the three lights and orient them in a similar manner so that the surfaced sides face the head in the center, as in Figure 10.113.

3. Make the bounce card surface about 500% luminous.

4. Turn off the fill and rim lights completely.

5. For they key light, turn off Affect Diffuse and turn it back to a spotlight.

   The key will now only cast specular light and will have no effect on diffuse shading (radiosity does not take specularity into account, so you still need this one light to create specular highlights).

6. Go into the Global Illumination panel and activate radiosity. Lower the tolerance to 1.5, increase the sample rate slightly, and lower the minimum evaluation spacing parameter to 5mm.

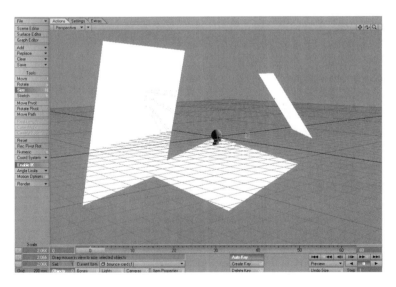

Figure 10.113   These three luminous squares will be used to provide all the diffused light for the radiosity render.

7. Press **F9** to render this (make sure Anti-aliasing is at least set at Enhanced Low and that Motion Blur is on). It might take a while to finish.

   When it's done, have a good look at the results. The subtle differences in the shading make all the difference. In general terms, the image is a big improvement.

There will be some problems, though. The radiosity technique that LightWave uses tends to produce slightly smeary artifacts and you will notice the odd shading discrepancy here and there. You can get rid of these, however. In general, lowering the tolerance and minimum evaluation spacing and increasing the sample rate will produce more accurate results, though unfortunately at the expense of rapidly increasing render times. Using radiosity for all the lighting in a scene like this tends to be prohibitively expensive in terms of the time it takes.

The best solution is to combine some direct illumination from standard lights with radiosity fill light:

8. Clear the bounce card next to the key light and reactivate Affect Diffuse for the key.

9. Press **F9** to re-render the scene. Save your work.

The results this time should be much more acceptable. The artifacts from the radiosity are, in fact, still present, but they are much less noticeable when mixed in with some direct illumination from a standard light. You can even lower the radiosity quality a bit (lower the sample rate and put tolerance up to 2 or 3) without much noticeable difference.

Figure 10.114 shows a comparison between a fully radiosity illuminated head (on the left) and one lit by the key with radiosity fill and rim light (on the right). The render on the right took about one-third the time as the one on the left and has fewer radiosity artifacts, especially around the eyes.

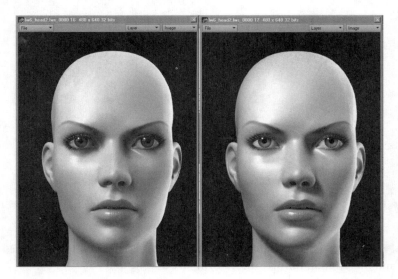

Figure 10.114   For the optimum balance between image quality and speed, mix radiosity fill lighting with shadow-mapped spots or area lights for the key.

Post-Processing: Finishing Touches

No matter how good a rendering engine is (and LightWave has one of the best), you can almost always get a bit more out of an image by using a few post-processing techniques. This is not cheating. All that matters is the final image, not how you get there, and 2D post processing is just as valid as modeling, lighting, or surfacing. In fact, try to think of it as the natural final step in the entire 3D process.

Some things are just easier to do in post. Things such as altering the final tonal and color qualities of an image are much quicker to do in a 2D image application than by constantly tweaking things in LightWave. Plus you have the advantage of being able to change your mind or try a variety of options quickly without having to go back and spend a long time re-rendering a sequence.

Most rendered output also tends to look quite hard-edged—even with radiosity. By adding subtle blooms and glows to bright parts of the image after rendering and even faking a bit of depth of field, you can get a much softer, more photographic feel.

Lastly, post-processing is a great way to make your images more distinctive. It can be hard sometimes to get away from the signature that rendering engines tend to impose. Post processing opens a whole new set of tools to enable you to find a unique look to what you do.

For an example, have a look at Figure 10.115 and compare it with the final rendered result in Figure 10.111. The changes are subtle (less so in color), but they do make a difference.

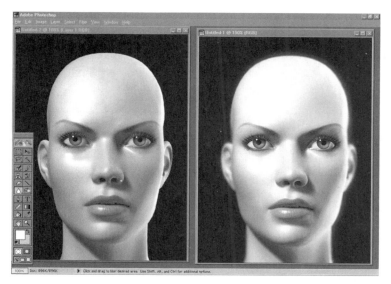

Figure 10.115   A few minutes in Photoshop can transform the final rendered output.

Save the last render and try the following in Photoshop, but remember that this process is fairly subjective. Find settings that suit your personal tastes.

Exercise 10.28   Applying Post-Process Effects

Add some "bloom" to the highlights. This also tends to give your images more of a feeling of atmosphere about them.

1. Copy the whole image and then paste it into a new layer.
2. Set this layer's Apply mode to Screen and reduce the opacity to around 50%.
3. Apply a Gaussian blur at around 10 pixels.

    You should now have a subtle glow over the whole image (the size of the glow is controlled by the blur radius).

4. To control the effect, play about with the Curves command. Generally you want to push up the blacks so that the bloom concentrates around the bright parts of the image.
5. Merge down the bloom layer once you're happy.

Next, try playing with the tonal contrast of the whole image. There are several ways to do this:

- Use the contrast and brightness controls
- Use the Levels panel
- Use the Curves panel

Generally, the Curves graph gives you the most control. Most images can benefit by compressing the tonal range slightly. Have a look at the Curve graph in Figure 10.116. Push both the extreme black and white points in slightly by making the curve into an "s" shape.

Tip

While Adobe Photoshop was used to post-process this single image, you can use Eyeon Software's Digital Fusion to produce the same effects on a complete animation. Other packages such as NewTek's Aura 2, and Adobe's After Effects 4.1 can also provide post-process techniques.

Do the same for the color values; again, you have more than one option:

- Hue and saturation controls
- Color balance
- Use the RGB channel options in either Levels or Curves

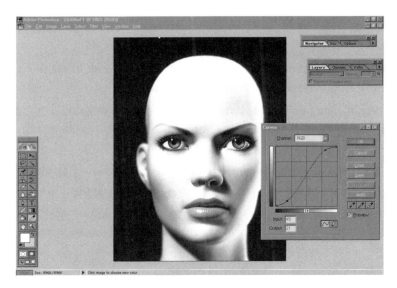

Figure 10.116   Adjust the Curve graph to compress the tonal range in the image.

Using the color balance panel is a good way to work because it enables you to effect the color on specific tonal ranges differently, which can often give some nice effects. Play around with this (for example, push the shadows toward red/yellow and the highlights toward blue/cyan). Try to find settings that create a distinct mood.

Lastly, use the Blur tool to simulate depth of field. Soften the outer extremes of the head—around the ears, back of the skull, and lower neck. Although probably not a good idea on an image sequence where you would want to use proper 3D depth of field for consistency, this can give a nice effect on a still, making the center of the face leap out at the viewer.

Note

Appendix C " Plug-Ins and References," discusses third-party plug-ins, such as Worley Laboratories' Polk plug-ins. One of the Polk plug-ins is called Confusion, and it enables you to set depth-of-field effects in your animation based on the position of a null object. You could use it on the face model to make the eyes the focal point, while slightly blurring the back of the head.

Rendering Summary

A quick recap on the main points of this section:

- Choose your mapping types carefully. Layer different kinds of maps to suit different areas and blend them using alpha layers.

- Texture mapping does not require amazing painting skills (although they certainly help). Carefully modulated but reasonably simple structured textures will often suffice.

- Always try to use geometry templates to guide you when making the maps. Crop the images to suit the templates. That way, you can quickly auto-size textures to fit.

- Use the Photoshop layers feature. Making changes and mixing elements to create multiple map types becomes a lot easier.

- Use VIPER to quickly make changes to surfaces.

- Make your lighting interesting by using a careful balance of key, fill, and rim lights. Try to maintain some contrast in your images.

- Control how soft your lighting is by changing light types. Generally, area lights are superior if you can afford the rendering time.

- Radiosity opens a whole new raft of lighting options and can create wonderfully realistic illumination. But watch out for the down sides: shading artifacts and huge render times. Try to use a variety of lighting techniques and settings to get the right balance between realism and speed.

- Treat post-processing as part of the whole 3D process. Final tweaks are often much easier to do after rendering and can give you that extra 5%.

Further Reading

Here is a list of recommended books that deal in-depth with many of the more general issues dealt with in this chapter:

The Artist's Complete Guide to Facial Expression
Gary Faigin
Published by Watson Guptill

Utterly indispensable. If you have the slightest interest in representing the human face in any medium, you need this book.

Drawing the Human Head

Burne Hogarth

Published by Watson Guptill

Although aimed at traditional artists, any digital sculptor will find a wealth of good material to help him or her understand the human head here.

Painting with Light

John Alton

Published by University of California Press

Classic text on cinematography and lighting.

The Next Step

Make more fantastic models and try your luck at using the techniques in this chapter to create animals, aliens, and more. Study the people around you anytime you can. Notice their differences and their similarities. Take a look at different eye shapes, facial tones for texturing, and anything else that might stand out to you. Through keen observation and practice in LightWave Modeler, you can build anything you want.

Summary

This chapter instructed you on just how powerful the SubPatch feature is in LightWave. You followed this real-world project to learn about proper modeling, texturing, and image mapping. You also learned how important lighting is to your final work. It's up to you to experiment and take the information listed here even further. For now, turn the page and learn how to make the beauty you modeled come to life.

Chapter 11

Character
Construction

You might be the type to dive right into

character animation in LightWave, or you

might be the type who thinks you'd never

use the character animation tools in this

software. But the reality is, the tools available in LightWave 6 to create movable characters can be used for animations other than those involving characters. In addition, these tools are different from those in previous versions of LightWave. So whatever your situation might be, you should read through this chapter, as it will provide you with a solid understanding of these new tools and how to use them in your animations.

Project Overview

The focus of this chapter is character animation. Now, rather than bore you with technical babble about offsets and muscle structures, this chapter discusses the following:

- Bones
- Skelegons
- Bone Weights

You'll see a basic bone setup and how problematic bones used to be in LightWave. You'll see how a few bones have more control than you can imagine, due to LightWave 6's Weight Map tool. You'll set up a bone structure for a full human character using Skelegon tools in Modeler, and then you'll take that model into Layout and give the character motion.

Bones and Bone Weights Compared

Before you begin the first exercise, take a quick look at the following examples to help you differentiate between bones and bones with weights. Bones are a deformation tool. Represented by a tie-shaped outline in Layout, a bone can deform the points of an object. Because points make up polygons, the polygons are, in essence, manipulated. The purpose of bones is to create a skeletal deformation of a solid object to give it movement and life. Without the use of bones, objects would need separate limbs to move independently of each other. A human, for example, does not have any joints at the elbows, wrists, knees, and so on. For the arms and legs to bend, a bone structure must be set up to deform the polygonal mesh. Because a robot would have joints at the elbows, wrists, and knees, bones are not needed. The individual objects attached in a hierarchy can be moved independently. Figure 11.1 shows a bone in Layout.

Bones are much simpler to work with than you might imagine. However, you must follow some rules to make them work properly. First, bones must be associated with an object. The following exercise provides the steps to do just that.

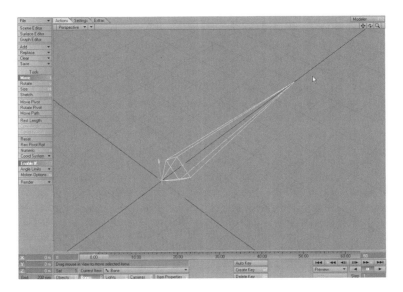

Figure 11.1   This is a bone.

Exercise 11.1   Creating Bones in Layout

As mentioned, bones must be associated with an object. This is because the purpose of bones is to deform an object. Given that, bones have no purpose by themselves other than as a representation in Layout. Even then, an object needs to be added to create bones.

1. Start Layout, select Add, then Add Object, and then Add Null. Rename the null if you like, but the default name "Null" is fine.

    This null object is your base object. Even though bones need to be associated with an object, the object can be just a single-point object.

2. With the Null object selected, click Add, then Add Bone, and Add Bone again. LightWave asks you to rename the bone. Just click OK for now.

    You'll see a 1m bone, like the one in Figure 11.1, but sticking out down the Z axis from the null object at the 0, 0, 0 axis. Figure 11.2 shows the example.

    Next you will set up a chain of bones using child bones.

3. With the first bone still selected, choose Add, Add Bone, and Add Child Bone. Click OK, as you don't need to set a name when the requester asks you to.

    You'll see a bone attached to the end of the previous bone. Figure 11.3 shows the additional bone.

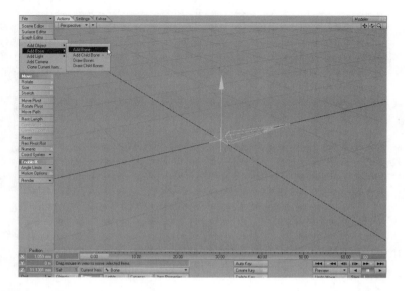

Figure 11.2   Adding a bone to a null object creates a 1m bone heading down the Z axis.

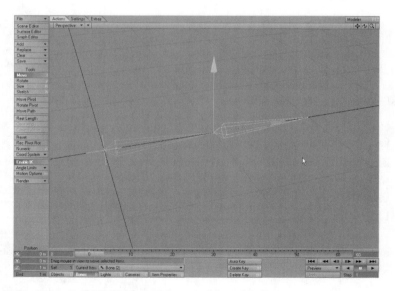

Figure 11.3   You can add child bones to create a hierarchical structure.

4. Add one more child bone as you did in Step 3. After it is added, select the first bone and rotate it.

You'll see the child bones rotate as well. If you select and rotate the second bone, the child of that bone rotates.

This hierarchical structure is explained in detail in Chapter 13, "Inverse Kinematics." For now, you can think of this structure as similar to your own arm. The shoulder is connected to the upper arm, which is connected to the forearm, which is connected to the hand, and so on. If you move the shoulder, the other bones move too.

Note

Using the Scene Editor, you can recolor the bones for easier visibility and better organization in Layout. The color change does not affect the bone's influence, only its visibility.

This example showed you how to create bones in Layout. The null object that you assigned bones to can be anything you want, from a character, to a snake, to a piece of paper. Anything you want to deform can have bones added to it.

Note

For bones to deform an object, the object must be made up of multiple polygons. A solid object such as a box with six sides will not deform well with bones. If the box were subpatched or subdivided into multiple segments, it would be more malleable and, therefore, could be deformed by bones.

Exercise 11.2   Adding Bones to an Object

This exercise uses the same techniques as those in Exercise 11.1 to add bones in Layout. This time, however, you'll add bones to a character's head and see the effects.

1. Select Clear Scene in Layout. Load the 11SimpleGirl.lwo object from the book's CD-ROM. This is the head of a girl. Bones need to be added to move her head and flip her ponytail.

2. Go to the Side view in Layout (Viewport 3). From the top of the Layout window, change the Maximum Render Level to Vertices. You can find this on the small drop-down list, as pictured in Figure 11.4.

   Changing the view to Wireframe helps visibility with setting up bones. LightWave 6 enables you to see the bones, regardless of whether or not the object is solid. You'll work with the solid object in a moment.

3. For now, with the head object selected, select Add, then Add Bone, and then Add Bone again. Name the bone "Neck" when prompted. This is the first bone in the head structure.

4. Using the comma key (,), zoom out to make sure the object and the bones are all in view.

   You'll see that the bone is huge in comparison to the head, as shown in Figure 11.5. This is because bones by default are 1m in length. The head object is 100mm in size. Not a problem, though. The bone is not yet active and can be changed.

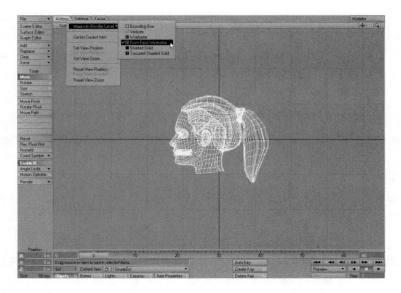

Figure 11.4   Change the visibility of the object from solid to Wireframe directly in Layout through the Maximum Render Level settings.

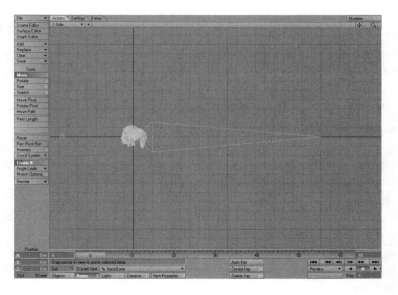

Figure 11.5   Bones by default are 1m in length—much larger than the head object!

To reset the bone to the proper length, you must change the rest length, not the size. This can't be stressed enough. The rest length is the final length of the bone before it is made active—in other words, its resting position. The number-one mistake LightWave animators make with bones is changing the size to set up a bone, instead of the rest length. If you change the size of the bone now, after it is activated, it will change the size of the object with which it is associated.

5. Select Rest Length from the Actions tab, and click and drag the bone down to 0.025m.

You can see the rest length in the bottom-left corner information window. Figure 11.6 shows the bone's new rest length.

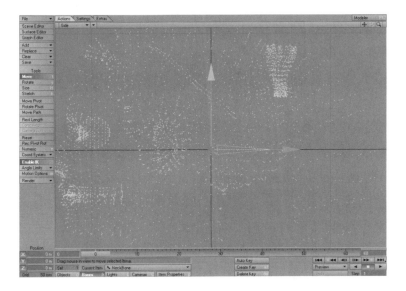

Figure 11.6   The rest length is changed to make the bone the appropriate length for influence. The Rest Length tool, not the Size tool, is used to do this.

Now it's time to position the bone in the neck area, as this is the area you want this bone to affect.

6. Select Rotate (**y**) and rotate the bone –90 on the Pitch. You can grab the green handle if you have Show Handles enabled from the Display Options panel. Move the bone to the base of the neck, and create a keyframe at frame 0 to lock it in place. Figure 11.7 shows the bone in position.

Setting up that first bone is the hardest part. Now that it is in place, you can set child bones.

7. The head bone is a child of the neck bone. Make sure the neck bone is selected and press the shortcut equal sign (=) key to add a child bone. Name the bone "head_bone" when prompted.

You'll see a bone added to the top (or end) of the neck bone, as shown in Figure 11.8. Notice that this bone's rest length matches the neck bone, as does its rotation.

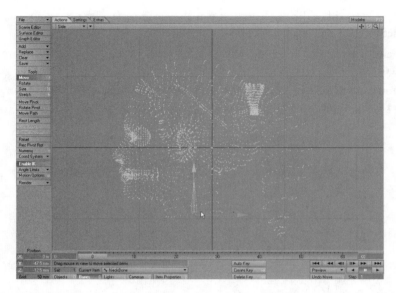

Figure 11.7   After the rest length has been changed, the bone is rotated and moved into position for the head.

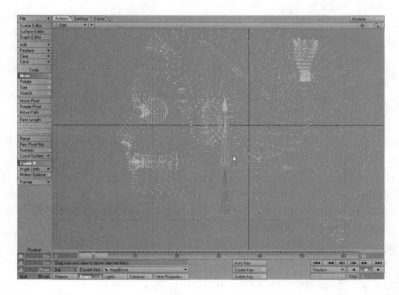

Figure 11.8   After it is added, a child bone takes on the rest length and rotation of the parent bone.

8. Because the head area needs more influence from the bone, change its Rest Length to fit the head.

9. Add a child bone for the head bone and name it "ponytail bone." Rotate the ponytail bone about 138.0 degrees on the Pitch, and move it so that its base (the fat end) is at the base of the ponytail of the head object. You also might need to adjust the rest length if the bone is too long for the ponytail. Figure 11.9 shows the bone in position.

Note

A child bone does not need to touch its parent, as is the case here. But if the head bone moves, the ponytail bone still moves with it.

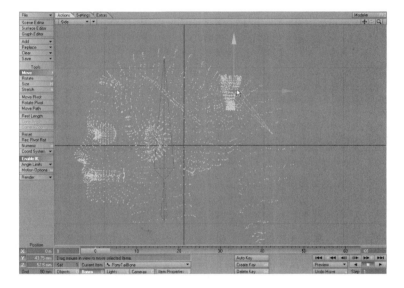

Figure 11.9   A child bone is created for the head bone and has its rest length adjusted and moved into position for the ponytail of the object.

10. Add a child bone to the ponytail bone. Adjust the rest length, and rotate the bone so that it fits into position, not extending out of the ponytail. You don't need to rename it. LightWave will name it ponytail_bone(2).

    Now the bones are in place, but they are not yet influencing the model. This is because they are not active.

11. Activate the bones by pressing the **r** key, which tells LightWave this is where you want the bones to rest and begin working.

    Because ponytail_bone(2) was the last bone you created, it should still be selected.

12. With it selected, press the **r** key.

    Do you see what happened? The head object went crazy! This is not a problem. Many animators stop here and freak out. You did nothing wrong.

What's happening at this point is that the bone you've set into position is now active and influencing the model. But, it is the only bone influencing it, so the model is deforming based on the position of this bone only. When you activate the other bones, the model will return to its proper shape and position.

13. Use the up arrow to select the next bone, press **r**, and repeat the bone activation by pressing **r** for each bone.

When you activate ponytail_bone(1), the head bone, and the neck bone, the model will return to its original shape, as shown in Figure 11.10. This is because all bones are now active and properly influencing the deformation of the model. When only one bone was active, such as the ponytail bone, the entire head was being influenced by only one bone.

Note

You can differentiate between an inactive bone and an active bone by their visibility. Dashed lines represent an inactive bone. When the bone is active, solid lines represent it. And remember, you can change the color of these lines with the Visibility commands in the Scene Editor.

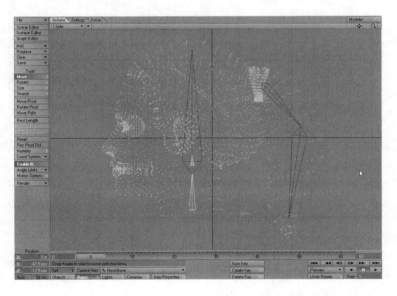

Figure 11.10   After all bones are activated, the model is positioned properly and no deformations occur.

14. Go back to the Camera view and change the Maximum Render Level in the scene to Shaded Solid. Select the head bone, press the **y** key to rotate the bone. You'll see the head deform.

15. Move the camera around to view the side of the head. Create a keyframe to lock it in place at frame zero. Select ponytail_bone(1) and rotate it.

Notice how the head and face deform when this bone is used. Figure 11.11 shows the example of rotating only the ponytailbone.

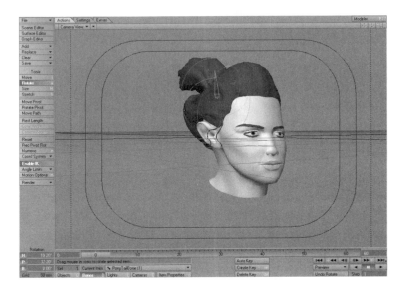

Figure 11.11   Although the bones are set properly, the influence of the ponytail bone is too much for the head model. Just rotating the ponytail bone deforms the head, which is not desired.

Often, adding bones in Layout for skeletal deformation is all you need for things such as cloth, breathing creatures, or exaggerated movements. In objects such as this simple girl head, however, the deformation is not right. To correct this unwanted deforming, you would place more bones as "anchor" bones to hold the head in place. You could also increase the falloff of the bone influence, or set a limited range. Although these techniques work just fine, they can be labor intensive. They also increase the complexity of your hierarchy. LightWave 6, however, can solve all your problems with Bone Weights.

Bone Weights

Bone Weights is a Modeler tool that enhances a Weight Map with a specific falloff range. This technique is used for setting up limited ranges of influence on bones. The Bone Weights feature automates the process of creating Weight Maps that approximate what the normal bone influence would be. However, you must have Skelegons already in place. After a Weight Map is created, you can adjust the maps to suit your needs through the Bone Weights feature. It basically gives you a starting point when creating Weight Maps for your bones. Figure 11.12 shows the Bone Weight panel in Modeler, found under the Additional list of tools.

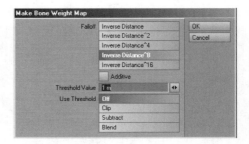

Figure 11.12   The Bone Weights panel in Modeler enables falloff and influence control of your bones.

The first step in understanding the use of Bone Weights is to explore LightWave 6's Weights in Modeler. Weight Maps were demonstrated earlier in the book; they enable you to scale the falloff of various tools in LightWave. With a Weight Map, a bone affects points according to the weight you set. The result is a controlled influence that eliminates the problem you saw in Exercise 11.2 and Figure 11.11.

Falloff

The Falloff selections within the Bone Weights panel determine how the influences of bones fade with distance. The settings work mathematically, and the default is Inverse Distance^4. This exponential value of ^4 sets a fair amount of falloff for a bone, whereas a higher value of ^16 will have a greater (or faster) falloff. Exercise 11.3 uses a falloff setting so that you can see the effects.

Additive

The Additive selection within the Bone Weights panel tells LightWave to add weight to any existing value. Therefore, in the case of the simple head object in the previous exercises, the ponytail bones were named the same. Because their names were the same, LightWave added the weight values to both. Using Additive quickly sets up Bone Weights without renaming every bone.

Threshold Value

The Threshold Value is similar to Limited Region for bones in Layout. It is an encapsulated region around a bone, and the value set (such as 1m) determines the size of the region.

Using Threshold

This setting takes the weight value of the set threshold distance as Off, Clip, Subtract, or Blend. Off ignores the Threshold Value set. Clip applies the weights outside of the Threshold value distance. Subtract subtracts the weight from all values making the weights run smoothly at 0, and negative at the threshold. Finally, Blend subtracts the Threshold Value, and then clips the negative weights to 0. This setting often is the most useful.

More information and specific details are highlighted in the "LightWave Motion: Animate and Render" manual that came with your LightWave 6 software. For now, this next exercise guides you through the use of setting up Bone Weights in Modeler, and then applying them in Layout. The result is perfect deformations, unlike the bone setup outlined in Exercise 11.2.

Exercise 11.3   Applying Bone Weights

Bone Weights enable you to specify regions of influence. Much of the time when creating character animation, you'll be building your model from the ground up. You can assign Weight Maps as you go. But you can also use existing models, either from a previous project, by another artist, or perhaps from this book's CD-ROM.

1. Open Modeler, and load the 11BoneHead_A.lwo from the book's CD-ROM. This is the same simple head object you used in the previous exercises, but renamed for clarity. Figure 11.13 shows the model loaded. Press the **a** key to fit the model in view to match the figure.

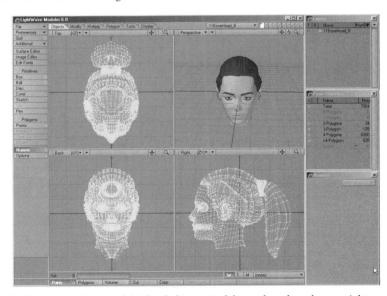

Figure 11.13   An existing model is loaded into Modeler and ready to have weights assigned to it.

Note

Figure 11.13 shows the Modeler interface sized to the left a bit, with the Layers (Display tab), Numeric (**n**), and Statistics (**w**) panel left open on the right. You can set up your view like this if you want.

In Exercise 11.2, you created four bones: one bone for the neck, one bone for the head, and two bones for the ponytail. You only need to set up some Weight Maps for these areas, and your model will deform properly in Layout.

2. Choose Polygon Selection mode by clicking the Polygon button at the bottom of the Modeler interface. Open the Statistics panel for Polygon by pressing the **w** key.

3. In the Polygon Statistics panel, click the second to last small triangle at the bottom of the panel.

   You'll see a list of surfaces. These are all the polygon surfaces assigned to the current model.

4. Select Hair_PonyTail as shown in Figure 11.14. You'll see the listing appear under the Name column.

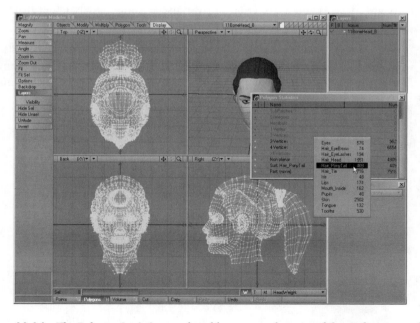

Figure 11.14   The Polygon Statistics panel enables you to select any of the surfaces created for the object.

5. Click the white plus sign to the left of the name.

   You'll see the polygons surfaced as Hair_PonyTail become selected. Figure 11.15 shows the selection.

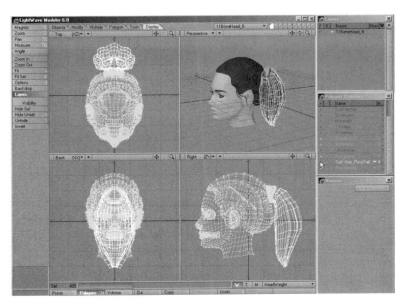

Figure 11.15   Clicking the plus sign next to a name in the Statistics panel selects only that named polygon.

6. With the ponytail polygons selected, select the W at the bottom of the Modeler interface (next to T and M) to choose Weight mode. In the drop-down list next to these choices where it reads (none), select New. Figure 11.16 shows the selection.

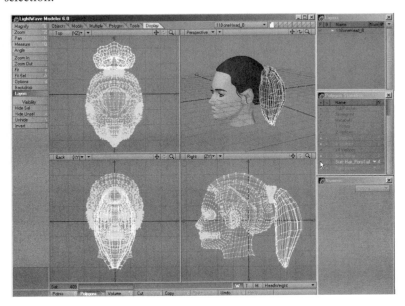

Figure 11.16   Assigning a Weight Map to selected polygons is done by selecting New from the W drop-down list.

The Create Weight Map panel comes up. You can now assign a Weight Map to the selected polygons. Remember, the selected polygons are for the ponytail.

7. Change the Name to ponytail_weight. You don't need to call it "weight," but it helps to keep things clear when many weights and surfaces are similarly named. Keep Initial Value checked, and leave 100% applied, as shown in Figure 11.17.

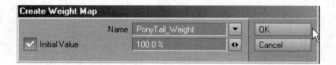

Figure 11.17   When you assign a Weight Map, you can also set the name of the weight. This is a good habit to get into for organization.

You've now set a Weight Map for the ponytail, but if you remember, there are two bones in the ponytail.

8. Before you deselect all the ponytail polygons, deselect just the top half and only leave the bottom portion of the ponytail polygons selected, as shown in Figure 11.18.

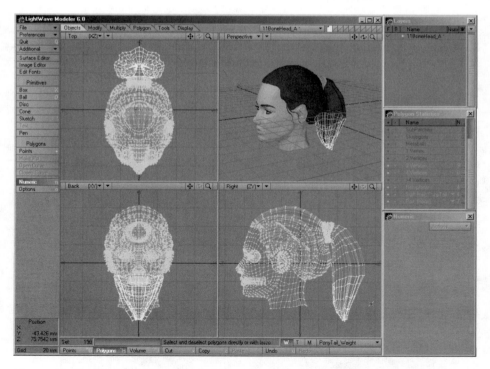

Figure 11.18   You can assign a Weight Map to just half of the ponytail by selecting just the desired polygons.

9. Select New again from the W command to Create Weight Map for this selection. Name the new Weight Map PonyTailEnd_Weight, as shown in Figure 11.19.

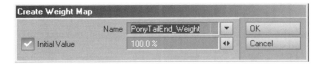

Figure 11.19 Renaming each Weight Map you create will save time later in Layout when assigning bones to the weights.

You can assign Weight Maps to selected polygons or points. But if you apply a Weight Map to selected polygons, you are really applying the weight to the points of the selected polygons.

10. So, switch over to Point mode by selecting the Point button at the bottom of the Modeler interface or pressing the **Ctrl+g** key combination. This tells Modeler you're now working with points.

11. With the right mouse button in the Right view, lasso around the points of the entire head (including the ponytail), except for the bottom two rows of points of the neck. Figure 11.20 shows the selection.

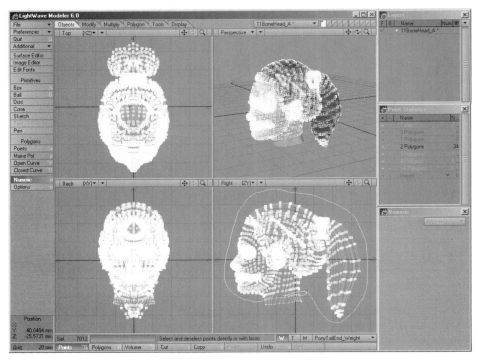

Figure 11.20 You can assign Weight Maps to points as well as polygons. Here, the points of the entire head are selected for a Weight Map to be applied.

12. From the same drop-down list next to the W, choose new, and Create Weight Map. Set the Name to Head_Weight.

13. Instead of deselecting and reselecting points, press the **Shift** key and the single quote (') key.

    This reverses the selection. The only points not selected are those that make up the neck area. These are the points you want.

14. After the neck points are selected, create a weight map for them and name them Neck_Weight. When completed, save your object as HeadWeight or something similar.

15. Go to Layout and load the 11Exercise11_2b.lws scene from the book's CD-ROM. This is the scene from Exercise 11.2. If you remember, rotating just the ponytail bone deformed the head and face.

16. Select the SimpleGirl object, and select Replace from the Actions tab, then Replace Object, then Replace With Object File, as shown in Figure 11.21.

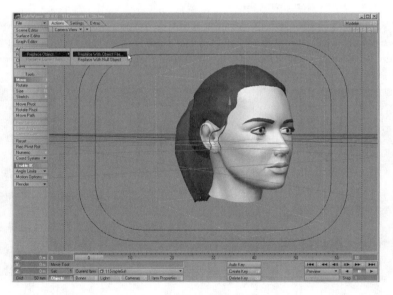

Figure 11.21   Updating an object is easy to do by using the Replace with Object File in Layout.

17. Select the 11BoneHead_B.lwo object. This is the girl head object with Weight Maps assigned.

    By replacing the existing head, the bones will now be assigned to the weighted head. All you need to do is tell the bones to use the Weight Maps.

18. Be sure the 11BoneHead_B object is selected, then press the Bones button at the bottom of the Layout interface (or press **Shift + b**). You're now working with the

bones of the head object. The neck bones should be selected; if they aren't, select them. Press the **p** key to go to the Item Properties panel for Bones.

19. In the middle of the panel, select Neck_Weight for Bone Weight Map, as shown in Figure 11.22.

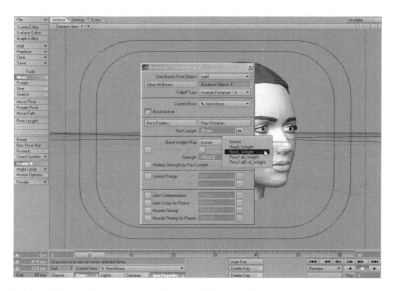

Figure 11.22   The Weight Maps created in Modeler can be assigned to bones through the Bones Properties panel in Layout.

20. While still in the Item Properties panel for bones, press the down arrow key on the keyboard to select the HeadBone. To verify your selection, you can move the Properties panel aside to view both the panel and Layout. Set the Bone Weight Map to Head_Weight. Can you now see why appropriately naming the bones and the weights is important?

21. Assign the rest of the Bone Weight Maps to the ponytail bones.

    Figure 11.23 shows the HeadBone rotated in one direction, while the first pony-tail bone is rotated in the opposite direction. Notice that the head object no longer gets squashed, or deforms oddly. When the ponytail bone is moved, only the ponytail moves, not the head polygons nearby, as was the case in Exercise 11.2. Welcome to Bone Weights.

You might have noticed that some other selections were available in the Bones Properties panel, such as Use Weight Map Only, and Weight Normalization. If you want your Weight Maps to be the only control over influence, you can activate Use Weight Map Only. When you do, the Weight Normalization becomes active, and if you select it, bone influences are scaled on distances and the Weight Map.

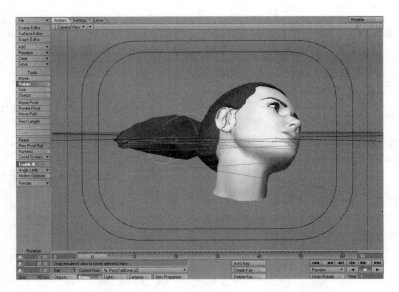

Figure 11.23   Bone Weights applied to the model allow much greater control over bone influences.

The subtlety of using Weight Maps with bones is that you can define the falloff influence of a bone. This exercise created all Weight Maps with 100% initial value, which tells the models to rely on the bone falloff with this value only. You can have even more power over your models with Weight Maps because you can absolutely control the bone influence. For example, you can use one of the weight tools to drop off the weighted influence from 100% to 0 toward the top. Try experimenting with the scenes on the book's CD-ROM and change the influences to see what sort of results you can come up with.

Skelegons

Skelegons are also new in LightWave 6. You'll grow fond of this term as you work through this next section because Skelegons are polygons that resemble bones. In Modeler, you can create and modify Skelegons as if they were polygons and then convert them to bones in Layout. The benefit of this is the ability to set up bones for a character in a perspective view with modeling tools such as Drag and Rotate. Even more, the skeletal structure you create for a character is saved with the object! In previous versions of LightWave, you needed to save a scene to hold the object and skeletal hierarchy. Now it's all saved with the object. This means you can set up full bone structures for characters and load them individually into a single scene.

When you create a character with Skelegons, you can change the model at any time, and adjust its skeletal structure. In addition, you can create one base skeletal structure and use it over and over again for future characters. The next exercise gets you right into it, by setting up Skelegons for the body of the head you worked with earlier in this chapter.

 Note

Be sure to always save a copy of your model with Skelegons. When you convert Skelegons to bones, they can't be changed back to Skelegons.

Draw Skelegons

There are a couple of ways to create Skelegons in Modeler. You can build them point-by-point, and convert single-line polygons to Skelegons, such as two points connected with a line polygon or a curve. This is useful for creating Skelegons from existing models. The Draw Skelegons feature is fast and easy, however, and it's the focus of this next exercise.

Exercise 11.4   Creating Skelegons in Humans

This exercise uses an existing model to demonstrate how quickly and easily you can set up a full hierarchy for a human character. Using the Bone Weight information from the previous exercises, and the Skelegons information provided here, you'd be animating a fully-articulated character in no time.

1. In Modeler, clear out any work after you've saved it by selecting Close All Objects from the File menu. Load the 11InDress.lwo object from the book's CD-ROM. This is a woman figure in a simple orange dress. Figure 11.24 shows the model loaded with the Layers (Display tab), Numeric (**n**), and Statistics (**w**) panels open.

2. Go to a new layer and place the woman object in a background layer.

3. From the Additional drop-down list, select DrawSkelegons as shown in Figure 11.25.

 Note

It's a good idea to edit the menu layout and set up a group of Skelegon tools that you use often. Refer to Chapter 1, "Introducing LightWave 6," for more information on customizing buttons and menus.

4. Move the mouse over the Back view (Viewport 3) at the bottom left of Modeler, and press the **0** key on the numeric keypad to make the view full-screen. Use the comma key (**,**) to zoom in. You can move the view over a bit to concentrate on the upper right of the woman's body. Now, click and drag up, just above the woman's waist, as shown in Figure 11.26.

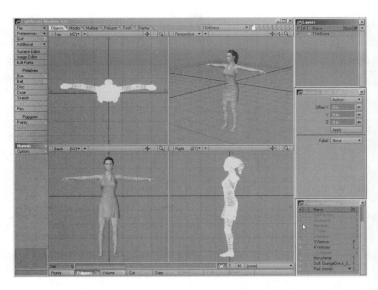

Figure 11.24   The woman object loaded into Modeler.

Figure 11.25
The DrawSkelegons command is in the Additional drop-down list, found in the Objects tab.

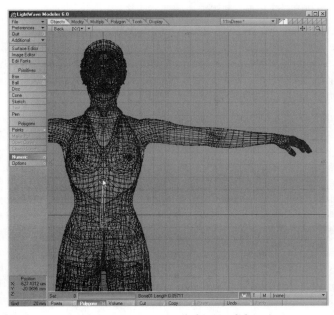

Figure 11.26   Drawing Skelegons is as easy as clicking and dragging.

5. With the numeric window open (**n**) you can set a name for
the Skelegon, as well as a Weight Map assignment. This
Weight Map setting does not create a Weight Map, but only
saves you the trouble of setting the bone to use the Weight
Map later in Layout. Name the first bone "Pelvis" and set the
Weight Map to Pelvis_Weight, as shown in Figure 11.27.

Figure 11.27
The Numeric:
DrawSkelegons panel
enables you to set a Name
and a Weight Map for the
current Skelegon.

> **Note**
>
> The Use Digits selection in the numeric DrawSkelegons panel tells
> Modeler to sequentially name the Skelegons as you create them.
> Sometimes, you might not set a name for each Skelegon, so
> Modeler will name them Bone.00, Bone.01, Bone.02, and so on.

6. Click in the middle of the chest of the woman object.

You'll see the Skelegons draw automatically, creating a child
bone, as shown in Figure 11.28.

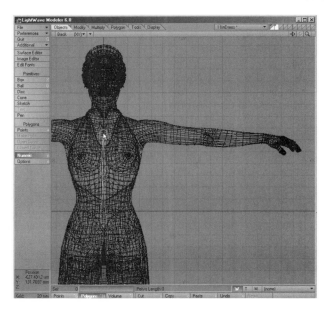

Figure 11.28 You can quickly add Skelegons by clicking in the desired locations.

The small circles around the ends of the Skelegons are the controls for that
bone. If you are in DrawSkelegons mode, clicking outside this circle will draw a
Skelegon attached to the one before it. If you need to adjust the Skelegon, be
sure to click within the circles.

7. Click on the right shoulder, on the elbow, on the wrist, and once more on the middle of the hand. Press the spacebar when finished to turn off the DrawSkelegons tool and to keep the bones. You can set names and weights later for individual bones with the Skelegon Tree. Figure 11.29 shows the Skelegons down the right arm.

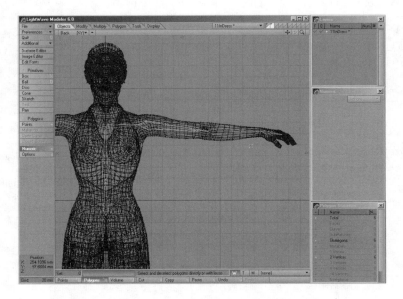

Figure 11.29   In no time at all, you can begin creating a skeletal structure with DrawSkelegons.

8. From the Additional drop-down list, select Skelegon Tree. When the panel comes up, drag the corner to expand the size of the panel slightly.

You'll see a hierarchy of bones named Pelvis (the first Skelegon you drew) with Weight Maps. Figure 11.30 shows the Skelegon Tree.

You know that the first bone is the pelvis bone, so you don't need to rename it.

9. Double-click the second bone indented in the list, under the Skelegon heading in the Skelegon panel. This calls up the Rename Skelegon command. Rename this bone "Chest," as it was created in the chest area of the object.

10. Double-click the second bone in the list under Weight Map to rename it. This is the Weight Map for the chest.

11. Continue renaming the Skelegon and the Weight Map accordingly. Figure 11.31 shows the Skelegon Tree with the bones and weights renamed.

12. Save your object. Saving the object also saves the bone structure.

From here, you can create the Skelegons for the legs. However, the upper-body bones are children of the pelvis bone, but don't worry.

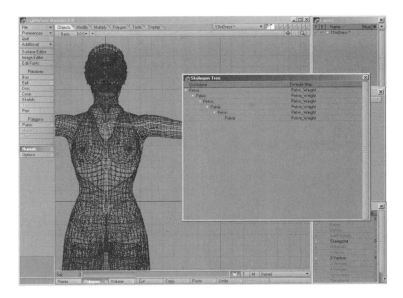

Figure 11.30   The Skelegon Tree helps you manage your Skelegon structures.

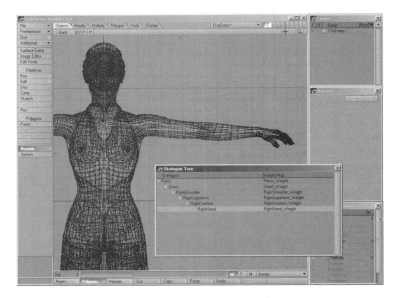

Figure 11.31   You can rename all bones and Weight Maps in the Skelegon Tree.

13. Select DrawSkelegons from the Additional list, and draw out a bone for the right hip, as shown in Figure 11.32.

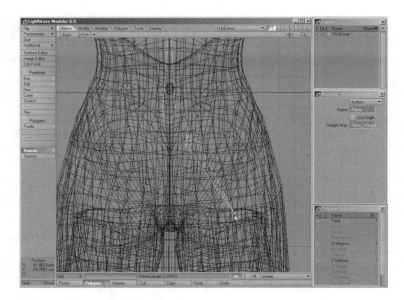

Figure 11.32   A new hierarchy of Skelegons is created for the leg.

14. As you did with the arm, continue drawing Skelegons down the leg by clicking on the knee, ankle, and foot. Press the space bar to turn off the DrawSkelegons tool. Figure 11.33 shows the Skelegon structure down the leg.

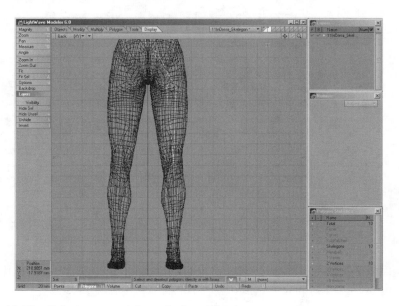

Figure 11.33   Skelegons created down the leg of the character.

In the real world, moving the pelvis of a person would influence the thighs. Because you have a main pelvis bone in the middle of the character, you need to attach the right thighbone to it.

15. Go to Point mode, and select the point at the fat end of the thighbone, and then select the point at the fat end of the pelvis bone, as shown in Figure 11.34.

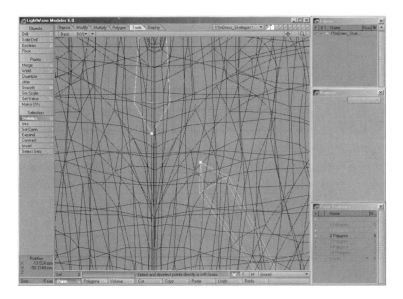

Figure 11.34   The two points at the end of the bones are selected to be joined.

16. Weld these together by pressing **Ctrl+w**. Now the thighbone and its children are a child of the pelvis bone. Save the object.

You've successfully created a bone structure for a human character. What? It's not complete, you say? No problem. You don't have to draw Skelegons again because Skelegons are a polygon type. In the next exercise you can apply Modeler tools to them and adjust their position, size, and so on.

Exercise 11.5   Adjusting and Positioning Skelegons

This exercise shows you how to take an existing Skelegon structure and adjust the position and size of each Skelegon. In Exercise 11.4, you created the Skelegons from only one view, and if you remember, this is 3D animation, which means you have two other axes to worry about.

1. In Modeler, select Close All Objects from the File menu to create a clean workspace. From the book's CD-ROM, load the 11HalfSkel.lwo object into Modeler. This is the woman figure in the dress with Skelegons in another layer. The Skelegons cover only half of the woman's body.

2. Move the mouse over the Perspective view (Viewport 2) and press the **0** key on the numeric keypad to bring this view to full frame. Select layer 2 (the bones) as the foreground, and layer 1 (the woman object) as the background. Figure 11.35 shows the setup.

Figure 11.35   The bones might line up in the Back view when created, but in looking at the setup from Perspective view, they need some adjustment.

3. Select the Drag tool (**Ctrl+t**) to start adjusting the bones. Rotate the Perspective view so that you have more of a top-down view. Click and drag on the end of the bone near the hand. Drag until the bone is lined up inside the hand. Do the same for the elbow, dragging the end point to the elbow joint. Figure 11.36 shows the two bones adjusted.

4. Go back to the Quad view by pressing **0** on the numeric keypad. Depending on your skill, you might have an easier time adjusting the Skelegons from orthogonal views. Adjust the remainder of the Skelegons in the upper body so that they fit appropriately, such as the shoulder bone and upper arm bone.

5. In the Right view, drag the bones to fit the knee and feet more accurately, as shown in Figure 11.37.

6. For the foot bone, drag the end point on the last bone to the tip of the foot. There's no need to rotate or redraw the Skelegons.

7. Save the object when all the bones are centered within the object and adjusted to your liking.

8. Select all the bones in Polygon mode, except for the pelvis and chest bones. Press the **c** key to copy them, and then press the **v** key to paste them into a new layer. Figure 11.38 shows the selection.

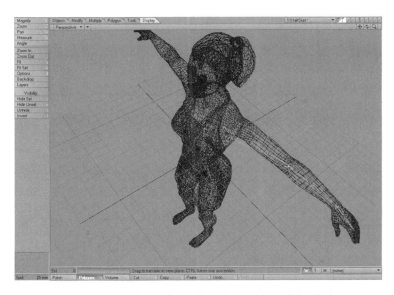

Figure 11.36   The Drag tool can be used to adjust the position of the Skelegons.

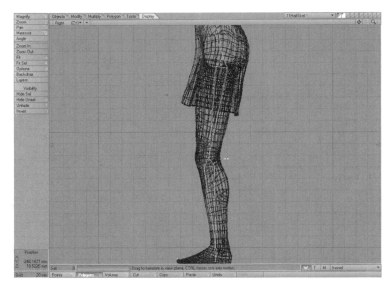

Figure 11.37   In the Right view, bones can be adjusted easily with the Drag tool.

9. Select the Mirror tool, and click the Y axis to Mirror the bones over the Y, duplicating them for the X axis. You can adjust the Mirror tool through its numeric panel for more precise control. Also, feel free to add the background layer as reference for mirroring. Figure 11.39 shows the mirrored bones.

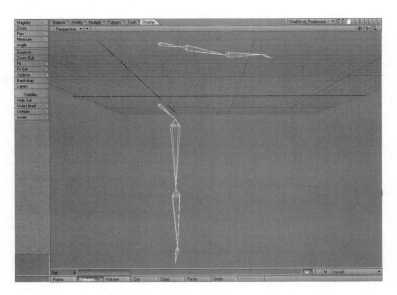

Figure 11.38   The bones for the right arm and leg, copied and pasted to a new layer.

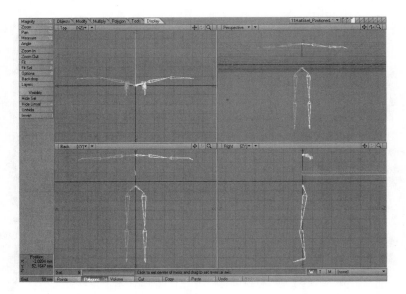

Figure 11.39   The bones for the arms and legs of the character are easily copied via the Mirror tool.

You now have a complete bone structure for the left side of the character.

10. Cut and paste this layer to the second layer—the layer with the pelvis and chest bones. Zoom into the Back view, select the points at the top of the left and right hipbones and the base of the pelvis, and weld them together with the Weld tool

(**Ctrl+w**). Do the same for the shoulder bones and the top of the chest bone. Figure 11.40 shows the selection of the chest and shoulder bones welded.

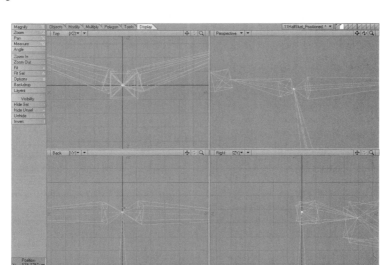

Figure 11.40   The points of the two shoulder bones and the tip of the chest bone are welded to become one hierarchy.

11. Save the object.

Note

Depending on how perfect your model is, you might need to use the Drag tool on the mirrored bones for fine-tuning their positioning.

Using Skelegons in Layout

The final part of this chapter takes you back into Layout, where you convert these Skelegons to actual bones and make them control your model. You will assign the Weight Maps created to each Skelegon as well. However, it's not necessary to move the Skelegons to the Modeler layer that contains the object, which will be influenced. The Skelegons can keep their own layer, thanks to LightWave 6's MultiMesh object format. Beyond this exercise, you can select portions of the model to assign Weight Maps, then apply the bones in Layout. Just like you did in Exercise 11.2, you can simply go further and select the regions of points on the full woman object, assign a Weight Map, and apply the Bone Weights. If you remember, applying Bone Weights to the head and pony-tail on the object enabled you to control the influence of bones—you can do the same throughout the body.

Exercise 11.6   Converting Skelegons to Bones in Layout

You'll find that the more you practice creating Skelegons, the less likely you'll be to set up bones directly in Layout. The functionality of Skelegons far exceeds that of just ordinary bones. It is those ordinary bones that deform the objects, however, and you need to convert the functional Skelegons to bones before you can see the results.

1. Open Layout, and load the 11HalfSkel_Positioned.lwo object from the book's CD-ROM. This is the simple girl object with a separate layer of Skelegons.

2. From the Current Item list, select the 11HalfSkel_Positioned object, not Layer 2. Select the Bones button at the bottom of the Layout interface. The Current Item list will show none, that there are no bones. Press the **p** key to enter the Bones Item Properties panel.

3. At the top of the Bones Item Properties panel, change the Use Bones From Object selection to 11HalfSkel_Positioned:Layer2, as shown in Figure 11.41.

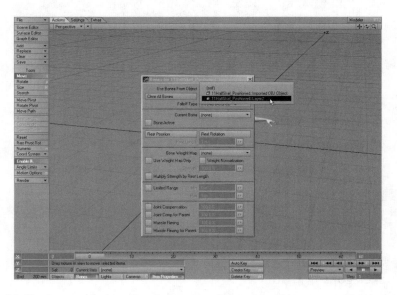

Figure 11.41   Because the bones are in a separate layer of the object, you need to instruct Layout where the bones are.

4. Close the Item Properties and return to Layout. Select the 11HalfSkel_Positioned:Layer2 object. From the Settings tab, select the CVT Skelegons button, and Layout will convert the Skelegons to bones. Figure 11.42 shows the buttons.

5. With Bones selected at the bottom of the interface, select the Pelvis bone. Press **y** to rotate, and rotate the bone.

   The object moves with the chest and arms accordingly.

Figure 11.42
To use the Skelegons created in Modeler in Layout, they need to be converted to bones with the CVT Skelegons command.

The exercise here is basic and straightforward. However, much of your character work does not need to be more complex than this. You can go further by adding Skelegons for the fingers in the hands, and perhaps in the toes as well. At any time, LightWave 6 enables you to bring this model back to Modeler, make adjustments, and add more Skelegons or Weight Maps. Figure 11.43 shows the object with a few bones rotated.

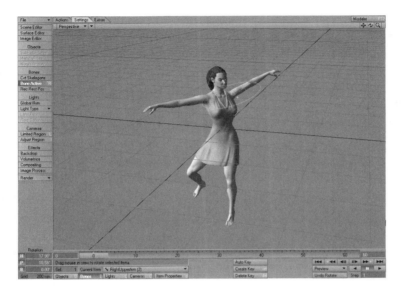

Figure 11.43   With Skelegons now converted to bones, the character can have motion.

The Next Step

This chapter introduced you to bones, Skelegons, and how to create both. You saw how to set Bone Weights to control the influences of bones. With this knowledge, load some of the full characters from the book's CD-ROM, and set up full bone structures with Weight Maps. Position bones using the Drag tool, and use the Mirror tool to copy the Skelegons. See what kind of other uses you can apply these tools to, such as animals, aliens, or your own fascinating creatures.

Summary

Skelegons and Bones are powerful animation tools in LightWave 6. One chapter can't present all the different possibilities of these tools. With the right project and a little time, however, you'll be setting up skeletal structures faster than you could have imagined. But where can you go beyond this? You can turn to Chapter 12, "Organic Animation," and make your characters not only move with bones, but also talk with Endomorphs.

Part III

A Project-Based
Approach to
Animating Scenes

Chapter 12

Organic Animation

Throughout *Inside LightWave [6]*, you've learned different techniques, tips, and tricks. You've learned about keyframing and the Graph Editor. You've learned about organic modeling and lighting. This chapter takes you a step further into organic animation. Organic animation in LightWave 6 is more than just moving a leaf from point A to point B. It is the blending of points and the changing of shapes.

Project Overview

The goal of this chapter is to help you create talking characters. The Endomorph technology in LightWave 6 that you'll learn about in this chapter has many uses, but its primary function is for character animation. You learned how to make a beautiful human face in Chapter 10, "Organic Modeling." Now you learn how to bring that face to life. This chapter covers:

- Creating Endomorphs
- Grouping points and polygons
- VMap tools
- MorphMixer for lip sync

Preparing for Facial Animation

Although there is not enough room in this book to describe the entire process of creating facial expressions, movement, timing, and the art of character animation, there is enough space to stress the preparation you can take before you embark on such endeavors. Facial animation is one of the most difficult aspects of 3D animation. Human facial expression has so many nuances that we take for granted every day. But if you stop to look, really look, you'll find that with a few key facial expressions, you can make a character come to life in LightWave 6.

A number of books on the market deal specifically with character animation and the human form. Many of these books discuss facial muscle structure and illustrate various facial positions. This chapter takes a different approach and uses a simple method—do it until it looks right. Although most of your preparation requires manipulating the 3D model, you should take some time and visit your local library or bookstore to study the human form. This, along with just watching people's movements and expressions, is the best preparation you can arm yourself with. From there, it's up to you to create facial animation.

Endomorph Technology

The Endomorph technology in LightWave 6 is not only smart, it's also helpful and user friendly. Endomorphs enable you to create a 3D object in Modeler and build an unlimited number of morph targets into the object. A *morph target* is a change in the position of the points or polygons of an object. You can use morphs to change a straight road into a curved road, or a car into a boat, and so on.

In previous versions of LightWave, to create a morph you needed separate objects. The Endomorph technology in LightWave 6 enables you to create all your morph targets with one single object. You can change the base model and add polygons to it. Adding polygons to a morph previous to the Endomorph technology resulted in crazy morphing results. Endomorphs solve many of the production headaches of morph targets, as you'll discover in this chapter. Endomorphs are an extension of LightWave 6's VMap capabilities. Weight and UV maps generally use the same feature. The difference is in how the information is interpreted. With Endomorphs, different point position sets are defined.

Note

Although you can edit your model with Endomorphs, you still need the same number of points and polygons to properly morph between targets.

Animating Faces

Facial animation is the number one reason Endomorph technology exists. If you remember the Morph Gizmo plug-in in earlier versions of LightWave, you'll understand what the new technology of Endomorphs and MorphMixer can accomplish. Animating faces can be a complex, arduous task. You need to understand the timing of eye movements, phonetics of speech and everyday expressions. However, you can easily set up facial animation in LightWave 6 by sometimes just looking in the mirror. It's often difficult to picture, say, the facial expression when someone says the word "trumpet." But if you look into a mirror and say it, you have your animation reference. Animators who keep mirrors at their desks are not usually that vain. By keeping a mirror at your desk, you have an encyclopedia of facial expression animation references.

Full Bodies and Endomorphs

Because many of the demonstrations of the Endomorph technology depict a face, it shouldn't go unmentioned that a body can be attached to the face. The process of setting up bones for a character is only enhanced by the animation created with Endomorphs. Using full bodies with Endomorphs is easy. When setting up morph targets for a face, just make sure it's a face on a body. In another layer, the body can have a full bone structure set up with Skelegons. By bringing the object into Layout you have a full character, bone structure, and morph targets all in one model. You can animate to your heart's content.

Creating Endomorphs

Creating Endomorphs is easier than you might think. By using some of LightWave 6's grouping technology in the next exercise, you'll be able to adjust and manipulate your model into just about any expression you like.

Exercise 12.1   Creating Selection Sets

In Chapter 10, you learned how to create a beautiful female head model. This chapter takes that model even further by creating blinking eyes, facial expressions, and a few mouth phonetics. The first step is to create a Selection Set. This is not always needed to create Endomorphs, but it can be very helpful.

1. Open Modeler and load the 12StartHead.lwo. This is a copy of the head model built in Chapter 10.

2. Be sure you have a default quad view in Modeler to match this exercise. You can see from Figure 12.1 that the model has multiple layers. The layers contain eyes, teeth, a tongue, and the head itself. Select the first layer, the head.

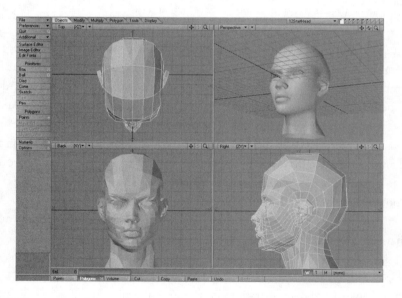

Figure 12.1   A copy of the model created in Chapter 10 is loaded and ready for some Endomorphs.

The first step in creating Endomorphs for this model is the setup of Selection Sets. Selection Sets enable you to select a range of points and give them a group name. To select a particular polygonal region in previous versions of LightWave, you needed to create a separate surface name, even if the surface attributes were the same. Now you can group selections within one surface.

3. Zoom into the lips of the head object by pressing the period key (.). Move the mouse pointer over a specific area in a viewport, and press the **g** key. This instantly brings to the center the area where the mouse is. Use this with the Zoom tool to get the lips to full view.

4. Switch to Point mode at the bottom of the Modeler interface. Selection Sets work with points, and although you can select polygons and create a Selection Set just as easily, point selection can be more precise.

5. Click and select a point or two on the bottom lip of the head. If you work in a shaded mode such as Texture, it's a bit easier to make the selection. Figure 12.2 shows the selection.

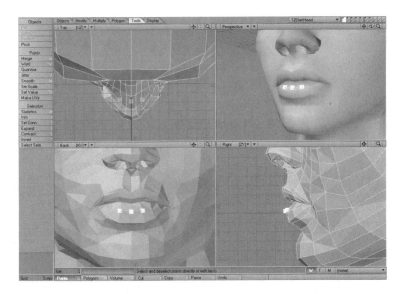

Figure 12.2   Selecting a couple of points on the bottom lip is all you need to do to get started.

6. Because the original model's lips are close together, selecting just the bottom is difficult and time consuming. Instead, use the Expand Select command, found in the Tools tab or by pressing **Shift+}**. (That's the right bracket key, two keys over from the p key.) Expand Select one time and notice that points are being selected outward from the initial few first selected.

Note

The points in Figure 12.2 might seem a bit large to you. This is because the Simple Wireframe Points option is on in the Display Options panel. This enables you to change the visible size of the points in Modeler. You also can turn on the Simple Wireframe Edges option as well. Figure 12.3 shows the Simple Wireframe Points option.

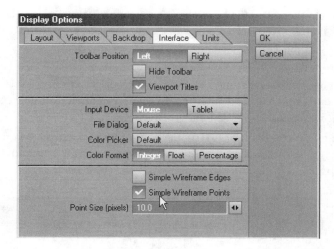

Figure 12.3   Simple Wireframe Points is on to make the points more visible in Modeler's views.

7. Continue using Expand Select until the entire bottom lip is selected, as in Figure 12.4.

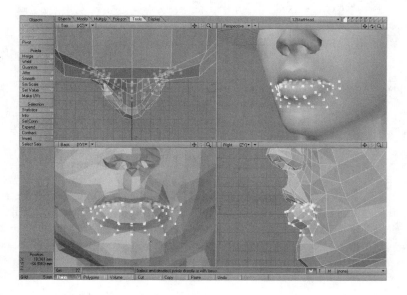

Figure 12.4   Using Expand Select, the points in just the lower lip are easily selected.

8. Zoom out slightly to fit the jaw into view. In the Right view, while holding down the **Shift** key, select the points that make up the jaw area of the head object. If you're working in shaded mode for this view, switch to wireframe to be sure you select the points on both sides of the head. Figure 12.5 shows the selection.

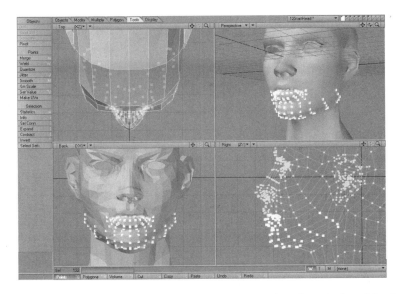

Figure 12.5   The points in the bottom lip and jaw are now selected, ready for a Selection Set assignment.

9. This group of points can now become a Selection Set. While the points are still selected, choose the Selection Sets command from the Tools tab. Enter the name Jaw for the Point Set, as in Figure 12.6. You do not want to remove points. Click OK, and the Selection Set is created. Deselect the points.

   Remember to work with just the first layer, which contains only the head model.

Figure 12.6   After points are selected, the Selection Set tool enables you to name the group.

10. While in Point mode, press the **w** key to call up Point Statistics. Click and hold the bottom triangle in the list and you'll see the new Selection Set, as in Figure 12.7. Click the plus sign (+) next to the name to select the new Selection Set and add it to the list. (Clicking the minus sign deselects it.) As you create more point Selection Sets, the names you assign to them will be in this list as well.

Note

If you have older LightWave objects that use different surfaces to control selections, you can use the Surf-to-Parts (Surface to Parts) command. It can be found under the Additional list of tools, and it assigns a selection of polygons to a specific surface. This "parts" list is available in the Polygon Statistics panel, similar to the Selection Sets for points.

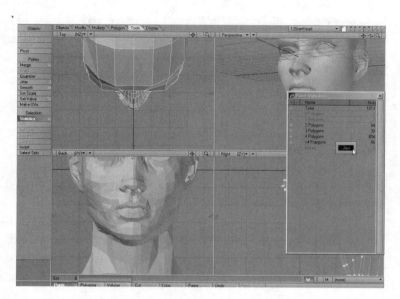

Figure 12.7 The created Selection Set is now accessible through the Point Statistics panel (**w**).

11. Create additional Selection Sets, such as for the eyelids, nose, and so on. Create these sets for areas that you want to easily select later. It doesn't affect your model in any way, but rather, defines areas of points for easy selection.

For the next exercise, you will work with a model from the book's CD. This is the same model you were working with in Exercise 12.1, but it has a few Selection Sets already applied.

Exercise 12.2   Building an Endomorph Character

Using a version of the same head object as in the previous exercise, this exercise shows you how to create the various Endomorphs for facial animation in Layout. Using the Selection Sets from Exercise 12.1 will help you get started.

1. Select Close All Objects from the File menu in Modeler to start clean, and then load the 12StartHead_Sets.lwo object.

   This is the head object you loaded in Exercise 12.1, but with Selection Sets applied to the eyes, upper lip, and lower lip. These areas are normally hard to select, and because the specific surfaces cover more area than is needed to adjust their position, a Selection Set is appropriate.

2. Open the Point Statistics panel, and click the bottom triangle to view the Selection Sets, as in Figure 12.8.

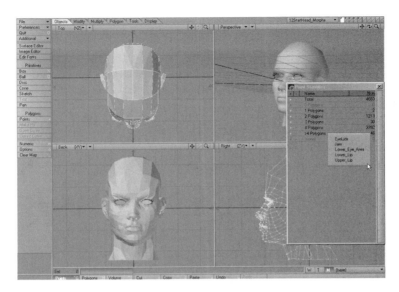

Figure 12.8   The Selection Sets for the head model are ready to be selected and used to create Endomorphs.

At the bottom right of the Modeler interface are the W, T, and M buttons, for Weight, UV Texture, and Morph.

3. Select the M for Morph. The drop-down list next to it says "base." The model you're viewing in this neutral position is the base model. Click and hold on this list and select "new." The Create Morph Map panel opens.

4. Type in the name Mouth.Open.

It's important to add the dot (.) between Mouth and Open. This creates a group and a slider for the MorphMixer plug-in in Layout. The Mouth becomes a group tab, and the Open becomes a control. You'll see these results later when the model is animated in Layout.

5. For now, keep the type to Relative, and click OK. Figure 12.9 shows the Create Morph Map panel.

Figure 12.9   Selecting "new" from the M list creates a new Morph Map, or Endomorph.

6. In the Point Statistics panel, select the Jaw Selection Set. Click the white plus sign (+) to the left of its name.

The points of the jaw are highlighted.

7. Press the **y** key to select the Rotate tool, and from where the joint of the jaw would be—in front of the ear—click and drag slightly to rotate the jaw, opening the mouth. You just created an Endomorph!

Figure 12.10 shows Modeler, with the Point Statistics panel open, and the Rotate Numeric tool. These are moved to the side so that all tools and the interface are visible.

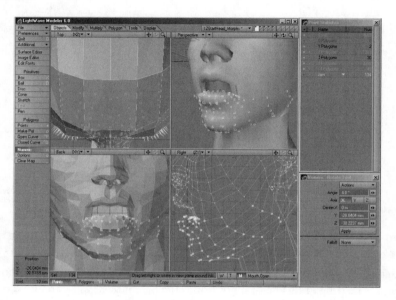

Figure 12.10   Use the Selection Set and the Rotate tool to easily open the character's mouth in preparation for setting up an Endomorph.

8. From the M drop-down list, select Base, and the mouth should return to its original position, closed. Then from the list, select the newly created Endomorph, Mouth.Open.

You'll see the mouth open.

9. Deselect the jaw points by clicking in a blank area of the screen, or by pressing the minus sign (–) next to the Selection Set name in the Point Statistics panel. Turn off the Rotate tool by pressing the spacebar.

10. From the M (Morph) list at the bottom right of the Modeler interface where you created your first Endomorph, select "new" again.

11. Name this new Morph Map Eyes.Blink, and click OK.

12. Select the Eyelids Selection Set from the Point Statistics panel. When the name is added to the list, press the white plus sign (+) next to the name to select the eyelid set.

13. Again, select the Rotate tool (**y**) and from the corner of the eye in the right view, click and drag to close the eyelids. You might need to move them forward slightly on the –Z axis to completely cover the eyeballs. Figure 12.11 shows the change.

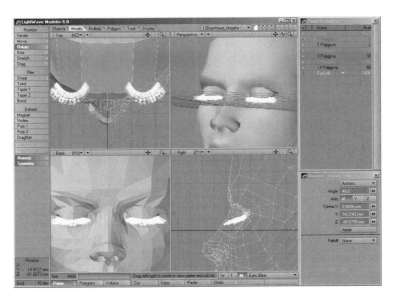

Figure 12.11   The Eyelids Selection Set is used to close the eyelids and create another Endomorph.

14. Turn off the Rotate tool, and deselect the eyelid points. Choose the base Endomorph to view the eyelids open, then choose the Eyes.Blink Endomorph you just created. You'll see the eyes open and close.

From this point on, you need to create the phonetics of speech. Doing so is easy with reference and Selection Sets. The model you've loaded for the previous exercise has the Selection Sets you need to begin shaping the mouth into proper phonetics. A model with many Endomorphs already made is on the CD. The file is labeled 12CoverHead_Morphs.lwo. This model has Selection Sets as well as a full set of Endomorphs. When you get a chance, load this model into Modeler and look at the different Endomorph positions.

Before moving on to the next section, make a note of the following things to remember when creating Endomorphs:

- Always select "new" from the M list before creating an Endomorph. If you don't, you will end up making adjustments to an already set morph target.

- Use the something-dot-something naming convention to properly set up group assignments for the MorphMixer in Layout. Examples are Mouth.Open and Mouth.Closed. The Mouth becomes a group, and the Open and Closed become slider controls.

- Although phonetic speech is complex, you can convincingly get away with making only vowel sounds and facial expressions. For example, A, E, I, O, and U, along with a smile, open mouth, frown, and grin, can create enough combinations of morphs for lip-syncing.

- Try using the Bkd-to-Morf command from the Additional drop-down list to create a Morph Map from a background object. For example, if you have multiple morph target objects—say, from a previous version of LightWave—you can combine these targets into one target with Bkd-to-Morf. With the LightWave 6 Endomorph in the foreground and the morph target in a background, you can apply the tool to create a new Morph Map.

- Use the VMap Copy command from the Additional drop-down list to copy one Endomorph to another. For example, you've created an Endomorph of a great smile. It took some time to get it just right. The next Endomorph you need to create is similar to this smile. If you select "new" to create a new Endomorph, your model will jump back to the base model.

  Instead, run VMap copy, as seen in Figure 12.12, and select the Morph Map you want to copy as the Source VMap, then type in a new name. Click OK, and you'll see the new name in the morph list. Select it, and make any minor adjustments.

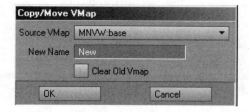

Figure 12.12   The VMap copy tool enables you to copy any of your morph maps.

- You can clear a map, morph or otherwise, by selecting the Clear Map From Vertices command, also found in the Additional drop-down list. Select the Morph Map you want to remove, then run the command, or press the underscore (_) key.

- When creating phonetics for speech, don't just move the lips. Too often, animators forget about the rest of the face, making their characters look stiff and unnatural.

Figures 12.13, 12.14, 12.15, and 12.16 show different facial expressions you can use as references.

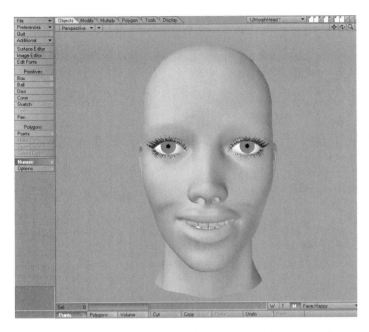

Figure 12.13   A smile. Notice how the lower lids of the eyes ride up, as do the cheeks. The facial expression is more than just a change to the mouth.

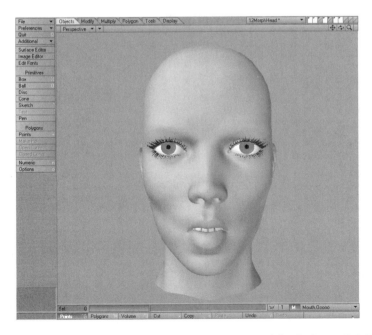

Figure 12.14   A pucker. This expression is a morph target used for the letters P, B, U, Q, G, or O.

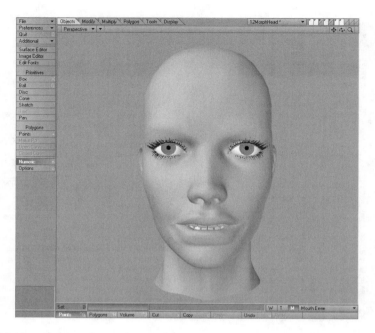

Figure 12.15   The same face making the E sound. This can be a morph target for E, I, C, S, T, V, Z, or D

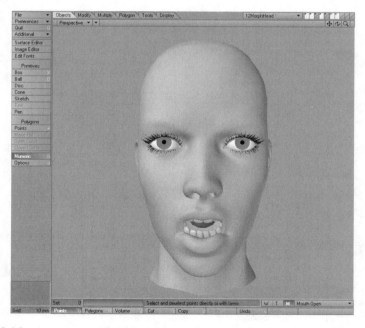

Figure 12.16   An open mouth. This can be used as a morph target for A, H, J, K, R, or Y.

These figures and letter references are not rules but merely guidelines. Remember that you can use just a percentage of a morph target or blend targets to create different facial expressions. The examples here are good for many situations, but if you are creating a larger production, or something that is higher profile (such as a network television show), you should consider modeling many morph targets. Although the vowel sounds can suffice for most everyday projects, taking the time up front to create morph targets of the full alphabet (a, b, c, d, and so on) will pay off in the long run. With all 26 letters of the alphabet created as morph targets, as well as many expressions (sad, happy, angry), you will never be at a loss for achieving the right look.

From this point on, take some time and make many Endomorph targets with different vowel sounds. Along with applying Selection Sets to points, the best way to shape the face of a character is to do it point by point. It is situations such as this when modifying detailed areas of a character benefit from good modeling. Overbuilt models will give you more headaches than you can imagine. Making morph targets and phonetics for faces is exceedingly easy when the character is built with SubPatches, which you'll do in Exercise 12.3.

Endomorphs in Layout

As much fun as you had creating different expressions for your character, when it comes to facial animation, the real fun is in Layout. LightWave's Layout gives you the tools you need to create talking characters. In the next exercise, you will load an audio track from the book's CD-ROM directly into Layout, and animate the cover model of this book to the sound track. You'll use a displacement plug-in called MorphMixer, as well as the Graph Editor.

Before you begin, there are some new things in LightWave 6 that can make your life much easier when it comes to bones, characters, and parented objects. It has always been a challenge in previous versions of LightWave to have eyeballs attached to a character head whose motions are controlled by bones. LightWave 6 enables you to parent anything you want to bones. When you bring in a MultiMesh object, such as the head for this tutorial, there are separate layers with the head, eyeballs, teeth, and tongue. These layers can be parented to the head, but if the head has bones deforming it, the parented objects will not be deformed. This is because bones deform the points, not the polygons, of an object. Instead, you can parent the eyeballs directly to the controlling bone. To do this, select the item you want to parent, such as the eyeball, and press **m** on the keyboard to open the Motion Options panel. At the top for Parent Item, select the appropriate bone. After it is parented, the eyeball will deform with the bone, but it can still be animated on its own for, say, rotating eyes.

Another way to associate parented items with a boned layer is to use the bones for every layer. For example the head in the scene you'll load has two bones in it, just like the examples in Chapter 11, "Character Construction." The bones are associated with the head object. The other layers, such as the eyes, tongue, and teeth, have no bones. Essentially, every layer from Modeler is treated as an independent object. You can associate any layer of the object, such as the eyeballs, to the bones of the head. For example, if you select the eyeball layer of the object, then switch to Bones mode, you'll see that the current item listing for bones reads (none). Even so, pressing the **p** key brings you into the Bones Properties for the eyeball layer. At the top of the interface, you can specify to Use Bones From Object, such as the head. Figure 12.17 shows the panel.

> **Note**
>
> Applying the Use Bones From Object method is great, but you will not be able to independently animate these associated objects. The bones from the selected object will solely influence them.

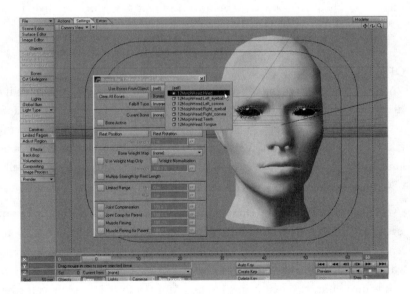

Figure 12.17   You can assign any layer of an object to Use Bones From Object.

Exercise 12.3   Creating Talking Characters

For this exercise, be sure to save any work you've done, and then Clear Layout. Also, save any work you might have in Modeler and close the program. Using audio in Layout requires more system resources than normal, and because you won't need any program other than LightWave Layout, close them all now.

I. In Layout, load the 12HeadParenting.lws scene. This is a version of the cover head that you can use for setting up lip sync. The eyeballs, tongue, and teeth are parented to the head. Figure 12.18 shows the scene. Note that the camera is cheated over to the left to leave room for use of the MorphMixer panel.

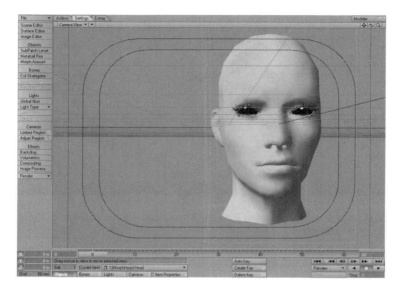

Figure 12.18   The 12HeadParenting.lws when loaded. The Display SubPatch Level is set to 1 for faster updates in Layout.

2. Select the Objects button at the bottom of Layout.

3. Press the **p** key to enter the Object Properties panel.

You'll see in the Geometry tab that the Display SubPatch Level is set to 1 for faster display in Layout, but the Render SubPatch Level is set to 4, creating a high-quality model when rendering.

Also in the Geometry tab of the Item Properties panel for the head, you'll find the Subdivision Order drop-down list. This is important for SubPatched objects in Layout. Figure 12.19 shows the list.

These settings tell LightWave when you want the SubPatch data calculated. By default, the value is set to First, meaning LightWave will subdivide the object before applying effects such as displacement. Figure 12.20 shows the head model morphed with the Subdivision Order set to First.

With Subdivision Order, you can choose from First, After Morphing, After Displacement, After Bones, After Motion, and Last. Figure 12.21 shows how the same model looks in Layout with Subdivision Order set to Last.

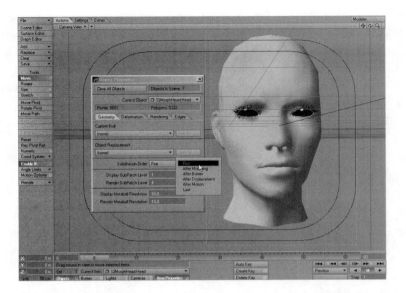

Figure 12.19   The Subdivision Order list within the Geometry tab of the Item Properties for an Object.

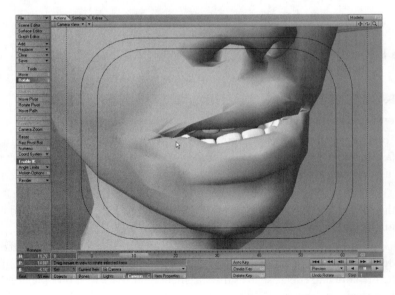

Figure 12.20   With the Subdivision Order set to First, your object will be subdivided and then morphed (for lip-syncing). With this order, your morph is stretching the final model, resulting in a cracked surface. Note the corners of the mouth in this image.

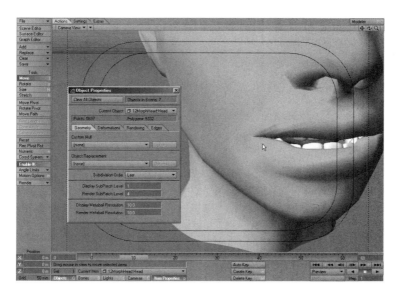

Figure 12.21 With Subdivision Order set to Last, the cracked surface at the corner of the lips is no longer there.

As you can see, changing (or setting) the Subdivision Order is important to your projects.

4. For this exercise, set the Subdivision Order to Last for best results.

Note

Using Subdivision Order set to Last, your system performance will suffer slightly. Be patient.

5. Set your Current Object to 12MorphHead:Head from the top of the Object Properties panel, and then select the Deformations tab. From the Add Displacement list, select LW_MorphMixer. Figure 12.22 shows the selection.

You should see the words "Mixing 11 MORPHs in 3 Groups" under the Name column.

6. Double-click this to open the MorphMixer panel. Figure 12.23 shows the MorphMixer interface.

You can see in the image that there are three groups across the top. If you remember, creating new Endomorphs with the Mouth.Open style, the Mouth portion of the name is now a tab or group. You can see that sliders have been created for the second part of the name. Mouth is the group, and Open is the control slider.

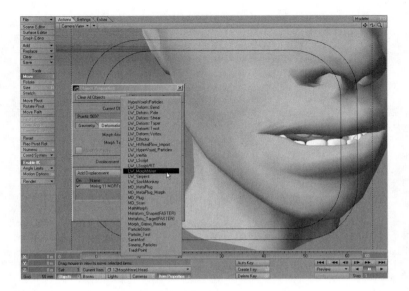

Figure 12.22   Selecting the displacement plug-in LW_MorphMixer applies the MorphMixer to your object.

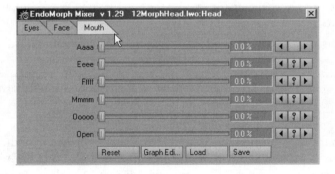

Figure 12.23   The MorphMixer interface shows all the Endomorphs created in Modeler.

7. Close the Object Properties panel, leaving only the MorphMixer panel open. Move the panel down to the left so that the model in Layout is in view, as in Figure 12.24.

Note
If you have a dual-monitor setup, now is the time to use it.

8. Click in the Layout window, and then press the **d** key to call up the Display Options panel. Set the Bounding Box Threshold to 6000 or higher.

With a SubPatched head object of 1 and a threshold of 6000, the head object will remain solid while using MorphMixer.

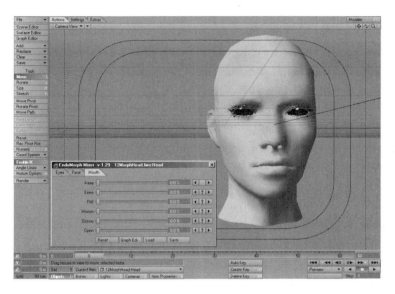

Figure 12.24   LightWave 6's non-modal panels enable you to keep the MorphMixer window open and move it aside while working.

9. Back in the MorphMixer panel, click and drag the slider labeled Open from the Mouth group.

Watch the mouth open on the character. You'll also notice that a small key mark has been added to the end of the slider, telling you a keyframe has been made. Figure 12.25 shows the mark.

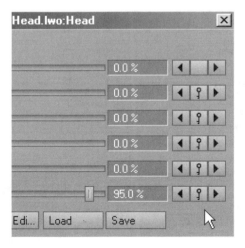

Figure 12.25   Clicking a slider button and either sliding it or not creates a keyframe, which is represented by the small key mark in the MorphMixer window.

The timeline slider in Layout was at frame 0. By moving the slider for Open in the MorphMixer window, you instantly created a keyframe of an open mouth at frame zero.

10. Now, move the timeline slider in Layout to frame 10. Back in the MorphMixer panel, click the Face tab.

You'll see four sliders for the face: Frustrated, Grin, Happy, and Sad.

11. Drag the Frustrated slider to 100%.

You'll see the model update in Layout. You now have made a combination of Mouth.Open and Face.Frustrated Endomorphs. If you make a small preview in Layout, you can see the face with an open mouth at frame zero, and a frustrated look at frame 10.

These are the basics of setting up MorphMixer with an Endomorph character. Try different settings, different timings, and different combinations of morphs to see what you can come up with. Also, take your time to get a feel for how the sliders work in combination with other groups in the model.

Exercise 12.4   Animating with Audio

This exercise uses LightWave's audio feature to do more with Endomorphs and the MorphMixer plug-in. What good is a cool morphing plug-in without audio to sync it up to?

1. With the 12HeadParenting.lws scene from Exercise 12.3 loaded, open Layout's Scene Editor. From the Audio drop-down list at the top of the interface, select Load Audio, as in Figure 12.26. Load the bald.wav audio file from the book's CD-ROM.

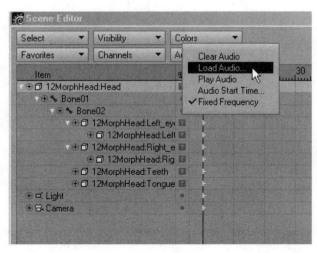

Figure 12.26   You can load a .WAV file into Layout to time your animations, or to lip sync characters to.

2. Click the Fixed Frequency option in the Audio drop-down list to keep the audio playing at the right pitch in Layout. Also from the Audio drop-down list, select Play Audio.

You should hear "I'm bald and I'm beautiful." This is the audio file you'll animate to.

3. Close the Scene Editor.

If you look at the timeline in Layout, you'll see a visual representation of your audio, as in Figure 12.27. This is a helpful guide when lip-syncing characters.

Figure 12.27 Adding audio to Layout is represented by a visual graph in the timeline.

4. Open the MorphMixer panel to animate the face of the character.

5. Move the panel to the side but above the Layout timeline. You'll be using both the Layout timeline and the MorphMixer panel. Drag the Layout timeline back and forth and you'll hear the loaded audio. Listen carefully. What is being said and at what frame? Repeat the words and pay attention to the shape of your mouth.

To say the first word of the audio, "I'm," the mouth starts open, then closes just four frames later.

6. At frame zero, slide the Mouth.Open slider to about 65%. You can just type 65% into the MorphMixer panel as well.

7. Now move the Layout timeline to 4.

You'll hear the "m" part of "I'm," and you can start to hear the "b" sound of "bald," the next word in the audio track.

8. At frame 4, bring the Mouth.Open slider back to zero.

A keyframe is automatically created for you.

Now, around frames 6 to 11, the "bal" of "bald" sound is happening. Here, you can accentuate the "m" part of "I'm" before the character opens her mouth again to say "bald." This also buys some time between words, without creating a stiff face.

9. At frame 8, move the Mmmm slider to about 40%, and the Oooo slider to 30%.

You'll see that the mouth of the character changes slightly. This adds a nice, soft transition between morph targets and avoids linear change between keyframes.

10. At frame 13, bring all sliders back to 0% to close the mouth for the "d" in "bald."

11. Move the Layout timeline to frame 21 or so and you'll hear the "and" part of the phrase. Create a keyframe at 20 to keep the mouth closed from frame 16, its last keyframe, to frame 20. Then at frame 22, drag the Open slider about 40%. Also, set the Oooo to 0%.

As you can see, you can get away with making a character talk without many phonetic morph targets. If you create the vowel sounds, you can re-create most speech patterns. Of course, a full Endomorph with proper phonetics is always best if you have the time.

12. At frame 22, the audio begins to say "and I'm," so set a keyframe at 20 with the mouth closed, then opened slightly at frame 23 or 24.

This will keep the mouth closed right until the time it should speak and then close slightly after frame 22.

13. From here, move the Oooo and the Open slider to shape the character's lips to the "beau" sound of "beautiful." This is the next syllable the character will say at about frame 23 or so.

14. Bring the Oooo slider up slightly and the Open slider down at frame 46 or so, for the "eauti" part of "beautiful."

From this point, you can drag the Layout timeline, listen to the audio, adjust the Endomorph, and continue making the character talk. Here's a rule to work by: Do it until it looks right! There's no set formula for creating the perfect Endomorph character. Use your morph targets together to make your character look and act the way you want. After you have the mouth positions set, you can go back to frame zero in the Layout timeline, and then start adding other Endomorph groups. For example, as the character begins talking, choose the Eyes.Blink Endomorph and make her blink. Move through the timeline listening to the audio, and when you feel that the character should blink, set the Endomorph. Remember, you need to set a keyframe to keep the eyes open until the blink occurs. If not, the blink will begin from the last keyframe, which could result in a blink taking many seconds! Most blinks happen in about three frames. Three frames to close, three frames to open.

Continue just like you have in these steps. Drag the Layout timeline slider, and then adjust your morph target. You'll be doing this over and over to make sure your audio is in sync with the character's face. It becomes quite repetitive, and sometimes confusing, when you hear the same audio track over and over. When this happens, take a break and come back to the animation. You'll be better for it. You also can make a preview of the animation for better playback. Do this by selecting Make Preview from the Preview drop-down list at the bottom right of the Layout interface.

Endomorphs and the Graph Editor

There might be a time when the MorphMixer panel is just not enough. This is when you could use LightWave 6's Graph Editor. At the bottom of the MorphMixer interface is a button labeled Graph Editor. Entering the Graph Editor through the MorphMixer panel automatically loads the channels of the Endomorphs. This enables you to see and grab the keyframes and adjust the values in real time. Figure 12.28 shows the Graph Editor, as accessed through the MorphMixer.

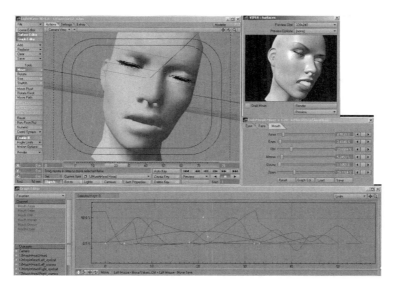

Figure 12.28   The Graph Editor might be your choice for better control or just timing adjustments for your morphs. Here, LightWave Layout has been sized down, the MorphMixer panel moved to the right, and the Graph Editor moved to the bottom. This configuration enables you to see all your controls at once.

By accessing the Graph Editor through the MorphMixer window, you can see each channel of motion. You also can see the keyframes created by MorphMixer. Using the Graph Editor for Endomorphs enables you to precisely control keyframes by adding them, deleting them, or adjusting values. Of course, you'll have real-time feedback in Layout. Using the Graph Editor to tweak your lip-syncing projects is highly recommended, as you can cross-reference channels with others. For example, in Figure 12.28, the Mouth.Aaaa channel is selected, and you can see the curve with keyframes in the curve window. The other channels are visible in the background. This is beneficial because you can see if a facial expression is overriding a mouth position, or perhaps an eyeblink is drifting over too many frames.

Note

When you have the MorphMixer panel open as well as the Graph Editor, you can instantly update the channels in the Graph Editor by clicking the specific group tab in the MorphMixer panel. For example, if the Mouth tab is selected and the Graph Editor is opened from the MorphMixer panel, the Mouth channels are visible. Clicking the Eyes tab in the MorphMixer panel, then clicking the Graph Editor button again updates the channels in the Graph Editor.

In addition to using the Graph Editor to edit and create keyframes for your Endomorph character, you can use Modifiers to automate Endomorphs. The following exercise shows you how to add Modifiers to Endomorphs.

Exercise 12.5   Adding Endomorph Modifiers

1. Load 12HeadOsc.lws into Layout. Go to the Objects Properties panel and select the 12MorphHead object. Add and open the MorphMixer plug-in.

2. Select the Eyes group, and click the Graph Editor button from within the MorphMixer panel.

   The Graph Editor opens, and the Eyes.Blink channel is in the Curve Bin.

3. Click the Modifiers tab in the Graph Editor and from the Add Modifier list select LW_Oscillator. After it's loaded, double-click the oscillator listing to open its control panel.

4. In the Oscillator panel, change the Cycle time to .5, making the blinks occur every half-second. All the other settings are okay at their defaults. You can, however, change the Damping to 25% or so, to make the oscillator modifier fade off toward the last frame of the animation. If you set a value for Damping, you'll see the change reflected in the curve line in the Oscillator panel.

5. Close the Oscillator panel, and press the Play button in Layout.

   You'll see the character blink repeatedly, and you didn't set up keyframes.

Using Modifiers with Endomorphs is much more powerful than the basics in this exercise. You can easily create repeating motions with offsets. You can modify an Endomorph in Modeler, and assign the change to the modified channel. For example, you've set up the LW_Oscillator plug-in for the eyes. Perhaps your client wants you to make the ears wiggle while the eyes blink. Instead of adding another channel to the ears, you can assign the ear selection to the Eyes.Blink Endomorph in Modeler. Saving the changed object updates Layout, in turn updating the channels the LW_Oscillator modifies. You must have the LightWave Hub running for updates between Modeler and Layout.

> **Note**
>
> You need to remember that a keyframe will drift if it is not locked down. For example, if you want the character to blink 16 frames into the animation, setting only a keyframe at frame 16 will make a blink that's 16 frames long—very slow. Instead, remember to create a keyframe a few frames before the blink, so the eyes stay open until it's time for them to blink.

Experiment with other modifiers, such as the LW_AudioChannel modifier. This modifier enables you to load an audio clip and assign it to a channel. If you selected the Mouth.Open channel and applied the LW_AudioChannel modifier, LightWave would move the Endomorph based on the strength and weakness of the audio waveform. You might need to adjust the values to get the right effect.

The LW_AudioChannel modifier is really useful for things such as animated VU meters (VU is short for "volume units," a measure of average audio power). It also is useful for any movement that needs to be modified to match a sound. You can load a music file with the LW_AudioChannel (double-click to open the controls), and assign a rotation channel to it.

Additional Lip-Sync Tools

LightWave 6 has just about everything you need for quality character animation work. Its methods, however, might not be suited for you. If that's the case, there is another program that works with LightWave, but it is a standalone application. Magpie Pro, from Third Wish Software, offers the user an integrated set of tools for lip-syncing characters. It uses prerendered thumbnail images and can also reference an .AVI file. You can even load 3D objects into Magpie Pro as well. Figure 12.29 shows the Magpie Pro interface.

Magpie Pro can be used to scrub the audio track and manually fill the exposure sheet frame by frame to obtain a highly detailed animation, or it can automatically analyze the audio and fill the exposure sheet. Magpie Pro's audio support is excellent, providing real-time feedback of your character lip-syncing.

Besides synching character mouths to audio tracks, Magpie Pro can be used to sync almost anything to the audio. It also can be used as a timing tool without the need for an audio track. Magpie Pro provides export options to many 3D animation programs, generating animation files with the preview contents. Another cool feature of Magpie Pro is that you can print the exposure sheet of your audio track as reference for setting up animations and timing. The software exports its information for LightWave 6. Check out Magpie Pro at http://www.thirdwish.simplenet.com.

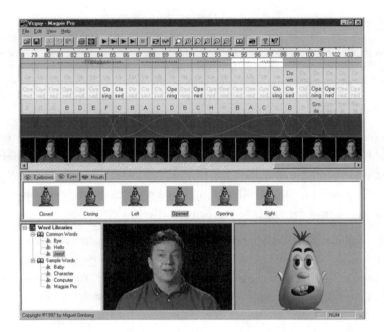

Figure 12.29   Magpie Pro is a third-party software application that can enhance your lip-syncing capabilities.

The Next Step

There are 10 various .WAV audio clips on the book's CD-ROM. These are here for you to use to animate your characters. Use the models on the CD to make Endomorphs, and try animating them to the audio provided. The details in this chapter have given you enough references and examples so that you can build your own characters with expression and personality and make them come to life. Remember that using the audio feature in Layout can be for more than just lip-syncing. You can use the audio feature to time your animations. By listening to the audio track, you can quickly determine what position a character should take. More importantly, you'll know exactly when to change the character's position because it will be based on the timing of audio. Use the bones in the sample animation to move the character's head around after you assign morph targets for speech. When the animation is timed up, you can render it and, in your favorite editing solution, such as the Video Toaster, attach the audio clip you've been using as a reference to the final animation. They will time up perfectly.

Note
Rendering animations with an audio clip loaded does not save the audio with your file.

Summary

Throughout this chapter, tips and tricks were mentioned to help you become a better animator. No single book can do that, nor can a library of books. It's up to you to take this knowledge of Endomorphs, SubPatches, and MorphMixer and put it all together to create the type of characters you've always wanted.

Chapter 13

Inverse Kinematics

For years, character animation has been the veritable Holy Grail of 3D animation. Until recently, only an elite few could do it, and those who were good at it were in high demand. To reach a competitive level of character animation required expensive software running on even more expensive workstations. However, with today's advances in technology, more and more of these high-end tools are becoming available to the general public. LightWave 6 offers character animation tools that not only rival the big boys, but also surpass them on many levels. One such tool is the new hybrid kinematics engine for character setup and animation. Figure 13.1 is a character rigged with LightWave's hybrid kinematics.

Figure 13.1   This character was set up with a mixture of kinematics systems in LightWave 6.

The basic method for manipulating a character is with forward kinematics (FK). FK systems have been around for awhile, and since the early days of animation they have been the main technique for character manipulation. Recently, a more powerful and easy-to-use kinematics system was developed: inverse kinematics (IK).

Although IK has many benefits over FK, due to its lack of proper integration into animation software, many animators still prefer using FK. Several animation packages limit the amount of control available to IK setups. Some software even gives preferential treatment to one kinematics system over the other. Obviously, limiting the power of one system in favor of another is not the best solution. LightWave 6 was built around a hybrid IK/FK engine that seamlessly integrates IK and FK systems in a user-friendly environment. This new hybrid system is one of the fastest and most powerful systems available.

This chapter introduces you to the world of IK, and through the use of exercises it teaches you the techniques involved with utilizing IK in character animation. Specifically, this chapter discusses:

- Basic inverse kinematics usage
- Character setup
- Rigging a real character
- Configuring inverse kinematics chains

Understanding Kinematics

Kinematics is the study of motion without consideration of the forces acting upon it. Essentially, it is the study of raw motion—motion in its most basic form. Kinematics in 3D animation is not too different from its real-world counterpart. In 3D animation, kinematics refers to the basic technique of manipulating items or placing items into motion. The actual method used to manipulate the item is called a kinematics system.

Kinematics systems come in two basic flavors: forward and inverse. Each system is unique and can be used for your benefit. Because LightWave 6 enables the use of both FK and IK, you should familiarize yourself with each system.

Forward Kinematics

FK, a technique more commonly known as keyframe animation, is the default method of motion in LightWave. The actual term "forward kinematics" is rarely mentioned unless it's being referred to in hierarchical or character animation. The main advantage of FK is its accuracy. In FK you place the items exactly where you want them placed. FK doesn't require any additional setup to begin using it. You are animating with FK when you begin directly keyframing objects. FK also has a huge disadvantage; it is time consuming. After all, it is basically the technique of hand-positioning each object in a hierarchy—starting with the root object and then moving forward through the chain, rotating and keyframing each item to form the desired pose. Every time you need to change something you must re-keyframe all the items in the chain.

If you were to animate a character's arm with FK, you would first create the arm in a hierarchical form. This arm would consist of fingers parented to a hand, the hand parented to a forearm, and the forearm parented to an upper arm. The pivot point for each item would be located at the joint between the child and its parent, resulting in rotation that is similar to that of a real arm. Due to the nature of parent/child relationships, any time a parent item is manipulated, its movement is directly translated to its children. To animate this arm, you would start by rotating the upper arm into position, followed by the forearm, the hand, and finally by the fingers. Figure 13.2 shows the technique of using FK to animate such an arm.

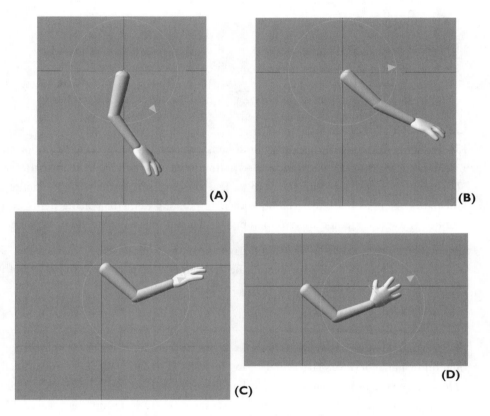

Figure 13.2   When positioning this bone structure (A) with FK, the upper-arm bone is first rotated into position (B), followed by the lower arm (C), and finally by the hand bone (D).

With FK, a keyframe must be created for each item in the hierarchy every time you change something. Imagine animating a complex character with nothing but FK. Obviously this is not the ideal way to animate. A faster, easier-to-use, and much more flexible kinematics system was developed: IK.

Inverse Kinematics

IK—or, as it is more descriptively called, goal-driven animation—operates on the principle of manipulating a single "goal object" to position an entire object hierarchy.

In essence, it is the opposite of FK. Rather than working from the root item forward through the hierarchy, you use a goal object to manipulate the hierarchy from the end, through the root item.

Where FK requires the keyframing of multiple items, IK only requires you to keyframe a goal object to control the entire hierarchy. The obvious advantage of this is the amount of time saved during animation. You now have free time to focus on much more important things, such as timing. A few more initial steps are involved in setting up an IK system, but the time saved in keyframing outweighs the extra expense of setup.

To animate the above-mentioned arm with IK you would only need to add a goal object, and then set up controllers for each joint. After the joints are set up, you can control the entire arm just by moving the goal object (see Figure 13.3).

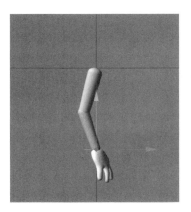 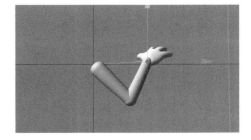

Figure 13.3   Inverse kinematics is controlling the arm. The null object at the joint between the hand and the forearm serves as the goal object.

The easiest way to understand each kinematics system is through the following analogy: If you were to pull on someone's finger, his or her arm would follow wherever you moved the finger. Every joint in the arm would automatically rotate to allow the finger to reach its goal. This type of movement is basically real-world IK. However, if a person were to reach out for a glass of water, their brain would tell their upper arm to rotate a certain amount, followed by the rotation of the forearm and of each joint thereafter, until it reaches the glass. This movement is FK.

Think of FK as an "internal force" driving the movement of the hierarchy to the desired position, and IK as an "external force" pulling the hierarchy into position.

As you can see, both techniques are quite useful and each offers its own set of advantages and disadvantages. The benefits of each system are far too great to consider throwing one out in favor of the other. FK will definitely work better than IK in certain situations, and vice versa. In a perfect world you could use both at the same time. LightWave 6 brings you as close to a perfect world as you can get with its new hybrid IK/FK engine, which enables you to mix IK and FK in the same character, chain, or even bone!

Basic IK Usage

The hierarchical structure used in an IK system is called an IK chain. IK chains in LightWave can be composed of any item capable of existing in a hierarchy. When using an IK chain, LightWave internally computes the rotations of each item in the chain based on the position of a goal object (see Figure 13.4). The result of this internal calculation is called a solution. The process of reaching the solution is referred to as solving, or being solved for.

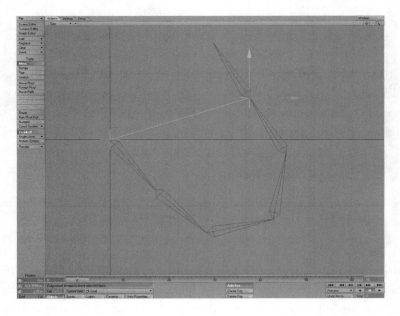

Figure 13.4   Manipulating the goal object in this IK chain automatically creates the rotations for each bone.

Unfortunately, an IK chain can often have more than one solution, which could result in errors. To help avoid these errors, the chain must be cheated slightly using "preferred angles." A slight bend at the joints in a chain tells LightWave this is the "preferred angle" of rotation (see Figure 13.5). LightWave will then try to rotate the items based on that angle. Even with preferred angles, solutions can still get messy and sometimes require the setup of angle limits.

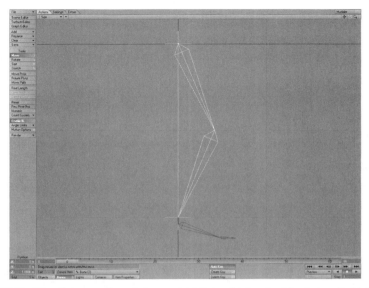

Figure 13.5   The slight rotation of the two highlighted joints in this chain tells LightWave to rotate the chain based on this "preferred angle."

LightWave has the ability to use multiple IK chains in the same structure. This enables the creation of complex systems. Multiple IK systems in the same skeletal structure offer a greater level of control over an object. For instance, a biped character will commonly have separate IK chains for each legand arm (see Figure 13.6). You could then animate the entire character simply by moving the goal objects.

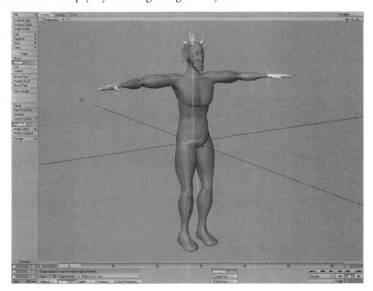

Figure 13.6   This character contains four IK systems, all in one complete bone structure. The arms and legs are all controlled by IK.

Constraining Rotations with Angle Limits

Many times when setting up a character you will want to limit the range of motion a joint can rotate. The classic example of this is the human knee. If you were to set up an IK chain similar to a human leg, you wouldn't want the lower leg to overextend itself beyond the normal range of motion. Without angle limits, the results could look quite painful. Figure 13.7 demonstrates the benefits of using angle limits in an IK chain.

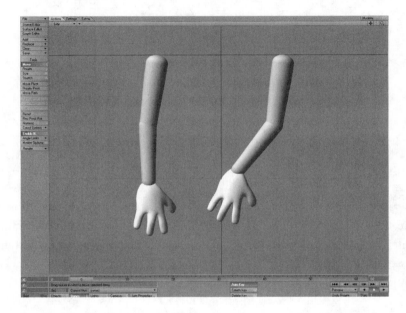

Figure 13.7   The arm on the left is using angle limits to prevent rotation beyond the arm's fully extended position. The arm on the right has no angle limits and shows just how painful a broken elbow could be.

You can set up angle limits interactively for each joint with the Record Angle Limits button in the Actions tab. When recording angle limits, you can control which rotation channels receive the limits through the use of local constraints. If only the pitch is activated, the recorded limit will affect only the pitch channel.

You also can set up angle limits in the Controllers and Limits section of the Motion Options panel. Setting up limits in the Motion Options panel is the most precise method, as you can directly input the minimum and maximum rotational limits for each channel (see Figure 13.8).

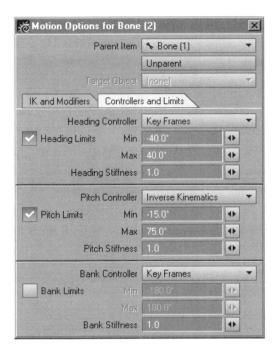

Figure 13.8   You can directly input values for the angle limits in the Motion Options panel. Here, you can see that minimum and maximum values have been set for the Heading Controller and the Pitch Controller.

The Motion Options Panel

LightWave 6 offers one of the most powerful IK engines on the market, and you can harness most of this power in the Motion Options panel. The Motion Options panel is the centerpiece of IK setup. Here you will find most of the controls you'll use to set up, control, and activate IK chains. Like all other panels in LightWave, the Motion Options panel is laid out in an easy-to-understand format.

The first tab is the IK and Modifiers tab (see Figure 13.9). This is where you set up the basic functionality of your chain. Here you select goal objects, activate full-time IK, and set the goal strength for IK chains. Full-time IK means that when IK is applied to elements in your scene, LightWave will always be calculating. Turning this feature off tells LightWave to calculate the IK solution when movements and keyframes are created. You would turn this off for extremely complex kinematic setups that require large amounts of processing information. Most IK solutions work just fine with full-time IK active.

The second is the Controllers and Limits tab (see Figure 13.10). The controllers determine what will control the rotation channels of each item. Each item has three controllers: a Heading Controller, a Pitch Controller, and a Bank Controller. Using the pop-up menu, you can configure each controller to utilize FK or IK independently.

Figure 13.9   The IK and Modifiers tab is where you set up basic IK information.

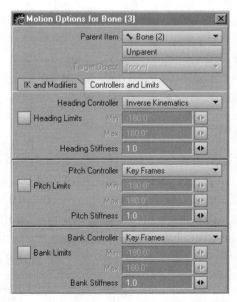

Figure 13.10   The Controllers and Limits tab is where you set up rotation controllers. Here, only the Heading Controller has inverse kinematics applied. The Pitch and Bank Controllers are set to use keyframes.

Goaled Items

Before an IK chain will function, LightWave needs an item in the chain that will point to a goal object and position the items farther up the chain. This "pointer" can be any item as long as it resides in the hierarchy to be controlled by IK. You can configure a pointer item in the Motion Options panel by specifying a goal object for it. When given a goal object, LightWave automatically understands that this item will point to the rest of the chain. These "pointers" are often called goaled items because they have a goal to follow. Figure 13.11 shows proper setup of a goaled item.

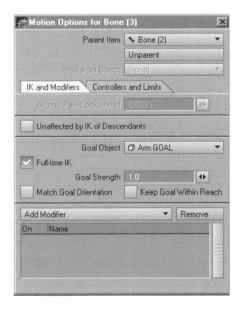

Figure 13.11   Goaled items are configured in the Motion Options panel by specifying a goal object to follow.

Under normal circumstances the pointer item is usually the last item in the chain. However, this is not always the case. LightWave allows the use of multiple goals in the same chain, so one pointer might be at the end of a hierarchy pointing to one of the goals, while another pointer is in the middle of the hierarchy pointing to a different goal. The location of the pointer is determined by the design of your IK chain and will vary with different setups.

Exercise 13.1   Creating a Basic IK Chain

As always, the best way to learn something is to sit down and try it, so fire up the computer and get to it! You'll find that many 3D applications tend to make IK as confusing as possible. IK in LightWave is simple, easy to understand, and straightforward.

LightWave is not only one of the fastest IK engines around, but it is also the easiest to set up.

It might seem like many steps are involved with setting up a simple IK chain. You will soon realize that many of these steps are there because of the flexible choices LightWave offers. It is this flexibility that makes LightWave one of the best character animation systems available. This exercise shows you how to set up IK with a chain of bones in Layout. Note that this is only one example, and this IK information can apply to your objects as well, not just to bones. To see just how simple setting up an IK chain is in LightWave, follow these steps:

1. Start Layout, or if you were already running Layout just clear the scene by choosing Clear Scene from the File pop-up menu.

2. Select Add, Add Object, and then Add Null from the Actions menu. When prompted for a name, type Root.

   This will create a null object named Root, which will serve as the root or base object of the hierarchy.

   In LightWave, bones require an object to reside in; therefore, an object must be created before any bones can be added. Under normal circumstances your bone structure will exist inside a seamless object. The seamless object would serve the same purpose as the null does in this example. For this example, a set of five bones will be used. The number of bones is irrelevant and is just an arbitrary number for demonstration purposes. You should try this exercise again on your own with more than five bones.

3. Create five bones by pressing the equal (=) key five times. Accept the default bone name each time you are prompted to enter a name.

   Using the equal (=) key, bones are automatically created in a hierarchical format, as in Figure 13.12. Each bone is parented to the bone before it. By default, each bone's rest length is set to 1.000, and they are drawn pointing down the Z axis.

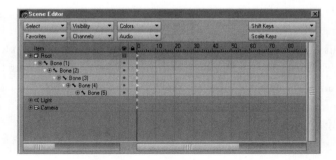

Figure 13.12   A parent/child relationship was established between each bone in the scene. This relationship is what forms the hierarchy. The first bone is parented to the root object, the second bone is parented to the first bone, and so on.

4. Create another null by selecting Add, Add Object, and then Add Null from the Actions menu. Give this null the name Goal. This null object will function as the goal object of the IK chain.

Note

Naming the null object Goal has no effect on the IK chain. It could be given any name; however, using descriptive names makes setup a little easier. You should get into the habit of giving everything a descriptive name.

5. Move the goal null 4m on the Z axis. Press the **n** key to activate the numeric input fields. Enter 4m for the Z value. Moving this null is not necessary for IK to work; however, doing so prevents the bone chain from jumping to attach to the goal when the IK is activated.

The goal null will now jump to 4m on the Z axis. Your scene should now resemble Figure 13.13.

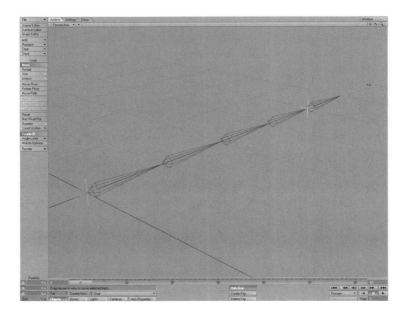

Figure 13.13   Properly laid out, the chain is now ready to be configured for IK.

Note

Notice that the goal was placed at the pivot point of the last bone rather than at the end of the hierarchy. LightWave uses the pivot point of the bone to reach for the goal. Just like parenting or targeting in LightWave, IK goals point to the pivot point of Layout items, such as bones.

In the next few steps you will configure the IK for the bone hierarchy.

6. Select the last bone in the hierarchy. This bone will be the item that points to the rest of the IK chain.

7. With the last bone still selected, enter the Motion Options panel by pressing the **m** key. The Motion Options panel is where you set up most of the controls for the IK chain.

8. Choose the null object named Goal from the Goal Object pop-up menu.

    This will tell LightWave to use the goal as the goal object for the IK solution.

9. Activate Full-Time IK in the Motion Options panel. Full-Time IK forces LightWave to continuously solve for an IK solution. Figure 13.14 shows what the setup for Bone (5) should look like.

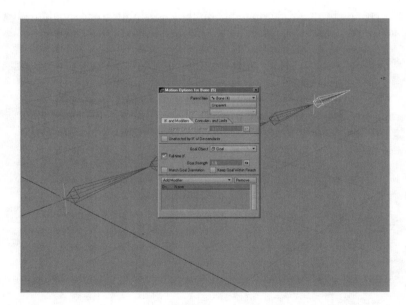

Figure 13.14   The bone has been given a goal object, and Full-Time IK has been activated.

  Note

LightWave's default IK mode is with Full-Time IK deactivated. In the default mode, LightWave calculates IK only while you are physically moving the goal object. If you advance a frame without keyframing the items in the chain, the chain jumps back to its previous pose. The default IK mode is designed to let you pose your character with IK while you use FK to create keyframes. This is useful for quickly posing a character and works much like a puppeteer.

When using Full-Time IK, LightWave will continuously solve for an IK solution. It enables you to animate the goal object. You move a goal and the chain follows, and that's all there is to it. If AutoKey is activated, you won't even need to create keyframes; just move the goal around. You will find that you use Full-Time IK more often than not.

You now have a completed IK chain. The solid blue line extending from the root object to the goal object indicates the completed IK chain. This IK chain in its current state is worthless, however. Before the IK solution will actually control the bones, each bone needs to have a controller set to use IK. You set up these controllers in the Controllers & Limits tab of the Motion Options panel.

Controllers enable you to set up each channel of the current item to be controlled by FK or IK. Although the setup of the controllers at first might seem like an excessive amount of work, it is actually a blessing in disguise. These controllers are one of LightWave 6's great strengths in character animation, as you can mix and match FK and IK in the same item. To set up the controllers for the bones, follow these steps:

10. With the Motion Options panel still open, select the next bone up the chain. Switch to the Controllers & Limits tab.

    Three pop-up menus will appear. These enable you to specify what controls each of the current items' rotation channels.

11. Choose Inverse Kinematics under the Pitch Controllers pop-up. Your setup should look like Figure 13.15.

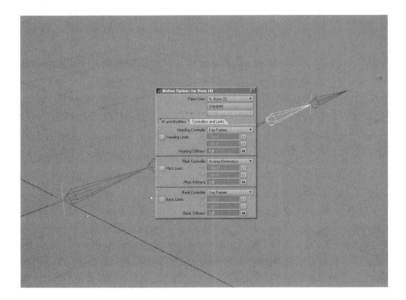

Figure 13.15   The Pitch Controller for each bone is set to Inverse Kinematics.

12. Set the Pitch Controller for all the other bones in the chain to Inverse Kinematics. Save your scene!

The IK chain is now completely functional. Select the goal object and move it around in the scene. The bones will now follow the goal, similar to Figure 13.16. Notice that regardless of the goal's X position, the chain only follows on the YZ axis. This is because the chain is planar or 2D. It's planar because you set IK to control the pitch.

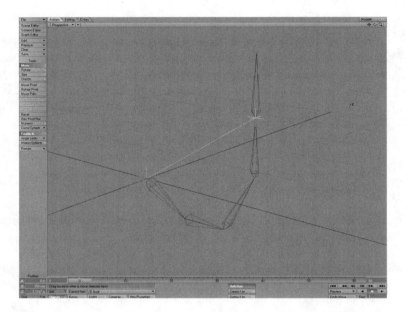

Figure 13.16   Inverse kinematics is being used to manipulate these bones' pitch axis.

Experiment with the basic IK chain by activating IK on different rotation controllers. Apply IK to the heading or bank controllers for each item in the scene. Does the IK chain move differently with the other controllers activated? Experimenting with different configurations will give you more insight into how IK works. You'll also find that the most common IK controls are heading, pitch, and X, Y, Z movements, but not often the bank rotations.

Joint and Chain Types

IK consists of two basic joint types: 3D and planar (2D). Joint types in LightWave are determined by their controller's setup. An IK chain can consist of multiple joint types throughout. With the two basic joint types alone, almost any naturally occurring joint can be replicated in LightWave.

Planar Chains

A chain composed of 2D joints is called a planar IK chain. 2D joints are probably the most commonly used types of joints in character animation. Planar joints are often referred to as hinge joints because they rotate much like a hinge. The elbow and knee joints in human skeletal structures are planar joints. Planar chains are the easiest types to work with because they are limited to one axis around which to rotate. Figure 13.17 shows a planar joint in action.

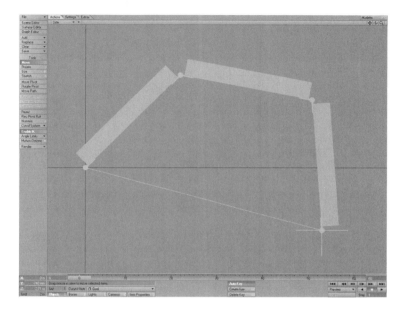

Figure 13.17   A planar joint is limited to rotate around one axis and is often referred to as a hinge joint.

To create a planar joint in LightWave, activate IK for only one rotation controller. This will limit the rotation to one axis controlled by IK.

3D Chains

A 3D chain occurs when all the joints of the chain are set to rotate on more than one axis (see Figure 13.18). The joints of a 3D chain are sometimes called ball joints. A 3D joint will have two or more controllers set to Inverse Kinematics. 3D joints occur everywhere in nature, and you will use them often when setting up characters. The human shoulder is considered to be a 3D joint. Due to the rotational freedom of 3D chains, they are also the most difficult to work with.

Rigid IK Structures

Up until now, you have dealt with IK being used exclusively with bones. The nice thing about IK in LightWave is that it will function with any hierarchical structure, not just with bones. In LightWave, items capable of being parented to other items (except for lights) can participate in an IK chain. IK systems composed of objects rather than bones are referred to as rigid.

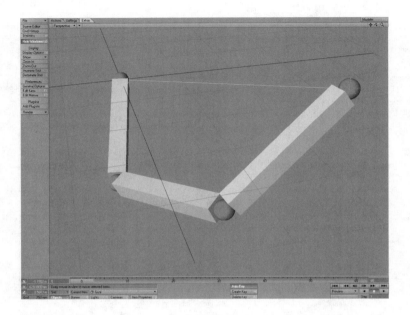

Figure 13.18   3D chains are useful for manipulating objects such as a robot animal's tail.

A rigid IK system physically moves the objects rather than deforming them with bones. Rigid IK systems are great for creating mechanical movement such as that of a robot or a hydraulic actuator. You create a rigid IK system in the same manner as you would an IK system for bones, except you use a hierarchical structure of objects instead of bones.

Exercise 13.2   Creating a Rigid IK System

To better understand how a rigid IK system is used, follow the steps in this exercise. This exercise will help you set up a rigid IK system to simulate a robotic arm.

1. Clear the scene and load the RobotArm.lwo object from the content CD. RobotArm is four separate objects within the same file. Press the **3** key to switch to the Side View mode. The default position of the arm is shown in Figure 13.19 when the object is loaded.

   The RobotArm object consists of five separate objects saved as one object file. Each object has its own pivot point positioned in Modeler to give proper rotations for each joint. The object structure for the robot arm is as follows:

   - RobotArm:Base—The Base is the platform that the robot arm rests on. It is not controlled by IK but can be manipulated through regular keyframe animation. It is the root object in the hierarchy.

- RobotArm:Stand—The Stand is the portion of the robot arm that holds the actual arm in place. In the real world, the stand has a motor at its base to rotate its heading, and it has a motor at the top that rotates the Primary Arm. The robot arm's Stand should have its heading controlled by IK.

- RobotArm:Primary—The Primary Arm is connected to the motor on the Stand. As such, it can only be rotated up and down. You will need to configure the pitch controller of the Primary Arm to use IK.

- RobotArm:Secondary—The Secondary Arm is attached to a motor located at the end of the Primary Arm. It is also rotated only on its pitch, and should be controlled with IK.

- RobotArm:Grabber—The Grabber is the hand of the robot arm. In this case, it contains a tool used for soldering rather than a physical hand. The Grabber can only be rotated on its pitch axis, but it will be the goaled item in the hierarchy and won't need IK controllers.

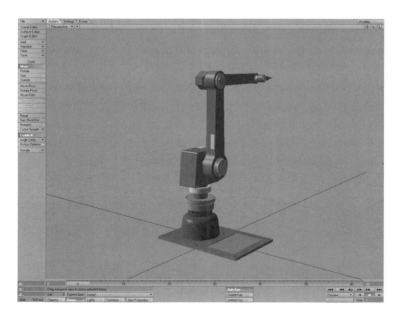

Figure 13.19   RobotArm ready to be animated with inverse kinematics.

You should configure the joints of the robot arm according to the information listed above. Before configuring the joints, you will need to add a goal object for the arm to follow.

2. Select Add, Add Object, and then Add Null to add a null to the scene. When prompted to enter a name for the null, enter Goal. This null object will serve as

the goal object of the robot arm. To manipulate the robot arm, you will just drag the goal around.

3. Click the Keep Goal Within Reach option. The exact positioning isn't all that important, but this option will keep the goal object attached to the IK chain, which helps keep your scene organized.

You need to configure the joints for the arm segments. After they are configured, you can animate the entire arm by dragging the goal object around. The next steps will show how to configure the joints:

4. Select the RobotArm:Stand object. Open the Motion Options panel (**m**) and switch to the Controllers & Limits tab. Using the Heading Controller's pop-up list, choose Inverse Kinematics. Leave all the other settings unchanged. The stand will now rotate around its heading when the goal object is moved.

5. Keep the Motion Options panel open, move it off to the side, and select the RobotArm:Primary object in the Layout interface. Use Inverse Kinematics to control the pitch of the primary arm by choosing it from the pitch controller pop-up.

6. Like the primary arm, the secondary arm can only be rotated on its pitch. Select the RobotArm:Secondary object and set the pitch controller to use IK.

7. Switch back to the Inverse Kinematics and Modifiers tab of the Motion Options panel. Select the RobotArm:Grabber.

This object will point the rest of the chain by following the goal object.

8. To configure the grabber as the goaled item, simply select the goal null from the Goal Objects pop-up list.

This will tell LightWave to follow the goal with the RobotArm:Grabber object and that the grabber is the end of the IK chain.

Note

Because the RobotArm:Grabber object is a rotatable part of the structure, you can also parent a null object at the very tip, and goal that item instead. The benefit is that you will have more control over movements.

9. Finally, activate Full-Time IK for the grabber. Make sure that Show IK Chains from the Display Options panel (**d**) is active, and you'll notice the light-blue line drawn from the RobotArm:Base to the goal object indicating a complete IK chain (see Figure 13.20).

A rigid IK chain now controls the RobotArm. Manipulating the goal will move the RobotArm. Notice how the arm moves similar to that of a real robot arm. This is due to the rigid IK solution. Although a similar setup could be achieved with bones, it isn't necessary and wouldn't give the rigid-looking results.

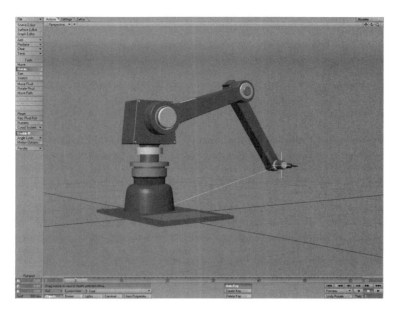

Figure 13.20   Indicated by the line from the base to the goal object, an IK chain is set to control the RobotArm.

Introduction to Character Setup

The proper setup of a character is the most important step to an enjoyable experience in character animation. If you overlook something in the initial stages of setup, you might have hell to pay later when animating the character.

Setting up a character is often called rigging. Rigging is basically the process of configuring a character with animation controls. These controls can be based on FK, IK, or a combination of both. The next few sections of this chapter will focus on the rigging of a human-like skeletal structure and guide you through the process of setting up the animation controls.

The Importance of Preplanning

Character setup can be complicated and, like other aspects of 3D animation, is greatly simplified through some preplanning. Whether you are rigging a simple biped character or a multi-legged centipede, preplanning will be your most important resource.

When planning, gather as much information about your character as possible. The amount of preplanning you need to do varies upon the type of character you want to animate. Research the type of character that you are going to animate to determine how it moves, what range of motion it has, how its joints work, and what traits you want to integrate. The more research you do up front, the more time you will have available to animate.

After you've done your research, it's time to figure out the best setup to use for your character. If your character has a seamless skin, you will more than likely be animating it with bones. A segmented character will probably best be animated with a rigid kinematics system, but you might want to use bones with it as well. If you are using bones, you need to figure out the best placement of the bones to give you the best deformation. For more information on bone setup, see Chapter 12, "Organic Animation."

After you have a basic setup, be it with bones or object segments, you need to determine which joints will be 3D and which need to be planar. Also think about which portions of your character are going to be controlled by what kinematics system. Many factors are involved in good character setup, and figuring out some basic information in advance is essential.

Schematics, like blueprints, can be useful tools during both the preplanning and rigging stages. Using a schematic will help you determine parent/child setup, joint types, and goal placement, as well as many other important factors.

For the purpose of this exercise, you will set up a simple biped skeleton. Because this chapter focuses on the actual kinematics setup, the bone structure has already been created for you. You should closely examine the skeletal structure and determine what animation controls need to be set up. Figure 13.21 shows the skeletal structure in its default pose.

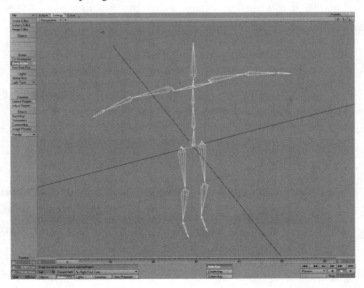

Figure 13.21   The bone structure has been created in an "arms wide open" pose to aid in the setup of the animation controls.

While looking at the skeleton, ask yourself:

- What types of joints need to be set up?
- Is inverse kinematics the ideal system for this character, or should forward kinematics be used? Maybe both systems should be used?
- Where is the best position for the goal objects?
- What range of motion does the character need?

This character was designed to offer a generic range of humanlike motion. After the character is rigged, you can make it walk, run, sit, wave, dance, or perform any other basic primary motion. The skeletal structure could also be modified to offer a precise range of motion for specific tasks.

In 3D animation, it can often be helpful to make different variations of an object designed with different types of motion in mind. If you wanted to make a generic walk cycle, a simple skeleton with basic kinematics control would be more than adequate. However, if you wanted to animate a character with complex motion (such as falling down stairs or washing a car), you would need to design the rig accordingly.

Preparing the Object

After planning the character's setup, the next step is to set up basic controls. The character you will be working with is a basic skeletal structure designed to exploit the setup of IK in LightWave. The actual bone structure is not necessarily the best layout for all characters, but the techniques used in rigging the structure are essential to every character.

Exercise 13.3   Setting Up Basic Controls

1. Clear the scene and add in a null object by selecting Add, Add Object, and then Add Null from the Actions tab. Give this null the name WHOLE_MOVER, and press Enter to accept the name. Load in the IKSkeleton object from the book's CD-ROM. Notice that the object is an empty bounding box. The object is actually a group of skelegons that will need to be converted into usable bones.

> **Note**
>
> The IKSkeleton object is a group of skelegons arranged in a biped skeletal structure. It consists of 30 skelegons ready to be rigged with animation controls. After you feel comfortable with the setup of this structure, you can use it as the skeleton for any of your characters with only a few minor modifications.

2. Press the Cvt Skelegons button located in the Settings tab.

This will convert the skelegons in the object to regular bones so that they are usable in Layout. After pressing the Cvt Skelegons button, you will be prompted that 30 bones were created. The converted skelegons should look like Figure 13.22.

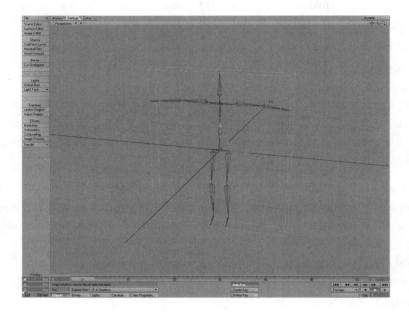

Figure 13.22   This is the IKSkeleton after the skelegons have been converted to regular bones.

Due to the nature of parenting skelegons in Modeler and LightWave's use of pivot points, a few bones need to be tweaked before setting up the animation controls. Click the Bones button at the bottom of the Layout interface, and then look closely at the Left.Arm.Upper bone. It isn't properly aligned with the collarbone; instead, it is located at the tip of the shoulder's control bone. This is a result of parenting skelegons in Modeler.

When you parent a skelegon to another in Modeler, it will be shifted to the tip of the parent skelegon. Usually, this would be perfectly acceptable, but because the Left.Arm.Upper bone needs to be aligned with the collarbone, yet remain the child of the shoulder's control bone, you will have to correct it in Layout. Correcting this is as simple as zeroing out the position values of the shifted bones.

Tip

By using the middle mouse button (if you have one) to select objects or bones in Layout, you do not need to be as precise selecting Layout items. You can easily select items by clicking near them. Deactivate the Left Mouse Button Item Select feature in the General Options panel (o), which helps keep your selections deliberate. Often, with the Left Mouse Button Item Select feature enabled, you inadvertantly select different Layout items while trying to move or rotate. Instead, use the middle mouse button. Cool!

3. Select the Left.Arm.Upper bone, either by middle-clicking the bone itself or by choosing it from the Scene Editor. Press the **n** key to activate the numeric input fields. Enter 0 for all the fields so that the bone's position is indicated as:

   X 0

   Y 0

   Z 0

   The bone will jump back to its proper place and remain parented to the appropriate bone.

4. Repeat this procedure for all the misplaced bones and be sure to save your scene. The bones that need to be fixed are:

   Left.Arm.Upper

   Left.Leg.Upper

   Right.Arm.UpperRight.Leg.Upper

After you finish zeroing out the shifted bones, the skeleton will be ready for setup. The actual rigging process will take a little while to complete, so sit back and enjoy the ride.

Placing Goal Objects

Goal objects are the manipulators for IK chains. They can technically be any objects, but null objects are commonly used because they don't render and are easy to manage. The IKSkeleton will consist of four independent IK chains. It will have a chain for each arm and one for each leg. You will need to create goal objects for each IK chain.

Exercise 13.4   Creating Goal Objects

1. Choose Add, Add Object, and then Add Null from the Actions tab. When prompted for a name, enter LeftARM.GOAL. This null object will serve as the goal object for the left arm IK chain.

   Rather than adding all the nulls at the same time, it is best to configure one side of the character first and then clone the nulls for use on the other side. This will ensure exact goal placement for a symmetrical character.

2. Select the LeftARM.GOAL. This goal needs to be placed into position at the joint between the Left.Arm.Hand and the Left.LowerArm bones. Move the goal into position by either dragging it into a rough position or by entering the following values in the numeric field:

   X   760mm

   Y   600mm

   Z −   121mm

Note

It isn't always necessary to place the goal in an exact position, as the IK chain will jump to the goal when activated. However, keeping your scene clean and precise will make animating much more enjoyable.

3. Clone the LeftARM.GOAL by first selecting the LeftARM.GOAL, choosing Add, and then Clone Current Item. Set Number of Clones to 1 in the dialog that appears, and then click OK or press Enter.

   Doing so will create an exact copy of the LeftARM.GOAL. The clone will be used as the goal object for the right arm.

4. Choose Replace, and then Rename Current Item from the Actions tab. Rename the currently selected null RightARM.GOAL.

5. With the RightARM.GOAL still selected, position it on the opposite side of the character between the Right.Hand and the Right.Forearm bones. The easiest way to do this is to add a negative (−) sign to the X value. The positional values for the RightARM.GOAL should be as follows:

X	−760mm
Y	600mm
Z	−121mm

   You now have the two goals for the arm IK chains in position. When the setup is complete, moving these two goals will give you a full range of motion for the arms. Although all the other goals will be parented to the WHOLE_MOVER null, it is essential that you do not parent the arm goals, as they will be controlled by the Keep Goal Within Reach command discussed in the next exercise. If you've followed along exactly, your scene will look like Figure 13.23.

   Now you are ready to create the goals for the legs. The legs will be a little more complicated than the arms due to the need for two extra goal objects. The extra goals will help keep the feet planted on the floor and give a broader range of motion for the legs. Again, creating the goals for one side and then cloning them for the other side will make things a little easier on you.

6. Add a null object and name it LeftLEG.MASTER. This null will be the main goal you use to manipulate the left leg. Parent this goal to the WHOLE_MOVER null.

7. Add another null object, but this time give it the name LeftLEG.GOAL. The LeftLEG.GOAL will be a descendent of the LeftLEG.MASTER, and as such will inherit its rotations to give a greater level of control for the feet.

8. Using the Scene Editor, drag the LeftLEG.GOAL on top of the LeftLEG.MASTER so that it becomes a child of the LeftLEG.MASTER. When dragging an item in the Scene Editor, you will see a small yellow line directly under the selected item. This line helps you parent items to each other. When the line is slightly offset from the item you want to be the parent, let go of the mouse button (see Figure 13.24).

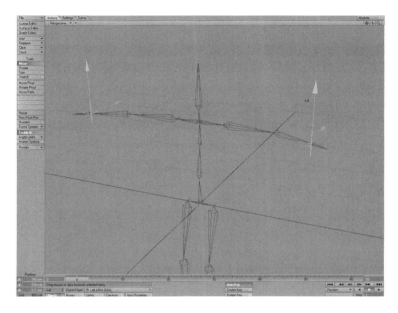

Figure 13.23   The IKSkeleton's arm goals have been placed in the proper positions.

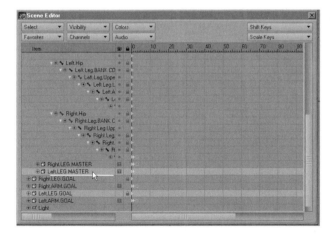

Figure 13.24   The Scene Editor enables you to parent an item to another simply by dragging
it on top of another item.

9. Select the LeftLEG.MASTER object. Move this object to the joint between the
Left.Foot and Left.Toes bones. If you want you can enter the following values in
the numeric field:

X   100mm

Y   −1m

Z   −108mm

Note

The LeftLEG.MASTER is the main item you will use to manipulate the left leg. It is essentially the ball of the foot. Using the goal in this position will give you greater flexibility when posing the feet. Things like heel and toe control are gained using this setup.

Now you will position the LeftLEG.GOAL object at the ankle.

10. Select LeftLEG.GOAL and move it 100mm on Y and 108mm on the Z axes.

This will place it at the joint between the Left.LowerLeg bone and the Left.Ankle bone. The values for the LeftLEG.GOAL's position should look like this:

X	0m
Y	100mm
Z	108mm

That wraps up the goal positioning for the left leg. To create the goal objects for the right leg, follow these step:

11. Select the LeftLEG.MASTER object and clone it by choosing Add, and then Clone Current Item. Cloning does not clone descendents, so you will need to clone the LeftLEG.GOAL separately.

12. With the LeftLEG.MASTER (2) selected, choose Replace and then Rename Current Item from the Actions tab. Name this object RightLEG.MASTER.

13. As you did with the arm goals, give the RightLEG.MASTER a negative (–) value on its X channel.

The negative value will move it across the median into the exact same position on the opposite side of the character. The position values for RightLEG.MASTER should be as follows:

X	–100mm
Y	–1m
Z	–108mm

14. Now select the LeftLEG.GOAL object and clone it. Rename it RightLEG.GOAL and, using the Scene Editor, parent it to the RightLEG.MASTER object. Save your work.

You can also parent an item using the Motion Options panel (press the **m** key) and choose the desired parent object from the Parent Object pop-up list. Notice that it jumps into the proper position on the right side of the object.

That concludes the goal creation and positioning portion of this exercise. Figure 13.25 shows what the scene should look like if you are following along exactly.

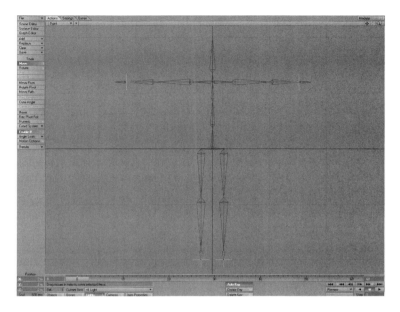

Figure 13.25 This is the complete IKSkeleton with goal objects positioned and is ready to be rigged with animation controls.

Configuring the Joints

The only thing left to do is configure the joints and activate the goal objects.

If you closely examine the skeleton, you will notice some awkwardly placed bones at the shoulder and hip joints. These are the control bones mentioned earlier in this chapter. In certain instances, a bone's rotation channels won't allow the desired range of rotation for a specific joint. An example of this would be a bone that is slightly rotated on its pitch. The heading and bank channels would then be based on the angle that the bone is pitched. If you wanted to rotate the bank of the bone in a planar fashion around the Z axis, you'd be out of luck. This is where control bones come into play. Parenting the pitched bone to a control bone (which is lying flat on the XZ axis) will enable you to control the bank angle of the pitched bone in the desired manner by rotating the control bone on its bank channel.

> **Note**
>
> Another solution to control bones in LightWave 6 is to use the Record Pivot Point feature found under the Actions tab in Layout. Clicking it for a selected item, such as a bone, records the current pivot point eliminating the control bones.

Figure 13.26 shows a control bone in action. Control bones can be an invaluable resource when used properly. Always remember that with LightWave nothing is set in stone and you should experiment with different techniques to get your desired results.

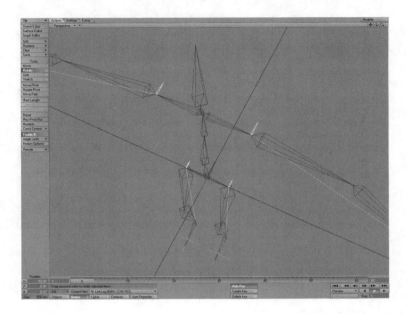

Figure 13.26   Control bones can be used to give a third degree of rotation to a planar joint when desired.

Keeping the types of joints found in the human skeleton in mind, it's time to set up the joints of your character, starting with the arms. The shoulder is usually a 3D or ball joint and can rotate into almost any position. The next joint in the arm is the elbow. The elbow is a planar (2D) joint, also referred to as a hinge joint because, like a hinge, it can only open or close on one axis. With the exception of the fingers, the last joint in the arm is the wrist, which is also a 3D joint. Following along with the next few steps will assist you in configuring the joints.

Exercise 13.5   Setting Up Joints

1. Select the Left.CollarBone and press the **m** key to bring up the Motion Options panel. This bone will be controlled by FK, so you don't need to set up any controllers for it. This bone also will serve as the terminator for the IK in the left arm, so activate Unaffected by IK of Descendents.

2. With the Motion Options panel still open, advance to the next bone by pressing the down arrow key. This bone is the Left.Shoulder.IK-ONLY bone. Select Controllers and Limits in the Motion Options panel.

This shoulder bone is a control bone for the rest of the arm. It will be controlled exclusively with IK.

> **Note**
> LightWave 6 makes extensive use of non-modal panels such as the Motion Options panel. These panels can remain open while you work. It is recommended that you keep the Motion Options panel open while rigging your characters. You should place it so that you can still see your scene while you set up all your bones.

3. Choose Inverse Kinematics from the Heading and Bank Controllers pop-up menus. Leave the Pitch Controller set to Key Frames.

4. Once again, advance to the next bone, which should be the Left.Arm.Upper bone. Select Inverse Kinematics for the Heading Controller.

The upper arm bone functions like that of a 3D or ball joint. Rather than using IK for all its controllers, the bone will share rotations with the shoulder control bone to simulate a 3D joint (see Figure 13.27).

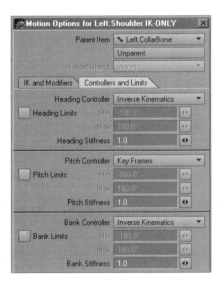 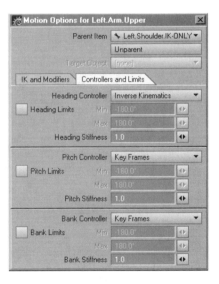

Figure 13.27   Inverse kinematics is controlling the heading and bank of the shoulder control bone (left) and the heading of the Left.UpperArm bone (right) to form a simulated 3D joint.

The next bone is the Left.LowerArm bone. This bone represents a humanlike forearm. The joint between it and the Left.Arm.Lower bone simulates an elbow. Because an elbow is a planar (2D) joint, it will only be rotated on one axis.

5. Choose Inverse Kinematics for the Heading Controller.

Moving right along, you should now be at the final bone of the arm the hand bone. The hand bone will be rotated exclusively with FK. It will also serve as the "pointer" bone for the IK chain.

6. To set up the Left.Hand bone as the pointer bone, switch back to the IK and Modifiers tab of the Motion Options panel. Under the Goal Object pop-up menu, choose LeftARM.GOAL.

   This tells LightWave to use the LeftARM.GOAL as the goal object for this IK chain.

7. Activate Full-Time IK for the hand bone by pressing the Full-Time IK button under the IK and Modifiers tab of the Motion Options panel. This forces LightWave to continuously calculate a solution for this IK chain.

8. Select Keep Goal Within Reach under the IK and Modifiers tab to lock the goal to the IK chain.

Note

Keep Goal Within Reach is a new feature in LightWave that locks the goal to the IK chain. With this activated, the goal object cannot be moved beyond the reach of the IK chain. This is a wonderful feature that is used primarily in single-goal IK chains.

9. The left arm is now complete. Repeat Steps 1 through 8 for the items on the right side of the character, and save your work when you're done. When they're completed, the upper body will be ready to animate. Figure 13.28 shows the scene in its current state.

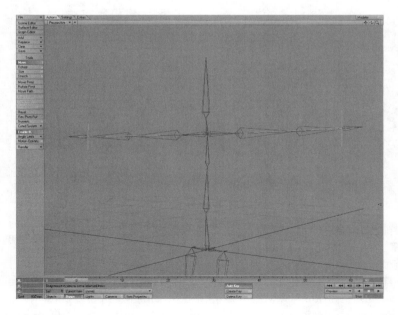

Figure 13.28   All the joints in the upper body have been configured and are ready to be animated.

You are now ready to set up the legs. Once again, look at the real-world equivalent of the leg joints and determine the type of joint needed in the IKSkeleton. The joint between the hip and the upper leg is a 3D joint. The IKSkeleton will use a planar joint for the upper leg in combination with a bank control bone to create a 3D joint. The next joint in the leg is the knee, which is a planar joint. Although it's slightly limited in range of motion, the ankle is also a 3D joint. Knowing this information, follow the next few steps to complete the leg setup:

Exercise 13.5   Applying IK to Legs

1. Select the Left.Hip bone. The hipbones are not controlled by IK. Activate the Unaffected by IK of Descendents function found in the Motion Options panel (**m**) to terminate the IK chain at the end of the hipbones. .

2. Select the Left.Leg.BANK CONTROL bone. You can use the up and down arrow keys to move through the bone hierarchy. Select Inverse Kinematics as the Bank Controller for this bone. Controlling only the bank of this bone will give you good results when moving the leg side to side.

3. Again, press the down arrow key to select the next bone, which is the Left.Leg.Upper bone. This bone is the equivalent of the human thigh. Set it to only be controlled by IK on its pitch. Leaving the heading controlled by FK will give you the ability to point the knee. Although it isn't necessary for this bone right now, you could set up the pitch angle limits to constrain the rotation of the upper leg.

4. Select the Left.Leg.Lower bone and activate Inverse Kinematics for the pitch controller. Leave all the other controllers set to Key Frames.

5. With the Left.LowerLeg bone still selected, activate Pitch Limits under the Controllers and Limits tab of the Motion Options panel. Enter 5.0 in the Min field, and enter 145.0 in the Max field.

> **Note**
>
> Applying pitch limits to this bone will prevent the bone from rotating beyond its natural range of motion. You don't want your knee to rotate backward, do you? Ouch!!! Remember that IK is not perfect and can occasionally come up with multiple solutions for a chain, even though it was created using a preferred angle. Setting angle limits will help reduce strange IK solutions.

6. Select the Left.Ankle bone. The anklebone will point to a goal object and terminate an IK chain that will exist in the foot. Switch to IK and Modifiers in the Motion Options panel and activate Unaffected by IK of Descendents. Choose LeftLEG.GOAL from the Goal Object pop-up menu, and finally activate Full-Time IK for this bone.

You should see a blue line indicating a complete IK chain appearing between the hipbone and the anklebone.

7. Look directly under the Goal Object pop-up menu, and you will see a Goal Strength field. Enter a value of 50.0 into the field.

Note

The Goal Strength field enables you to input the strength that an IK chain reaches for its goal. Imagine the goal strength setting as a magnet between the goaled bone and the goal. As the value increases, so does the strength of the bond between the two items. Goal strength's main purpose in life is when there are multiple goals in the same chain. When you have multiple goals in the same chain, you can give one preference by increasing its relative goal strength. Multiple goals in the same chain with the same strength can result in erratic responses as the IK tries to calculate them both. Experiment with different goal strengths for each pointer bone to come up with different results.

The LeftLEG.GOAL will control all the items in the leg, from the hip to the ankle. The LeftLEG.GOAL is parented to the LeftLEG.MASTER, so you won't ever directly control the LeftLEG.GOAL. The LeftLEG.MASTER will also be the goal object for a small IK chain in the foot section of the leg. To finish setting up the legs, follow these steps:

8. Select the Left.Foot bone. Open the Motion Options panel and switch to the Controllers and Limits tab to configure the controllers for the foot. Activate Inverse Kinematics for the pitch controller only. Leave everything else like it is.

9. Now select the Left.Foot.Toes bone. It is a pointer bone and doesn't need any controller adjustment, so switch to the IK and Modifiers tab. From the Goal Object pop-up menu, choose LeftLEG.MASTER.

10. Enter 200.0 into the Goal Strength field of the Left.Toes bone.

That completes the setup of the IKSkeleton's left leg IK chain. The setup of the IKSkeleton is almost complete. The only thing left to set up is the right leg. The right leg uses an almost identical setup as the left leg. To set it up, follow these steps:

11. Select the Right.Hip bone. Activate the Unaffected by IK of Descendents (located in the Motion Options panel) to terminate the IK chain at the end of the hipbones.

12. Select the Right.Leg.BANK CONTROL bone. Select Inverse Kinematics as the Bank Controller for this bone.

13. Select the Right.Leg.Upper bone. This bone will function as the thigh bone. Set it to be controlled by IK on its pitch. This setup enables you to point the knee using FK by rotating the heading.

14. Select the Right.Leg.Lower bone and activate Inverse Kinematics for the pitch controller. Leave all the other controllers set to Key Frames.

15. With the Right.Leg.Lower bone still selected, activate Pitch Limits under the Controllers and Limits tab of the Motion Options panel. Enter 5.0 in the Min field, and enter 145.0 in the Max field.

16. Select the Right.Ankle bone. Switch to IK and Modifiers in the Motion Options panel and activate Unaffected by IK of Descendents.

17. Choose RightLEG.GOAL from the Goal Object pop-up menu. Activate Full-Time IK for this bone and enter a value of 50.0 in the Goal Strength field.

18. Select the Right.Foot bone. Open the Motion Options panel and switch to the Controllers and Limits tab to configure the controllers for the foot. Activate Inverse Kinematics for the pitch controller. Leave everything else as it is.

19. Now select the Right.Foot.Toes bone. This is a pointer bone and doesn't need any controller adjustment, so switch to the IK and Modifiers tab. From the Goal Object pop-up menu, choose RightLEG.MASTER.

20. Enter 200.0 into the Goal Strength field of the Right.Toes bone.

That's all there is to it. You now have a completely set-up kinematics skeletal structure. Provided you followed step by step with the exercise, your scene should look like Figure 13.29.

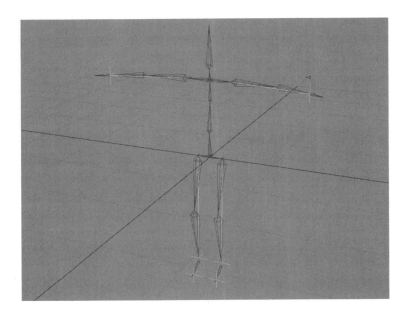

Figure 13.29   This is the completed IKSkeleton skeletal structure.

Enhancing the Setup

You can take this setup to the next level with some minor adjustments to the scene. To further enhance the IK Skeleton setup, try the following:

- Lock some of the bones with the Scene Editor to prevent accidental selection. You can do this by clicking next to the desired bone in the Scene Editor under the Lock column. A small padlock-type icon identifies this column.

- Deactivate the motion channels for all the bones in the scene. This will keep you from accidentally moving a bone. You can do this by clicking the X, Y, or Z buttons on the bottom left corner of the Layout inteface, next to the numeric information panel.

- Deactivate all the rotation channels for the bones that you aren't manipulating with FK. You can do this by clicking the H, P, or B buttons on the bottom left corner of the Layout inteface, next to the numeric information panel.

- Set up angle limits for joints in the skeleton. Properly set-up angle limits will prevent unwanted rotations. You can do this in the Motion Options panel, under the Controllers and Limits tab.

- Turn AutoKey on! With AutoKey on, you can animate the character without manually creating a single keyframe. To use AutoKey, remember that AutoKey Create must be active in the General Options panel (**o**). Then, click the AutoKey button on the Layout interface to activate.

Rigging a Real Character

Now that you have a firm grasp of the basic techniques involved in character setup, it's time to put your knowledge to work by rigging a usable character. As you will soon see, properly setting up a character will give you a pleasurable animation experience. After all, animation is supposed to be fun, isn't it?

The character you will be rigging is a robotic-insect hybrid that was created for a couple of effects shots in an upcoming sci-fi film. The IKBot was designed as a surveillance device for a race of aliens from a planet far, far away. The script called for insect-like creatures to scurry across the floor in a few scenes. Due to the nature of the shot, extreme modeling and surfacing detail was not necessary. Instead, good high-quality insect-like movements were needed. So a rig was integrated into the base object to give a wide range of motion. Figure 13.30 shows the IKBot in action.

Figure 13.30   Here is a sample shot of the IKBot. A scorpion-like tail was added to the creature to make it appear more menacing in the film.

Although the IKBot has six legs, with LightWave the setup is still relatively simple. Using cloning for the goal objects will simplify the setup. An interesting feature of LightWave 6's IK system is the ability to mix bones and rigid IK in the same chain. This capability alone opens some unique possibilities. You will use this feature to rig the scorpion tail on the IKBot. So let's get started.

Exercise 13.6   Setup of the IKBot

The IKBot's rigging is based around the same principles of IK that you learned in the previous exercises. For the film, the IKBot needed to be placed in a variety of poses, so creating multiple versions of the character for different ranges of motion was out of the question. The hybrid IK/FK engine in LightWave 6 will enable you to create a single character with a relatively simple rig to accomplish every shot. Follow these steps to rig up your own IKBot.

1. Start with a fresh scene by choosing Clear Scene from the File pop-up menu. The scene you'll end up with after you finish setting up this character can easily be integrated into other scenes with the Load Items From Scene command.

2. Select Add, Add Object, and then Add Null to add the most important object in the scene, the root null.

   This null will be the root object of the IKBot and will enable you to move the entire character anywhere in the scene, maintaining any walk cycles or positioning information you've created.

Note

It really isn't necessary for this null to be added as the first item in the scene, but doing so will keep things tidy. A good habit to get into is adding items to a scene in a logical order. This will make it easier to select items using the up and down arrow keys as well as make for a clean setup. Keeping your scene clean will add years to your life of animating.

Now it's time to bring in the actual IKBot.

3. Select Add, Add Object, and Load Object. When the load requester pops up, navigate to the book's CD-ROM and load the IKBot-Scorpion object. Objects can also be loaded by pressing the (+) on the numeric keypad.

Note

The IKBot-Scorpion is a layered object that makes use of LightWave's powerful layered object format. The object consists of the body, which contains a few skelegons, six separate legs, each containing skelegons set up on their own pivot points, and each segment of the tail as a separate object to be used as a rigid IK chain. The hierarchical structure of all the objects was established in Modeler through the use of the Layers panel. All the individual objects are contained in one object file.

Several of the object pieces contain skelegons that need to be converted to bones so that they can be used in Layout.

4. Select the item containing the skelegons and press the Cvt Skelegons button found under the Settings tab. Do this for each object listed here. The objects that need to have their skelegons converted are:

- IKBot-Scorpion:Body, containing seven bones
- IKBot-Scorpion:Leg.Front.Left, containing six bones
- IKBot-Scorpion:Leg.Front.Right, containing six bones
- IKBot-Scorpion:Leg.Mid.Left, containing six bones
- IKBot-Scorpion:Leg.Mid.Right, containing six bones
- IKBot-Scorpion:Leg.Back.Left, containing six bones
- IKBot-Scorpion:Leg.Back.Right, containing six bones

Now you are ready to add in the goal objects. It's not necessary that you add the goal objects as the next step, but doing so will make the controller and IK setup of each chain go a bit faster.

The goals for this character will be null objects.

5. Add in the first null object by selecting Add, Add Object, and then Add Null. At the name prompt, enter Leg.Front.Left.GOAL. This null will be the basis for all the other goals in the legs.

6. Move Leg.Front.Left.Goal to the end of Leg.Front.Left. Select Move (or press the **t** key), press **n** to activate numeric input, and then enter the following values in the number fields:

    X   871mm

    Y   0mm

    Z   −80mm

After you've positioned the object, you can clone it to create the other goal objects.

7. With Leg.Front.Left.Goal still selected, choose Clone Current Item from the Add pop-up menu. LightWave will ask how many clones you want to create; enter 5. This will make five clones of the current item.

8. Press the down arrow key to advance to the next item. This will select the Leg.Front.Left.Goal (2) object. Choose Rename Current Item from the Replace pop-up menu. For the name, enter Leg.Front.Right.Goal. Proceed to the next object and repeat this step, renaming all the cloned null objects to match their respective legs that they will control. You should end up with:

    Leg.Front.Left.Goal

    Leg.Front.Right.Goal

    Leg.Mid.Left.Goal

    Leg.Mid.Right.Goal

    Leg.Back.Left.Goal

    Leg.Back.Right.Goal

All those goals are nice, but they won't be effective until you position them in the right places. Logically you would place the Leg.Front.Right.Goal at the tip of the Leg.Front.Right object. The easiest and most accurate way of placing all these goals is through numeric input.

9. Press the **n** key to activate numeric input. Enter the following position values for each null:

    Leg.Front.Right.Goal:

    X   −871 mm

    Y   0 m

    Z   −80 mm

Leg.Mid.Left.Goal:

X   871 mm

Y   0 m

X   0 m

Leg.Mid.Right.Goal:

X   −871 mm

Y   0 m

Z   0 m

Leg.Back.Left.Goal:

X   871 mm

Y   0 m

Z   84 mm

Leg.Back.Right.Goal:

X   −871 mm

Y   0 m

Z   84 mm

Only one more goal object needs to be created, and it is for the IK chain in the tail.

10. Select Add Object and then Add Null from the Add pop-up menu. Enter Tail.GOAL when prompted for a name.

11. Press the **t** key to activate the Move tool. Activate the numeric input fields (**n**) and enter the following:

X   0 m

Y   220 mm

Z   1.236 m

These settings will place the Tail.GOAL at the joint between the last segment of the tail and the Stinger segment.

Save your work. With all the goals in place, your scene should now look like Figure 13.31.

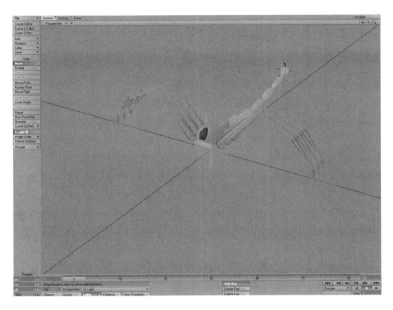

Figure 13.31   The goals have all been placed in their proper spots. Changing the display colors of items in a scene can help you remember how you set it up. From the Scene Editor, you can set important goals to the color red if you want.

Configuring the IK Chains

After you've created and placed the goal objects, you need to set up the IK chains. The IKBot makes full use of LightWave 6's hybrid IK engine, and because of this you can pose the legs with both IK and FK. Even with this basic IK setup in the legs, you are given much control over the character. By simply rotating two bones in the legs, you can change the IKBot from the ominous look of a spider to a pose resembling that of an ant, all while maintaining full control of the legs with IK (see Figures 13.32 and 13.33).

The process of configuring a character for IK is easier by leaving the Motion Panel open. By keeping it open, you can work with various parts of the character, and set up the IK accordingly without constantly opening and closing the Motion Options panel. Seeing which objects and bones you're working with while assigning IK as well as seeing the IK effect is essential to your productivity.

Applying IK to the Legs and Hips

Looking at Figure 13.34, you can see the structure of the legs. Each leg contains six bones. Are you sure there are six? There only appear to be five. The sixth bone is a null bone at the end of the chain that will serve as the pointer for the IK; its rest length has been scaled down to keep the bone out of the way.

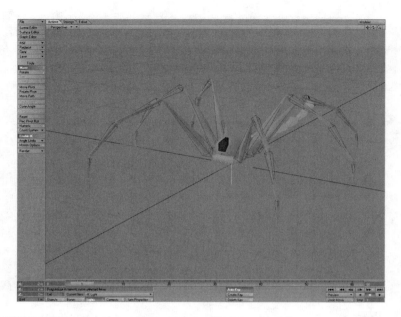

Figure 13.32   This is the IKBot in the normal spider-like pose.

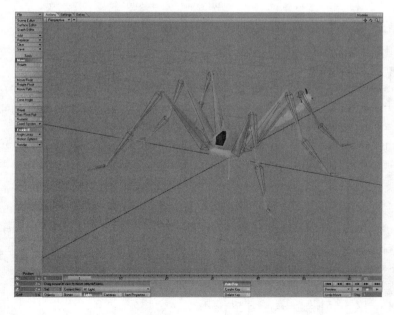

Figure 13.33   The two forward kinematics bones at the ends of each leg were rotated, giving the IKBot an ant-like pose.

Note

Null bones will commonly serve as the pointer items in your IK chains. A null bone is a bone that has no effect over the deformation of an object. You create null bones as you would any other bone; however, you either leave the bone inactive or scale down its rest length to make it null.

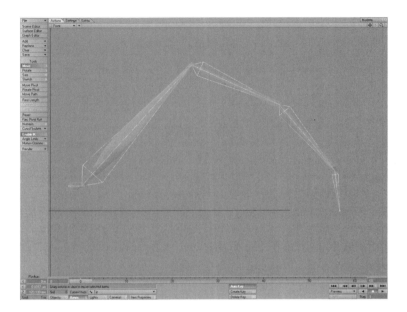

Figure 13.34   This is the complete structure of one of the legs.

Starting from the root, the bones composing the legs are as follows:

- Hip.Socket—This bone is the root bone of the leg hierarchy. You will never move this bone. It is the terminator of the IK chain and will keep the socket of the leg in place.

- Leg.Upper—This bone will deform the upper portion of the leg. It is the main bone that will control most of the positioning of the structure. IK will control this bone on the heading and pitch channels, leaving the bank channel to FK.

- Leg.Mid—Deforming the mid section of the leg will also help position the other bones in the hierarchy. Its pitch channel will be controlled by IK, and you won't ever want to control this bone by hand.

- Leg.Lower—The next section of the leg is deformed with this bone. This bone will greatly affect the pose of the leg, although, it is controlled entirely by FK. No IK controllers need to be set up on this bone, and you will control its pitch by hand.

- Foot—The last true bone in the hierarchy will also be controlled exclusively by FK. This bone deforms the last segment of the leg. You will be able to manipulate this bone with FK on the pitch channel.

- Tip—This is the final bone of the hierarchy. It is a null bone and will have no deformation effect on the leg. It is the item in the hierarchy that will point the chain's IK. You will give this bone a goal object to follow.

With this information, you can begin rigging the legs. This exercise will show you how to configure one complete leg. You will then need to use the same procedure to set up all the other legs.

Exercise 13.7   Rigging the Legs and Hips

1. Select the Hip.Socket bone in the Leg.Front.Left object. Because this is the first item in the leg hierarchy, it's best to start with this object and move forward through the structure.

2. Press the **m** key to bring up the Motion Options panel. Make sure you are in the IK and Modifiers tab. The Hip.Socket is the terminator of the IK Chain, so activate Unaffected by IK of Descendents. Leave all the other settings unchanged.

3. Keep the Motion Options panel open and press the down arrow key to move to the next bone in the hierarchy—the Leg.Upper bone. This bone doesn't need any direct IK setup, but it does need to be controlled by IK, so switch to the Controllers and Limits tab. Use the pop-up menus and select Inverse Kinematics for both the heading and pitch controllers. Keep the bank controller set to Key Frames so that you can manipulate it with FK.

4. Proceed to the next bone, which is Leg.Mid. Activate Inverse Kinematics for the pitch controller. You will not be using any of the other channels for this bone, and later you will use constraints to prevent accidental movements.

   The next two bones don't need any setup at all, so proceed to the tip bone. This is the pointer bone of the IK chain and needs to have some direct IK setup.

5. With the tip bone selected, switch back to the IK and Modifiers tab. Choose Leg.Front.Left.GOAL from the Goal Object pop-up menu. Activate Full-Time IK so that LightWave will continuously solve for this chain. Finally, enter a value of 50.0 in the Goal Strength field.

Although Goal Strength is typically used to mix the IK strength between multiple goals in the same chain, it can also be used to make the chain "stick" closer to an individual goal.

That's all there is to setting up a leg. To set up all the other legs, repeat the above procedures. Remember to point each leg to the proper goal; this is where descriptive names come in handy. There is still some more work to be done to the legs before you start playing with them, but first you need to rig the tail.

Rigging the Tail

Here comes the good stuff. The tail is going to use a complex IK structure unique to LightWave 6. Although the setup is considered complex, it is still extremely easy to set up in LightWave.

The actual tail was designed to be a rigid IK structure so that it would rotate in segments, much like that of a real scorpion. Unfortunately, a simple rigid IK system wouldn't affect the body of the IKBot at all, and everyone knows that the body would move a little to compensate for the motion of the tail. The solution to this is to actually connect the tail into the skeletal structure of the IKBot's body. After it is configured, you can use a single goal object to manipulate the tail and deform the body accordingly.

All the segments of the tail were set up and parented to form a hierarchical structure in Modeler. Modeler doesn't enable you to parent items to bones, so the connection between the tail and the bones in the body will need to be set up in Layout.

Exercise 13.8   Configuring the Tail with IK

1. Select the first segment of the tail, ever so conveniently named Tail.Segment.1. Open the Motion Options panel, and using the Parent Item pop-up menu, parent Tail.Segment.1 to the bone named Abdmn06.

   Oops, the tail jumped off into the distance. If you remember from the previous exercises, this is a result of the location of pivot points.

2. To correct this, simply zero out the position values for Tail.Segment.1 by typing the following in the information panel at the bottom left of the Layout interface. Select Move, and then press the **n** key (for numeric) and enter the following:

   X 0 m

   Y 0 m

   Z 0 m

> **Note**
>
> The Abdmn06 bone is actually a null bone that serves as a placeholder for the tail. Hence, the tail was parented to it. Parenting in LightWave uses an item's pivot point for positional information. As such, the tail took on the pivot point of Abdmn06 as its own local center. The default position of the tail was "x" distance from the median of all the axes, so when you parented the tail to Abdmn06 the location that the position information was based on is shifted to the pivot point of the Abdmn06 bone. The tail maintains the same distance from the local center, so it appears to jump. When you zero out the positional data of the tail, it jumps back to the pivot point of the Abdmn06 bone. Because the pivot point of a bone is located at its fat end, a null bone was created to place the tail in the desired spot.

Now that the hierarchy has been established (see Figure 13.35), you can begin setting up the controllers for the tail.

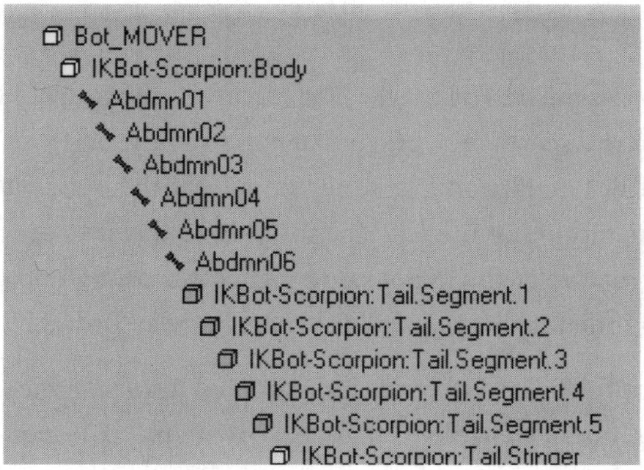

Figure 13.35   Here you can see the hierarchical setup of the IKBot's tail structure. Notice how the first segment of the tail is parented to the last bone of the abdomen.

Although the tail is a combination of rigid- and IK-driven bone deformation, you still set up the IK information as you would any other chain. To set up the tail's controllers, follow these steps:

3. Select the IKBot-Scorpion:Body, and then select the bone named Abdmn01. This bone will terminate the IK chain for the tail, so turn on Unaffected by IK of Descendants in the Motion Options panel.

4. Activate Inverse Kinematics for the pitch controller of bones Abdmn02 through Abdmn05 by selecting each bone and, in the Motion Options panel, choosing Inverse Kinematics from their pitch controller's pop-up menu.

> **Note**
>
> Abdmn06 is just a null bone, which has no effect on the geometry, so it doesn't need any setup.

5. Select Tail.Segment.1 and set up Inverse Kinematics for its pitch and heading controllers. This setup will have the biggest impact on posing the rest of the chain.

6. For Tail.Segment.2 through Tail.Segment.5, apply inverse kinematics controllers on their pitch and bank channels.

    This will enable the tail to be moved on the X axis while keeping its scorpion-like appearance.

7. Select the Tail.Stinger segment. This object will be the goaled item in the chain and will point the rest of the hierarchy to an IK solution. Set this up by choosing Tail.GOAL from the Goal Object pop-up menu in the IK and Modifiers section

of Motion Options. Activate Full-Time IK and then enter a value of 50.0 in the Goal Strength field.

That completes the entire IK setup for the IKBot. You should now have a scene that looks like Figure 13.36. Now for those of you who like to animate in a totally immersive environment, follow the next few steps and set up constraints for the IKBot.

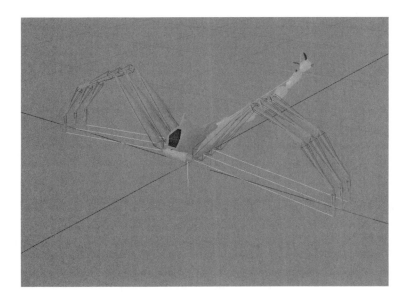

Figure 13.36   The IKBot has been completely rigged with IK.

Constraints

A complex character such as the IKBot can be confusing to work with after it has been set up. So many individual parts can easily be selected and manipulated, which could cause disastrous results to your scene. To prevent this from happening, you need to set up local constraints as well as lock items in the Scene Editor.

Local constraints are the little buttons in the lower left-hand corner of Layout next to the numeric input fields (see Figure 13.37). They are indicated by an X, Y, or Z or by an H, P, or B, depending upon what tool you have activated. These constraints can function in two modes. The first is activated, which enables the item to be manipulated for that channel. The second mode is deactivated, which locks the item from being manipulated on that channel.

If an object's local constraint is on for the X channel and off for all the other channels, your ability to manipulate that object is constrained to the X channel. Using these buttons, set up constraints for each leg. The following list indicates the way the constraints should be set up for a complete leg. You should apply these settings to all the other legs.

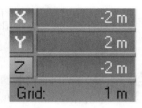

Figure 13.37
Motion channels can be activated or deactivated with these buttons.

- Object: Leg.Front.Left—You should turn off all the channels for this object so that it can't be accidentally moved or rotated on any channel.

- Bone: Hip.Socket—Turn off all the channels for this bone as well.

- Bone: Leg.Upper—Turn all the position channels off. Turn off H and P of the rotation channels, leaving B on. Because the object is being controlled by IK, it doesn't need to be hand-manipulated on the H and P channels. The bank controller is set to Key Frames, so leave this channel on and you can rotate the bank by hand.

- Bone: Leg.Mid—This bone is controlled by IK on its pitch channel. You don't want to control any other channel, so turn off all the position and rotation channels.

- Bone: Leg.Lower—Turn off everything except for the P rotation channel. This bone is set to use forward kinematics exclusively; however, you will only want to control its pitch by hand.

- Bone: Foot—Like the previous bone, turn off all the channels except for P. Because these bones are children in the hierarchy, they will automatically follow the IK solution, yet they aren't directly controlled by IK.

- Bone: Tip—Remember that this is a null bone, and as such it won't be manipulated at all. Turn off all the channels for this bone.

With all these constraints in place, you are now free to animate the IKBot. It is recommended that you save the scene before manipulating anything. With the scene saved in this current state, you can easily bring the IKBot into any other scene using the Load Items From Scene command.

You can still do a few other things to the scene to make a more user-friendly animation environment. Using the Scene Editor you can lock items so they can't be selected. This will make it easier to select the goal objects without inadvertently selecting something else. It is also recommended that you color-coordinate all the items in your scene. Setting up the display colors in the Scene Editor will make it easier to understand the scene. You can also set up angle limit constraints to the segments in the tail to prevent them from going through the ground plane. If you're feeling really risky and have a good understanding of the expressions engine in LightWave 6, you can rig some expressions into the character to automate some of the animation tasks. A couple of different IKBot scenes are on the CD-ROM that you can dissect or play with to better understand how they were set up.

The Next Step

LightWave gives you flexibility for experimenting and for trying new techniques. Use this flexibility to your advantage. The information covered in this chapter is not the only way to complete a kinematics setup. Take this basic information and build on it. Mix techniques together or create your own. LightWave 6 gives you the freedom to create. The information in this chapter can be used for a countless number of projects, from animated ropes to slithering snakes, crazy aliens, or even animals. IK is useful for robotic movements, characters, and even everyday occurrences such as blowing curtains. You can use IK with bones to animate things such as water surfaces, or image-mapped tubes to simulate a twisting tornado. The ideas are endless, but with the right information you can create anything!

Summary

IK often seems overwhelming. But after reading through this chapter, you can see that in a matter of steps, you've broken through the barrier and set up simple objects such as a robotic arm, and complex creatures such as a scorpion. Bones and objects can both be set up to work with IK, and it's now up to you to go to the next level and set up IK on one of your own creations. The following chapters can help you use expressions and compositing for your characters, so read on!

Chapter 14

Expression Animation

In this chapter, you will learn how to use

expressions to enhance and simplify your

animations. *Expressions* are the individual

pieces that make up a special subset of

animation known as procedural animation. In its simplest form, an expression links one item's motion to that of another with a mathematical formula. At its most complex, it could make virtual worlds rise and fall with the touch of a button.

In LightWave 6, there are several ways to harness the power of expressions. A true expression is a mathematical formula that defines the behavior of one item by the behavior of another item. In LightWave 6, this method is available through the Channel Express modifier plug-in. In this chapter, you will use Channel Express to accomplish a task for which it is uniquely suited. In fact, everything accomplished in this chapter could be done using this method, but this is not necessarily the fastest or easiest method to accomplish your goals.

A true expression requires you to define behaviors using formulas that could be quite lengthy and complex. To free you from this burden, LightWave 6 provides other plug-ins that automatically handle these situations. These could be called expressive plug-ins. Although technically not "true" expressions, these plug-ins are used to carry out the same duties of an expression, but in a simpler manner. Although a true expression is broad enough to deal with almost any situation, these plug-ins are made for a specific job.

Although this chapter uses these expressive plug-ins, along with true expressions, you should realize that all these plug-ins are a form of expression and should be thought of as such. This chapter will instruct you on the following:

- Using Channel Express
- Using Cycler
- Applying ChannelFollower

Project Overview

Animating with expressions is one of the unique experiences in 3D graphics. It has no parallel in any other form of animation. Being able to take advantage of the power of expressions can take your animation to a new level of realism and usability.

Expressions (like computers) are at their most useful when they are employed to automate repetitive or complex tasks. Animation of mechanical objects such as gears, pulleys, and wheels is often quite simple, yet when combined in large numbers and complex relationships, the task of animating each piece becomes tedious and inspiration-sapping. Linking these objects through expressions frees the animator from worrying about each piece, allowing the creative flow to continue uninterrupted.

Characters and other organic shapes can benefit from expressions as well. Imagine being able to automatically keep the hips of a character centered between its feet, or have a character's eyes automatically turn in the same direction as the head a split-second beforehand. All these things, and more, are possible through expressions.

LightWave 6 gives you the power of expressions in every channel of data, from position and rotation, to surface and light color, even to morph data. In this chapter, you will construct and animate a futuristic spacecraft as it prepares for takeoff and leaps into the noonday sky. You will use expressions to control or drive:

- A complex landing-gear retraction
- The wing extension
- The engine rotation
- The engine exhaust size and luminosity
- Surface motion

Examining the Model's Parts

Figures 14.1 and 14.2 show the major parts of the model you're going to build and animate. These are

- The fuselage
- The wings
- The engines
- The front landing gear and door
- The rear landing gear and doors
- The rear horizontal stabilizers

The landing gear of an aircraft such as this is the perfect case for the use of expressions. Each of the three gear sets is made up of eight separate parts, each of which must be animated to extend or retract the gear. This is *not* something you would want to do repeatedly. So, you will use the expressive plug-in Cycler to make the process nice and easy. You also will be using the expressive plug-in ChannelFollower to further simplify the set-up process.

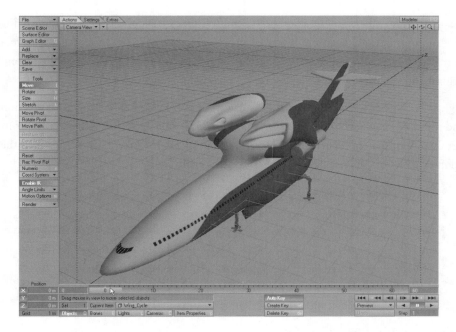

Figure 14.1   United Aerospace Z77 Spaceliner in storage mode. Note the major parts and compare them to those in Figure 14.2. In this configuration, the wings are retracted and the engines are folded on top. The landing gear is extended.

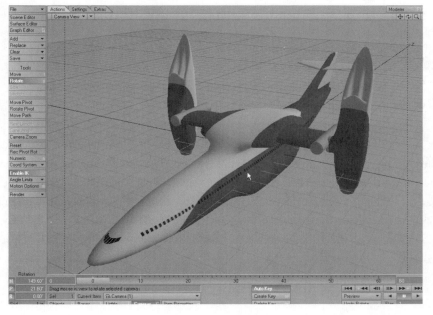

Figure 14.2   United Aerospace Z77 Spaceliner in flight mode. In this mode, the wings are fully extended and the engines are set to their upright configuration for flight. The landing gear is retracted.

Using Cycler and ChannelFollower

Cycler works by using a control object to "cycle" or repeat another object through a defined range of keyframes. It associates the action of one item with a repeatable action of another. You define the start and end keyframes for the object and tell Cycler the low and high values that the control object will go through. As the control object, such as a null object, goes from its low value to its high value, the controlled object cycles from its first defined keyframe to its last. For example, you can use Cycler to define the rotation of wheels on a car. With the plug-in setup, you can animate the car, resulting in turning wheels.

ChannelFollower enables you to let one motion channel of one object "follow" a motion channel of another object. One application of this is a character's eyes; one eye is animated with keyframes while the other follows the exact rotation of the keyed eye, but from its own location.

In this case, you will animate the unfolding sequence for each part of the landing gear and use Cycler to link their motion to a single control object. You will use ChannelFollower to duplicate the motion of the port side gear on the starboard side, eliminating the need for keyframes on that side completely. You also will drive the animation of the front gear from the port side. From then on, all you'll need to do to extend or retract the entire gear assembly is move one null.

Note

Procedural animation (that is, using expressions or other math to control object motion) has its own set of terms with which you should be familiar. An item that is procedurally animated could be said to be dependent upon another object, which is often called the control object. It also could be said to be linked to that object, though "link" most often means a simple, direct relationship, as in one object exactly following another, or mirroring its motion. Another way to express a mathematical relationship between two objects is to say that the control object drives the dependent object. Because this is the way you will encounter them in the real world, this chapter uses all these terms interchangeably so that you can begin thinking about using them.

Before you start setting up your landing gear with Cycler, you need to import your objects and set them up properly. Thanks to the magic of LightWave's new multilayered object format, this is extraordinarily simple. However, the following techniques are good to know, and you should get into the habit of doing them.

Exercise 14.1   Preparing Objects for Animation

1. In a blank scene, add a null and name it Z77_Global.

2. Add another null to the scene. Name this one Z77_Control. Parent this null to Z77_Global.

Note

This two-extra-nulls setup is common in production environments. Having a global null enables you to move and rotate the entire motion path of the ship at any time. The need for this may not be readily apparent, but should you ever need it, you will be glad you have it.

Also, you will be animating the motion of the ship with the Z77_Control null instead of the actual fuselage object. This is for two reasons:

- It gives you more control, enabling you to easily rotate the ship independently of its motion path (this is possible with LightWave's new channels, which allow independent position, rotation, and scale keyframes. However, it is not always the fastest way of accomplishing the same goal).

- It sidesteps an issue in LightWave's expression engine. As of this writing, the expression engine would not correctly deal with objects that had spaces in their names (such as cloned objects, Null (1), Null (2), and so on, or multilayered objects, into whose names Layout places a colon (:). This would cause the engine to fail on the name "Z77:Fuselage." A fix for this is expected soon and might already be available.

Because you already know what items of the ship you will need to control, you can make control nulls for them. Of course, you could create them at any time, but creating them now will put them at the top of the object list, making them easier to find and access.

3. Add the following four nulls, all parented to Z77_Control:

- Wing_Cycle

- Landing_Gear_Cycle

- Engine_Rotator

- Throttle

Now you can bring in and prepare your objects.

4. Load the ..\..\Objects\Z77\Z77.lwo spacecraft file.

5. Parent the Z77:Fuselage object to the Z77_Control null.

Because the complete hierarchy and all pivot locations were created in Modeler, you don't have to do anything more to prepare the objects. Figure 14.3 shows the Spaceliner as it loads into Layout. Your scene is now ready to animate!

6. Save your scene.

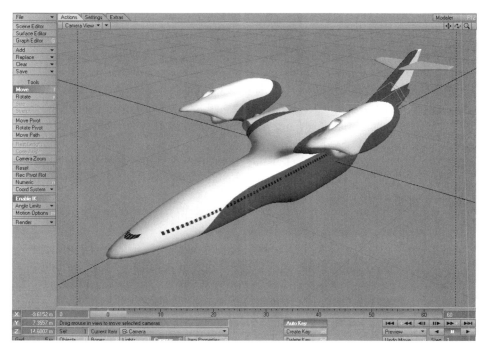

Figure 14.3 The Z77 Spaceliner as it loads into Layout. Notice the gear is retracted and the wings are extended at this point.

Exercise 14.2   Animating the Port Side Landing Gear

The landing gear is loaded into Layout in the retracted position. For the port side gear, you'll need to move each piece out to the extended position and set keyframes. You'll also need to make sure that everything happens in order so that none of the pieces are colliding.

> **Note**
>
> You will animate so that the gear legs are completely extended by frame 30. This is really an arbitrary number; any would do. However, because 30 frames equal one second in video, animators generally have an easier time thinking in multiples of 30. This also will give you sufficient time to get all the steps in order. For example, the doors must open before the gear extends.

You'll start by animating the port side gear, and then use ChannelFollower to drive the starboard side and front gear.

1. Select the object Z77:Gear_Door_Rear_Port.

2. Go to frame 10.

3. Rotate the object to 120 degrees on the Bank axis. Set a keyframe.

   This opens the gear door by frame 10. Begin animating the gear legs at frame 5, which should give sufficient time to avoid collisions between the objects.

4. Go to frame 5 and select Z77:Gear_Hip_Port. Press Enter or click Create Key to bring up the Create Motion Key dialog. Click the button marked Selected Items and scroll down to Current Item and Descendants. Press Enter or click OK.

   This creates a keyframe at frame 5 for the Z77:Gear_Hip_Port object and all its descendants, which will cover the entire port rear gear assembly.

5. Press Del or click Delete Key to bring up the Delete Motion Key dialog. Notice that LightWave already has Current Item and Descendants selected. Enter 0 in the Delete Key At field. Press Enter or click OK.

   This deletes the keyframe at frame 0 for your items and eliminates the possibility of any unwanted motion before frame 5.

6. Go to frame 15. Move Z77:Gear_Hip_Port to –900mm on the Y axis. Press Enter or click Create Key to bring up the Create Motion Key dialog. Click the button marked Current Item and Descendants and scroll down to Selected Items. Click OK to create the key. Now rotate the object to 60 degrees on the Heading axis. Set a key for this position at frame 25.

7. Select Z77:Gear_Thigh_Port. Set its Pitch to –35. Set a key at frame 15.

8. Set its Pitch to 15, and create a key at frame 25.

9. Select Z77:Gear_Calf_Port. Set its Pitch to 75. Set a key at frame 25.

10. Select Z77:Gear_Toe_One_Port. Create a keyframe at frame 20. Delete the keyframe at frame 5.

11. Rotate Z77:Gear_Toe_One_Port to 90 degrees in Pitch. Create a keyframe at frame 30.

    You have three other toes, each which will move at the same time and in a similar manner to the toe you just animated. This is a perfect use for ChannelFollower.

12. Start by selecting Z77:Gear_Toe_Two_Port.

13. Open the Graph Editor.

14. Because the proper rotation for this foot is along its Heading, select the Z77:Gear_Toe_Two_Port.Rotation.H channel in the Curve Bin. Click the Modifiers tab.

Note

If you cannot see the entire channel name in the Curve Bin, you can drag the bar that divides the Curve Bin from the Curve Window to give the Curve Bin more space.

15. Click Add Modifier and select ChannelFollower. Double-click the ChannelFollower listing to bring up the interface.

Figure 14.4 shows the ChannelFollower interface as it opens. The top of the interface is an expandable list of all the items in your scene. Clicking the triangle to the left of any item gives you the channels associated with that item. The channel you select here becomes the "driving" channel, the channel that the selected object will follow.

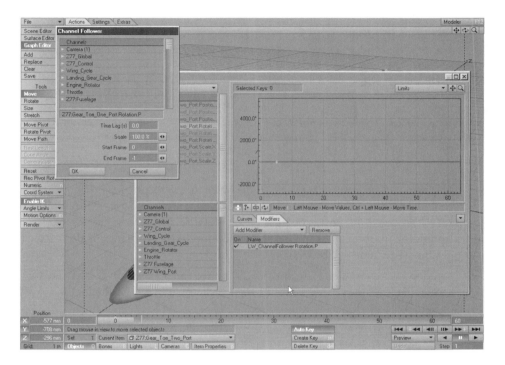

Figure 14.4   The ChannelFollower interface.

Below that is the Time Lag setting. This enables you to set a time, in seconds, which the selected object will wait before following the driving channel.

Beneath Time Lag is the Scale value. The driving channel's value is multiplied by this value to determine the followed value. For instance, if you had a gear that turns once, 360 degrees, but the object you wanted to drive needed to turn twice, your Scale would be set to 200%. 360 degrees × %200 = 720 degrees.

Below Scale are the Start Frame and End Frame values. These numbers set the range of keyframes in which ChannelFollower will be active. For instance, if you only need to have a ball follow a hand for the frames between 47 and 92, you would specify 47 as your Start Frame and 92 as your End Frame. By default, the values are set to 0 and –1, which means that ChannelFollower will be active at all times through the scene.

Now, it's time to drive the other three toes by Z77:Gear_Toe_One_Port.

16. In the item list, scroll down until you find the Z77:Gear_Toe_One_Port object. Click the triangle on the left side to reveal all the channels available for the object.

17. Double-click the Rotation.P of Z77:Gear_Toe_One_Port.

> **Note**
>
> Because of the new way of handling channels in LightWave 6, items can have more than just the standard position, rotation, and scale channels. An object, for instance, can have a surface color, dissolve, or morph channel associated with it. Lights can have color, intensity, and cone angle channels. This nearly unlimited expandability has necessitated a change in channel names to a more programmatic style. Specifically, the X, Y, and Z channels are now known as Position.X, Position.Y, and Position.Z, respectively. Heading, Pitch, and Bank are now known as Rotation.H, Rotation.P, and Rotation.B. However, referring to an item's Pitch, while not *technically* correct, is still a common and useful method. It's good to understand that these different names still refer to the same things. Therefore, this chapter will refer to these different naming styles interchangeably.

The name of the channel is placed in the box beneath the item list. The reason you are looking at the pitch of Z77:Gear_Toe_One_Port to drive the heading of Z77:Gear_Toe_Two_Port is because of the way it was modeled. The proper "unfolding" motion of Gear_Toe_Two is accomplished by rotating it along its heading. The same will be true for Gear_Toe_Four.

You don't want any Time Lag, but you do need to alter the Scale. If you were to leave it like this, the toe would rotate the wrong way, going into the foot instead of out.

18. Set the Scale to –100% so that the toe rotates in the opposite direction. Click OK and close the Graph Editor.

19. Now scroll through your animation slowly and watch the second toe move exactly when and where it should, following its neighbor perfectly.

20. To complete the foot, repeat Steps 16–18 with Z77:Gear_Toe_Three_Port and Z77:Gear_Toe_Four_Port.

Z77:Gear_Toe_Three_Port's Pitch channel will be driven by Z77:Gear_Toe_One_Port's Pitch channel and have a Scale of –100%.

Z77:Gear_Toe_Four_Port's Heading channel will be driven by Z77:Gear_Toe_One_Port's Pitch channel and use all the default settings.

21. Save your scene.

This completes the animation of the port side landing gear. In the next exercise, you will assign ChannelFollower to the starboard and front gear objects. Figure 14.5 shows the landing gear in its extended position.

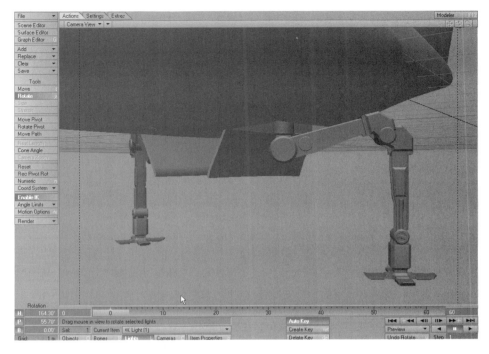

Figure 14.5   A close-up of the rear landing gear in its extended position.

Exercise 14.3   Using ChannelFollower to Link the Starboard and Front Gear Objects

1. In the Graph Editor, make Z77:Gear_Hip_Star follow both Z77:Gear_Hip_Port's Y channel and its Heading channel. Make the Y channel follow Z77:Gear_Hip_Port's Y channel with a Scale of 100% and the Heading channel follow Z77:Gear_Hip_Port's Heading channel with a Scale of –100%. Click OK and close the Graph Editor.

2. Make Z77:Gear_Thigh_Star's Pitch channel follow Z77:Gear_Thigh_Port's Pitch channel.

3. Similarly, make Z77:Gear_Calf_Star's Pitch follow that of Z77:Gear_Calf_Port.

4. Set each Starboard Toe object so that it follows its Port counterpart:

   Z77:Gear_Toe_One_Star's Pitch follows Z77:Gear_Toe_One_Port's Pitch, with default settings.

   Z77:Gear_Toe_Two_Star's Heading follows Z77:Gear_Toe_Two_Port's Heading, with a Scale of –100.

   Z77:Gear_Toe_Three_Star's Pitch follows Z77:Gear_Toe_Three_Port's Pitch, with default settings.

Z77:Gear_Toe_Four_Star's Heading follows Z77:Gear_Toe_Four_Port's Heading, with a Scale of –100.

5. Finally, set Z77:Gear_Door_Rear_Star's Bank channel to follow the Bank channel of Z77:Gear_Door_Rear_Port, with a –100% Scale.

   Now, on to the front gear. These objects also will be dependent upon the port gear, but because they are in a slightly different configuration, they will not all be a direct copy as were the starboard gear objects. You will have to adjust the Scale for every object except the toes, which move identically to the others.

6. Select Z77:Gear_Hip_Front. Set ChannelFollower on its Y channel to follow the Y channel of Z77:Gear_Hip_Port. Set the Scale to 106%.

7. Set Z77:Gear_Thigh_Front's Pitch channel to follow the Pitch channel of Z77:Gear_Thigh_Port, with a –100% Scale.

8. Set Z77:Gear_Calf_Front's Pitch channel to follow the Pitch channel of Z77:Gear_Calf_Port, with a –100% Scale.

9. Set Z77:Gear_Toe_One_Front's Pitch channel to follow the Pitch channel of Z77:Gear_Toe_One_Port, with a –100% Scale.

10. Set Z77:Gear_Toe_Two_Front's Heading channel to follow the Heading channel of Z77:Gear_Toe_Two_Port, with a –100% Scale.

11. Set Z77:Gear_Toe_Three_Front's Pitch channel to follow the Pitch channel of Z77:Gear_Toe_Three_Port, with a –100% Scale.

12. Set Z77:Gear_Toe_Four_Front's Heading channel to follow the Heading channel of Z77:Gear_Toe_Four_Port, with a –100% Scale.

13. Set Z77:Gear_Door_Front_Port's Bank axis to follow the Bank axis of Z77:Gear_Door_Rear_Port, with a 100% Scale.

14. Set Z77:Gear_Door_Front_Star's Bank axis to follow the Bank axis of Z77:Gear_Door_Rear_Star, with a –100% Scale.

15. Save your scene.

Now the animation of the landing gear is complete. Although the initial setup here might have seemed a bit tedious, the enormous benefit of doing it this way is that to make any changes to the animation, you'll have to change only the port side.

Exercise 14.4   Setting Up Cycler on the Port Gear

In this exercise you will set up Cycler on the port gear so that you can control it with a single null.

1. Select Z77:Gear_Hip_Port, and go into the Graph Editor.

2. Select the Position.Y channel.

3. Click Add Modifier and select Cycler. Double-click the Cycler listing to bring up the interface.

Figure 14.6 shows the Cycler Controller interface in its default state.

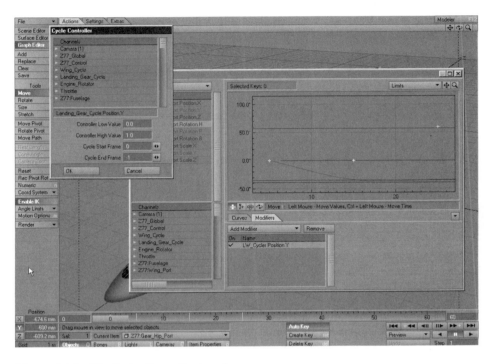

Figure 14.6   The Cycler Controller interface.

Although the Cycler interface looks a great deal like the ChannelFollower interface, in that it has the same item lister window to pick the dependent object, the parameters for it are a bit different.

The Controller Low/High Value that you see in the Cycler interface defines the range of motion over which the controller object will move to cycle the dependent object. If you think of your control object as a "handle," this would define the starting and ending positions of the handle.

As the "handle" moves from its starting position to its ending position, it will cause the dependent object to go through the animation contained between two frames. Those frames are the Cycle Start and End Frame.

For this exercise, the Start Frame will be 0, and the End Frame will be 30, even though some of the objects start after 0 and end before 30. This is because after you have your Cycler link, the animated frames don't have any real meaning in time. They will animate according to the control object, losing any values they had on their own. What becomes important at this point is the proportion of the animations of the objects.

The gear doors open between frames 0 and 10, which is one-third of the total length of the gear extension sequence of 30 frames. If you defined the Cycler start and end frames as 0 and 10, the doors would take just as long to open as the entire gear assembly does to extend, which would pretty much mess up the entire sequence.

To avoid this, every object in the sequence will have the same start and end frames, which will keep all the objects moving in their original, correct proportions.

4. Find and double-click Position.Y for Landing_Gear_Cycle, making it the active controller object.

5. Set the Cycle Start Frame to 0 and the Cycle End Frame to 30. Leave the Low and High Value at 0 and 1, respectively. Click OK and close the Graph Editor.

Note

The controlling parameter here, Position.Y, is really completely arbitrary. Any channel would work. The Low and High values are also arbitrary.

The Y position of the control object is often used because it makes it easy to think of the controller as a "handle," or a slider on a mixer. But a slider might also go "left to right" along the X axis. It's best to choose something that's easy for you to think about and remember and stay consistent with it.

Repeat Steps 4 and 5 for the rest of the port gear assembly, and remember, you still want Position.Y as the controller:

Z77:Gear_Hip_Port Rotation.H

Z77:Gear_Thigh_Port Rotation.P

Z77:Gear_Calf_Port Rotation.P

Z77:Gear_Toe_One_Port Rotation.P

Z77:Gear_Door_Rear_Port Rotation.B

7. Save your scene.

Congratulations! You've completed the entire setup! All that remains is to animate the control null, which you will do from frames 0 to 60 to show that the gear is now really controlled with the null.

Exercise 14.5   Animating the Control Null

1. Move Landing_Gear_Cycle to 1.0 meters on the Y axis. Set a key at frame 60.

You have set up a relationship of the null object's Y position from 0 to 1 with the other objects' motion on frames 0 to 30. Now you can animate the motion that would normally occur over frames 0 to 30 by keyframing the Y position of the controller null.

2. Make a preview to see the fruits of your labors!

3. Delete the key at frame 60, and set the Y value of Landing_Gear_Cycle to 1.0 meters at frame 0.

This puts you at your starting point for the final animation.

4. Save your scene.

Exercise 14.6   Setting Up the Wing Extension

The next step in your setup is to animate the wings and engines to move from their retracted, folded positions to their extended positions. You can see these respective positions in Figures 14.7 and 14.8.

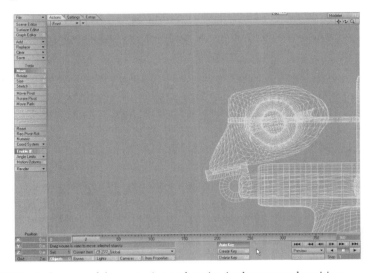

Figure 14.7   A close-up of the port wing and engine in the retracted position.

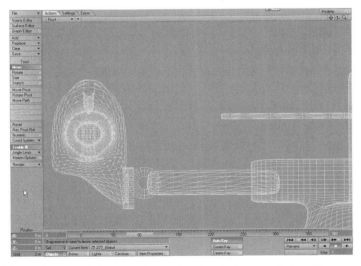

Figure 14.8   A close-up of the port wing and engine in the extended position.

You'll use ChannelFollower to mirror the port side motion on the starboard side, just like you did for the landing gear, and you'll also use Cycler to make them animate to a control null.

But first, you need to set up the wing extension, which you can do by following these steps:

1. Select Z77:Hinge_Port in Layout.

   The Hinge objects rotate the engines from folded to extended position.

2. Because the Z77:Hinge_Port is already at the ending position, make a key at frame 30. Now, rotate it to –78 degrees on the Bank axis, and set a key at frame 0.

3. Select Z77:Wing_Port. Move it out to –2.4 meters in the X axis, and set a key at frame 30.

   Now you need to set up ChannelFollower on the starboard side hinge and wing.

4. Select Z77:Hinge_Star, and open the Graph Editor. Select the Rotation.B axis, and click the Modifiers tab. Click Add Modifier, and select ChannelFollower. Double-click ChannelFollower to bring up its interface.

5. Find and double-click the Rotation.B axis of Z77:Hinge_Port. Set the Scale to –100%.

6. Now select Z77:Wing_Star. Add ChannelFollower to the Position.X channel. Set it up as you did for the last object, but use Z77:Wing_Port's Position.X channel as the control object. The Scale should still be –100%. Click OK and close the Graph Editor.

   Now the starboard wings and engines should extend along with the port. The next step is to set up Cycler to control the wing extension sequence just like you did for the landing gear.

7. Select Z77:Wing_Port, and open the Graph Editor. Select the Position.X axis, and click the Modifiers tab. Click Add Modifier, and select Cycler. Double-click Cycler to bring up its interface.

8. Find and double-click the Position.Y channel of Wing_Cycle, to set it as the control object.

9. Set the Cycler Start Frame to 0 and the Cycle End Frame to 30. Click OK and close the Graph Editor.

10. Repeat Steps 7–9 for the Bank channel of Z77:Hinge_Port.

11. Save your scene.

That completes the wing extension setup. Now whenever you want to extend or retract the wings and engines, all you'll have to do is animate the control null between 0 and 1 on the Y axis. You'll be doing this in your final animation. For now, make sure that Wing_Cycle is set to 0 on the Y axis at frame 0.

The next step in your animation setup is to assign a controller for the engine's rotation. The engines on this ship will rotate to point straight up for takeoff. You could use ChannelFollower to have one engine follow the other, but instead, you're going to use it to have *both* engines follow a null. This will centralize the control, freeing you from having to remember which engine is keyframed and which is driven by the expression.

Exercise 14.7   Assigning a Controller for the Engine's Rotation

1. Select Z77:Engine_Port, and open the Graph_Editor. Click the Rotation.P channel, and then click the Modifiers tab.

2. Click Add modifier and select ChannelFollower. Double-click ChannelFollower to bring up its interface.

3. In the item lister, find and double-click the Rotation.P channel for the object Engine_Rotator. Click OK and close the Graph Editor.

4. Repeat Steps 1–3 for Z77:Engine_Star.

   Now the engines will follow the Pitch rotation of Engine_Rotator. You need to do one more thing to make your life a bit easier. Because only a certain 90 degrees of rotation is valid for the engines, you can set rotational limits on Engine_Rotator to make sure you never put them in a position in which they shouldn't be.

5. Select Engine_Rotator. Press **m** or click Motion Options to bring up the Motion Options panel.

6. Click the Pitch Limits button to activate the limits.

7. Set the Min to –90 degrees and the Max to 0 degrees. (pitch stiffness is strictly for inverse kinematics and won't affect you here).

8. Save your scene.

Now you can quickly and easily move the engines into their launch or flight positions.

At this point, you need to show that the engines are on and working. You'll use volumetric lights to simulate the exhaust flames coming out of the back of the engines. You'll set the minimum and maximum throttle settings, and then you'll use Cycler to set up a throttle control null, much as you did for the landing gear and wings.

First, you'll need to set up the exhaust flames.

Exercise 14.8   Setting Up the Exhaust Flames

1. Click Add, Add Light, Add Distant Light.

2. Name the light Exhaust_Flame_Port. Click OK to continue.

3. Parent the light to Z77:Engine_Port.

4. Move the light to these coordinates:

X   −2.78m

Y   2.1m

Z   −920mm

Create a key at frame 0.

5. Rotate the light −180 degrees on its Heading.

6. Open the Item Properties for the light.

7. Set the color of the light to:

Red   106

Green   179

Blue   255

You want the light to have an intensity to work properly with the volumetrics, but you don't actually want it to give out any light to its surroundings.

8. Set the Light Intensity to 200% and uncheck Affect Diffuse and Affect Specular.

9. Click the box to activate Volumetric Lighting, then click Volumetric Light Options.

This brings up the Volumetric Options panel. Figure 14.9 shows this panel.

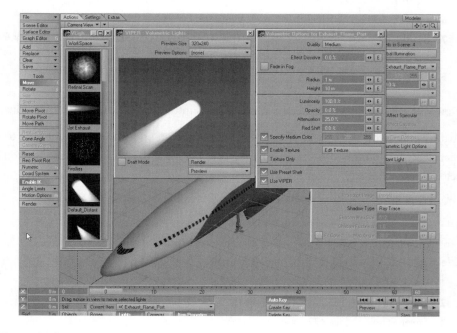

Figure 14.9   The Volumetric Options panel as it opens.

10. Set the Radius to 200 mm.

11. Click the E beside Height.

    This is the first parameter you'll set up for animation.

    You should now be in the Graph Editor, with only the channel Volumetric Options.Height displayed in the Curve Bin and graphed in the main window.

12. Click the plus sign representing the keyframe at frame 0, and set its value to 0.

13. Now click the button marked with a key located below the main window.

    This puts you into keyframe editing mode.

14. Click in the window on the line that represents frame 30 to create a key at that frame. Now, set its value to 8.

    You've now established that at frame 0, the volumetric light representing the engine exhaust will have a length of zero, and at frame 30 it will have a length of 8 meters. These represent our minimum and maximum throttle values. All that remains is to use Cycler to link these values to the Throttle control null as you did for the landing gear.

15. Click the Modifiers tab. Click Add Modifier and select Cycler. Double-click Cycler to bring up its interface.

16. Select the Position.Y channel of Throttle as the control object, and set the Start and End frames to 0 and 30, respectively. Click OK to continue. Close the Graph Editor.

    Now as you move the Throttle null from 0 to 1 on the Y axis, the length of the exhaust flame will go from 0 to 8 meters. But in addition to making the flame longer, you also want it to become more intense as the throttle power is increased. This you can set with the Luminosity parameter.

17. Back in the Volumetric Options panel, click the E beside Luminosity.

    This brings you back to the Graph Editor, this time with Volumetric Options: Luminosity as the selected channel.

18. Click the dot representing the keyframe at frame 0, and set its value to 0.

19. Now click the button marked with a key located below the main window.

    This puts you into keyframe editing mode.

20. Click in the window on the line that represents frame 30 to create a key at that frame. Now, set its value to 500.

21. Click the Modifiers tab. Click Add Modifier and select Cycler. Double-click Cycler to bring up its interface.

22. Select the Position.Y channel of Throttle as the control object and set the Start and End frames to 0 and 30, respectively. Click OK to continue. Close the Graph Editor.

    As the Throttle is moved up in the Y axis, the exhaust flame will get longer and more intense, giving exactly the effect you want!

23. Save the scene.

Next you need to add a little texture to the flame to make it look like it's moving.

Exercise 14.9   Texturing the Flame

1. Click Edit Texture to open the Texture Editor. Figure 14.10 shows the texture window.

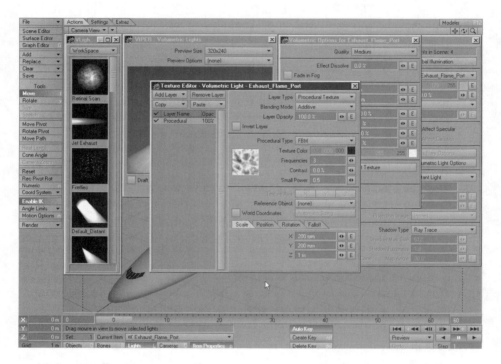

Figure 14.10   The Texture Editor window as launched from the Volumetric Options panel.

2. Set the Layer Type to Procedural Texture.

3. Set the Procedural Type to FBM.

   FBM stands for "Fractional Brownian Motion" and is one of the new texture types added in LightWave 6. It also was one of the volumetric textures in HyperVoxels 2.0.

4. Set the Texture Color to Red: 0, Green: 0, Blue: 0, which is pure black.

> **Note**
>
> Because volumetric lights are an *additive* effect, the pure black color will effectively make holes in the effect, because adding zero to anything does not change the value.

5. Keep the default settings of Frequencies: 3, Contrast 0.0%, and Small Power 0.5 the way they are.

6. Beneath the Scale tab, set the X and Y values to 200 mm, and the Z value to 1 meter.

7. Click the Position tab, and then click the E beside the Z value field.

    This brings up the Graph Editor.

8. Make sure TextureLayer.Positon Z is selected in the item lister on top.

9. Click the small key icon beneath the main display window to activate key create mode.

10. Click+left mouse button above the line marking frame 30.

    This will create a key at that frame. If you didn't get it exactly at 30, don't worry. Go back to Drag mode by clicking the Drag icon just to the left of the key icon. You can Ctrl+left mouse button-click the key and drag it forward or back in time until the key is on frame 30. Or, you can use the minislider beside the Frame field below, or enter the frame directly into the field.

11. Set the key's value to 100 meters.

12. Now set the channel's Pre and Post Behaviors to Offset Repeat.

    Offset Repeat will repeat the channel motion starting from where it left off. Your texture will move outward from the engine 100 meters, then Offset Repeat will make it move another 100 meters, and then another, and so on and so forth, giving the texture a constant velocity, much like the texture velocity in previous versions of LightWave.

13. Close the Graph Editor. Close the Texture Editor.

14. Be sure that Enable Texture is checked, and close the Volumetric Options panel.

    All that remains is to clone this engine light to the other side.

15. Make sure you have Exhaust_Flame_Port selected.

16. Click Add, Clone Current Item.

17. Click OK to clone the light once.

18. Select Exhaust_Flame_Port (2). Click Replace, Rename Current Item and rename the light to Exhaust_Flame_Star.

19. Now, change this light's parent from Z77:Engine_Port to Z77:Engine_Star.

20. Change the X coordinate of this light from −2.78 meters to 2.78 meters and create a key at frame 0.

21. Save the scene.

You now have nice-looking engine flames that you can easily control with the Throttle null. Take a look at what you've created by moving the Throttle null to 1.0 on the Y axis and creating a key at frame 30. Move the camera around so that it shows the rear of the engines and do a test-render.

Up until this point, you've created "handles" to animate large groups of objects automatically. Expressions are extremely handy for doing just that, but they also are useful for making automatic adjustments to objects.

Next you will set up the rear stabilizers to automatically respond to the motion of the ship. In a real ship, the control surfaces would move in response to the pilot's commands, causing the ship to move. In this case, because you have no actual pilot, you're going to do just the opposite to make it *appear* as though a pilot is inside.

Using Channel Express

Channel Express is the purely mathematical way to do expressions in LightWave 6. Any channel data of any kind, be it position or rotation information from an object, a light's intensity, or the zoom factor of a camera, can be used as input data. This data can be operated on with any number of built-in mathematical operations.

Channel Express also contains four slots to do extra computations. The results of these computations are stored in four variables: A, B, C, and D, which can then be used in the main operation.

You will use these all in concert to make the stabilizers anticipate the motion of the hull, and to rotate in such a way that they appear to be causing the motion.

Exercise 14.10   Using Channel Express to Automate Stabilizer Motion

1. Select Z77:Stab_Port from Layout. Open the Graph Editor. Select the Rotation.P channel. Click the Modifiers tab. Click Add Modifier and select Expression. Double-click Expression to open the interface (shown in Figure 14.11).

   The Expression field in the Channel Express interface is where you will input the mathematical formulas that will modify the motion of this channel. The formula could be as simple as adding two channels of data, or it could include complex trigonometry. But whatever it is, this is where the final value of the channel will be determined.

   Just below the Expression field is the Additive button. When activated, it *adds* the final calculated value in the Expression field to the keyframed value rather than *replacing* the value.

   Below the Additive button is the Test Expression button. This is a handy little button that enables you to test your expression to make sure everything is correct without leaving the panel. If you want to check the syntax of your expression, just click the button and it will tell you if it's okay, and if not, what's wrong. It can't tell you if an expression is going to do what you want, but it will at least tell you if it's possible to be executed.

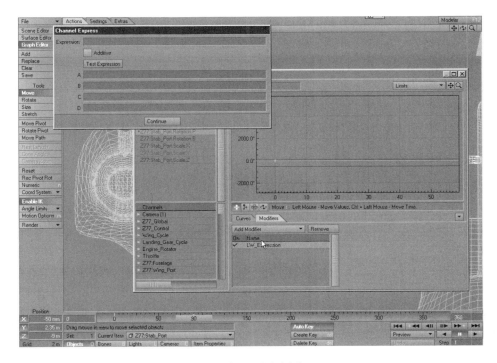

Figure 14.11 The Channel Express interface as it initially opens.

Below the Additive button are the four variable slots. Each is calculated in the same way as the main expression field. However, each result is assigned to the letter variable beside it. These can then be used in the main expression field. This helps to keep the main field less cluttered and just generally easier to deal with. The variables also are calculated successively so that A can be used in the calculation of B, B in C, and so forth.

Back to the problem at hand. The best way to calculate the rotation of the stabilizers is to find the difference in rotation of the hull over a period of time, and to apply the reverse of that to the stabilizers. You also might multiply the value to make it look a bit more obvious. Remember, you want it to look realistic, but the overriding goal is still to make it look *cool*. It's okay to take some artistic license to further that goal.

The first thing you need to calculate is the difference in Pitch value of the hull over a period of time.

2. In the field beside A, enter this formula:

Z77_Control.rot(Time+.5).p

This formula returns the Pitch of your control object at a half-second from the current frame, telling you what the rotation *will be*.

3. In the field beside B, enter this formula:

   Z77_Control.rot(Time).p

   This tells you what the current Pitch of the control object is.

   Now, you want to calculate the difference in Bank.

4. In the field beside C, enter this formula:

   Z77_Control.rot(Time+.5).b

   This formula returns the Bank of your control object at a half-second from the current frame, telling you what the rotation *will be.*

5. In the field beside D, enter this formula:

   Z77_Control.rot(Time).b

   This tells you what the current Bank of the control object is.

6. Now, in the main field, enter this formula:

   (B–A)+(D–C)/2

7. Click Continue and close the Graph Editor.

8. Save the scene.

The main formula first takes the *difference* in the Pitch of the control object between a half-second in the future and the current time. (On a real airplane, this would be simulating the elevators of the plane, the control surfaces that alter the pitch of the plane.) To that it adds the difference in the Bank of the control object divided by two. (This simulates the function of the ailerons of the airplane, whose job it is to bank the craft.) You divide the Bank difference by two because Bank is more likely to have quick changes over the course of an animation. This helps to limit how much of an effect it can have. Figure 14.12 shows the Channel Express interface.

 Note

> Keep in mind that this is only a simulation of a real effect, and it will give you pretty decent results so long as you keep the animation of the control null within reasonable limits. Expressions are "dumb"; that is, they don't know what effect you are trying to achieve. They only calculate values. Because 3D animation has no limitations under the laws of physics, it's possible, and quite easy, to make an animation that would, for instance, rip the wings right off your ship.

Now it's time to animate the control null to show off your automatic control surface.

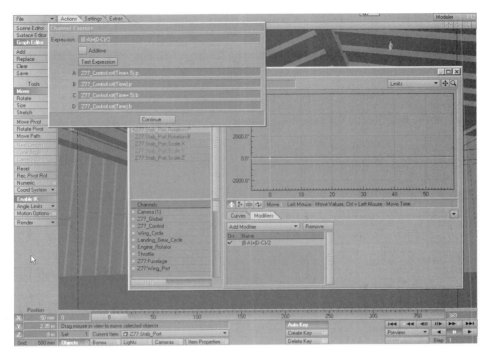

Figure 14.12   The Channel Express interface with the expression completed.

Exercise 14.11   Animating the Vehicle to Test Your Expressions

1. Select Z77_Control and give it these rotational values at these keyframes:

    Frame 10: Heading: 0 Pitch: 0 Bank: 17

    Frame 20: Heading: 0 Pitch: 0 Bank: −30

    Frame 30: Heading: 0 Pitch: −20 Bank: 0

    Frame 40: Heading: 0 Pitch: 15 Bank: 0

    Frame 60: Heading: 0 Pitch: 0 Bank: 0

2. Now create a preview, and you should see the port stabilizer moving up and down in response to the hull's motion!

    Now you need to set up the rotation for the other stabilizer. Unlike the previous cases, where the motion of the starboard side is basically a copy of the port side, the expression for the starboard side stabilizer is partially opposite.

    The Pitch component of the starboard stabilizer motion will be identical to that of port side. However, the Bank component will be exactly opposite. You will need to alter your expression to reflect that.

3. Select Z77:Stab_Star. Open the Graph Editor. Select the Rotation.P channel. Click the Modifiers tab. Click Add Modifier and select Expression. Double-click Expression to open the interface.

4. In the field beside A, enter this formula:

   Z77_Control.rot(Time+.5)).p

5. In the field beside B, enter this formula:

   Z77_Control.rot(Time).p

6. In the field beside C, enter this formula:

   Z77_Control.rot(Time+.5)).b

7. In the field beside D, enter this formula:

   Z77_Control.rot(Time).b

8. Now, in the main field, enter this formula:

   (B–A)+(C–D)/2

9. Save the scene.

As you can see, the only difference between this and the original expression is that you are subtracting C from D, rather than D from C. This makes the bank component the opposite of its port counterpart.

Now, make another preview and have fun watching just about the only time math will ever be cool! After you're done watching, delete all the keyframes you made earlier for Z77_Control. You're going to want a clean slate for your final animation.

Putting It All Together

The final part of your project is to put all these things to use to make your ship fly with the controls you've created.

Note

From this point on, the animation is mostly subjective. There's nothing that says you have to follow the instructions precisely, or at all, for that matter. However, if you do follow the instructions as they are laid out for you, you'll be assured of making a pretty cool animation, and maybe learning some helpful hints and tricks along the way.

Exercise 14.12   Preparing the Spaceliner for Takeoff

1. From the File menu, use the Load From Scene command and load the Hangar_Setup.lws from the book's CD-ROM. This scene file can be found in the

Scenes/Chapter14 directory. The Load From Scene command loads the elements of one scene into the current scene. Lights are included with this scene, so when LightWave asks if you want to load lights as well as objects, click Yes. Now, to the right of the time slider, set the end frame to 360.

This scene contains a hangar setup for your ship. Included in the setup are two top doors set to animate with a Cycler null, and lights for both the inside and the outside of the hangar.

The hangar should load in so that the landing gear of your ship is sitting right on the floor; so everything should be right in the proper place and ready to animate.

The first thing to do is animate the hangar doors opening.

2. Select Hangar_Door_Cycler and move it to 1.0 meters on the Y axis. Create a keyframe for this object at frame 240.

Note

One of the most important parts of animation to master is a sense of weight. A sense of the weight of an object is one of the unconscious signals sent to the viewer that can create—or if done wrong, destroy—the realism of a scene. One of the basic rules of weight is that bigger things move slower than smaller things. You can see this in every part of life and in all good animation.

In the case of your hangar doors, you want them to seem quite large. To do so means to animate them opening slowly. You'll give them 240 frames, about 8 seconds, to complete their cycle. But they'll be clear of the opening at about frame 120, so even as the doors are opening, you can continue to work with the spacecraft.

The next steps are to animate the wings opening, engines rotating to launch position, and engines cycling up to full power.

3. Select Wing_Cycle and move it to 1.0 meters on the Y axis. Create a keyframe for it at frame 90.

4. Select Engine_Rotator and create a keyframe at this position at frame 90.

5. Delete its keyframe at frame 0.

6. Rotate it on its Pitch to –90 degrees. Create a keyframe at frame 150.

7. Select Throttle and create a keyframe at frame 150.

8. Delete its keyframe at frame 0.

9. Move it to 1.0 meters on the Y axis. Create a keyframe at frame 180.

10. Save your scene.

Now you'll actually animate the entire ship rising up from the ground, and make the landing gear retract.

Exercise 14.13   Animating the Ship

1. Select Z77_Control from inside Layout and create a keyframe for it at frame 180.
2. Delete its keyframe at frame 0.
3. Move it to 10.0 meters on the Y axis and create a key at frame 270.

   Normally, objects like this start out slowly and accelerate, so you'll need to adjust the Tension of the Y channel to reflect that.
4. Open the Graph Editor.
5. Click Z77.Control.Position.Y in the Curve Bin. This should display the Y channel, which should be a straight green line.
6. Select the first keyframe by clicking the small white cross at frame 180.
7. Click the Curves tab, and adjust the Tension to 1.0.
8. Close the Graph Editor.

   You'll come back to the animation of the main ship. Right now you need to retract the landing gear.
9. Select Landing_Gear_Cycle. It should already be at 1.0 meters on the Y axis. Create a keyframe in this position at frame 180.
10. Delete its keyframe at frame 0.
11. Move it down to 0 on the Y axis, and create a keyframe for it at frame 240.

    Now you'll continue with animating the main ship.
12. Select Z77_Control and rotate it to 130 degrees on the Heading and 11 degrees in Pitch. Create a key at frame 330.
13. Now move it to 11 meters on its X axis, 20 meters on Y, and 13 meters on Z.
14. Rotate it to 135 degrees on its Heading, and 22 degrees on its Pitch.
15. Create a key at frame 360.
16. Save the scene.

This completes the animation of the objects in the scene to the end of the shot. Now, you'll set up your camera for a dramatic presentation.

Exercise 14.14   Virtual Cinematography I

1. Move the camera to:

X	−4
Y	−1.5
Z	15m

2. Rotate the camera to:

   H   160 degrees

   P   –12 degrees

   B   0 degrees

3. Create a key at frame 0.

4. Move the camera on the X axis to –9.5 meters.

5. Rotate the camera on its Heading to 142 degrees. Create a key at frame 180.

6. Save the scene.

This makes a nice camera move that helps to add depth to the shot from the parallax between the ship and the hangar around it. It also gets you in great position to observe the takeoff of the ship, which happens next.

In practical (real) filmmaking, the cinematographer or director generally frames the shot as he or she wants it to look at the beginning, and if the subject moves, the camera operator rotates the camera so that it keeps the subject in frame, even if it's not the original frame. He or she just keeps it looking nice throughout the shot.

In 3D, it's not quite as easy as just watching what happens and moving the camera. You don't have the benefit of real-time feedback, but you do have the added bonus of being able to control time and go back and fix errors. Practical cinematographers would probably gladly trade with you for those capabilities.

The trick is to *think* like a real cameraperson; to see the view through the virtual camera as he or she would through a real one. A couple of basic rules will help guide you in deciding where and how to place and move the camera.

- Real camerapeople do not have the benefit of looking into the future to see where their subject is *going to be*. They can only focus on where it is *now*. They cannot anticipate the movement of their subject, so they cannot move the camera before the subject moves. They must respond to that motion. The camera anticipating a subject's motion is an obvious sign that what you are viewing is CGI, and is something to be avoided if possible.

- Real cameras must obey the laws of physics. If your virtual camera does not at least try to act in the same way, it is another telltale sign that could pull the viewer out of the illusion and ruin the effect. Now, if the subject matter is appropriate, by all means, throw physics out the window. There's no way to truly, realistically move a camera in a person's bloodstream, for example. Physics have no place in an animation such as that.

An easy way to begin acting like a virtual cinematographer is to drag the time slider until your subject begins to move out of frame, then adjust the camera to put it back in frame at that point. Usually, for slower-moving subjects, letting the subject get about halfway off-screen will give a good effect, allowing the camera to seem to react to the subject, rather than the other way around. For faster movers, it might be better to let it go all the way off-screen before adjusting.

And if, in the final animation, the subject does go off-screen a little, don't panic. It's not necessary to have the subject dead center at all times. Because you pour so much time and energy into the objects you animate, the natural reaction is to make sure it gets as much screen time as possible, but this isn't always the best course of action. Examine some of the better effects films of the past decade or so and see for yourself.

In this case, around frame 290 is where you're going to want to make an adjustment.

Exercise 14.15   Virtual Cinematography II

1. Drag the time slider to frame 290 and notice how the ship moves completely off-screen and begins its rotations.

2. Now rotate the camera to 145 on its Heading, and −35 on its Pitch. Create a key.

    This should pretty much center the ship in frame at that time and as you scrub through the animation, you'll see that it keeps it pretty well in frame throughout, without anticipating too much.

    With only 70 frames remaining in the final animation, it's probably best to just set a key at the final frame.

3. Move the time slider to frame 360. Rotate the camera to 139 degrees on its Heading, and −32 degrees on its Pitch. Create a key.

4. Save the scene.

Finished! Now create a preview and marvel at what you've accomplished! At this point, you might even want to render the animation in its entirety.

The Next Step

This chapter is a good example of the power of expressions to simplify and enhance your animations. The simplification comes from going from animating many objects at a time to animating just one. The enhancement comes from being freed from the tedious work, enabling you to put more into your animations. It's also an example of a fairly typical setup a technical director might run into at a production studio.

But don't think that this is the end of the animation. You should continue from this point, fleshing it out in any way you can. Here are some suggestions:

- A shake as the engines run up to full power
- Flares in the engine nozzles
- Debris kicked up by the engines
- More pieces to the set, such as barrels, crates, service vehicles, and so on

Summary

This chapter has introduced you to the world of procedural animation. You've learned to use true expressions and their plug-in counterparts. You've seen how expressions can be used to simplify tasks that would otherwise be quite daunting, and to automate tasks that would otherwise become quite tedious. This chapter is but a scratch on the tip of the surface of a rather vast iceberg, but it should have given you a good solid understanding of the basics of expressions and procedural animation. From there, you can go on to test the boundaries of this seemingly limitless way of working. But remember, in the end, expressions are best used to make you job easier. Use the extra time they buy you to take your work to a whole new level!

Chapter 15

LightWave 6 Compositing

Compositing enables you to seamlessly blend 3D computer-generated images either with other 3D computer-generated images, or with 2D images, such as photographs of real settings or people. Most of the visual effects created for film and video consist of 3D animation and digital effects composited over live-action photography. Using compositing, you can make it seem as though an object is there when it actually isn't. Another important aspect of compositing with LightWave is that it enables you to do more, especially if your system is not as fast as you'd like it to be. Compositing in this sense enables you to blend multiple images together.

Understanding Compositing

From the optically composited spaceships of *Star Wars* to the digital dinosaurs of Disney's *Dinosaur*, compositing has come a long way. The technology has evolved from purely optical techniques to completely digital methods, but compositing will always be an important part of animation and visual effects.

Indeed, the enormous importance of compositing has led to the development of many high-powered, complex, and *expensive* programs dedicated to the task. But LightWave comes with its own, rather extensive, set of tools for compositing in LightWave and for exporting images to be composited in other software packages.

In this chapter, you will examine several different compositing techniques. You will use compositing to

- Place a 3D object against a cloudy sky
- Place a 3D object in front of and behind a mountain
- Place a 3D object in front of and behind a building, and with shadows
- Place a 3D car on a road with real cars
- Examine the basic techniques for doing two-pass compositing

Beginning Compositing: Background and Foreground Images

Compositing can be an extraordinarily complicated process, combining hundreds of separate 2D and 3D elements into one final image. However, many times it's just as simple as a 3D object against a background image.

A background image, or background plate, as it is commonly called, is a 2D image. It is usually a digitized photograph or sequence of film, though not necessarily so; sometimes other rendered 3D footage is used as the background image. A 3D object is placed against this to make it appear that the 3D object was there when the photograph was taken. An example of this would be the aforementioned creatures in Disney's *Dinosaur*.

Real settings were filmed with a regular camera, the footage was digitized, and then the 3D dinosaurs were placed against the footage to make them appear to be in the picture.

Naturally, a situation like this is a bit more complex than the simple explanation above. But the background image is the beginning of every composite scene.

In LightWave, the background image has its place in the Effects panel, under the Compositing tab. This is where you will begin the first exercise.

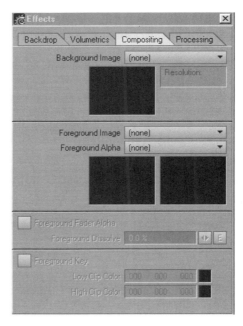

Figure 15.1 The Effects panel, under the Compositing tab. Most everything needed for compositing in LightWave can be found here.

Exercise 15.1   Placing a 3D Object Against a Cloudy Sky

1. From Layout, open the Image Editor.
2. Load the image Cloud_Sky_BG.tga, as in Figure 15.2.
3. Open the Effects panel.
4. Click the Compositing tab.
5. Click the list beside Background Image, and select Cloud_Sky_BG.tga.

Note

In addition to using the Image Editor to load and manage images, you can also go directly to the Compositing tab and select Load Image from the Background Image drop-down list.

Figure 15.2   A nice bright sky, shot with clouds, acts as a backdrop for compositing.

  6. Render a frame. You'll see the cloud image and nothing else.

Only the cloud image is displayed in the render, as nothing else has yet been added to the scene. There are a few important things to note at this point:

- When using a background image, this image overrides any backdrop color or gradient backdrop.
- 3D objects will not reflect the background image. It does not "exist" to the rendering engine.
- The background image is not affected by fog, though it can be used as the fog color instead of a solid color.
- By default, the background image will not be refracted by transparent objects. However, you can set this option for each surface in the Surface Editor.
- The background image will always be centered and stretch itself to fill the camera's entire field of view. This also is true of the foreground image, which you'll get to shortly.

The next step is to add a 3D object into the scene.

  7. Load the object Gnat.lwo from the book's CD-ROM.
  8. Select the camera. Move it down on the Y axis about 7m. Rotate the camera up on the pitch about 30 degrees so that the ship looks similar to the one in Figure 15.3.
  9. Press **F9** and render a frame.

Now the 3D object is composited against the background image, the most basic of all compositing situations. Figure 15.4 shows the rendered image.

Figure 15.3   Move the camera until the view looks roughly like this.

Figure 15.4   A backdrop image has been set in LightWave and an object has been loaded. When rendered, the space fighter is composited over the cloud image.

This technique will work for any situation in which a 3D object does not need to go behind a 2D image. You will need to use a foreground image for situations in which a 3D object needs to go behind a 2D image.

The foreground image behaves in most ways like the background image. The main difference is that whereas the background image appears *behind* the 3D objects in the scene, the foreground image is applied *on top of* the 3D objects.

Exercise 15.2   Applying Foreground Images

1. Continuing from the previous exercise, in Layout, clear the scene.
2. Load the image Mountain_Sky.tga image from the book's CD-ROM.
3. Under the compositing tab in the Effects panel, set Mountain_Sky.tga as the Background Image.
4. Load the object Gnat.lwo from the book's CD-ROM.

Note

LightWave also offers you the capability to view the background image in the Layout window, to aid in positioning your 3D objects.

5. Press the **d** key to open the Display Options panel.
6. Beside Camera View Background, click the item selector and drag down to Background Image.
7. Close the panel.

You should see the background image pop-up into the Layout screen when you select Camera view.

8. Move and rotate the object until it appears, as in Figure 15.5. The exact placement isn't important. What is important is that the ship is placed so that it is roughly split across the top line of the mountains—part of it is across the mountains and part is across the sky.
9. Press **F9** to render a frame.

You'll see that like the previous example, the 3D object is pasted over the background image.

Now you will add the foreground image and see how that changes your final output.

10. Under the Compositing tab in the Effects panel, set Mountain_Sky.tga to Foreground Image. Do not change the background image.
11. Press **F9** to render a frame.

You'll see that the 3D object is now gone, having been covered by the foreground image, which in this case is the same as the background image, as in Figure 15.6.

Figure 15.5 By setting the Camera View Background to see the backdrop image, you can easily position the spaceship object in Layout.

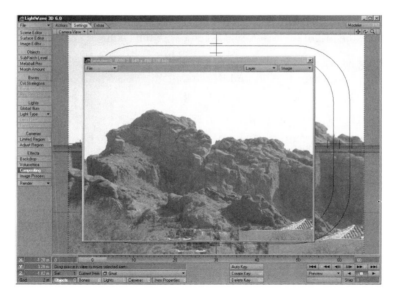

Figure 15.6 The spaceship object is obscured from view when a foreground image is applied in the Compositing tab.

As you also can see, this isn't terribly useful. All you end up with is the foreground image, which you already had. To be useful, parts of the foreground image must be *cut out* to reveal the 3D objects behind it.

LightWave provides two means to accomplish this. The first is the Foreground Key, and the second the Foreground Alpha.

Foreground Key and Foreground Alpha

In the next exercise, you'll start with the Foreground Key. The Foreground Key is nothing more than a color-keying system such as the blue- and green-screen systems used by TV weathermen and in visual effects throughout the industry. It works by *keying out*—removing—a range of colors that you specify. LightWave gives you two colors, a Low Clip Color and a High Clip Color.

The Low Clip Color is generally the darkest, most saturated color you would want to remove from your foreground image. The High Clip Color is the brightest, least saturated color you'd want to take out. Any colors between these two colors are removed from the foreground image before it's pasted over the rendering.

Exercise 15.3   Setting Up a Foreground Key

In this exercise, you will *key out* the sky and leave the mountains. To do this, you want to pick the darkest, most saturated color in the sky, and set this to be the Low Clip Color. And you'll set the brightest, least saturated color for the High Clip Color.

1. Starting where you left off in Exercise 15.2, under the Compositing tab in the Effects panel, check Foreground Key to On.
2. Set the Low Clip Color to R:129 G:192 B:204.
3. Set the High Clip Color to R:255 G:255 B:255.
4. Open the Render Options panel. Make sure that Show Rendering In Progress in checked On.
5. Press **F9** to render a frame and watch as it renders. Figure 15.7 shows the render.

    As LightWave renders, you should see the foreground image render first, but you'll notice that it doesn't render the sky because those colors fall within the range between the Low Clip Color and High Clip Color that you specified. You'll then see the Gnat ship object render in the blank area above the mountains. Finally, the Background Image is put in behind that.

This is a good technique to use when your foreground image will support it. In this case, the image was a good candidate for this technique because the area you needed to key out was a single large area with very little variation in color, and it was a very different color than the rest of the picture.

However, not all images are this easy. And for images that are more complex, or when you just want more control, LightWave offers you the Foreground Alpha.

Figure 15.7   Using a Foreground Key and setting the Low and High Clip Colors drops out the sky of the Foreground Key, enabling you to see the object and the background image.

An *alpha* is a grayscale image that is used to tell a program where certain things should happen. In the case of a surface texture, an alpha image would tell the surface where to apply a texture map. It could tell a surface where to be transparent and where to be opaque. And in the case of a foreground image, it determines where the image will appear and where it won't.

Exercise 15.4   Using Foreground Alpha

1. Continuing from the previous exercise, load the image Mountain_Sky_Alpha.tga from the book's CD-ROM.

2. Under the Compositing tab in the Effects panel, and beside the Foreground Alpha image, click the selector and choose Mountain_Sky_Alpha. If you want, you can always load an image from here as well.

3. Click the checkbox beside Foreground Fader Alpha.

    This will tell LightWave to ignore the areas of the foreground image that the Foreground Alpha has marked pure black. Otherwise, those areas will be added to the image, making that part of the image much too bright.

4. Press **F9** to render a frame. Figure 15.8 shows the rendered image.

Figure 15.8   Using a Foreground Alpha image gives you precise control over where the composited foreground image will be clipped.

Now you can see that the rendered image appears much as it did with the Foreground Key, but this time using an alpha image. Using an alpha image gives you much more flexibility in determining where your foreground image appears. It is also more accurate than using a range of colors to clip the image. However, both methods are suitable depending on the project.

Using alpha images when compositing gives you the most control over your scene because the alpha can be used to shape the foreground image into any shape you desire.

The situation you've just outlined in the previous exercise would be fine if your 3D object only needed to be behind the mountains and in front of the sky. But if your object needed to start out behind the mountains, rise up above them, and then swoop down in front of them, it wouldn't work. The foreground image would be pasted on top, no matter what.

Another, more common situation is having a 3D object cast shadows and otherwise interact with your 2D images. This kind of seamless compositing is the mainstay of the visual effects industry. Without it, the movies and television shows you watch every day would be tremendously different.

As you might have guessed, LightWave has the answer to compositing and casting shadows—Front Projection Image Mapping.

Intermediate Compositing: Front Projection Image Mapping

Front Projection Image Mapping is one of the most powerful compositing tools LightWave has to offer. It enables your 3D objects to interact with your 2D images in almost every way that they can interact with other 3D objects.

Front Projection Image Mapping works by, you guessed it, projecting an image onto an object. It's "projected" from the camera's point of view such that it would appear exactly as if it were a background or foreground image. It's difficult to explain but easy to understand when you see it for yourself.

Exercise 15.5   Applying Front Projection Image Mapping

1. Start with a clean workspace in Layout by selecting Clear Scene from the File menu.

2. Load the object Front_Projection_Odd.lwo from the book's CD-ROM.

3. Open the Surface Editor, and make sure the Front Projection surface is selected. Click the T button beside the Color channel to open the Texture Editor.

4. Select Load Image from the Image list, and Load the image Hotel.tga from the book's CD-ROM.

5. In the Texture Editor, click the drop-down list beside Projection and select Front, as in Figure 15.9.

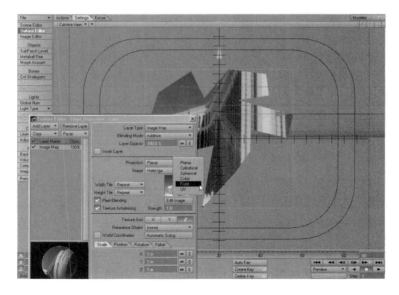

Figure 15.9   In the Texture Editor, you can tell LightWave to map an image as a Front Projection Image for compositing by selecting Front from the projection list.

6. Make sure you have Image set to Hotel.tga.

7. Uncheck Pixel Blending and Texture Antialiasing to produce a cleaner rendered image. (Because you are going to match this mapped image with the same image in the background, you want them to match perfectly.) Also, set Width Tile and Height Tile to Reset. You do not want the image to repeat.

8. Click Use Texture and return to the Surface Editor.

9. Set the surface's Luminosity to 100%.

   This will make the image self-illuminating and help you match the backdrop. LightWave can't cast light onto a backdrop image, but because the front projection image is on a polygon, you do not want LightWave's lights to be its only light source.

10. Set the surface's Diffuse to 0% to tell the surface not to accept any light from the scene. The luminosity setting will make it visible.

11. Render a frame. Figure 15.10 shows the render thus far.

Figure 15.10   As it stands now, the render looks like nothing more than a regular image map on an odd polygon. But wait!

You can see that the 2D image of the hotel and sky appears wherever the object is. The image was mapped on the object from the point of view of the camera, exactly as a foreground or background image would appear. Moving the object does not move the image; it only moves that part of the image that is shown. Similar to rotating the object, the region defined by the shape of the object is the region of the image that will be shown, no matter what position it's in.

Note

To illustrate this point more fully, feel free to move, rotate, size, and stretch the object. Render a frame. It will always show a portion of the image no matter where you place it or what angle it's at.

Theoretically, if you were to set this same image to be the background image of the scene, the images should blend seamlessly. In fact, this is the case.

12. Under the Compositing tab in the Effects panel, click the selector beside Background Image and select Hotel.tga.

13. Render a frame.

If you have Show Rendering In Progress still turned on, you will see LightWave render the object and then fill in the background image around it. Now you can't distinguish between the two. Figure 15.11 shows the example.

Figure 15.11   When the hotel.tga image is placed as the background image, the front projection mapping seamlessly matches up with the image-mapped polygon.

It's this ability to blend seamlessly that gives Front Projection Image Mapping its power. Now you'll examine how to really use that power.

Exercise 15.6   Creating Shadows for Compositing

Front Projection Image Mapping is unique in the way it maps the texture image, but in every other way it's just a normal surface texture. It can receive shadows, reflect other objects, and be transparent. By using these characteristics, you can make the objects appear to interact with the scene.

1. Picking up from Exercise 15.5, clear the object Front_Projection_Odd.lwo. You can quickly do this right in Layout by pressing the dash (-) key.

2. Load the object FPIM_Square.lwo from the book's CD-ROM. You can quickly do this by pressing the plus (+) key on the numeric keypad.

3. Load the object Gnat.lwo.

Now that you have the two components of the scene, you need to place them in the proper position.

The FPIM_Square.lwo object is going to be the *stand-in* for the hotel. Because you can't cast shadows on background images in LightWave, the FPIM_Square.lwo object is a flat polygon that will catch the shadows. Using Front Projection Image Mapping as in the previous exercise, you can match the polygon to the backdrop.

You don't have an exact 3D model of the hotel to use, and for what you're going to do, you don't need one. The square here will do perfectly fine. The Gnat.lwo object is once again going to be the subject.

The first step in doing a shot such as this is to establish your camera angle. There are various techniques you can use, and even some programs dedicated to the task. However, you're going to start out simple, and you'll see that in certain cases, it isn't even that important.

When trying to match the camera to a real picture, the first things to look for are reference points. Usually, the best reference points to use are those on the ground, or even the ground itself. But you'll notice that in this picture you do not see the ground at all. This is both bad and good; it's bad because it doesn't give you any easy reference, and it's good because if you don't have to see the ground, you don't have to be as precise in the setup. Precision eats up time, and time is money. Hence, the less precision you can get away with, the better.

Therefore, without the ground to use for reference, all you're left with is the building itself. Looking at the angle, it's safe to say this picture was taken by someone on the ground. From counting the window divisions, which you can safely assume to be whole stories, you can guess that the building is somewhere on the order of 300–400 feet tall, given a story is about 10 feet. Again, precise measurements aren't necessary in this instance, so don't sweat about the details. You just want a good idea to start with.

Comparing the height of the building, which is about 400 feet, to the height of a human, which is about 5–6 feet, you see that the building is about two orders of magnitude higher than a person. What does this mean to you? It means that the height of the camera in the scene doesn't really matter, so long as it's quite close to zero. As a matter of fact, you're going to leave it at zero and eliminate that variable altogether.

So you have the coordinates for the camera's position: 0,0,0. The next thing to figure out is the angle at which the camera is pointed. You'll need a reference to do that. The perfect reference is the FPIM_Square object.

The FPIM_Square object is going to be standing in for one of the walls of the hotel. Knowing this, you know that it has to be about 400 feet high. Knowing that the size of the square is 1 meter, you need to scale it up about 120 times.

4. Stretch FPIM_Square.lwo to 120.0 on the Y axis and 120.0 on the X axis.

   Now you should position the stand-in object so that it's about the right size and angle to match the hotel.

5. Open the Display Options panel and set the Camera View Background to Background Image.

6. Move FPIM_Square.lwo to –60 meters on the X axis and 220 meters on the Z axis.

7. Open the Scene Editor and set the FPIM_Square.lwo object to Bounding Box.

   This will enable you to see the background image through the object.

8. Rotate the FPIM_Square.lwo object to 36 degrees on its Heading.

   As you can see in Figure 15.12, this aligns the top edge of the object with the top edge of the hotel. This alignment will not change when you rotate the camera on its pitch, so you can leave it here without worrying about adjusting it later.

Figure 15.12   Make the top left edge of the object parallel to the top left edge of the hotel.

Now the object is in good position, and you can rotate the camera to match the square to the building.

9. Rotate the Camera to –14 degrees or so on its Pitch.

   This will roughly align the top edge of the object with the top edge of the hotel. You don't have to be precise because you have another way of aligning the edge.

10. Do a test render by pressing **F9** so that you'll have something to compare to, as in Figure 5.13. Save the scene.

Figure 15.13   After pitching the camera, you'll see that the stand-in object is more closely aligned with the top edge of the hotel. Notice how the box edge outline is lined up along the left side of the building.

What you see is the object aligned properly but extending off the edge too far. If you were to Front Projection Image Map the hotel's image as it is now, it's possible that the Gnat could cast a shadow onto the sky, which is obviously no good. You could tweak the scaling of the object until it fits perfectly to the building. The problem is, that's a lot of work, and there's still the issue of the irregular edge at the top of the hotel. No amount of tweaking and scaling would fit the square to that shape. So you need to call on the help of Clip Maps.

Clip Maps

A Clip Map is a special kind of image map. It can be applied every way a normal texture can, but it works in a much different way. A Clip Map is an image map that determines where an object will exist. It's very similar to transparency, but instead of determining where an object is clear or opaque, it actually determines whether the object is there.

Exercise 15.7   Working with Clip Maps

In this exercise, you're going to use a Clip Map to "trim away" the unwanted parts of the polygon and make it conform to the shape of the building. You've got an image already prepared for this.

1. Load the image Hotel_Alpha.tga from the book's CD-ROM.

   This image is much like the alpha image you used before. Like transparency, for a Clip Map, white denotes where the object *won't* be, and black where it *will* be. Also, white denotes where an object is fully clipped out, and black where it's not clipped at all. To make sure everything lines up perfectly, you're going to Front Projection Image Map the Clip Map onto the polygon.

2. Select the FPIM_Square.lwo object and open the Object Properties panel (**p**) for it.

3. Click the Rendering tab.

4. Click the T beside Clip Map to open its Texture Editor.

5. Set the Projection type to Front.

6. Select Hotel_Alpha.tga as the Image.

7. Uncheck Pixel Blending and Texture Antialiasing to produce a cleaner rendered image. Also, set Width Tile and Height Tile to Reset. You do not want the image to repeat.

8. Check Invert Layer. You need to do this from time to time if your black areas are white and your white areas are black.

   This will make it so that the white areas are left in and the black areas are clipped out. Notice that the white area in the preview image is the exact shape of the hotel. This assures you that the object behind the stand-in object, the Gnat ship object, will appear behind the hotel when using Front Projection Image Mapping. The ship will not be composited correctly if the stand-in object is not aligned with the backdrop image.

Note

To create the stand-in objects for compositing and Front Projection Image Mapping, you can load the desired backdrop image into Modeler and create polygons that are the exact size and shap, based on the image. Chapter 10 explains the use of backdrop images in Modeler for reference.

9. Press **F9** to do a test render. Figure 15.14 shows the scene thus far.

   Now you should see the hotel image, with an area of plain gray where the polygon is, and the polygon should be perfectly fit to the edge of the hotel. Behold the power of the Clip Map!

   Now you can put the Gnat into place and continue on.

10. Move the Gnat object to –45 meters on the X axis, 64 meters on the Y, and 200 meters on the Z.

11. Rotate the Gnat 36 degrees on its Heading.

    This should set the ship to be exactly perpendicular to the wall, and just above it.

12. Scale the object to 3.000.

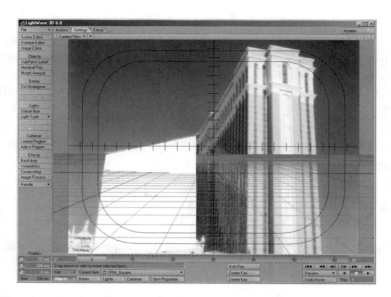

Figure 15.14   Position the stand-in object, and it's almost ready to catch some shadows!

This will put the Gnat a little bit out of realistic scale but make it a lot easier to see in the composite.

Figure 15.15   Now the Gnat hovers over the edge of the hotel, just waiting to be a part of the scene!

Exercise 15.8   Compositing Light Shadows

The next step is to match the virtual LightWave light to the real light in the scene. Like camera matching, there's no certain way you have to go about doing this, but there are generally much more obvious reference points for light matching, and they're called *shadows*. Let's take a look at how you can match them.

First, you need to be able to see both the real and virtual shadows.

1. Go back to the Object Properties panel for FPIM_Square.lwo.
2. Set the Dissolve to 50%.
3. Check the Render Options panel. Make sure Trace Shadows is turned on.
4. Do a test render. Figure 15.16 shows the partially dissolved stand-in object.

Figure 15.16   The stand-in object is dissolved out 50%, enabling you to see the position of the sunlight to cast appropriate shadows from the Gnat ship object.

Now you can see the large shadow on the side of the hotel juxtaposed with the shadow cast by the ship on the polygon. You should also be able to see that they don't even come close to matching. For the rest of the composite to hold up, it is essential that they match very closely.

5. Rotate the Light to –10 degrees on its Heading and 45 degrees on its Pitch.
6. Save the scene, and then do a test render. Figure 15.17 shows the shot with the light adjusted and the shadow of the ship in place.

Figure 15.17   When the light is adjusted to match the original hotel image and Ray Traced Shadows is turned on in the Render Options panel, the Gnat ship casts a nice shadow on the stand-in object.

There, that's better. Now the shadow seems to line up nicely with the large one on the wall of the hotel.

You might be wondering why you haven't yet set up the Front Projection Image Map of the hotel onto the polygon. As you'll see, it will be necessary to precisely balance the diffuse and luminosity values of the polygon's surfaceto make the compositing seamless and the shadow values match. Because the brightness of the polygon is partly determined by the angle of the light in the scene, it is best to get the light situated first, and only then begin to adjust the surface values.

Exercise 15.9   Matching Front Projection Images

1. Continuing with the scene from the previous exercise, go back to the Object Properties panel for FPIM_Square.lwo.
2. Under the Rendering tab, set the Object Dissolve back to 0%. Close the Object Properties panel.
3. Open the Global Illumination panel.
4. Set the Ambient Intensity to 10%.

    With the polygon fully back in place, it's time to surface it.

5. Open the Surface Editor. Select the FPIM_Square surface.
6. Click the T beside the Color channel to open its Texture Editor.

7. Set the Projection type to Front.

8. Select Hotel.tga as the Image.

9. Uncheck Pixel Blending and Texture Antialiasing to produce a cleaner rendered image. Also, set Width Tile and Height Tile to Reset. You do not want the image to repeat.

10. Press **F9** to render. Figure 15.18 shows the changes.

Figure 15.18   After the front projection mapping is applied to the FPIM_Square object, the ship looks like it's casting a shadow onto the building.

Now the hotel image is projected onto the polygon, matching up nicely with the rest of the image, but the brightness isn't quite right. Here's where you have to eyeball it. You have to play with the Diffuse and Luminosity values until the polygon matches the background image and the shadow values of the objects match those in the image.

11. Click Use Texture to exit the Texture Editor.

12. Set the Luminosity of the surface to 41%.

13. Do a test render. Figure 15.19 shows the change.

Now the values of the polygon surface and the background image match seamlessly. But the shadow is a little too light. You need to set the Luminosity lower and the Diffuse value higher.

14. Set the Luminosity to 10%.

15. Set the Diffuse to 153%.

You might need to play with the values slightly until you get the right balance of shadow and light.

Figure 15.19   Adjusting the luminosity of the FPIM_Square balances the brightness of the front projection image. But the shadow is lighter than the shadow on the building.

16. Do a test render. Figure 15.20 shows the final render with matched shadows.

Figure 15.20   The finished render with properly matched shadows.

Now, this is what you want! The shadow has a pretty nice value, closely matching the shadows the hotel casts on itself. This scene would be good enough for any situation in which the ship flies over this side of the hotel.

This is as far as you're going to take this project, but there is a lot more you could do with it to flesh it out. For example, you could:

- Set other walls in place to receive shadows, or even model an entire stand-in hotel.
- Model the hotel's windows to receive not just shadows, but also reflections.
- Add more lights to more fully simulate the light in the scene.
- Add a bit of fog to help blend the ship into the background even better.
- Add post-processing filters such as film grain. A bit of film grain usually helps to really *set in* the objects.

Situations like you've just seen, casting shadows on vertical walls such as the hotel, are fairly common. But what's even more likely is what you'll examine next.

Exercise 15.10   Casting Compositing Ground Shadows

Having a 3D object cast a shadow onto "real" ground is probably the most common compositing situation you'll have to deal with. Fortunately, it doesn't have to be a chore! Most every principle you just learned will translate directly. You'll follow the exact steps you just followed:

> Position the camera.
>
> Position the stand-in.
>
> Position the subject.
>
> Adjust the lighting.
>
> Adjust the surface of the ground plane.

In this exercise, you're going to place a 3D car among some "real" cars and make it fit right in.

1. Clear the scene.
2. Load the image Car_Street.tga from the book's CD-ROM.
3. Load the Car_Ground.lwo object from the book's CD-ROM.
4. Also, load the Rental_Car.lwo object.
5. Under the Compositing tab in the Effects panel, set the Background Image to Car_Street.tga.
6. In the Display panel, set the Camera View Background to Background Image. Figure 15.21 shows the scene at this point.

Figure 15.21   The elements are in place in Layout for casting ground shadows over a real image with a 3D car.

7. Open the Scene Editor and select the Car_Ground.lwo object.

8. Click Visibility, and choose Show Selected Items As > Bounding Box.

This will enable you to see where the ground object is without obscuring the view of the background image.

Now you need to move the camera so that the car lines up correctly with the other cars in the background image. And like the previous example, there are no hard and fast rules on how to do it. You'll just eyeball it, following a good procedure.

The first thing to do is set the height of the camera. If you know the position the camera was in when the shot was taken, by all means, use it. If you don't, you'll have to guess. Unlike the previous example, the height of the camera will matter a great deal. In this case, it is known that the picture was taken with a digital camera, and a person was holding the camera at the time. That means that the height of the camera should be about the height of a person—usually between 1.6 and 1.8 meters (or 5 feet, 7 inches). A good combination of camera and object movement helps get things lined up.

9. Move the camera to 1.7 meters on its Y axis.

Now you need to move the camera so that the car is lined up like the other cars. But because you're using realistic measurements for the camera's height, you'll need to adjust the scale of the car so that it's more realistic.

10. Size the car up to a factor of 1.2 in all axes. Do this by selecting the rental car object, choosing Size (**Shift+h**), and then pressing **n** to edit the numeric values in the bottom-left corner of the Layout interface.

Now it's time to position and rotate the camera. This is still the most difficult part, but here are some tips that might help you:

- Enlarge your grid size until the grid turns into just one line. This is your horizon line. Line this up with the real horizon first.

- Use your grid to help. Try to find straight lines on the ground in the picture and match the grid to those. In this case, you'll use the lines on the road.

- The hardest part is matching the zoom. Unless you know the lens length from the real camera, you'll just have to guess and work it out through trial and error.

A good guess for the lens length in this case is 35mm. This is a common setting for normal cameras, so it seems reasonable.

11. Set your camera's Focal Length to 35mm. You can do this through the Camera Properties panel. Instead of Zoom Factor, change the value to Focal Length from the drop-down list and then enter 35. LightWave will add the mm part.

12. Move the camera to 2.4 meters on the X axis and −7 meters on the Z axis.

13. Rotate the camera to −13 degrees on its Heading and −5.5 degrees on its Pitch.

14. Now Move the Rental_Car object to −1.8 meters on the X axis and 11 meters on the Z axis. Rotate the car around on its heading so that it's driving in the correct direction on the street. You should have something like Figure 15.22.

Figure 15.22   The car in position. Notice how it seems to fit in the scene already, and the lines of perspective match. This is key. These settings were found through trial and error. And that's really the only way to do it. But after you've found that spot, and all the lines of perspective are correct, you'll know it.

Now you need to move the ground under the car. This is much easier.

15. Move the Car_Ground object to –1.8 meters on the X axis and 11 meters on the Z axis.

16. Size the object to a factor of 20 on all axes.

Now that you've got the ground, you need to map the image on.

17. In the Surface Editor, select the Car_Ground surface.

18. Click the T beside the Color channel to open its Texture Editor.

19. Set the Projection type to Front.

20. Select Car_Street.tga as the Image.

21. Uncheck Pixel Blending, Width Repeat, Height Repeat, and Texture Antialiasing.

22. In the Render Options panel, make sure that Trace Shadows and Trace Reflection are turned on.

23. Press **F9** for a test render. Figure 15.23 shows the scene at this point.

Figure 15.23   With the camera aligned and the front projection map on the ground, the composited scene is coming together.

Now you've got the ground correctly mapped, so it's time to add the lights. To speed the process, there's a light kit already made for you. A light kit usually refers to a pre-made lighting setup that you will use by invoking the Load Items From Scene command. In this case, the light kit consists of a Key light, a Fill light, and a Ground Fill light. The Key light represents the main source of light in the shot, which in this case is the sun. The way to find the proper angle for the Key light is to line up the shadows cast by the 3D object with those already in the background plate. In this case, the most prominent shadows are those cast by the cars onto the road. This is what you need to match. The Key light in the light kit should match nicely.

The Fill light is a light that is generally opposite of the Key light. It represents bounced light and/or the light from the sky. Sometimes more than one Fill light is necessary if there are obvious sources of reflected light. Generally speaking, Fill lights should not affect specularity and should not have shadows of any kind.

The Ground Fill is a light that represents the light bouncing straight off of the ground. It should be set to a color that is representative of the ground in the scene—a dark gray in the case of a road, a brighter tan were it a desert scene. Ground Fill, like regular Fills, should not have shadows or affect specularity.

Note

It's good to be careful with the values of these shadowless Fill lights. They can easily overbrighten your objects. Generally, they should be a very low value. 25% or less is usually enough.

24. Select File, then Load Items From Scene. Load the scene Compositing_Lights.lws. When prompted, click Yes to "Load Lights from Scene". After this scene is loaded, you'll have three additional lights. Select the light named just "light," and press the dash (-) key to delete it. This leaves just the Key_Light, Fill_Light, and Ground_Light.

25. Do another test render.

    Looking better now. The ground is still a little dark, so bump up the Diffuse.

26. Open the Surface Editor.

27. Select the Car_Ground surface.

28. Set the Diffuse value to 110%.

29. Do a test render. Figure 15.24 shows the car composited over the street.

    Now that's more like it! The Front Projection Image Mapped ground plane blends seamlessly with the background image, and still catches the shadow. A little more tweaking will have the shadows lined up and in place.

Note

To add realism to the shot, turn on Trace Reflections in the Render Options panel and tell the car's various surfaces, such as the windows and bodypaint, to reflect the backdrop image, Car_Street.tga.

Now, like in the hotel example, this situation, although useful, is somewhat limited. Specifically, this trick would not work if the ground were not perfectly flat; an uneven surface would receive light unevenly, thereby keeping it from blending seamlessly with the background image.

Figure 15.24   With proper lighting and diffuse on the ground, and with Ray Traced shadows turned on from the Render Options panel, the car is starting to blend well with the other cars.

30. Select the Car_Ground object.

31. Select Replace Object, and then Replace With Object File.

32. Choose Car_Ground_Rough.lwo from the book's CD-ROM.

33. Press **F9** to render, and take a look at Figure 15.25.

Figure 15.25   A bumpy ground is added for additional realism in the composite.

Examining this test render, you can see that the edge of the object now stands out as the geometry of the object causes it to receive light unevenly. Even the middle of the object looks wrong as the shading causes parts of the road to darken. Unfortunately, there's no way to conquer this problem using anything you've learned up until now. To get around this, you're going to have to do a two-pass composite.

> **Note**
>
> Whenever possible, study the surroundings of the original image. Pay attention to light conditions, camera height, shadows, and other key elements. These references can help you when putting together composited images.

Advanced Compositing: Two-Pass Compositing

If it were only possible to "catch shadows" in the manner you had done in the previous exercises, you would be very limited in what you could accomplish with compositing in LightWave. Fortunately, LightWave has what you need to composite rendered shadows.

Exercise 15.11   Using Shadow Density for Compositing

1. In the Render Options panel, make sure Render Display is set to Image Viewer.

2. Do another test render by pressing **F9**.

3. Now, in the Image Viewer, switch between viewing the Image and the Alpha. Figure 15.26 shows the example.

   You'll see that in the alpha image, everything is black except where the car and ground plane are, where it's white.

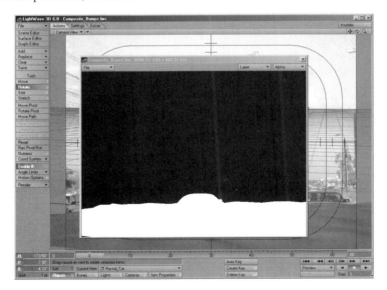

Figure 15.26   LightWave's Image Viewer from the Render Options panel enables you to view the alpha of any render image.

4. Make sure the Car_Ground_Rough object is selected, choose Replace Object, and then Replace With Object File.

5. Choose Car_Ground_Alpha.lwo.

6. In the Surface Editor, select the Car_Ground_Alpha surface.

7. Click the Advanced tab.

8. Beside Alpha Channel, click the Surface Opacity button and select Shadow Density, as in Figure 15.27.

9. Close the Surface Editor and render a frame.

Figure 15.27   The Surface Editor's Advanced tab. Setting the Alpha Channel to Shadow Density means that only the shadowed portion of the ground object will be a part of the alpha.

Now when you examine the alpha of the render, you'll see something very different! Instead of the ground plane being all white as it was before, it's now mostly black, except where the shadow of the car hits. There it's a range of grays, as in Figure 15.28.

What you've done is change the object surface so that the rendered alpha of the object is determined not by opacity of the surface, as it would normally be, but by the density of the shadow hitting it. This means that in the alpha channel of the rendered image, only those parts of the object that are shadowed will show up, and the strength of the alpha will depend on the strength of the shadows. Therefore, if you were to color the surface of the object black (as you have done), the resulting render would have a black shadow with the proper shape and transparency levels.

Figure 15.28 Using the Shadow Density option will show the alpha shadow of the car.

Exercise 15.12   Compositing Multiple Images

At this point, you could take the rendered image to another package, such as NewTek's Aura 2.0 or Adobe's After Effects 4.1, for compositing. But the beauty is, you don't have to. You already know that you have the tools necessary to accomplish this composite right in LightWave 6.

1. Continuing with the scene from the previous exercise, render and save both the RGB image and the alpha image. Chapter 17, "Output and Rendering," describes this process in more detail.
2. Load these images back into LightWave.
3. In the Object Properties panel, set the Dissolve of both the Car_Ground and Rental_Car objects to 100%.
4. Go to the Effects panel, under the Compositing tab.
5. Beside Foreground Image, select your rendered RGB color image.
6. Beside Foreground Alpha, select your rendered alpha image.
7. Check Foreground Fader Alpha On.
8. Do a test render. Figure 15.29 shows the render.

If you watch the render, you'll see the foreground image get overlaid on the background image. As predicted, the shadow looks correct, taking the shape of the object and the density of the shadow. And because no other part of the road is rendered, it's perfectly seamless. Remember, you dissolved out the objects, and what you're seeing in the render are rendered images composited together.

This was a simple example with a single frame, but everything in it applies properly to image sequences as well.

Figure 15.29   When you use just a rendered color image and a rendered alpha image, you can easily composite the car in LightWave over the background image.

The Next Step

The exercises in this chapter have not only introduced you to the compositing tools in LightWave, but have also given you the knowledge to create your own composited images and animations. From here, you can build your own 3D objects, such as cars, spaceships, or people, and experiment with compositing them into real-world images. You can use the color photographs on the book's CD-ROM for your projects. Take a look in the Extras folder, and you'll find royalty-free images, which you can use in the same manner as the images from the exercises in this chapter. Try using some of the city photographs to fly objects in front of and behind buildings while casting shadows. Use other images to make a 3D character walk down a long sidewalk. From here, experiment and practice whenever you can. If you have a digital camera, keep it with you at all times to create your own images for compositing.

Summary

Compositing is an art unto itself. Production houses often have entire departments devoted to the task, and thousands of dollars in software.

As you've seen, LightWave has plenty of compositing power. These examples are only the tip of the iceberg, but hopefully they'll give you a good working knowledge of the fundamentals of compositing, from which you can learn further on your own.

Note

Many thanks to all the great artists who contributed images for this chapter! Lynn Wilczek provided us with the photograph of the hotel building; Pat Brouliette contributed the photos of the cloudy sky, the moutain, and the street with cars.

Chapter 16

Broadcast Animations

Anyone will tell you, the bread-and-butter animation jobs are flying logos. And although you might wince at even the mention of the term, flying-logo animations pay the bills in many animation studios around the globe.

Project Overview

This chapter takes you full-speed ahead into a complete broadcast animation, that goes far beyond the typical chrome flying logo you might be used to. LightWave 6 has a powerful rendering engine and tons of texture tools that will make your job easier, especially when creating flying logos. Figure 16.1 shows a still from the finished animation that you will create.

Figure 16.1   You will create a rich, colorful broadcast animation, a still from which is shown here, by using LightWave 6 and following the steps in this chapter.

In this chapter, you'll learn how to model text and elements that can give your animations depth and character. No one cares to see a simple flying logo anymore, so it's your job to stay ahead of the curve. To do so, this chapter also instructs you on techniques used by professionals. You'll put things in constant motion, not just move them from point A to point B. This chapter gives you the knowledge and, hopefully, the excitement to create stunning broadcast graphics and animations. It covers the following:

- Modeling text and elements for a broadcast animation
- Creating a mood or feeling with color and style
- Using transparency, glow, and bloom enhancements
- Creating continuous and multiple motions

Broadcast-Style Graphics

News programs and entertainment television shows have one thing in common—broadcast-style graphics and animations. Such graphics and animations are bold, colorful, and downright cool to look at. Creating graphics and animations for broadcast can be fun and lucrative. Major television markets have high budgets for animation packages, which consist of a main title and bumpers—short versions of the main title that are used to go in and out of commercial breaks. These packages also can include variations on the main title theme for weather segments and news segments for news television stations. Animation packages must represent the feeling and style the broadcaster is trying to convey. This could be serious and strong, classy and cute, or the best way, sharp!

Creating a Broadcast Treatment

For this project, your client wants you to create a bold and colorful animation treatment that represents a proud, growing company. The term "treatment" refers to a full set of animations, such as a broadcast package. This animation treatment will include moving backgrounds and title and segue animations. These animations will be given to a video editor who will blend them with video and audio.

The company's colors are red and blue, with some white. This can be limiting, if you let it. Red is always a hard color to work with, especially when it comes to graphics for videotape. It is a "hot" color that tends to bleed or smear when recorded to tape. Not to worry, though, you'll be able to work around it with LightWave. Blue, on the other hand, is a marvelous color to work with, and you can use it to your advantage with this project. Blue doesn't smear when recorded to tape, and it is comfortable to look at. The client has only a red, white, and blue printed logo for you to go by when creating your animation treatment; that's all. It's up to you to bring it to life—time to be an animator.

Exercise 16.1   Creating the Main Title Elements

Broadcast treatments vary animations based on a theme or an initial animation. This exercise shows you how to begin creating the elements for that main title animation. Follow these steps:

1. Open LightWave's Modeler.

   The main logo is nothing more than an S with an exclamation point in the middle. Not too complex, but it can still look cool in an animation. Figure 16.2 shows the logo you will create.

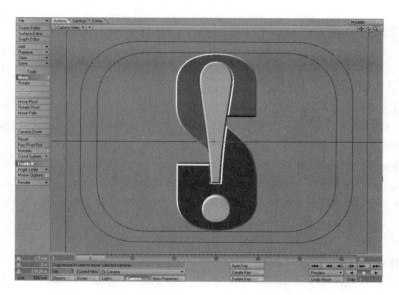

Figure 16.2   A simple logo is the focus of this broadcast treatment. The elements you add will enhance it.

2. From the Objects tab, click the Edit Fonts button.

   This calls up the Edit Font List panel, as shown in Figure 16.3.

Figure 16.3   The Edit Fonts button calls up the Edit Font List panel, where you can import fonts into Modeler for 3D creation.

Now it's time to select your fonts. The main font chosen for this project is Impact, shown in Figure 16.4. If your system doesn't have this font, use something similar.

IMPACT

Figure 16.4   The Impact font is a common system font on many computers. Use this font or something similar.

3. To select the main font, click the Add True-Type button and choose Impact from the list. You need to add the fonts into Modeler before you can select them and create your text. The Impact font will be used to create the main logo.

When working with the Edit Font List panel, you can add as many fonts as you like and any of them can be selected from the Font drop-down list, as shown in Figure 16.5.

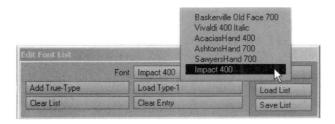

Figure 16.5   You can load as many fonts as you like and later select any of them from the Font drop-down list, in the Edit Font List panel.

4. Click the Add True-Type button again and add a basic Helvetica font.

This font will be used to create text elements used in the animation.

5. Click the Save List button, and save this list of fonts as BroadcastFonts or a name representing your project. Click OK to close the Edit Font List panel.

By saving this list, you can now load it and work with just these fonts on future projects.

Now enter your text. Access the Text tool first to align and size the text.

6. Press **Shift+w** to call up the Text tool in Modeler. (You also can access this tool under the Objects tab.)

7. Click the Back view (Viewport 3).

A small, L-shaped bracket appears, as shown in Figure 16.6. You will use this L-shaped bracket to align and size your text.

8. Type the letter S and an exclamation point (!).

Note

When you enter text, it will appear in the last font you loaded into your Font list. Don't worry—just use the up arrow on your keyboard to cycle through the Font list and click your desired font. You'll see your typed text change font styles, without having to go back into the Edit Font List.

9. Change the font to Impact.

If you click and drag on the top of the L-shaped bracket, you can size the type. If you click and drag the bottom corner of the L-shaped bracket, you can position the text. For this exercise, you don't need to resize much.

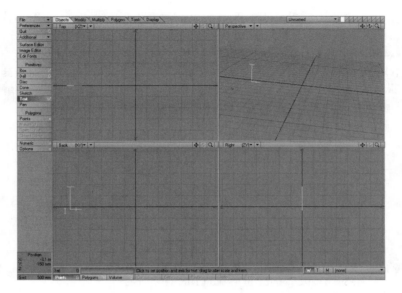

Figure 16.6   When you use the Text tool, an L-shaped bracket appears, enabling you to align and size your text.

10. To keep the Impact font, click the Text tool.

Note

When you select the Text tool from the Objects tab, your keyboard essentially becomes a typewriter, enabling you to type and create fonts. Because of this, keyboard equivalents are temporarily suspended, requiring you to use the mouse to turn off the Text tool.

With the S and exclamation point created, you can begin creating the main part of the logo.

11. Select the exclamation point, cut and paste it into a separate layer, and select the layer with the exclamation point.

12. Make the layer with the S object a background layer and press the **a** key to activate the Fit All Views command.

This enables you to line up the exclamation point with the S. Figure 16.7 shows the example.

13. Position the exclamation point so that it is centered in the S. (You'll probably need to use the L-shaped bracket to size down the exclamation point a bit so that it fits.) Figure 16.8 shows the new position.

14. Press the double quotation mark key (") to instantly flip or reverse the foreground and background layers.

Reversing the layers will enable you to cut the background object out of the foreground object, which is discussed in the next exercise. Pressing the double quotation mark key saves you the time it takes to click the Layers button.

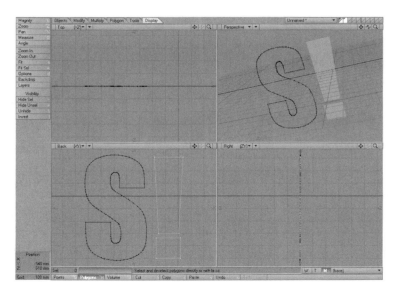

Figure 16.7   The exclamation point is in a top layer, and the S object is in a background layer.

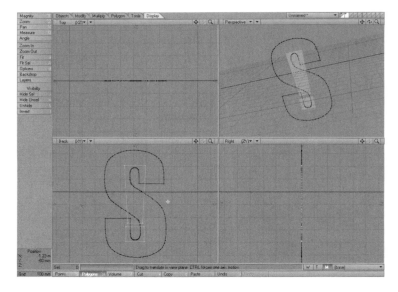

Figure 16.8   Because the S object is in a background layer, the positioning of the exclamation point is easy to set.

15. Save the file as S_temp.lwo.

Exercise 16.2   Cutting Out a Background Object from the Foreground Object

Now it's time to cut the background object out of the foreground object, a step for which you will use LightWave's Template Drill command. To use the Template Drill command, or any Boolean operation, the main object should be in a foreground layer. Objects that will be used to "cut" another object should reside in a background layer. LightWave's Template Drill feature enables you to do this. Just follow these steps:

1. Press **Shift+r** to call up the Template Drill command (also found under the Tools tab).

   A template drill is useful for flat objects such as the ones you're working with here.

2. With the exclamation point in the background layer and the S object in the foreground layer, perform a Template Drill on the Z axis, as a Tunnel operation.

   This tunnels the exclamation point through the foreground object, creating a cutout in the shape of the exclamation point.

   You should see a hole in the S shape of the exclamation point, as shown in Figure 16.9.

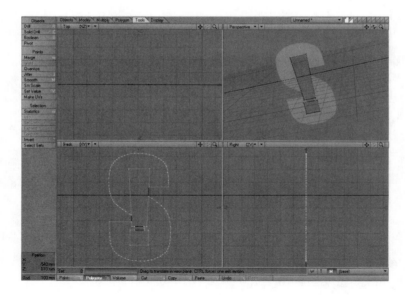

Figure 16.9   The Template Drill command enables you to cut one flat object out of another.

3. With the S object layer active, select Extrude from the Multiply tab, or press **Shift+e**. In the right or side view, click the logo and drag to the right. You'll see the object extrude, as shown in Figure 16.10.

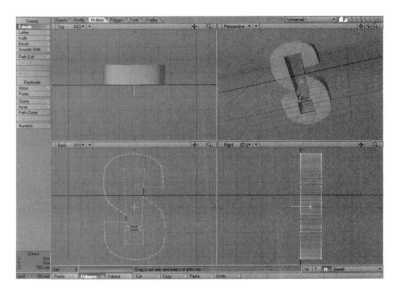

Figure 16.10   Using LightWave 6's Extrude tool is as simple as clicking and dragging. Here, the S object has been extruded from the Right, or side view (Viewport 4).

4. Perform the same Extrude operation on the exclamation point. Save this as S.lwo.

Exercise 16.3   Surfacing and Beveling the Objects

From here, you can surface and bevel the objects, following these steps:

1. Go to the S object layer, and press the **q** key to call up the Change Surface command.

2. Type the name S_Sides and uncheck Make Default.

3. With the right mouse button in the Right view, drag around the front-facing polygons of the S object (the –Z axis). This is often referred to as Lasso selection. (Make sure you are working in Polygon mode, at the bottom of the Modeler screen.) Figure 16.11 shows the example.

Because you named the entire object S_Sides in Step 2, you now only need to select the front polygons of the object to create the bevel and face surfaces. Selecting just the front polygons with the Lasso tool is much easier than trying to select all the side polygons of the object.

4. With the face of the S object selected, press **q** again to access the Change Surface command, and name the selection S_Bevel.

5. Press **b** to activate the Bevel tool.

6. Click the face of the object in the Back view (Viewport 3), and drag to the right to interactively bevel the S object. Be careful not to overlap the bevels. You can undo what you did by pressing **u**. Figure 16.12 shows the beveled S.

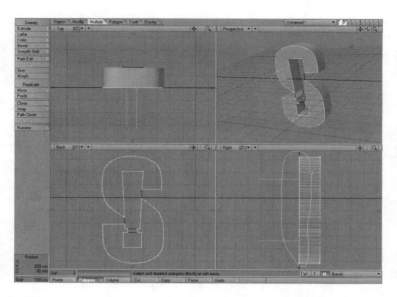

Figure 16.11   Using the right mouse button, you can select the front polygons by lassoing around them from the Right view.

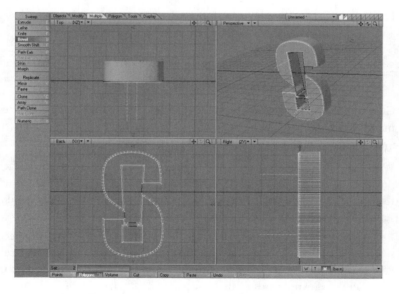

Figure 16.12   The Bevel tool is used to add a soft bevel to the S object.

7. While the front polygon is still selected, press **q** one more time, and name this surface S_Face. Then, deselect the polygon and save the object.

8. Perform the same selection and surfacing steps on the exclamation point, but name the surfaces Ex_Sides, Ex_Bevel, and Ex_Face, or something similar.

9. When complete, cut and paste the exclamation point into the S object.

 You might want to move the exclamation point forward just a bit so that it's sticking out of the S.

10. Save the object as S.lwo. Figure 16.13 shows the final S and exclamation object before any surfacing. A final version of this object is on the book's CD and is labeled 16Sfinal.lwo.

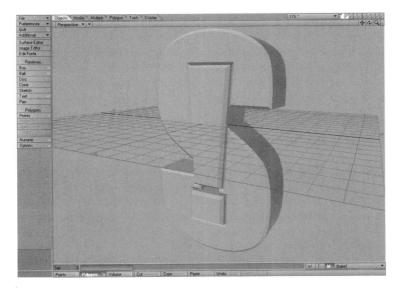

Figure 16.13   The extruded and beveled exclamation point is cut and pasted to the S object to create one complete object.

The preceding exercises showed you how simple it is to create and model 3D text. Although the fonts were simple, beveling them adds a soft, subtle touch and even gives your models a touch of class. When it's time to surface this object later in this chapter, you'll see how the bevels you've created help make the logo stand out. But before you do that, you should create the background text elements that will make up the complete logo. The next exercise takes you through those steps.

Creating a Broadcast Animation Environment

The environment in which the animation takes place is just as important as the logo itself. A simple logo on a black background is not nearly as effective as a logo with complementing objects, colorful backgrounds, and enhancement elements. This next exercise discusses how to create the enhancements that will give the full animation some depth.

Exercise 16.4   Creating Animation Elements

Broadcast animation elements are the extra pieces you'll need to help sell the logo concept. Remember: You're doing more than just creating an animated logo, you're creating a theme, or mood, that needs to be conveyed to the viewer. Follow these steps:

1. In Modeler, make sure any work is saved, and press **Shift+n** to create a new object.

   Part of the company's logo is the slogan "Solution Summit." That's not much to go on, but there are ways to transform two words into a complex animation.

2. Load a Helvetica or Arial font if you didn't do so in Exercise 16.1. This is the secondary font used in the animation.

3. Create the text "Solution Summit" with the Text tool and then extrude and bevel the text. Figure 16.14 shows the new text.

Figure 16.14   Additional text is made, extruded, and beveled. This is an additional animation element.

4. Save the extruded "Solution Summit" text.

   This will become one element you'll use later. Because this is the only text or slogan in the animation, you need to copy it and modify it in some way to create additional elements, so don't close the object just yet. You'll come back to it in a moment.

5. Select one other font to use in this animation. The standard Times Roman font, or a font that isn't as blocky as the Impact or Helvetica font, should work.

6. Create a new object and use this new font to create an additional font element, spelled out as "Dialog 98," similar to what you did with the S and exclamation point. However, make this object thinner—do not extrude it as much—as shown in Figure 16.15. Save the Dialog text object.

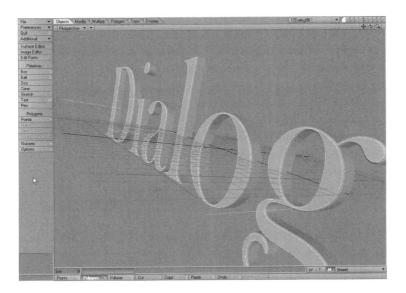

Figure 16.15   A Times Roman font is used to create an additional font element for the animation (a similar font can be used instead). The element is extruded about 50mm in depth on the Z axis.

7. To create outline fonts for the animation, create a new object, select the Text tool again, and type "Solution Summit" in Times Roman font. Do not extrude the font this time, but do change the surface name (**q**) to Summit_Outline. Save your work.

Exercise 16.5   Creating the Background for the Animation

Now that the outline fonts have been created, you need to create something soft and transparent for the background of the animation. Follow these steps:

1. Create a new object, and using the Box tool, create a large, flat box in the Back view, roughly 25m in size.

2. Be sure that your mouse is in the Back view and press the **up arrow** on the keyboard about 10 times to add segments to the object on the Y axis. Now press the **right arrow** key about 10 times to add segments on the X axis.

Note

While a primitive object is being created, you can use the up and right arrow keys in a particular view to add segments to it. Using the down and left arrow keys removes segments.

3. Press the **spacebar** to turn off the Box tool. Change the surface name to FlatBox or something similar.

   You should now have a large, flat box in the back view with multiple segments, as shown in Figure 16.16.

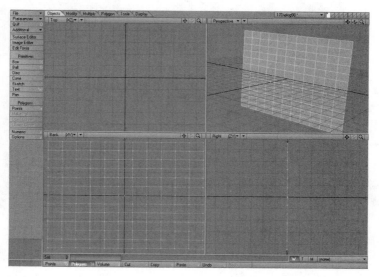

Figure 16.16   This large, flat box will become a large background element in the animation.

4. Copy the flat box by pressing **c** on the keyboard.

5. Select the first Solution_Summit text object you created in Step 3 by choosing it from the object drop-down list, at the top right of the Modeler interface, as shown in Figure 16.17.

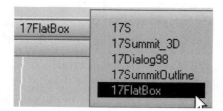

Figure 16.17   Selecting objects you've created for this project is easy. Find them in the drop-down list at the top right of the Modeler interface.

6. With the Solution_Summit text as the current object, select an empty layer and press the **v** key to paste the flat box object you copied in Step 4. Make the Solution_Summit text a background layer, as shown in Figure 16.18.

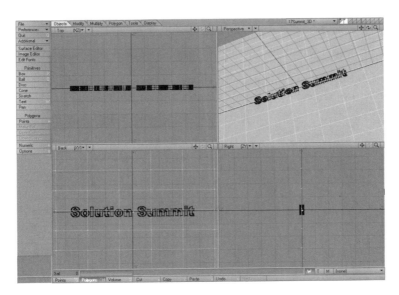

Figure 16.18   Although each Modeler object has its own layer set, you can use different objects on the layers for Boolean operations.

7. With the text in a background layer and the flat box in a foreground layer, be sure they are intersecting, as shown in Figure 16.19.

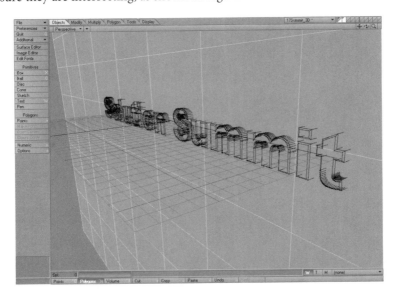

Figure 16.19   To perform Boolean operations, a background layer holding the "cutting" tool must intersect the foreground layer. This will cut the object in the background layer out of the object in the foreground layer.

Now you want the Solution_Summit text to cut a hole in the flat box.

8. From the Tools tab, select the Solid Drill tool (or press **Shift+c**).

The Solid Drill tool is used to perform slicing or cutting operations between a flat and extruded object.

9. Select Tunnel for the Operation, as shown in Figure 16.20, and click OK. In a moment, you'll see the Solution_Summit text cut a hole in the flat box.

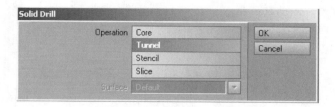

Figure 16.20   The Solid Drill tool can be used to core, tunnel, stencil, and slice objects that are both flat and extruded.

10. Increase the Size of the Solution_Summit text, about double its current size. Move it up to the top of the flat box (referenced in a background layer) and off to the side.

11. Use the Solid Drill tool again to cut a hole in the flat box. Do this a few times until you have something similar to Figure 16.21.

Figure 16.21   Use the same Solution_Summit text object to cut different sizes out of the flat box object.

> **Note**
>
> Don't be afraid to overlap text when preparing to cut the holes out of the flat box. Also feel free to let the Solution_Summit text bleed off the edge, as shown in Figure 16.21. Think outside the box!

12. Once you have the flat box cuts created, press the **x** key to cut the object from the Solution_Summit object layers.

13. To save each object individually, press **Shift+n** to create a new object, and then paste (**v**) the flat box with cut-outs. Save the object as flat_box2.lwo or something similar.

> **Note**
>
> If you left the flat box in its layer, next to the Solution_Summit text, both objects would be part of the saved Solution_Summit text. Although you can animate these separately in Layout, you also can save them separately to keep more organized.

Only a few more steps, and you'll be able to see how this all comes together. This next exercise guides you through some final steps to enhance the broadcast elements and prepare them for animation. You'll be modifying the original models so that they fit the final look of the animation, which in this case has many curves (refer to Figure 16.1 in the front of the chapter).

Exercise 16.6   Enhancing Broadcast Animation Elements

1. Select the flat box object, and in the Right view (Viewport 4), bend it forward on the –Z axis.

2. Rotate the flat box object from the Top view so that it curves around the Y axis. Figure 16.22 shows the bent object.

3. Select Save Object As from the File menu, and save it as CurveBox.lwo.

4. Select the first Solution_Summit object, the extruded one. In an empty layer for this object, create a flat box with multiple segments along the X axis, as shown in Figure 16.23.

5. Change the surface name for this box to SummitBKD.

   This is a flat box that will give the "Solution Summit" text some dimension.

6. Be sure the flat box is centered with the object (as shown in Figure 16.23), and then cut and paste it into the Solution_Summit layer to make one solid object.

7. Bend this object back on the Z axis about 90 degrees, as shown in Figure 16.24.

8. Rotate it back around the Y axis so that it is curved equally on both sides, as shown in Figure 16.24, then press the **F2** key to automatically center it on the XYZ axis.

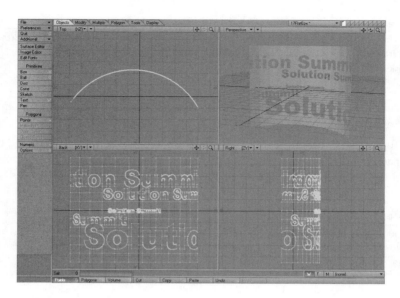

Figure 16.22   The Bend tool is used to curve the flat box.

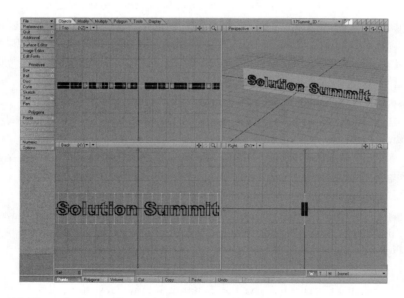

Figure 16.23   A flat box, with multiple segments on the X axis, frames the Solution_Summit object.

Note

Remember that you should be using the Default LightWave Modeler configurations for these exercises. Default Modeler has the Center function assigned to the F2 key.

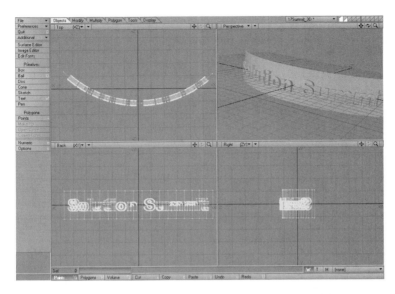

Figure 16.24 The "Solution Summit" text with a background plate, and bent to a 90-degree angle.

  9. Save the Solution_Summit object in its bent position, and make sure all the other objects you've created are saved as well.

  10. Select the Dialog98 text, bend it 90 degrees on the Z axis, and resave.

This tutorial stepped you through the creation of simple text using LightWave's Text tool and generic system fonts. You saw that by adding a few boxes and using a few of LightWave's tools such as Solid Drill and Bend, the objects begin to look less boring. But wait, this next part shows you how to texture, light, and set up the animation.

Broadcast Animation Setup

Setting up an animation can be simple or complex, depending on what you want to do. Broadcast-style animations generally have a lot of parts that need to move, and stay moving, throughout the animation. Considerations should be made as to what objects are moving, and how they are moving. The following exercise steps you through:

- Loading the objects you've created into Layout
- Adjusting pivot points for proper rotations
- Positioning the objects
- Creating object surfaces

Exercise 16.7   Setting Up Broadcast Animation Objects

Although you can load any object at any time into Layout, it's usually helpful to load the objects in the order that you'll use them. In this case, there are only a few objects to load, so you can simply load the objects in the order that they were created.

1. Open Layout and select Add, Load Object from the Actions tab.

2. Load the CurveBox, the Dialog98 text, the big S logo, the Summit 3D logo, and the SummitOutline object.

Note

If you want to, you can use the objects on this book's CD for this tutorial.

3. Go to the Camera view, and move into the frame to see the S object full frame, as shown in Figure 16.25.

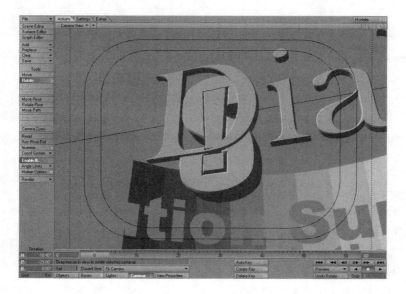

Figure 16.25   Because the S object is the main focus of the animation, the first Layout step is to move the camera into view.

4. Move the camera down about 2m on the –Y axis and rotate it up so that you are looking up at the S logo.

   Moving the camera beneath the objects helps give the logo a more powerful presence.

5. Create a keyframe at zero to lock the camera in place.

   The Dialog98 font is on top of it—this is okay for now.

6. Select the CurveBox object and move it back and up to fill the frame.

7. Select the Dialog98 object and move it forward, away from the S object. (You probably should size down the Dialog98 a bit to keep it in view.) Figure 16.26 shows the changes.

Figure 16.26   The CurveBox object is moved back and up to fit the frame, while the Dialog98 object is sized down slightly and moved in front of the S object.

Note

When you select your objects and move them, they may seem to move really fast. If so, you need to adjust Layout's Grid Square Size. Do this by pressing the left bracket key ([) to size down the grid. The right bracket key (]) increases the size of the grid. You also can manually set a grid size in the Display Options panel (d). A smaller grid enables you to move your objects with more control.

8. Select the SummitOutline object, and move it into view. You may need to size it down to make it fit between the camera and the S object.

9. Create a keyframe to hold it in place. You don't need to see the entire SummitOutline object, only a portion of it, as shown in Figure 16.27.

10. Select the Summit3D text object and Size it down so that it fits into camera view.

11. Create a keyframe to hold its new size in place.

12. Save your scene. It's not nearly complete, but saving is only one step, whereas setting everything back up to this point is many steps. Save often!

13. Press the **2** key on the numeric keypad.

This brings you to the Top view in Layout, looking down at your scene. Use the comma (,) key to zoom out to see all the elements. Figure 16.28 shows the Top view. Be sure to save your work thus far.

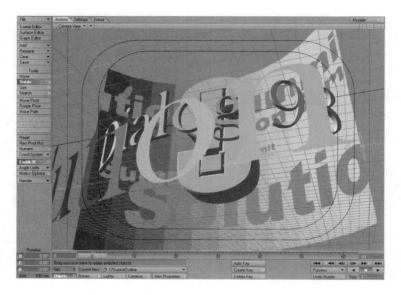

Figure 16.27   The SummitOutline object is sized down and brought forward in front of the camera, but not entirely.

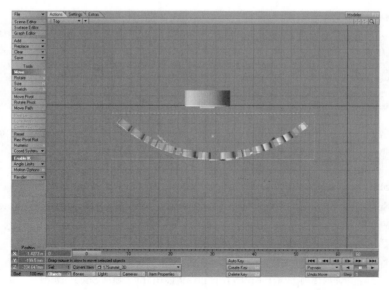

Figure 16.28   The Top view in Layout gives you a complete overview of your scene.

14. In Top view, select the CurveBox object. Resave the file.

The Layout window changes and looks as though nothing is there. This is because the pivot point of the object is near the object, which is off to the back of the scene beyond the grid square. The curve box needs to rotate slightly on its heading around the S logo object. For it to rotate properly, you need to adjust the pivot point, which you'll do in the next exercise.

Exercise 16.8   Using the Hub to Adjust Objects

LightWave 6 offers a lot more control than in previous versions. The previous exercises guided you through the creation of objects and elements in Modeler and how to move them into Layout. And although you can make adjustments to the Pivot Point in Layout, it is sometimes easier to reset the object in Modeler. LightWave 6 makes this easy to do through use of the Hub.

LightWave 6 now allows you to adjust pivot points in Modeler as well as Layout. The advantage: more control. But, you can also simply move the objects in Modeler and resave, which resets the pivots. This is much easier than moving pivot points in Layout.

1. Save your current scene from the previous exercise, and jump back to Modeler.

2. Select Close All Objects from the File Menu in Modeler. Don't save when it asks you. You already have the objects saved.

3. Select the drop-down object list.

   This list of objects represents the objects currently loaded into Layout, thanks to the Hub. You can select any of them to instantly import into Modeler and make changes. Figure 16.29 shows the list.

Figure 16.29   When objects are loaded in Layout, you'll be able to see them from the Object list in Modeler. This is LightWave 6's Hub at work.

4. Select the S object to import it into Modeler, press **F2** to make sure it is perfectly centered on the 0 XYZ axis, and press **s** to save the object.

   This object does not need its pivot point adjusted, as it can rotate upon itself in the animation.

5. Select the CurveBox object. Use the comma key (,) to zoom out a bit and move the object about 10m away from the center 0 axis, based on a 500mm grid in Layout, as shown in Figure 16.30.

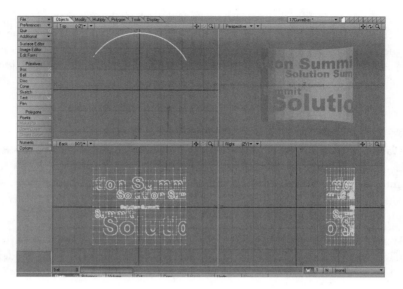

Figure 16.30   Moving the CurveBox object back into the Z axis leaves its pivot on the 0 axis.

> **Note**
>
> By moving the CurveBox back on the Z axis, when it is rotated in Layout it will rotate around its pivot point at the 0 XYZ axis. This is good because you want the object to encompass the scene, rotating around the S object that is centered at the 0 axis. Remember to save the CurveBox after you move it.

6. Select the Dialog98 object, and move it forward on the Z so that it, too, curves around the 0 XYZ axis. Remember to save. Figure 16.31 shows the Dialog98 object moved.

7. Continue selecting and modifying all the objects from the scene. If the object curves back on the Z axis, move it forward so that it pivots around the 0 XYZ axis. Save each object after you've adjusted it.

8. Back in Layout, load the scene you saved in Step 7.

   The scene will load with all the objects' adjustments you made in Modeler. If the objects in the camera look different than previously, reposition the camera so that it is focusing on the S logo object.

9. Look at the scene through the Top view, and you'll see the objects off of the 0 axis, where the S logo object is, as shown in Figure 16.32.

10. Move the objects into position again so that they can all be seen from the camera. Save your scene as Broadcast1.lws.

   The next step is to add surfaces to the objects and set up the lights! Figure 16.33 shows the scene before surfacing, with the modified objects in place.

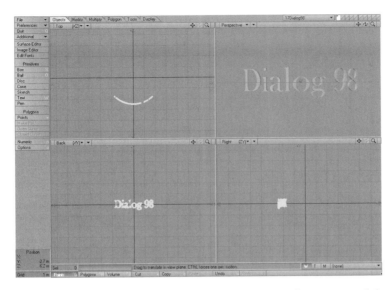

Figure 16.31   The Dialog98 object is moved forward so that it will rotate around the 0 XYZ axis.

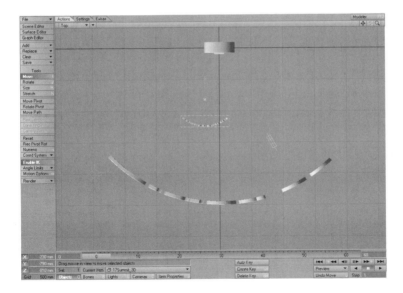

Figure 16.32   The adjustments to the objects made in Modeler can be seen in Layout from the Top view when the scene is reloaded. The objects will now rotate around the S logo object.

Figure 16.33   The curved objects are in place, ready to be surfaced and animated.

This exercise used LightWave's Hub to adjust models already loaded in Layout. By moving models back and forth between Layout and Modeler via the Hub, you can quickly update and modify your objects.

Too often, animators think that a really complex object will create a great animation, and at times, this is true. But it is not a rule. The simplest objects, even text, can look bold and beautiful if they are surfaced well.

Exercise 16.9   Creating Broadcast-Style Surfaces

Exercise 16.9 sets up the surfaces for the broadcast animation you've been creating throughout this chapter.

1. Load the scene you've been creating, or feel free to load the 16BroadcastSetup.lws scene from the book's CD-ROM.

2. Open the Surface Editor and choose Edit By Scene to make all surfaces from the entire scene visible.

3. From the Surface Name list, select Summit_Outline.

    This surface was named Summit_Outline because that's all you want from it—the outline.

4. Make the Summit_Outline surface color red. Under the Basic tab, you can click and drag on the individual RGB values for color. Or, click the small white color swatch to open the Color Requester.

5. Click the Advanced tab, and turn up Glow Intensity to 100%. Also in the Advanced tab, click Render Outlines, with a Line Size of 1.0.

This renders only a thin outline for the Summit_Outline surface. Figure 16.34 shows the Advanced tab.

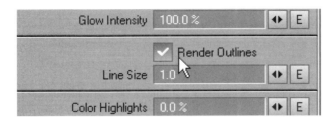

Figure 16.34   The Advanced tab in the Surface Editor enables you to add some settings, such as Glow Intensity and Render Outlines.

You should see the SummitOutline object in Layout only as a red outline now. The outlines add a nice touch and an added moving element to the scene. This object will be animated large, close to the camera. Refer to Figure 16.1 to see the red outlined text.

It doesn't matter which surface you set next, but when many surfaces are in a scene, you can work your way from back to front.

6. Select the surface that is part of the object and is farthest away from the camera in Layout and the FlatBox, from the Surface Name list.

This is a large, curved element in the background that should be transparent and streaked, sort of like smeared clouds.

7. To apply surface properties, first make the FlatBox surface soft white by clicking the small white box from the RGB Color selection in the Basic tab.

8. After the color is set, click the T button for Transparency to enter the Texture Editor.

9. Set the Layer Type to Procedural Texture.

10. To add this procedural to the blue surface, make the Blending Mode Additive. The Procedural Type should be set to Fractal Noise.

11. Set the Texture Value to 100%.

This tells LightWave to apply this transparency fractal noise texture to its full extent.

12. Set Frequencies to 5, which sets how often the pattern repeats within its size settings.

13. Set the Contrast to 2.5.

Because the Fractal Noise texture you're applying is created with grayscale values, the contrast setting alters the strength of the black and white variables. The small texture window within the Texture Editor can show you the change to this setting, as shown in Figure 16.35.

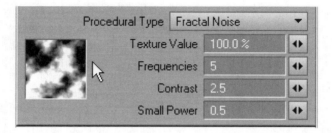

Figure 16.35   The best way to see how a value setting affects a surface is to view the changes with the small texture window preview.

14. Set the Small Power to 0.5.

This sets the spacing of the fractals.

The next step is to set the scale of the fractal noise texture. By applying a transparent fractal noise, you'll be creating soft, random transparencies throughout the surface, almost like soft holes. But, this surface needs to be streaked. So, instead of using the Automatic Sizing function, which would equally place the fractal noise pattern across the entire surface, you'll want to manually set the size.

 Note

The Automatic Sizing function can help you set the surface manually. Because it's hard to guess what size parameters to enter for the X, Y, and Z axes, Automatic Sizing can instantly find an approximate value for you to work with.

15. Click the Automatic Sizing button. You'll see the values adjust in the Scale tab at the bottom of the Texture Editor. This is what the Automatic Sizing feature has set for the surface.

16. Change the X value to 10m, making the texture very long from side to side. Change the Y value to 1m, a strong contrast from the X size. Lastly, change the Z Scale to 10m.

17. Select Use Texture to return to the Surface Editor. Save your work. Figure 16.36 shows just the CurveBox object with its surface applied.

Figure 16.36   Fractal Noise as a transparency texture streaks the curved, flat box to make a nice background element.

Exercise 16.10   Changing the Backdrop

To enhance the scene and the transparent surface you just set, you want to change the background color from the default black that LightWave uses.

1. Click the Settings tab at the top of the Layout interface and select Backdrop from the Effects group on the lower-left side of the screen.

2. Click Gradient Backdrop.

    The default gradient is a blue sky, with a dark-brown ground. You can set and blend four Gradient Backdrop colors. This setting applies an infinite and unseen sphere of color around the Layout, determined by the zenith, which is the top-most portion of the sphere, the sky in the upper middle, the ground in the lower middle, and the nadir, the bottom-most portion of the sphere. This color sphere is not an object you can see in Layout—only the color shows when rendering.

3. Leave the Zenith set to its default color of 0, 40, 80 RGB, and set the Sky to 15, 70, 120 RGB.

    This adds a medium blue color to match the client's logo colors for the project.

4. Set the Ground color to the same value as the Sky: 15, 70, 120 RGB.

    This blends the sky into the ground without showing a visible horizon line, like the default settings do.

5. Set the Nadir color to a brighter blue: 30, 130, 220 RGB.

6. Save your scene as Broadcast2.lws, and remember to select Save All Objects from the Actions, Save command. It's always good to save your work in stages, just in case you need to go back to previous work.

Saving your objects saves any surface settings you've applied. Saving your scene saves the objects you've loaded, the backdrop colors you've applied, and any other scene parameters.

Note

In the LightWave 6 Display Options panel, you can tell Layout to show a colored background. Although you can't show the Gradient Backdrop you've created here, you can uncheck Gradient Backdrop, set a Backdrop Color (in the Backdrop Effects panel), and turn on Backdrop Color for the Camera View Background in the Display Options panel.

Now that you've set up two simple surfaces and a backdrop, you need to move on to the main portion of the animation—the logos. There's nothing too special about setting up a surface for a logo, but it's something that you might have to do over and over again in your job. Plus, the techniques here can be applied to all kinds of surfaces, not just logos. This next exercise guides you through the process of surfacing one of the main logos in the scene. From there, you'll light the scene and put everything into motion.

Exercise 16.11   Surfacing Text Objects

You'll have to create text at one time or another during your career as an animator. Whether it's a main title animation, broadcast logo, or credits for an animated movie you've created, text is an important element to 3D animation.

You can continue working with the scene you saved in the last exercise, or feel free to call up the 16BroadcastSetup.lws scene from the book's CD-ROM. If you use the scene from the CD, all the objects will be a default gray color without any surface attributes. The surfaces applied in the previous exercise are not applied to the objects in this scene. You can use this scene as a template for practicing surfacing. Start with the Solution_Summit object surfaces. This object has four surfaces, two text sides, a text bevel, and a text face.

1. To start surfacing the sides, select SolutionSummit_Sides from the Surface Name list in the Surface Editor. Make the Color Red.

2. Set both the Specularity and Glossiness to 50%.

These settings create some nice highlights, but don't make the text too shiny. This surface now needs some type of reflection.

3. Change the Diffuse to 75% and the Reflection setting to 25%.

This tells the surface to use 75% of the scene's lights and to reflect 25%.

4. Click Smoothing.

   You've told the surface to reflect 25%, but you still haven't told it what to reflect.

5. Enter the Environment tab in the Surface Editor, and set the Reflection Options to Spherical Map.

6. Under Reflection Map, select Load Image, and load the ColoredReflection.jpg image from this book's CD-ROM. This is the image the surface will reflect. When finished, go back to the Basic tab.

7. Copy this surface and apply it to the SolutionSummit_Face. Do this by right-clicking the SolutionSummit_Sides name in the Surface Name list and selecting Copy. Then, right-click the SolutionSummit_Face surface, but select Paste. All the settings are applied.

Warning

Be sure to unclick Smoothing. Because the face of the object is flat, you don't need to apply smoothing. If you do, the surface of your object might appear streaked and cause oddities when rendered.

Figure 16.37 shows the surfaced sides and face of the text object.

Figure 16.37   You can use the same surface settings from the side surfaces on the face of the object.

The bevel is used to make the object stand out, and to help give it a more polished look. The bevel should not be the same color as the sides for the face of the object and should provide a contrast between the two.

8. Set the color of the SolutionSummit_Bevel surface to a soft gray.

9. Change the Diffuse level to 40% and Reflection to 60%.

    This makes most of this surface appear as a reflection, like shiny metal.

10. Go to the Environments tab and set a Reflection Image the way you did in Step 6, using the same reflection image.

    Often, using the same reflection on different colored surfaces helps give the full animation some diversity while keeping a consistency throughout.

11. When you have this surface set, copy and paste it to the SummitBKD surface.

    This is the surface behind the logo—the logo background plate. Because this surface and the bevel surface are curved, be sure to turn on Smoothing. Figure 16.38 shows the rendered object. Be sure to save your work and remember to select Save All Objects to save the surface settings with the objects.

Figure 16.38   Fractal Noise as a transparency texture streaks the curved, flat box to make a nice background element.

From this point, you can set the rest of the surfaces on your own. The other surfaces throughout the scene should be similar to the ones you just set in the previous exercise. The colors are red and blue, and some white. You can add a metallic color such as the SolutionSummit_Bevel surface to add some variations. For example, the Dialog98 surfaces can be set to a nice variation of the SolutionSummit_Bevel surface. The large S object surfaces can be copies of the SolutionSummit_Sides and face surfaces. By setting up one surface, you can quickly and easily copy and adjust the surface to complete your scene. After you've surfaced all the objects, be sure to save them.

Glowing Surfaces

The surfaces you set for the text in the previous sections are typical to the types of surfaces you would set for just about any kind of logo. Color, reflection, and some shininess would all be a part of it as well. But you can enhance the final look of the animation with Glow. Glow softens any of the animations you create, especially broadcast-style animations, by creating a bright halo around the applied surface. Adding glows is easy—follow these tips to add Glow to your scene:

- Set the amount of glow for each surface through the Advanced tab in the Surface Editor. You can set the Glow Intensity for the surface anywhere from 0 to 100%.

- Under the main Settings tab in Layout, you can access the Image Process panel. Here, you must check Enable Glow to activate any Glow Intensities you've set.

- You can set the Intensity for all surfaces with Glow Intensity set through the Image Process panel. A typical glow setting is 50%–60%.

- Because Glow adds a soft haze when applied, you can set the amount of the Glow Radius through the Image Process panel as well. A good average to work with is 10 pixels.

Try adding glow to every surface in your scene, and then activate the Glow Intensity feature through the Image Process panel. See what kind of results you come up with.

Applying Transparency

Besides adding glowing surfaces to enhance a broadcast animation, the addition of some transparency further enhances the look. Figure 16.39 shows logo treatment. Notice the SummitBKD surface that forms a ring around the center of the animation. The sides are soft and the surface slightly see-through. By not adding completely solid objects to the entire scene, all the elements start to work together. And, if the project you're creating is limited in color and depth, transparent objects can help add significant variances to any surface without changing any colors. You can add transparency by:

- Entering the Shaders tab in the Surface Editor, and adding a Shader modifier, such as Edge Transparency.

- Double-clicking the Edge Transparency shader to set Transparent edges to your surfaces.

- Setting the overall transparency of any surface by changing the 0% Transparency in the Basic tab up to 100% transparent.

Adding a Fast Fresnel Shader

LightWave's Fast Fresnel shader offers you the ability to add more real-world surfacing properties to your animation. The Fresnel effect is universally known in studios and can be designed in animation for maximum light control by adding the Fast Fresnel shader plug-in in the Surfaces panel. The Fresnel effect happens when certain surface properties such as reflection, light diffusion, or specularity appear changed based on the angle of viewing. A glass window, for example, will appear more or less reflective depending on the angle in which you are looking at it. The same can be said for reflective metallic objects, such as a logo. Apply LightWave's Fast Fresnel shader through the Shaders tab to some of the surfaces in your scene to see the results.

Lighting Broadcast Animations

Lighting any scene in LightWave can be fun, but also time-consuming. If you're not familiar with traditional lighting techniques and principles, it might take you a bit longer to get up to speed. But lighting for broadcast-style graphics is not difficult. These types of animations can be lit with basic two- or three-point lighting schemes.

Exercise 16.12   Lighting Broadcast Animations

You can be as creative as you want with your lighting. However, knowing a few simple rules might help you with this exercise, as well as others. Good lighting also produces another important element in your animations—shadows. Shadows are as important as the background elements you modeled for this project. By setting up the proper lights, you can create shadows throughout your scene that add depth and interest for the viewer. Follow along with this next exercise to set up lights in a broadcast text animation.

1. Load into Layout the scene you've been creating throughout this chapter. You also can use the 16BroadcastLightMe.lws scene from the CD-ROM.

   A default Distant light is always in the scene. This scene has transparencies and glows, so adding a ray-traced shadow to the mix will not help with rendering. Instead, spotlights can add soft shadows with fast rendering.

2. Select the default light, and press **p** to enter the Light Properties panel.

3. Change the Light Type to Spotlight. Make both the Spotlight Soft Edge Angle and Spotlight Cone Angle 40 degrees. Spotlights shine a round cone of light. The angle in degrees is the size of the cone, zero being no cone, and 40 about average.

   The Spotlight Soft Edge Angle will add a nice edge falloff to the light. This light will be the key light for the scene. The default color is white, but no light is ever a pure white.

4. Change the Light Color so that it is slightly off-white. The Light Intensity should be at 100%.

5. Because this is the main light for the scene, move it up and to the left, in front of the objects.

This position also will help cast decent shadows from foreground elements to the background elements, helping to add depth to the animation. Figure 16.39 shows the position through the Perspective view in Layout.

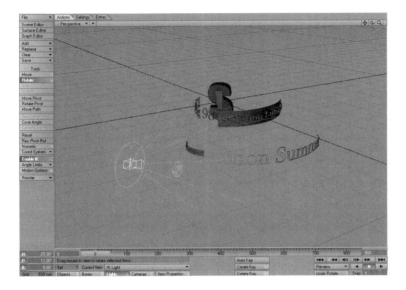

Figure 16.39   The main light for the scene should be set above and in front of all the elements.

The next light can be added to help create some distance to the scene. You don't want it to look like there is just one big, hot light shining on the objects. By adding a soft blue light off to the side, you enhance the feeling of distance and depth.

6. Add another spotlight and move it off to the right side of the elements. Make the color soft blue, and set the Light Intensity to 75% or so—you don't want this light to overpower the main light.

7. Add a colored backlight to the animation. Save your scene and objects.

This can be a red colored light that simply adds more dimension through color and shadows. Place it above and behind the objects like a hair light, to light the top of the objects. You also can try the opposite position, underneath the objects to light the bottom. Test a few options to see which you like best.

Lighting can definitely be a lot of fun when it comes to 3D animation, but the Ambient Intensity is also important. For this broadcast-style animation, one last setting can make the elements pop off the screen more than they already are.

From the Settings tab, go to Global Illumination and set the Ambient Intensity to 0% (default 25%). Too much ambient light can flatten your scene, and take away effects of your lighting. Ambient light is the area in the animation not directly hit by any of your lights. As a rule, 0% to 5% is a good Ambient Intensity value.

There's only one more thing to do before you can render this animation—make it all move!

Movement and Timing

When it comes to broadcast-style animations, your goal should be to keep everything moving. Watch any of the major television productions—the titles are always moving. Perhaps the main title flies in and sits, but the background or foreground elements are in motion from the time the animation fades in from black, to the time it fades out. This is easy to do, especially on the animation you've created in this chapter.

Exercise 16.13   Putting Elements in Motion

Earlier in this chapter, you adjusted the positions of the objects in Modeler and resaved them. You did this to change their pivot points so that when it came time to animate, your job would be much easier. Because this animation consists of a main logo surrounded by curved text elements, the elements need to slowly rotate. The objects are curved and ready to be put in motion.

1. Start by selecting the S object from the elements you've created in this chapter. Or, if you're using the scene from this book's CD-ROM, select the 16Sfinal.lwo object.

2. Press **y** on the keyboard to switch to Rotate mode. Rotate the S to the right on its heading about 45 degrees. Create a keyframe at 0 for it.

3. Next, rotate it back and about –45 degrees. Create a keyframe at frame 800.

   This makes it move over the course of 28 seconds. Your animation might not be 28 seconds long, but the object will stay moving, so if you render 600 frames (20 seconds at 30 frames per second), your object will still be moving as the animation ends.

4. Select the Summit3D object.

   This is the theme of the client's logo, and should be more prominent in the animation; therefore it's closer to the camera.

5. To add more elements to the scene, clone this object, and move it up to the top of the frame. Feel free to make it larger to add variation to it. Figure 16.40 shows the cloned object.

Figure 16.40 Cloning object elements adds another level of movement and complexity to your scenes.

6. To continue adding rotations, select the first Summit3D object, and rotate it on its Heading about –35 degrees. Create a keyframe at 0 for it. Then, rotate it on its Heading the other way, +35 degrees. Create a keyframe for it at frame 800.

7. Create keyframes for the other elements.

They all animate on their headings. Simple rotations for each object—that's all there is to it. Save the scene as Broadcast3.lws or something similar to keep the motion changes you've made.

Too often, animators feel the need to move things fast and furious. If you're keyframing, things should move fast, right? Wrong. The most creative broadcast animations involve slow, colorful, moving elements, which is what you've created here. Remember to not overdo it. Subtle and classy is what you want for these types of animations. You can load the 16BroadcastFinal.lws scene from the book's CD and take a look at the final scene with lights and movements. Something should always be moving, and movements should not be sudden. After you've set everything in motion, all you need to do is render it out.

Rendering for Broadcast

Rendering your animations is your final step to get this animation finished and out the door. But, how you render it is crucial to the overall success of the project. Broadcast rendering needs to be of high quality, but not nearly the quality of that for film. Rendering for film requires almost four times the resolution than for broadcast. What does that mean to you as an animator? It means longer render times! Rendering for broadcast only requires you to set up a few key items within LightWave, and does not take forever to render.

Resolution Settings

The first step to rendering for broadcast is to determine where your animation is going. That is to say, are you going to use an animation recorder to play the animation to tape? Are you rendering directly to tape? Or is the animation going to stay digital and be edited together in a non-linear editor? This is key to setting up the proper resolution for your animation. If you are rendering for an animation recorder, such as the Perception Video Recorder from Digital Processing Systems, you need to render in a different resolution than if you're rendering to a Stratosphere non-linear editor from Accom.

Video resolution should be determined and set in the Camera Properties panel. You can choose a preset resolution from the drop-down list, such as D1 NTSC. This sets up your animation for a render with a pixel width of 720 and a pixel height of 486. It also sets the pixel aspect ratio to 0.9, the proper aspect ratio for NTSC video. If you are working with a PAL setup, you can select the D1 PAL Resolution setting, which sets a pixel width of 720 and a pixel height of 576. The pixel aspect ratio would change to 1.0667.

If you need to set a custom resolution, as you would for the Perception Video Recorder, you can manually adjust the width and height values to create a custom resolution. The PVR resolution setting is 720 × 480. To decide what resolution you need, it's best to check with your client, or video editor. Or, check the documentation of the recording device you choose to use. They will usually list the resolution needed to bring in animations, video clips, and so on.

Antialiasing Settings

After you have a proper resolution determined, you need to set up antialiasing. Antialiasing is a smoothing process in LightWave Layout that ranges from Low and Enhanced Low, to Extreme and Enhanced Extreme. For a broadcast-style animation, an Antialiasing setting of Enhanced Medium works well. This smoothing process takes away the sharp, jagged edges in the final rendered animation and makes the overall appearance clean.

Field Render and Motion Blur

When you're creating animations for film and special effects, you should always add a little motion blur. It makes your objects look more realistic and lifelike. But when it comes to broadcast-style animations, nothing works better than field rendering for selling the whole package. Field rendering draws two fields of video for every frame. What this means is that fast motions do not blur and textures remain visible. Field rendering keeps animated text in broadcast logos clean and smooth. Without field rendering the animation might not look as sharp, and almost blurry if the motions are too fast. Be sure to apply Field Rendering to your broadcast and text animations for the best possible quality.

The Next Step

The techniques in this chapter can be applied to many everyday animations, from text, to effects, to image processing animations. You can modify the techniques in this animation by using different text and different colors. By doing so, you suddenly have an entirely new animation. Instead of the large S in the middle of the elements, how about adding some effects, such as fire? Figure 16.41 shows the same techniques adjusted with different colors and fonts to create another similar animation.

Figure 16.41   The techniques in this project can be used to create other animations. Here, the text and colors are modified and the center logo is changed to a fire to create a different look and feel while keeping the same broadcast-style animation.

After you have worked through the exercises and are comfortable with the techniques and principles applied, try creating your own broadcast-style animation. Perhaps you can animate your company logo? Another way to practice these types of animations is to copy the big boys. Watch television, watch satellite and cable channels. Set a tape and start recording title animations for your own reference. There is a ton of high-quality work being broadcast everyday, each of which is a spark for a new idea for your next project.

Summary

When you can, experiment with different motions and adjust the timing of your animations. You can refer to Chapter 4, "LightWave 6 Layout," of this book for more information on adjusting timing and keyframes. Now, if you are the type of person who likes to really get into a program and create custom programming scripts, read the next chapter, Chapter 17, "Output and Rendering."

Part IV
Animation Post

Chapter 17

Output and Rendering

After you've set up your animations, you

must have asked yourself at some point,

"Now what?" This chapter shows you

the methods and options available for

rendering and outputting your animations. Specifically, this chapter provides you with information on the following:

- The LightWave 6 rendering engine
- Camera settings for rendering
- Rendering options

LightWave 6 gives you a variety of rendering methods, so dive right in. Figure 17.1 shows the LightWave Render Options panel in Layout.

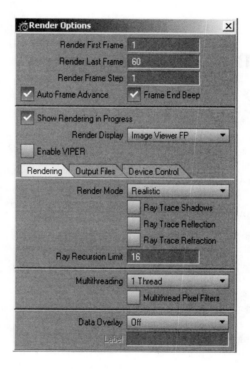

Figure 17.1   The Render Options panel in Layout.

LightWave 6 Render Engine

You will find that the LightWave 6 render engine is one of the best in its class. It's fast, efficient, and, most importantly, good at what it does. As you can see from the cover of this book, the quality of the renders LightWave can produce is unparalleled. Through the software's radiosity rendering, area lighting, and shadow options, the LightWave 6 rendering engine can deliver astonishing results. Chapter 9, "Environmental Lighting," discusses lighting further. Before you can get to this render level, it's good for you to know the process of setting up an animation to render.

Camera Settings for Rendering

Before long, the steps involved in rendering an animation will become second nature to you. You'll be jumping between the Render Options panel and the Camera Properties panel at the blink of an eye, making sure you have all your settings in place. Figure 17.2 shows the Camera Properties panel. This panel is mentioned in this chapter because the settings here are directly related to the output of your animation.

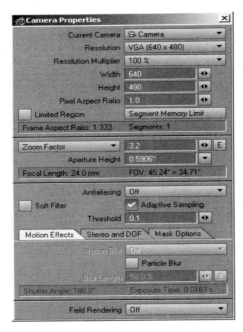

Figure 17.2   The Camera Properties panel goes hand in hand with the Render Options panel. Here, you define the current camera's resolution for rendering, antialiasing settings, and aspect ratio.

When your animation is complete, you should open the Camera Properties panel and check out your settings. For proper camera placement, these values should be set up before you begin animating, and it's always a good idea to double-check them before you render. In addition, it is here that you set up any motion blur, field rendering, or antialiasing.

Exercise 17.1   Everyday Rendering: Part 1

This exercise guides you through the kind of rendering most commonly used by LightWave animators: rendering that generates animations for video or computer work. If, however, you are using LightWave for rendering anything other than video or computer work, such as film or print, the information here still applies, and the difference is noted.

1. In Layout, load the 17Render.lws scene from the book's CD-ROM.

    This scene is set up with a few simple objects so that when you render, you'll have more than just a black screen. Figure 17.3 shows the scene setup.

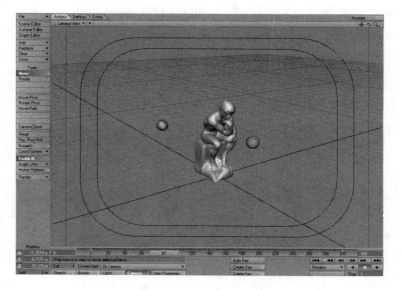

Figure 17.3   For rendering purposes, use the 17Render.lws scene from the book's CD-ROM.

The first thing to do when you're ready to render is enter the Camera Properties panel. You are ready to render when you have all your lighting, textures, and motions in place. This scene has all of these in place.

2. Select the camera and press the **p** key to enter the Camera Properties panel.

    The Current Camera at the top of the panel should read Camera because only one camera is in the current scene.

3. Set the Resolution to D1 (NTSC) for video resolution. Change the Resolution Multiplier to 100% for equal size. You'll see the Width and Height values change when you do so.

    Figure 17.4 shows the information area in the Camera panel that displays the Frame Aspect Ratio and the Segments.

Figure 17.4   The information area within the Camera Properties panel shows how many segments LightWave is currently rendering each frame with.

4. Make sure your Segments have a value of 1 by increasing the Segment Memory Limit.

   If the Segments value is higher than 1, your render times could increase. Don't worry, though. If you are short on system memory, you can use less RAM for rendering. Therefore, the Segments will be greater than 1—say, 3 or 4.

   At this point, you want to tell LightWave to use more RAM for rendering.

5. Click the Segment Memory Limit button, and change the value to 20000000 (20MB).

   LightWave now has more memory with which to work and will render your frames in single segments.

6. When asked if you want this value set at default, click Yes.

   The Zoom Factor should have been set up before you began creating your animation. If you change it now, you might have to change your shots and reset the keyframes.

7. Leave the Zoom Factor set to 6. The Aperture Height should be left at the original setting as well.

> **Note**
>
> While you're working, it's not necessary to have Antialiasing on. But you *definitely* do want this on for your final renders. Although you have the choice of Low to Extreme settings, it's recommended that you render all your animations for video in at least Enhanced Low Antialiasing. Medium or Enhanced Medium Antialiasing can provide you with a cleaner render. High Antialiasing is overkill and a waste of render time for video. It might actually make your images look blurry.

8. Click Adaptive Sampling.

   Activating this setting tells LightWave to look for the edges to antialias in your scene. The Threshold value compares two neighboring pixels and a value of 0 sees the entire scene. A good working value is .12. You can set the value higher, which will lower rendering time. For this scene, you do not need any motion blur.

9. Do not change the Stereo and DOF settings as well as the Mask Options. This scene will not use these. You can read more on these settings in Chapter 6, "LightWave 6 Cameras."

10. Go back to the Motion Effects tab and select Even First for Field Rendering.

Because the 17Render.lws scene has textures applied to the thinker model and wireframe balls rolling, you want to keep these elements sharp during their motions. Field rendering will render two fields of video for every frame rendered, with the even field first. Figure 17.5 shows the selection.

Figure 17.5   Field rendering is selected and set to Even First in the Camera Properties panel. This tells LightWave to render the even fields of each frame first.

11. Close the Camera panel and save your scene. All your settings will be saved along with it.

The Camera panel should be visited at least twice during an animation, if not more: once to set up the camera and zoom factors before beginning animation setup, and once before you are ready to render to set up antialiasing, motion blur, field rendering, and proper resolution size. From here, you can set up the Render panel.

Exercise 17.2   Everyday Rendering: Part 2

The Camera and Rendering panels go hand in hand. This chapter is designed to show you the proper steps to take to set up an animation for rendering. This exercise continues where the first exercise left off.

1. Load the 17Render2.lws scene from the book's CD-ROM and go to the Render Options panel. You can find this panel by selecting the Render drop-down menu in Layout. The first selection in the list is Render Options.

Figure 17.6 shows the Render Options panel. This is where you tell LightWave what to render and where to save it. You'll see Render First Frame, Render Last Frame, and Render Frame Step values. If your LightWave animation in Layout has a first frame of −30 and a last frame of 300, it will not render those frames unless they are entered here.

The frame numbers you assign to your timeline in Layout do not automatically apply in the Render Panel.

2. Leave the First Frame set to 1, and make the Last Frame 300 (10 seconds). Frame Step should be at 1 to render every frame. A Frame Step of 2 would render every two frames, and so on.

3. Turn on Automatic Frame Advance.

This tells LightWave to advance to the next frame and continue rendering.

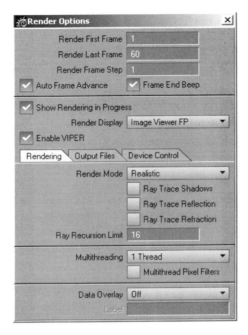

Figure 17.6   The Render Options panel is home to all the controls you need for setting up renders.

Note

Frame End Beep is useful for monitoring the completion of your rendered frames, but is not necessary.

4. Uncheck Show Rendering in Progress to turn it off.

   Although it is useful for monitoring your rendering, Show Rendering in Progress will slow down the rendering process if left on for longer animations.

5. Turn off the Render Display.

Note

The Image Viewer FP render display remembers your rendered frames. Turn this on while performing test renders on individual frames (**F9**), and leave it open. You can select any of your previously rendered images from its Layer list. You also can view the alpha channel in this viewer and save an image.

6. Turn off Enable VIPER.

   VIPER is needed when setting up surfaces and other VIPER-ready features in Layout, but for final rendering this should not be applied. Leaving VIPER on while rendering multiple frames increases render times and memory usage.

The Rendering tab is where you tell LightWave what parameters to use for rendering, such as ray tracing. Here, you can tell LightWave to calculate Ray Traced Shadows, Ray Traced Reflections, and Ray Traced Refraction.

7. Turn Off Ray Traced Shadows, as well as Ray Traced Reflections and Ray Traced Refraction. These options are not needed in this particular case. Unless you are applying Ray Traced Shadows with lights, reflections, or refraction to a surface, these options will increase render times.

8. The Render Mode is usually set at Realistic and is not often changed. However, you do have the option to render Wireframe or Quickshade versions of your animations here.

9. Set the Ray Recursion Limit to 12.

   The Ray Recursion Limit, which doesn't often change, determines the number of times LightWave calculates the bounced rays in your scene. In the real world, this is infinite, but in LightWave, you can set a Ray Recursion Limit up to 24. This increases render times. A good working value is 12. However, this can be a real timesaver while using the Ray Traced Reflection option, by setting a low value of 1 or 2.

10. If your computer has more than one processor, select 2, 4, or 8 for Multiprocessing. If you have only 1 processor, set the Multiprocessing to 1. And if you have multiple processors and have applied pixel filter plug-ins such as HyperVoxels, make your processors work for you by clicking Multithread Pixel Filters.

11. Set Data Overlay to display the Frame Number, SMPTE Time Code, Film Key Code, or Time in Seconds on the bottom-right corner of your animation.

    This is good for reference test renders. In addition, when one of these values is set, you can add a note in the Label area. This is good to do for test renders for clients that have a history of not paying and/or stealing your work.

12. After you've set all the render options, be sure to save your scene. It's a good habit to get into before any render, even single frame renders.

Those are the main parameters you need to set up to render an animation. But you still need to tell LightWave where to save the files and what type of files to save. The next section discusses the various file formats and processes for saving your animations.

Saving Renders

Within the Render Options panel is another tabbed area entitled Output Files. This area is where you tell LightWave what type of file you want to save and in what format it should be. Figure 17.7 shows the Output Files tab within the Render Options panel.

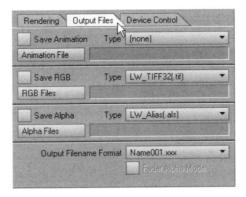

Figure 17.7   The Output Files tab within the Render Options panel is where you tell LightWave what type of file to save and where to save it.

The first area within the Output Files tab is the Save Animation selection. This confuses many people. You are creating an animation in LightWave, right? Save Animation! Makes sense—but it means something a little bit different. Clicking Save Animation enables you to save your rendered frames as one animation file, such as an .AVI, QuickTime, or .RTV (Video Toaster) format. It will save one complete file. You can select different types of animations to save from the Type selection option.

Using Save Animation is great for previewing QuickTime movies, or when using Aura and Video Toaster. But you can also save out individual frames as well—and at the same time. If you select the Save RGB button, you're telling LightWave to save the individual frames as they are rendered. Similar to Save Animation Type, you select a variety of RGB formats in which to save your animations by selecting one from the Type drop-down list, as pictured in Figure 17.8.

Finally, in the Output Files tab, you also can save out the alpha channels of individual frames. Figure 17.9 shows the alpha channel of frame 100 of the 17Render.lws animation.

This is great for later compositing in a post-production environment. Remember, all these file types can be saved with one rendering. You can save a QuickTime or .AVI or .RTV, plus the RGB files and the alpha all at once. Pretty cool, huh?

When all this is set—the camera resolutions, the rendering information, and the output file information—you're finally ready to render your animation. Pressing the **F10** key will render your animation. Congratulations!

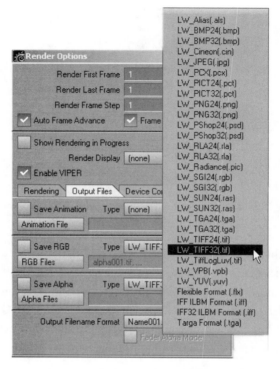

Figure 17.8   LightWave 6 gives you a slew of formats to save your RGB frames. This is the best way to render your animations if you do not use Video Toaster NT. The individual frames can later be imported into a variety of programs.

Figure 17.9   You can save the alpha channel information of individual frames in the Output Files tab.

Tip

You might have a high-resolution frame that needs to render over a long period of time. You can tell LightWave to automatically save this frame by setting up the Render Options as if you were rendering a full-length animation. Set the RGB format, output file-name, and location for saving, and then click Automatic Frame Advance. Make the First Frame and the Last Frame the same frame you want to render—say, frame 10. LightWave will render that frame and save the RGB, and because it's also the Last Frame, rendering will stop.

Render Selected Objects

If you click the Render drop-down list in Layout, you'll see the Render Selected Objects selection. Because LightWave enables you to select multiple objects, you can save significant rendering time with this option. In the Scene Editor or in Layout, holding the Shift key and clicking objects will select them all. Rendering selected objects has two useful functions:

- It saves render time by rendering only the objects you're interested in at the moment.

- It enables you to render multiple passes of the same animation with or without certain objects. This is great for special effects or compositing, or even before and after type animations.

Network Rendering

LightWave enables you to render over a network of computers, not just the individual machine on which you're working. Whether you have a few computers or hundreds of computers at your location, you can use all of them for rendering the same animation.

Stealthnet

LightWave 6 offers a powerful new rendering solution for today's animation studios. Stealthnet is designed for studios that have just a handful of computers. Its networking capabilities are based on TCP/IP, so you are not limited to just the machines on your network. Perhaps you are working at home one day and you finish a project for a client. You can use Stealthnet to send the animation over your ISDN, DSL, or other high-speed network connection to render on your office machines.

However, a few things need to be in place before you begin rendering with Stealthnet. *Inside LightWave [6]* recommends that you thoroughly go through the "LightWave

Motion: Animate and Render" manual that came with your software. In it, you'll find the correct, most up-to-date data on setting up a Stealthnet environment, from the Stealthnet Server to the Render Agent.

ScreamerNet

ScreamerNet has been a part of LightWave for years and is still available in LightWave 6. With ScreamerNet, LightWave needs to be installed on only a single machine. This distributive rendering can send your animations to other machines on your network that have a ScreamerNet process running. The process of setting up the original ScreamerNet or ScreamerNet II is involved, so please refer to your LightWave manuals for proper instruction.

ScreamerNet also is useful on a single machine for batch-processing your animations. Think about setting up four versions of your animated logo to render one right after the other. Because LightWave saves the Render Options information within a scene file, ScreamerNet knows where and what to save from your specific animations. You can even run ScreamerNet without running LightWave. Use ScreamerNet to batch-render animations without loading your scenes. The distributed rendering section of your LightWave manuals can instruct you further on the proper command lines to set up this process.

The Next Step

You can refer to this section of the book often when it's time to render your animations and images. But then the question arises, what to do next? WShen your animations are complete, the next step is to bring them into a digital animation recorder and lay them off to tape, or edit your final animations with audio and effects in a non-linear editor. Next, in Chapter 18, "Animation Editing and Demo Reels," you will learn about adding the finishing touches to your rendered animations.

Summary

Rendering your animations has to be done. Someday, you might not need to ever render, as processors and video cards become increasingly powerful. For now, though, LightWave still has to render, just like any other 3D application. But you'll find that the rendering engine inside LightWave 6 is one of the best around. It's strong and stable, and most importantly, it produces beautifully rendered images.

NewTek has added many OpenGL enhancements so that you can see what's going on directly in Layout, such as lens flares, reflections, texture, and fog. These speed up your workflow, but also give the poor F9 (Render Current Frame) key a break. Work through the exercises in this book, and make your own animations anytime you can. You can't be in front of your computer 24 hours a day—well, maybe you can, but you shouldn't. When you leave, set up a render. Don't just wait until the animation is "perfect." Render often and see how your animation looks. You might find new ways to enhance it and make it even better. Or, you might just find that it's perfect the way it is.

Chapter 18

Animation Editing and Demo Reels

As an animator, not long ago you had to know only animation and didn't have to concern yourself with any other job function. Today, however, because software and hardware tools have become more sophisticated and easier to use, you are not only an animator, but also an editor, cameraman, audio engineer, and modeler.

Out of these ancillary functions, that of editor is perhaps most crucial. Why? Because the post-production process doesn't just clean up an animation, it can improve it. If you can edit your animations, you can create a better presentation for your client.

Because knowledge of editing is so important to producing high-quality animations, this chapter introduces you to animation editing concepts. Useful information also will be provided to help you create the best and most effective demo reel, whether you're a freelancer selling your skills to new clients, or you're applying for a full-time job. Specifically, this chapter discusses:

- Editing with Video Toaster NT and Speed Razor
- Audio issues
- Creating a demo reel

Enhancing Animation with Editing

Knowledge of animation editing is crucial in today's marketplace. For example, say a client asks you to create a full corporate logo treatment. The client provides you with print material for their upcoming sales and service conference that will have more than 1,200 attendees. They are producing several videos that involve interviews with corporate executives and members of the service team and need an animation that incorporates their logo treatment, but as a soft animated backdrop that needs to be placed behind the video interviews. They also need a "walk-in" graphic, which is a looping animation that will play on monitors and projection screens as conference attendees gather for the meeting, as well as a similar "walk-out" graphic that also incorporates the main theme of the conference with the logo.

To create all these animations in LightWave (or any other 3D application), you'll need a lot of render time. At 30 frames per second for video, and with probably more than 30 minutes of animation, chances are you can't handle that much render time, your client won't be willing to pay for it, or both. The solution is editing. By editing your animations, you can lengthen them, shorten them, loop them, and distort them to create various looks. When you render one element of the animation, you can use it countless times to create additional elements.

Bringing your LightWave animations into the editing environment is easier today than ever before. You can acquire a high-quality, non-linear editing system for less than

$4,000. A few years ago, comparable systems cost \$20,000 or more. Editing solutions such as Adobe Premiere, Discreet's Edit, or In Sync's Speed Razor are excellent post-production software tools for editing animations. To perform broadcast-quality video editing on your computer, you will most likely need a video card.

This chapter focuses on the non-linear editing software Speed Razor, from In Sync. Speed Razor works with many types of boards, including Truevision's TARGA and DPS' Perception. The board discussed here is NewTek's Video Toaster for Windows NT. This D1 uncompressed board works directly with LightWave. D1 is a broadcast resolution setting of 720 × 486 pixels. Most non-linear editing systems compress video so that it takes up less drive space, and so a computer system can handle the transfer of high amounts of data. With an uncompressed non-linear system such as the Video Toaster, the video and animation files you work with are uncompressed, which is as good as you can get.

File Formats for Editing

You can render your animations in a number of formats, including such movie formats as .AVI and QuickTime. But for serious projects, it's often good to render in RGB frames. As mentioned in Chapter 17, "Output and Rendering," RGB frames enable you to save individual frames of an animation in a variety of formats. The rendered frames can be used individually in a paint program such as Adobe's Photoshop, or the images can be brought back into LightWave as a sequence for added render effects. You can use them in NewTek's Aura, a paint, animation, and compositing program discussed in Appendix C, "Plug-Ins and References," and you can bring them into Speed Razor for editing. The best plan of attack when working with the Toaster and Speed Razor, however, is to use NewTek's own native .RTV format. This is an uncompressed file that LightWave, Aura, and the Video Toaster all use. Saving an animation in .RTV format will generate one animation file. Saving an animation as RGB frames generates individual frames of the entire animation.

Within LightWave's Render Options panel, you can choose Save Animation. There, you can select the .RTV format, and LightWave will save each frame to a single file.

Note

You can still save RGB frames while saving an .RTV file for editing. However, if you do have Video Toaster, RGB frames work best. The .RTV format is proprietary for Video Toaster.

Editing with Video Toaster NT

When NewTek introduced the original Amiga-based Video Toaster in 1990, it forever changed how video production and graphics were produced. The Video Toaster was developed specifically to get video into your system in real time so that you could get to work editing. This means that the editing software has immediate access to the actual video stream, allowing features such as real-time DVEs (digital video effects), both full-screen video previewing (called ToasterVision) and on-screen video monitoring (called ToasterScope) on your PC monitor, and *much* more.

Now available on the NT platform, the Video Toaster NT for Windows is the ultimate in quality and performance and can give you the most bang for your buck when it comes to non-linear systems. For the LightWave animator, the Video Toaster NT is ideal because it interacts with LightWave and Aura, both of which utilize the .RTV format.

Hard-Drive Concerns

Although uncompressed video files need high bandwidth and lots of storage, you can use everyday, high-quality hard drives as video drives. This is a cost-effective approach, because you can get a high-quality hard drive without spending thousands of dollars on a large SCSI RAID array.

Instead, under Windows NT and Windows 2000 technology, you can "stripe" drives. Using multiple Ultra 66 IDE hard drives, you can create enough speed and storage to handle uncompressed video and animation. IDE (Integrated Drive Electronics) is a standard electronic interface used between a computer motherboard's data paths or bus and the computer's disk storage devices. When you stripe drives under Windows NT and Windows 2000, if each drive is fast enough you will require only two drives to achieve the 22MB/second sustained data rate needed by the Video Toaster NT. If the drives are not fast enough, you must add an additional drive to the striped set. You keep adding drives until the set is fast enough. A good working system includes four 30GB hard drives with a speed of 7200RPM. A 30GB IDE hard drive costs less than $350.

The process of striping drives is simple. You tell the computer to look at all the particular drives and read them as one. For example, four 30GB drives striped together show up on the computer system as one 120GB drive. Check your system and hardware for more information on striping drives. Windows NT, Windows 2000, and Macintosh computers have many non-linear animation solutions available that require a striped set of drives.

Speed Razor Editing

Editing in the Video Toaster is done with Speed Razor from In Sync. Figure 18.1 shows the Speed Razor interface.

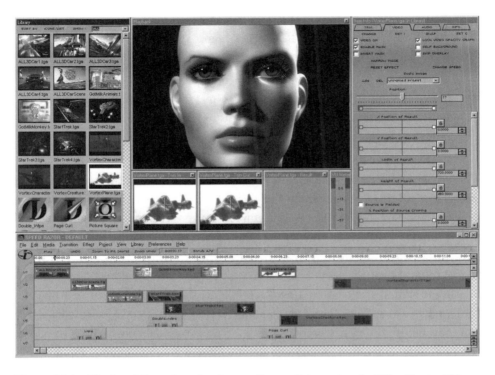

Figure 18.1 The Speed Razor interface for non-linear editing, using the Video Toaster NT from NewTek.

The following steps explain how to import your animations into Speed Razor for editing.

1. From LightWave's Render Options panel, select the Output Files tab.

2. Select Save Animation, and set the Type to NewTek-RTV-NTSC.

3. Click the Animation File button to designate a location for the .RTV file. It's a good idea to point to your video drives for best playback results.

4. Make sure Auto Frame Advance is on, and render your animation by pressing the **F10** key.

   When it's complete, you'll have one file containing the full animation.

 Note

For more information and specifics on rendering, refer to Chapter 17.

5. To load the animation in Speed Razor, click the blank gray area in the Library window and select Add Media from the pop-up menu that appears. Point to the

rendered animation file, select it, and click Open. Your rendered animation in .RTV format is now ready to be edited. Be sure to save your work!

If you are using another non-linear application other than Speed Razor and Video Toaster, you can use the similar methods to edit your animations. Be sure to save the animation in the appropriate format for your specific video board. Most non-linear editing software programs require you to load media into a bin or library. From there, you drag the media into a timeline and begin editing.

With the single .RTV file inside Speed Razor, you can duplicate it, process it, change the speed, blend it with other animations and video files, or just fade it in and out. These features are important to have when working on complex projects, and especially when creating a demo reel.

Non-Linear Editing

Non-linear editing was conceived by George Lucas, and eventually matured into the EditDroid system at Lucas Film Ltd. This was 1980, and in the 20 years since its inception, non-linear editing has become standard in post-production facilities. It also is becoming a viable production tool for animators like you.

Non-linear editing is the process of working in a tapeless environment. Unlike traditional editing, which is done in a linear process one clip after the other, with non-linear editing you can work on any portion of a production at any time. For example, your boss has made you videotape a long lecture. In reviewing the footage, your edit project requires that you edit together clips from the end of the lecture, then from the front, and then from various sections in between. On a traditional tape-to-tape editing system, you would need to constantly fast forward and rewind to the appropriate sections of the video tape. With a non-linear editing system, after the footage is in the computer (which does not have to be captured in any specific order), you have instant access to any part of the video.

Timeline Editing

The timeline in Speed Razor or any non-linear system is where you can create your production. When you import animations into the editing software, it is treated like a video clip. Most systems, including Speed Razor, enable you to load clips, stills, video, or animation into a library or bin. Think of this as a big bowl where your footage files live. Dip your hand into the bowl and grab a clip. Drop that clip into the timeline and begin editing. The timeline enables you to see your edits, the length of your video clips, and the audio through an opacity graph. Here, you can repeat clips, such as a looping animation. From the library of clips, you can use any clip as many times as you like without any loss of quality. The digital content remains intact as many times as you use it.

Adding Audio to Animation

During the editing process with Speed Razor or any non-linear editing solution, you also can add audio to your animations and video clips. Although you can load .WAV files into LightWave for lip sync and timing purposes, you cannot render an animation with audio. However, the same audio file used to help create the animation can be loaded into your non-linear editor and added to an audio track along with your animation clip. You load audio into Speed Razor the same way you load an animation clip: select Add Media from the Library and select the specific file to import music, sound effects, or dialog. Other non-linear systems work in a similar fashion.

You can drag and drop the audio clip into the timeline for an added element of your final animation. Sound is incredibly important to the work you're doing. Certain music can evoke creativity when it comes to 3D imagery. Consider animating to music whenever you can to help you visualize color, light, and movement. Thinking ahead to your final project destination is always a plus. Don't think of the animation—think of the editing, the sound effects, and the music. All these combined will help make a dynamite final project.

Syncing Audio Lip Sync

If you used an audio clip in LightWave to animate your character, either for motion or lip sync, you can use that same audio clip when editing the rendered animation. After the final animation is rendered, you can bring it into Speed Razor. Using the same audio file, you can sync up the audio track with the animation to the exact frame. Speed Razor enables you to trim your imported clips to specific in and out points. This includes animations, video, and audio. For example, if your character begins talking immediately when she opens her mouth, you know that is where the audio should start. In your non-linear editor, find the beginning or start point of the animation and the audio file, create in-points, and you'll easily sync up your audio.

Using LightWave 6's Endomorph feature and audio files (discussed in Chapter 12, "Organic Animation") along with Speed Razor, you can literally create your own movies and demo reels!

Creating a Demo Reel

Your demo reel speaks for you. If you have eight degrees in computer science but only a spinning cube on your demo reel, you won't be hired as an animator. The reel speaks for itself.

What makes a good demo reel? Contrary to what you might think, it's not about just the animation, but rather, the entire reel.

The first thing you must understand when you put together your demo reel is that the people looking at it don't care about you. They don't care about the nights you stayed up creating the complex filtration plant, or the weekends you missed while animating a detailed skyscraper. All they care about (at first) is your reel. From there, you will be evaluated. Often, people say that to get a great job you need to know the right people. In the real world, *whom* you know can help you land the interview and, perhaps, get the job, but *what* you know will keep you there. Here are the key things you need to remember when creating a demo reel:

- It's not necessary to show your entire animation. Show only highlights. Tease the viewer with your best stuff.

- Keep your demo reel to about 2.5 to 5 minutes in length. Often, less is more.

- Do not title sections of the tape, such as "Character Work" or "Logos." Viewers aren't stupid. They'll know a logo when they see it. This also eats up some of that 5-minute limit.

- Audio is key. Find a unique and killer audio track to accompany your reel. Do not use copyrighted music. Potential employers viewing the tape might not appreciate you stealing music and will wonder what you might do when working for them.

- Find a cool musician to write you a piece of music. Offer him/her credit at the end of your reel in exchange for usage. This is free promotion for the musician and cool original music for you.

- If you are Joe Blow and sending a reel to get a job, do not put "JB Design Company" on the reel. If you have a company, why are you looking for a job?

- Use your best stuff, and don't feel the need to include long explanations of techniques unless asked.

- Do not thank your Mom and Dad, or anyone else, for that matter, on the reel—this is not professional.

- Avoid the term "FX." This abbreviation for "effects" is in about half of the company logos in business today. Try to be more original. Separate yourself from the pack. Be smart, and think about what you would like to see if someone sent you a demo reel.

What if you don't have enough material for a demo reel? A great (albeit time-consuming) solution to this is to create a demo reel that showcases what you can do, instead of what you've done. For example, you can title the demo reel with a clever logo animation using Inverse Kinematics and machinery. This alone shows your ability to create logos and industrial-type animations. Add some character animation that shows off your skills. Have your character introduce him or herself to the viewer, or act as your agent and tout all your wonderful animation. This character could dominate the entire reel by doing such things as singing, riding a bike, or anything else you can imagine. Be creative and original when putting together a demo reel. Think about what would pique your interest if you received a demo reel in the mail. Consider making animations specifically for the demo reel. Remember, with animation, you have the power to create just about anything you want, so don't let the lack of jobs stop you from creating a dynamic demo.

Media Types

How should your demo reel be delivered? That is, what format should you use to show your reel? Most often, a VHS tape will be the best plan of attack. Any serious employer will have a VHS machine available for viewing tapes, especially if he is recruiting. Also, VHS tapes are cheap, lightweight, and inexpensive to mail. If you have access to BetaSP, this will make your animations look and sound much better than VHS, but it's also more expensive. BetaSP tapes can cost anywhere from $8 to $25, depending on length and brand. The person viewing the tape might not have access to a BetaSP machine, so don't send this format unless it is requested.

Digital media also is another way to deliver a demo reel to your clients. You can put streaming video or QuickTime movies on a website for someone to look at, avoiding all mailing costs. Or, instead of downloading from the Internet (because not everyone has a fast connection), you can mail a CD-ROM with your digital files. If you are clever enough to create an auto-play CD with Director from Macromedia, you can customize a menu interface, enabling the viewer to look at your bio, photos, demo materials, and so on. This method is probably one of the best because it can show all your abilities in one consolidated, user-friendly application. It also can show your knowledge of Director and your graphics talents.

Note

If you don't have access to a non-linear editing system, you can use LightWave! If you have all the source frames, such as an animation rendered out as RGB frames, you can piece your demo together using source frames as background images. If you have Aura 2, it is even easier because you can use the timeline. Aura 2 also has audio support. Save out an .AVI and voila! Ready for broadcast over the Internet or CD-ROM recorder.

The Next Step

Many of the chapters in this book took you from start to finish with a particular project. As you build your skills and work more with LightWave 6, piece your projects together with editing. Add music, digital video effects, dissolves, and even titles. Taking your animations to the next level with editing and post-production will make your work stand out even more.

Summary

The finishing touches you add to your animations and the demo reels you create with them can make or break you. The ability to post-process animations enables you to have more flexibility over the final look of your projects, from adding glows, to duplicating frames, and mixing live video with animation. The demo reel you present to a client or prospective employer is a direct representation of you and your abilities. Make it better with post-production effects. Remember, just because you might be going after a job in 3D animation does not mean using 2D and editing effects on your 3D animation is off limits. Use all the tools you can to get the job done.

Part V
Appendixes

Appendix A

Expressions in LightWave 6

Expressions. The very name conjures up the vision of hours spent writing complex formulae and long scripts of archaic commands intelligible only to computers and perhaps a few "math geeks" (the type who love to sit around and endlessly debate the finer points of differential calculus). Many animators suspect that behind that steep learning curve might be something useful to their animation work, but the time spent trying to learn expressions seems too forbidding. Indeed, it seems some animators fear they would lose their creative edge were they to try to comprehend the mathematics behind expressions, as if the left side of their brain would simply gobble up the right side and leave them without a shred of creativity left.

This need not be so, as the few elite animators who have made the leap from keyframe-only animation to expressions can attest. It can actually allow more time to focus on the creative aspects of animating, rather than being swamped in the minutiae of keyframing every last envelope and motion. So, swallow your fears and your 'artiste' snobbery and be prepared to embrace a new freedom in your animations.

Project Overview

Expressions capabilities are certainly not new to LightWave—indeed, MathMotion and MathMorph, introduced in LightWave 5.0, can be considered very limited expressions engines. In addition, several third-party plug-ins have brought expressions capabilities to LightWave as far back as version 5.0. LightWave 6 is the first version of the software to include more substantial expressions capabilities "right out of the box". The purpose of this chapter is to introduce you to some of the fundamentals of expressions design and function. Specifically, this chapter

- Defines expressions
- Discusses expressions plug-ins
- Explains expressions syntax
- Details common expressions concepts
- Discusses advanced mathematical expressions

Definition of Expressions

The first questions that might come to your mind are, "What are expressions?" and, "Why should I use them?" The simplest definition for expressions is that they are a means of mathematically relating the value of one item (or a group of items) to the value of another item in your animation. Most often, expressions are used to automate the control of a motion based on some other set of motions in your animation, but an expression can just as easily control the value of an enveloped setting on a panel, such as light intensity or camera zoom.

Because expressions enable you to automate parts of your animations, their use enables you, the animator, to focus on the bigger picture, rather than losing your focus trying to manage dozens (or perhaps hundreds) of keyframes and enveloped values in your scene.

When evaluating a scene for possible inclusion of expressions, you should ask yourself the following questions:

- Could parts of the animation benefit from automation—that is, do some items in the scene depend on the motion of other items in a relatively straightforward fashion?

- Are multiple items not directly related to each other by parenting that nonetheless need to move together as a cohesive whole?

- Will the time spent designing an expression to automate pieces of the scene really save time in the end—that is, would you spend more time designing the expression than it would take to hand-keyframe (or envelope) a part of your animation? Starting as a novice in expressions, the answer to this last question might initially be "no," yet it might still be beneficial to try the expressions route. After all, you have to start somewhere.

As you gain more expertise in expressions design, you can more intelligently decide when and when not to use expressions in your work.

A Simple Expressions Example

One simple example of when you might want to use expressions is to rotate the wheels of a car. The equation that relates a car's wheel rotations to its motion is actually quite simple. It states that one rotation should occur every time the distance traveled is equal to a multiple of the circumference (distance around the outside edge) of the tire (see Figure A.1). The circumference is simply the diameter of the tire times the mathematical constant "Pi." Hence, the equation:

Number of rotations = distance traveled / (Pi × diameter)

This particular relationship is not new. In fact, it has been discussed at length several times in various online LightWave discussion forums. At that time, animators were forced to drag out their calculators and input the various values for the wheel rotations while trying to obtain some sort of measure of the distance the car had traveled. Or they had to "eyeball" the wheel's motion, trying to keyframe it so that it looked right. Using expressions, an animator can animate the car and have the wheels come along for the ride, as it were.

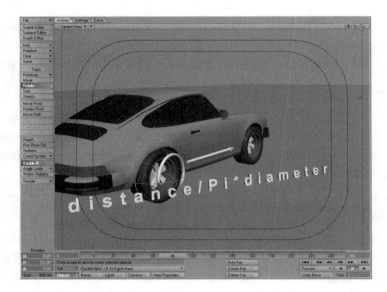

Figure A.1   The mathematical relationship between distance traveled and wheel rotation.

One thing to bear in mind is that expressions are not a substitute for a physics simulation engine. Although it is certainly possible to add the equations for simple physics-based motions to expressions, they would quickly bog down even attempting a moderately complex physical simulation. Such simulations are best left to more dedicated dynamics plug-ins and programs. Expressions usually work at a more basic level, enabling users to define mathematical relationships between items that will likely represent a gross simplification of the underlying physical reality. For instance, the real reason a car's tires rotate is a combination of the forces of friction, thrust, weight, torque, and pressure, yet it makes more sense to invoke the end result of all those physical equations: a simple distance/rotation relationship.

When discussing expressions, the question naturally arises, "Do I need to be a math genius to use expressions in my animation?" For basic expressions use, the answer is "no;" however, to truly unleash the power of expressions in your animation, it helps to have a good grasp of some math concepts, such as the basics of algebra and even some trigonometry.

Note

If you've been doing 3D animation for any length of time, you already know more mathematics fundamentals than you might think. 3D Cartesian coordinates (XYZ coordinates), Euler rotation angles, spline interpolation—all these are mathematical concepts. So don't let the idea of brushing up on a little math scare you away from a powerful method of animating. When you begin to understand the power of using expressions in your animations, you'll wonder how you ever survived without them.

Expressions Plug-In Interfaces

Throughout this chapter, you will be introduced to a variety of expressions concepts, using both the internal LightWave expressions system and one of the leading third-party expressions engines for LightWave—Relativity. A working demo of Relativity is included on the CD for use with the exercises that employ Relativity. Relativity is included in this discussion for three reasons. First, it is an expressions system with which this author is intimately familiar. Second, it is a well-established standard in the LightWave community and is in use by most LightWave production facilities in the country, especially the larger, more established facilities. Third, being an older and more "battle-tested" system, it supports many features not yet supported by the native expression system in LightWave 6.

The LW_Expression Interface

The LightWave 6 expressions system is currently available only through the LW_Expression plug-in, which is included in LightWave 6 and can be applied as a channel modifier in the Graph Editor (see Figure A.2). This enables the expression to affect any enveloped value, be it a motion channel or an enveloped value assigned on a panel. Its interface consists of a main expression slot and four "scratch variables" that enable you to type in sub-expressions, which can then be combined to build up the main expression typed into the expression slot.

While designing an expression, you can click the Test Expression button to see if your expression is following the correct syntax. Unfortunately, the errors returned in the case of an incorrect expression are rather ambiguous, often leading to a bit of head scratching to determine where the error has occurred. Worse, invalid syntax can sometimes lead to a crash, so save often when designing an expression lest you lose a good amount of hard-earned work. The entire expression syntax is defined in a rather terse section in the manuals.

The Relativity Interface

You can access Relativity from three different areas of LightWave's interface. First is the "original" Relativity motion plug-in available as a Motion Option modifier on the Motion Options panel (the Motion Options panel can be invoked by pressing the **m** key). Relativity also has a channel modifier component (Rel_Channeler) available under the Graph Editor. Finally a morphing/displacement plug-in component of Relativity is available from the Deformations tab on the Object Properties panel.

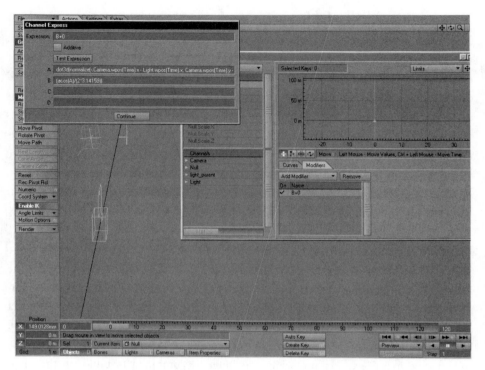

Figure A.2   The expression interface (through the LW_Expression plug-in) in LightWave.

The Relativity motion plug-in interface has slots for each motion channel, X through Z scale, along with a separate panel that has room for a total of 18 scratch variables (see Figure A.3). From a pop-up list next to each motion and scratch variable slot, you can access the Professors (analogous to wizards in other applications). These enable point-and-click setup for many common expressions. You also can switch between items from the pop-up list in the upper left corner while the Relativity interface is up, and you can copy, paste, save, and load expressions between these items. There also is space for comments, so you can remind yourself how and why you set up the expressions the way you did. The Rel_Channeler plug-in, by contrast, has a single expression channel but retains the full complement of scratch variables (see Figure A.4).

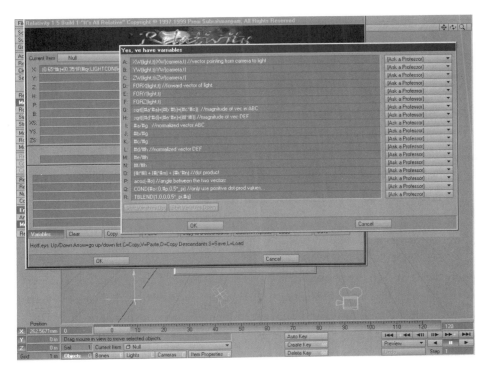

Figure A.3   The Relativity motion plug-in interface.

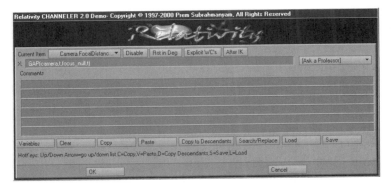

Figure A.4   The Relativity Channeler plug-in interface.

Note

In the standard LightWave interface, there is no assigned hotkey for the Graph Editor. Because access to the LW_Expression and Rel_Channeler plug-ins require using the Graph Editor, assigning a hotkey will save a lot of time and mouse motion. A suggested hotkey is the **g** key.

Relativity also installs a number of generic plug-ins (you might want to edit your LightWave menus to place these generics on the main interface). These generic plug-ins enable you to do the following:

- Globally enable or disable all instances of Relativity.
- Save out a motion file with motion plug-in data applied.
- Globally access all instances of the Relativity morph, Relativity Channeler, and Relativity motion expressions from a top-level interface.
- Set up several useful global scenes with multiple interacting copies of Relativity.
- Freeze all Relativity-defined motions in the scene.

Expressions Syntaxes

At the heart of each expressions plug-in is a simple programming language with a set of rules known as its syntax. This set of rules governs how the expression engine interprets your commands and turns them into something useful within your animation.

LW_Expression Syntax

The LW_Expression syntax has a lot of similarities to the syntax of LScript, which in turn has a lot of similarities to C and C++. The LW_Expression syntax uses an object-oriented, structured approach to its data, where you can envision a number of items clustered together into common structures, called objects. An object can be a literal item in your scene, such as a camera, light, bone, or mesh object, but it also can be an abstract object, such as a vector, string, or scene object. As an example of how the syntax works, say you wanted to access the X motion of object "MyObject." You would type the following expression into the expression slot of the interface:

    MyObject.pos(Time).x

Say you wanted to divide that position by the number of frames per second defined in your animation; you would need to access the fps member of the scene object:

    MyObject.pos(Time).x/Scene.fps

Say you wanted to access the heading rotation of your object, you would type

    MyObject.rot(Time).h

Which can alternatively be written as

    MyObject.rot(Time).x

This last expression can be a little confusing at first (how can you use 'x' to access the 'h' channel also?), until you begin to understand how the different data types in the syntax operate. The LW_Expression syntax supports six basic elements:

Methods (or functions). A method is anything that requires a series of one or more arguments, enclosed in parentheses and separated by commas, to define its value. An example of a method is the pos(Time) method. It has a single argument, which it expects to be a double that resolves to a time value. In the LW_Expression syntax, a method might return any one of the four types: int, double, vector or string.

Operators. These can take the form of simple mathematical operators (+, −, /, ×) or logical operators ("(?:)", <, >). What they actually do is dependent upon the data type that they're operating on. The data types—Ints, Doubles, Vectors, and Strings—are listed below.

Ints. These are integers, such as 2, 5, 645—basically any number that does not have any numbers after its decimal point.

Doubles. A double is any non-integer number, such as 1.0425. The name "double" is a carryover from C/C++ programming, where it defines a double-precision (or double-length) floating point number. It is entirely possible to have a double that has only zeros after the decimal point (such as 34.000), making it functionally an integer, but it is still a double by definition of its data type. Aside from numeric constants, three undocumented double variables are available to expressions:

- Time: the current time
- Frame: the current frame
- Value: the default value of the channel at the present time

Vectors. A vector is nothing more than a set of 3 doubles tied together, much like a coordinate position in Layout. It has three members, X, Y, and Z (or H, P, and B) The traditional mathematical definition of a vector is a direction in space. The programming definition is more abstract—it is any set of three doubles that can be manipulated simultaneously by a method or an operator (such as '+','−','/', and so on). Many methods can return a vector as their type, which can then be passed into another method or expression that expects a vector. It is also possible to define a temporary vector on the fly by enclosing three numbers in a pair of "<>" symbols. An example is <3 × 2, 4 − 5, 2>, which would define a vector with elements 6,−1, and 2.

Strings. A string of characters, such as a name, line of text, etc.

Hence, using the preceding data type definitions, it's clear that rot(Time) is a vector method (that requires some argument in parentheses to define itself—in this case, you inserted "Time"). This method can be accessed from any object, light, bone, or camera name (in this case, you chose MyObject.rot(Time)). Because vector types have 3 members, X, Y, and Z, you can access the first rotation member (which is really the heading) by using "MyObject.rot(Time).x".

An important concept to note in expression design is that time is not a constant. It is simply another variable that can be manipulated in your expression at will. You could have just as easily typed "MyObject.rot(Time/2).x" and gotten the X position of MyObject at a time equal to half of the present time (that is, if the current frame was 60, your expression would be looking backward to the X value of MyObject at frame 30).

Expressions can also be nested as arguments in methods and nested within parentheses. Hence, the following expression is perfectly valid, although what it does is a bit unclear:

(8 + MyObject.rot(Time/(2 + Light.coneangle.rad)).x) × (4 −(2 × MyOtherObject.pos(Time).y))

Breaking Down an Expression

To interpret what such lengthy expressions might actually do, first you need to define a set of fixed values to "lock down" all the variables. These values are, in essence, imaginary and can be substituted with other values as needed. In fact, substituting several sets of values can help you understand more clearly how the expression behaves. Take the following expression example:

(Time/2.0) × Light.coneangle.rad + ((2.0−Time)/2.0) × Light2.coneangle.rad

Three variables need to be defined: the current time, and the cone angles of the lights "Light" and "Light2". Start with the following values:

- Time: 0.0
- Cone angle of first light: 35 degrees
- Cone angle of second light: 20 degrees

Substituting these into the above expression yields

$(0.0/2.0) \times 35.0 + ((2.0 - 0.0)/2.0) \times 20.0$

Performing the operations in the innermost parentheses yields

$0.0 \times 35.0 + (2.0/2.0) \times 20.0$

Again, performing operations in the remaining set of parentheses yields

$0.0 \times 35.0 + (1.0) \times 20.0$

Now, perform all multiplication and division operations first (this is using standard mathematical operator precedence). This yields

$0.0 + 20.0$

Finally, perform all additions and subtractions. This yields the final result of

20.0

It is left as an exercise for the reader to determine what values this expression will have with the same angle values and time values of 1.0 and 2.0, respectively.

When designing expressions in the LW_Expression plug-in, keep in mind that the meaning of an expression is defined by its contents. If an expression contained only vector data types, its type would also be a vector. So, for example, the expression would be a vector expression, and actually have no meaning all by itself:

$<1.0,2.0,3.0> + <4.0,5.0,6.0>$

All this does is ask the engine to store the values 5.0, 7.0, and 9.0 somewhere in memory for safekeeping. For the expression to actually have any meaning when modifying a channel's value, you would need to select something to be the final value for the expression. Hence, the following expression would actually modify your channel value, specifically to the number 9.0:

$(<1.0,2.0,3.0> + <4.0,5.0,6.0>).z$

The LW_Expression plug-in expects that the contents of each field (both scratch variable and expression slots) ultimately resolve into a single numeric value.

Before going any further, and before the discussion gets any drier, it's time to practice using a few expression examples. Load up Layout and get ready to "express yourself."

Exercise A.1   Creating a Simple Expression

1. Add a null object to Layout.

2. Without changing the selected item, bring up the Graph Editor.

3. Add the null's Position.Y channel to the channel bin.

4. Click the Modifiers tab located beneath the graph display.

5. Select the LW_Expression plug-in from the drop-down menu.

6. Double-click the LW_Expression line in the Modifiers pane.

   This brings up the interface for this plug-in.

7. In the expression field, enter the line sin(Time and press Enter.

   You should get an error indicating that it was expecting a closing parenthesis.

8. Click OK and go back to the expression editor window.

9. Add a closing parenthesis to the expression, press Enter, and then click the Test Expression button.

   It should now indicate that the expression is OK. Close the expression window.

   In the graph display, you should notice a dashed line slightly above the solid line. The solid line represents the keyframed value for this channel, while the dashed line represents the expression-modified value for the channel.

10. To better see the graph, select Numeric Limits from the Limits pop-up menu on the upper right corner of the Graph Editor window and enter the following: Min Frame: –228, Max Frame: 283, Min Value: –2.8066, Max Value: 2.7074.

    You should now see a solid keyframed line with a dashed sine wave superimposed over it.

11. Exit the Graph Editor and play back the animation.

    If you have a standard 60-frame scene, you won't see much motion. The null will rise and start to fall, and then the animation will repeat. The null is rising and falling with a small part of what's known as a sine wave. To get more of the wave to affect the null during the animation, you need to edit the expression to make the time value increase more rapidly.

12. Bring up the Graph Editor window again and double-click the line reading sin(Time) in the Modifiers bin. Change the expression to sin(4 × Time), press Enter, and click Continue. Play back the animation again and notice it fluctuate more rapidly now as the argument of the sine function increases more quickly, but the animation seems discontinuous as it wraps back around from the end frame to the beginning frame.

    The sine function technically is measuring a trigonometric property of an angle value. As the angle value changes from 0 to 360 degrees, the sine function draws out a continuous wave, with a nice loop point where the angle changes from 360 degrees back to 0 degrees. Hence, to smooth out the beginning and end points of the animation, you need the argument of the sin() method to progress evenly from 0 to 360 degrees over the 60 frame time period. You might think that simply multiplying the Time value by 180 (causing the value inside the parentheses to progress from 0 to 360 over 2 seconds) might do the trick; however, the sin() method requires that its argument be expressed in radians. Fortunately, there's a conversion method for turning degrees into radians, and vice versa.

13. Change the expression to sin(rad(180 × Time)) and play back your animation.

Your null should now complete a single sine-wave cycle before the animation restarts at frame 0.

Although illustrative of a basic expression, it is rare that you will need a sinusoidally oscillating null in your animations. This next exercise will focus on a more practical application of expressions, using a null to control the focus of the camera.

Exercise A.2   Camera Focal Distance via Expressions

1. Load the example scene ball_focus_native.lws from the book's CD-ROM.

2. Press the **c** key to switch to camera editing, and press the **p** key to bring up the Camera Settings panel.

3. Click the Stereo and DOF tab and click the E button next to the Focal Distance field.

4. Add the LW_Expression plug-in to the channel and type in the expression vmag(extent(Camera.wpos(Time), focus_null.wpos(Time))).

5. Close the Graph Editor panel and drag the frame slider, watching the changes to the camera Focal Distance value as the null moves through the scene.

This expression measures the distance between the camera and the null and applies that distance value to the channel. Because it is a bit more complicated than the first example, here is a breakdown of what each component of the expression does:

- Anything.wpos(Time) will return the world coordinate position of an object at the current time. Note: wpos is a vector method, so it can be inserted into any method that expects a vector for an argument.

- extent(vector1, vector2) will create a new vector between the two points in space represented by vector1 and vector2, which, in this case, are the world coordinate positions of the camera and null.

- vmag(vector) measures the length of its argument, vector.

The combined result of all these pieces is an expression that measures the distance between the camera and the focus null, allowing easily animateable rack-focus effects. Wherever the null is positioned, that area of space will be sharply focused, with the focus becoming blurred closer and further from the null (see Figure A.5).

Figure A.5   Using an expression with a null object to precisely place the focal distance.

None of these examples has yet used the scratch variable slots, which will be revisited in a later exercise.

Relativity Syntax

The Relativity syntax has its origins in simple mathematical expression languages used in applications such as math function plotters and the like, which is also the origin of the "Math-" plug-ins (MathPlot, MathMorph, MathMotion). The syntax is a bit simpler than LW_Expression, made up of five basic elements:

Numbers   Any hard-coded number, such as 2.45.

Operators   Numeric operators, similar to their counterparts in the LW_Expression syntax.

Variables   There are two types of variables: the standard X, Y, Z, and T (which represent the current X, Y, Z positions and the current time) inherited from the "Math-" plug-ins, and Relativity's own internal variables, #a, #b,..., #r, which represent the scratch variable slots. In addition, Relativity supports a few special variables:

- #frm: current frame
- #fps: frames-per-second value
- #ex: numeric tag of the present object or channel
- #def: default value for the present channel

Functions   Similar to "methods" in the LW_Expression syntax, they consist of a name (all in caps), followed by a series of arguments separated by commas and enclosed in parentheses. Exactly what each argument does is defined by what the function expects. Rather than having functions clustered into objects (such as MyObject.pos(Time).x in the LW_Expression syntax), functions are instead free-floating entities. In Relativity, to get the X position of MyObject at the current time, you'd type X(MyObject,t).

Object names   Object names are used as arguments in functions to specify an object. Relativity supports names of cloned objects (MyClone (1)) and layered sub-objects. There are also several predefined object names (valid only from the motion plug-in version of Relativity):

- SELF: References the object itself. This can be useful for writing expressions that can be copied and pasted between objects and yet retain the same meaning.
- PARENT: References the object's parent.

Exercise A.3   Revisiting the Camera Focal Depth Expression

This exercise will familiarize you with the Relativity Channeler plug-in and its syntax.

1. Load the scene ball_focus_rel.lws from the included CD-ROM.
2. Select the camera and press the **p** key to bring up the Camera Settings panel.
3. Select the Stereo and DOF tab and click the E next to the Focal Depth field.
4. Select the Modifiers tab and select Rel_Channeler from the drop-down menu.
5. Bring up the Relativity interface and type the following in the X field:
   GAP(camera,t,focus_null,t
6. Click OK.

   Relativity should alert you to the fact that you have unbalanced parentheses in your expression and bring the interface back up.
7. Give the expression an ending parenthesis (so it looks like GAP(camera,t,focus_null,t)), and click OK.
8. With the Camera Settings panel still open, drag the frame slider back and forth to see the value change in the Focal Depth field.

Notice how Relativity includes a pre-built GAP function that performs the task of measuring the distance, rather than having to hand-roll an expression to create a vector between the two objects and take a vectorial magnitude of it. GAP expects as its first and third arguments the names of two items in LightWave (they could be objects, lights, bones, or cameras), and as its second and fourth arguments, a time value (in this case, you entered the variable "t" to get the current time). Relativity includes many prebuilt functions (such as GAP) to help ease the process of expression design.

Some Common Expression Concepts

Now that you have begun to familiarize yourself with basic expression syntax, it is time to turn to more practical expression applications—applications that you are more likely to encounter in your day-to-day animation. These include rotational motions, interpolated motions, logic-based motions, cycling motions, expressions using fractal noise, and physics-based expressions.

Rotational Motions

One of the simplest expression-based motions is rotational motion, where an expression drives an object's rotation based on the motion of other objects (or possibly the object itself) in the scene.

Tire Rotations

At the beginning of this chapter, you were introduced to one of the classic uses for expression-based motion, rotating the wheels of a vehicle in response to its motion see Figure A.6). The concept behind this kind of expression is simple: as the wheel moves forward, it needs to rotate so that an equal amount of its outside edge (its circumference) travels along the ground. Hence, if a wheel travels forward .4 meter, .4 meters of its outer edge will have been in contact with the ground. If the outer edge were a total of 1.2 meters around, the wheel would need to rotate 1/3 of a complete rotation, or 120 degrees over the .4 meters.

In general, it is difficult to get a good measure of the circumference of a virtual wheel, it being much easier to measure the wheel's diameter. There is a simple mathematical relationship between the diameter of a wheel and its circumference, the mathematical constant Pi (equal roughly to 3.1415927). Hence, given a wheel with diameter 1.607, its circumference is $1.607 \times 3.1415927 = 5.049$ meters. Thus, every time the wheel moves forward by 5.049 meters, it should rotate one complete revolution, and if you divide the total distance traveled by this number, that should give you exactly how many revolutions (or fractions thereof) need to take place.

Figure A.6   Expression-driven rotation. Notice how the motion blur on the rear wheels indicates that they are rotating, as opposed to the front wheels, which are not.

Exercise A.4   Setting Up Wheel Rotations

This exercise will help familiarize you with the expressions for setting up wheel rotations.

1. Load the scene stone_wagon.lws on the included CD-ROM. Notice the rather primitive vehicle setup.

2. Select the axle01 object and bring up the Graph Editor.

   In this scene, the wagon was originally constructed facing into the X axis. For ease of setup, it was parented to a null and rotated 90 degrees on its heading so it is facing into positive Z. Hence, the wheels need to rotate on their bank to rotate properly.

3. Select the Rotation.B channel and apply the LW_Expression plug-in to the Modifier list.

4. Enter the expression 360.0 × (master_parent.pos(Time).z) in the expression slot, press **Enter**, and click Continue.

5. Play back the animation in the preview window.

   The wheels rotate, but not correctly, because the expression did not yet incorporate the circumference of the wheel.

6. In Modeler, the diameter of the wheel object was measured, and it came out to 1.607 meters. To incorporate this into the expression, change it to read 360.0 × (master_parent.pos(Time).z/ (1.607 ¥ PI)). Play back the animation.

   The wheels rotate the correct number of rotations, but they're rotating backward. To fix this, you will need to make the bank rotation expression negative.

7. Add a "−" sign at the beginning of the expression to make the rotation negative. At this point, your expression should play back correctly.

   In Relativity, the expression might look like

   −360 × Z(master_parent,t)/(1.607 × _pi)

Note

If you attempt to animate the stone wagon along a nonlinear path, the LW_Expression system will not be able to properly apply rotations to the wheels. It does not have a facility for measuring the non-linear path distance traveled by an object. For more complex animations of this nature, it is recommended that you use the LW_Cyclist plug-in, or Relativity, which both have features for measuring path distance traveled.

Relative Rotation

Another variant of the rotational expression is that of relative rotation based on the rotation of another object. This is most often needed for gear rotations, where one gear needs to drive the rotation of another gear, but this can be applied in any situation where the motion of a smaller wheel-like object relates directly to the rotation of a larger one, or vice versa.

The concept behind this form of expression is simple. Given two objects of different size, as one object rotates, another object needs to rotate a fraction (or a multiple) of the rotation of the other object. The classic case is a set of gears. Say, for example, that you have a gear with 14 teeth and a larger one with 28 teeth. It would stand to reason that every time the larger gear rotates once, the smaller gear would need to rotate twice. This relationship can be expressed by a simple formula:

(rotation of smaller gear)=2 × (rotation of larger gear)

But where does the "2" come from? It is derived from the larger gear's tooth count divided by the smaller gear's tooth count ($28/14 = 2$). Hence, if we defined t_0, t_1, r_0, and r_1, as the tooth count of the first gear, the tooth count of the second gear, the rotation of the first gear, and the rotation of the second gear, respectively, the formula can be generalized to

$$r_0 = (t_1/t_0) \times r_1$$

Converting the original example of the 14-tooth and 28-tooth gears into the LW_Expression syntax yields

(28.0/14.0) × BiggerGear.rot(Time).y

In Relativity it yields

(28.0/14.0) × P(BiggerGear,t)

This same formula can be used with wheels of differing diameters that need to rotate together (different sized pulleys, for example). Simply replace the gear tooth counts with the respective diameters. The example scene planetary_gears.lws on the included CD-ROM shows a set of gears (found in many automobile transmissions) known as *planetary gears*. Browse through the various Relativity expressions attached to the gears as Motion Options modifiers to see how they interact.

Interpolated Motions

Interpolation is the process of defining in-between values between a set of known values. Splines are a form of interpolation, using a set of cubic interpolation equations to smoothly connect keyframes or adjoining points in an envelope. In a similar fashion, interpolation expressions can define the behavior of a motion or envelope between key values. They are often the workhorses of expression design, helping to express situations such as "if I rotate my object this way, I want this motion to happen, and if I rotate it that way, I want another motion to happen, with a smooth variance in between those two extremes." Some good applications for interpolation might be

- Muscle flexing, where a muscle needs to relax and contract with the rotation of a joint

- Pistons or springs contracting and expanding with joint rotation

- Tentacles wriggling based on the motion of a null

- Tossing a child object from one parent to another

- Moving double-armed joints, such as the joints on many desk lamps

These represent a mere handful of the kinds of situations that can benefit from interpolation expressions.

Value-Based Interpolated Motions

Figure A.7 illustrates a hypothetical set-up where an animator desires a bank change from 20 to 40 degrees as the X value of some object (this could be the object itself or another object) ranges from 2 to 9. This is a classic case of linear interpolation, where you desire a formula that connects the line between the two endpoints. Notice how the line continues beyond the end points, following the same path (these areas beyond the end points can be defined as over-interpolated areas). The definition for this formula, while a mathematical one, is not very complex. Given endpoints x_0, y_0 and x_1, y_1, and some value x in between x_0 and x_1, the interpolation formula is

$$\text{Value} = (x_1 - x) \times y_0/(x_1 - x_0) + (x - x_0) \times y_1/(x_1 - x_0)$$

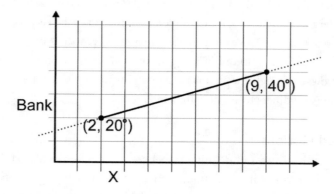

Figure A.7   A hypothetical example of a linear interpolation graph.

Applying this formula to the hypothetical example in Figure A.7, x_0 is 2.0, y_0 is 20.0, x_1 is 9.0, and y_1 is 40.0, giving the formula

$$\text{Value} = (9.0 - x) \times 20.0/(9.0 - 2.0) + (x - 2.0) \times 40.0/(9.0 - 2.0)$$

Converting it into the LW_Expression language, you might have the following:

> A: 7.0 (that is, 9.0 – 2.0)
> B: MyObject.pos(Time).x
> Expression: (9.0–B) × 20.0/A ++ (B–2.0) × 40.0/A

Note

A bug in early versions of LW_Expression caused it to inexplicably choke on the B–2.0 part of the expression. Changing this to B ++ –2.0 does the same thing mathematically but does not cause the first version of the LW_Expression parser to reject it.

This might be a good time to try debugging this expression to truly see if it works as expected. Substituting in 2.0 for the X position and changing A to 7.0, you end up with

$$(9.0 - 2.0) \times 20.0/7.0 + (2.0 - 2.0) \times 40.0/7.0$$

$$= (7.0) \times 20.0/7.0 + 0 \times 40.0/7.0$$

$$= 20.0 + 0$$

$$= 20.0$$

When X equals 9.0, you have:

$$(9.0 - 9.0) \times 20.0/7.0 + (9.0 - 2.0) \times 40.0/7.0$$

$$= 0 \times 20.0/7.0 + 7.0 \times 40.0/7.0$$

$$= 0 + 40.0$$

$$= 40.0$$

When X equals 5.5 (which, incidentally, is the halfway point between the two endpoints), the expression becomes

$$(9.0 - 5.5) \times 20.0/7.0 + (5.5 - 2.0) \times 40.0/7.0$$

$$= (3.5) \times 20.0/7.0 + (3.5) \times 40.0/7.0$$

$$= 0.5 \times 20.0 + 0.5 \times 40.0$$

$$= 10.0 + 20.0$$

$$= 30.0$$

This is the desired behavior. The interpolation function connects the beginning, middle, and endpoints exactly. Given any other point in between, the interpolation will calculate that value as well.

Exercise A.6   Interpolation Expressions in Action

This exercise will familiarize you with interpolation expressions in action.

1. Load the scene mech.lws from the included CD-ROM and drag through the frames.

   Notice how the mech has a simple walk cycle assigned to it, yet the toes remain still whether they're up in the air or on the ground. This is a perfect place to put an interpolation expression.

2. Select the mech_leg01:front_toes01 object and notice its default rotation value (24.10 degrees).

3. Go to frame 6 and rotate the toe object along its bank, noting how far you can rotate it before it comes close to the ground (approximately 45 degrees).

4. Select the foot01_goal object and notice its Y position at frames 0 and 6 (730 millimeters and 1.14 meters, respectively). Note: 730 millimeters = 0.73 meters.

5. Select the mech_leg01:front_toes01 object and bring up its Graph Editor. Select the Rotation.P channel and apply the LW_Expression plug-in to it.

6. Type in the following expression:

   Expression: $(1.14-B) \times 24.1/A + (B +-0.73) \times 45.0/A$

   A: 1.14–0.73

   B: foot01_goal.pos(Time).y

7. Drag the Frame Slider and notice how the toe now bends as it lifts off the ground.

8. Perform Steps 2 through 6 with the rear toe object, substituting rotation values as required.

   The scene mech_blended_toes.lws on the CD-ROM shows an example set-up with the interpolation expressions in place for the mech's left foot.

Time-Based Interpolated Motions

The preceding interpolation expression is an example of a value-based interpolation, where one value varies linearly along with some other value. This is often adequate for defining simple reactive behaviors in your animations. There are cases, however, where a value will need to vary in a non-linear fashion with another value. While there are other possible interpolation formulae (quadratic and cubic interpolation, for instance), one of the best methods of connecting nonlinear values together is by using splines. Implementing splines directly in an expression is well beyond the scope of the current crop of LightWave expressions engines. The solution is actually quite simple: use

LightWave's internal splines by keyframing a number of frames, and then use interpolation to pick time values along the timeline (remember, time is not a constant). The following exercise should help familiarize you with this concept. It is also designed to introduce you to the powerful point-and-click expression design system within Relativity—the Professors.

Exercise A.7   Compressing Pistons

1. Load the scene mech_pistons.lws from the included CD-ROM.

   Notice how the pneumatic pistons are rotating rather wildly during the walk cycle. There is actually a method to this madness.

2. Select the object mechleg01:foreleg01.

3. Bring up its Motion Options panel (**m**), switch the tab to Controllers and Limits, and change the bank controller from Inverse Kinematics to Keyframes.

   The next few steps involve re-keyframing the rotation of the foreleg. Before doing this, it's important to store the rotation of the leg at frame 0 somewhere so that it can be restored when you finish with this exercise.

4. Go to frame 0, press Enter to bring up the Create Motion Key dialog, change the frame value to 24, and press Enter again.

   This will store the keyframe from 0 to frame 24.

5. Back at frame 0, rotate the foreleg to 0 degrees on its bank and keyframe it there. At frame 10, rotate it to its maximum bank rotation (–50 degrees) and keyframe it there. Go into the Graph Editor and make these two bank keyframes linear.

6. Drag the Frame Slider from frames 0 through 10.

   The rotations of the pneumatic tubes are actually keyed correctly now when the leg rotates. When inverse kinematics IK is enabled, the foreleg moves differently and, thus, masks the piston rotations.

7. Reverse all the steps you did in Step 4, re-keyframing the rotation at frame 24 at frame 0, deleting the keyframes at frames 10 and 24, and turning on IK as the controller for the bank of the foreleg object.

8. With the foreleg object still selected and the Motion Options panel still up, change to the IK and Modifiers tab and double-click the line beginning with "Relativity 2.0 Demo…" in the modifiers pane (Relativity has already been applied in this scene).

   This will bring up the Relativity interface. Notice that the After inverse kinematics button is enabled for this object. This instance of Relativity will actually not have any expressions applied to it. It is there simply to capture the post-IK motion of the foreleg object so that it can be passed on to other instances of Relativity that are interested in this motion.

9. Click the Current Item pull-down and select the mechleg01.lwo:upper_pneumo01 object.

10. Next to the B: field (the Bank expression), click the Ask a Professor pull-down menu and select the Dr. Blend Machinist professor.

   Blend Machinist is the professor designed to aid in the creation of interpolation (blending) expressions in Relativity.

11. Enable the Truncated Blend and Blend Time buttons.

   This should enable the beginning and end frame fields. By selecting Blend Time, you are instructing the professor that you want to set up a time-interpolated expression.

12. In the Beginning and Ending Frame fields, enter the values 0 and 10 (these are the frames over which the pneumatic rod has been keyframed).

13. Select B for the value to be tracked for the blend, and from the Pick Object button, select the mechleg01.lwo:foreleg01 object as the object to track.

14. For the Lower and Upper Blend Trigger values, enter 0 and –50, respectively.

   These are the bank angle limits that will control the interpolation.

15. Click OK.

   You should now see the following expressions in your interface:

   Variables panel (click the Variables button to see this panel)
   A: TBLEND(0.000000,0,0.333333–50,B(mechleg01.lwo:foreleg01,t))

   Main panel:
   B: B(SELF,#a)

   The expression in "A:" creates a blend (or interpolation) between the values 0 and 0.3333 (equivalent to 10 frames or 1/3 of a second) when the bank value of the foreleg object ranges from 0 to –50. This value, in turn, goes into the Bank expression, causing it to query the keyframed bank angle of the piston between frames 0 and 10.

> **Note**
>
> Be sure the Rot in Deg button is enabled for this expression, to allow all rotation values to be indicated in degrees rather than radians.

16. Click the Copy button to copy the expressions to the buffer.

17. Change the Current Item to mechleg01.lwo:lower_pneumo01, and click the Paste button to paste the expression from the buffer.

Because this expression contains SELF in it, it will automatically import the bank motion of the lower_pneumo01 object to which it now belongs.

18. Change the current item to mechleg02.lwo:upper_pneumo02 and paste the expression. Then click the Search/Replace button and use it to search for 01 and replace it with 02. Double-check the Variables panel to ensure that the expression has indeed changed.

19. Copy this new expression to the buffer and paste it into the expressions for mechleg02.lwo:lower_pneumo02.

20. Exit Relativity and play the animation.

Both pneumatic piston pairs should now react properly to the motions of their respective legs (see Figure A.8).

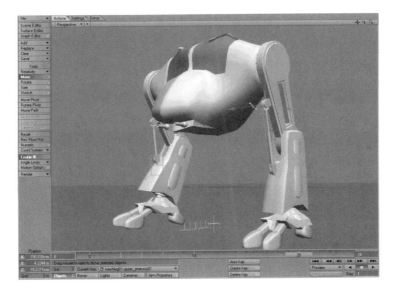

Figure A.8   Interpolation expressions have effectively automated the toes and pistons of this mech as it walks.

Logic-Based Expressions

Perhaps one of the most powerful features of expression-based animations is the ability to give them a rudimentary capability to "think". The previous expressions examples are applied blindly over space and time without regard to the circumstances under which they're used. For instance, a linearly interpolated motion can over-interpolate, continuing to follow the formula beyond the endpoints of its defined range of behavior. Given a set of criteria, you might want your expression to decide between several possible outcomes. This is the essence of logic—reasoning to a conclusion. Indeed, the TBLEND() function used in the previous exercise is a simple form of logic—it will interpolate the values only as long as they're between the expected endpoints.

When designing logical expressions, it is often easiest to place sub-expressions that represent behavior choices in scratch variable slots. Unfortunately, because the LW_Expression has such a limited number of scratch variables, building a readable logical expression of more than two or three choices becomes difficult at best. Relativity, with its 18 scratch variables, can theoretically enable you to select between two full sets of position, rotation, and scale behaviors; or three full sets of position and rotation behaviors.

In the LW_Expression syntax, the operator for performing a logical choice is similar to the conditional statement in the C programming language. It has the basic form:

(value1 (<)(=)(>) value2 ? true result : false result)

It compares two values using the greater than ('>'), less than ('<') or equals ('=') symbols and then returns one of two answers. If the condition is true, it takes on the value of the true result; if false, it returns the false result. Here are some examples of the conditional in action:

- (3.4 < 4.5 ? 2.0 : Light.rot(Time).z) returns 2.0
- (3.4 > 4.5 ? 2.0 : Light.rot(Time).z) returns the light rotation
- (Null.pos(Time).x < 4.0 ? 3 × sin(Time) : 2.5) returns 3 × sin(Time) if the null's x value is less than 4.0; returns 2.5 otherwise

In Relativity, the primary logical function (although there are several) is the COND() function. It has a similar structure to the previous conditional:

COND(value1 (<)(=)(>) value2, true result, false result)

Converting the above logical expressions to the Relativity syntax, you have

- COND(3.4 < 4.5, 2.0, B(light,t))
- COND(3.4 > 4.5, 2.0, B(Light,t))
- COND(X(null,t) < 4.0, 3 × sin(t), 2.5)

Examining the two syntaxes side-by-side illustrates an important point—namely, expressions are often interchangeable between different engines with a minor amount of rewriting. Their underlying principles remain the same, even though the punctuation and syntactical grammar might differ.

Exercise A.8   Creating a Logical Expression

In Exercise A.6, you created an interpolation motion for the toes of the mech object. If you closely examine the resulting motion, it might seem that the toes don't seem to open deliberately enough as the foot descends. It's almost as if the presence of the ground is pushing the front toes up. Perhaps a bit of logic can be used to alter the descent motion without changing the behavior of the foot as it ascends.

1. Load the scene mech_blended_toes.lws from the included CD-ROM and play the animation for a moment, noting the toe motion with respect to the ground.

2. Select the mechleg01:front_toes01 object and bring up its Graph Editor. Select the Modifiers tab and bring up the interface for the expression on the Rotation.B channel.

   This should resemble the interpolation expression you created in Exercise A.6.

   Due to the nature of logical expressions, it is often a good idea to design them in several intermediate steps, so you can carefully examine the results to be sure they are behaving as expected.

3. Clear out the fields and enter the following expressions:

   A: foot01_goal.pos(Time).y

   B: (foot01_goal.pos(Time+(1/Scene.fps)).y–A)/(1/Scene.fps)

   Expression: $(B < 0.0 ? 10.0 : 20.0)$

   The "A:" sub-expression is the Y position of the foot01_goal at the present time. The "B:" sub-expression is a velocity expression (velocity will be covered in depth in a later section of this chapter) that should be positive $(B > 0.0)$ if the foot is ascending, and negative $(B < 0.0)$ if the foot is descending. The expression itself selects between these two cases and returns a value.

4. Drag the frame slider and notice how the bank angle changes from 20.0 as the foot ascends to 10.0 as the foot descends.

5. Type the following expression in the C slot:

   $$(1.14 - A) \times 24.1/(1.14 + -0.73) + (A + -0.73) \times 45.0/(1.14 + -0.73)$$

   This is a simple interpolation expression between the angles 24.1 and 45.0 as A varies between 0.73 and 1.14.

   To achieve a faster opening motion as the foot descends, you can set up an interpolation expression that reaches its endpoint sooner—say, perhaps, at 0.85.

6. Type the following in the D slot:

   $$(1.14 - A) \times 24.1/(1.14 + -0.85) + (A + -0.85) \times 45.0/(1.14 + -0.85)$$

7. Change the main expression to:

   $(B < 0.0 ? C : D)$

8. Drag the frame slider.

The bank angle of the toe object should open more rapidly as the foot descends. But there is a problem—as the foot hits the ground, the bank angle decreases to 15.45 degrees, causing the toe to stick up. This is a classic case of over-interpolation. The rest elevation of the null is at Y=0.73, yet the expression ends at 0.85. From 0.85 down to 0.73, the expression keeps rotating the toe farther than the specified ending angle.

To fix this, you will need to add some logic to the descent interpolation expression.

9. Change the descent interpolation expression from:

$$(1.14 - A) \times 24.1/(1.14 + -0.85) + (A + -0.85) \times 45.0/(1.14 + -0.85)$$

to:

$$(A > 0.85 \, ? \, (1.14 - A) \times 24.1/(1.14 + -0.85) + (A + -0.85) \times 45.0/(1.14 + -0.85) : 24.1)$$

You just added some logic that states "if A [that is, the Y position of the null] is greater than 0.85, use the interpolation expression. Otherwise, hard-code the angle to 24.1 degrees."

10. Play the animation and observe the improved motion for the front toes.

The scene mech_logic.lws on the included CD-ROM shows the scene with logical expressions added to the front and rear toe objects of the mech's left foot.

Cycling Motions

Aside from rotation and interpolation expressions, one of the most universal applications for expression design is the cycling motion, be it a walk cycle or some other motion that needs to repeat with varying frequency. The basic premise is that an object, or set of objects, needs to repeat its/their motion every time a certain event happens. This event can be the passing of a certain amount of time (which can be handled well by using LightWave's internal Repeat End Behavior), or by some sort of motion, such as traveling enough distance for a walk cycle to repeat (see Figure A.9).

Cycling motions are beyond the scope of what can be reasonably done using the LW_Expression plug-in because it has no method for measuring path length traveled by an object moving non-linearly. Instead, this role is usually given to the LW_Cyclist plug-in. Although it could be described as a "canned" expression, it is not very flexible when compared with a full-fledged expression system.

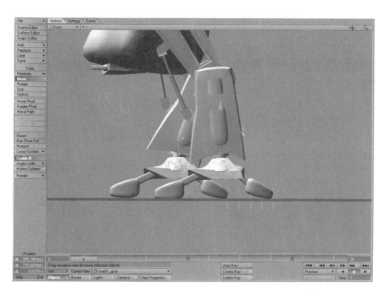

Figure A.9   Set-up for a walk cycle. Notice the placement nulls at the rear toe of the mech.

Creating an Expression Walk Cycle

Before performing the next exercise, load the tutorial scene mech_cycle.lws from the included CD-ROM to see an example of a walk cycle prepared for cyclic animation.

First, notice how everything (including the IK goals) is parented to a master null called mech_master and the cycle is performed "walking in place". This allows the entire mech animation to be encapsulated within the space of the master null. After the expression is set up, the master null will then be animated to replay the cycle automatically.

Second, notice how the beginning and endpoints of the animation (frames 0 and 24) are keyframed to look identical. This is important to achieve a proper match between the beginning and end of the cycle. If they were different, the cycle would appear to "skip" as it reached the end and wrapped back around to the beginning. As a side note, the animation was set up using a multiple of 6 frames—this is a little secret used by some character animators, making it easier to define midway points through the stride.

Third, notice how a set of marker nulls is placed along the ground where the feet land and slide backward. Expressions were used to place these nulls at one-quarter, one-half, and three-quarter points between the front and back null. This gives you markers to ensure that the feet maintain an even velocity across the ground. Without using markers during the keyframing process, it would be harder to ensure that the feet move at an even velocity across the ground. Another possible method of maintaining proper foot-ground contact would involve detaching a copy of the foot object and keyframing it from the front to the rear position during the cycle. The detached foot can serve as a reference, enabling you to properly align the motion of the parented foot.

Exercise A.9 Creating a Basic Walk Cycle

In this exercise, you will create a cycling expression that will allow the walk cycle to replay automatically with the mech's motion.

1. Load the scene mech_cycle.lws from the included CD-ROM.

    A number of instances of Relativity were already applied to objects in the scene, but their expressions are blank.

> **Tip**
>
> Use the REL:Global_Motion_Access generic plug-in to quickly navigate between all the motion expressions applied in the scene.

2. Select the object rear_mark and notice its X position.

    This is a measure of how far one foot travels backward when it's resting on the ground. Write it down somewhere, as this value will be useful for setting up the expression.

3. From the REL:Global_Motion_Access generic plug-in, move down until you get to the foot01_goal" object. Select Dr. Cycler from the Ask a Professor menu next to the X slot.

4. In the Dr. Cycler's panel, enter the following values:

    Motion channel to cycle on: X

    Object to pull the cycle from: SELF

    First frame/last frame of cycle: 0 and 24, respectively

    Object's motion to drive the cycle: mech_master

    Function of driving object to be used: Oriented distance

    Optional stride length: multiply the X value of rear_mark by 2 and enter that value into this slot. You should have entered 2.4588.

5. Leave all other fields at their default values and click OK.

    This should have created the following expression:

    XCYCLE(SELF,(ODIST(mech_master,t))/ 2.4588,0.000000,0.800000)

6. Next to the Y slot, open the Dr. Cycler panel, change the Motion Channel selector at the top to Y, and click OK.

This should set up a Y cycle identical to the previous X cycle.

7. Repeat Step 6, setting up expressions for the Z, H, P, and B slots.

8. Click OK to return to the main Layout window. Keyframe the mech_master null so that is has motion in the X direction to see the result of the cycle.

   Although the goal moves, the foot does not rotate properly. It needs to have the cycle applied to it as well.

9. Open the REL:Global_Motion_Access generic plug-in and re-select the foot01_goal object. Copy its expressions and paste them into the mechleg01.lwo:foot01 object. Play back the animation.

   It's getting a little closer to what it needs to be. The cycle still looks incorrect with the body not moving in-sync.

   To complete the cycle setup, you will need to apply the same cycling expressions to the mech's body, the goal for the second foot, and the second foot itself.

10. Copy the expressions from the foot01_goal object to the mech's body, the goal for the second foot, and the second foot object. Play back the animation.

    Now the mech should appear to walk properly and automatically as the master null moves.

    Notice how you applied the same expression to all the various moving parts on the mech, regardless of whether an individual part only needed to cycle on a few motion channels.

11. Examine which motion channels are needed for each object by watching what values actually change during the walk cycle (for example, the IK goals don't need to cycle on their rotations) and clear the expressions slots not needed for a particular object.

    This can optimize your scene, allowing it to play back slightly faster.

Step 11 involved a process known as *optimizing* your expressions. By looking for unnecessary expressions and eliminating them, you create a sleeker system. To further optimize this particular expression system, notice how they all have a common function, ODIST(mech_master,t). This particular function measures the path length that the mech_master traveled up to the current frame, and can take a small amount of time to compute.

Each separate instance of Relativity has to recompute this value for each frame, making a total of five separate times that the same value is calculated. This is a waste of valuable CPU cycles and slows down the interactivity of the expression. Instead, you could take that sub-expression and apply that to the X channel of a null and have all the other expressions reference that value. The expression on the null would only calculate its value once per frame and then pass that on to the other expressions needing it. The scene mech_final.lws on the included CD-ROM shows this optimization in action.

Adding Noise to Expressions

One criticism of expression-based animation, especially cycle-based animation, is that it often has a mechanical quality to it because the expression repeats itself exactly every time. Fortunately, for a mech, having a mechanical feel to the animation is not necessarily a bad thing. For more organic characters, this mechanical quality can be unwanted. You can employ several methods to give your expression a more organic feel. One method is to vary the velocity along the keyframed path by adding extra keyframes and adjusting the Tension, Continuity, and Bias values at strategic points in the animation. This would cause the character to step just a little faster or slower, depending on its overall speed. Another method is to add a little fractal noise to the expressions to prevent the cycle from repeating itself exactly every time.

Relativity supports a special function, NOISE( ), that enables you to convert any continuous value into a fractal pattern. Figure A.10 shows a null object whose Y value is being modified by the expression

NOISE(X(null,t))

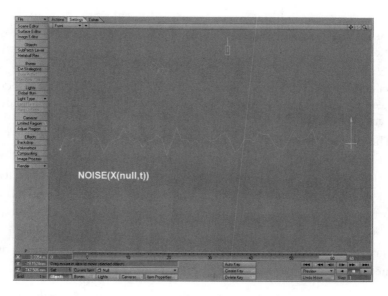

Figure A.10   Using fractal noise to vary the motion path of an object.

Fractal noise has a very important quality for use in expression design—namely, that two input values close together will have similar output noise values, but two input values further apart will have less similar output values. This can be used to make the fractal variance more or less smooth as needed. By taking the input argument of the

NOISE( ) function and scaling it down, the fractal noise will become smoother. By scaling it up, it will become rougher. Figure A.11 illustrates the effect of multiplying the X(null,t) function by 0.2 and 2, respectively.

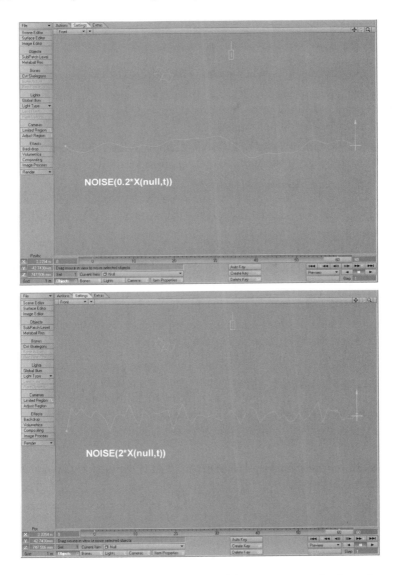

Figure A.11   The effect of multiplying the input of the NOISE expression by various values.

Fractal noise can be put to great use in animations, from adding a little camera shake to create a more hand-held feel to the camera's motion, to shaking things around in a virtual earthquake. In this case, you are going to use it to vary the height of each step in the walk cycle, thus giving it a more organic quality.

Exercise A.10   Using Noise to Create Organic Motion

In thisexercise, you will use fractal noise to add a subtle uncertainty to the height of each step taken by the mech.

1. Load the scene mech_noiz.lws from the included CD-ROM.

   The mech has a standard walk cycle expression applied to various parts so that as the mech_master null is moved, the mech appears to walk. Notice also how the cycles repeat rather monotonously.

2. Invoke the Generic plug-in REL:Global_Motion_Access and select the foot01_goal object. It should have cycle expressions on its X and Y motion channels.

3. Using cut and paste, copy the text from the Y field into the A slot on the Variables panel (accessed by clicking the Variables button on the main Relativity panel).

4. Using the Y values for the foot01_goal from Exercise A.6 (0.73 and 1.14), set up a blend expression in the B variable slot that blends from 0 to 1 as the goal moves from its minimum to its maximum elevation:

   TBLEND(0,0.73,1,1.14,#a)

5. In the C variable slot, create an expression that multiplies the value in the B variable slot by a noise function. A suggested expression is

   abs(0.6×#b × NOISE(0.3×X(distobj,t)))

   This expression takes the distance traveled by the distobj null and converts that into a noise value. It then multiplies it by 0.6 times the value of the blend in the B variable slot and converts it into positive numbers (the abs() function converts negative numbers into positive numbers and leaves positive numbers unchanged).

6. In the Y motion channel slot, clear the YCYCLE() expression and replace it with the expression *#a–#c.*

   This should subtract the noise value in the C variable slot from the actual cycle value in the A variable slot.

7. Play back the animation and notice how the left foot now makes subtly different steps with each cycle, compared to the mechanical steps taken by the right foot (see Figure A.12).

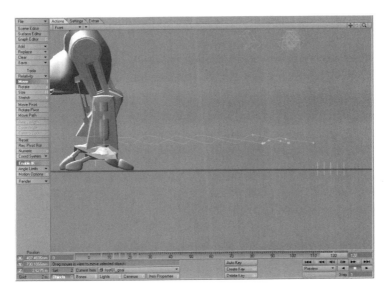

Figure A.12   Applying noise to break up the monotony of a cycle. Notice how one cycle repeats evenly every time, while the other cycle has some randomness to it.

More Advanced Mathematical Expressions

The previous expressions examples were not very math-heavy, involving rather simple relationships and the formulas that defined them. Perhaps the most mathematically intense expression covered to this point was the interpolation function. This next section will dive into some slightly more intense mathematics. It might make for some dry reading, but the nuggets contained therein will be worth the effort.

Relativity was used to do most of these expressions, as the simpler language (and greater number of variable slots) makes it easier to break down the expressions into digestible portions. The LWExpression syntax, although capable of doing much the same math, in many cases more tersely, suffers in readability from that very terseness. Where applicable, alternative example scenes using the LW_Expression syntax are provided for further inspection.

Vectors

During the previous discussion of the LW_Expression syntax, you were introduced to the concept of a vector. For expression programming purposes, a vector is nothing more than a collection of three independent double (floating-point) numbers, known as components. The classical definition of a vector, on the other hand, is a set of three components that define a direction in space. It does not have a specific starting or end point, only a direction where it points. Some examples of vectors might be the points on a compass, such as north, south, east, and west. It doesn't matter where you are on a map, north always points in the same direction. 3D coordinates can also be considered a vector. They indicate which direction they are from the origin and how far away they are located. One standard mathematical convention for writing vectors is a set of three numbers enclosed by triangular brackets:

<x, y, z>

Another is in the form of a matrix column vector:

[x]

[y]

[z]

When illustrating vectors graphically, they are most commonly represented by an arrow pointing in the vector's direction (see Figure A.13). The point of the vector is known as the head, and the other end as the tail.

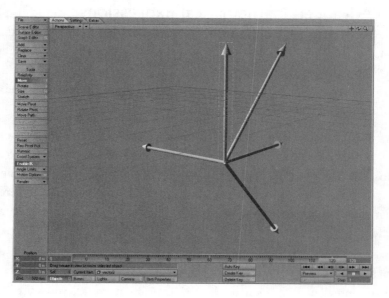

Figure A.13   Graphical representation of vectors.

In contrast to a vector, a scalar is a single numeric value. Things such as weight, speed, and mass, are all examples of scalar values, as well as single arbitrary numbers such as 4.3565, or Pi.

Every item in LightWave has a set of three vectors—the forward, right, and up vectors, which encapsulate all the 3D rotations and scaling applied to that object. For items such as the camera and light, their forward vectors can be an easy way to determine exactly where the camera or light is pointing.

Vector Math

This next section is designed to familiarize you with some basic vector concepts: addition and subtraction of vectors, and multiplication of vectors by scalars.

To add two vectors together, simply add the individual components of the vectors to each other, the first component of the first vector to the first component of the second vector, and so on. Mathematically, you would represent it as follows:

$$<x_1, y_1, z_1> + <x_2, y_2, z_2> = <x_1 + x_2, y_1 + y_2, z_1 + z_2>$$

For example, say you wanted to add the vectors $<1,-3,5>$ with $<2,4,6>$. The result would be:

$<1,-3,5> + <2,4,6>$

$=<1 + 2, -3 + 4, 5 + 6>$

$=<3,1,11>$.

Graphically, you can represent vector addition by taking the second vector, aligning its tail with the head of the first vector, and then drawing the addition vector from the tail of the first vector to the head of the second vector, as illustrated in Figure A.14.

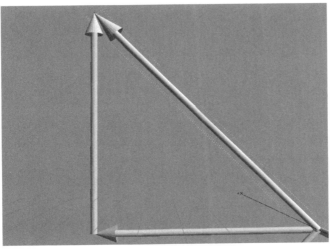

Figure A.14   Addition of two vectors. The selected vector object represents the addition of the horizontal vector with the vertical vector.

To subtract one vector from another, subtract the components of the second vector from the first:

$$\langle x_1, y_1, z_1 \rangle - \langle x_2, y_2, z_2 \rangle = \langle x_1 - x_2, y_1 - y_2, z_1 - z_2 \rangle$$

Hailing back to the previous example, if you subtracted the second vector from the first, the result would be

$$\langle 1, -3, 5 \rangle - \langle 2, 4, 6 \rangle$$
$$= \langle 1 - 2, -3 - 4, 5 - 6 \rangle$$
$$= \langle -1, -7, -1 \rangle.$$

Graphically, vector subtraction can be represented by aligning the heads of both vectors with each other and then drawing the subtraction vector from the tail of the first vector to the tail of the second (see Figure A.15).

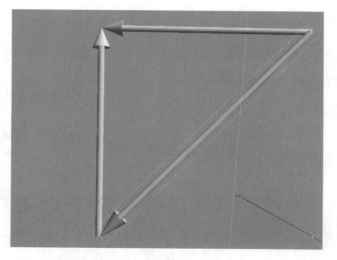

Figure A.15   Subtraction of two vectors. The selected vector object represents the subtraction of the vertical vector from the horizontal vector.

When you multiply the three components of a vector each by a single number (that is, a scalar number), you perform the process of scaling a vector, which behaves exactly the same as if you evenly scaled a 3D model of a vector object (see Figure A.16). The tip points in the same direction, but the overall length of the vector is changed. For example, if you multiplied the vector $\langle 1, 1, 1 \rangle$ by 0.5, the resultant vector would be $\langle 0.5, 0.5, 0.5 \rangle$. It still points in the same direction, but has a shorter length.

Note
You could just as easily scale a vector up and make it longer.

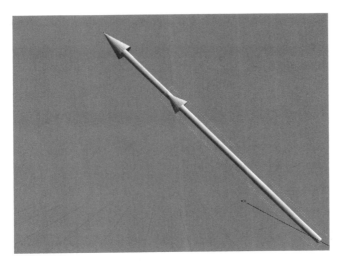

Figure A.16   The effect of scaling a vector. The selected vector object represents the longer vector scaled down by a value.

Measuring Vector Length and Normalizing Vectors

In the previous section the length of a vector was mentioned several times, which leads to the question, "How do you measure the length of a vector?" Perhaps you recall in your distant past discussing a concept known as *Pythagorean Theorem*. For those who don't remember, it states that, "The square of the length of the hypotenuse of a right triangle is equal to the sum of the squares of the other two sides." It can also be restated as "The length of the hypotenuse of a right triangle is equal to the square root of the sum of the squares of the other two sides." So, given a right triangle with its horizontal side of length x and its vertical side of length y (this happens to define a vector lying in the X-Y plane <x,y,0>), the length of the vector can be written as

$$\sqrt{(x \times x + y \times y)}$$

Note that "$\sqrt{}$" is the square root symbol. This same formula can easily be extended to a 3D vector <x,y,z>:

$$\sqrt{(x \times x + y \times y + z \times z)}$$

For example, say you wanted to find how far the point <2,3,9> was from the origin. The length would be

$$\sqrt{(2 \times 2 + 3 \times 3 + 9 \times 9)}$$
$$= \sqrt{(4 + 9 + 81)}$$
$$= \sqrt{(94)}$$
$$= 9.695$$

In the LW_Expression syntax, the vmag() method will calculate the length of a vector object.

Often, a vector of length 1 (or a unit length vector) is needed for various formulas. The process of scaling a vector into a unit length vector is called *normalization.* To normalize a vector, you will need to divide each of the vector's components by the vector's length. Taking the previous example vector <2,3,9> whose length was already determined to be 9.695:

<2/9.695, 3/9.695, 9/9.695>

= <0.206, 0.3094, 0.9283>

If you calculate the length of the vector that was just normalized, it would come to 0.99995, which is pretty close to 1. The LW_Expression method normalize() can be used to automatically normalize a vector. The next section will show some practical applications of vector normalization in expression design.

Dot Product

In 3D animation, one of the most used vector formulas is known as the dot product. Every pixel of your LightWave renders uses the dot product at least once to determine the illumination of lights on a piece of geometry. The dot product of two vectors is defined as

$$<x_1, y_1, z_1> \text{ dot } <x_2, y_2, z_2> = (x_1 \times x_2) + (y_1 \times y_2) + (z_1 \times z_2)$$

For example, the dot product of the vectors <1,–3,5> and <2,4,6> is

<1,–3,5> dot <2,4,6>

$= 1 \times 2 + -3 \times 4 + 5 \times 6$

$= 2 + -12 + 30$

$= 20$

In the LW_Expression syntax, there is a dot3d() method that will automatically calculate the dot product of two vector objects.

Notice that the result of the dot product is not a vector, but rather, a single number (that is, a scalar). At first glance, there doesn't seem to be anything terribly useful about getting the number 20 out of two vectors. It's when a certain well-known mathematical theorem is invoked that the dot product gains usefulness. This theorem states that the dot product is equal to the length of the first vector, times the length of the second vector, times the cosine of the angle between them. In mathematical notation, where the vertical bars "||" represent vector length (or magnitude), and "<A>" is used to represent a vector. This theorem can be written

$$<A> \text{ dot } <B> = |<A>| \times |<B>| \times \cos(angle)$$

Thus, you can take the dot product of two vectors, divide that by the length of the first vector, divide that by the length of the second vector, and you will end up with the cosine of the angle between them. If the vectors are prenormalized, their lengths are equal to 1, and thus the dot product itself is the cosine of their angle. If you then took the inverse cosine (or arccosine) of the dot product, you would get the actual angle between the two vectors. The example scene vectors.lws on the included CD-ROM shows a number of vector functions (addition, subtraction, scaling, normalization, dot, and cross products) in action. Take a look at the various nulls in the scene to see the expressions in action.

The next exercise will show an application of the dot product (and its ability to calculate the angle between vectors) in expression design.

Exercise A.11   Expression-Driven Lens Flares

This exercise originated from a discussion regarding the design of expressions that could react to lights in a scene. Specifically, given a number of characters with lighted helmets or flashlights going down a dark cave. As the lights shone into the camera, it would be interesting to have their lens flares automatically ramp up. Another interesting light effect might be to have a character's pupils automatically dilate as a light is shone on them. All these are within the realm of possibility using expressions.

1. Load the scene flashlight.lws on the included CD-ROM and render a few frames.

   The lens flare value is constant. As an animator, you could always manually envelope the lens flare to get the effect you desire, but if the flashlight motion had to change, you would then need to re-envelope it. If you had several such lights in the scene, revisions would become a very time-consuming affair indeed.

2. Select the light named Light and open its Graph Editor. Select the Light.Flareintensity channel, click the Modifiers tab, and then double-click the Rel_Channeler line to bring up its interface.

3. Bring up the Variables panel.

   Here you are going to design the bulk of the expression. In the A, B, and C slots, you will construct a vector pointing from the light's position to the camera's position.

4. Enter the following values into the A, B, and C slots:

   A: XW(camera,t)–XW(light,t) //vector pointing from the light to the camera

   B: YW(camera,t)–YW(light,t)

   C: ZW(camera,t)–ZW(light,t)

In the D through F slots, you will grab the forward vector of the light.

5. Enter the following values in the D through F slots:

   D: FORX(light,t) //forward vector of light

   E: FORY(light,t)

   F: FORZ(light,t)

In slots G and H, you will set up expressions to calculate the magnitudes of the vectors in ABC and DEF.

6. Enter the following values in the G and H slots:

   G: sqrt((#a × #a)+(#b × #b)+(#c × #c)) //magnitude of vector in ABC

   H: sqrt((#d × #d)+(#e × #e)+(#f × #f)) //magnitude of vector DEF

In slots I, J, and K, you will set up expressions to normalize the vector in ABC.

7. Enter the following values in the I, J, and K slots:

   I: #a/#g   //normalized vector ABC

   J: #b/#g

   K: #c/#g

In slots L, M and N, you will normalize vector DEF.

8. Enter the following values in the L, M, and N slots:

   L: #d/#h //normalized vector DEF

   M: #e/#h

   N: #f/#h

9. In the O slot, take the dot product of vectors IJK and LMN by entering the following:

   O: (#i × #l) + (#j × #m) + (#k × #n) //dot product

10. In slot P, take the arccosine of the dot product in O and convert it from radians to degrees by entering the following:

   P: 360 × (acos(#o))/(2 × _pi) //angle between the two vectors

Note

The dot product will be positive if the light and light-camera vectors roughly face in the same direction. If they were more than 90 degrees apart, the dot product would be negative. This would correspond to the flashlight facing away from the camera, in which case you would not want the lens flare to shine at all, hence all angles greater than 90 degrees are useless for this expression.

11. Use a logical expression in the Q slot to limit the angle between 0 and 90 degrees:

> Q: COND(#o>0,#p,90) //only use positive dot-prod values...

12. In slot R, set up a blend from 1 to 0 depending on whether the angle is 0 (the light is facing directly into the camera) or 90 (the light is facing away from the camera):

> R: TBLEND(1,0,0,90,#q)

With all the calculations in place in the variables slots, it's time to generate the actual expression. You could just put "#r" in the main expression slot, but that would end up looking unnatural. If you ever tried shining a flashlight at your face, you would notice that as your eye went from the outer edges of the light cone to the center, there was a sudden jump in intensity as the center of the beam shone at you.

13. Enter the following expression to make the lens flare gradually ramp up with a sudden jump as the camera falls within the light cone of the spotlight:

> X:((1.0 × #r)+(0.20 × IF(#q<(360 × LIGHTCON(light,t)/(2 × _pi)))))

The "IF(#q..." part of the expression will become 1 when the value of q is less than the light cone angle converted to degrees. Otherwise, it will be zero and thus eliminate the extra jump of 20% of the lens flare intensity envelope.

The example scenes flashlight_rel.lws and flashlight_native.lws on the included CD-ROM show completed scenes with the lens flare ramping expression applied in both Relativity and the LW_Expression plug-in (see Figure A.17).

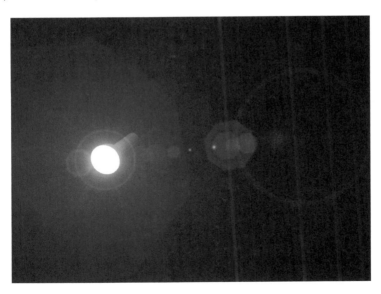

Figure A.17 A lens flare being automatically ramped as the light shines toward the camera.

Physics-Based Expressions

As was stated at the beginning of this chapter, it is generally beyond the scope of the present crop of expressions engines to do an even moderately complex physics-based simulation. For instance, a seemingly simple simulation where a ball needs to roll down a hill-shaped path realistically with gravity would be difficult to achieve with either LW_Expression or Relativity. However, This does not mean that you cannot add physics-based behavior to your expressions. The following section will show you how to use some simple physics to spice up your animations.

Velocity

One of the simplest physical concepts is velocity—the rate of change of position over time. If an object does not change position over a period of time, it has no velocity for that time period—it is at rest. Given two positions in time for an object—say, $<P_0>$ and $<P_1>$ (notice that these are expressed as vectors) at times t_0 and t_1—the velocity can be written as

$$<V> = (<P_1> - <P_0>)/(t_1 - t_0)$$

Or, alternatively as

$$\text{Velocity} = \text{distance traveled/time}$$

For example, say an object is at position $<1,2,3>$ at 0.1 second and position $<4,6,0>$ at 0.2 second. The object's velocity can be calculated as

X velocity = $(4 - 1)$meters/$(0.2 - 0.1)$seconds =

3 meters/0.1 second = 30 meters/second.

Y velocity = $(6 - 2)$meters/$(0.2 - 0.1)$seconds =

4 meters/0.1 second = 40 meters/second

Z velocity = $(0 - 3)$meters/$(0.2 - 0.1)$seconds =

−3 meters/0.1 second = −30 meters/second

Notice that the velocity in each direction had to be calculated separately. Velocity is a vector quantity and can also be negative in one or more directions. Speed, on the other hand, is a scalar quantity that is equal to the length (or magnitude) of the velocity and can never be negative. The speed of the object in the previous example would be

$\sqrt{(30 \times 30 + 40 \times 40 + -30 \times -30)}$

$= \sqrt{(900 + 1600 + 900)}$

$= \sqrt{(3400)}$

$= 58.3$ meters/second

With a simple definition of velocity under your belt, another question might arise—
"Given an object's position and a predefined velocity, is it possible to predict where that
object will be at a later time?" The equation for velocity can be rearranged as

$$\text{Distance traveled} = \text{velocity} \times \text{time}$$

Alternatively, by rearranging the first velocity equation (with $<P_0>$ and $<P_1>$ in it), you
can determine what the second point will be, given the first point, the velocity, and the
time elapsed

$$<P_1> = <P_0> + <V> \times t$$

Notice how this is essentially adding one vector ($<P_0>$) with the velocity vector ($<V>$)
scaled by the time value (time is a scalar).

For example, using the velocity value from a previous example ($<30,40,-30>$ meters/sec-
ond), a starting point of $<0,0,0>$, and an elapsed time of 2.5 seconds, your object will be
at position:

$$X = 0 + (30 \text{ meters/second} \times 2.5 \text{ seconds}) = 75 \text{ meters}$$

$$Y = 0 + (40 \text{ meters/second} \times 2.5 \text{ seconds}) = 100 \text{ meters}$$

$$Z = 0 + (-30 \text{ meters/second} \times 2.5 \text{ seconds}) = -75 \text{ meters}$$

Say you wanted to convert this into an expression. The following would work in
Relativity:

Variables panel:

A: 30 //x velocity

B: 40 //y velocity

C: –30 //z velocity

Main panel:

X: X(SELF,0) + #a × t

Y: Y(SELF,0) + #b × t

Z: Z(SELF,0) + #c × t

In LW_Expression, you would need to apply three separate instances, one to each channel. The expressions would take the form

D: 30

Expression: Value + D × Time

Exercise A.12   Velocity-Based Thrusters

In this exercise, rather than creating a dull scene of an object moving with a simple velocity expression, it hearkens instead back to one of the "original" uses of LightWave—space ships. This exercise will use a ship's speed to automatically ramp thruster lensflares and adjust the scale of a pair of hypervoxel point cloud thrusters.

Figure A.18   A shuttle's hypervoxel/lens-flare thrust being controlled by expressions.

1. Load the scene thrust_shuttle.lws from the included CD-ROM, and render a few frames.

   Notice how the (rather hastily built) shuttle has a pair of lensflares and a set of point clouds (that feed the hypervoxels filter) attached to its rear to provide nifty thrust effects.

   You want to set up an expression based on the shuttle's speed, but before doing that, you need to get an idea of how fast the shuttle is moving. This is why there is a null named speednull in your scene. It is there for writing test expressions and watching their values.

2. Select the generic plug-in Rel:Global_Motion_Access, and select the speednull object.

3. In the X slot of the speednull's interface, type the following expression:

   X: SPEED(master,t+0.2)

4. Click OK. Select the speednull object in Layout, and drag the frame slider.

   The X value should vary between 7 and 21 meters/second. The SPEED expression that you typed looks ahead by 1/5 of a second (about 6 frames if you're working at 30fps) into the future. The reason being, you want your thruster element expressions to *anticipate* the motion of the shuttle. That way, as the lens flare ramps up and the thrusters lengthen just prior to the shuttle picking up speed, it will appear they caused the speed increase.

Because the speed of the shuttle will be controlling the scale of the thruster hyper-voxel point clouds, you will probably want the lower limit roughly around 1.

5. Edit the expression for the speednull to

    X: SPEED(master,t+0.2)/7.0

6. Drag the frame slider around again. The X value of the speednull should vary approximately between 1 and 3.

    Now that you've gotten a reasonable test expression, it's time to apply that to the thruster point clouds.

7. From the REL:Global_Motion_Access generic plug-in, select the speednull, click Copy to copy the expression, and then click Paste to paste it into the expressions for one of the thrust objects.

8. Highlight the text in the X slot and cut it to the Windows (or Mac) clipboard (in Windows, press **Ctrl+x**). Copy the clipboard contents to the A variable slot.

9. In the XS motion channel slot, type *#a* to apply the speed expression to the X scale channel.

10. Copy this new expression, and then paste the expressions to the other thrust object.

11. Click OK and play back the animation with one or the other thrust object selected (they are set to 100% dissolved to prevent the points from rendering directly in the scene).

    Notice how they spread out more behind the shuttle just prior to it speeding up.

12. If you think they need to scale up more, edit the expressions to multiply the *#a* by some value. To really bring out the thrusts' scaling, you can multiply #a by itself (that is, #a × #a).

13. Bring up the REL:Global_Motion_Access plug-in again, and copy the expressions from one of the thrust objects. Close the Motion_Access interface, and open the REL:Global_Channl_Access plug-in.

14. Select one of the FlareIntensity channels, and click Paste.

    This will paste the contents of the buffer to the A slot.

15. In the X: expression slot, enter

    X: 0.30 × #a × #a

16. Click OK. Select the light's panel, and go to Lens Flare Options to see the changes to the lens flare intensity value as you drag the frame slider.

17. Copy the expressions from one FlareIntensity channel to the other.

18. Render a few frames (or the entire animation if you so desire) to see the result.

The example scene thrust_shuttle_final.lws on the included CD-ROM shows the completed scene with all Relativity expressions in place. The scene thrust_shuttle_native.lws shows the same scene using the LW_Expression plug-in.

Acceleration and Gravity

Seldom does an object simply travel through space at a constant velocity, especially objects that you might encounter on a day-to-day basis. Our world is governed by the law of gravity—what goes up must come down (often landing on one's foot). What, exactly, is gravity? By its simplest Newtonian definition, gravity is a force that acts upon objects with mass, causing them to accelerate. In our everyday lives, the acceleration caused by Earth's gravity is constant—roughly 9.8 meters/second^2. Were you far enough out into space, the gravity of Earth would be reduced proportionally.

This leads to the next question, "What is acceleration?" Acceleration can be defined as the rate of change of velocity over time. Hence, given velocity $<V_0>$ at time t_0 and velocity $<V_1>$ at time t_1, acceleration can be written as

$$<A> = (<V_1> - <V_0>)/(t_1 - t_0)$$

Notice that acceleration is also written as a vector quantity, and thus has three distinct components, the acceleration in the X, Y, and Z directions.

For example, if an object were not moving at all at time zero and then was moving at −9.8 meters/second in the Y direction one second later, its Y acceleration rate is:

Acceleration in Y = (9.8 m/s − 0 m/s)/(1s − 0s)

= 9.8 m/s/s or 9.8 m/s2

Now, given a constant acceleration rate, how far does an object move? Without going into a lot of mathematical manipulation, the formula for distance traveled under constant acceleration is

Distance = 1/2 × acceleration rate × time × time

or

1/2 × $<A>$ × t2

Assuming that the example object started its free-fall at Y = 10 meters, it will be at

Y = 10 m − 0.5 × 9.8 m/s^2 × 1.0s × 1.0s

= 10 meters − 4.9 meters

= 5.1 meters

For an object moving along a ballistic trajectory (that is, something that's been thrown up into the air somehow), you will need to combine its initial position and its initial velocity equation with the acceleration equation. Say the previous example object is launched into the air traveling 2 meters per second. With no acceleration, its position would be found using

$$Y = 10m + 5m/s \times time$$

With acceleration applied, its position can be found using

$$Y = 10m + 5m/s \times time - 0.5 \times 9.8 \ m/s^2 \times time^2$$

Picking an arbitrary time, at 4 seconds, the object will be at

$$Y = 10m + 5m/s \times 4 - 0.5 \times 9.8m/s^2 \times 4s \times 4s$$

$$= 10 \ m \ + 20 \ m - 78.4 \ m$$

$$= -48.4 \ m$$

The following exercise will show you how to apply acceleration to your expressions.

Exercise A.13   An Acceleration Expression

In this exercise, you will be applying an acceleration expression to a number of objects to simulate an explosion under the influence of gravity (see Figure A.19).

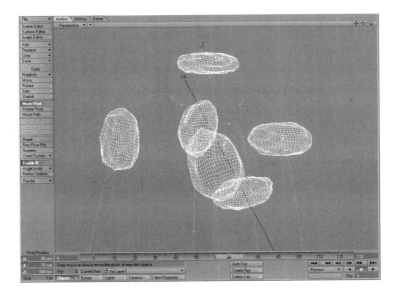

Figure A.19   Using an acceleration expression to simulate a ballistic trajectory under the influence of gravity.

1. Load the scene explode.lws from the included CD-ROM.

   Notice how each rock segment has been given a simple velocity motion expression, using its position relative to the origin to determine its velocity. Strategic placement of pivot points can ensure that none of the debris objects end up accidentally intersecting. These expressions use a single null trigger as a timekeeper. The trigger null, in turn, has an event-based expression on it that triggers when the null named TNT gets close to Y=0.

2. Select the Relativity interface for rox:layer2 and add the following to the end of the Y expression:

   $-0.5 \times \_moon\_grav \times X(trigger,t) \times X(trigger,t)$

   This adds an acceleration component to the expression equivalent to the moon's gravity.

3. Play back the animation and watch the rock fall to the ground.

   Copy and paste this expression to the other rox:layer objects.

   It is left as an exercise for the reader to add logic to prevent the pieces from falling through the floor, and to add randomized rotation.

The Next Step

This chapter has attempted to introduce you to some of the fundamentals of expressions design. This is in no way an exhaustive list. Rather, there are plenty of expressions types, and their applications are beyond the scope of a single chapter (the sample documentation included with the Relativity demo can expose you to more expressions types). Indeed, many applications for expressions have not even been dreamed up. It is up to you, the animator, to find those applications and use them to their fullest. The key thing to remember in expressions design is to look for things that can be automated in your scene—things that would either require painstaking setup to achieve in the first place, or would be difficult to revise after the fact (revisions are often a way of life in the animation world).

As you learn to spot these areas in need of automation, try to avoid the disease of "over-designing", turning expressions into a be-all/catch-all part of your design. Sometimes, rather than setting up a character's nose to twitch when a null moves from one position to another, it might be easier just to directly keyframe the nose twitching. Good design skills will help immensely in deciding when to use expressions. Be prepared to spend volumes of time learning the art behind the magic of expressions, but as you do so, you will become a better animator.

Summary

No doubt you may be experiencing a mild headache trying to absorb all the concepts outlined in this chapter, especially if you tried to take it all in one sitting. It is recommended that you go over concepts in this chapter several times, focusing on ones that did not seem quite clear the first time through. After you've gotten a pretty good handle on those, you might want to try using the online Relativity manuals included with the Relativity demo. They have more expressions examples and tutorials for you to try. Expressions can be a very rewarding aspect to animation, often bringing a new "gee whiz" factor into play as you watch your character ambling nimbly along, or watch your tank menacingly bear down on the enemy with the simple animation of a null object. And don't worry; if the left side of your brain increased in volume by a cubic centimeter or two, your secret will be kept safe.

A p p e n d i x B

LScript

Like most people, you probably have to spend time every week purchasing groceries at your local supermarket. After a short while, however, the entire process becomes routine; in fact, with the exception of your sometimes-varying tastes in cuisine, this activity follows a set pattern. You drive to the store, gather your sustenance, pay for it (most times using the same method of payment), and then drive home using the same route that you took to get there. Now, imagine that the actual process of purchasing those groceries once a week could be automated, that the routine portions could be described in such a way that they could be replayed exactly, with each replay achieving the same result. Encompassing the routine actions of the process in this fashion would leave you free to worry only about the more important goal of the activity: What should you have for lunch for the rest of the week?

This type of instructional—or *procedural*—replay is the basis of programming. Programming can be a complex or simple activity, often directly proportional to the scope of the procedures being described. It is the case, however, with any organized activity—be it programming or grocery shopping—that the inner workings might seem forbidding until you actually take the time to understand the rules and procedures.

This chapter focuses on scripting, which is actually a form of programming that provides a higher level of abstraction. As it relates to computer languages, a higher level of abstraction means that more can be accomplished in fewer lines of code. Scripting with the LightWave 6 LScript system can help the animation programmer (or scriptwriter) to concentrate on the task to be accomplished instead of what tools to use.

This chapter covers the essentials of LScript and how to use the LightWave scripting language in your projects. Specifically, the chapter covers the following topics:

- LScript features
- Creating and executing LScripts
- LScript for LightWave Modeler
- Scripting LightWave Layout
- The LScript Integrated Development Environment

LScript Features

LScript provides access to the underlying programmatic interface to LightWave. This access provides greater control over LightWave's operation than is sometimes possible through its user interface. LScript's programmatic access is similar in nature to that provided by LightWave's plug-in Application Programming Interface (API). Indeed, LScript is a series of plug-ins that function directly atop this API.

However, LScript offers this API-based access without requiring the user to become familiar with the complexities and overhead of the underlying plug-in interface or the traditional tools needed to employ it. For instance, no platform-specific software compiler (an additional software purchase, in most cases) is required to use LScript. Of more importance is the fact that, except in certain limited cases, LScripts are completely platform independent: Scripts developed on any LightWave platform are instantly usable on any other LightWave platform.

LScript provides many features to the LightWave scripter. Here is a partial list of those features, some of which are discussed later in this chapter:

- Familiar, modernized language syntax advanced enough for seasoned software developers, yet simple enough for the programming novice.

- Structured programming controls and constructs for cleaner, easier-to-understand script writing.

- Scripting of eight Layout plug-in architectures: Item Motion, Displacement Mapping, Image Filter, Procedural Texture, Object Replacement, Layout Generic, Layout Master, and Channel Filter.

These are only a small percentage of the features that LScript offers the LightWave user. As you begin to use the LScript software, referencing its documentation and reviewing the work of other LScript writers, you will likely begin to realize the true power of scripting. Scripting can enable you to solve more day-to-day animation problems on your projects, and can be a tremendous aid in streamlining many tedious tasks.

Creating Scripts

When you are ready to create your first LScript, you will need a means of creating text documents. LScripts are nothing more than text files, which are common elements of any computer operating system. All LightWave-supported operating systems provide some type of built-in software for creating and editing text files. For instance, the Microsoft Windows operating systems (Windows 95, Windows 98, Windows NT) provide an application called Notepad that you can use to manage your LScripts. Windows-based word processors such as WordPad and Microsoft Word are also acceptable for use in creating LScripts, as long as you remember to save your files as text-only documents. UNIX operating systems often provide the vi text editor as part of their command set, and more powerful text editors, such EMACS, are freely available. The Macintosh operating system includes a text-editing application called SimpleText that can create and edit your LScripts.

As an alternative to those utilities included with your operating system, you can use the LScript Editor. This software is part of a new suite of utilities introduced in LightWave 6—collectively known as the LScript Integrated Development Environment, or LSIDE, and specifically designed to aid those LightWave users who create and maintain LScripts. The LScript Editor includes features designed to support LightWave LScripts, and is discussed briefly at the end of this chapter.

Saving Scripts

After you have created a script, you will need to save it to disk. It is really up to you where on your disk scripts will reside; LScript doesn't care. However, to make your life easier, you should probably store all your scripts in the same directory (or, within subdirectories of the same directory if you feel the need to organize them further).

A good place for this storage is within the LightWave installation directory. Creating such a directory, perhaps called "NewTek\Lscripts," not only gives you a location to consolidate your scripts, but also keeps them within the LightWave umbrella. Because each LScript architecture will remember, and return to, the location on disk where the last script was selected, centralizing this location will also enhance your workflow.

When naming your scripts, you should use the standard LScript extension for your script files. This extension, .ls, is used by many file requester dialogs within LightWave when you are asked to both locate scripts and add new plug-ins to the system.

Executing Scripts

After you've created your script, LightWave 6 provides two methods to execute it. The first, and more traditional, method requires that you activate the LScript plug-in for the architecture to be used. After the LScript plug-in is enabled, you will need to activate the plug-in's interface by double-clicking on the active plug-in under LightWave 6, or by clicking the Options button next to the active plug-in under previous versions. This causes the enabled LScript plug-in to post a file requester dialog that enables you to locate and select the script to be executed. This method of running a script is the only one available in versions prior to LightWave 6.

New to LightWave 6 is the capability to install and execute LScripts as though they were plug-ins. This capability simplifies the process of using LScripts. When installed, LScripts will appear in plug-in drop-down menus, and can be selected and enabled like other plug-ins in the list. However, before you actually install an LScript in this way, you will first want to ensure that it will execute properly, with no errors in its syntax. While developing and testing your LScript, you will probably want to use the more traditional method of execution until you are satisfied with your script's performance.

To aid in this installation mechanism for LScripts in LightWave 6, you should include at the beginning of your script a pragma directive that identifies the architectural type of the script. A pragma is a message you send to LScript that provides instructions on how it should behave in certain, predefined situations. To identify your script for installation into LightWave 6, you will need to include the @script pragma with the correct architecture type.

```
// identify as an Image Filter LScript
@script image
...
```

The @script pragma accepts one of the following architecture identifiers: modeler, displace, generic, motion, image, replace, master, channel, or shader.

Note

The @script pragma is a new preprocessor addition to LScript v2.0.

Up next is your introduction to the underground realm of LightWave power and control: the basics of scripting with LScript for Modeler.

LScript for LightWave Modeler

All Modeler scripts are required to contain a single user-defined function, identified as main. A user-defined function (hereafter referred to as UDF) is a group of script lines, enclosed in a well-defined and uniquely identified structure, that can be invoked (or called) to have its script code executed. This function name is a marker for the LScript for Modeler scripting plug-in, letting it know the entry point of the script, which is the location where execution of the script should begin. Each such function in your script must be identified with a unique name so that it can be easily distinguished from any other function. However, the required entry-point function in Modeler LScripts must be named main so that LScript can locate it.

Functions have bodies or sections of script code that are enclosed between body markers. In LScript, body markers are identical to those used in C—opening and closing curly braces ({}). All UDFs require these body markers, regardless of how many script commands are embedded between them.

Armed with this basic knowledge, you can now create a template that will be used for your first Modeler LScript:

```
main
{
}
```

Now, if you are interested in doing nothing more than running the LScript Modeler plug-in, you can save this complete (yet useless) LScript to a disk file and execute it.

> **Note**
>
> LScript is case sensitive. This means the case of a character is significant when LScript interprets a script. For instance, had you used all uppercase characters when naming the Modeler LScript entry-point identifier (MAIN instead of main), LScript would not have recognized it.

Variable names and other such identifiers can suffer from this case-sensitivity problem, too. For example, assume you assigned the number 6 to a variable named num. If, on the next script line, you try to display the value of a variable named Num to the user, you will find that what is actually displayed is the value nil instead of the number 6. This occurs because you have inadvertently created a new variable called Num whose value is initially set to nil by LScript (remember that explicit variable declarations are not required in LScript).

Using Explicit Declaration

The combination of LScript's flexibility where variable usage is concerned and its case sensitivity can cause problems with first-time scriptwriters. The Num-versus-num case just presented was a simplified and easy-to-detect instance. More subtle problems—much harder to locate and eradicate—can occur as a result of this type of situation. This is especially true as your scripts become larger, and the usage of a variable does not immediately follow its initialization.

You can override LScript's default variable-handling behavior by placing the interpreter into a state where both variables and arrays must be explicitly declared before they can be used. Had you activated this state in the Num/num example, LScript would have generated a compile-time error message regarding both variables, informing you that undeclared variable references appear in the script.

Use of this explicit declaration state of LScript is recommended for beginning scriptwriters. It can sometimes aid in preventing potential problems that can occur with variable usage. You activate explicit declaration requirements by placing the @strict pragma directive at the top of your LScript. The following code fragment shows the @strict pragma in use with the Num/num case. Refer to the LScript online documentation for more information regarding use of pragma directives.

```
@strict
...
main
{
    ...
    var num = 6;
    info(Num);      // this line will now generate an "undeclared
                       ↪variable" error

    ...
```

The example scripts in this chapter will not employ the @strict pragma directive. The scripts included in this chapter were tested to ensure their functionality and usability, so they can be used directly without such safety measures.

"Hello" LScript!

One of the traditional tests of any computer language is "Hello World!" This is a simple and unscientific test of the complexity of a language. The test shows how many lines of code are required to display the message "Hello World!" The fewer lines of code compared to other languages, the higher the level—or more abstract—the language. So, this chapter's first complete LScript will adhere to this tradition and test this complexity.

```
main
{
    info("Hello World!");
}
```

This LScript will post an informational window with the message "Hello World!" displayed. Clicking the OK button on the window will end the script.

To execute this simple script from LightWave Modeler, select the LW_LScript plug-in from Modeler's Additional menu. When activated, this plug-in will prompt you to locate the script to be executed. Navigate to the location on disk where you saved the "Hello" script. Execution of the script will begin immediately after you select it and click the OK button (or double-click the file).

This first script, while an authentic and complete LScript, was not very practical. So, to illustrate the power and simplicity of LScript, the next section will create an LScript that performs a function that is difficult to accomplish manually: creating single-point polygons from the points of an object.

Creating Single-Point Polygons from the Points of an Object

For this exercise, your script will need to switch Modeler into a mode known as Mesh Data Edit. Your script must be in this mode to use LScript commands and functions designed to operate directly on mesh data. In Mesh Data Edit mode, you can freely add and delete lower-level mesh data such as points, polygons, and curves. By entering this state in Modeler, you are beginning a "transaction" on the state of the mesh in Modeler. The changes you make during this transaction period are not applied to any existing mesh, but rather, are accumulated until the end of the transaction. When you end the Mesh Data Edit mode, you have the power to apply or discard the changes you made during the transaction.

Within the scope of LScript's built-in commands and functions, some cannot be used in Command Sequence mode, some cannot be invoked during Mesh Data Edit transactions, and others can be used regardless of the state in which Modeler is currently functioning. Refer to the LScript online documentation provided by NewTek for more information concerning which LScript commands can be used during which Modeler states.

The `editbegin()` LScript command is used to begin a Mesh Data Edit transaction in Modeler, and the companion command `editend()` completes the transaction, placing Modeler back into its default Command Sequence state.

The following exercise shows you how to set Modeler into Mesh Data Edit mode using LScript, while at the same time test for the presence of points in the active mesh layer.

Exercise B.1   Testing for the Presence of Points

1. To get your starting points for this exercise, load an object into LightWave Modeler and press the **k** key to remove all the polygons from the object.

2. Using the LScript Modeler template, insert the `editbegin()` command into the body of the `main()` UDF. Use the following code listing as a guide:

```
main
{
      count = editbegin();
      ...
}
```

An integer value representing the number of points in the currently active foreground layer(s) is returned by `editbegin()` when you switch into Mesh Data Edit mode. This value will be used to determine if there are any points in the active layers and as a limit for some looping code.

3. Use the following code to check for the existence of points, and cancel the script if none is present:

```
main
{
      count = editbegin();
```

```
        if(count == 0)
        ...
}
```

In the final step of the this exercise, the `if()` control tests for the presence of points in the active layers. If none is present, the variable count will hold a value of zero (0), the equivalent of a Boolean false for testing purposes. The `if()` control is used to make a decision based on the Boolean value (either true or false) of an expression. If the expression count == 0 results in a Boolean true value, the active foreground layers contain no points.

> **Note**
> The script code above uses a C/C++ operator (==) to test for equality. As you learn more about LScript, you will find that many operators and controls in LScript are taken from or modeled after the C language.

After you introduce a decision control into your script, you must provide a path for logic to follow depending on the outcome of the expression test. If the expression proves false (that is, points are available in the foreground layers), you will want the script to continue its execution. If the expression proves true, however, no points are available, and therefore, no data is available to process. The script should be terminated immediately.

In the following script fragment, if `editbegin()` returns zero (0), the user is informed that there are no points to process, and the script is cancelled. Because this will require two executable statements (one to display a message and one to halt the script), they will need to be enclosed within body markers.

```
main
{
    count = editbegin();

        if(count == 0)
        {
            error("No points to process!");
            return;
        }
        ...
}
```

The `error()` function is one of three message-display routines available in LScript (along with `info()` and `warn()`), and is used to let the user know that you cannot continue processing. A return command is then executed, which has the effect of terminating the script. If a script executes all the way to the end of the `main()` UDF, an implicit return command is executed for you by LScript, also terminating the script.

Note

You may notice that when the script is terminated using return, it leaves Modeler in Mesh Data Edit mode (that is, no corresponding editend() call is made). This is not a problem because LScript cleans up many things if you leave in a hurry without cleaning up after yourself. If you fail to reset Modeler into Command Sequence mode upon exit, LScript will detect this condition and correct it for you. This is also the case with other state-driven conditions, such as data requesters.

Now that you have taken care of the more-obvious error checking, you can move on to the real processing of the script. When the script switches into Mesh Data Edit mode, behind the scenes LScript has done some work for you. In particular, two new internal linear arrays are created, one called points[] and one called polygons[]. These arrays contain the point and polygon identifiers of the data in the active layer(s). Whenever your script communicates with Modeler regarding a particular point or polygon, it must provide the correct identifier, so these convenience arrays will certainly come in handy. Because the goal is to process all points found in the currently active foreground layer(s), you can simply use all the point identifiers made available in the points[] array.

To process all available points, your script will need to loop through the points[] array from the first element to the last. LScript provides two primary looping controls, the for() loop and the while() loop. Both are modeled after their C counterparts, with the for() loop control being somewhat more complex in its structure. Being new to scripting, you will likely want to opt for the simpler of the two. However, the for() control will be used in subsequent examples to give you exposure to its usage.

Exercise B.2   Processing the Available Points

1. Initialize your counter variables outside the loop itself using a variable called pnt to hold the integer value of the current loop iteration. This variable also will serve as the index value into the points[] array.

```
main
{
    count = editbegin();

        if(count == 0)
        {
          error("No points to process!");
          return;
        }

    pnt = 1;
        while(pnt <= count)
        {
          ...
        }
    ...
}
```

As you retrieve each point identifier, you will perform whatever processing is necessary on that point. In the case of processing points into polygons, that will require the use of multiple lines of script code, so you will need to enclose them in body markers. The expression you will evaluate in the while() control will simply ensure that you do not use an index value greater than the size of the points[] array, which would generate a run-time error and terminate the script.

2. Because you are using a while() loop control, increment the pnt loop counter somewhere inside the loop body.

```
        . . .
                pnt = 1;
                    while(pnt <= count)
                    {
                        . . .
                        ++pnt;
                    }
                . . .
```

Warning

If you neglect to increment the value in the pnt counter variable, you will create a condition known as an "infinite loop." This is a situation where the loop never ends. In such a situation, your only recourse is to forcibly terminate Modeler.

Note

In Step 2, you used a C-like increment operator (++) to add one (1) to the pnt counter variable as the last action of the loop itself. You also can use a more traditional and BASIC-like method of incrementing the counter, pnt = pnt + 1. Both expressions produce the same result.

3. Using the pointinfo() LScript function, find the location of the current point so that you can duplicate it as a single-point polygon. Pass the point identifier taken directly from the points[] array as the parameter required by pointinfo().

```
        . . .
                pnt = 1;
                    while(pnt <= count)
                    {
                        loc = pointinfo(points[pnt]);
                        . . .
                        ++pnt;
                    }
                . . .
```

4. The addpoint() function creates a point in Modeler's mesh space at the location specified by the value contained in the loc variable. If the call to addpoint() is successful, it will return to the identifier for the new point. Save this new point identifier for later use with other functions.

```
. . .
              pnt = 1;
                  while(pnt <= count)
                  {
                     loc = pointinfo(points[pnt]);
                     pid = addpoint(loc);
                     . . .
                     ++pnt;
                  }
        . . .
```

> **Note**
>
> Because of the nature of a Mesh Data Edit transaction, new points and polygons added during such a transaction are not automatically appended to the `points[]` and `polygons[]` arrays. You must take care to preserve these returned identifiers while you are within you data-editing session if you need to use them with other data-edit functions. These new identifiers will, however, be available in the `points[]` and `polygons[]` arrays in any subsequent transactions you initiate.

At this stage in your script, you have added a new point that occupies the same three-dimensional position as another point. If you were to execute your script now, you would effectively duplicate the existing arrangement of points in the active layer(s). You would have two points for every one you had originally.

In the next exercise, however, you will add script code to distinguish this new point from the original. Not only will it become visible when rendered in Layout (the original point would be invisible), it will no longer be a point at all. You will promote this single point into a polygon.

Exercise B.3   Making the Point into a Polygon

1. Call the LScript `addpolygon()` function, and provide to it as an argument the identifier of the point you just added to the transaction.

```
. . .
              pnt = 1;
                  while(pnt <= count)
                  {
                     loc = pointinfo(points[pnt]);
                     pid = addpoint(loc);
                     addpolygon(pid);
                     . . .
                     ++pnt;
                  }
        . . .
```

2. Add to your loop the command `rempoint()`, which will permanently delete the original point, leaving only the new single-point polygon in its place.

```
. . .
            pnt = 1;
                while(pnt <= count)
                {
                   loc = pointinfo(points[pnt]);
                   pid = addpoint(loc);
                   addpolygon(pid);

                   rempoint(points[pnt]);

                   ++pnt;
                }
            . . .
```

3. Add the editend() command as the last action for the script to perform before it completes, which will terminate the Mesh Data Edit transaction you initiated with editbegin().

```
main
{
     count = editbegin();

          if(count == 0)        // what?   no points?
          {
             error("No points to process!");
             return;       // terminate script
          }

          pnt = 1;
              while(pnt <= count)
              {
                 loc = pointinfo(points[pnt]);      // where is it?
                 pid = addpoint(loc);
                 addpolygon(pid);       // new single-point polygon

                 rempoint(points[pnt]);      // delete original point

                 ++pnt;
              }

          editend();       // apply changes
}
```

You can verify the actions of this script by first checking the count of polygons in the object before and after you execute the script. You will see that the number of polygons has increased by the number of points that were processed by the script.

If your script fails to call editend(), or you pass to the function a value that can be evaluated as a Boolean false, all the work you performed during the Mesh Data Edit transaction will be discarded. This mechanism is provided to allow a script to abort changes it may have made to any existing mesh data in Modeler. As mentioned before, changes you make during this state will be accumulated by Modeler, and not actually applied to any existing data as changes and additions are made. It is not until you give Modeler the "A-OK" that the changes you have made will be applied.

Calling editend() with an expression that evaluates to a Boolean true (which is the default if no parameter is provided) is the equivalent of giving Modeler permission to modify your existing mesh data.

More functionality can be added to this basic script, such as placing the new single-point polygons into a separate layer without destroying the original points. Such enhancements would make it more functional and convenient to use. On your own, try adjusting this script to make it more effective for your needs.

The following list explains in detail some of the commands that you used in the exercises in this section. For more information, see the LScript online documentation from NewTek.

- pointinfo(). Returns a vector, which is one of LScript's internal data types. This vector contains the location, on the X, Y, and Z axes of the point you identify. A vector data type is not restricted to merely containing axis data and can hold any three numeric quantities.

- addpoint(). Creates a point in Modeler's space at the specified coordinate.

- addpolygon(). Returns the identifier of the new polygon just created.

- rempoint(). Deletes a point from the existing mesh data. This command cannot be used to delete points that have been added during the same Mesh Data Edit transaction.

- editend(). Terminates the Mesh Data Edit transaction you started with editbegin().

Using a Requester

So far, you have seen how LScripts can interact with Modeler to affect its behavior. However, you can add another dimension to your LScripts by enabling them to interact with the script users as well. You can accomplish this by using a dialog-generating interface, known as the Requester. The Requester allows the scriptwriter to post a dialog window that can gather data and operational instructions from the script user through the use of Requester controls. As you will see in this section, creating and managing a Requester from LScript is quick and easy.

Because you will concentrate on the Requester in this exercise and less on actual processing of the script, you will begin with the complete processing code of the script to be used. The script, called "Snap!," will make points selected by the user move location on any axis. The location and axis to be used will be specified by the user ? location Requester panel. The following listing shows the processing code that "Snap!" the relocate selected points. Most of this processing code should already be familiar to taken largely from the Points-to-Polygons LScript you created in the previous s

```
main
{
     ...
     selmode(USER);
     count = editbegin();

          if(count == 0)       // are any points selected?
          {
             error("No points to process!");
             return;       // terminate script
          }

          pnt = 1;
               while(pnt <= count)
               {
                  loc = pointinfo(points[pnt]);       // where is it now?
                  ...
                  ++pnt;
               }

          editend();       // apply changes
}
```

Notice that a new command, selmode(), has been added to the script code. This command acts as a filter, telling Modeler which types of data you want to work with. This can be either data that has been explicitly selected by the user (USER), or all data that is currently in the mesh regardless of what might be currently selected (GLOBAL). In the case of "Snap!," you are interested only in those points that might have been selected explicitly. As far as Modeler is concerned, if no points (or polygons) are selected explicitly by the user, all are selected implicitly.

When your script interacts with the user, it will gather from that interaction a number of items that will be used as operational parameters when moving a point. It must know which axes will be used (or ignored), and it will need to know where on each axis the point should be placed.

The following exercise takes you through the steps to script the Requester.

Scripting the Requester

To initialize some working variables that will be used both by the Requester and processing code, add the following working variables to your "Snap!" LScript:

```
...in
```

```
        useX = false;
        locX = 0.0;
        useY = false;
        locY = 0.0;
        useZ = false;
        locZ = 0.0;
        . . .
        selmode(USER);
        count = editbegin();

                                                    . . .
    }
```

2. Add some Requester code. Posting a data Requester in LScript begins with a call to reqbegin().

```
        . . .
        locY = 0.0;
        useZ = false;
        locZ = 0.0;

        reqbegin("Snap!");
        . . .
```

3. Begin adding controls. In your "Snap!" script, allow the script user to indicate each axis to use as well as a location along that axis by creating six controls, two for each axis, using the appropriate LScript control-creation function:

```
        . . .
        reqbegin("Snap!");

        c1 = ctlchoice("Use X?",useX,@"Yes","No"@);
        c2 = ctlnumber("X Location",locX);
        c3 = ctlchoice("Use Y?",useY,@"Yes","No"@);
        c4 = ctlnumber("Y Location",locY);
        c5 = ctlchoice("Use Z?",useZ,@"Yes","No"@);
        c6 = ctlnumber("Z Location",locZ);
        . . .
```

LScript's Requester offers a number of different control-creation functions, and each describes the type of control to be created. In the preceding script fragment, two basic types of control are created: a choice control and a numeric edit field control. Each control type you create will have differing parameters and data types (although all take the control title as their first argument). For more detailed information about all the Requester control types available, see the LScript online documentation from NewTek.

4. Post the panel to the users with a call to reqpost(), allowing them to edit the

values to suit their needs:

```
...
c5 = ctlchoice("Use Z?",useZ,@"Yes","No"@);
c6 = ctlnumber("Z Location",locZ);

        if(reqpost())
        {
            ...
        }
        else
                return;
        ...
```

Notice that the preceding script code uses an else clause to provide a logic
pathway if the return value from reqpost() proves to be other than true. If
reqpost() should return false, this is an indication that the user has clicked the
Cancel button on the Requester panel and you should simply terminate the
script, allowing LScript to perform any necessary state clean up. Also, you should
take note that because you used only a single line of script code, you did not
need to enclose the return command within body markers.

If the user clicks the OK button on the Requester panel, your script will need to
query each control on the Requester for their new values. The values themselves
might not have changed from those you originally used to initialize the controls,
but it makes your script much simpler if you assume they have.

5. Query each Requester control you created by employing the LScript getvalue()
   Requester function:

```
...
c5 = ctlchoice("Use Z?",useZ,@"Yes","No"@);
c6 = ctlnumber("Z Location",locZ);

        if(reqpost())
        {
            useX = getvalue(c1);
            locX = getvalue(c2);
            useY = getvalue(c3);
            locY = getvalue(c4);
            useZ = getvalue(c5);
            locZ = getvalue(c6);
        }
        else
        return;
        ...
```

6. Issue the LScript command reqend() to allow LScript to close the Requester
   panel and free up any internal resources it might be using. Closing the Requester
   panel now also enables you to initiate a Mesh Data Edit transaction later in the
   script.

```
      ...
        useZ = getvalue(c5);
        locZ = getvalue(c6);
      }
      else
            return;

   reqend();
      ...
```

7. Update your processing code to employ the new data.

The complete "Snap!" LScript adds the final script code to the processing loop to place the currently selected point(s) into the new location indicated by the working variables. If the script user does not alter any values in the Requester panel, any selected points will simply be moved to their current locations—in effect, nothing will happen.

```
main
{
      useX = false;
      locX = 0.0;
      useY = false;
      locY = 0.0;
      useZ = false;
      locZ = 0.0;

      reqbegin("Snap!");

      c1 = ctlchoice("Use X?",useX,@"Yes","No"@);
      c2 = ctlnumber("X Location",locX);
      c3 = ctlchoice("Use Y?",useY,@"Yes","No"@);
      c4 = ctlnumber("Y Location",locY);
      c5 = ctlchoice("Use Z?",useZ,@"Yes","No"@);
      c6 = ctlnumber("Z Location",locZ);

            if(reqpost())
            {
               useX = getvalue(c1);
               locX = getvalue(c2);
               useY = getvalue(c3);
               locY = getvalue(c4);
               useZ = getvalue(c5);
               locZ = getvalue(c6);
            }
            else
                  return;

      reqend();

      selmode(USER);
      count = editbegin();
```

```
            if(count == 0)        // are any points selected?
            {
              error("No points to process!");
              return;        // terminate script
            }

    pnt = 1;
        while(pnt <= count)
        {
          loc = pointinfo(points[pnt]);      // where is it now?

              if(useX == 1)
                    loc.x = locX;
              if(useY == 1)
                    loc.y = locY;
              if(useZ == 1)
                    loc.z = locZ;

          pointmove(points[pnt],loc); //move the point to 'loc'

          ++pnt;
        }

        editend();
    }
```

The following list explains in detail some of the new commands that you used in this exercise. For more information, see the LScript online documentation from NewTek.

- `selmode()`. Filters the types of data you want to work with. This is data that has been explicitly selected by the user if you specify USER mode, or all mesh data that is currently contained in active foreground layer(s) regardless of what might currently be selected if you enable GLOBAL mode.

- `reqbegin()`. Accepts a character-string parameter that will be used as the title of the Requester window, and performs necessary internal preparation for adding controls to the Requester.

- `ctlchoice()/ctlnumber()`. Accepts a variable number of parameters and returns a numeric control identifier. This control identifier is used subsequently to retrieve the value contained by the control.

- `reqpost()`. Returns a Boolean value to indicate which button the user clicked to terminate the Requester, either OK or Cancel. If OK was clicked, `reqpost()` returns a Boolean true value, otherwise a Boolean false is returned indicating the user's wish to halt processing. The `reqpost()` call can be used as the expression to be evaluated by the `if()` control.

- getvalue(). Accepts a single parameter that is the identifier of the control to be queried and returns the data that is contained within that control. The data type returned is identical to that used to initialize the control, so you can easily assign the return values directly to your storage variables.

- reqend(). Allows LScript to close the Requester panel and free up any internal resources it might be using. Also changes the state of LScript out of the Requester, subsequently enabling LScript to launch into other states (such as a Mesh Data Edit transaction).

Closing Thoughts on Modeler LScript

A good rule of thumb to keep in mind as you are writing scripts is to start out simple and add functionality in a modular fashion. If you go back and review the "Snap!" script, you will see that it was created in steps. Components were added as they were needed in the location where they needed to be, building on work that was already accomplished and tested.

Certainly, if you were to first look at an LScript in its entirety—especially one that performs a complex task—it can seem daunting. If, however, you consider each script as a collection of components or sections—a section to gather user input, a section to add points, a section to write data to a file, and so on—you will find that no script is as complex or mysterious as it might at first seem.

Thinking in terms of discrete, modular script sections will help you better understand the construction of LightWave Layout scripts. A discussion of this topic begins in the next section.

Scripting LightWave Layout

There is a fundamental difference between the philosophies governing the design of Modeler and Layout plug-ins. Within Modeler, plug-ins are given control of Modeler's CPU time and are expected to complete all their processing before returning control to Modeler. Layout differs in that, with the exception of the Generic class, plug-ins are expected to activate and then remain passive until Layout calls on them to perform processing appropriate to the current state of Layout's execution. This state varies, being a file save of the scene at one point and the rendering of an animation frame at another. Layout plug-ins must be prepared to activate at any time and to process appropriately based on Layout's current state.

LScripts designed to execute under one of Layout's plug-in architectures must follow this convention as well. However, because of its built-in convenience, LScript does not require the scriptwriter to include code to support a particular Layout execution state if it is not appropriate for the script. LScript provides an internal function for Layout to execute instead, enhancing the practice of building scripts modularly—you can add these state functions incrementally as you complete and test others.

LScript extends scripting capabilities to eight of Layout's plug-in architectures:

- Image Filter
- Object Replacement
- Procedural Texture
- Item Motion
- Displacement Mapping
- Generic
- Channel Filter
- Master

Note

The Master and Channel Filter classes of plug-ins are new in LightWave 6.

However, before you begin delving into the scene-related scripting classes, a brief detour through the exception, Layout Generic, is in order.

Layout Generic Scripting

Unlike other Layout plug-in types, the Generic plug-in class is unassociated with a scene, and as such does not adhere to the callback mechanism enforced on other Layout plug-ins. This plug-in class is structurally similar to Modeler plug-ins in that they have a single entry point and are expected to complete all processing during their first and only invocation. In addition, because of their lack of association with a Layout scene, Generic plug-ins have the capability to load and save scene files directly into Layout during their execution.

LScript Generic scripts not only have access to all the internal features of LScript, but they also have the power to access objects, along with their attributes, in a currently loaded Layout scene. New to LightWave 6, LScript Generic scripts have full access to Layout's new Command Sequence interface system. If you add to all this the Generic capability to load and save Layout scene files, it becomes easy to see how LScript Generic scripts can be exceptionally powerful.

LScript Generic (known as LS/GN) scripts have a single point of entry. Like LScript for Modeler's main() user-defined function, LS/GN scripts have an entry point identified as generic(). The following listing provides an example.

```
generic
{
}
```

In this section, you will create an LS/GN script that creates, from scratch, a base Null object that contains a five-bone chain with Inverse Kinematics enabled. In addition, the script will create a goal object (another Null) to which the IK-enabled bone chain will be targeted. As a final action, the script will give the "goal" Null object motion so that you can immediately see the IK chain in action when the script completes. This new script will be called "IKwik." Not only would such a script be useful in providing quick IK chains in your project, it also serves as a practical example of how scripts can be used to encapsulate the steps required to perform routine tasks. Although the IK chain created by "IKwik" is simple, you can easily alter the script to create IK chains that are more complex and, more importantly, address your specific project needs.

Because you've switched to Layout scripting, your goals are now different. In Modeler, you were concerned with editing mesh data—altering existing data and creating whole new objects. In Layout, however, animation of objects has become your primary concern. Now that your goals differ, your available functions for achieving those goals will also differ. Although a core set of functions and commands is available in LScript (and therefore available to all scripts, regardless of application or architecture), Layout LScript requires a different set of functions and commands to facilitate Layout's animation-oriented goals.

Indeed, these functions and commands can even vary by architecture (Displacement Mapping, Channel Filter, and so on). For example, to construct the IK-enabled chain of bones in Layout, the "IKwik" script will employ a collection of commands that are available only to the Layout Generic and Master plug-in architectures. These commands, equivalent in nature to the Command Sequence functions available under Modeler, allow the script to select functions directly available on Layout's user interface. Like other LScript functions, some of these Layout Command Sequence functions also can be passed parameters.

The "IKwik" script will enable its user to specify the number of bones that will be generated in the IK chain. To facilitate this, a Requester will be used. Posting a Requester in

Layout scripting involves script code that is nearly identical to that used by Modeler. In fact, you can copy and paste requester code from a Modeler script and it will work identically under Layout. However, Layout presents some special conditions that the LScript for Layout software is designed to handle—specifically, the availability of Requester controls that are designed for conditions found only in Layout. Although such controls will not be used in the "IKwik" script, it is important that you are aware that additional controls are available to Layout LScripts. Descriptions of these Layout-specific Requester controls can be found in the LScript online documentation provided by NewTek.

The following exercise takes you through the creation of the "IKwik" script, which includes steps on creating a Requester panel in Layout LScript.

 Note

The Layout Command Sequence system is new to LightWave 6. Although other scripts presented in this chapter should run correctly with previous versions of LScript, the "IKwik" script will function correctly *only* with LScript v2.0—which itself will function correctly only with LightWave 6. This is because the script accesses the new Command Sequence feature found in LightWave Layout.

Exercise B.5   Creating the "IKwik" Script

1. Ensure that your "IKwik" script will function only with LScript v2.0 by placing the @version pragma directive at the start of the script. Also, add the @script pragma at this time as an aid should you later decide to install this script:

```
@version 2.0
@script generic

generic
{
        . . .
```

2. Using the reqbegin() command, add Request code so that the script can gather operational information from the user regarding how many bones it should create in the IK chain:

```
. . .
generic
{
        reqbegin("IKwik");
        . . .
```

3. The number of bones to be added is an integer value, so use the ctlinteger() control-creation function:

```
. . .
        reqbegin("IKwik");
```

```
            boneCount = 5;

    c1 = ctlinteger("Bone chain count",boneCount);
    ...
```

4. Post the Requester and query the control values just as you would under LightWave Modeler:

```
    ...
        c1 = ctlinteger("Bone chain count",boneCount);

            while(true)
            {
              if(reqpost())
                    boneCount = getvalue(c1);
              else
                    return;

              break if boneCount > 0;

              warn("Bone chain count cannot be less than 1");
            }

        reqend();
        ...
```

Notice that in this code fragment the script code to manage the Requester panel is placed into a while() loop. You did this because when you enable the user to enter or alter operational values, you run the risk of receiving data that might not be valid for the purpose of your script. To address this, some validity, or sanity, checks will ensure that the operational values provided do not adversely affect the operation of the script at some later point.

Immediately following the retrieval of the value contained in the Requester control, a sanity check is performed on that value. If the value in the boneCount variable is appropriate for the purposes of the script (that is, it is a positive, non-zero integer value), the while() loop is terminated by the break keyword. However, if this sanity check fails, a warning message is posted to the user concerning the situation. According to the logic flow of the while() loop, the user is placed back into the Requester panel while this condition persists so that he or she can enter a correct value or terminate the script by pressing the Cancel button.

5. Using the Command Sequence function AddNull(), begin creating objects in Layout. Begin with the goal Null object, followed by the base Null object:

```
    ...
        reqend();

    AddNull("Goal_Null");
```

```
AddNull("Base_Null");
. . .
```

The Layout Command Sequence system applies its processing implicitly to whichever object is currently selected in the scene; in other words, you do not explicitly specify the object to be affected when you call a Command Sequence function. As you will see later in the construction of this script, a function is available for explicitly selecting objects within the current scene. However, as functions such as AddNull() create new objects in the current scene, Layout's current selection changes to the new object. Therefore, Command Sequence functions that follow the addition of a new object will operate directly on that new object.

6. Add an unparented bone to the currently selected base Null object using the AddBone() Command Sequence function. Calling AddBone() consequently makes this new bone the currently selected object in the scene:

```
. . .
AddNull("Base_Null");

AddBone("Base_Bone");
. . .
```

7. Activate support for Inverse Kinematics in the bone by explicitly specifying that Inverse Kinematics will be responsible for managing the heading and pitch channels for the object. Do this by calling the HController() and PController() Command Sequence functions with a value of 4.

The value of 4 corresponds to the fourth item in the Controllers and Limits pop-up menu for controlling an object's rotational channels. By default, the rotational channels of an object are controlled by keyframes (the first item in the pop-up menu).

```
. . .
AddBone("Base_Bone");
HController(4);
PController(4);
. . .
```

To position the goal object accurately, the script must maintain the complete length of the bone chain as bones are added.

8. Maintain the length of the bone chain using the bonePos variable. Initialize this variable to a default rest length of 1 meter to accommodate the base bone just added:

```
. . .
PController(4);

bonePos = 1.0;
. . .
```

9. Add the remaining bones to the object using a `for()` loop to iterate over the size of the `boneCount` variable. The bone-adding activities within the loop are similar to those used to add the first bone; however, use the `AddChildBone()` Command Sequence function instead to ensure that the bones added are properly parented in the chain:

```
. . .
        bonePos = 1.0;

            for(x = 1;x <= boneCount;x++)
            {
                AddChildBone("Child_" + x);
                HController(4);
                PController(4);

                bonePos += 1.0;
            }
        . . .
```

Notice that the name of each child bone is constructed using LScript's string math capabilities. The prefix value `"Child_"` is added to the value of the loop counter variable x, resulting in bone names such as `"Child_1"`, `"Child_2"`, and so on.

In most IK chains, any bone that targets a `goal` object should be rather small. This helps visually to manage the chain, and reduces the influence of the targeting bone.

10. Reduce in size to 10 centimeters the last bone in the chain (left selected in Layout when the `for()` loop terminated), and adjust the `bonePos` variable accordingly:

```
        . . .
                bonePos += 1.0;
            }

        BoneRestLength(.1);
        bonePos -= 0.9;
```

11. Make some final IK-related settings to the target bone to activate the Inverse Kinematics feature of the bone chain:

```
        . . .
        BoneRestLength(.1);
        bonePos -= 0.9;

        GoalItem("Goal_Null");
        FullTimeIK();
        UnaffectedByIK();
        . . .
```

12. Finally, position at the end of the bone chain the `goal` Null created at the beginning of the "IKwik" script. In addition, give this object some keyframed motion, using the `Position()` and `CreateKey()` Command Sequence functions, to

enable the user to scrub through the frames in the scene and see the Inverse
Kinematics at work in the bone chain.

Here is the complete "IKwik" Layout Generic script with the final code added:

```
@version 2.0
@script generic

generic
{
        reqbegin("IKwik");

           boneCount = 5;

        c1 = ctlinteger("Bone chain count",boneCount);

           while(true)
           {
             if(reqpost())
                   boneCount = getvalue(c1);
             else
                   return;

             break if boneCount > 0;

             warn("Bone chain count cannot be less than 1");
           }

        reqend();

        AddNull("Goal_Null");       // this will be dealt with later

        AddNull("Base_Null");

        AddBone("Base_Bone");
        HController(4);
        PController(4);

        bonePos = 1.0;    // bones are initially 1 meter in length

           for(x = 1;x <= boneCount;x++)
           {
             AddChildBone("Child_" + x);
             HController(4);
             PController(4);

             bonePos += 1.0;
           }
```

```
        BoneRestLength(.1);      // make the last bone really small
        bonePos -= 0.9;        // adjust goal's initial position

        GoalItem("Goal_Null");
        FullTimeIK();
        UnaffectedByIK();

        scene = getfirstitem(SCENE);

        SelectItem("Goal_Null");
        Position(0.0,0.0,bonePos);
        CreateKey(0);
        Position(0.0,3.0,0.0);
        CreateKey(30 / scene.fps);       // convert to time index
        Position(0.0,0.0,-bonePos);
        CreateKey(60 / scene.fps);

        GoToFrame(0);     // reset slider to frame 0
    }
```

The following list explains the new commands introduced in this exercise. For more information, see the LScript online documentation from NewTek.

- AddNull(). Creates a Null object in the current scene using the specified name. Leaves the newly added Null selected.

- AddBone(). Adds an unparented bone to the currently selected Layout object. The newly added bone becomes the selected object.

- AddChildBone(). Adds a new bone to the currently selected bone, effectively making it a child of that bone.

- HController()/PController(). Selects the type of controller for the heading and pitch rotational values of the selected object. The companion function BController() can be used to select the type of controller for the object's bank rotational value.

- BoneRestLength(). Sets the rest length for the currently selected bone.

- GoalItem(). Provides the identity of the Layout object to which the currently selected object should be targeted in an Inverse Kinematics situation.

- FullTimeIK(). Enables the full-time IK setting of the currently selected object.

- UnaffectedByIK(). Enables the Unaffected by IK of Descendants setting of the currently selected object.

- SelectItem(). Changes the selection state of objects in the current scene to match only that of the object identified. Objects can be identified by unique name, object identifier, or indexed type.

- `Position()`. Moves the currently selected object to the X, Y, and Z location specified.
- `CreateKey()`. Creates a keyframe for the currently selected object, at its current location, at the specified time index. As illustrated in the "IKwik" script, frame numbers can be converted into time indices by division of the current frames-per-second setting of the scene.
- `GoToFrame()`. Positions the scene's frame scrubber at the specified frame index.

To execute the IKwik script, select the LW_LScript plug-in from the Generic menu of the Layout Plug-In options panel. As with Modeler LScript, a file requester dialog will be displayed so that you can select the Generic script to be executed—in this case, the IKwik script. The script is executed as soon as you make your choice.

IKwik has shown you the power that LScript Generic script can provide. It can create and manage objects in LightWave, allowing it to act as a supervisor for scenes. It offers a powerful interface to the LightWave Layout system, while maintaining the simplicity of structure provided by LScript for Modeler.

You will next create a Master LScript to intercept the creation of Nulls in a scene and apply a plug-in to alter its appearance.

Using LScript Master to Apply Plug-ins

LScript Master Class (LS/MC) is an event processing architecture. As actions take place within Layout—an object is loaded, a keyframe is created, and so on—notification of these actions is sent to an active Master Class plug-in. In this section, a Master Class LScript will be constructed that will monitor the events taking place in Layout. When it detects that a Null object has been added, it will, depending on the name of the new object, apply a CustomObject plug-in the Null to alter its appearance in Layout. This LScript will be called "Null-2-Custom."

All non–Generic LScript for Layout scripts conform to the notion of callbacks, as was discussed earlier. Each LS/MC script you create will contain at least two UDFs that LScript will invoke at appropriate times. The first is identified as `create()`, and is invoked when the LScript for Layout script is first activated. It is called only once, and is intended to be a location and a time when one-time setup of the script is to be performed. The second UDF, called `process()`, is where processing will take place, and the frequency of processing will depend on the type of processing taking place. In the case of "Null-2-Custom," this equates to each time an event occurs in Layout. Other Layout plug-in architectures will have their own conditions for processing, such as the Image Filter plug-in type (discussed in the next section), which has its process() UDF called when each frame of an animation is completed. Regardless of the frequency involved, however, it is within this particular UDF that the main processing of each script takes place.

As you become acquainted with other architectural types of Layout LScript, you will find that other user-defined functions are used as callbacks, varying with the type of the architecture. For instance, the flags() UDF, employed by several Layout plug-in architectures, is called only once, like create(), and is used to return a list of operational settings, or flags, that specify to Layout how the plug-in wants certain conditions to be treated. In the case of LScript Procedural Texture (LS/PT) scripts, the flags() UDF is used to indicate the exact attributes that the script will be modifying for the surface of the object. You can find information about flags(), and other callback UDFs, in the LScript online documentation.

 Note

The Layout Master Class plug-in architecture is new to LightWave 6. Consequently, the "Null-2-Custom" script will function correctly *only* with LScript v2.0—which itself will function correctly only with LightWave 6. The "Null-2-Custom" script also employs language features—such as post-conditional code execution, and regular expressions—that are available only in LScript v2.0.

Exercise B.6   Creating the "Null-2-Custom" Script

1. Begin your "Null-2-Custom" script by adding some pragma directives that establish the script's dependence on LScript v2.0:

```
@version 2.0
@script master
...
```

2. Add the create() UDF.

   In the "Null-2-Custom" Master script, the create() UDF will do nothing more than establish the description of the plug-in. This step introduces a command unique to LScript for Layout, called setdesc(), that enables you to set the text of the description displayed by Layout on the plug-in panel for this particular plug-in. If you want, you can use this command to display operating parameters to the Layout user without the need to bring up the Options panel. However, for the purposes of the current script, simply displaying the title for the script will be sufficient.

```
@version 2.0
@script master
```

```
create
{
        setdesc("Null-2-Custom");
}
. . .
```

3. The meat of the script will be created in the process() UDF.

   LScript will call the process() UDF with two parameters. The first is an integer code representing the type of the event that has occurred. As of this writing, two event types have been defined for the Master Class: NOTHING, and COMMAND. Of course, "Null-2-Custom" will focus only on the COMMAND types of events.

   When the event code is COMMAND, the second parameter will be a character string that contains the command name that was executed and, optionally, any parameters that might have been required. A space character separates these two elements.

```
. . .
create
{
   setdesc("Null-2-Custom");
}

process: event, command
{
   if(event == COMMAND)
   {
      . . .
   }
}
```

4. So that the event that occurred can be evaluated, extract the tokens in the command string (provided as a parameter to process()). To accomplish this, apply a regular expression to the character string to identify the tokens in the string, and to separate them into individual containers that the script can access.

```
      . . .
      if(event == COMMAND)
      {
         command ~= s~([a-zA-Z]+) (.+)~;
         . . .
      }
      . . .
```

Several components of this new line of script code bear explanation. First, a new assignment operator (~=) has been used. This operator is intended for use exclusively with regular expressions (also to be discussed shortly). When used with a search regular expression, as is the case in the preceding code fragment, it will not actually alter the data contained in the variable on the left of the assignment (that is, no assignment actually takes place). Instead, some background processing is performed, and the tokens that were matched by the expression itself, if any, are placed into locations where they can be subsequently accessed. When used with a search-and-replace regular expression, however, this assignment operator *will* alter the data contained in the variable on the left, depending on the success of the pattern match.

> **Note**
>
> Regular expressions have been an integral part of computer operating systems since their introduction in the UNIX operating system nearly 30 years ago. Their usage has been most prominent in the shell process (or command line interpreter) provided by all modern computer systems, but their implementation has been varied—from full implementation under UNIX, to the limited wildcard filename matching employed by Windows. LScript uses an implementation of regular expressions that falls nearer the level found in the UNIX operating system.

Search regular expressions, as introduced in the code fragment in Step 4, are used in LScript by surrounding them with the s~<pattern>~ characters (for search-and-replace regular expressions, the sequence would be

```
r~<pattern>~<string>~).
```

The tilde characters (~) mark the beginning and the end of the pattern that is to be used. A detailed discussion of the construction of regular expressions is well beyond the scope of this chapter; a great deal of information is available on the subject on the Internet, or within books specifically written about them. However, the expression used in Step 4 is simple enough that an explanation of its functioning can be included.

The initial pattern, "[a-zA-Z]+", specifies a range of characters to be matched. In this case, any character that exists in the English alphabet, regardless of its case, will successfully match the set (denoted by open and close brackets). The plus sign (+) that trails the range is a metacharacter whose meaning reads "one or more instances." So, any sequence of one or more upper- or lowercase alphabetic characters will match this first pattern. In the case of the command string provided to process(), this is how the "verb" of the command will appear in the string. The space that separates the patterns is interpreted literally—in other words, within the string being processed, there must be a single, literal space character that separates the other characters that will match the patterns provided. The final pattern includes a period (.) metacharacter whose meaning reads "any character except a newline." By suffixing this metacharacter with the plus sign, the pattern becomes "one or more instances of any character except a newline."

The parentheses surrounding each pattern are not a functioning part of the pattern, but are used to identify patterns whose matching values should be remembered. The regular expression works identically without these parentheses;

however, the tokens that ultimately matched the patterns of the expressions will not be available to you later. They are used in "Null-2-Custom" because the matching values need to be examined as part of the script's processing.

5. Assign to individual variables the tokens that matched the regular expression. This is done because of the volatile nature of the container that holds them.

```
. . .
      if(event == COMMAND)
      {
        command ~= s~([a-zA-Z]+) (.+)~;
        (verb,object) = this;
        . . .
      }
      . . .
```

The assignment in the preceding code fragment includes two variables on the left side. In normal situations, only one variable can be used to contain a value on the right side of an assignment. However, when one or more variables appear on the left of an assignment *enclosed in parentheses*, an associative assignment is taking place. An associative assignment in LScript, simply put, means that each variable on the left is associated positionally with a value that is generated by the expression on the right. So, the first value generated by the expression on the right of the assignment would be deposited into the first variable found on the left, the second value deposited into the second variable, and so on. If there are more variables than values in the assignment, the unassigned variables are set to the value nil.

You also might have noticed that a variable is being used on the right side of the assignment that has not existed or been referenced in the "Null-2-Custom" script. This is not a mistake in the script. Instead, the this variable is an implicit container in LScript v2.0 whose purpose is to capture and hold any generated result from the last expression LScript evaluated. This behind-the-scenes processing that LScript performs has definite advantages in certain situations—for instance, acquiring the tokens that matched patterns in a regular expression. When the search regular expression on the preceding line matched values in the command variable, those matching values were deposited into the this container by LScript as an array of values. The associative assignment then places the first token into verb, and the second token (if any) into object.

Note

When LScript evaluates the next expression, the value in the this container will be overwritten with the new results—if any—generated by that expression. Keep this in mind when your script depends upon the value(s) contained in this.

6. Check for the "AddNull" event using the command in the verb variable.

```
. . .
      command ~= s~([a-zA-Z]+) (.+)~;
      (verb,object) = this;
```

```
                    if(verb == "AddNull")
                    {
                       ...
                    }
                    ...
```

When the `"AddNull"` event occurs, the object variable will hold the name of the new Null object. "Null-2-Custom" will examine this name, and decide which plug-in to apply based on it.

```
        ...
                    if(verb == "AddNull")
                    {
                      plugin = nil;
                      plugin = "LW_Ruler" if object == "Ruler";
                      plugin = "LW_CameraMask" if object == "CameraMask";
                      plugin = "LW_EffectorNull" if object == "Effector";
                      ...
                    }
                    ...
```

In the preceding code fragment, the `plugin` variable is set to the name of a specific CustomObject plug-in depending on the name of the Null object that was added. If the name of the Null does not match any of the filter names, the `plugin` variable will continue to hold the value of `nil`.

Note

For "Null-2-Custom" to apply a plug-in server to an object, the plug-in to be applied must first be installed in Layout. The CustomObject plug-ins referenced by "Null-2-Custom"—LW_Ruler, LW_CameraMask, and LW_EffectorNull—should be included when you install LightWave 6 onto your computer. However, you might need to explicitly load them into Layout using the "Add Plug-ins" system to make sure they are available to "Null-2-Custom."

7. Because the `plugin` variable was assigned the name of a LightWave CustomObject plug-in, use that name in a call to the `ApplyServer()` Command Sequence function.

Here is the entire "Null-2-Custom" LScript Master script with the remaining script code added:

```
@version 2.0
@script master

create
{
  setdesc("Null-2-Custom");
}
```

```
process: event, command
{
  if(event == COMMAND)
  {
    command ~= s~([a-zA-Z]+) (.+)~;
    (verb,object) = this;

    if(verb == "AddNull")
    {
      plugin = nil;
      plugin = "LW_Ruler" if object == "Ruler";
      plugin = "LW_CameraMask" if object == "CameraMask";
      plugin = "LW_EffectorNull" if object == "Effector";

      if(plugin)

        ApplyServer("CustomObjHandler",plugin);
    }
  }
}
```

To enable the "Null-2-Custom" script, select the "LW_LScript" plug-in from the Add Layout or Scene Master menu of the Layout Plug-In options panel. A file requester dialog will be displayed so that you can select the "Null-2-Custom" Master script.

As you can see, the LScript Master Class architecture has the capability to call on Layout's Command Sequence system just as the LScript Generic architecture does. This capability to "push the buttons" of Layout's user interface represents one of the most powerful additions to the Layout plug-in API since its creation. However, you have only touched the tip of the LScript Master Class plug-in's tremendous potential with the "Null-2-Custom" script. Many powerful "supervisory" features can be added to LightWave Layout through this plug-in architecture.

Next, you will practice altering the appearance of a completed frame of rendered animation using the LScript Image Filter scripting architecture.

Making Some Noise with LScript Image Filter

Now you proceed into the world of LScript Image Filter, or LS/IF. In this architecture, you will post-process rendered frames of animation just prior to their final destination, whether that destination is a disk file, animation file, or visual display to the user. For this exercise, you will create an LS/IF script that will add an amount of noise, or snow, to each frame of rendered animation. Because each frame will have its own randomly applied noise factor, the effect will create an additional layer of animation to the project. This LS/IF script can be useful for applying a certain amount of grain to the visual appearance of your animation, providing the look and feel of age, as happens to celluloid film as time passes.

The structure of LS/IF scripts is similar to that of LScript Master Class (LS/MC). Like that architecture, it employs both `create()` and `process()` UDFs. The LS/IF script created in this section will also employ the `options()` UDF, wherein the user can alter the operating parameters of the Noise LS/IF script.

In the `create()` UDF, the LScript `recall()` function will be used to retrieve values that might have been stored previously on behalf of the script. Later in the script, the companion function `store()` will place values into storage after they have been altered by the user. Subsequent invocations of "Noise" will retrieve the user's last settings, adding a nice element of continuity.

Exercise B.7   Creating the "Noise" Script

1. Add some global variables to your script, along with the `create()` UDF.

Global variables are those that belong to the script as a whole, not to a particular UDF. Their visibility, or scope, is universal, meaning that all UDFs can read from or write to them as though they were their own, but their values will persist across UDF invocations.

```
noiseColor;
noisePercent;
noiseVariance;

create
{
  noisePercent = recall("noisePercent",.2);
  noiseVariance = recall("noiseVariance",.2);
  noiseColor = recall("noiseColor",<200,200,200>);

  setdesc("Noise (LS/IF)");
}
...
```

2. Invoke the `process()` function to process the image.

LS/IF `process()` functions are called by LScript with a number of parameters. These parameters provide information, such as the image's dimensions, so the script can access pixel information correctly. You will use this information heavily in `process()`.

```
...
   setdesc("Noise (LS/IF)");
}

process: width, height, frame, starttime, endtime

{
  red[width] = nil;
  green[width] = nil;
  blue[width] = nil;
  beenThere[width] = nil;
  out[3] = nil;
  ...
}
...
```

Note

By definition, every row of an image must pass through each Image Filter plug-in applied to it. If an Image Filter plug-in neglects to read and then write any of the image information, those areas in the final image will be filled in with a default color of black (<0,0,0>). LScript extends its conveniences to remove this burden from the scriptwriter. Your script need not process every—or, indeed, any—pixels in the image to ensure that they appear in the final image. LScript will implicitly forward for you any pixels that your script does not explicitly alter.

3. Add the main processing loop, which cycles through all the rows of pixels that are available in the image buffer:

```
...
  beenThere[width] = nil;
  out[3] = nil;

  moninit(height);
  ...
      for(i = 1;i <= height;++i)
      {
        ...
        if(monstep())
              return;
      }

  monend();
}
...
```

4. Enter into the process() UDF the script code to acquire, modify, and forward pixel data. Use the row-at-a-time processing function provided by LS/IF, called processrgb(). This command processes all four default pixel buffers at the same time, which achieves significant gains in processing speed.

```
...
  moninit(height);
    ...
        for(i = 1;i <= height;++i)
        {
          red = bufferline(RED,i);
          green = bufferline(GREEN,i);
          blue = bufferline(BLUE,i);
          alpha = bufferline(ALPHA,i);
          ...

          processrgb(i,red,green,blue,alpha);

          if(monstep())
              return;
        }
    ...
```

The remainder of the process() UDF for the LS/IF "Noise" script consists of the script code you need to randomly insert noise into the image. The settings found in the global variables for the script (potentially set by the user) are used to determine where and how a pixel will be shaded. The method used is largely just a determination of how many pixels per row will be altered, and of those, which will have the noise color and which will have a variant of that color. All these factors can be affected indirectly by values entered by the user in the options() UDF, which will be added in Step 7.

When a pixel is selected for alteration, your script will need to keep track of it in an array so that time is not wasted processing the same pixel again. Because pixels are selected randomly in each row, not tracking those pixels already modified would likely result (incorrectly) in lower densities of noise.

5. Use the beenThere[] array to track the modified pixels:

```
        ...
            blue = bufferline(BLUE,i);
            alpha = bufferline(ALPHA,i);
            ...

        beenThere[] = nil;
            for(j = 1;j <= max;++j)
            {
              pixel = random(1,width);
              while(beenThere[pixel])
                  pixel = random(1,width);

              beenThere[pixel] = true;
              ...
```

6. To complete the process() UDF, add the script code that is responsible for actually altering selected pixels to simulate video noise:

```
...
alpha = bufferline(ALPHA,i);

max = random(1,integer(width * noisePercent));
beenThere[] = nil;

    for(j = 1;j <= max;++j)
      {
        pixel = random(1,width);
        while(beenThere[pixel])
              pixel = random(1,width);

        beenThere[pixel] = true;

        switch(random(1,3))
        {
          case 1:
                red[pixel] = noiseColor.x - vary;
                green[pixel] = noiseColor.y - vary;
                blue[pixel] = noiseColor.z = vary;

                break;

          case 2:
                red[pixel] = noiseColor.x;
                green[pixel] = noiseColor.y;
                blue[pixel] = noiseColor.z;

                break;

          case 3:
                red[pixel] = noiseColor.x + vary;
                green[pixel] = noiseColor.y + vary;
                blue[pixel] = noiseColor.z + vary;

                break;
        }

        if(red[pixel] < 0) red[pixel] = 0;
        if(red[pixel] > 255) red[pixel] = 255;

        if(green[pixel] < 0) green[pixel] = 0;
        if(green[pixel] > 255) green[pixel] = 255;

        if(blue[pixel] < 0) blue[pixel] = 0;
        if(blue[pixel] > 255) blue[pixel] = 255;
      }
```

```
                      processrgb(i,red,green,blue,alpha);

                  if(monstep())
                        return;
            }
            ...
```

7. To complete the "Noise" LS/IF script, add the `options()` UDF.

LScript invokes this UDF when the user clicks the Options button to the right of the plug-in button (or, in LightWave 6, by double-clicking the active plug-in entry). It is in this UDF that requester code is placed for acquiring data from the user.

```
noiseColor;
noisePercent;
noiseVariance;

create
{
   noisePercent = recall("noisePercent",.2);
   noiseVariance = recall("noiseVariance",.2);
   noiseColor = recall("noiseColor",<200,200,200>);

   setdesc("Noise (LS/IF)");
}

process: width, height, frame, starttime, endtime
{
   red[width] = nil;
   green[width] = nil;
   blue[width] = nil;
   beenThere[width] = nil;
   out[3] = nil;

   moninit(height);

   vary = noiseVariance * 75;

      for(i = 1;i <= height;++i)
      {
         red = bufferline(RED,i);
         green = bufferline(GREEN,i);
         blue = bufferline(BLUE,i);
         alpha = bufferline(ALPHA,i);

         max = random(1,integer(width * noisePercent));
         beenThere[] = nil;
```

```
for(j = 1;j <= max;++j)
{
  pixel = random(1,width);
  while(beenThere[pixel])
       pixel = random(1,width);

   beenThere[pixel] = true;

   switch(random(1,3))
   {
     case 1:
           red[pixel] = noiseColor.x - vary;
           green[pixel] = noiseColor.y - vary;
           blue[pixel] = noiseColor.z - vary;

           break;

     case 2:
           red[pixel] = noiseColor.x;
           green[pixel] = noiseColor.y;
           blue[pixel] = noiseColor.z;

           break;

     case 3:
           red[pixel] = noiseColor.x + vary;
           green[pixel] = noiseColor.y + vary;
           blue[pixel] = noiseColor.z + vary;

           break;
   }

   if(red[pixel] < 0) red[pixel] = 0;
   if(red[pixel] > 255) red[pixel] = 255;

   if(green[pixel] < 0) green[pixel] = 0;
   if(green[pixel] > 255) green[pixel] = 255;

   if(blue[pixel] < 0) blue[pixel] = 0;
   if(blue[pixel] > 255) blue[pixel] = 255;
                 }
```

```
                    processrgb(i,red,green,blue,alpha);

                        if(monstep())
                            return;
                }

        monend();
    }

    options
    {
      reqbegin("Noise");

      c1 = ctlnumber("Noise amount (%)",noisePercent * 100.0);
      c2 = ctlnumber("Noise variance (%)",noiseVariance * 100.0);
      c3 = ctlrgb("Noise color",noiseColor);

          if(reqpost())
          {
              noisePercent = getvalue(c1) / 100.0;
              noiseVariance = getvalue(c2) / 100.0;
              noiseColor = getvalue(c3);

              store("noisePercent",noisePercent);
              store("noiseVariance",noiseVariance);
              store("noiseColor",noiseColor);
          }

      reqend();
    }
```

Running the "Noise" script requires the use of the Image Filter LScript plug-in. This can be found within the Image Filter plug-in menu of the Image Processing Layout panel. Select the LW_LScript plug-in from the list, and select the "Noise" script to activate it.

Certainly, more can be added to this LS/IF script. "Noise" can be enhanced to add scratch lines to your images, increasing the illusion of age. Other channel information can be accessed and used to provide you with more detail about the structure of the image itself. For instance, the Alpha channel data can be accessed to enable you to create even more special effects with the image's pixels.

LScript Image Filter scripting provides a great means of prototyping image processing techniques. Many different techniques can be created, such as embossing or edge detection, using the conveniences provided by LScript.

Next, the LScript Item Motion scripting system will be used to put a new "spin" on things in your animation project.

Spinning Your Wheels with LScript Item Animation

For your scripting exercise, you will create an LScript Item Animation (LS/IA) script. Item Animation (also known as Item Motion) plug-ins have the power to alter an object's position, rotation, and scaling factors on a frame-by-frame basis. Using Item Animation, you can completely replace the keyframed motion of an object with your own.

In the exercise in this section, you will create an LS/IA script called "Spinner" that produces accurate revolutions-per-minute rotations on an object. This can be useful for items such as propellers, wheels, and machinery. For instance, if you needed to create animation showing the internal workings of an automobile engine, you would want the camshaft connections of the individual pistons in the engine to rotate at the same RPM setting. "Spinner" can help ensure that your engine won't look like its nuts and bolts are in need of tightening.

"Spinner" will begin much like the other Layout LScripts you've created in this chapter, with global variables and a create() UDF. However, you will move a step higher in your usage of LScript by employing the preprocessor to establish some macro definitions. The macro identifiers will be replaced wherever they are encountered later in the script by their assigned values. Macros are handy for centralizing script values, enabling you to change them in one location while the preprocessor propagates that change throughout the script code.

Exercise B.8   Creating the "Spinner" Script

I. Add the following create() UDF elements to your "Spinner" script to initialize most of the global variables you will use:

```
@define CW    1;
@define CCW   2;

rpm, rot, fps;
degreeIncr;
toH, toP, toB;
direction;

radrev = 2*PI;

create
{
  scene = getfirstitem(SCENE);
```

```
    fps = scene.fps;

    rpm = 100;
    toH = false;
    toP = false;
    toB = true;
    direction = CW;

    totaldegrees = rpm * 360;
    degreeIncr = totaldegrees / (fps * 60);

    rot = nil;

    setdesc("Spinner: ",rpm," rpm/",(direction == CW ? "cw" : "ccw"));

}
...
```

Note

As a result of changes made to the plug-in API in LightWave 6, LScript v2.0 can option-ally provide to the `create()` UDF the Object Agent for the Layout object to which the Item Animation script has been applied. However, including this parameter to `create()` will render the "Spinner" script capable of functioning only under LScript v2.0. This para-meter has been omitted from the script to keep it as compatible as possible with all ver-sions of LScript.

2. Begin your `process()` UDF.

A delayed-initialization variable, called `rot`, is used in the script. This global vari-able was set to `nil` in the `create()` UDF, so you can check to see if it has been initialized the first time the `process()` UDF is invoked.

```
...
    totaldegrees = rpm * 360;
    degreeIncr = totaldegrees / (fps * 60);

    rot = nil;

    setdesc("Spinner: ",rpm," rpm/",(direction == CW ? "cw" : "ccw"));
}

process: ma, frame, time
{
    if(rot == nil)
    rot = ma.get(ROTATION,time);
    ...
}
...
```

The `rot` variable will be used to hold the initial rotation settings (heading, pitch, and bank) for the object, giving you a launching point for any subsequent rotations that you will apply. This has been done to prevent a violent snap of the object as would happen if it were to have to adjust to new rotational parameters that might be radically different from its current settings. This method enables the animator to set a keyframe for a starting rotational position without having it instantly replaced by "Spinner" with a different value.

Along with the current animation index, values provided as both floating-point time and integer frame, LScript passes to the process() UDF an Object Agent that provides the script with an interface to read and affect the Layout object's Item Animation settings. Your script will use this Object Agent to access and alter the object's rotation values based on settings provided by the user in the options() UDF.

3. Check to see which rotational axis (heading, pitch, or bank) has been selected for spinning, and apply the rotation setting based on the direction selected. This will be either clockwise (CW) or counterclockwise (CCW):

```
...
  if(rot == nil)
        rot = ma.get(ROTATION,time);

  if(toH)
  {
    if(direction == CW)
        rot.x -= rad(degreeIncr);
    else
        rot.x += rad(degreeIncr);
  }

  if(toP)
  {
    if(direction == CW)
        rot.y -= rad(degreeIncr);
    else
        rot.y += rad(degreeIncr);
  }

  if(toB)
  {
    if(direction == CW)
        rot.z -= rad(degreeIncr);
    else
        rot.z += rad(degreeIncr);
  }
  ...
```

4. Wrap rotation values, keeping them in the range of 1 to 360 degrees:

```
  ...
        rot.z -= rad(degreeIncr);
    else
        rot.z += rad(degreeIncr);
  }
```

```
    if(rot.x > radrev)    rot.x -= radrev;
    if(rot.x < 0)         rot.x += radrev;
    if(rot.y > radrev)     rot.y -= radrev;
    if(rot.y < 0)          rot.y += radrev;
    if(rot.z > radrev)      rot.z -= radrev;
    if(rot.z < 0)           rot.z += radrev;
    ...
```

There is an upper limit to the number of revolutions LightWave Layout will track for an object. The script does not know how long the animation will last, nor where this limit might be and how Layout will react if it is reached. This code will ensure that the value will never reach or exceed this limit.

5. For your `process()` UDF, update the object's rotational values by using the `set()` method provided by the Item Animation Object Agent:

```
...
    if(rot.z > radrev)    rot.z -= radrev;
    if(rot.z < 0)         rot.z += radrev;

    ma.set(ROTATION,rot);
}
...
```

6. Add the finishing touches to your "Spinner" LS/IA script using the `options()` UDF:

```
// direction?
@define CW    1
@define CCW   2

// some globals

rpm, rot, fps;
degreeIncr;
toH, toP, toB;
direction;

create
{
  scene = getfirstitem(SCENE);
  fps = scene.fps;

  rpm = 10;
  toH = false;
  toP = false;
  toB = true;
  direction = CW;

  // calculate the per-frame degree increment
  // to achieve the required RPMs

  totaldegrees = rpm * 360;
```

```
   degreeIncr = totaldegrees / (fps * 60);

   rot = nil;

   setdesc("Spinner: ",rpm," rpm/",(direction == CW ? "cw" : "ccw"));
}

process: ma, frame, time
{
  if(rot == nil)
       rot = ma.get(ROTATION,time);

  if(toH)
  {
    if(direction == CW)
         rot.x -= degreeIncr;
    else
         rot.x += degreeIncr;
  }

  if(toP)
  {
    if(direction == CW)
         rot.y -= degreeIncr;
    else
         rot.y += degreeIncr;
  }

  if(toB)
  {
    if(direction == CW)
         rot.z -= degreeIncr;
    else
         rot.z += degreeIncr;
  }

    if(rot.x > 360)        rot.x -= 360;
    if(rot.x < 0)          rot.x += 360;
    if(rot.y > 360)         rot.y -= 360;
    if(rot.y < 0)           rot.y += 360;
    if(rot.z > 360)         rot.z -= 360;
    if(rot.z < 0)           rot.z += 360;

    ma.set(ROTATION,rot);
}

options
{
  reqbegin("Spinner");

  c1 = ctlinteger("RPMs",rpm);
  c2 = ctlchoice("Direction",direction,@"CW","CCW"@);
```

```
        c3 = ctlcheckbox("Effect heading",toH);
        c4 = ctlcheckbox("Effect pitch",toP);
        c5 = ctlcheckbox("Effect bank",toB);

        if(reqpost())
        {
          rpm = getvalue(c1);
          direction = getvalue(c2);
          toH = getvalue(c3);
          toP = getvalue(c4);
          toB = getvalue(c5);

          // update the working values to catch any changes

          totaldegrees = rpm * 360;
          degreeIncr = totaldegrees / (fps * 60);

          rot = nil;

         setdesc("Spinner: ",rpm," rpm/",(direction == CW ? "cw" : "ccw"));
        }

        reqend();
    }
```

To use "Spinner," select the object to which it will be applied and press the **m** key to bring up the Motion Options panel for the object. From the Add Modifier menu of the IK and Modifiers tab, select the LW_LScript plug-in. Once enabled, activate the file requester dialog by double-clicking the plug-in entry in the panel, and select the "Spinner" script. You can then double-click the "Spinner" entry to activate the script's options() UDF and enter values more appropriate for your needs.

The "Spinner" script provides a set-it-and-forget-it solution to accurately rotating items in an animation. Although a similar effect can be achieved by repeating the motion of an object, such repetition would not always provide an accurate simulation of the real-world revolutions-per-minute rotations offered by "Spinner."

An LS/IA script can also modify other items, such as an object's position and scaling factors. Some amazing effects can be achieved by manipulating this combination of object attributes.

This section has covered, rather quickly and directly, some of the more-popular Layout scripting architectures. You have created some comparatively simple-but-practical Layout LScripts, studying along the way some of Layout's peculiarities as they differ from Modeler LScript and pertain to plug-in development.

Creating or affecting animation programmatically can bring into existence visuals that are beyond the capabilities of LightWave 3D as it comes out of the box. Any one of these particular Layout scripting architectures can achieve such results in and of themselves; by working in combination, whether directly or indirectly, the potential is staggering and the results can be equally so.

The LScript Integrated Development Environment

The LScript Integrated Development Environment (or LSIDE) is the collective term used to describe a suite of three standalone applications that were developed specifically to aid the LScript developer. This suite of applications includes the LScript Editor, the LScript Debugger, and the LScript Interface Designer. Each LScript-support application is described briefly in this section.

It is important to note that each application was developed using the LightWave toolkit—the same toolkit that is responsible for ensuring that LightWave looks and behaves identically across all the LightWave-supported computer platforms. This commonality in LSIDE's look and feel means that, like LightWave, you need only learn the tools once, not each time you use them on a different computer system.

The LScript Editor

Although it can be used as a general-purpose text editor, the LScript Editor was specifically designed with script editing in mind. Several features of the editor are designed to work with LScripts, and, to serve as aids in the development of your scripts. Among these features are color-based syntax highlighting of script code (visible in Figure B.1), LScript templates for quickly beginning a new LScript project, and syntax checking of script code *directly within the editor.*

Although it is a standalone application, the LScript Editor integrates with the LScript Debugger. If the Editor has the script currently being processed by the Debugger as one of its loaded documents, the Editor will synchronize the current line of that document with the current line of the Debugger. This can enhance your workflow by enabling you to quickly locate and edit the line and begin debugged if there should be a problem. Changing the script in the Editor does not change the script in the Debugger, however. They are, at the time, two separate documents. You would need to reinitialize LScript with the changed script for the changes to become visible in the Debugger.

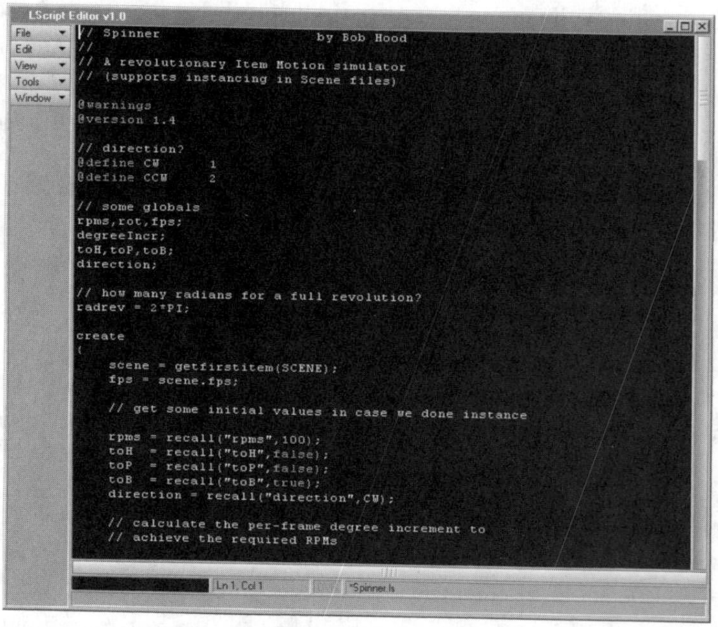

Figure B.1   The LScript Editor interface.

The LScript Editor also integrates with the LScript Interface Designer. When the LScript Interface Designer generates code, that code will be delivered automatically to the LScript Editor, if it is running, as a new, unsaved document. From there, you can edit the generated code, or perhaps integrate it with an existing script, before saving it to disk.

The LScript Debugger

As you can see from Figure B.2, the LScript Debugger has a user interface similar to the LScript Editor. However, this application is used to debug LScripts symbolically as they execute within LightWave. It supports many of the features found in professional debuggers, including break points and stepping over and into functions.

In addition, the LScript Debugger enables you to "watch" variables in your script. Watching a variable enables you see the value of that variable as the script executes. When the value of the variable changes within the running script, the value displayed in the Debugger's watch window will reflect the change.

LScripts can initiate a debugging session using the LScript v2.0 debug() command (this is visible in Figure B.2). If the Debugger is already running and not already in use by another script, this command will cause the script to engage the Debugger. If it is not already running, LScript will attempt to locate and execute the Debugger binary to facilitate a debugging session. To successfully launch the Debugger, its binary must reside in the same directory where LightWave's binaries are installed (typically NewTek\Programs).

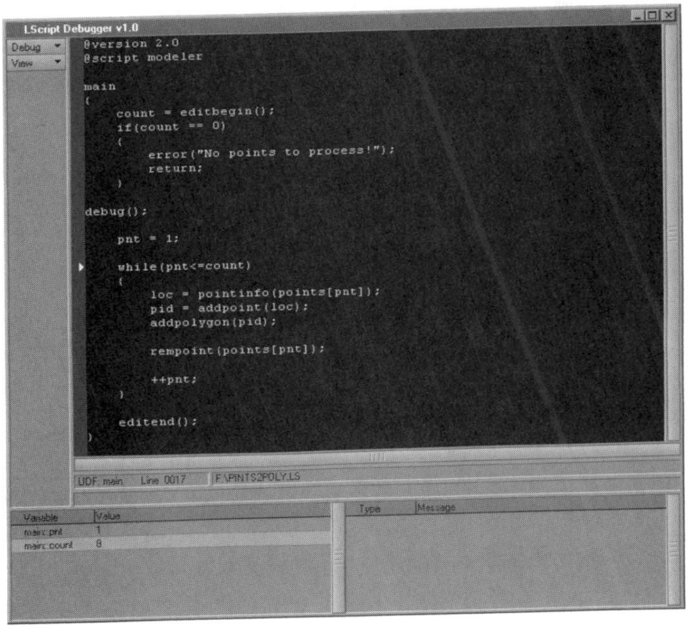

Figure B.2 The LScript Debugger in session.

The LScript Interface Designer

The LScript Interface Designer (see Figure B.3) enables Requester panels to be designed using the What-You-See-Is-What-You-Get (WYSIWYG) method. You can add a wide range of controls to the Interface Designer's virtual Requester panel. You can move controls by dragging them with the mouse. Although LScript does not directly support it, you can even resize the controls for use with other Requester-based applications (such as a C plug-in that uses LightWave Panels directly).

Controls can be managed using the hierarchical parenting tree. Controls can be parented to other controls, enabling you to drag whole groups of controls on the screen at the same time. In the case of Tab controls (visible in Figure B.3), other controls can also be parented directly to the individual tabs of the Tab control, effectively placing them on that particular "page."

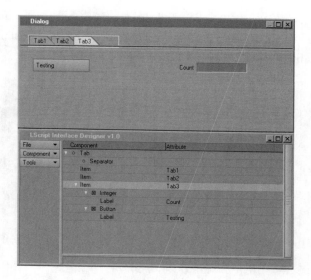

Figure B.3   The LScript Interface Designer.

When your Requester panel is complete, you can save it to disc for later reconstruction in the Interface Designer. More importantly, however, you can ask the Interface Designer to generate code that will reconstruct your Requester panel in a number of different formats and languages—including code for use with LScript, and even LightWave Panels! Code that you generate using the Interface Designer is delivered directly to the LScript Editor as a new document if the Editor is running at the same time.

Summary

This chapter merely touched the tip of the LScript iceberg. Other LScript for Layout architectures were left unexamined, as were more advanced uses of the LScript software system—enough to fill several chapters. However, the intention here was not only to show you the usefulness and power of the LScript scripting software, but also to whet your appetite to begin writing your own useful scripts.

Along with the LScript online documentation provided by NewTek, an excellent source of reference for the budding LScript writer is the large number of existing LScripts. Examining the works of others can always teach you things more quickly and efficiently than learning through your own means of trial and error.

You can find the LScript documentation (in HTML format) and many sample LScripts on the LightWave 6 CD-ROM. You can also find more information about the LightWave LScript system by visiting NewTek's web site at http://www.newtek.com. Scripting utilities, additional documentation, mailing-list information, an patch releases of the LScript system are available at the LightWave Outpost Website, http://www.lightwave-outpost.com.

Appendix C

Plug-Ins and References

LightWave 6 gives you the power to create

just about anything you can imagine.

Included with LightWave 6 are a number of

useful plug-ins, some of which are actual

programs integrated into LightWave. This appendix introduces you to a number of plug-ins, including:

- Motion Designer, a soft-body dynamics engine that can produce realistic motions such as clothing, draperies, or even moving body parts.
- Particle Storm SE, LightWave 6's particle generation system.
- HyperVoxels 3, which is included in LightWave 6 and enables you to create fire, smoke, explosions, lava, or liquids.

This chapter also discusses some popular and useful plug-ins from third-party developers and ends with references and Internet resources that can help you take your LightWave experience further.

Plug-Ins

LightWave plug-ins are programs that work within Layout and Modeler to extend the functionality of the program without requiring upgrades. Plug-ins are useful for all kinds of things, such as motion, displacements, shading, image manipulation, and much more.

Types of Plug-Ins

When a plug-in is created, it is designed to work in LightWave in a specific way. This means you need to access the plug-in in a specific location, such as a Pixel Filter plug-in or a Shader plug-in. The following is a list of plug-in types available in LightWave 6 (all except the last are available in Layout):

- Shader plug-ins in the Surface Editor
- Graph Editor plug-ins
- Custom Null Object plug-ins
- Object Replacement plug-ins
- Displacement Object plug-ins
- Motion plug-ins
- Pixel Filter plug-ins in the Effects Panel
- Image Filter plug-ins in the Effects Panel
- Volumetric plug-ins in the Effects Panel
- Environment plug-ins in the Effects Panel

- Layout and Scene Master plug-ins
- Generic plug-ins
- Loader and Saver plug-ins
- Texture plug-ins
- Modeler plug-ins

As you can see, plug-ins reside in many locations in LightWave Layout. When it comes to LightWave Modeler, plug-ins are found in only one location, the Additional drop-down list. This enables you to create shortcuts and screen buttons for your favorite tools. The Additional drop-down list in Modeler also is home to any Modeler tool that does not have a home in the panels or tab areas.

Adding Plug-Ins in Layout

Don't worry about trying to add plug-ins to any of these specific areas. When the plug-in is created, the developer determines what type of plug-in it will be. When the plug-in is added to Layout or Modeler, the plug-in is installed in the appropriate place. To add plug-ins in Layout, select the Add Plug-ins button from the Extras tab. You can also select the Plug-in Options panel from the Extras tab, and select Add Plug-ins there, as in Figure C.1.

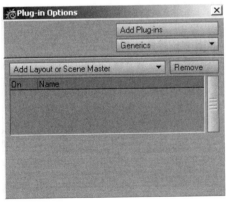

Figure C.1   Adding plug-ins in Layout can be done through the Plug-in Options panel.

To add a plug-in, click the Add Plug-ins button at the top of the Plug-in Options interface. Point the directory to the appropriate plug-ins, which are identified by the .p extension, and click OK in the load browser to add a plug-in. A note appears telling you how many plug-ins have been loaded (some plug-ins contain multiple plug-ins in one plug-in .p file). As soon as plug-ins have been loaded, close Layout to save the plug-in information to the LightWave configuration (lw.cfg) file. The next time you start Layout, the plug-ins will be already loaded. You do not need to load them each time you run LightWave and LightWave does not need to scan a directory for them either. To load plug-ins in Modeler, all you have to do is select the Add Plug-ins command from the Preferences drop-down list.

You should remember a few things when it comes to loading plug-ins in LightWave:

- When you're in Layout, be sure to load plug-ins with an empty scene. Not doing this could cause problems with your LightWave scene setup.

- Plug-ins only need to be loaded one time. But you need to quit Layout and Modeler to record to the configuration file. This tells the programs which plug-ins are loaded.

Note

LightWave 6 enables you to load multiple plug-ins at once. Select the first plug-in in a directory, hold down the Shift key, and select the last plug-in in the list. This selects them all. If you add a Modeler plug-in to Layout, or a Layout plug-in to Modeler, LightWave will ignore the action. You also can re-add plug-ins for updates if needed.

Motion Designer

Motion Designer is a powerful new addition to LightWave Layout's Generic plug-in class. It can be found under the Generic plug-in–type list, within the Plug-in Options panel. When you select the plug-in, the Motion Designer interface appears, as in Figure C.2. This is a plug-in that you will grow to love (if you don't already)! Motion Designer is a soft-body dynamics simulation program that enables you to create realistic cloth-type motions. But you're not limited to just cloth. You can make body parts wiggle, such as the belly of a cartoon-style fat man; or dangle, such as the big jowls of a dog. This next exercise introduces you to a few of the key features in Motion Designer, and how to implement this plug-in into LightWave.

Note

To save time when using a Generic–type plug-in such as Motion Designer, create a button for it in Layout using the custom controls. Press **F2** to configure menus.

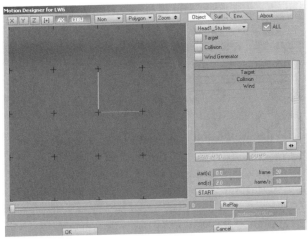

Figure C.2   A Generic plug-in type, Motion Designer is a program that runs within LightWave 6 and enables you to create soft-body dynamics such as cloth.

Exercise C.I   Using Motion Designer with LightWave 6

This exercise gives you the basics to begin creating your own cool animations or enhancing some existing ones with Motion Designer. Begin this exercise in Layout.

1. From the CD that accompanies this book, load the ABFlag.lwo object found in the Appendix directory, within the Projects folder.

   This is a simple flag object that has been subdivided into about 170 polygons. Figure C.3 shows the flag object loaded in Layout.

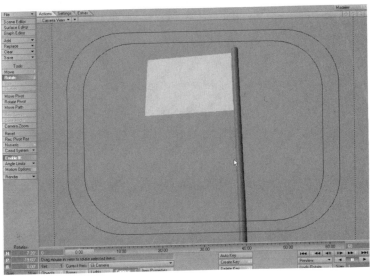

Figure C.3   A subdivided box attached to an elongated disc makes a flag and flagpole, ready to be animated with Motion Designer.

2. With the object in good view, run the Motion Designer plug-in from the Generic plug-ins drop-down list, within the Plug-in Options panel.

The ABFlag.lwo object loaded in Layout shows in the object list in Motion Designer, as in Figure C.4.

3. With the flag object as the current selection in Motion Designer (see Figure C.5), click the Target button.

The representation of the object appears in the Motion Designer layout.

By clicking the Target button, you've told Motion Designer that this is the Target object to which you'll be applying effects.

4. At the bottom right of the Motion Designer interface, set the end(s) selection to 10 to tell Motion Designer that you want to create a 10-second animation.

5. Set the frame/s selection to 30, for 30 frames per second. You'll see the frame value adjust to 300.

6. Select the Surf (for Surface) tab at the top of the Motion Designer interface.

You'll see a number of values appear in the list, which control many factors for the object, such as Stretch Limit, Resistance, and more.

7. Make sure Flag is selected from the drop-down list just under the tab selections.

This is the flag surface of the object, the surface you want to animate.

8. For this example, you can use a preset of these values by selecting the cotton (thin) selection from the Material lib selections, as in Figure C.6.

Figure C.4
Motion Designer sees what objects are loaded into Layout. You can select any of them and apply the Motion Designer plug-in.

Figure C.5
Clicking the Target button shows a representation of the selected object in Motion Designer's layout window.

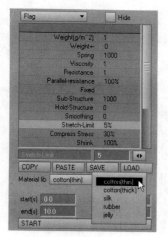

Figure C.6   Select a preset cotton material for the flag object.

9. After you've selected the cotton (thin) preset, change to the FlagPole surface, as in Figure C.7.

Note

The FlagPole surface does not need Motion Designer applied to it. The flagpole would not animate in the real world like thin cotton, and for Motion Designer to properly apply realistic effects on the surface of an object, that surface must be attached to another.

Figure C.7
You can choose which surface to apply effects to using the Surface tab.

10. Double-click the Fixed setting in the list to read On, as shown in Figure C.8.

Figure C.8   You can assign various parameters to every surface of your objects in Layout, through Motion Designer. Here, the FlagPole surface is told to be Fixed, meaning that it has no dynamics applied.

You've now told Motion Designer that you want the preset material of thin cotton applied to the flag surface, and you fixed the flagpole surface, essentially applying no effects to it.

Click the Env. (Environment) tab.

This area of control tells the selected surfaces how to move—what effects you want to apply, such as gravity and wind. There are three places to set values for each parameter. These values are for the X, Y, and Z axes.

Begin by setting the value of –2.0 in the middle value box (the Y axis) for gravity, as in Figure C.9.

value you set told Motion Designer to apply gravity on the negative Y axis, downward. A positive value of 2.0 would apply the gravity upward. The value a decent setting for thin cotton, but the higher you set this value, the more you'll apply.

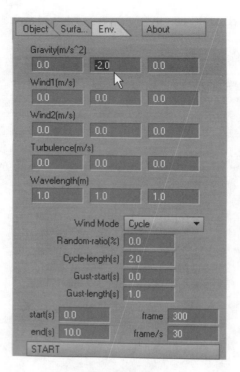

Figure C.9   A value of –2.0 is set for Gravity on the Y axis for the flag surface.

13. To see how the gravity affects the flag object, click the Start button. Fig
    shows gravity taking effect on the flag.

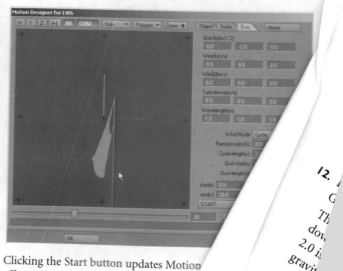

Figure C.10   Clicking the Start button updates Motion
    effects of the Gravity setting.

Now it's time to add some wind.

14. The flag is on the left side of the pole, or the negative X axis. For the Wind1 setting, set a value of –1.5 in the first value area. Click the Start button to see the effects.

    You'll see that there is motion on the flag to the left, but the gravity still pulls the flag down, making it just hang there. This is because the Gravity setting is greater than the Wind1 setting.

Note

You can abort a preview by pressing the Ctrl key.

15. Change the Gravity to –3.0, and the Wind1 to –4.0 Add some gravity to the Z axis with a setting of 2.0. The Z axis setting is the field all the way to the right, or the third field. Click the Start button again to see the effect. The flag now flies out and away from the flagpole.

16. The flag seems to be stretching a bit. This is easily corrected by going back to the Surface tab and selecting the Flag surface. Change Viscosity by selecting it, then changing the value in the box to 10, as shown in Figure C.11. Also change the Stretch Limit to 5%.

    The Viscosity setting is a sort of stiffness, or how thick the surface is. Changing the value to 10 made the flag less flimsy. Changing the Stretch Limit to 5% limited how much the surface can stretch, or pull away from the flagpole surface.

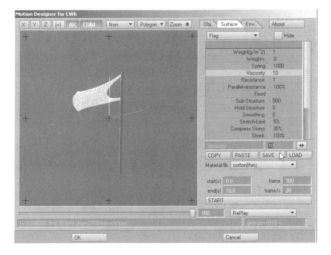

Figure C.11 Because of Motion Designer's interactive interface, you can see the effects of your settings in real time. Adjustments can be made to the surface parameters, as shown here.

Now it's time to add a few more settings.

17. Go back to the Environment tab.

18. To make the flag flap some more, make sure the Z axis Gravity is set to 2.0. Add wind to the flag by setting Wind1 on the Y axis to 2.0, and Z axis, 3.0. Click the Start button to see the effects.

To use the file in Layout, you must first generate the Motion Designer file.

19. Click the Start button and let the preview run until finished. Then, go back to the Object tab in Motion Designer and click the Save MDD button. Save the file as flag.mdd.

20. Click OK to Close Motion Designer. Make sure the flag object is selected in Layout, and press the **p** key to enter the Object Item Properties panel. In the Deformations tab, choose MD_Plug plug-in from the Add Displacement drop-down list, as in Figure C.12.

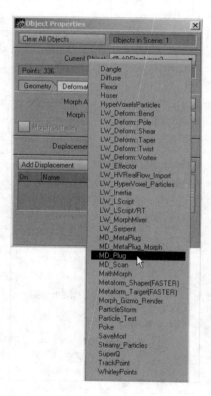

Figure C.12 MD_Plug is the Displacement Map plug-in used to assign the Motion Designer file to the object.

21. Double-click the plug-in in the list, after it has been loaded, to open its interface. Click the right-triangle next to MDD Filename, and load the .MDD file you saved from Motion Designer. Figure C.13 shows the interface with the file loaded.

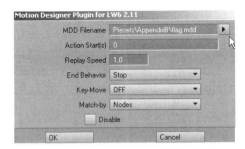

Figure C.13   Load the .mdd file generated by Motion Designer into the Displacement Map plug-in.

22. This plug-in interface enables you to control the End Behavior for the motion. Set this to Repeat so that your flag keeps on waving. You also can set a starting time if you want to, as well as Replay Speed. For now, just click OK to close the plug-in interface. Then close the Object Properties panel for the flag.

23. Finally, make a preview in Layout to view your motion. Don't forget to set the end frame to 300 for your Layout scene. Remember, you made the Motion Designer file 300 frames long.

This exercise gave you a brief overview of Motion Designer, a useful and fun plug-in that ships with LightWave 6. But don't think waving flags is all that can be done with this tool. The flag you created in this exercise was stationary. But Motion Designer is smart enough to compensate the real-world properties you apply to moving objects as well. You can easily parent this flag to a soldier's hand and make it wave. All the gravity and wind parameters you set up would apply themselves to the motion of the waving flag, creating a realistic motion.

But in addition to just flags and motions, you can create cloth on digital characters. Motion Designer enables you to apply collision to a surface so that a long jacket or a flowing cape on a character hangs and bends properly to fit the model without intersecting. Some cool tutorials and examples for Motion Designer can be found at http://www2m.biglobe.ne.jp/~ino-dx/md/indexe.htm.

Particle Storm SE

LightWave 6 includes another Generic plug-in type called Particle Storm SE. This is Dynamic Realities' Particle Storm 2 program, integrated with LightWave. Similar to Motion Designer, it is a program within LightWave that requires you to create a desired effect and save out the motion data. That data is then loaded and applied in Layout to an object as a Displacement Map plug-in.

Particle Storm can be used for creating any number of animations, from simple rain, to explosions, to stormy seas, and more. You can use Particle Storm to generate flocks of birds, or even bullets shooting from a gun. This exercise introduces you to the basic principles of Particle Storm by teaching you to generate a fountain of particles. In the next exercise, you'll use LightWave 6's HyperVoxels3 to turn the particle data into water.

Exercise C.2   Using the Particle Storm SE Plug-In

This exercise gives you enough information on the basics of Particle Storm, such as how to run it, create and control particles, and then apply those particles in Layout.

1. Clear Layout. From the Plug-in Options panel, select ParticleStorm2(SE) from the Generic plug-in list. Figure C.14 shows the plug-in interface.

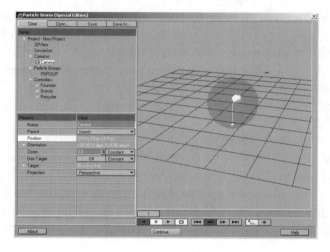

Figure C.14   The Particle Storm 2 SE interface.

2. Click the Play button (right-triangle icon) at the bottom of the Particle Storm interface.

   You'll see Particle Storm generating particles in the Layout window. This is the default.

3. Make the length of the particle stream longer by selecting Simulation from the Items list in the top left of the Particle Storm interface. Change the Property Value of Stop Time to 300 for a 10-second animation. Figure C.15 shows the interface.

Now you can begin working with the Particle Group.

4. Select the PGroup in the Item list, under Particle Groups.

   This is the group of particles you saw flowing when you clicked the Play button.

5. In the Property field, click under the Value heading to change the PGroup Name to Fountain, as in Figure C.16.

Figure C.15   Changing the Stop Time value extends the particle animation length. The Start and Stop time values become available when the Simulation setting is selected.

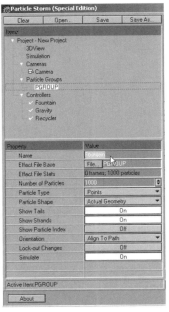

Figure C.16   PGroup is a default name, and you should change this to match your current scene. Later, when using the particle effects in Layout, you can easily find and apply the effects.

6. Click the File button for the Effect File Base property. When the panel opens, select a file location, and enter the name "Fountain." Click OK.

You've now told Particle Storm where to save the effect object file and the particle data (coming up later). All the other settings for the particle group are fine for this exercise. But what these settings do is control the number of particles and what type of particles you want—points, in this case.

7. Select the Fountain listing in the Item list for Controllers, as in Figure C.17.

The controller settings enable you to set the position of the particle group, the orientation, the scale, and so on.

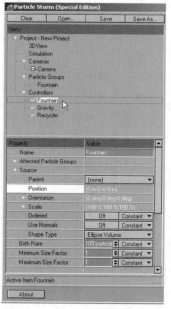

Figure C.17   Select the Fountain Controller to adjust its properties.

8. Because you'll want this fountain to stream upward, select the Orientation property and expand its settings by clicking the white triangle to the left. You'll see the settings for Heading, Pitch, and Bank, as in Figure C.18.

9. Change the Pitch setting to –90, making the particle group rotate upward. Click the Play button to see the particles stream.

You'll notice that as soon as the particles are emitted, they fall. This is because the Gravity setting is too strong.

10. Select the Gravity listing from the Item list under Controllers. The Strength defaults to the world's gravity of 9.81 meters per second, squared. The fountain you want to create can be less affected by gravity, so change the setting to 1. Note that you don't have to enter anything other than 1. Particle Storm adds the m/s/s. This stands for meters per second, squared.

Figure C.18   The small white triangle expands the settings for orientation.

11. Click the Play button again and you'll see that the particles now stream and float before falling.

12. The stream of particles is somewhat wide, so go back to the Fountain controller, and expand the Scale by changing the X, Y, and Z Scale to 5% from the existing 100% setting.

> **Note**
> You don't have to start and stop playing the particle stream. You can click the Play button once, and let the particles play as you make changes. You'll see the effects of your changes in real time.

Now it's time to make the particles shoot higher.

13. With the Fountain controller still selected from the Item list, first change the Birth Rate to 50 to distribute 50 particles per second of the original 1000 particles. Change the Minimum Speed to 2 (meters per second) and the Maximum Speed to 3 (meters per second). You might need to drag the scrollbar to see the additional parameters.

14. Tighten the spread of the particles by changing the Maximum Angle to 20.

Take a look at the particles playing in the Particle Storm preview window. They should stream up, then fall outward and down.

One last setting finishes this fountain and then it is ready for Layout. You want the particles to hit a ground plane, so you need to add a collision object.

15. Select the Controllers listing in the Items list. Right-click and hold to select Collision, as shown in Figure C.19.

Figure C.19   Right-clicking the Controller listing enables you to add more controllers to the particle group. Here you're adding more collision.

16. Select the Collision Detection from the Controller list to edit its settings. Expand the Collision Shape properties and set the Y position to –1.

This lowers the ground plane underneath the fountain.

17. Set the X Scale to 400%, the Y Scale to 100%, and the Z Scale to 400%.

This makes a large ground plane.

18. Change the Shape Type to Box. Figure C.20 shows the settings.

19. Press the Play button on the particle storm interface.

You'll see the particles stream up, fall, and now bounce on the ground. When they collide, the particles turn red. This indicates a collision.

Note

You can apply other controllers as well, such as Death Wish, which enables you to make the particles dissipate over a specific time. You can add wind, or perhaps flocking. Experiment with these to see what kind of different effects you can come up with.

When you like what you see, save the effect.

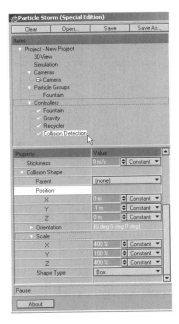

Figure C.20   A collision detection object is made in the form of a box and enlarged to catch all the fountain's particles.

20. To save, right-click the Fountain under Particle Groups. Holding the right mouse button, select Create Effect Object, as shown in Figure C.21.

This is a null object Particle Storm generates to initialize the particles in Layout. You'll be prompted with a message when the effect object has been created.

Note
You can specify where clicking the Effect File Base button for the Fountain group located in the Properties settings will create the Effect Object.

21. Drag the slider back to frame 1. Click the Record button (the red dot, on the bottom right of the interface). Turn off the Loop button to the right of the Play button, and then click the Play button.

You're now recording the particle storm data to the location specified in Step 6.

22. When Particle Storm plays through the full 300 frames, click the Continue button to close the plug-in and return to LightWave Layout.

You've now created the particle storm data. Now you need to apply this data in Layout.

23. First, load the effect object created from Particle Storm. For the time being, load the Fountain.lwo from the book's CD-ROM. This is the file created for this tutorial. You'll see a null object load into the middle of Layout. Make sure it's selected, and press the **p** key to enter the Item Properties for it.

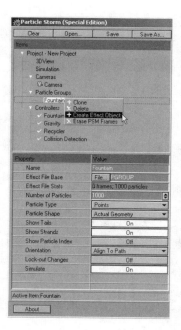

Figure C.21   The first step in saving from Particle Storm is to create an Effect Object for the particle group.

24. In the object's Item Properties panel, select the Deformations tab. Then, from the Add Displacement list, select ParticleStorm. This is the displacement plug-in for the Particle Storm program. Once loaded, double-click it in the list to open the Particle Storm Effect Object Options panel, as in Figure C.22.

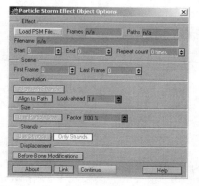

Figure C.22   The Particle Storm Effect Object Options enables you to apply the Particle Storm data to an effect object in Layout.

25. Click the Load PSM button and select the Fountain.psm file you created, or load the one located in the Objects/AppendixC/ParticleStorm directory on this book's CD.

    This is the particle data recorded in Particle Storm.

26. Click Continue to close the panel, close the Item Properties panel, and return to Layout. Change the final frame on the Layout timeline to 300 to equal the particle storm animation length. Click the Play button to see the particles stream, now in Layout. Save your scene.

That's it! That is the process of creating particles, adjusting them, and bringing them to Layout. From here, you can do a number of things, such as attach the particle effect object to another object to create a fountain object or the blowhole on the top of a whale. You can add to the particle stream with additional controllers such as wind, flocking, or swarming.

The next exercise uses the particle scene you just created to create a water fountain using LightWave 6's new HyperVoxels3 plug-in.

Exercise C.3   Using the HyperVoxels3 Particle Effects Engine

HyperVoxels3 is the next generation of LightWave's own particle effects engine. Although it does not generate particles like Particle Storm, it can take any point or particle (null objects included) and transform it into a surface, volume, or sprite object type. A surface object type will create blobs that can mold and blend together, such as lava, marshmallow creme, or, in this exercise, water. A volume object type enables you to create smoke, clouds, explosions, and gases using the same points or particles. Sprite object types are softer than volume type HyperVoxels, and are useful for smoke-type effects.

1. In Layout, load the ParticleFountain.lws scene from this book's CD-ROM. This is the scene created in Exercise C.2 for the Particle Storm plug-in. Drag the timeline slider back and forth, and you'll see the particle fountain in action. Leave the slider at frame 100.

2. From the Settings tab in Layout, select Volumetrics to bring up the Volumetrics tab within the Effects panel. From the Add Volumetric drop-down list, select HyperVoxels Filter to add HyperVoxels3 to the Add Volumetric list. Double-click the file in the list to open the HyperVoxels3 interface, as shown in Figure C.23.

3. Under Object Name, you'll see the Fountain object name ghosted out. Select it, and click Activate. You can also just double-click the name.

A check mark appears in front of the name and the other settings become active as well.

4. At the bottom of the HyperVoxels interface, click the Open VIPER button to use LightWave's interactive preview render. This is extremely helpful when setting up HyperVoxels. When it opens, you'll see HyperVoxels go to work on your particles, and create tiny white balls, as shown in Figure C.24.

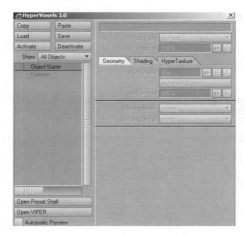

Figure C.23   The HyperVoxels3 interface is accessed through the Volumetrics tab in the Effects panel.

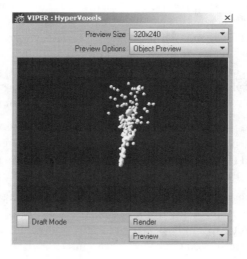

Figure C.24   HyperVoxels works best when you can see what you're doing. Using VIPER makes life much easier!

Note

Remember that LightWave 6's panels are nonmodal, meaning you can rearrange your panels so that VIPER and the HyperVoxels3 interface are both in view and open at the same time.

The Geometry tab should be highlighted in the HV3 interface. An Automatic Size was applied when the Fountain object was activated. For water, you'll need to change this.

5. Change Particle Size to 500mm.

6. Change Size Variation to 100%, allowing a random variation between all the particles. Then set Blending Mode to Additive.

This makes a mix of particles that blend.

7. Now click the Shading tab.

The Surface Editing settings are built into HyperVoxels, so the settings you're used to applying on other surfaces also can be applied to your particles!

8. Change the Color to a watery color of 197, 215, 235 RGB. The default Luminosity is 0%, while Diffuse is 100%; leave these set. Set the Specularity to 100% and Glossiness to 40%. Set Transparency to 100%. Set Refraction to 1.2 (for water), and click Full Refraction at the bottom of the interface.

9. Click the T button to set a transparent texture.

The Texture Editor interface appears. You want to set a Gradient Layer Type, with Additive as the Blending Mode.

10. Change the Input Parameter to Incidence Angle. This sets the gradient based on the incidence angle of the surface to the camera.

Add a key within the Gradient at 10%, with an Alpha of 100% and Parameter of 11.0. Change the default key to 0, and add a key at the bottom, at 100. Figure C.25 shows the Texture Editor settings.

By varying the transparency, based on the surface's angle to the camera, you mimic real-world effects. Take a look through a window and you'll see that as you move more in front or more to the side, the transparency varies. You also can apply the surface shader plug-in FastFresnel (pronounced *fre-nel*) to achieve this same effect. Any time you are setting a reflective or transparent surface, you should apply the FastFresnel plug-in.

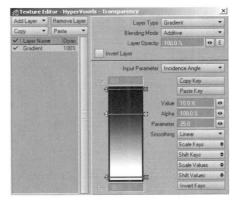

Figure C.25 Gradient textures can be used to help create watery HyperVoxels particles.

11. Close the Texture Editor window and switch to the Environment tab. Make sure the Reflection Options are set to Ray Tracing and Backdrop. You can see your updates thus far in VIPER.

12. Close the HyperVoxels interface and return to the Effects panel. Go to the Backdrop tab and click Gradient Backdrop. Close the Effects panel and return to Layout. From the Render Options panel, click on Trace Refraction. Press **F9** and check out the water!

13. Tweak from here by adding geometry around the fountain and a better backdrop. Render out a preview of this to see how the particle motion looks with HyperVoxels applied.

> **Note**
>
> Remember that you can use VIPER's preview to see how the HyperVoxels look in motion! When the HyperVoxels interface is open with VIPER, select Make Preview from the Preview drop-down selection on the VIPER window.

HyperVoxels is extremely powerful. This exercise only introduces you to navigation and procedure for applying HyperVoxels. Try loading the TextureFountain.lws scene from this book's CD. This is the exact same scene demonstrated here, except that Object Type is set to Volume. So instead of solid blobs blending with a Surface Object Type, a smoky soft fountain is created with the Volume Object Type. Experiment with HyperVoxels on existing objects. It applies itself to the points of the object, enabling you to make your object looked like it was "slimed" (that is, if you're a *Ghostbusters* fan).

Third-Party Plug-Ins

LightWave 6 not only has internal plug-ins available to you, but also has third-party plug-ins as well. These plug-ins add increased functionality to your animations.

Worley Laboratories

Often considered the best in the business, the Worley Laboratories plug-ins bring your animations to new levels of professionalism. The small price and huge toolset provided by Steve Worley are unprecedented in the 3D animation community.

Sasquatch Hair and Grass Plug-In

This long-awaited plug-in took more than four years to develop. It enables you to apply hair and fibers to selected surfaces. What's cool about this is that the fibers react to gravity, weight, wind, and more. They can receive shadows, and work with LightWave's surface settings. Figure C.26 shows the Sasquatch interface. Figures C.27 and C.28 show example renders.

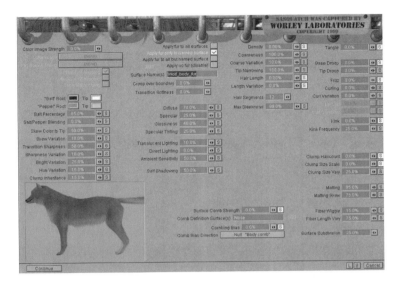

Figure C.26   The Sasquatch interface gives you all the control you'll need for creating just about any type of fiber.

Figure C.27   A cool-looking wolf thanks to Sasquatch.

Figure C.28   Hairy animals aren't the only things you can create with Sasquatch. This jungle shot uses Sasquatch for leaves, grass, and general foliage.

The best thing about Sasquatch is that it is a Pixel Filter plug-in. This means that there is no geometry in your LightWave scene to slow down your workflow. The fibers are created during the render process. In addition, you can multithread pixel filter plug-ins in LightWave 6, so if you have two or more processors, you can render these effects even faster. Check this one out at www.worley.com.

The Taft Collection

The Taft Collection from Worley Labs is a set that provides six powerful plug-ins for Layout. The plug-ins enable you to do things that are nearly impossible otherwise.

- **Camera Match.** Aligning LightWave objects with photographs is much harder to do than it may seem. For example, if you render a LightWave object so that it matches the view of a camera in a photograph, you can perform many tricks including compositing and photo-texturing with Sticky Front Projection (explained next). But matching a photograph's view is much harder. Taft's Camera Match plug-in solves the task of matching a 3D object with a real photograph by using mathematical optimization. What it does is find the absolutely best match for your scene. If you ever composite, Camera Match will not just save you days of tedious frustration, but will enable you to do shots that are simply impossible manually. Camera Match is designed for use only with photographs, not animations. Animated camera tracking is significantly different and more specialized.

- **Sticky Front Projection.** A streak of dirt, a rust stain, or even a crack in plaster can add realism to your LightWave scenes, but they take time and effort to re-create. Image maps can help considerably, but simple mapping often is not enough. One answer to this problem is "image-based rendering," which uses real photographs and simple geometry to build photoreal objects. The difficult part is applying the photograph to the object to match its shape and surface. This is exactly the task of Worley's Sticky Front Projection. You also can build object surfaces with multiple photographs.

- **Whirley Points.** Many real-world objects bend and deform when they're moved, such as the way paper flutters when you drop it, or when a cloth wrinkles, or a double chin bounces while walking. These effects of "soft dynamics" are every-where in the real world, but not often seen in 3D animation. LightWave 6 comes with Motion Designer for full dynamics simulation, but often you will want something simpler, more interactive, and faster to apply, test, and tweak. Whirley Points applies fast, real-time dynamics to your object (or parts of your object). It features an interactive OpenGL preview of your object motion, showing the result of your settings in real time.

- **Tracer.** Imagine firing 100 shots out of an animated gun, one at a time—how long will it take you to set up those keyframes? And what happens when you want to change your aim later? And what if you wanted to add a second gun? As powerful as LightWave 6's Graph Editor is, there is no way to automate this process. Keyframing those simple shots can take days. Tracer is designed for automatic weapons fire enabling you to shoot thousands of rounds or launch fireballs, sizzling lasers, flame, or old-fashioned lead at your favorite targets.

- **HeatWave.** The real world has billions of details that people are used to seeing in any image or animation. Your goal as an animator is to re-create enough of those details to convince the viewer. One of the details that can add that subtle realism effect is air shimmer, often seen in hot environments. With HeatWave, you can make hot pavement, fires, jet exhaust, and deserts. Its animated effect is simple to apply and animate, and its real-time preview gives you instant feedback to design the exact effect you need.

- **Hoser.** It can be difficult to animate tubes, ropes, tails, cords, tentacles, antennae, strings, ducts, pipes, vines, cables, and hoses. The Hoser plug-in simplifies this process. Instead of wrestling with IK and bones, just apply Hoser for instant, easy, interactive control of your object. You can move or rotate either end of the object and Hoser will make sure your tube behaves. Here are a few examples of the types of objects you can control:

- Scuba air hoses
- Car suspension springs
- Octopus tentacles
- Snakes
- Animal tails
- Telephone or electrical cords
- Sailing ship rigging

The Taft Collection should be every LightWave animators next purchase. Visit www.-worley.com for more information and example animations.

The James K. Polk Collection

This collection of useful plug-ins from Worley Labs will help you more than you can imagine. Like the Taft collection, the Polk collection is a set of plug-ins designed to take difficult to nearly impossible animation tasks and make them painless. Here's what this set of plug-ins can help you accomplish:

- **Acid.** This shader enables you to change a surface's texture and bump mapping based on effectors.
- **Poke.** This is a displacement plug-in with history.
- **Blink.** Automates irregular but periodic motion.
- **Parent.** Enables dynamic parenting of objects and bones over time.
- **Link.** Enables easy control of complex cycled motion.
- **Lens.** Corrects or adds lens distortions to LW imagery.
- **Wheelie.** Rotates wheels automatically.
- **Speedlimit.** Forces objects to stay within defined speeds.
- **Track.** Enables any object to align any axis to point at any other item.
- **Limiter.** Restricts object movement to prevent out-of-bounds motions.
- **Dangle.** Animates dangling chains, ropes, and cables automatically.

- **Flexor.** Allows smooth, dynamic bending of objects.

- **Diffuse.** Enables gaslike diffusion of particles over time.

- **HSVBoost.** This surface shader allows hue, saturation, and value manipulation.

- **Enviro.** Makes QuickTime Virtual Reality (maps QTVR), as well as spherical, cubical, and orthogonal views of your scene.

- **Vfog.** Creates faster ground fog than LightWave's built-in fog.

- **DropShadow.** Creates simple 2D blurred shadows.

- **Confusion.** Renders depth of field effects in your scene.

- **Whip.** This is a simple physics simulator for adding dynamic hinges and joints.

- Plus 10 other bonus plug-ins.

Gaffer

This plug-in from Worley Laboratories has been used by the LightWave community for years. Gaffer is a plug-in shader for LightWave 3D that performs a similar job as a real gaffer; it is a tool for controlling lighting and shading. It changes the algorithm LightWave uses to determine the appearance of a lit surface. Gaffer's new model is not a minor change in the shading options of LightWave; it is a considerable extension. It adds new specular and diffuse shading options, per-surface light exclusion, boosting controls, area light shadows, bloom around bright reflections, and a new tool for compositing shadows into a background plate. Gaffer has been developed in close cooperation with several major Hollywood studios. Their need for photorealistic rendering drove the development of a tool to give them more control over their objects' appearance. Gaffer gives you control over:

- **Selective Lighting.** Exclusion of lights on any surface, negative lights, and new falloff options.

- **Advanced Specularity Control.** Multiple specular reflections, with independent intensity and color control.

- **Anisotropic Specularity.** Nonuniform specularity from brushed metals, hair, and threads.

- **Advanced Diffuse Shading.** Diffuse transmission, and a new model for rough surfaces such as rock.

- **Advanced Shadowing Options.** True photoreal area light shadows.

- **Shadow Compositing Modes.** Seamless integration of shadows into plates.

- **Specular Bloom.** Automatic glows around the brightest reflections.

For information on Gaffer, Polk, Taft, and Sasquatch, visit www.worley.com to find examples and buy online.

MetroGrafx/Binary Arts

A long-time creator of cool plug-ins, such as FiberFactory, Wobbler, Sparks, PointAt, and Extract Audio, MetroGrafx's Jon Tindal has released FiberFactory3. This hair-generating plug-in for LightWave 6 helps you build 3D hair in Modeler and render it in Layout. The trick is with a Pixel Filter plug-in that doesn't require you to build enormous amounts of geometry—you only need very little. Figures C.29 and C.30 show the FiberFactory3 interfaces.

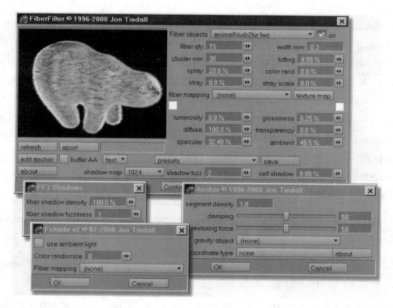

Figure C.29   FiberFactory3 enables you to render hair in Layout with color, reflections, and shadows.

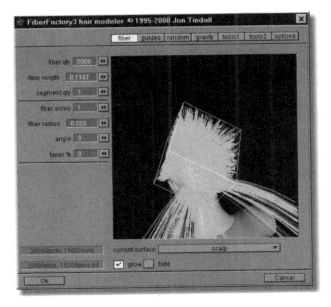

Figure C.30   FiberFactory3 enables you to create hair in Modeler.

For more information on MetroGrafx plug-ins, visit www.metrografx.com.

project:messiah

project:messiah, from Station X Studios, is a user-focused character animation plug-in for LightWave 6. Some features include:

- Fast inverse kinematics
- Fast bones
- Fast expressions
- Easy character setup
- Real-time interactivity
- Local/world coordinates on-the-fly
- Forward/inverse kinematics
- Procedural/keyframe animation blending
- Multitarget effects

Figure C.31 shows the project:messiah interface. For more information, visit www.-projectmessiah.com.

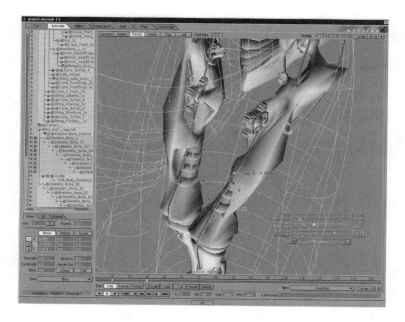

Figure C.31   Here is project:messiah's easy-to-use interface.

Internet Resources

As you can see from the plug-in examples listed here, all references point to the Internet. As a LightWave animator, it is vital for you to be online. No matter how little or how often you animate, you are doing yourself a great disservice by not accessing the resources on the Internet.

Here is a list of LightWave-related sites to visit:

www.flay.com   www.sharbor.com

www.newtek.com   www.worley.com

www.projectmessiah.com   www.metrografx.com

www.joealter.com   www.danablan.com

www.agadigital.com   www.dougworld.com

www.wwug.com/forums/lightwave/index.htm

If you visit www.flay.com, you can always find the most up-to-date information on LightWave and the LightWave community. You should also subscribe to the various LightWave 3D mailing lists. These lists have constant activity and talk ranges anywhere from nonsense to serious technique. Visit www.egroups.com and search for LightWave. You'll see which LightWave group is good for you. Lastly, if your Internet provider has a news service (which most do), visit comp.graphics.apps.lightwave for the LightWave newsgroup. Visitors often include representatives from NewTek and various high-profile studios. It's a great place for quick tips and techniques.

Summary

This appendix just skims the surface of the amount of information available to you. The tools for LightWave 6 and 3D animation are plentiful, and you should gobble up whatever you can. Information is like money—you can never have too much of it!

Appendix D

What's On the CD-ROM

The accompanying CD-ROM is packed with all of the exercise files to help you work with this book and with LightWave 6. The following sections contain detailed descriptions of the CD's contents. In addition, a number of "extras" have been provided for your enjoyment.

For more information about the use of this CD, please review the ReadMe.txt file in the CD-ROM's root directory. This file includes important disclaimer information as well as information about installation, system requirements, troubleshooting, and technical support.

Technical Support Issues

If you have any difficulties with this CD, please check out our tech support website at http://www.mcp.com/support.

System Requirements

This CD-ROM was configured for use on systems running Windows NT Workstation, Windows 95, Windows 98, Windows 2000, Macintosh, SGI, or UNIX.

Loading the CD Files

To load the files from the CD, insert the disc into your CD-ROM drive. If autoplay is enabled on your machine, the CD-ROM setup program starts automatically the first time you insert the disc. You may copy the files to your hard drive, or use them right off the disc.

Note

This CD-ROM uses long and mixed-case filenames, requiring the use of a protected mode CD-ROM driver.

Exercise Files

This CD contains all the files you'll need to complete the exercises in *Inside LightWave 6*. These files can be found in the root directory's Projects folder. Please note, however, that you'll not find any folders for chapters 1, 6, 18, or Appendix B; these chapters contain exercises for which you do not need to access any project files. You may find, however, that some chapters have CD files that are not mentioned in the book; these are what we're calling "bonus stuff" and are varations on the book's projects. To properly access the project files, do the following:

1. In LightWave's Layout, press the **o** key to call up the General Options panel.

2. At the top of the panel, select the Content Directory button.

3. A system file dialog box titled Set Content Directory will open. Select your CD-ROM drive, go to the Projects folder, and click Open.

4. Your content directory is now set for working through the exercises. The content directory path should look something like this: "\X:\Projects\", where X is your CD-ROM.

When you select Load Scene, LightWave will open to the Projects folder. There, you'll see folders named Scene, Objects, and Images. Within these folders are the individual chapter folders. Selecting Load Object within LightWave will point to the Objects folder within the Projects folder.

Third-Party Programs

This CD also contains several third-party files and demos from leading industry artists and companies. These programs have been carefully selected to help you strengthen your professional LightWave skills.

Please note that some of the programs included on this CD-ROM are only demo versions of the particular software. Please support these independent vendors by purchasing or registering any shareware software you use for more than 30 days. Check documentation provided with the software on where and how to register the product.

Here's what you'll find on the CD in addition to all the project files:

- Ernie's Wright's Unwrap Plug-In for Modeler. Chapter 10 uses this plug-in, and it is free, not a demo. Versions on this disc are for all supported LightWave platforms.

- FiberFactory3 Demo from Binary Arts/Metrografx. Try out this cool hair-generating plug-in for Modeler and Layout.

- Marlin Studios Textures (www.marlinstudios.com). Tom Marlin has provided a sample of many of his popular textures for you to use. You won't find these anywhere else!

- Relativity, the expression plug-in from Prem Subrahmanyam (www.premdesign.com). Appendix A guides you through the use of Expressions with this demo.

- Bill Fleming of Komodo Studios (www.komodostudio.com) has provided a great sample of his excellent 3D models for LightWave.

- James Hans from Infinite Detail (www.infinite-detail.com) has provided models and textures worth thousands of dollars.

- Credo Interactive, Inc. Life Forms 3.9 demo is a great way to manage and edit motion capture data. Try this out!

- A few extra images for reflections maps or compositing from Dan Ablan.

- A bunch of extra models from Dan Ablan for you to study and work with.

- A LightWave 6 screensaver and LightWave 6 logo backgrounds for your desktop.

We've worked hard to make sure the contents on this CD are just as useful as this book. The combination of the two make this a tremendous resource. Enjoy!

Index

J-K

L

P

New Riders Professional Library

3D Studio MAX 3 Fundamentals
Michael Todd Peterson
0-7357-0049-4

3D Studio MAX 3 Magic
Jeff Abouaf, et al.
0-7357-0867-3

3D Studio MAX 3 Media Animation
John Chismar
0-7357-0050-8

3D Studio MAX 3 Professional Animation
Angela Jones, et al.
0-7357-0945-9

Adobe Photoshop 5.5 Fundamentals with ImageReady 2
Gary Bouton
0-7357-0928-9

Bert Monroy: Photorealistic Techniques with Photoshop & Illustrator
Bert Monroy
0-7357-0969-6

CG 101: A Computer Graphics Industry Reference
Terrence Masson
0-7357-0046-X

Click Here
Raymond Pirouz and Lynda Weinman
1-56205-792-8

<coloring web graphics.2>
Lynda Weinman and Bruce Heavin
1-56205-818-5

Creating Killer Web Sites, Second Edition
David Siegel
1-56830-433-1

<creative html design>
Lynda Weinman and
William Weinman
1-56205-704-9

<designing web graphics.3>
Lynda Weinman
1-56205-949-1

Designing Web Usability
Jakob Nielsen
1-56205-810-X

[digital] Character Animation 2 Volume 1: Essential Techniques
George Maestri
1-56205-930-0

[digital] Lighting & Rendering
Jeremy Birn
1-56205-954-8

Essentials of Digital Photography
Akari Kasai and Russell Sparkman
1-56205-762-6

Fine Art Photoshop
Michael J. Nolan and Renee LeWinter
1-56205-829-0

Flash 4 Magic
David Emberton and J. Scott Hamlin
0-7357-0949-1

Flash Web Design
Hillman Curtis
0-7357-0896-7

HTML Artistry: More than Code
Ardith Ibañez and Natalie Zee
1-56830-454-4

HTML Web Magic
Raymond Pirouz
1-56830-475-7

Illustrator 8 Magic
Raymond Pirouz
1-56205-952-1

Inside 3D Studio MAX 3
Phil Miller, et al.
0-7357-0905-X

**Inside 3D Studio MAX 3:
Modeling, Materials, and
Rendering**
Ted Boardman and Jeremy Hubbell
0-7357-0085-0

Inside Adobe Photoshop 5.5
Gary David Bouton and Barbara
Bouton
0-7357-1000-7

**Inside Adobe Photoshop 5,
Limited Edition**
Gary David Bouton and
Barbara Bouton
1-56205-951-3

Inside AutoCAD 2000
David Pitzer and Bill Burchard
0-7357-0851-7

Inside LightWave 3D
Dan Ablan
1-56205-799-5

Inside LightWave 6
Dan Ablan
0-7357-0919-X

Inside trueSpace 4
Frank Rivera
1-56205-957-2

Inside SoftImage 3D
Anthony Rossano
1-56205-885-1

Maya 2 Character Animation
Nathan Vogel, Sherri Sheridan,
and Tim Coleman
0-7357-0866-5

**Net Results: Web Marketing
that Works**
USWeb and Rick E. Bruner
1-56830-414-5

Photoshop 5 & 5.5 Artistry
Barry Haynes and Wendy Crumpler
0-7457-0994-7

Photoshop 5 Type Magic
Greg Simsic
1-56830-465-X

Photoshop 5 Web Magic
Michael Ninness
1-56205-913-0

Photoshop Channel Chops
David Biedny, Bert Monroy,
and Nathan Moody
1-56205-723-5

<preparing web graphics>
Lynda Weinman
1-56205-686-7

Rhino NURBS 3D Modeling
Margaret Becker
0-7357-0925-4

Secrets of Successful Web Sites
David Siegel
1-56830-382-3

Web Concept & Design
Crystal Waters
1-56205-648-4

**Web Design Templates
Sourcebook**
Lisa Schmeiser
1-56205-754-5

The New Riders [digital] Series

New Riders' [digital] series applies traditional artistic principles to the world of digital animation and effects. Our authors believe that knowing how to use the technology is only the beginning of creating computer-generated art: Understanding how to make art evoke passionate responses is the real key to success. That's why our [digital] books are non-software specific, showing you how to use the technology to expand your existing artistic repertoire.

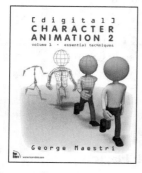

[digital] Character Animation 2, Volume I: Essential Techniques
George Maestri
ISBN: 1-56205-930-0

An expanded update of the original bestseller, this step-by-step, full-color guide helps you create convincing computer-generated characters in 3D. Apply conventional character animation techniques such as walk cycles and lip sync to computer animation, and make your characters look real.

[digital] Lighting & Rendering
Jeremy Birn
ISBN: 1-56205-954-8

This book contains strategies for lighting design that are relevant to any digital artist. It presents computer lighting models, how they differ from real-world lighting effects, and how to approach 3D lighting objects differently from lighting live scenes.

[digital] Textures & Painting
Owen Demers
ISBN: 0-7357-0918-1

Following the highly acclaimed design of George Maestri's techniques-based *[digital] Character Animation*, this full-color book combines traditional texture creation principles with digital techniques, all in a non-software-specific environment.

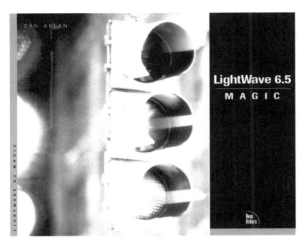

The *Inside LightWave 6* CD

The CD that accompanies this book contains valuable resources for anyone using LightWave 6, not the least of which are:

- **Project files.** All the example files provided by the author are here, to help you with the step-by-step projects.

- **LightWave-related third-party software.** This includes several LightWave demos and plug-ins.

For a complete description of everything that's included, please see Appendix D.

Accessing the Project Files from the CD

To load the files from the CD, insert the disc into your CD-ROM drive. If autoplay is enabled on your machine, the CD-ROM setup program starts automatically the first time you insert the disc. You may copy the files to your hard drive, or use them right off the disc.

NOTE: This CD-ROM uses long and mixed-case filenames, requiring the use of a protected mode CD-ROM driver.

Technical Support Issues

If you have any difficulties with this CD, you can access our tech support website at http://www.mcp.com/support.